ARSENAL

official

Hamlyn Illustrated History
ARSENAL
1886–1998
Phil Soar
Martin Tyler

HAMLYN

Records by John Burt and Daniel Feinstein with assistance from Jonathan Culverhouse and Kevin Connolly.

Additional Text: Peter Arnold and Adam Ward

This edition published in 1998 by Hamlyn an imprint of Reed Consumer Books Limited, Michelin House, 81 Fulham Road, London SW3 6RB and Auckland, Melbourne, Singapore and Toronto

First published 1986
Revised and updated 1994, 1995, 1996, 1997, 1998

A catalogue record for this book is available from the British Library

ISBN 0 600 59512 9

Copyright © 1998 Hastings Hilton Publishers Limited

Produced by Mladinska knjiga
Printed in Slovenia

PICTURE ACKNOWLEDGEMENTS

Allsport/Russell Cheyne 171, /Shaun Botterill 170, 177, /Clive Brunskill 189 top, Arsenal Football Club 8, 10 bottom, 11, 14, 16, 19, 24 left, 25 top and bottom, 32 (all three), 34 top, 42, 45 top and bottom, 46-47, 48 top and inset, 66 bottom left and right, 72 top left, 78, 79, 80, 82 top, 84 top, 85, 86 top and bottom, 88 bottom, 89 (all three, 93 top, 96 bottoom, 99, 107 bottom, 108 top, 110, 112, 117, 119 (all three), 120, 122, 125, 126-7, 130 top and centre, 131 bottom left, 134, 136 top and bottom, 137 top right and bottom, 138 top and centre, 131 bottom left, 134, 136 top and bottom, 99, 107 bottom, 108 top, 110, 112, 113, 117, 119 (all three), 120, 122, 125, 126-7, 130 top and centre, 131 bottom left, 134, 136 top and bottom, 137 top right and bottom, 138 top and bottom 139 top and centre, 141, 142-3, 143, 144-5, 199, /Ben Radford 197; Colorsport 151, 154, 155 centre and bottom, 159 top and bottom left, 163, 164-5, 166-7, 169 bottom, 173, 174, 184, 187 bottom, 187 top, 188, 189 bottom, 190, 191, 192, 193 below, 193 top, 194, 195 top, 195 below, 196, 197, 198, 198, 200, 201, 202, 203, 204 Top, 205, 206 Bottom, 206 Top; Daily Express, London 2; Football Association 67 (all four); The Guardian, London 66 top, 123; Hulton Deutsch Collection 10 top, 16-17, 21 bottom, 31 top and bottom, 40 top and bottom, 43 bottom, 44, 19, 50, 51, 54-5, 56 top, 57 top and bottom, 58, 59, 61, 71 top, 83, 87 top and bottom, 88 top and centre, 90, 94 top and bottom, 97 centre; Mark Leech 176,/ John Motson 72 bottom left and right; The Photo Scource 13, 14-15, 62, 63, 64-5, 68 top, 69 top and bottom, 71 bottom, 73, 74 top, 75 77 93, 93 bottom, 94 centre, 95, 96 top, 103 top and bottom, 114, 115, 116; Doug Poole 168, 169 top; Popperfoto 97 top and bottom; Press Association 106, 129, 130 bottom, 131 top, 133 top and bottom, 139 bottom, 148, 157 top and bottom; Royal Ordnance 24 right; Sunday Times 80-1, 107 top, 108 bottom; Syndication International 124, 128, 131 bottom right, 137 top left, 140, 142, 153 top and bottom, 152, 259 bottom right; Bob Thomas Sports Photography 161 top, 162,/Bob Thomas 181,/Clive Brunskill 179 top and bottom, 182, /Fresco 180,/M Thompson 186 top and bottom;

It has not been possible to trace the original copyright owners of some of the photographs used in this history. Any questions relation to photographs used should be addressed to The Hamlyn Publishing Group Limited, We apologise should we have inadvertently infringed copyright.

Colour Photography by Colorsport. Colour photographs from the Double season are the property of Arsenal Football Club.

Contents

INTRODUCTION 6

· CHAPTER 1 ·
Herbert Chapman 9

· CHAPTER 2 ·
Royal Arsenal 23

· CHAPTER 3 ·
Woolwich Arsenal 32

· CHAPTER 4 ·
The Arsenal 42

· CHAPTER 5 ·
Legendary Arsenal 50

· CHAPTER 6 ·
Allison's Arsenal 82

· CHAPTER 7 ·
Whittaker's Arsenal 98

· CHAPTER 8 ·
Arsenal's Double 118

· CHAPTER 9 ·
And So to Anfield... 149

· CHAPTER 10 ·
Wenger's Double 197

· CHAPTER 11 ·
The Arsenal Record Match by Match 207

INDEX 239

Introduction
and Acknowledgements

It was the 92nd minute of the very last match of the 1988–89 season, probably the most significant and dramatic in English football history. For only the third time in the 101-year existence of the Football League the two leading teams were playing for the Championship on the final day of the season. Uniquely, there were no other games this day. It really was the last game of the season. Arsenal were winning 1–0 at Anfield, in any other circumstances an outstanding result. But here, at that moment, it meant that Liverpool were going to win the League and the Double by a single goal. Both clubs had the same number of points but Liverpool had a goal difference advantage of just one. It would be Liverpool's second Double in four seasons, an astonishing achievement in a season which will always be remembered primarily for the Hillsborough disaster.

It was all over bar the presentation of the trophy to Ronnie Whelan. A late injury to Kevin Richardson had taken the match into injury time. There were just seconds for the Kop to wait before they acclaimed their double-Double winning team as, perhaps, the greatest English club side ever.

And then Alan Smith, as he had been doing all night, cleverly picked up a pass from Dixon and moved it deftly on to Michael Thomas, some yards out from goal on the right side of the pitch. Thomas moved forward, went past Nicol by taking a rebound off the defender's body and sped into the penalty area. Grobbelaar, hero of so many similar situations, a keeper who had saved from the same Thomas just 10 yards out a few minutes before, came out and spread himself. Nicol and Houghton flung themselves at the Arsenal man. But Thomas deftly flicked the ball to his right, over Grobbelaar's body and into the corner of the goal. 2–0. Seconds left. Pandemonium. Arsenal were Champions by virtue solely of scoring more goals. On points and goal difference Arsenal and Liverpool had identical records. If goal average rather than difference had still been the arbiter, Liverpool would have been Champions and so winners of the Double. No Championship has ever had a closer finish. None has gone to the last 30 seconds. None has deprived a team of the Double in such an impossible-to-script manner.

History takes many years in the making and as long in the writing. It is probably too early to place Michael Thomas's goal securely in its rightful context. But it is already arguable that it will become the most famous goal ever scored in League football — comparable with Geoff Hurst's second in the 1966 World Cup final or Blackpool's fourth in the 1953 FA Cup final.

It was a game and a finale which no fantasist would have dreamed of writing. It was surely enough that these two teams had come together to decide the Championship in the very last game of the season, a season forever to be remembered for Hillsborough. For the season to end that way, with just seconds remaining, and at that venue, was to live and rewrite every boy's childhood fantasies.

It was inevitable that there should be reminders of another goal in another game against Liverpool. The comparisons were close: a yellow and blue shirted young star scoring in the dying minutes of the last match of the season; red shirted Liverpool were the opponents and the Double was at stake. But Charlie George lay down after his goal in 1971, while Michael Thomas turned a flying somersault of, in all probability, utter astonishment. And Arsenal were to win their Double of 1971, while Liverpool were to lose theirs of 1989. To have played each other twice for the Double; that alone is worth its place in the history books, particularly this book which was created to celebrate the first hundred years of Arsenal's history.

One hundred years is a long time. How long can perhaps the best be judged when we realise that 1886, the moment of Arsenal's birth, was also the year that the world's first motor car was built. And, even then, the fifteen young men who founded Royal Arsenal were probably well into their thirties before they actually saw a motor vehicle and certainly grandfathers before they would have seen an aeroplane.

Much can happen in a century. Too much to record fully here. To give our story meaning we must seek out landmarks, find moments when it is possible to explain much in a short space of time, perhaps even in a single game. That is why we begin our story not with 1886, or even the magical Double of 1977, but with the FA Cup final of 1930. The story is more precise even than that. It homes in on the two captains that day, Tom Parker and Tom Wilson, walking onto the field together. In that one innocent gesture they told so much; in a way they revealed the underlying story of inter-war football. And that is the heart of Arsenal's story; a tale essentially of the 1920s and 1930s.

By some chronological freak, Arsenal's world changed at the turn of the 1930s. The glories that followed can probably be traced to a dramatic few minutes against a team of Second Division nobodies at Elland Road, the first of the games which are the real cornerstones in the Highbury story. Forty-one years later, on another ground in Yorkshire, those few minutes were to be eerily rerun. If we must pick landmarks, if that is how this history should be told, then these few minutes from these two matches shine like beacons from the dusk of history. It is these two games, rather than the 1971 FA Cup final or the last game of the 1989 League Championship, which will be the centrepoints of our story.

Both were semi-finals. Both games had seen Arsenal, at half-time, 2–0 down and virtually out. Both finished 2–2. The first game eventually led to the 1930 final, the game which defined an era. It was Arsenal's first ever trophy and from it they went on to the glories of the next ten years. Without that conclusion, it is entirely possible the Arsenal of today would be no more significant than a middle of the road club.

The second game was dramatic for its dénouement, a last minute Peter Storey penalty which was perhaps the second most important goal in the club's long history. It was to lead to the 1971 FA Cup final and the Double, a feat Herbert Chapman's team of the 1930s could never achieve. We say this was the second most important goal for one simple reason. Peter Storey's penalty was not so much the moment the Double was won, but was certainly the moment it could have been lost; The Double is a central, vital and highly emotional part of the Arsenal story. But it is ultimately not as important as 1930. With or without the Double, Highbury would still be Highbury. The ground, the club and the worldwide reputation were built by Herbert Chapman, Tom Whittaker and the teams of the 1930s. The Double was the icing on an already substantial cake.

This book is about those men and those landmarks, and about more moments and matches and the players that created them. In particular it is about Herbert Chapman, the greatest manager the game has ever seen.

A first-class football club is a complex organism. It is of course about players, directors, grounds and games, but it is also about the far greater numbers who watch each week. A soccer team is often a deeply significant part of a man's three score years and ten. Having been born under the star of a football club, it is almost impossible to stray elsewhere in the mind, no matter where he may go physically. That one team will always slightly increase the pulse rate at 5pm on a Saturday evening. The heights of exultation that a Cup final or, in Arsenal's case, the Double, can bring to tens of thousands should not be doubted or devalued. For many it will be one of the two or three most emotional and moving moments they will ever experience in their lives.

All football clubs have their peculiarities; Arsenal's most interesting is one of location and historical accident. Football in England has long been about provincialism. Arsenal are not (at least since their move from Woolwich) a provincial club. Chapman's efforts, coupled with the lack of any alternative, allowed them to become the capital's club, at a time which corresponded with London imposing its economic as well as political dominance over the rest of a depressed and uncertain nation. It was this historical good fortune which was ultimately to determine the character of Arsenal. A team supported by rich and poor, but somehow, then and now, the rich relation. Herbert Chapman chose his time and his location well.

Since their foundation in 1886 Arsenal have played around 6,000 first-class games. We cannot talk about them all, but we can at least record them. At the back of the book you will find a complete match-by-match, week-by-week record (up to August 1997) of every first-class game the club has played. We have chosen 1919, the year the club's modern history began with that sensational start to their record-breaking unbroken spell in the First Division, as the year from which we cover not only all the games and their results, but also all the team line-ups and goalscorers. The statistical part of the book has been a massive undertaking for all concerned and we should like to thank John Burt, who provided the original material, and checked and corrected it; Daniel Feinstein, who prepared the players' records which give every first-class appearance since the club was founded; Kevin Connolly for his updates; Roger Walker for his work on the typography and layout; and Jonathan Culverhouse for his expertise.

Numerous people assisted us in our research and talked to us of their own experiences and recollections, including many Arsenal players, past and present, who kindly took time to help. There are simply too many to thank here. Instead we would like to mention just a handful — Bertie Mee, Don Howe, Don Roper, Billy Wright, Ken Friar, David Miles, and especially Bob Wilson who made his own archives available to the authors. At Hamlyn, we would like to mention our art director Chris Pow, editors Sarah Bennison and Peter Arnold, picture researcher Jean Wright, Diana Godwin-Austen, supporters Charles Fowkes and Terence Cross.

But above all others we would like to record our debt to Tony Bagley. It was he who originally commissioned the book, argued about its contents and enthused over its preparation. A great lover of the game, he sadly died before the book's completion.

Phil Soar and Martin Tyler

HERBERT
CHAPMAN

· CHAPTER 1 ·
Herbert Chapman

The beginning of everything can really be traced to 2.45 pm on Saturday 26 April 1930. The place was London's vast Empire Stadium. Two men stood together in the Wembley tunnel, tense with just fifteen minutes to go before the start of only the eighth FA Cup final to be played there.

Soon they were to emerge into the sunlight together, the first captains ever to lead out their teams side-by-side for a major football match. One of those men was Tom Wilson, captain and centre-half of Huddersfield Town, the dominant team of the age. In the brief decade since the First World War, Huddersfield had won a unique hat-trick of League Championships and reached four FA Cup finals. But, though no one could have believed it that day, the parade had already passed Huddersfield by. They would never again win a major honour.

The second man, Tom Parker, captained Arsenal, a north London club of no great distinction which, in nearly 50 years, had won absolutely nothing. And yet in the decade that remained between that April day in 1930 and the start of another world war, Arsenal, originally Royal Arsenal, later Woolwich Arsenal, briefly The Arsenal, would win five Championships, match Huddersfield's League hat-trick and reach two more FA Cup finals. By 1939 they would have become the richest, best supported and most successful club side in the world, a bright shining star that has yet to be dimmed in the football firmament.

For that fleeting moment in 1930 the pendulum stood still. Midway between the two world wars the centre of gravity of English football gently moved south. And, as if to mark such a uniquely symbolic game, the teams not only took the field together but crowded into the same dressing room at the end to congratulate the winners and even shared the same celebration dinner that night at the Cafe Royal.

There had to be more to it than that, of course; much more, certainly another reason for such a peculiarly portentous day. The reason was to be found in the slightly portly, commanding figure of the 52-year-old Arsenal manager, Herbert Chapman. It was he who had earlier led Huddersfield to their hat-trick in the mid-1920s, left that team before the end of it and moved to small, struggling, trophyless Arsenal. When he arrived at Highbury in May 1925 he

had said it would take five years to build a winning team. Here he was at Wembley, literally five years to the week later, presumably intending to make good his boast.

In retrospect, with the useful hindsight of half a century, it is easy to see what happened and provide explanations for why it happened. But it was not so clear then. Huddersfield were clearly the better team of the two; Arsenal were in the bottom half of the First Division and had survived several close shaves on their way to the final. If the Gunners had lost that day it is not unreasonable to argue that the whole history of Arsenal FC might have been very different. There may never have been the 1930s; we may never have had reason to speak of the marble halls of Highbury; Arsenal may have remained, at best, as they had since their 1927 FA Cup final defeat, a middle of the road First Division club. The 1930 FA Cup final might have been remembered primarily for the dramatic appearance of the *Graf Zeppelin*, another peculiarly poignant moment in this symbolic final midway between the two wars. The hopes and fears of years gone by, and of years to come, rested heavily on the shoulders of Tom Parker and Herbert Chapman that day.

It is the measure of this one game, of its remarkable portents, of the future that it promised for one of the two clubs and the past chapter that it closed for the other, that virtually the whole history of inter-war football can be told in its 90 minutes.

And, by the same token, the history of Arsenal FC, which remains in essence a tale of the 1930s, can be related in the day's dominant figure – Herbert Chapman. That is why we must start our story of Arsenal Football Club on this one day, with the life of that one man, and with one single, all-encompassing football match.

Saturday 26 April 1930 had begun fine and warm; temperatures were in the sixties, perfect for the 55th FA Cup final. The morning papers had said King George V would not be well enough to attend, but he surprised everyone by arriving to a rousing reception for his first outdoor appearance since an illness 18 months ago. The leading story in *The Times* that day had been the arrival home from India of the Prince of Wales, his plane actually touching down in front of the cameras in Windsor Great Park. But even

The bust of Herbert Chapman which stands in the legendary marble halls of Highbury, specifically inside the entrance to the East Stand. Modelled by the famous sculptor Jacob Epstein, it was commissioned and paid for by twelve of Chapman's friends including his physiotherapist and spiritual heir Tom Whittaker. The twelve would meet each year on 4 January, the anniversary of Chapman's death, to talk and lay a wreath on his grave in Hendon churchyard. The rituals of this 'HC Club', as it was called, were to continue until the death of its last members.

The Times took a more than passing interest in the day's football, pointing out to its readers that. . . 'The broadcast from Wembley Stadium this afternoon will begin at 2.30 pm with community singing conducted by Mr T. P. Radcliff and accompanied by the band of the Welsh Guards. At 2.45 pm Mr George F. Allison will open the commentary on the Cup final match between The Arsenal and Huddersfield Town, and this is expected to last until about 4.45 pm. The position of the ball in the field of play and the score will be called at intervals by Mr Allison's assistant in the stand.'

George Allison was, as it happened, also an Arsenal director and the club's second biggest shareholder. It was only the fifth time that a game had been broadcast live and the effects of this exciting new medium, wireless, were far

Arsenal team was Charlie Preedy in goal, Tom Parker and Eddie Hapgood at full-back, Alf Baker, Bill Seddon and Bob John the half-backs, and Joe Hulme, David Jack, Jack Lambert, Alex James and Cliff Bastin the forwards. Nine of the eleven had been brought to Highbury by Chapman himself and, with the substitution of Moss for Preedy, Roberts for Seddon and Charlie Jones for Baker the team was probably close to the greatest one of an era that lives on in the memories of those fans still alive over fifty years later.

Huddersfield were, at the time at least, a rather more distinguished eleven. Former England captain Roy Goodall was at full-back, the magnificent centre-half Tom Wilson (a famous Huddersfield surname) remained as stopper, and the right-wing pair of Alex Jackson and Bob

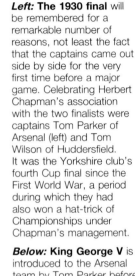

Left: **The 1930 final** will be remembered for a remarkable number of reasons, not least the fact that the captains came out side by side for the very first time before a major game. Celebrating Herbert Chapman's association with the two finalists were captains Tom Parker of Arsenal (left) and Tom Wilson of Huddersfield. It was the Yorkshire club's fourth Cup final since the First World War, a period during which they had also won a hat-trick of Championships under Chapman's management.

Below: **King George V** is introduced to the Arsenal team by Tom Parker before the 1930 final. In the picture (left to right) are Bill Seddon, David Jack, Jack Lambert, Bob John, Alex James and, shaking hands with the King, Cliff Bastin. Bastin was one month past his 18th birthday, then the youngest player to appear in a Cup final. He sent his winners' medal to his schoolteacher in Exeter.

from being fully felt. For one thing, the Football League still organised a full programme on Cup final day. The crowds who stayed away to listen to the radio missed some good matches — Wolves drew 4–4 with Bradford Park Avenue, Fred Cheesmuir of Gillingham scored all six goals in his side's 6–0 defeat of Merthyr Town and Lincoln City beat New Brighton 5–3. Sheffield Wednesday stayed five points clear at the top of the First Division with a 1–0 defeat of Grimsby. Arsenal were little concerned about League results. With just two matches left of the season they were in twelfth place and the Wembley crowd of 92,488 was understandably only interested in what was about to happen there and then. Only one London club had won the FA Cup in the twentieth century (Spurs) and the capital had still never applauded a League Championship winner.

As a match, it was one of the better finals. The

Whatever the result, the 1930 final would always have been known as the Graf Zeppelin final. Towards the end of the first half the airship, pride of a German nation slowly rebuilding its self-confidence, suddenly appeared like a great cloud at 2,000 feet. It dipped in salute to the King and passed on. Most of the players apparently carried on oblivious. The picture, which shows W.H. (Billy) Smith (no relation to the bookshops) centring from the left, reveals only Huddersfield left back Spence and David Jack (far right) looking up.

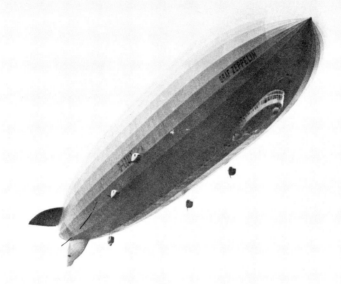

Kelly was the best in the country. 'Flying Scotsman' Jackson, scorer of a hat-trick in Scotland's famous 5–1 defeat of England at Wembley two years earlier, had also scored nine of Huddersfield's eleven goals on the way to the final. Eddie Hapgood was given the job of shadowing him wherever he went, Bob John taking the role of subduing Kelly. The defensive plan worked superbly, though it was in no sense a one-sided game.

Memories, however, are not made of defensive tactics but of goals, and never more so than in Cup finals. The first remains one of Wembley's most famous. In the team coach on the way from the club's hotel in Harrow, Alex James had spoken to winger Cliff Bastin: 'If we get a free-kick in their half early on, I'll slip it out to you on the wing. You give it me back and I'll have a crack at goal.' Most of the players thought James was joking – since joining the Gunners from Preston he had ceased to be anything other than a very occasional goalscorer. But in the 17th minute just such a free-kick occured; James was fouled 40 yards from goal, sprang to his feet and looked at referee Tom Crew, who nodded to the Scotsman to take the kick without any ado. Out went the ball to the left-wing, off hared Bastin, drawing Goodall out towards him. At just the right moment Bastin slipped the ball back inside for James, following through, to hit it into the corner of the net. The Huddersfield players protested briefly, but the referee had been quite correct in allowing the instant restart. It was, said *The Times:* 'The skill and bold tactics of James that turned the scale in favour of his side. . . to his remarkable control of the ball, he added the craft that both sees and makes openings.'

Some minutes later, in yet another incident redolent with symbolism, the *Graf Zeppelin,* Germany's giant airship and pride of a nation slowly rebuilding its self confidence, suddenly loomed over the stadium like a massive cloud. Flying at 2,000 feet, well below the legal limit, it dipped its nose in salute to the King and flew on. The players barely noticed; those that did were apparently annoyed at the break in their concentration.

Huddersfield attacked for the rest of the game, greatly helped by Arsenal's erratic goal-keeper, Charlie Preedy, who was deputising for the injured Dan Lewis. In the programme pen-notes he had explained how he liked coming out to meet the ball at the earliest opportunity. Unfortunately he appeared not to have explained this to his defence, used to playing in front of a more conservative keeper. Said *The Times* on Monday: '. . . at times Preedy took risks which hardly deserved to succeed as they did. Three times he let the ball slip from his hands as he was trying to clear.'

The Arsenal goal led something of a charmed life, often unguarded after a Preedy dash had failed to connect with the ball, and the Gunners' centre forward Jack Lambert spent much of the second half virtually alone on the centre line as his colleagues defended frantically. With just seven minutes left, a sudden long clearance from James found Lambert in the centre circle. Somehow he slipped between Goodall and Spence and the centre forward hared nearly half the length of the pitch towards the Huddersfield

Below: **Alex James'** (out of picture) **famous goal** in the 17th minute of the 1930 final. Fouled 40 yards out, he sprang to his feet, looked at referee Tom Crew and got a nod to restart instantly. He passed to Bastin (behind the near post) who slipped the ball back inside for James to score. The goal was a complete surprise, partially because James rarely scored, but more because of the speed of the free-kick. James had learned this habit in Scotland, where referees allowed it, and Chapman had become very irritated with him trying it south of the border. Because the officials usually called him back, Chapman had ordered James to desist. It was not the only controversial decision Tom Crew made that day. At half-time he sent a telegram to the manufacturer of the ball saying: 'I've chosen your ball.' It was later suggested that Cup final referees tended to expect some favour in return and the issue later lead as far as the resignation of the FA's treasurer.

Above: **David Jack heads wide** during the 1930 final. In 1923 Jack recorded the first goal ever scored at Wembley – for Bolton versus West Ham in the White Horse final. He also scored the only goal of the 1926 final and secured winners' medals in both games. He would presumably not have been nervous before the match, but most of the Arsenal team were. The appropriately named Highbury groundsman, Bert Rutt, had played gramophone records to the team in the dressing room for an hour before, hoping to take their minds off things. They were also to be encouraged through the game by the two mascots which became their supporters' trademarks during the 1930s – the bugler and the lucky white duck.

goalkeeper, Turner, who seemed suddenly dazed by this disastrous turn of events. Lambert shot from the edge of the area past the badly placed keeper, the ball hit the back of the net and Lambert turned, arms outstretched, expecting to greet his onrushing colleagues. But there was no one there; the rest of the side were still in their own half. So Lambert set off alone, applauding himself as he went, to provide one of football's more enduring memories at the end of one of football's most famous matches. It is probably no exaggeration to say that this game, which ended 2–0, along with the FA Cup final and semi-final in the Double year of 1971, is the most memorable in the history of Arsenal Football Club. It was not only the moment when the greatness began, it was also the moment when everything could so easily have slipped away.

The 1930 FA Cup final was the forerunner of two more in the decade that followed — 1932 and 1936 — and of five League Championships, 1931, 1933, 1934, 1935 and 1938. By the time Hitler's war began, Arsenal were without doubt the greatest, the most famous, the most widely supported football club in the world. In the half century since only Liverpool have managed a comparable dominance, and even then, it has to be said, without quite the same national promi-

nence or emotional commitment, for and against. One cannot begin to compare, for instance, Liverpool's two defeats by Brighton in the 1983 and 1984 FA Cups with the sensation caused by Walsall when they knocked the Gunners out of the same competition fifty years before. Since the 1930s the glories have inevitably been fewer, the trophies more widely spaced, but the reputation and image that Herbert Chapman built remain essentially as he left them. And so dominant is Chapman in Arsenal's history that, although it was nearly half a century before the club won a major prize, it is surprising to recall that it is also more than fifty years since Chapman died so tragically in 1934.

The history, status and wealth of the club is so bound up with this one man that it is surely necessary to go back and discover what we can about him, to find what it was that he brought to Highbury which was to generate such an amazing transformation and leave such a lasting legacy. The story of Arsenal must inevitably begin with the story of Herbert Chapman.

Herbert Chapman was born eight years before Arsenal, on 19 January 1878 in Kiveton Park, a small mining village on the borders of South (then West) Yorkshire and Nottinghamshire. His father was an illiterate miner who had five other sons and one daughter. Herbert was an

Charlie Preedy's handling, both safe (*left*, with Bill Seddon and Tom Parker looking on) and unsure (*below*, completely missing a corner) was to be one of the features of the game. Preedy was a late season replacement for the unlucky Dan Lewis, who had given away the dramatic only goal of the 1927 final, and the deputy had a reputation for erratic behaviour. Jack Crayston, who made his debut in a Third Division game against Preedy (then with Wigan), wrote afterwards: 'It was an odd start to my career; the goalkeeper played the deuce of a fine game against us – at right back!'

exceptionally bright child in an age when working class children had virtually no opportunities, so much so that he eventually reached Sheffield Technical College to complete a course in Mining Engineering. He was to use his academic qualifications, and hold down various jobs in industry, for nearly all of his life. Indeed, it was not until Huddersfield first became League Champions, when Chapman was already 46, that he finally turned his back on an engineering career.

He was a moderate footballer, a roly-poly inside forward or wing half, but nothing like as good as his brother Harry, who was a forward with the Sheffield Wednesday Championship winning sides of 1903 and 1904. Herbert remained an amateur through most of his playing career, which took him through a remarkable range of clubs and locations. In the ten years between 1897, when he was 19, and 1907, when he became player-manager of Northampton, he played for Stalybridge Rovers, Rochdale, Grimsby, Swindon, Sheppey United, Worksop, Northampton, Sheffield United, Notts County and Spurs.

In most of these towns he also took an engineering job, which was wise as his playing career could only be described as unmemorable. But ten clubs in as many years also had its advantages. He got to know people in the game throughout the country, he saw numerous styles of management (most of them poor) and he began to develop his own theories about how best to run a football club and win football matches. His longest spell in a single place was

Cliff Bastin was less humorous after the final: 'I am all in favour of a goalkeeper who advances at the right time (as Preedy had written in the programme notes for the final). On this particular occasion, however, Charlie was advancing all the time – whether it was the right or wrong time was purely incidental.' Arsenal survived Preedy's forays, though on several occasions he was to miss the ball completely when way outside the goal. Preedy was actually a taxi-driver. After the game it became a Highbury joke that: '…there's never one around when you need one.'

two years at White Hart Lane and, though he was usually in the reserves, the potential for a major club in North London (Arsenal were still south of the river) cannot have escaped his attention.

When he took over at Northampton in 1907 they had just finished bottom of the Southern League. In 1908–09 Northampton were Champions. Chapman finished playing the same year and in 1910 Northampton were fourth, in 1911 second and in 1912 third. By that time Chapman had returned to his native Yorkshire as manager of Second Division Leeds City. His first job was to canvass for votes at the League's AGM, where City were facing re-election. The club improved dramatically, just missing out on promotion in 1914 and then, in the rather different atmosphere of wartime football, being good enough to win the unofficial League Championship of 1918. Chapman had taken over the management of a munitions factory in 1916, a move which was probably and paradoxically to save his future career for, in 1919, Leeds were summoned before a League commission to answer allegations of making illegal payments between 1916

and 1918. This had always been, in theory, a major offence in the eyes of the League but was a much more sensitive issue in wartime. The club refused to release their books and were simply thrown out of the League. The club's officials, including their ex-manager, were suspended and Chapman remained in various industrial jobs for the next two years, suffering at least one spell of unemployment.

Chapman probably knew about the payments involved (he had been fined by the League once before, though on something of a technicality, in 1912) but as he was not at the club during the critical period the judgement seemed a little harsh. It was, understandably, to have a lasting effect on him and its echoes were to affect Arsenal in a truly dramatic way a decade later. That part of the story must, however, wait its turn.

When Leeds City were ejected from the League in 1919, Second Division neighbours Huddersfield Town sensibly decided to move up the road to Elland Road in their place ('From Leeds Road to Leeds City' went the headlines). Town were based in a rugby league stronghold,

had little support to speak of and were literally facing collapse. But in a classic instance of out of adversity coming strength, meetings of supporters rejected the decision to move towns (though the League had already approved), raised cash and reinvigorated the board. Co-incidentally there was a miraculous transformation on the field. Within a year Town were promoted to the First Division and were playing in the first post-war Cup final. Late in 1920 the Huddersfield secretary-manager, Ambrose Langley (an old playing colleague of Chapman's brother Harry) approached the then unemployed Chapman with an offer of a job as his assistant. Langley had been one of the main advocates of the move to Leeds and he was obviously aware that his own days must be numbered. Chapman had now been out of football for more than four years and the League cancelled his suspension without question, but it shows just how far his star had fallen that the appointment did not receive a single mention in even the local press.

Within a month Langley handed over the reins to Chapman (this must have been agreed in advance), within three years Huddersfield were League Champions and within five they had completed the first League hat-trick in history.

By that time, however, Chapman had again left Yorkshire and returned to North London. Though Arsenal advertised their manager's job in *The Athletic News* on 11 May 1925, Chapman had already been approached. Arsenal chairman Henry Norris offered him £2,000 a year to take the job, easily the highest salary in the game, and Chapman took little persuading. His days at Tottenham had shown him the potential of London, and when he had visited Highbury before the war he had been particularly struck by the adjacent underground station, only 12 minutes from Piccadilly. In a period of mounting unemployment he was also conscious of the better opportunities his two teenage sons would have in the capital.

So what sort of man was Herbert Chapman?

The image that has come down to us over half a century is that of a strict authoritarian, the man who once refused to allow Joe Hulme to spend a weekend at home in Lancashire (though Arsenal were playing at Bolton) because Hulme's two goals on the Saturday were not enough, the man who insisted none of the staff at Highbury left at 6.00 pm before asking whether there was anything more he wanted them to do. But if he was an authoritarian, it was in a far more authoritarian age. Jobs were scarce, jobs at football clubs were good ones, particularly at Highbury. A player earned £8 per week, four times as much as the average working man. To be the most successful club in Britain, you had to have the best. There was no gainsaying that, and it applied across the board. Early on he called the fifty club stewards into his office and told them he was ending the various free perks they received. He wanted everything above board. Though his teams were tough, he was never an advocate of unfair play. There are two celebrated

incidents when Chapman immediately transferred players who had been guilty of very bad tackles – Islip from Huddersfield and Black from Arsenal.

He was a committed man. He wanted to build the greatest of all football teams. Bernard Joy said of him: 'There are two kinds of visionary; those that dream of a whole new world, and those who dream of just one thing. Chapman's vision was of the greatest football team in the world. His genius was in actually creating something close to that.'

His players, in their reminiscences, seem to regard him with affection rather than fear; some go even further. Cliff Bastin wrote in 1950: 'There was an aura of greatness about him. He possessed a cheery self-confidence. His power of inspiration and gift of foresight were his greatest attributes. I think his qualities were worthy of an even better reward. He should have been prime minister, and might have been but for the lack of opportunities entailed by his position in the social scale.' An extreme view perhaps (and an inaccurate one as Ramsey Macdonald was PM at the time) but Chapman believed that his players were worthy of the very best, hence the tremendous facilities at Highbury and, in particular, the medical and physiotherapy side, years before its time, run by Tom Whittaker. He also insisted on his players having part of their earnings saved by the club. 'He was not a bully,' said Bastin, '. . . he gave few words of praise and fewer of blame.' The signing of Bastin himself also shows other essential elements in Chapman's success as a manager — his absolute commitment to the job and his willingness to back his judgement and take chances.

Chapman had first seen Bastin at Watford when the manager and George Allison had gone not to watch Bastin at all but to size up a member of the home side named Barnett. Bastin, playing for Exeter in a Third Division South game, was then only 16 but his amazing ball control and composure struck Chapman instantly and Barnett was completely forgotten. In the inter-war period youngsters developed much more slowly and it was very rare to see a teenager even in the Third Division. But Bastin was a natural (when he eventually arrived at Highbury the commissionaire wouldn't let him in, thinking he was a boy seeking autographs). Chapman set off immediately the following morning for Devon. Bastin, always a phlegmatic man, was unimpressed by Chapman's overtures, even though he had played just a handful of matches for his local club, Exeter City. He was more concerned with a tennis match he was due to play that afternoon. But Chapman persisted and persisted. 'I had visions of a lifetime spent sitting there listening to him,' said Bastin a quarter of a century later. Bastin, of course, eventually gave in, signed and became one of the all-time great names in British football, uniquely winning every honour in the game before his 21st birthday.

It was a good example of Chapman personally overseeing Arsenal as a close, family club. He had a very happy home life of his own. His wife was a teacher from the same Yorkshire village, and they had four children. His commitment to his family can be judged by the answer he gave immediately when asked what the proudest moment of such a successful life had been: 'When my son Ken qualified as a solicitor.' Oddly neither of his sons was to play soccer, but both were accomplished at rugby. Indeed, Ken, the eldest, was to become President of the Rugby Football Union. Perhaps the proximity to such tremendous success was a disincentive rather than an encouragement.

When Chapman joined Arsenal in 1925 he had been playing and managing in the senior game for nearly 30 years, apart from his four-year break. While it would be wrong to say that his conception of the ideal tactical approach was fully formed, it is certainly the case that, over this period, his successes had been based on certain constant themes.

Chapman was, above all else, a believer in great players. He brought Clem Stephenson to Huddersfield as soon as he became manager, and later won the signature of Alex Jackson. At Arsenal he immediately insisted on having Charlie Buchan, later David Jack and Alex James, among the greatest, if not the greatest, players of their generation. He believed that a great player could fit into any tactical system, and was to prove it, even with the complex Alex James. The fact that a player, like Stephenson or Buchan, might even be past his best was not in itself important.

It is arguable that Chapman was actually not a great tactician — when the offside law was changed from three defenders to two in 1925 Chapman was rather slow to spot the changes required to deal with the extra freedom it gave to attackers. The introduction of a centre-back and midfield link was suggested by Charlie Buchan, who could see the problem from the field, and it took Arsenal some time to settle down to the new system. Where Chapman was obviously magnificent was in fitting the man to the system required; to pursue the example, he then found and developed Herbie Roberts into the definitive stopper centre-back.

If there is another, simple key to understanding Chapman's view of the game it is perhaps in the phrase: 'A team can attack for too long.' He is first quoted as saying that when at Northampton in November 1907, after his side had attacked for most of a cup match but Norwich had stolen a 1–0 victory. Chapman soon instructed his wing halves not to press forward behind the attack quite so readily, and that the whole team should sometimes drop back to open out the game, bring the opposition forward and create the opportunity for a counter-attack.

Chapman was to say the same 25 years later: 'You can attack too long, though I do not suggest that the Arsenal go on the defensive even for tactical purposes. I think it may be said that some of their best scoring chances have come when they have been driven back and then have broken away to strike suddenly and swiftly.' That almost sums up a general view of Arsenal in the 1930s, the 'lucky' Arsenal of myth and legend. As with most myths, there is certainly something in it. The speed of Bastin and Hulme, the strength of Lambert and later Drake, the cunning of James, were all essential pieces of a clear plan. But in 1930–31 Arsenal scored 127 First Division goals — three per game. They can't all have come from breakaways.

Chapman has been misinterpreted in saying that a team goes on the pitch with one point and, if it doesn't concede a goal, keeps that point. He did indeed say almost exactly that, but not as an advocate. In fact he was criticizing the fact that so many teams, particularly in the early 1920s when goalscoring was at an all-time low, were basically defensive, off-side orientated tactical units. He once even advocated 11 up and 11 down as a means of forcing teams to look for

ARSENAL FOOTBALL CLUB
-F.A. CUP WINNERS-
-1929-30-

To Mrs Birago. From the Players with thanks for many kindnesses received.

The victorious 1930 team, all of whom signed this picture. Standing, left to right: Alf Baker, Jack Lambert, Charlie Preedy, Bill Seddon, Eddie Hapgood, Bob John. Middle row: Herbert Chapman, David Jack, Tom Parker, Alex James, Tom Whittaker. Front: Joe Hulme and Cliff Bastin.

goals. There is no doubt, nonetheless, that Chapman was one of the first to put to really good effect the very obvious truth that the best side is the one which scores most goals, not the one which attacks longest or which the crowd thinks has shown most endeavour. This was a surprisingly difficult point for many fans to appreciate in the 1930s, and beyond.

Chapman was never reluctant to admit the necessity of strong defence above all else. As he wrote in 1933: 'I confess I am out to win, and so are my players. It is laid down by law that the team who scores the most goals wins. To accomplish this, you must be sure that the defence is sound. All this, I know, is elementary but it is also the rock bottom of football.' Arsenal's system was designed on a pivotal principle, wrote Chapman: 'First, as to the attack, we have ceased to use our wing forwards in the old style, in which they hugged the touchline. Not only is it the aim of Hulme and Bastin to come inside when the Arsenal attack, but also the aim of the wing halves. This gives us

seven men going up on goal. Now, as to defence, the team swing the other way, but the same principle applies so we have eight defenders when the goal is challenged. The defence pivots towards the position of attack, the opposite back coming in to support the centre. It is, of course, essential that the two insides should come back and it is on this account that you get what is called the W-formation. The two wing halves are therefore the key men, either in defence or attack, and no defence can be sound unless it has the support of two inside forwards.'

All of this is relatively familiar today, going under terms such as 'closing down space' or 'getting behind the ball'. In the 1930s it was genuinely still a mystery. Programmes were always printed with a 5-3-2 formation (five forwards and two full backs) and crowds continued to believe that this is how teams like Arsenal played right through to the 1950s — despite the clear weekly evidence to the contrary in front of their eyes.

Because Arsenal so completely dominated

English football in the decade after the 1930 Cup final, it is perhaps worth examining exactly what it was about the manager, the club and their tactics that brought such astonishing success.

First of all, it is nonsense to suggest that Chapman arrived at Highbury with a plan in mind and then went out to find the players to fit it. If anything, the reverse was the case. Between his arrival in 1925 and his first game in charge, three months later, the offside law was changed and a whole new era had begun. Chapman had achieved considerable success in refining and exploiting the old system and it would be unrealistic to have expected him, or any other manager, to understand all the implications of the law change overnight. His Leeds and Huddersfield teams had been tight, defensive units, and his roving centre half at Leeds Road, Tom Wilson, was a key, if now obsolescent figure. When Charlie Buchan forced the third-back tactic on the team (the phrase 'policeman' came in later) the other changes required were reasonably obvious — the full backs moving out to mark the wingers and one of the inside forwards dropping back to become the midfield link. Arsenal may have adapted to these changes better than most other clubs but there was nothing secret or particularly subtle about them and, by the end of Chapman's first season (1925–26), most of his opponents were using the same formation. The tactical reason for Chapman's successes definitely lay elsewhere.

While it is undeniably true that the use of Alex James as the link-man was the *key* to Arsenal's success, its *essence* was further forward. The added dimension in Arsenal's game was actually the use of the wingers Cliff Bastin and Joe Hulme, and the club's relative decline towards the end of the 1930s was due more to the fact that these two could not be replaced than for any other reason.

Chapman did not plan it that way. By the late 1920s it had simply become apparent to him that, in the astonishingly fast Hulme and the cool clever Bastin, he had two players of very unusual quality. The basic difference in Arsenal's game from that point on was they they generally played only three real front men. There was always a strong centre forward (Jack Lambert being the most celebrated), and behind him David Jack was a goalscorer of quality but not a true front-runner. The wingers did not play in the manner of their equivalents at other First Division clubs. Their role was not, in other words, to hug the touchline, beat the full back, get to the goal-line and cross for the centre forward to head home. They were both capable of doing this, but Chapman saw it as essentially wasteful. A normal winger spent too much time waiting. He must be used more extensively and far more effectively.

The result was that both Hulme and Bastin would cut in far more often than they would go outside, that Alex James's most famous pass would become the ball *inside* the full back, and that both wingers became goalscorers of impor-

tance (in the great era between 1929 and 1935 Bastin scored 116 League goals and Hulme 75; an average between them of almost exactly a goal a game — meaning Arsenal expected one or other of their wingers to score every week). As long as no other club played this way, it was always likely to work. The opposing full backs had 40 games a year dealing with conventional wingers going outside; twice a season they met Arsenal and had to deal with a totally different threat. But, and here is the rub, Chapman could only do it because he had Hulme and Bastin and, eventually, Alex James to feed them. His competitors couldn't match his success simply because they didn't have the players; nor could his successor George Allison continue it, because ultimately he couldn't replace them.

Chapman did not create all of this overnight. Parts of his post-1925 system — the stopper centre half, the midfield link — were quite straightforward and the manager's strength here was finding the perfect men for the job. The more subtle development involving the wingers was probably largely chance but, having seen the potential, Chapman worked at the conclusions and maximised them. He didn't just win an odd League Championship, he completely dominated the game. What happened, bluntly, was that he moved one player back through each department of the team. The stopper centre half actually meant a line of three at the back rather than two. The need to replace the centre half in midfield meant one of the inside forwards had to fall back to create three in midfield and four up front. This is where most teams left it — at 3-3-4. As they continued to use conventional wingers they had to have at least two goalscoring forwards — otherwise there was no one for the wingers to serve. Chapman went further by dropping another man some way back as well, creating a system far closer to 3-4-3 than 3-3-4.

The benefit (as was also to be seen in the 1970s when 4-4-2 became the norm) was that the extra man in midfield helped Arsenal gain much more possession of the ball. In purely technical terms, it was a defensive alteration. It moved a man backwards. But Arsenal could make it work and scored a lot of goals because they had the genius of James, Hulme and the phenomenal goalscorer Bastin. Any other club trying the same thing was almost certain to fail for precisely those reasons. Hence, in general, they didn't try.

Chapman knew it was a scheme perfectly geared for scoring goals on the break. It was arguably the ultimate fulfilment of his old belief that '. . . you can attack for too long.' It was, in many ways, an away team's approach (in the six great seasons between 1929–30 and 1934–35 Arsenal won 187 points at home and 147 points away) but, at the same time, it in no way blunted the greatness of the other parts of the team when they wanted to attack and faced opponents who were their inferior. Their goalscoring record was second to none in the 1930s. Nevertheless, one can see the seeds of the tactics of the 1960s (using wingers in such unconventional ways

reserve, third and junior teams all tried to play, within their capabilities, to the same pattern. The reasoning was obvious — if a reserve came into the first team he would be familiar with the behaviour of the players around him. This was obviously most important in defence, but was not insignificant in attack. The club's classic moves, the ball from James inside the full back, or the cutting in of the wingers and the playing of the ground ball sideways, would not have come naturally to any player had they not also played that way in the reserves.

To ensure the tactical messages came across, Chapman turned part of his desk into a plan of the field, with models to represent the players. When players came to see him, it was easy to discuss moves, ideas and developments in a practical way. Chapman introduced weekly team talks for the whole side; everyone was invited to contribute, and it was from these meetings that many of the best ideas emerged.

One needs to put all this in perspective if one is to understand its significance. This was an era when directors chose the team, whether or not they knew a thing about the game. There was no such animal as team manager — technically he was secretary-manager, deputed basically to run the club. Attempts to integrate tactics, combine the best team (as opposed to the eleven players the directors might have thought were best in eleven individual positions) and develop a pattern of consistency were largely outside the control of the average manager, or were easily frustrated if he tried. Chapman, having seen over his playing career how not to run a whole range of clubs, was probably the first real professional in a world of semi-amateurs. These were the days when success was a Cup semi-final here and there, finishing fifth or sixth in the League now

found remarkable echoes in Alf Ramsey's seminal Ipswich side of 1962) and one can surely understand how the cries of 'Lucky Arsenal' arose from the unsophisticated and unseeing terraces of the era. Chapman's instinct for both fitting the right man to predetermined parts of a plan, while being able to adapt and develop other parts of that plan to the particular skills of the men available was, of course, the mark of footballing genius.

Another important part of Chapman's philosophy was that the whole club should play to the same system — in other words the first,

and again, and bringing in large enough crowds to balance the books. If further proof is needed, and with the possible exceptions of Wolves' Frank Buckley and Charlton's Jimmy Seed, who now can name any other manager of the inter-war era?

What was really remarkable about Chapman was his influence on, or attempts to influence, the game outside the playing area as well. Many of his proposals were firmly opposed by the FA, to whom he must have seemed a constant irritation. He introduced numbering on the Arsenal shirts on 25 August 1928, when the Gunners visited Hillsborough. This was the first time a team had ever been numbered and the FA told him to desist. He had a minor revenge by having the reserves continue to wear the same shirts. He introduced a 45-minute clock and was told to stop that (it was simply turned into the 60-minute clock still standing on the southern terracing), he wanted to start floodlit matches (midweek games then kicked off at 3.00 pm with the obvious loss of revenue) but was not allowed to, and Arsenal proposed the 10-yard penalty semi-circle ten years before it was finally adopted. Other ideas he put forward have still to come to fruition — goal judges (which he felt very strongly about), two referees rather than one, and far more clubs promoted and relegated (although the number was increased from two to three in 1973–74). He was a keen advocate of a single England manager, rather than a selection committee. In 1932 he wrote: 'The idea may be startling, but I would like the England selectors to bring together 20 of the most promising young players a week under a selector, coach and trainer. The idea would be to practise definite schemes and . . . at the end have them hold a conference at which views might frankly be exchanged. I would keep these players together during the season, . . . if this proposal were carried out, I think the result would be astonishing. I may say that I have no hope of this international building policy being adopted.' Note that not even Chapman dared suggest that a single manager actually pick the players. It was, of course, 30 years before these ideas began to be put into practice, and we are still some way from the ultimate conclusion but, surprisingly, the FA did give Chapman a chance to carry out some of his ideas in 1933. He travelled with the England party to Italy and Switzerland and, despite the objections of some of the selectors, was allowed to act as team manager, giving pre-match talks and trying to decide tactics in advance. With several Arsenal players in the team, this was obviously reasonably practical and the tour was a success — England drawing 1–1 with future world champions Italy in Rome and beating a strong Switzerland side 4–0.

The idea was not repeated, though there is no reason to suppose it might not have been eventually because Stanley Rous, secretary of the FA from 1934 and later, of course, President of Arsenal, was very much in favour. Chapman's death might have ended a good idea prematurely; with no obvious candidate to take his place the possibility died with him. It is arguable that, had Chapman lived longer, the principle might have been accepted and the whole history of post-war English international football could therefore have been very different.

The exploits of Arsenal as a team are covered elsewhere in this history, but to end a celebration of Herbert Chapman, the man who made the team and the club we know today, we should perhaps mention the most symbolic and yet most visible of all the man's achievements. When he took Leeds City to Highbury for the first time (on 6 December 1913) he had been particularly struck by the fact that the club had an underground station virtually in the ground. It was minutes from Piccadilly on the quickest and most direct of all the tube lines. The station, on what was then the Great Northern, Piccadilly and Brompton Railway, was actually opened in December 1906, when Chapman was playing for Spurs. There was only one problem, the station was called Gillespie Road. This was obviously a major advertising opportunity missed; what if all of the millions of people who travelled by the Piccadilly Line or looked at maps of the underground could see the name Arsenal right in front of their eyes? There was not much Chapman could do about it when he arrived at Highbury, but by 1932 the club was celebrated enough, and well supported enough, that he could invite the London Electric Railway (as it was by then called) to discuss the matter. Changing the name was not as simple as it sounds. In those days the destination was printed on each ticket, not to mention on all of the maps, in all of the time tables, and in all of the carriages. The LER was also no doubt wary of numerous other clubs requesting similar things (Chelsea are close to Fulham Broadway, then called Walham Green, though Fulham FC are not, West Ham are actually nowhere near the station of that name). On the other hand, Arsenal drew so many supporters that, Chapman argued, actually promoting the name might bring more passengers for the LER. Initially the railway proposed a compromise of Highbury Hill, but Chapman persisted and, on 5 November 1932, Arsenal became a fixture on maps throughout London. It remains the single greatest tribute to the skill, persuasion and perseverance of the man and Arsenal celebrated the honour with a 7–1 win at Molineux on the same day.

By the time Arsenal's half century came around Chapman was gone, dying from pneumonia at the age of 55. His bust, by the famous sculptor Jacob Epstein, was later placed in the magnificent entrance hall of the new East Stand, from where, for the last half century, he has watched over the club he raised to greatness. There are few clubs who can say with any certainty that they have already had their greatest manager and most influential era. It may not even be true of Arsenal, but it seems unlikely that there will ever be another Herbert Chapman.

· CHAPTER 2 ·
Royal Arsenal

Right: **The first badge adopted by Royal Arsenal FC,** probably around 1888. It was essentially the coat of arms of the Borough of Woolwich. The vertical columns are not chimneys but cannons. Until the end of the nineteenth century Woolwich was an entirely separate town and not in any real sense part of London. It was mentioned in the Domesday Book in 1086 and the first known reference to the famous ferry (for centuries the lowest public crossing point of the Thames) was as early as 1308, when the rights to operate it were sold for £10. The military connections began with the Royal Dockyard (thriving by Henry VIII's time), and then developed with the Arsenal, the Royal Military Academy, the Royal Artillery Regiment and the various military hospitals which still dot the local landscape. At the time of the club's foundation there were no fewer than 28 military units based in the area. It is easy nowadays to forget that the club is called Arsenal because it was an offshoot of the single most important military town in England at the end of the last century.

All in all, 1886 was a memorable year for football. Blackburn Rovers completed the last ever hat-trick of FA Cup wins, winning a replay against West Bromwich Albion 2–0 on Derby Racecourse in the first final to be played outside London. It was the initial year of professionalism and, though the Scots banned their clubs and players from any involvement with English professional teams, there did not seem to be any obvious ill-effects south of the border. But when James Forrest, a professional with Blackburn Rovers, played at half-back for England in Glasgow the Scots objected and the England selectors made Forrest wear a different shirt to distinguish him from the ten England amateurs. The Football Association was already 23 years old, the FA Cup fifteen, but the game was still very different from the one we know today. Apart from the centre line, there were no pitch markings; there was no need to provide a crossbar; there were no nets or penalties; a goalkeeper could handle the ball anywhere on the pitch, and the referee had no power to award a free-kick or even a goal unless the players appealed to him. There was not even any requirement that all members of a team wear the same coloured shirts.

In the wider world, 1886 was not particularly momentous. Prime Minister William Gladstone introduced his first Irish Home Rule Bill, saw it defeated in the Commons and was replaced by Lord Salisbury, after whom the new capital of Rhodesia was to be named. Great Britain extended her African empire even further by annexing Zanzibar, and the Severn railway tunnel, then the longest in the world, was opened. Frances Burnett wrote Little Lord Fauntleroy, Robert Louis Stevenson published

Dr Jekyll and Mr Hyde and, on the sporting front, the foundation of the Lawn Tennis Association remains the most significant fact that the history books record.

But, tucked away in a backwater on the borders of rural Kent and the southern sprawl of the largest city in the world, other events were taking place of which the newspapers and public at large were, understandably, totally ignorant.

It was a small group of Scotsmen which was really behind what happened at the Woolwich Arsenal towards the end of 1886, first among them one David Danskin from Kirkcaldy in Fife. What he actually did was to found a works football team. At that time Kent was firmly rugby and cricket country, both alien games to a lowland Scot like Danskin. The only local clubs which can claim a prior place in football history are Blackheath and Blackheath School, both attenders at the historic first meeting of the Football Association in 1863. Both quickly defected to play rugby and Blackheath are, oddly, the only founder members of the FA still in existence. The local cricketers were no more sympathetic to Danskin — earlier in 1886 one Joseph Smith had tried to persuade the cricket club at the Woolwich Arsenal to allow part of their pitch to be used for football, but they would not hear of it. None of this was perhaps too surprising. The Arsenal, one of the government's main munitions factories, was rather out of place in both Kent and the Home Counties, as were many of the men who came to work there.

The real spur came with the arrival in Woolwich of two Nottingham Forest players, Fred Beardsley and Morris Bates. Forest were already one of the leading sides in the country, having been the first northern club to reach the semi-finals of the FA Cup, which they did in 1879, 1880 and 1885. On that last occasion they had forced the great Queen's Park to two matches with Fred Beardsley as their goalkeeper. Nottingham also had (and still has) an ordnance factory next door to the old Forest ground at Trent Bridge, and no doubt this was where Beardsley and Bates had worked before they moved to similar jobs in Woolwich. Their arrival pushed Danskin and three friends, Elijah Watkins, John Humble, and Richard Pearce, into action. They asked around to see who might be interested and 15 men were prepared to pay

6d (2½p) each to start up a club. Danskin added another three shillings (15p) out of his own pocket (a tenth of the weekly wages of a working man at the Arsenal at that time) and the club bought a football with the money. Apparently they had 1s 3d (6p) change.

It is interesting to relate that Fred Beardsley had worked for a previous spell at Woolwich Arsenal, back in 1884, and had helped form another team then. Beardsley told his grandson, R. A. Beardsley-Colmer, many years later that this club had been called Woolwich Union and had played on 'Piggy' Walton's field in Plumstead. Beardsley was always a football fanatic — he changed jobs in 1887, going to work for Siemen's Engineering, but they quickly dis-

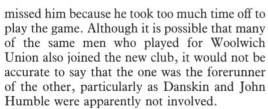

missed him because he took too much time off to play the game. Although it is possible that many of the same men who played for Woolwich Union also joined the new club, it would not be accurate to say that the one was the forerunner of the other, particularly as Danskin and John Humble were apparently not involved.

The likelihood is that there was more than one football team comprised of men from the Arsenal at that time. The better players probably turned out for several of them and the team that eventually became Royal Arsenal was no doubt a composite of some or all of these teams. The reason we today regard Danskins' Dial Square as the forerunner is that John Humble (and, to a lesser extent, Danskin himself) became the club's unofficial historian by virtue of eventually being associated with Arsenal longer than anyone else. Humble and Danskin naturally related their own experiences, the story of their earliest involvement with organised football in the Arsenal as they knew it. If another of the players, Beardsley for instance, had happened to

become honorary secretary, then he might have handed down a slightly different story for us to ponder today.

It is important to try and put ourselves in the position of those 15 founding fathers a century ago. As far as they were concerned, the team was a means of providing themselves with a little fun, exercise and, no doubt, a convivial social circle. They gave no thought to the future, of what their team might become. This was entirely sensible, for how could men who had yet to see a motor car and who would be grandfathers before they saw an aeroplane, possibly envisage an FA Cup final watched by thirty million people?

There were, to be sure, thousands of similar groups of young men dotted around the country whose identical efforts would never reach a history such as this. Naturally, only a tiny number of these sides were to rise, by good fortune and some genuine endeavour, to the national prominence of the next century.

The closest date we have for the initial subscriptions to Danskin's new club is October

Above left: **David Danskin effectively founded** the club by taking subscriptions in October 1886. This board was thought to have hung on the wall of the Royal Oak pub in Woolwich, where the club's name was changed to Royal Arsenal on 25 December 1886 and where its members regularly met. The sign found its way to Highbury in the 1950s.

Above: **Dial Square** today; for the first few weeks of the team's existence they had no name and were later referred to by Danskin as Dial Square simply because many of the 15 founders worked there. The workshop had been erected as long ago as 1717 and it was a worthy progenitor of such a famous club, for it had

Continued opposite ▷

Right: **A team line-up** at the Manor Ground in 1906. The framed figure is Fred Beardsley, then a director but earlier a key member of the 15 original founders. It was his arrival from mighty Nottingham Forest which prompted David Danskin to try to organise a team. Beardsley was the goal-keeper and one of his duties was to keep the goalposts in his garden, adjacent to Plumstead Common. It was also Beardsley who asked Forest for the loan of some old shirts. Instead they sent a full set of kit and Arsenal play in red to this day as a consequence of Beardsley's request. Beardsley had helped form an earlier club, Woolwich Union, at the Arsenal in 1884.

been designed by Vanbrugh, who also built Blenheim Palace for Marlborough and the facade of Kensington Palace for William and Mary. It acquired its name when the large sundial, still in place, was added in 1764.

Centre right: **John (or Jack) Humble,** for many years the club's secretary, chairman and director. At the age of 18 he walked to London from Durham, found a job at the Arsenal and became one of the 15 founders and Beardsley's understudy in goal. Largely responsible for recording the early details of the club, it was Humble who took it into the professional ranks of the League and who, after Chapman and Norris, must be regarded as the most important figure in its history.

1886, but it is unlikely that the founding of the Arsenal can accurately be attributed to any single day. Apart from the seven names mentioned earlier, others who paid at that point were named Price, Whitehead, Porteous, Gellatly, Ratcliffe and Brown (the other two must remain unrecorded by history). Danskin, Humble, Beardsley and Brown all lived to see Arsenal's first honour, the FA Cup victory in 1930. David Danskin himself was fortunate enough to witness all the successes of the decade that followed, writing to manager George Allison from his hospital bed after listening to the 1936 Cup final on radio, an arrangement surely not even vaguely imagined by his colleagues exactly half a century before when he put the whole thing in motion.

The first game of the new club was actually arranged against a team called Eastern Wanderers on 11 December 1886. There were one or two problems, such as the lack of a name, a pitch and any kit. For the time being the side, if it called itself anything at all, had simply used the name of one of the workshops within the Arsenal where many of the players were employed — Dial Square. The actual Dial Square had been erected as long ago as 1717, and acquired its name when a large sundial was built over its entrance in 1764. The facade of the building still exists, as does the sundial. The building is actually situated between Woolwich and Plumstead which in part explains why, despite their name, Woolwich Arsenal never played a single match in Woolwich itself.

Sadly, the historic first game did not take place anywhere near the Arsenal or Woolwich. The players crossed the Thames by the famous ferry to a piece of open ground someone had found on the Isle of Dogs. Elijah Watkins, whom Danskin had asked to be the first secretary, described it as follows: 'It eclipsed any

pitch I ever heard of or saw; I could not venture to say what shape it was, but it was bounded by back-yards for two thirds of the area and the other portion was . . . I was going to say a ditch, but an open sewer would be more appropriate. We had to pay handsomely to have . . . the mud cleaned out of our dressing-room afterwards!'

There was some dispute about the result, as there were no crossbars, hardly any pitch markings and the ball apparently spent a fair amount of its time in either the back gardens or the sewer. Nonetheless, Dial Square decided they had won 6–0 and met in the Royal Oak, next to Woolwich Arsenal station, on Christmas Day 1886 (a Saturday that year) full of enthusiasm. They immediately set about solving what they saw as their three major problems; a shortage of name, kit and somewhere to play. The name was easy — Dial Square was clearly far too unprepossessing and nothing less than Royal Arsenal would satisfy their ambitions. The name probably came from simply combining that of the pub they were sitting in with their place of work, though that was also referred to on occasions as the Royal Arsenal. It was to remain Royal until 1891, when Woolwich Arsenal was formally adopted though, strangely, the Football League insisted on calling the club Royal Arsenal until 1896.

The kit was almost as easy. Red was adopted because Beardsley and Bates already had shirts of that colour (first-class goalkeepers, like Beardsley, wore the same shirts as their colleagues until 1909), and in future players were supposed to provide their own shorts (several continued to wear knickerbockers) and real boots, as opposed to working boots with bars nailed across them. As the regal Royal Arsenal could not actually afford any of this kit, Fred Beardsley wrote to Nottingham Forest asking if

Right: **The main entrance** to the Woolwich Arsenal as it is today. Note the cannons on either side of the gateway. Most of the Arsenal is no longer in use and the club's grounds were one mile away in Plumstead anyway. Despite their name, Woolwich Arsenal never played a game in Woolwich itself.

Left: **After their 6-0 success** on the Isle of Dogs on 11 December 1886, the fifteen team members from Dial Square met in the Royal Oak (next, as the picture shows, to Woolwich Arsenal station) on Christmas Day 1886. It was there that they adopted the grand title of Royal Arsenal and, despite assumptions to the contrary, it is likely that the name came from a simple combination of the words in the picture – Royal from the pub and Arsenal from Woolwich. It is interesting that they were quick to drop Royal in 1891 when they turned professional.

they could help. Forest, who were the first team in the country to adopt uniform red when they began wearing caps of that colour in 1865, generously sent a complete set of red shirts and a ball and Arsenal have worn red and white, like Forest, for 100 years in consequence. The white sleeves, to add just a little extra distinction, were added by Chapman before a Highbury match against Liverpool on 4 March 1933.

Forest's ball was also useful, for the club didn't have one of those either, having lost the original somewhere along the line, but now all they lacked was somewhere to kick it. The only option was to use any convenient public land nearby and the obvious choice was Plumstead Common. This is not the flat, pleasant recreation area that the name conjures up, though it was also where Woolwich Union had played. Not only is it rather uneven and hilly, it was then also stony and rutted owing to it often being used by

the Royal Horse Artillery as a manoeuvring ground. While part of the old Common still exists, housing has been built on much of it in the intervening century and it is no longer possible to determine exactly where Royal Arsenal raised their goalposts. One thing we do know, however, is that the said goalposts were kept nearby in Fred Beardsley's back garden during the week. Many current League clubs started the same way. Spurs played on the Tottenham Marshes for five years before they were able to fence off an enclosure, being forced to do so by a combination of unruly spectators throwing mud at the players, their inability to take money and finding, on more than one occasion, that their carefully marked pitch had simply been stolen by another pair of teams.

The Reds (as they were then nicknamed) invited nearby Erith to Plumstead Common for a match on 8 January 1887, the first under the

Right: **Despite its name,** Plumstead Common is neither particularly flat nor particularly green. Very little of it remains undisturbed today and it was never a very good place to play football because of the ruts and damage caused by the Royal Horse Artillery, who used it for manoeuvres. It was, however, the closest public space to the Arsenal and that it why the team played on it during their first season, 1886-87. They played nine games after forming Royal Arsenal – winning six and drawing one. There is no record of exactly where their pitch was; indeed, it is possible that they played in different spots on the Common each week.

Left: **While playing on Plumstead Common,** the team would change in the local pubs. Of the three they were known to have used, only The Star, though altered, remains. The Common can be seen in the background, where the first ever game under the name Royal Arsenal was played (against Erith) on 8 January 1887.

without having kicked a ball, but that's another story). Within seven years of their foundation, Woolwich Arsenal were members of the Football League, a tribute to their entrepreneurial foresight rather, it must be said, than to their playing record.

The first few seasons, nonetheless, had their fair share of local success. As early as 1889 the club reached the semi-final of the London Senior Cup, where they were beaten 0–2 by Clapton. The following season they won the Kent Senior Cup, the Kent Junior Cup and, more significantly, the London Charity Cup. The latter was concluded with a 3–1 win over Old Westminsters (the old boys of Westminster School) at the Manor Field in front of 10,000 people. The team was Beardsley, McBean and Connolly (both full backs were from Kirkcaldy, Danskin's home town), Howatt, Bates (the captain) and Julian, Offer, Christmas, Robertson, Barbour and Fry. The Old Westminsters had their revenge in the London Senior Cup final, winning 1–0 in what was then the premier competition for clubs in the capital. These four competitions were no easy option, though it must be remembered that the London FA at this time was fiercely amateur and that Arsenal had the advantage of being a works team. Good players were found jobs at the Woolwich Arsenal by a sympathetic management and, on occasion, the club even bought out the contracts of footballing soldiers who they discovered stationed at the nearby barracks or enlisted with the Horse Artillery.

The next season, 1890–91, the Gunners won the London Senior Cup for the first time, beating Casuals 3–2 in the quarter-finals, Clapton 3–2 at the Oval in the semis (having been 2–0 down 25 minutes from the end) and St Bartholomew's Hospital 6–0 in the final, also at the Oval. This was the first really important

name Royal Arsenal, and their first formal 'fixture'. The first team ever to play under the name Arsenal was: Beardsley, Danskin and Porteous at full-back, Gregory, Price and Wells at half-back, and Smith, Moy, Whitehead, Crighton and Bee as forwards. Another eight fixtures had been completed by end of the season. The strength of Beardsley and Bates (who was known as the 'iron-headed man' because he regularly used his forehead, rare in an era of solid, heavy balls) was at the core of the team's early success, helped by the skills and occasional experience of several of the Scots, and they lost only two of their 10 matches that season.

Progress from here onwards was more than steady. Despite their humble origins, Arsenal actually had one of the fastest rises of all the early League clubs (Chelsea and Bradford City later went straight into the Football League

success for the club and, as the *Kentish Independent* reported: 'Excitement is a mild description for the scenes in Woolwich and Plumstead on the return of the football champions on Saturday night. A host of admirers met them at the Dockyard Station and drove them in open carriages, shouting and singing. There were celebrations everywhere all evening and, we fear, a good deal of drinking was mixed with the rejoicing and exultation.'

It was when they came up against the professionals, or even the leading amateur sides, that Royal Arsenal were made aware of their status. The club first entered the FA Cup, by far and away the most prestigious competition throughout the country, as early as 1889–90. Their first three ties were relatively easy, against Lyndhurst (an 11–0 victory in their first ever FA Cup match), Thorpe (who could not afford to come to London from Norwich for a replay after a 2–2 draw) and Crusaders. But Swifts beat them easily 5–1 in the next round and Derby County won 2–1 at the new Invicta ground in the first tie of the next season. Two Arsenal players, Peter Connolly and Bobby Buist, played so well in that game that John Goodall, the Derby captain and acting secretary-manager, offered them contracts. In the end they did not

The only known match report on the first ever meeting between Spurs and Arsenal, on 19 November 1887. The game was played on the Tottenham Marshes and Spurs won 2–1. As Arsenal arrived late the game lasted only 75 minutes but this was by no means unusual in those days, as can be seen from the second report. Since that day (and up to August 1985), the clubs have met 185 times, Arsenal winning 73, Spurs 78, with 34 draws. Note that Arsenal are already being described as 'lucky'.

This page: **The Manor Ground was Arsenal's main home** south of the river until 1913. They moved there on 11 February 1888. The site was next door to what is known as Royal Arsenal East (*upper left*), which explains why the club played in Plumstead rather than Woolwich. Plumstead station is behind the far embankment and the previous pitch (Sportsman Ground) was the next field on the left. Apart from the name of the main road (Manor Way) there is nothing left to give any indication that crowds of 25,000 once watched First Division football on this very site. It is now occupied by Manor Way, a roundabout, and the Plumstead Bus Garage. The game *above* was against Liverpool on 2 September 1905 (Arsenal won 3–1) and the view from exactly the same position

Right: **An altogether more impressive line-up,** taken in the summer of 1890. The trophies are the Ken Senior Cup, the Kent Junior Cup, the London Charity Cup (probably the Shield in fact) and a cup won in a six-a-side competition at the Agricultural Hall, Islington. The picture seems to have been taken at their new ground, the Invicta, to which they moved that summer. Founder David Danskin is second left on the bottom row. These are the only two known pictures of the club's founder.

Below: **The first known team picture,** probably taken before the London Association Cup match against Phoenix on 3 November 1888. The line up is, seated: Morris, Barbour, Brown, Connolly, Danskin, Chatteris. Standing: Horsington, Wilson, Beadsley, Bates, McBean, Scott. At back: Parr

today is seen *left*. The strange shaped roof of the engineering works on the horizon is the only remaining identifiable landmark. The embankment from which the picture *left* was taken and which can be seen in the centre of the picture *upper left* is not part of the railway but is, in fact, the Southern Outfall Sewer, the main liquid waste disposal for the whole of South London. When it was

constructed above ground at the turn of the century, it provided a perfect spot from which to watch the Reds (as they were then called) free of charge. As a result the club built a new, steeply banked terrace at the west and south ends of the ground, largely to cut off the view from the sewer bank. This was completed in 1904 and the many local soldiers who came to games quickly dubbed it

Spion Kop, after the famous Boer War battle in which hundreds of British soldiers had been slaughtered in crowded trenches on the top of a South African hill. The name Kop was later adopted on other grounds (most notably Anfield) but the one in Woolwich was the first large earth terrace and the original.

go, but the event set the alarm bells ringing in the Arsenal committee and was to begin the train of events which took Royal Arsenal into the Football League and also led to the foundation of the Southern League.

By this stage the club had settled at a formal address, the Invicta Ground (Invicta is the motto of the county of Kent). After playing on the Common in 1886–87, for the 1887–88 season they had occupied the Sportsman Ground in Plumstead, an old pig farm situated on the edge of Plumstead Marshes, but this pitch had a predictable tendency to become waterlogged. On the morning of their first home game against prime local rivals Millwall (to be precise on 11 February 1888), the committee arrived at the Sportsman Ground to find it under water.

Looking up Manor Road towards Plumstead Station, they noticed that the field next door, which was used as pastureland, appeared dry. Jack Humble rushed round to the owner, a Mr Cavey, and asked permission to use it. He agreed, Woolwich Arsenal drew 3–3, and for the next two years (1888–90) they played on the Manor Field, which they rather grandly called the Manor Ground. After the Cup successes of 1889 and 1890, they decided to move just across Plumstead High Street, to a new ground which already had a stand, terraces and dressing rooms — the Invicta. At the Manor Field, they had to rope off the pitch and bring in wagons (borrowed from the nearby barracks) if they expected a big crowd, which would mean around 500 to 1000. The players usually changed at the Green Man in Plumstead High Street or at the Railway Tavern beside the station (neither exists today), and often had to help with collecting the money.

All this seemed behind them at the Invicta, particularly when, on Easter Monday 1891, they attracted 12,000 fans to see a game against Scottish Champions Hearts. But when the landlord put a massive increase on the rent (from £200 to £350 per annum) hoping to exploit the club's election to the Football League in 1893, they could not pay and had to move again. The Invicta's owner was one George Weaver, of the Weaver Mineral Water Company, and after Arsenal left two rows of houses were built on the site named Mineral and Hector Streets. The old Manor Ground was repurchased and club and supporters worked through the summer of 1893 to get it ready for the Second Division. The club stayed there, opposite Plumstead Station, for 20 years until a final move far further afield than anyone could have envisaged in these early days.

Back in 1891, committee member and occasional goalkeeper John Humble was very shaken by the ease with which his better players could be lured away by a Football League club if they were playing well. As Royal Arsenal were nominally amateur (though their players were undoubtedly paid 'expenses') there was nothing to stop any of them accepting an offer from a professional club. The next step was a bold one, for everyone knew the obsessive hatred the London FA had of that evil northern virus professionalism, and few had yet dared challenge it. This was to be a problem for another decade and a half, eventually ending in virtually a complete break when the London, Surrey and Middlesex FAs formed the Amateur Football Association as an entirely separate body from the official FA in 1907.

Jack (as he was usually known) Humble deserves something of a diversion for, apart from being the most important influence on the club's history after Herbert Chapman and his chairman Henry Norris, he seems to typify the men who worked at the Arsenal and who founded the football club. He was born in a village called East Hartburn in County Durham in 1862. His father and mother died within three months of each other in 1880 and Jack and his elder bother decided to leave the relatively depressed North East. Not being able to afford the train fare, they walked from Durham to London and had both found jobs as engine fitters at the Arsenal by the time of the 1881 census. Their's was a hard but common story of the times. The Arsenal drew large numbers of poor men from the Midlands, the North and Scotland, of whom Danskin, Beardsley and Humble were unusual probably only in their devotion to, and skill at, football. Humble was to remain connected with the club for four decades, for much of that time the last link with the real working men who had founded the club.

At the 1891 AGM, held in the Windsor Castle Music Hall, Humble proposed taking the chance of going professional to ensure they kept their best players and this was carried by a large majority. Jack Humble declared at this meeting

that: 'The club (has been) carried on by working men and it is my ambition to see it carried on by them.' This was in objection to an additional proposal that a limited liability company should be formed simultaneously. Though this was to be adopted two years later, in 1893, it seems to have been regarded as a retrograde step, against the sporting ethos of the club and (rightly as it proved) endangering the control of the working men who had founded it. Humble, nonetheless, remained a director until a scandal in 1927 forced him, though wholly innocent, to resign.

The London FA were apoplectic about professionals in any form, and immediately banned Arsenal, their previous Cup winners, from all competitions under their auspices and expelled them into the bargain. The only modern-day equivalent is the reaction of the Rugby Union to anyone who has ever played rugby league or written a book (and taken payment) about his experiences as a player. But for Woolwich Arsenal (the AGM had also changed the name — presumably because calling a professional club Royal might have invoked even more fury from above) the arguments were not as arcane as they are today; the problems were very practical and very real.

They were effectively banned from playing in all competitions except the FA Cup or in friendlies against professional clubs from the North or Midlands. The FA Cup was therefore financially critical, but their first round tie in January 1892 took them to Small Heath (later renamed Birmingham) and they went down ignominiously 5–1. The following year was even worse — a first round proper 6–0 defeat by Sunderland.

There seemed only one solution — to try to form a southern version of the Football League, providing real competitive fixtures, and thus to staunch the ebb of support that the club was experiencing. In February 1892, just after their Cup ejection by Sunderland, Woolwich Arsenal called a meeting of possible southern members and, initially at least, there was real enthusiasm. Twelve sides were elected: Chatham, Chiswick Park, Crouch End, Ilford, Luton, Marlow, Millwall, Old St Mark's, Reading, Swindon, West

Above: **Between their foundation in 1886** and the move to Highbury in 1913, Arsenal played in four different locations in Plumstead. There is now no trace whatsoever of three of these pitches (the Common, Sportsman Ground and Manor Ground) and the only remaining trace of the fourth is some terracing in the back gardens of one or two houses in Hector Street, Plumstead. This was once the Invicta Ground (named after the motto of Kent) and was Arsenal's home between 1890 and 1893. When the club was elevated to the Football League in 1893, the landlord, one George Weaver, tried to increase the rent from £200 per year to £350. The club refused and moved back to the Manor Field. Weaver gave up his dreams of sporting glory (or profit) and built houses on the site, completely obliterating it except for these few feet of eerily nostalgic concrete.

Right bottom: **In April 1948** the Gunners invited the only three living members of their first professional team of 1891 to a game versus Chelsea. The three are (*left to right*) Bill Julian, Gavin Crawford and John McBean. Julian had gone to work at the Arsenal in 1889 and became the first professional captain two years later. The picture (*centre*) shows him in the kit of the era, though the star suggests he had just appeared as a guest for Luton. Gavin Crawford was a Scot who became the first professional imported by the club in 1891. John

Continued opposite ▷

Herts (forerunners of Watford) and Arsenal. If the inclusion of Old St Mark's and Crouch End suggests that the meeting was not particularly priescient, then this is further confirmed by the fact that Spurs came bottom of the poll, un-elected with just one vote (presumably their own). Nine years later Tottenham were to become the first Southern professional club to win a major honour, the FA Cup. The meeting was held on 24 February 1892 in Anderton's Hotel, Fleet Street. There was an obvious symbolic significance in the location, for it was in the very same hotel that the Football League itself had been formed four years before.

The London FA predictably exploded again, threatening to ban the other eleven clubs as well as Arsenal. Surprisingly, they all backed down, though the idea was successfully revived a year later by Millwall. Arsenal, with no one local to play against, were now getting desperate. There seemed only one gamble, and that a tremendous long shot at best. This was to apply for membership of the Football League, though the Woolwich club had never previously played in any league competition.

At the end of the 1892–93 season the Second Division was extended from 12 to 15 clubs. This created three vacancies, and two more surprisingly yawned when Bootle resigned and Accrington (a different club from the later, ill-fated, Stanley) refused to play in the Second Division after being relegated from the First. Newcastle United and Rotherham Town were given places without a vote, and Liverpool, Arsenal and Middlesbrough Ironopolis were elected at a later meeting. There were actually only seven recorded new candidates, the others being Doncaster Rovers and Loughborough Town. The simultaneous addition of Liverpool, Newcastle and Arsenal, who were to win an astonishing 26 of the next 80 Championships of the organisation they joined together, must surely be the most distinguished of all the League's annual elections. It was also clearly Arsenal's good fortune to have applied at a time

when there were so many vacancies. In a typical year they would have stood no chance, and even in a year with two new vacancies (the most at any normal time) they could have had little hope of success. On such random chances do great stories depend.

As there were no League clubs south of Birmingham and Burton, it was a considerable step for the League to take. Most journeys would be overnight, costs would be high, Woolwich Arsenal had no record of massive crowd support and they were hardly attractive visitors. On the playing front, the FA Cup was usually the acid test for new applicants, and here Arsenal could only be said to have failed dismally. They had never progressed beyond the first round proper and, oddly, were never to achieve even that small distinction in the remainder of the nineteenth century. Nonetheless, someone on the League Management Committee had the foresight to recognise the benefits. Firstly, if the League was ever to become a national institution, it must have members in London, the capital and the country's dominant city. Secondly travel was becoming less onerous. Cities like Manchester and Liverpool were now only four and a half hours from London by the fastest trains (even if Plumstead was nearly another hour on the other side). And thirdly, and perhaps the telling point in the end, to admit Arsenal would be to reward the club's brave stand on professionalism and to encourage others to do the same.

All in all, the summer of 1893 was a critical moment for the future of football. The Scottish FA finally accepted professionalism at their AGM the same month as Arsenal's admittance to the League, and 16 southern clubs were also persuaded to form the Southern League, though only half were professional at the time. All three decisions were major stepping stones on the road to legitimacy for the League and the FA in creating a general acceptance of professionalism and, a mere seven years old, Arsenal were playing a major part.

It was Arsenal's first significant contribution to the history of football. For the club and its board, however, one rather more immediate consequence of the club's arrival in the League, and the raising of the rent at the Invicta, was the decision to try and buy a ground of their own. The only way to raise enough money was to form a limited liability company, and this, despite those earlier objections, happened in the summer of 1893. The new company had a nominal capital of 4,000 £1 shares. In all 860 people subscribed for 1,552 shares (the rest were left unissued) and most of the shareholders were manual workers at the Arsenal who lived locally. There were only three holdings of 20 shares or more, the highest being 50 by a coffee house proprietor. The first board contained a surgeon, a builder and six engineers from the Arsenal. At that moment, without a ground, large crowds, or obvious playing resources, the problems were actually just about to begin.

· CHAPTER 3 ·
Woolwich Arsenal

The twenty years between Woolwich Arsenal joining the Football League in 1893 and their departure for Highbury in 1913 could not exactly be described as a period of unqualified success. Indeed, apart from the six-year spell following Harry Bradshaw's arrival as manager in 1901, it could better be termed one of financial struggle and footballing mediocrity. The Gunners were never a bad Second Division side. They chuntered along in mid-table until Bradshaw's arrival resulted in a fourth, third and second in successive seasons, the last gaining them promotion to the top division for the first time in 1904. They stayed there nine years, but never finished better than sixth and even that performance was not as outstanding as it sounds for they won 14, lost 14 and drew 10. Indeed, in only one of the nine First Division seasons between 1904 and 1913 did they win more League games than they lost.

The FA Cup is perhaps a better guide to their real status, for Arsenal were to go beyond the second round (the equivalent of today's fourth) only twice between 1893 and the First World War. Admittedly, these years, 1906 and 1907, were the highlight of the whole era, for Arsenal reached the semi-final in both seasons, but that proved the last gasp of the team Bradshaw built. He had already left, being lured away to Fulham in 1904, of whom we shall hear much more later.

So, 1904 to 1907 apart, the era was really the story of a struggle against geography and the rise of the other professional London clubs. Geography was perhaps the more insoluble of the two. Despite seeming to be relatively close to the middle of London, Woolwich is actually something of a backwater. No one passes through, it is difficult to reach from the eastern side, and the river effectively cut Arsenal's geographical circle of support by half. It was also a good 20 to 30-minute tram ride further out than the nearest major club (at the time Millwall Athletic), and was always a particularly inconvenient place to get to by rail, despite the Manor Ground being literally across the road from Plumstead Station.

George Allison was a junior sports reporter with Hulton's before the First World War and was given Woolwich Arsenal as his regular team. He told more than a few amusing stories about trying to get there: 'From Fleet Street to Plumstead was heavy going. Other sports writers were more than happy when I offered to undertake all the reporting of Arsenal's home games — meaning I wrote about them for most of the Saturday, Sunday and daily papers, often doing ten different reports (on the same) match. The payment I received softened the monotony of the long and tedious journey (Allison was, in consequence, often called George Arsenal by his colleagues). One could travel on the South Eastern and Chatham Railway from London Bridge, Cannon Street or Charing Cross. The trains stopped at every station. There were the same halts on the return journey, with the added difficulty that no one knew where the trains were going. I once travelled back with a soldier, who asked a porter on Plumstead Station where we were going. "London Bridge," he was told. At the next station he asked another railwayman. "Charing Cross," was the answer this time. He asked again at the next station and was given a third answer. Eventually he told one railway

Below: **Some of the early season tickets** from the Manor Ground covering seasons 1894-95, 1895-96 and 1896-97. The holder simply showed them on entry and the club was noted for encouraging their use – for many years Arsenal had more season ticket holders than any other club in the country.

FIRST TEAM.	GOALS FOR AGST				RESERVE TEAM.	GUALS FOR AGST			GOALS FOR AGST
SEPT. T 1 Rossendale ....Home		**JAN.** M 4			**SEPT.** T 3 15th Comp. R.A. ...Home		**JAN.** M 4		
S 5 *Manchester City ... Away		S 7 *Loughboro Town... Away			S 7 Thames Ironworks Home		M 9		
M 7 ‡Rushden ....Home		M 9			M 7		M 11		
T 10 Millwall ....Home		M 11			T 10		S 16 ‡Maidstone Invicta Away		
S 12 *Walsall..............Home		S 16 *Small Heath ....Home			S 12 Leytonstone .... Away		M 18		
M 14 *Burton Wanderers Away		M 18			M 14		S 23 ‡Faversham ......Home		
S 19 *Loughboro Town ...Home		S 23 *Newcastle United... Away			S 14 Thames Ironworks Away		S 30		
M 21		M 25			M 21		**FEB.** M 1		
S 26 *Notts County ....Home		S 30			S 26		S 6 Gravesend United Home		
		A.Cup, 1st round prop.			M 28		M 8		
OCT. S 3 ‡Luton ....Home		**FEB.** M 1			**OCT.** S 1				
M 5 *Rushden ....Away		S 6 *Grimsby Town ..... Away			S 5		S 13 ‡Folkestone ...... Home		
S 10 A.Cup Qual., 1st Round		M 8			S 10		M 15		
M 12 *Burton Wanderers Home		S 13 ‡A.Cup, 2nd round prop.			S 12		S 20 ‡Sittingbourne......... Away		
S 17 *Walsall..............Away		S 13 ‡*Leicester Fosse ... Away			M 12 ‡Maidstone Invicta Home		M 22		
M 19 ‡Wellingboro ....Home		M 15			M 19		T 25		
S 24 *Gainsboro Trinity...Home		S 20 *Burton Swifts......Home			S 24 Old St. Stephens ... Away		S 27 ‡Maidstone Ch. Inst. Away		
M 26		S 14 So'ton St. Mary's ...Home			M 26		**MAR.** M 1		
S 31 A.Cup Qual., 2nd Round		T 25 ‡Tott'nham Hotspur Away			**NOV.** M 2		S 6 ‡Ashford ....Home		
NOV. M 2 ‡Kettering .....Home		M 26			M 9		M 8		
S 7 *Notts County ....Away		**MAR.** M 1			S 14		S 13 ‡Sittingbourne........Home		
M 9 ‡Tott'nham Hotspur Home		S 6 *Newton Heath ...... Away			S 16		M 15		
S 14 *Small Heath ... Away		M 8 ‡Loughboro ....Home			S 21				
M 16		S 13 *Burton Swifts ...Home			M 23		S 20 ‡Cray Wanderers ...Home		
S 21 A.Cup, 3rd Round		M 15 So'ton St. Mary's ...Home			S 28 ‡Folkestone .... Away		M 22		
M 23 ‡Kettering ....Away		S 20 A.Cup, 3rd round prop.			M 30		S 27 ‡Dover .... Away		
S 28 *Grimsby Town ......Home		M 22			**DEC.** S 5 ‡Dover ....Home		M 29		
M 30 ‡Wellingboro .... Away		S 27 *Manchester City ...Home			M 7		**APL.** S 3		
DEC. S 5 *Lincoln City ... Away		M 29			S 12		M 5		
M 7		**APL.** S 3 *Newton Heath .....Home			M 14 ‡Ashford United...... Away		W 7		
S 12 A.Cup Qual., 4th Round		M 5			M 19		M 12		
S 19 *Blackpool ....Home		W 7 ‡Loughboro ....Away			**Xmas Day**		*Easter Holidays*		
Xmas Day		S 10 Assoc. Cup, Final			M 25 Gravesend United Away		F 16		
Boxing Day		*Easter Holidays*			**Boxing Day**		S 17 ‡Faversham .... Away		
S 25 *Lincoln City ....Home		F 16 *Newcastle United...Home			S 26		M 19		
S 26 *Gainsboro Trinity....Home		M 19 *Leicester Fosse....Home			**JAN.** F 1		S 24 Old St. Stephens ...Home		
		M 21 *Darwen ....Home					M 26		
JAN. F 1 *Darwen ...... Away		M 28 ‡Millwall ....Home					W 28		
S 2 *Blackpool .... Away		M 26 So'ton St. Mary's ...Home							
		W 28 ‡Gravesend United ...Home							

THIS LIST IS REGISTERED.]   * *English League.*   ‡ *United League.*   § *Kent League.*   WILSON, PRINTER, WOOLWICH.

official "You're a bloody liar, you don't know where it's going".'

When Woolwich Arsenal joined the League in 1893, they were London's only professional club. Fifteen years later, there were five in the Football League alone (Chelsea, Spurs, Fulham and Clapton Orient were the others — Spurs having already won the Cup), plus a range of good Southern League sides like Millwall Athletic and Crystal Palace not to mention excellent local amateur clubs such as Clapton and Dulwich. Amateur football remained strong in South London for many years, not only drawing support but also many of the good players who emerged. Arsenal's unique position had been eroded remarkably quickly.

Additionally, there was the Boer War between 1899 and 1902, an enormous blow to a club whose dependence on the military, in its earlier days, cannot be over-estimated. This took both players and support out of the area, particularly as the Arsenal itself introduced a Saturday afternoon shift. The tradition throughout the country at that time was for men to knock-off at Saturday lunch-time (there was no such thing as a full two-day weekend), have a drink and go to the game. The war was to prove almost as much a disaster for Arsenal as it was for the British troops in South Africa.

By the turn of the century the Reds (as they were then nicknamed) had so far managed to hold their own in the Second Division. The long distances were something of a help to them, for they rarely lost at home (only 13 defeats in the first five seasons). On the other side of the coin, they did not pick up many points away, never winning more than three games on the road in a single season until 1897–98.

There were occasional highlights — the very first game of their League career was on Saturday 2 September 1893 against another newly elected club, Newcastle. It ended 2–2, Shaw and Elliott being the scorers. Arsenal's first League win did not come until 11 September, at home to Walsall Town Swifts, when John Heath scored a hat-trick in a 4–0 home victory. Almost exactly two years earlier (on 14 September 1891) Heath had written his own ineradicable place in the history books when he scored from the first penalty ever awarded in an English first-class match (he was then playing for Wolves against Accrington). Newcastle scored six against the Gunners at the end of the month, and Burton Swifts did the same in November, but Arsenal returned the compliment twice during the season — against opponents Middlesbrough Ironopolis (away from home) and Northwich Victoria, both long since gone from the Football League. All in all,

Below: **The first team squad** at the start of the 1895-96 season; top: Boyle, Powell, Storer, Caldwell, Hollis; centre: Davis, Jenkyns, Ward; bottom: Mills, Hare, Buchanan, O'Brian, Mortimer. It was an average season, the side finishing seventh in the Second Division. John Boyle's season was particularly interesting – he played six times at half back and four times in goal. The club tried six men between the posts during the season in an attempt to replace the departed Storer.

Right: **Harry Storer, the first choice keeper** in 1894 and 1895. When he was chosen to represent the Football League against the Scottish League on 13 April 1895, he became the first Arsenal player to win representative honours. Storer is wearing the red and light blue striped shirt that the club briefly tried in 1895. As the idea was not pursued, one can only assume that just the single set of kit was ever purchased. Goalkeepers wore the same shirts as the rest of their team until 1909.

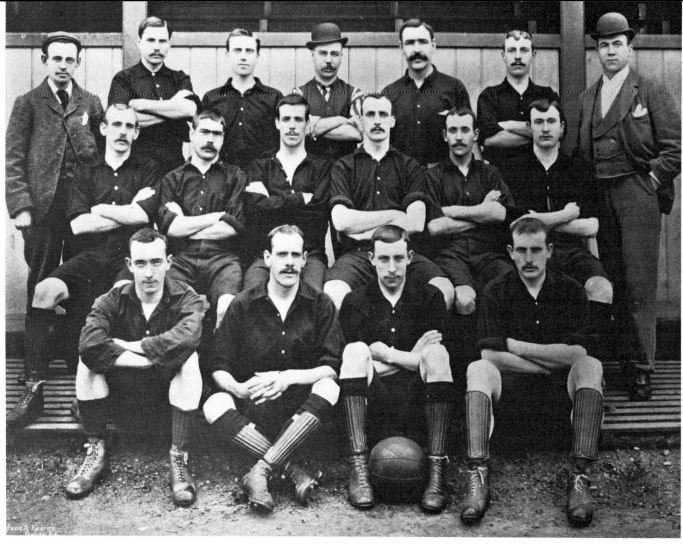

ninth place out of fifteen in their first season, with 28 points from 28 games, was acceptable, though Liverpool took all the attention by winning the division undefeated — the last time this was to occur in English football history.

The next few seasons were similarly unspectacular, though consecutive home games on 6 and 12 April 1895 did see a 7–0 victory over Crewe and a 6–1 victory over Walsall Town Swifts.

The club soon gained its first representative honours. Goalkeeper Harry Storer was chosen between the posts for the Football League against the Scottish League in April 1895 and the gloriously named Caesar Llewellyn Jenkyns became the first current full international when he represented Wales against Scotland on 21 March 1896. Typically, both men were too good for the club and had been transferred within a year. Also too good were, surprisingly, Loughborough Town, who beat the Gunners 8–0 away in a Second Division game on 12 December 1896. The Loughborough defeat came during a peculiar spell which has never been surpassed before or since by the club. Between October 17 and Christmas Day 1896, their League results went as follows: a 3–5 defeat at Walsall, a 6–1 win over Gainsborough Trinity, a 4–7 defeat by Notts County, a 2–5 defeat by Small Heath, a 4–2 win over Grimsby, a 3–2 victory over Lincoln, the 0–8 defeat at Loughborough, a 4–2 win over Blackpool and a 6–2 Christmas Day romp past Lincoln. In nine

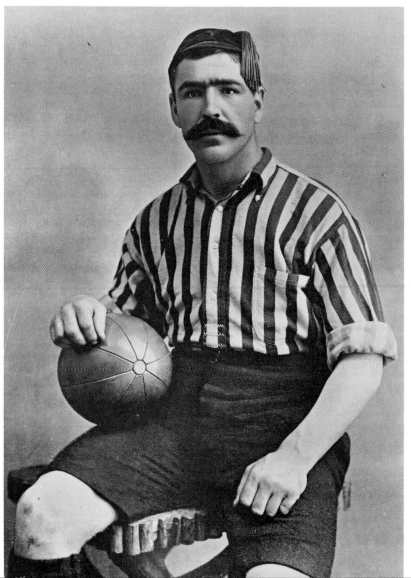

34

games they had scored 32 goals and conceded 34.

Imagine how enthusiastic fans would be today if they could count on seeing seven goals per game — and with very little idea of who would score the most. There was no obvious excuse for the Loughborough defeat (that team's only claim to fame nearly 100 years later) except that, perhaps, Arsenal's regular keeper Fairclough had been replaced by Leather. On the other hand Fairclough had conceded 23 goals on his last six appearances so this hardly counts as an excuse at all. Goalkeepers had long been Arsenal's achilles heel — as early as 1893–94 they had no recognised custodian and full back William Jeffrey played 12 games at left back and another 10 in goal!

The result at Loughborough remains Arsenal's record defeat, but the compliment was quickly returned on 12 March 1900 when Loughborough came to the Manor Ground and were themselves beaten 12–0. This is still Arsenal's record victory and is one of only 18 occasions when a side has scored a dozen goals in a Football League fixture. The peculiarity of having a record defeat and record victory against the same team, particularly only four years apart and against a club which left the League as long ago as 1900, is not surprisingly also unparalleled.

Sadly, these talking points only serve to brighten an essentially dour, unspectacular period. A disastrous FA Cup defeat by non-League Millwall (2–4 away) on 16 January 1896 proved one turning point for the committee. They decided to appoint a secretary-manager, one T. B. Mitchell from Blackburn, who was quickly succeeded by George Elcoat from Stockton. When Harry Bradshaw took over at the turn of the century the club were going nowhere very fast. He soon brought in the two most notable players of the period, an Australian left back, Jimmy Jackson, who became both club captain and a leader determined to control everything on the pitch, and a new goalkeeper from Sheppey United, Jimmy Ashcroft. When Ashcroft played in all three internationals in 1905–06, he became the first Arsenal player to be capped for England. Results and support improved slowly. By February 1903, over 25,000 were prepared to turn out to see Cup holders Sheffield United win a first round FA Cup tie 3–1 in Plumstead. The receipts were a healthy £1,000, the first time the club had passed the four-figure mark.

The following season, 1903–04, led to promotion. This was almost entirely the result of an excellent home record, with an astonishing goal average of 67 to 5. Not a match was lost at home (all were won but the last two) and there were 8–0 wins over Burton United and Leicester Fosse. The away record was not so impressive, with just six wins, but the overall goal tally of 91–22 could still be regarded as the best in the club's history, it being very difficult to compare seasons with differing numbers of matches. Proud Preston won the division a point ahead of Arsenal, with Manchester United another point behind third. The team which gained promotion was Jimmy Ashcroft (who played in every game), Archie Cross (a local lad from Dartford), captain Jimmy Jackson, John Dick, Percy Sands (an amateur schoolteacher who taught in Woolwich), Roddy McEachrane (a neat Inverness-born schemer who played left half), Tommy Briercliffe (signed from Blackburn), Tim Coleman, Bill Gooing (the centre forward, who was another ever present), Tommy Shanks (the leading scorer with 25 League goals) and Bill Linward (signed from West Ham). Of the twenty players to appear in the promotion season, only two had been with the club before Bradshaw's arrival as manager. Shanks was not only Arsenal's leading scorer, he was also the League's. Only two other Arsenal players have

subsequently led the Football League's lists in a single season — Ted Drake in 1934–35 and Ronnie Rooke in 1947–48.

Woolwich Arsenal's success quickly brought problems in its wake. Bradshaw was lured away to Fulham for a large salary before the next season had even begun and his Woolwich successor, Phil Kelso, was also to go to Craven Cottage five years later. Fulham have a strange affinity for Arsenal when choosing their managers — no less than nine of the first 14 at Craven Cottage either played for or managed the Gunners.

Kelso was a Scotsman, previously manager of Hibernian, and he reinforced the side, as many have done before and since, with his fellow countrymen. Initially gates were good (averaging over 10,000) and the club made a particular point of encouraging season-ticket holders, one result being that for a time they had more than any other club in the country.

Those supporters were well rewarded in 1906 when the club managed to get past the second round for the first time in their 20-year history and reach the semi-finals of the FA Cup. Nor was it an easy run: West Ham were beaten away after a home draw, then Watford 3–0, Sunderland (already having been League Champions four times) 5–0, a sensational result at the time, and then Manchester United 3–2 away in the quarter final. Charlie Buchan, a Woolwich lad, later wrote that he sold one of his school books to pay for his admission to that Sunderland game, and was beaten for it afterwards. He could not have realised that he was watching the two clubs which would span most of his famous career.

The semi-final was at Stoke, against all-conquering Newcastle. Between 1905 and 1911

the Magpies were to reach five FA Cup finals and Arsenal did not really stand in their way. Newcastle won 2–0 with goals from the great Colin Veitch and Jimmy Howie, though they then lost the final 1–0 to Everton. Arsenal had fielded one of their best ever forward lines and, early on, centre forward Bert Freeman hit the bar before Newcastle had scored. Arsenal could not hold Freeman for more than a couple of years, and had to sell him to Everton. He was to lead the Football League's goalscorers three times between 1908 and 1913 and finally won an FA Cup winner's medal when he scored the only goal of the game for Burnley v Liverpool in 1914. The two wingers were also internationals — Bill Garbutt on the right (capped for England later when with Blackburn) and the unpredictable Scot Bobby Templeton on the left. Templeton had won caps when with Aston Villa and Newcastle and is sadly perhaps best remembered for his part in the 1902 Ibrox disaster during the game there between England and Scotland. He had set off on one of his mazy runs down the wing and was doing so well that thousands on his side of the field pressed forward to get a better look. The movement caused a wooden stand to sway and collapse, and 25 people died as they fell through to the ground.

Considering that they had never before gone beyond the second round, it was a great surprise to see Arsenal pop up in the semi-final again the following year. This time their progress was easier, past Grimsby, Bristol City (at the time lying second in the First Division), Bristol Rovers and Barnsley. They met mighty Wednesday at St Andrew's in the semi-final and Arsenal went one up after only ten minutes when Garbutt headed in a Satterthwaite cross.

Left: **The Wednesday (they did not add Sheffield until 1929)** attack from a corner during the 1907 FA Cup semi-final at St Andrew's. It was the second consecutive year that Arsenal had reached the semi-final stage – a great surprise to their supporters as they had never previously gone beyond the second round. The Wednesday forward heading goalwards is actually Harry Chapman, Herbert Chapman's brother, and the Arsenal keeper is Jimmy Ashcroft. In the previous season, 1905-06, Ashcroft had become the first Arsenal player to be capped for England when he appeared in all three home internationals. Standing next to the goal-line is the famous 16-stone Charlie Satterthwaite; Satterthwaite's power became legendary after a 25-yard shot against Sheffield United hit the bar so hard that it bounced back, knocked the keeper out cold and still rebounded into the net. Against Wednesday, Satterthwaite provided the cross for Garbutt to open the scoring but Wednesday came back to win 3-1 and Arsenal had to wait another 20 years before they won a semi-final.

Football at Highbury.

TEAMS FOR TO-DAY.

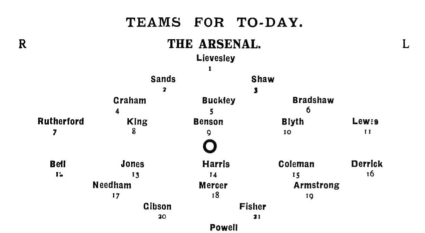

R   THE ARSENAL.   L

Lievesley
1

Sands   Shaw
2   3

Craham   Buckley   Bradshaw
4   5   6

Rutherford   King   Benson   Blyth   Lewis
7   8   9   10   11

O

Bell   Jones   Harris   Coleman   Derrick
12   13   14   15   16

Needham   Mercer   Armstrong
17   18   19

Gibson   Fisher
20   21

Powell
22

NOTTS FOREST.   R

Linesmen : J. North and W. H. Walton.

Referee : H. T. Yates.

Right: **Perhaps the most valuable of all Arsenal programmes** – that from the last game the club ever played in the Second Division. The match was against Forest on 24 April 1915 and, happily, the centenary year of 1986-87 marks 68 years in the top flight, equalling Sunderland's long standing record. The programme also announced manager George Morrell's resignation and the effective closure of the club and first-class football for the duration of the war. It turned out to be a remarkable game to match an historic moment. Arsenal won 7-0 with four goals for King and two for the out-of-position full-back Bob Benson. Within a year Benson was dead, collapsing during a wartime game at Reading and dying in trainer George Hardy's arms. The League table in the same programme showed Arsenal as sixth in the Second Division and this position was not altered in the official Football League records after the game had concluded the season. Arsenal were thus quoted, and printed, as finishing sixth in 1915 for the next 65 years until, in 1980, the Association of Football Statisticians pointed out that the 7-0 win had taken them over Birmingham on goal average and they actually finished fifth. In normal circumstances this might have seemed irrelevant but because of what happened in 1919 the repetition of the error for six decades was astonishing.

Then came tragedy; keeper Ashcroft was injured in a collison with centre forward David Wilson when coming outside his area to collect a loose ball (at this time keepers could handle anywhere in their own half) and Wilson scored from the free-kick which referee Jack Howcroft had controversially awarded Wednesday. The incident turned the game and Wednesday scored twice more (making it 3–1) to reach Crystal Palace for the final, which they won by beating Everton 2–1.

Nonetheless, it had seemed to be a very successful season for the Reds, perhaps a sign of things to come. They were seventh in the First Division, the reserves had won the London League and the South Eastern League, inside right John 'Tim' Coleman had played for England and full back Jimmy Sharp for Scotland. As it happened, it was actually the top of the roller-coaster, not part of a careful ascent. The club's support and finances were not strong enough to survive a decline in results, and, once things started to go wrong, they accelerated virtually out of control.

The problems were initially much more acute off the field than on it, where the side finished 15th, 6th and 18th between 1907–08 and 1909–10. Phil Kelso resigned, initially to run a hotel in Scotland, but almost immediately joined Fulham instead, replacing Harry Bradshaw (who had turned down a new contract and became secretary of the Southern League). The new Arsenal manager, George Morrell, found himself having to sell to survive. Within 12 months virtually all the important names had gone — Coleman, Freeman, Sharp, Ashcroft and

Garbutt. After leaving Woolwich for Blackburn, William Garbutt moved further and further afield. In 1914 he went to Genoa as coach, where his team won the Italian League the following year. By 1927 he was in Rome, and two years later went on to Naples. In 1935–36 he coached the Spanish champions Athletic Bilbao but the Spanish Civil War drove him back to Italy. During the Second World War he was hidden there by friends and in 1946 took up his old post again at Genoa.

Morrell's first full season in charge began on 2 September 1908. The first programme of the season was not shy about discussing the fact that the best players had all gone: 'Here we go again,' began the editor 'and the followers of Arsenal look forward to the advent of another season with a great number of the players on whom we rely practically unknown quantities. The "Reds" will look somewhat strange without such faces as Ashcroft, Sharp, Coleman, Freeman, Kyle and Garbutt but we believe capable men have been engaged to replace them and we look forward to a successful season.'

The hope was misplaced for it was to be nearly two decades before the 'Reds' had another genuinely successful year. Nonetheless, the editor did go on to comment: 'If we do not have a back of the same calibre as Sharp, we have one likely to prove a worthy successor in the person of (Joseph) Shaw.' Worthy indeed. Even the greatest of all the pre-war Gunners, Andy Ducat, eventually had to be transferred to Villa. Right-half Ducat appeared for England in all three internationals in 1909–10, when he was only 23, and after the war also played cricket for his country. Appearing at centre forward, Ducat scored a hat-trick in his first ever game for Arsenal, on Christmas Day 1905, versus the mighty Newcastle United, the best side of the era. It was particularly sad that his best playing days were lost to the First World War. For their part Woolwich Arsenal never recovered from those sudden sales in 1908, particularly missing keeper Ashcroft. The crowds melted away, as did the results, and by 1910 the club was effectively bankrupt and up for sale.

For the next decade the Arsenal story is really to be told off the field rather than on it. The main reason for this was one Henry Norris, the chairman of Fulham. As we have seen, the links between the two clubs were already close, if not necessarily friendly, and in 1910 Norris was able to use the Woolwich club's problems to effect a takeover of Arsenal as well.

Fulham had experienced a remarkably rapid rise since Norris became chairman. In 1902 and 1903 they won the Second Division of the Southern League, were then elected to the First and, under Bradshaw, won that Division in 1906 and 1907, upon which they applied to join the Football League and were immediately accepted. This was the first concrete evidence of Henry Norris' remarkable powers of political persuasion where the Football League was concerned. At the 1907 election Fulham easily received the

WOOLWICH ARSENAL FOOTBALL CLUB, 1910-11.

HARDY, (*Trainer*), · DICK, · THOMSON, · BATEUP, · COMMON, · RIPPON, · HEDLEY, · GRA.. · DUCAT, · GRANT, · McDONALD, · ROGERS, · SANDS, · LEWIS, McKINSON, GREENAWAY, HEPPINSTALL, Mr. G. MORRELL, (*Sec.*), LOGAN, NEAVE, SHAW, McEACHRANE.

George Morrell's hard-pressed team of 1910-11. This was the season the club went bankrupt and were bought by Henry Norris, who tried to persuade the League to let Arsenal and Fulham play alternate weeks at Craven Cottage. Virtually all of the players who had taken the side to the 1906 and 1907 semi-finals had been sold by Morrell, but one or two famous faces remain. Alf Common had been the first £1,000 footballer when transferred from Sunderland to Middlesbrough in 1905, while Andy Ducat was perhaps the greatest of all the pre-war Reds. Scoring a hat-trick versus mighty Newcastle on his debut, Ducat was one of the rare sportsmen to be capped for England at soccer and cricket.

highest number of votes (28) and replaced Burton United.

Norris was a self-made man, his fortune based on property development in south-west London. He was Mayor of Fulham for seven years, was knighted in 1917 and represented Fulham East in Parliament from 1918 to 1922. A dictatorial man, he ran his football clubs like his businesses. A thin autocrat with a walrus moustache, he welcomed neither criticism nor advice; nonetheless, he was influential and persuasive, as will be seen later. Over the years he developed very close friendships with members of the League Management Committee, particularly president John McKenna, and while an MP he was able to represent the interests of football, and himself, with some success.

Leslie Knighton, Arsenal manager to Norris' chairman between 1919 and 1925, has left us perhaps the best descriptions of Norris. Knighton said in his autobiography: 'I soon found out that everyone was afraid of Sir Henry. And no wonder! I have never met his equal for logic,

invective and ruthlessness against all who opposed him. When I disagreed with him at board meetings and had to stand up for what I knew was best for the club, he used to flay me with words until I was reduced to fuming, helpless silence. Then, as I sat not knowing what to say, and trying to bottle up what I was tempted to say, he would whip round and shout: "Well Knighton, we pay you a great deal of money to advise us and all you do is sit there as if you were dumb".' But afterwards, says Knighton: 'Sir Henry would ask my advice, smile, wheedle. . . . . and I was falling over myself to help him again. He did it with everyone. Those board meetings took years off my life.'

Like many influential Londoners with lower-class roots in the Edwardian era, Norris was sensitive to the fact that London appeared to be unable to compete with the provinces in what had become the national winter sport. For whatever personal reasons, he became determined to create a side capable of competing with the best from the North and Birmingham. His attention first turned to his local club, Fulham, but by 1908 he had obviously become convinced that they would never have a strong enough base for the success he sought.

Though Fulham had not been unsuccessful on the field, they, like Arsenal, were quite poorly supported. By 1910 the Cottagers had an accumulated overdraft of over £3,000 while the Woolwich club were to all intents and purposes completely bankrupt.

Though this was the year Norris took over Arsenal, he remained a Fulham director until the war. His co-director at Woolwich, William Hall, was also Fulham chairman until the same date and the two men obviously controlled both clubs. It was partially because of this that the League later insisted no one could have a controlling interest in two League members.

One may debate why Norris turned to Woolwich Arsenal rather than more promising sides to further his dream. The reasons were probably three-fold. The first was that the obvious alternatives were in the hands of equally autocratic men — Charlie Roberts at Tottenham and Gus Mears at Chelsea — and he was unlikely to wrest control of either club from them. The second reason was the Woolwich club's financial weakness and lack of a strong support base, which he would have known about from the two managers he had poached. And while this was not a long-term advantage, it did render the club susceptible to takeover. The third reason was, in the short term, crucial; Woolwich Arsenal were in the First Division and seemed to have established a relatively safe base there. In 1908 London had only Chelsea and Arsenal in the top Division.

Norris had no doubt been putting out feelers for some time, but it was not until the summer of 1910, with the Gunners having escaped relegation by only a couple of points, that he was able to take control. His initial plan was very simple — he wanted to amalgamate Woolwich Arsenal with Fulham, move them to Craven Cottage and have a First Division team play there. When the League said no, he proposed an even more financially attractive solution — Arsenal and Fulham could play at Craven Cottage on alternative Saturdays. The other London clubs objected and that was turned down as well. The League also pointed out the obvious disadvantages of having one man controlling two clubs (there was technically nothing to prevent this at the time) and Norris was in the position, having failed to achieve either of his objectives, of being informally forced to choose one club or the other.

In the end he came down in favour of the Woolwich club, no doubt because they were still in the First Division. Sadly, this was not to be the case for much longer. After a couple more years of mid-table insignificance, 1912–13 was a disaster. Arsenal finished bottom with only 18 points, 26 goals scored and three wins. The points, goals and wins were all the lowest ever recorded in the First Division and remained

records, though equalled, until the end of the two point system, after which the Stoke side of 1984–85 managed an even more disastrous season. In 1912–13 Arsenal won only one League game at home all season, still a record for any Football League club.

By the end of the 1912–13 season, the club was reported as having only £19 in the bank. The size of the disaster had been clear from the first few matches and Henry Norris and William Hall had been looking for some rapid solution to their plight throughout the year.

Their conclusion was as dramatic as it was simple. If the club was to have any chance of becoming the power in the land that Norris desired, then it would simply have to move.

There were four necessary guidelines for a new location. It should be within greater London so as not to lose all of the support the club had relied upon over the years; it should be in a heavily populated area, preferably not bounded by the river or any other restriction to access (while Arsenal had the river to the north, Fulham also suffered from it being immediately to the south-west); thirdly, it should not be too close to another major club; and, most important of all, it should be very easy to reach by public transport. In 1913 the last point was a prerequisite for any side which hoped to attract really big crowds. Among the open spaces that Hall and Norris negotiated for were ones in Battersea and Harringay, but they found nothing that met all of their requirements. Nor were they to, in the end, accepting that they would probably have to be in the north or west and therefore inevitably close to either Spurs or Chelsea.

Exactly when and how Highbury came into the reckoning is not known. The land in question was actually the site of St John's College of Divinity, but relatively little of it was built upon. Most was taken up by the two football pitches, two cricket pitches and various tennis courts used by the students. The keys to the site, as far as Hall and Norris were concerned, were its availability and the underground station. Negotiations were not exactly easy and went on for several months, Norris bringing all his considerable influence to bear on the very important Ecclesistical Commissioners. In the end, Arsenal paid a massive £20,000 for a mere 21-year lease and agreed not to stage matches on Good Friday and Christmas Day (this restriction was eventually lifted in 1925 when the club paid another £64,000 to buy the whole site outright). The college itself remained at the southern end of the ground until it burned down at the end of the Second World War, after which the large blocks of flats behind the clock were built.

The actual deed of transfer was signed by the Archbishop of Canterbury, but if Norris thought that this implied heavenly blessing for his plans then he was quickly to discover others disagreed. The objections to Arsenal moving to Highbury came from three main sources. The most pre-

dictable was from the other clubs, particularly Tottenham and Clapton Orient, then playing at Homerton. Both were within four miles of Highbury but Arsenal would be closer to the centre and, with that vital underground station, much easier to reach. Spurs had only joined the League five years before and had just spent enormous sums (around £50,000) on improving their ground. The old main stand at White Hart Lane (pulled down in 1981) had been finished only three years before.

Local residents joined in the outcry — it was one thing having a college of divinity on the doorstep, quite another to see it suddenly turn into a football ground. It is impossible to imagine such a transfer being approved today, but at that time there was very little in the way of planning permission required. If there had been, Norris would never have stood a chance, for Islington Council joined with the other objectors on the grounds that football clubs exploited their players for dividend purposes and because the value of the whole area would drop.

Tottenham, Orient, the local residents and even Chelsea appealed to the League Management Committee and a special meeting was

called in March 1913. It went on until two in the morning, by all accounts a not too friendly and highly argumentative debate. To cut a long story short, Arsenal won the day. This was arguably less because the Management Committee agreed with their plans (there is some evidence to suggest that one or two members didn't) than because they concluded they were: '. . . of the opinion that under the rules and practice of the League (we) have no right to interfere.'

Many clubs had moved in the past — very recently Notts County had crossed the Trent to Meadow Lane — but no one had ever objected before and the transfers had usually been local and to everyone's benefit. Nonetheless, the fact remained that clubs had never *asked* to move and the League had never claimed the right to prevent them. It was the club that was in membership, not the ground. Arsenal's case was, by any standards, different. It is only 10 miles as the crow flies from Woolwich to Highbury, but in terms of travelling times within greater London that is very different from Blackburn Rovers or Sunderland moving a mile up the road. In no previous case had there been a clear incursion into a competitor's catchment

Above: **The Manor Ground at Plumstead,** club home from 1893 to 1913. Because the ground was so hard to get to, few pictures of it were taken or survive. These two were taken during a game versus Bolton on 14 September 1912 and are interesting because they show the two stands. Arsenal lost the game 1-2, a familiar enough result as they won only one game at home all season (still a League record), won only three in all, finished bottom of the First Division and amassed only 18 points, also a First Division record until Stoke went one worse in 1984-85. This was the period when George Allison, then the programme editor among other roles, claimed he stood outside the ground with the sparse crowd jollying them to come in, and then rushed inside to shake their hands when they did. If that's true, it was all in vain. At season's end, in April

40

area, nor was there to be again. The only partly comparable example since is South Shields' move to Gateshead in 1930, and by then the League had already acted following the Arsenal furore to prevent clubs moving without permission.

The last first-class game at the Manor Ground was on Saturday 26 April 1913. The opponents were Middlesbrough and Woolwich Arsenal said goodbye to their name, their home and the south-east of London with a 1–1 draw, a rather better result than most that season for they had won only two games in all first-class competitions at the Manor Ground in the previous 12 months.

Woolwich was dropped from the name and, though the club apparently never officially called itself The Arsenal, that was to be the name under which it was publicly known until Herbert Chapman insisted on the single word some dozen years later. Oddly, the official *Football League Fiftieth Anniversary History* said: 'Thus the new Arsenal club was reborn and, on 3rd April of the following year (1914) it was given permission to drop the Woolwich from the name and was henceforth known as "The Arsenal".' This history then went on to point out that Sheffied Wednesday called themselves The Wednesday for many years, thus implying that the club had actually asked to be called *The Arsenal*.

Now the spending really began. In four months the new pitch was levelled (the north end had to be raised eleven feet, the south end lowered five feet), a new grandstand was partly built and turnstiles and terracing installed. It cost Norris another £80,000. Including bank guarantees and loans, by the time the first match was played at Highbury on 6 September 1913 he had found an astonishing £125,000 to put into the club. In 1986 terms that is well in excess of £2 million. Cash was so short that the builder of the stand agreed to take a percentage of the weekly gate in order to pay for its construction.

All Norris had to show for this investment at that time, of course, was a Second Division football team. The first game was against Leicester Fosse and the Reds did well enough, winning 2–1. Scottish international inside left Andy Devine scored the first goal, but it is centre forward George Jobey whose contribution that day has gone down in the history books. He sprained an ankle during the game and was helped off by trainer George Hardy. As there were no dressing rooms or running water (the single stand was not even half built), Hardy decided to take Jobey to the player's lodgings nearby. To do so, and not wanting the player to walk, he borrowed a cart from the local milkman David Lewis, who lived in Gillespie Road (and being Welsh, was known as Lewis the Milk), and Jobey was observed being trundled off home in conditions which were to change rather dramatically in the next 20 years.

All in all, the team did quite well in that Second Division season — finishing third and failing to go up only on goal average behind Bradford Park Avenue. The critical game was the last home match of the season, on 18 April against Clapton Orient, who were sixth in the division. In a bitter hangover from the controversy over Arsenal's move a year before, Orient fought like tigers to draw 2–2. The following week, though Arsenal won 2–0 at Glossop (the Hill-Wood family club), Bradford beat Blackpool 4–1 and were up.

But a far greater shock was about to face Norris. He desperately needed First Division football and seemed to have a team that might achieve it but, within a year of that first game at Highbury, Europe was at war. The result was disaster. Players, particularly the many with Woolwich Arsenal connections, went back to munitions work, others joined the forces, the crowds declined and the League, though it was contested in 1914–15, was something of an irrelevance.

The most notable players of the era were right back Joe Shaw, who was to stay with the club during and beyond the inter-war period as assistant manager and be a critical part of the glories that followed, and his full back partner Bob Benson. Benson was one of the many players who went back into munitions work and therefore lost his match fitness. Having gone to watch the club play at Reading in February 1916, Benson volunteered to take Joe Shaw's place as Shaw himself could not get away from his own job. Benson was clearly unfit, had to leave the field and, having gone to the dressing room, died a few minutes later in the arms of George Hardy. In a sad, but fitting, tribute he was buried in an Arsenal shirt.

Benson's was a personal tragedy and there were many more in that 'war to end wars'. For the club, having taken such a gamble only a year before, the war was a source of total despair. At the end of the 1914–15 season manager George Morrell was unceremoniously sacked to save money and, financially, things just got worse. By 1918 the club was £60,000 overdrawn and Norris was, not surprisingly, again desperate. His five years with Arsenal had so far been nothing but a catalogue of disasters.

On Saturday 24 April 1915 Arsenal had played their last game of the season against Nottingham Forest at Highbury. That very day's programme gave the details of George Morrell's departure and the club's plight. It was to be, nonetheless, their best display of the year, a convincing 7–0 win with Harry King scoring four goals, Jock Rutherford one, and the tragic Bob Benson, less than a year before his death, playing up front and getting two. Beyond that, it was not apparently a match of any great consequence — though one result was that Arsenal just squeezed into fifth place in the division. What no one knew at the time (and who can blame them) was that it was to be Arsenal's last game in the Second Division. Over 70 years later, Arsenal have still to make their next appearance in anything but the highest company.

1913, Woolwich Arsenal shut up shop, abandoned Plumstead, and headed north of the river to the hopes, dreams and destiny of distant Highbury.

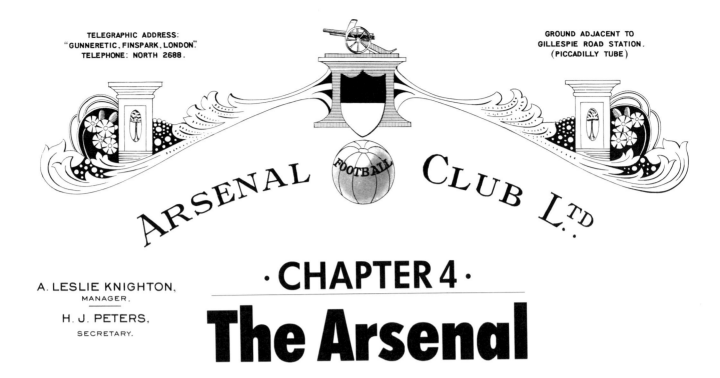

TELEGRAPHIC ADDRESS:
"GUNNERETIC, FINSPARK, LONDON".
TELEPHONE: NORTH 2688.

GROUND ADJACENT TO
GILLESPIE ROAD STATION.
(PICCADILLY TUBE)

ARSENAL FOOTBALL CLUB LTD.

A. LESLIE KNIGHTON,
MANAGER.

H. J. PETERS,
SECRETARY.

· CHAPTER 4 ·
The Arsenal

When the long, terrible conflict known then as the 'War to End All Wars' reached its exhausted conclusion in the November of 1918, first-class football had effectively ceased to exist. Three quarters of a million young British men had been killed, and of those no small number had been professional footballers.

Amid all this, The Arsenal's problems were clearly small ones, but to Sir Henry Norris they were real enough. When the war began the club had been fielding a side which should have quickly fought its way back into the First Division and hence helped with the £60,000 standing debt and Norris' immense £125,000 investment. But those players who survived the war were all five years older and there was absolutely no telling how any club would perform in the season that was to begin in September 1919.

It was at this point that Henry Norris set out on the single most outrageous enterprise ever to be conceived in the history of English football. His remarkable political successes in obtaining Fulham entry to the League and Woolwich Arsenal entry to North London were minnows compared with the audacious whale he was about to float. Nearly 70 years later there is still no convincing explanation of how Norris achieved his object and it is almost inconceivable that any other individual, before or since, could have carried it off at all. Norris's aim, very simply, was to talk The Arsenal back into the First Division.

In 1914–15 the team had finished fifth in the Second Division (for 60 years that League table was invariably copied showing Arsenal finishing sixth but, in actual fact, they finished just above Birmingham on goal average by virtue of that 7–0 win over Forest in their final game). Above Arsenal were Derby, Preston, Barnsley and Wolves. In 1919 it was decided to extend the First Division from 20 to 22 clubs. Extensions of the divisions had happened on several occasions since the League was founded in 1888 and the almost invariable procedure when extending the First Division was to re-elect automatically the bottom clubs from the previous season and promote the top clubs from the Second Division. Given the unfortunate intervention of the war, there seemed every reason to suppose that this is exactly what would happen, and little cause even to discuss it. And this was, indeed, what almost everyone assumed (and were told) would happen.

By chance, two other London clubs, Chelsea and Spurs, had finished nineteenth and twentieth in the First Division in 1915. Showing remarkable stealth and political judgement, Norris used the eight months between the end of the war and the Annual General Meeting in mid-1919 to canvass the other major clubs and various influential friends in the game. He had received his knighthood in 1917 and became a Tory MP in 1918, and one must assume that many were flattered by the attentions of this successful luminary in a game which then had few figures of note outside its own confines.

Norris seemed to have little to work on. But there was just one small chink of hope. At the end of the 1914–15 season it had become obvious that the League would have to be abandoned for the duration of the war. There had been allegations of some match fixing by one or two players (who had bet on the results) and, in one instance, this was proven after lengthy court cases. That particular game was Manchester United versus Liverpool, and United had won it 2–0 to finish 18th, just one point ahead of Chelsea. Though United would have dropped below Chelsea if Liverpool had beaten them, they would still have finished ahead of last

Above: **The official club letter-heading** used from 1921. Apart from the club badge and the pointed reference to the tube station, then called Gillespie Road, the document is interesting for what it does not say rather than what it does. In other words, though the press, public and even the Football League in its official records all insisted on calling the club The Arsenal, clearly Highbury itself was content with plain Arsenal. Herbert Chapman insisted on universal usage of the single word in 1927, intelligently realising that Arsenal would always come first in any alphabetical list of clubs. What he did not foresee was Aldershot joining the Third Division South in 1932. After the Second World War, interestingly, the official name reverted to The Arsenal and new share certificates were issued in that name (information courtesy of Malcolm Davis).

placed Spurs, but the whole business did serve to create an understandable uneasiness that the 1914–15 season was not quite all it should have been. It should be said that there was not the slightest suggestion that Spurs or Chelsea were ever involved in any wrongdoing at the time, and none has ever been suggested since.

What Norris said to the other chairmen has never been revealed, but his desperation for First Division status plus the size of the investment at risk clearly persuaded enough of them that he had a worthwhile case. Leslie Knighton described his chairman's technique at the time thus: 'His influence was enormous. (He would) speak to an important person there, suggesting

a favour, remind a certain financier who was interested that he had once done him a good turn and been promised something in return.'

When the AGM was convened, Norris' strategy became clear. It must have been agreed with League President 'Honest' John McKenna, a close friend of Norris and the owner of Liverpool, in advance. Firstly, Chelsea were detached from Spurs and their position taken separately. There was no vote, and the fact that Chelsea would have finished third from bottom in 1915 had Liverpool beaten United in the fixed match undoubtedly influenced the meeting. McKenna proposed they they be re-elected on the nod and this was accepted. Then Derby and

Above: **The date is 31 August 1913;** the view is from the corner of the North Bank across to the main stand and Avenell Road (which has clearly remained unchanged to this day). Six days later, on 6 September, the club played its first game at Highbury, beating Leicester Fosse 2-1. From the evidence of this picture, it is difficult to see how they managed it.

Right: **Some six months later,** on 14 February 1914, Huddersfield were the visitors in the first of many famous Highbury encounters between the two sides. Though this shot went wide, Huddersfield won 0-1. It was a costly defeat for Arsenal, as even a draw would have seen them promoted at the end of the season. They came third on goal average behind Notts County and Bradford PA. As can be seen, the main stand (actually the only stand until 1932) was now half built, though it had no walls. Massive tarpaulins theoretically kept out the rain. Norris had already spent £125,000 on leasing and levelling the land and was so hard pressed that the builder agreed to take a percentage of the gate receipts each week as his payment. This is one reason why the stand took so long to complete.

Preston, first and second in the Second Division in 1914–15, were elected to the First Division without debate. Then came the bombshell. McKenna, who might have been more reticent given that he was the force behind Liverpool FC, made a brief speech recommending that Arsenal be given the remaining First Division place because of their service to the League and their longevity, particularly pointing out that Arsenal had been in the League 15 years longer than Spurs.

The arguments were, of course, complete nonsense. The League is not run on the basis of the most experienced clubs being given the higher places, and, in any event, Wolves, who finished fourth, had been members of the League four years longer than Arsenal. Spurs chairman Charlie Roberts found it (not surprisingly) very difficult to counter the illogicalities of this Alice in Wonderland meeting in which he had suddenly, unexpectedly and inexplicably become entrapped. The vote was taken; Arsenal got 18 (the League minutes still insisted on referring to them as Woolwich Arsenal), Spurs got 8, Barnsley (who finished third) 5, Wolves 4, Forest (who finished 19th and had no claim to a place whatsoever) got 3, Birmingham 2 and Hull 1. Hence Arsenal were elected and Norris had his First Division club again. It is interesting to note that Arsenal got well under half the vote, suggesting that if Spurs had received advance warning they might have persuaded the five other clubs, who stood no real chance, to withdraw.

To this day it is impossible to explain what went on at that AGM. The most plausible explanation is actually the most irrational; the individual representatives assumed that, if McKenna was prepared to support so unlikely a cause, then he must have some very good, if well-hidden, reason for doing so. If there was such a reason, it has remained very well-hidden indeed, though it would clearly have been assumed to be something to do with the results at the end of the 1914–15 season. For the sake of completeness, it should be mentioned that for many years there were rumours of the involvement of significant sums of money. Nothing has ever been discovered in writing, of course, and there has never been any other documentary proof, so it must remain a mystery.

Paradoxically, it was a conclusion that probably favoured Spurs more than Arsenal. Only six years after failing to prevent the upstart's arrival on their patch, the Tottenham board went back to White Hart Lane pondering the injustice of it all. Their response was on the field. In 1919–20 they scored 102 goals and broke all the records for points (70) and wins (32). Straight back in the First Division, they finished sixth, and won the FA Cup at Stamford Bridge. Until Chapman was bedded in at Highbury, Spurs were clearly North London's leading club. There was, not surprisingly, a heavy residue of bitterness between the clubs, unparalleled before or since in the English game.

In September 1922 a particularly vicious match led to two sendings off (very rare at the time — twenty sendings off in a whole League season was high), censures, suspensions and an FA Commission of Inquiry.

As late as 1928, Arsenal were accused of throwing games at the end of the season to ensure Spurs went down. The games concerned in that 1927–28 season were both at home — a 0–2 defeat by Portsmouth (who finished 20th) on 28 March and, more relevantly, a 0–1 defeat by Manchester United (who finished 18th) on 28 April, the last week of the season. Both those clubs finished one point above Spurs, who had finished their programme early, and if Arsenal had managed even a draw with either Portsmouth or United then Spurs would have stayed up. On the other hand, the table in 1927–28 was astonishingly tight. Seven points covered Derby, who finished fourth, and Middlesbrough, who finished bottom. Arsenal, in 19th place, were only three points ahead of Spurs themselves and would therefore, one must assume, have endangered their own position by such unlikely behaviour. The Gunners rarely got the better of Spurs in the inter-war period anyway; between Chapman's arrival in 1925 and October 1934 Spurs did not once lose at Highbury.

The Arsenal did not exactly enjoy a successful spell for the few seasons after 1919, but at least they stayed where they were. It is a happy coincidence that the centenary is also the point that Arsenal equal the record for the longest unbroken spell of First Division membership. Sunderland stayed there from 1890 to 1958, a run of 68 years. Arsenal's 68th year comes in the second half of the season 1986–87.

Norris had appointed Leslie Knighton as manager in June 1919. Knighton, who had

The moment Henry Norris feared he would never see – Arsenal back in the First Division. Arsenal captain Joe Shaw (left) and his Newcastle equivalent Bill McCracken shake hands before the first post-War First Division fixture at Highbury on 30 August 1919. Arsenal's last League fixture had been four and a half years before in the middle ranges of the Second Division. The club's magical transformation from Second Division also-ran to membership of the elite without touching go is perhaps the most unlikely story in the history of English League football. Shaw, of course, went on to become team manager after Chapman's death, while McCracken retained a close affinity with Highbury. He was manager of the Hull side which, though at the wrong end of the Second Division, reached the semi-final of the FA Cup in 1930 and lead Arsenal 2-0 with only 30 minutes left. At the age of 90 he was invited to a reception at Highbury. Naturally the club offered to arrange hotels and transportation but McCracken politely refused, explaining that he had a breakfast appointment back home the following morning.

This page: **Before and after;** the top picture shows the ground as it was at the time of Leslie Knighton's departure and Herbert Chapman's arrival in 1925. The lower picture was taken just after the Second World War and shows the new East and West Stands. The first North Bank Stand was built in the 1930s but was destroyed in an air raid. The club rebuilt it to an identical design as soon as it could obtain permission (materials were scarce) after the war. Although the terracing looks similar in the two pictures, it was all built up quite considerably before the new stands were erected. One contractor who was dumping rubbish into a hole on the North Bank got too close to the edge and his horse and cart toppled in. It proved impossible to save the injured animal, which had to be destroyed where it lay and was left to be buried in the middle of the terracing. There is one other titbit of interest in the upper picture. Though there appears to be a full house for the game, and though there were no parking restrictions of any sort, there is not a single car to be seen anywhere.

previously had quite successful spells with Huddersfield and Manchester City, was, however, rarely allowed to manage. Among Norris' other edicts, Knighton was not allowed to sign players smaller than 5ft 8in, was not allowed to spend more than £1,000 on anyone (Norris was either not prepared to spend any more money or, more likely, was running short of it), was expected to sign and create a team of purely local players and, to compound all these problems, had to save money by abandoning the scouting system. The task tended to verge on the impossible and the playing record reflects this.

The best position between 1919 and Chapman's arrival six years later was ninth in 1921, the only time the club won more games than they lost. In the Cup Arsenal got beyond the second round just once, in 1922, when they lost to Preston in the quarter-finals after a replay. Knighton's last FA Cup game as manager (and probably one of the reasons behind his dismissal soon afterwards) actually provides one of the funniest stories in football history.

The Arsenal were drawn against West Ham in the first round in January 1925 and Knighton told how he was surprised to be approached by a Harley Street doctor who was also an Arsenal fan: 'I trust you agree that we have a poor chance of survival against West Ham, Mr Knighton,' said the doctor. 'What the boys require is something in the nature of a courage pill. They do no harm, but tone up the nerves to produce the maximum effort.' Knighton investigated the doctor, who was genuine, and his remedy, which did not appear poisonous or illegal, and decided to go ahead. The team were, naturally enough, reluctant. Knighton tried to reassure them by promising to take one of the pills himself. At 2 pm on the Saturday of the match they all took their pills. At 2.50 pm the referee came into the dressing room and told them he'd called the game off because of fog. 'Getting the boys back to Highbury that afternoon was like trying to drive a flock of lively lions,' said Knighton. 'The pills not only left us raring to go but also developed the most red-hot, soul destroying thirst I've ever known. We drank water until I thought the Thames would dry up.'

On the following Monday Arsenal went to Upton Park again and went through the same routine. Down went the pills. . . and down came the fog. The game was called off again. The after effects were the same.

On the Thursday the game finally began, the Arsenal team and their manager having taken their pills for a third time. By half-time the Gunners were running around like maniacs. 'They were giants suddenly supercharged. They tore away with the ball and put in shots like leather thunderbolts. They monopolized the play — and yet they couldn't score. . . For West Ham there was no defence against the pluck-pills. The ball crashed and bounced against the West Ham goal. The Arsenal players ran like Olympic sprinters, jumped like rockets to reach the high ones and crashed in shots from all

Key to photograph above: 1 Ratcliffe **2** Ewan **3** Buckley **4** Counley **5** Jim Peters **6** Bill Smith **7** Lewis **8** Peart **9** Kempton **10** Dunn **11** Wood **12** North **13** Plumb **14** Walden **15** George Hardy (trainer) **16** White **17** Blyth **18** William Hall **19** Sir Henry Norris **20** Jack Humble **21** C Crisp **22** G Peachey **23** Jewett **24** Butler **25** Paterson **26** Leslie Knighton **27** Graham **28** Baker **29** Williamson **30** Bradshaw **31** Rutherford **32** Joe Shaw **33** Hutchins **34** Pagnam **35** McKinnon **36** Hopkins **37** Voysey **38** Rosebotham **39** Rose **40** Groves **41** Greenaway **42** Burgess **43** Toner **44** Tom Whittaker **45** Coupland

The club line-up in 1920.
The picture is unusually interesting because, with the exception of Chapman, all of the major managerial and administrative names of the first half of the twentieth century happen to have come together at the same moment – Henry Norris, William Hall, Jack Humble, Joe Shaw, Leslie Knighton, Tom Whittaker and John Peters.

angles and distances. It is no disparagement to West Ham to say that they had the most incredible luck that half. Sometimes in Cup games, you must have noticed, fortune is completely one-sided.' The game ended as a goalless draw. But Knighton's troubles were only just beginning. 'I forgot my frightful thirst,' he recounts, 'croaking out congratulations and sympathy to the team. But you should have heard them! Running about had made their thirst and bitter throats a thousand times worse. That night those pills created a riot.'

An hour before the replay began at Highbury Knighton took out his box of pills. The team refused point-blank to go through it all again. They drew 2–2. The fifth attempt was at Stamford Bridge. There were no pills and no goals for Arsenal. With the last kick of the game, George Kay scored from a Jimmy Ruffell corner and West Ham won 1–0. The doctor never told Knighton what was in the pills, nor ever offered them again. He remained convinced that Arsenal would have won the Cup had they persevered. Assuming the doctor was right, Knighton would surely have stayed manager, Chapman would

presumably never have come to Highbury, and who knows where Arsenal would be today?

Knighton's team had its strengths, despite the poor playing record. Joe Shaw was still at full back, Scots utility player Billy Blyth was used anywhere and everywhere and Tom Whittaker was a very reliable, highly intelligent, wing half or full back until a knee injury in Woolongong, Australia, while on tour with the FA party, ended his playing career and directed him towards becoming the most famous trainer/ physiotherapist soccer has known. Knighton also made one or two clever and surreptitious signings. Alf Baker, later an England international at right half, signed for Arsenal after Knighton had met him at the pithead in Ilkeston (near Nottingham) to forestall other clubs waiting at Baker's home. Baker was to play in all eleven positions for the club during his career.

Another international who was whisked away for nothing from under the noses of others was Bob John. He came from Caerphilly, where Knighton painted a glowing picture of the glories of the capital (which John was, indeed, later to enjoy with the club) compared with

Cardiff, to whom John was pledged. He was in the Welsh national side within six months. Also from South Wales (though he was born in Bristol) came Jimmy Brain, who was to lead the attack for several seasons. Both Knighton and Peter McWilliam, manager of Spurs, reputedly had to disguise themselves when they visted South Wales because of the anger expressed when the two London clubs had stolen away Jimmy Seed, Cecil Poynton and Bob John, and Spurs were at a crucial disadvantage because all their negotiations for Brain had to be carried out in secret. It was a good time for South Wales football, of course. In 1923–24 Cardiff lost the championship to Huddersfield only on goal average, and would have won it had goal difference been operating then, or if a penalty given ten minutes from the end of their last League game had not been saved by Birmingham keeper Dan Tremelling. In 1925 and 1927 Cardiff were also to reach the FA Cup final, on the latter occasion defeating the Gunners. By that time, Chapman had effectively dispensed with almost all of Knighton's team, the only regular survivors being Baker, John and Brain.

Because of Norris' transfer edicts (he tried in both 1922 and 1924 to get the League to impose a limit on fees of £1,650 — rarely for a League AGM, they chose to ignore Norris' wishes), Knighton also had to indulge in some rather unusual transfers. Dr Jimmy Paterson was an amateur winger with Queen's Park in Glasgow, when his sister happened to marry the Arsenal club doctor, J.L. Scott. Paterson joined Scott's practice (based in Clapton) and also started to play for the club. Added to his then unique appearance (as a Scot) for the Football League against the Scottish League in 1921, he was presumably also the only man to have been a player for the club of which he was simultaneously one of the medical team.

A more celebrated transfer was that of the

Right: **Joe Shaw** at the time he entered the first team as a full back in 1908.

Below: **Forty-five years on,** in 1953, Shaw remained part of the Arsenal set-up. For most of that period he had been assistant manager and had been team manager in reality after Chapman's death in 1934.

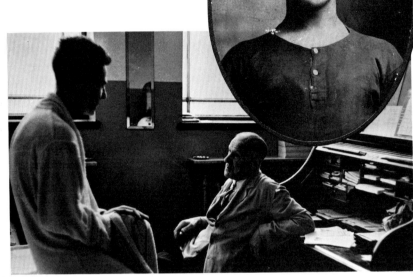

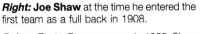

famous 'Midget' Moffat of Workington. Again, this is a story worth telling largely in Leslie Knighton's words.

Knighton had been told about Midget Moffat, the five foot tall Workington winger, by an old Huddersfield colleague, who had also warned him that other sides were beginning to take an interest. But chairman Norris had recently imposed one of his absolute edicts — no small men, all new signings had to be at least 5 feet 8 inches tall and weigh in at a minimum of 11 stone. Nonetheless, Knighton trusted his source enough to go to Workington by an overnight train and watch the player.

The manager was as mesmerised as the opposing full back: '. . . a tiny footballer

Left below: **The infamous Arsenal team bus** which was to begin Sir Henry Norris's slide into obscurity. The chairman is second from left, trainer George Hardy is on his right and manager Leslie Knighton on his left. The complex and lengthy series of FA hearings and High Court cases between 1927 and 1929 actually began with an accusation that Norris had sold the bus (for £125) and the receipts had somehow found their way into his wife's bank account. Norris did not deny this as such, but said it was repayment for the money he paid Charlie Buchan to come to Highbury in 1925 as well as being something of a consideration for the £17,000 the club actually owed him personally at the time (the club probably owed him rather more but whatever the sum it was enormous for the time). Further accusations and allegations followed and in 1929 Norris was eventually drummed out of the game he loved and had so influenced. The accusations were technically correct but essentially unfair. He had certainly done nothing that was not common practice elsewhere in the game. Norris' problem was the number of enemies he had made in various places, particularly with his amazing conjuring trick in 1919, and

Continued opposite ▷

spinning rings around two perfectly competent full backs, a midget with a kick like a horse,' Knighton said later. He immediately offered the player a job but Moffat strangely failed to turn up at Highbury the following day. Knighton arrived at the ground the subsequent morning to find the groundsman waiting for him. 'I've got a little tiny chap waiting for you. Says he's come to play for Arsenal. He's asleep in the dressing room.' And, said Knighton: 'There was Moffat, fast asleep on some kit in a corner, his shock of hair sticking out like a squirrel's tail.' Moffat had arrived at Euston and gone straight to Woolwich, thinking the club still played there (they had moved 12 years earlier). When he arrived it was dark. A road-sweeper explained things, and offered Moffat a lift on his cart all the way to Highbury.

Knighton took Moffat straight off on a continental tour to Scandinavia, where the winger was apparently a great success. Norris, who had been on a summer holiday in Nice, returned at the start of the new season to find a midget in his midst. 'Norris smiled and said nothing,' wrote Knighton, 'but, as always, he got his way. Moffat had to go, to Luton and thence on to Everton.'

Sadly, Midget Moffat rather sums up Knighton's career at Highbury — clever, thoughtful, but bound hand and foot by Norris' peculiar restraints. Whether Knighton would have been a more successful manager in different circumstances is difficult to assess; it certainly seems possible, for he went on to achieve a fair deal with Chelsea and Birmingham.

For his part, it appears that Norris could not work out what was going wrong. As far as we can tell, it doesn't seem to have occurred to him that his restriction on transfers could be affecting the team's potential. He saw the game with an outsider's eye — each of the players seemed good enough, why wouldn't they knit together properly, why did they keep losing by the odd goal? There were other pressures on Norris. As we have seen, Spurs had recovered well from the shenanigans of 1919 and were established as the leading, and best supported, club in the area

(between 1921 and 1925 Spurs finished sixth, second, twelfth, fifteenth and twelfth).

And Norris wasn't getting any younger. If he was ever to do it, to realise the dreams of the past two decades, it would have to be soon. He was no longer an MP, no longer Mayor of Fulham. Highbury had become his career and, in his own eyes perhaps, the remaining symbol to crown a successful life. If Arsenal were ever to achieve anything, there was now only one place to go and one man to go to. All the seeds of Norris' own personal tragedy had now been sown. They were to be reaped in the next five years.

Knighton was dismissed towards the end of the 1924–25 season. In his autobiography, the manager gives his own explanation of the event. Early on in his Highbury days, he had decided to get married. As his future wife lived in Manchester, and a house was available there, Knighton decided to move back north. Norris, according to Knighton, persuaded him to stay by offering his own apartment for Knighton's use (which Knighton accepted) and a benefit game in 1925–26, specifically the Arsenal versus Spurs match that season. This game could be expected to bring in perhaps £3000 to £4000 for Knighton, as a benefit then meant that the player or manager simply kept the takings of a regular season fixture. As it happened, the Arsenal-Spurs match proved to be the first of the 1925–26 season. Knighton believed that Norris fired him simply to avoid paying over the gate receipts of this game. Knighton actually wrote: 'I believe Norris sacked me to get round offering me the big benefit he promised. . . when I tackled him about it, he made it clear I had nothing but a verbal promise, but he offered me £500 "without prejudice".' It is worth mentioning that Norris remembered Knighton in his will nine years later, by which time Knighton appears to have forgiven him.

It is certainly an interesting story, but matters are rarely so simple and it does not ring entirely true. A more likely explanation surely lies in the fact that The Arsenal had been knocked out of the Cup by West Ham in the first round, and had finished 20th in the League. As it happens, they have never finished so low in the 60 years since.

Norris probably approached Chapman in April 1925. The chairman managed one final dig at everything he had railed against with a superfluous advertisement in the *Athletic News* on 11 May 1925. It read: 'Arsenal Football Club is open to receive applications for the position of TEAM MANAGER. He must be experienced and possess the highest qualifications for the post, both as to ability and personal character. Gentlemen whose sole ability to build up a good side depends on the payment of heavy and exhorbitant (sic) transfer fees need not apply.'

It was a final restatement of at least one of his beliefs before they were allowed to rest in peace. From this point on, Arsenal and Sir Henry Norris were in the hands of the first football professional.

· CHAPTER 5 ·
Legendary Arsenal

Herbert Chapman's first few months at Highbury were not exactly uneventful. In the close season the old offside law was changed. Previously to remain onside required three defenders between the frontmost attacker and the goal, and now this was reduced to two. This was in response to the deadening effect of the offside game, refined during the early 1920s by teams such as Newcastle and Notts County. The immediate effect was a flood of goals and a change in tactics which allowed far more goal-scoring in the English game until around the late 1960s. To take one good example of the effect of the change, Huddersfield's first two championships (1923–24 and 1924–25) under Chapman had been achieved with 60 and 69 goals scored. Chapman's two Championships with Arsenal saw the Gunners score 127 in 1930–31 and 118 in 1932–33.

Chapman does not appear to have developed any immediate tactical variations in the light of the new law. His first season started relatively poorly — the very first game was a 1–0 home defeat by Tottenham though this was followed by 1–0 away wins at Manchester United and Leicester. However, on 3 October 1925 came a truly critical match, a resounding 7–0 defeat at Newcastle. This defeat so upset Charlie Buchan, new to Arsenal from nearby Sunderland, that he demanded a tactical change by dropping the centre half (previously the free-ranging link between defence and attack) back between the full backs. The centre half could thus cut out forwards coming through the middle who hoped to exploit having to be behind only one defender rather than two. Apparently Newcastle, with Charlie Spencer at centre half, played this very system during their 7–0 win and Buchan, who had suggested the idea at every Arsenal team meeting since the opening day of the season, clearly thought himself vindicated.

A handshake begins one of the most symbolic games ever played at Highbury. The date was 29 August 1925, the captains Charles Buchan of Arsenal and Arthur Grimsdell of Spurs. It was Chapman's first game as Arsenal manager, Buchan's first as an Arsenal player and the first day of the revolutionary new offside law. A combination of the three, among other things, was to change Arsenal within a decade from First Division also-rans to the greatest side in the world. These things take time though — Spurs won this game 0-1.

Charlie Buchan is beaten to the ball by his old colleague and Sunderland keeper McInroy at Highbury on 20 November 1926. Arsenal lost the game 2-3 with Buchan and Ramsey getting the home side's goals. Buchan, born in Plumstead, had played four games for Arsenal reserves back in the Woolwich days but left over a dispute about 11 shillings (55p) expenses and made his name with the great Sunderland team of the pre-war era. He moved to Highbury in 1925, the transfer fee being perhaps the most celebrated of all time. Sunderland manager Bob Kyle had asked for £4,000, insisting that Buchan may be 33 but he would still score 20 goals in a season. Henry Norris asked Kyle to put his money where his mouth was and accept £2,000 down and £100 for every goal Buchan did score. Kyle accepted and did well on the deal, for Buchan scored 21 and Sunderland made a £100 bonus.

Charlie Buchan was a player Chapman would always listen to, a good example of Chapman's determination to bring the very best players, irrespective of age or price, to his clubs. He had used Clem Stephenson at Huddersfield in the same way in 1920 (Stephenson later took over from him as manager there) and Chapman also took the great Alex Jackson to Leeds Road. At Highbury he paid a record fee for David Jack and eventually captured Alex James, the outstanding schemer of the inter-war period.

Charlie Buchan was Chapman's first purchase at Highbury, and one that was to reverberate round the club for many years. Buchan had actually been born in Plumstead, had watched Arsenal as a boy, studied at Woolwich Polytechnic, and had played four games for Arsenal Reserves. He walked out on the club in 1909 when the notoriously mean George Morrell turned down an expense claim for 11 shillings (55p). He joined Northfleet, then Leyton, and was transferred to Sunderland (after turning down Norris and Fulham) for a massive £1,200 when aged only 18. He played in their Championship side of 1913 and in the Cup final that year, became captain of England and, after his retirement, became a very well known journalist and broadcaster, famous to the post-war baby boom generation for *Charlie Buchan's Football Monthly*. He was nearly 34 when he came to Highbury, and had, a couple of months before, already been the subject of an approach by Leslie Knighton, who had clearly decided to go out with a bang by (unbeknown to Norris) offering £7,000 for Buchan's signature. Buchan's main concern was his sports shop in Sunderland,

from which he took a great deal of income. The maximum wage at the time was only £8 per week and the need for sweeteners and compensations was not uncommon in persuading very good players to move.

Chapman was presumably a much more persuasive negotiator than Knighton, for Sunderland were eventually prepared to consider and accept a much lower fee. The signing has, of course, gone down as one of the most celebrated in football history and is worth recounting. Buchan was serving in his shop in May 1925 when in walked Chapman. 'I've come to sign you for Arsenal,' he told Buchan immediately, and the player assumed he was joking. On being told that Chapman had spoken to the club, Buchan telephoned Sunderland manager Bob Kyle, finding it difficult to believe that the club would release him so easily. It was another ten weeks before he put pen to paper and in the meantime the deal had been thrashed out. It was actually Norris, and not Chapman, who had insisted on handling the financial negotiations. Sunderland had asked for £4,000, but Norris was not prepared to pay that for a 33-year-old player. Norris had originally interviewed Buchan in 1910 when he was chairman of Fulham and Buchan was 18 — Norris offered 30 shillings a week and Buchan insisted on £2 so their paths diverged for 15 years. Kyle argued that Buchan might now be 33 but that he would still score 20 goals in his first season with Arsenal. Norris asked Kyle to put his money where his mouth was — £2,000 down and £100 for every goal scored. Kyle agreed and Buchan scored 19 League goals and two in the Cup. So Kyle got

his £4,000 and £100 interest on top. For Arsenal the deal was a publicity godsend, a ready-made headline every time Buchan scored. The crowd responded as well: 'There goes another £100,' they would chant whenever he got near goal.

Norris must already have given Chapman *carte blanche* on transfer fees, for within a few weeks the manager had also bought the Scottish international keeper Bill Harper from Hibs for £5,000. The Buchan transfer dragged on for those ten weeks because of the player's insistence on somehow being compensated for the likely loss of revenue from his shop.

Chapman, no doubt remembering only too clearly what had happened when Leeds City were suspended in 1919 and how difficult it had been for him to find work afterwards, would not get involved in any illegal payments but, according to Norris, pleaded for the chairman to meet Buchan's demands. The chairman later claimed that Chapman left the room when this delicate point was reached. The scene is interesting to imagine; the chairman, desperate for success and prepared to bend the rules; the manager, sensing and needing success just as much, but frightened to risk his livelihood and reputation again. The payments involved came to light as part of a much wider League commission two years later, which found Norris and William Hall guilty of various financial irregularities (it would be harsh to call them anything worse). Though the hearing was supposedly secret, the *Daily Mail* published the details and Norris sued the FA for libel in suggesting he had acted dishonestly. Norris had a reputation for being quick to take legal action, which he usually won, but in February 1929, the case having gone as high as the Lord Chief Justice, the FA were vindicated and were able to exclude Norris from any further involvement in football. No doubt the cluckings of chickens coming home to roost were heard loud and clear at FA headquarters; the ghosts and resentments of 1913 and 1919 had stalked London football as sharply as any other disagreement in the history of the game and there were many who were anything but displeased at the outcome.

The significant findings of the commission were that between 1921 and 1924 Norris' chauffeur had been paid by the club, and that in 1926 the club had paid for his motor car. During the case, Norris and Chapman clashed, the chairman saying that the manager and club had known about various payments and Chapman (perhaps again with his mind on 1919) denying it. Norris called Chapman a liar and particularly mentioned that £125 for the team bus was the sum he had given to Buchan, under the counter, to come to Highbury. It should be said that Buchan, in his autobiography, disputed this — though only in general terms: 'Let me say here that I made nothing out of my transfer. . . In fact, I lost rather a lot of money through changing quarters like that.' One is, nonetheless, struck by Buchan's careful choice of words, which seem chosen to cloud rather than clarify.

When asked why he had done it, Norris replied very simply and obviously: 'Because (otherwise) we would not have got the players.' It all sounds desperately petty now, but at the time there were many scores to be settled and, in the fashion of a true Greek tragedy, the opportunity was not regretted by some. It was a genuine tragedy for Norris; since 1910, in addition to the money he had found for the club via various business ventures and from his own companies, he had sunk over £15,000 directly from his own pocket and no one could seriously claim that he was alone or unique in his supposed misdemeanours. Most of the leading clubs were doing the same thing one way or another.

During the case Norris declared that: 'I only made one mistake in my career, and that was sacking Knighton.' Leslie Knighton took this as a signal compliment, but in its context one is tempted to believe that it was a none-too-subtle jab at Chapman. Nonetheless as a final epitaph to the man who, almost as much as Herbert Chapman, built the modern Arsenal, we should return to the manager he fired, Leslie Knighton: 'Despite everything,' said Knighton in his autobiography, 'I still say he was the best Chairman I ever had (Knighton managed eight clubs). He did miles more for football and for footballers than the public will ever know. If he had not been (such) a rebel against petty authority he would have risen to the greatest position in the game. A financial genius, football was his hobby and delight, even though only a bagatelle compared with some of his business deals. The game was immensely the poorer for his passing out of it, and it was a tragedy indeed that such a man should have gone under a cloud.' In a sense the greater regret was that the dreams were about to come true — the year after his exclusion saw the first major trophy at Highbury. Norris lived to see the FA Cup and League won before dying, an outcast from the game, just six months after Chapman on 30 July 1934. His estate, £71,733, was still the equivalent of a seven-figure sum today.

The new Chairman was Sir Samuel Hill-Wood, whose family had run Glossop North End before the war as a sort of works team, and with some success. Glossop, in Derbyshire, remains by far the smallest town ever to have hosted a First Division club. Hill-Wood had his own place in the sporting record books already. Playing for Derbyshire versus the MCC at Lord's in May 1900, he had scored 10 runs off a single ball, the highest ever recorded before or since from a single hit. He was content to leave the running of the club to a Herbert Chapman who was no doubt greatly shaken by the court case but mightily relieved at its outcome. It is certainly possible to put down Chapman's relative lack of success between 1927 and 1930, in part at least, to the tensions and pressures created within the club by this long-running and highly emotional affair.

But back to October 1925 and to the team

meeting after that appalling 7–0 thrashing by Newcastle; it was here Buchan persuaded Chapman that centre half Jack Butler had to drop back. The meeting was in the Royal Station Hotel in Newcastle and Buchan had started the debate by refusing to catch the train back to London. 'Oh no,' said Chapman. 'You're playing at West Ham on Monday. I know what you want so let's discuss it.' Buchan outlined his ideas to the team. He didn't actually want a centre half 'policing' the centre forward, rather a man given a geographical 'beat' on the edge of the area. The rest of the defence would wheel around him to provide support. Buchan then pitched hard to be given the now necessary roving inside forward job needed to replace the centre half's attacking role (he described it as being like the fly half in rugby) but Chapman refused, wanting Buchan to continue as a goalscorer up front. There was no other obvious candidate for the job, so Chapman apparently put it to Buchan: 'It's your plan Charlie, do you have any suggestions?' Buchan suggested occasional inside forward Scotsman Andy Neil, who, though not fast ('slow as the post', said Buchan) could kill the ball instantly and distribute it quickly and accurately with either foot. After some argument (obviously everyone's role was affected, and someone had to drop out for Neil) the plan was accepted and Neil took on the role for the following day's match at West Ham. The plan worked perfectly, Arsenal won 4–0 and, for a year at least, they barely looked back. Jimmy Ramsey and then Billy Blyth later took over the link man's job from Neil.

It would not be true to say that the new system was in any sense invented by Buchan and Chapman. As we have seen, Newcastle were already experimenting, as were Queen's Park and several other sides, including Spurs. What Chapman did do, of course, was to refine it and find the players to fit the positions as perfectly as was ever likely to be possible.

He quickly moved his full backs out to mark the wingers (that job had regularly been done by the half backs), dropped a second inside forward back halfway between the midfield line and the forwards, and decided that three very fast moving and adaptable forwards were probably the best attacking answer to the new defensive formations and the revised offside law. This was not developed overnight, but over a period of years, ending with the 3-4-3 or WM formation of the great Arsenal teams. The key was never the scheme itself, but the players who fitted into it.

Chapman had retained relatively few of the men he inherited from Knighton. Alf Baker continued at right half, Bob John for a time at left back and then at wing half. Bernard Joy said of John that: '. . . next to Joe Mercer, he is the finest wing half Arsenal have had and I have played alongside giants like Jack Crayston, Wilf Copping and Archie Macaulay. There was nobody like him for plucking the ball out of the air with his foot, whatever its height or pace, and bringing it to the ground. He did his job quietly,

efficiently and unobtrusively, and there lay his strength.' Charlie Buchan was equally unstinting in his praise of John, whom he regarded as the core of the Arsenal side: 'He deserves a place in any list of famous players. . . yet one rarely hears him mentioned nowadays (this was in 1955). You could depend on Bob in every game but this dapper player was not showy. He just got on with the job.' Bob John eventually played 421 First Division matches (a club record until surpassed by George Armstrong) over 16 seasons, won three Cup medals, three Championship medals and 16 caps. If there was a cornerstone of the great teams, it was surely Bob John.

Chapman moved Jimmy Brain, who had recently been playing as an inside forward, to centre forward and Brain immediately established a new club scoring record with 33 goals in 1925–26. By February 1926 another of the critical influences had arrived — right winger Joe Hulme. Reputed to be the fastest winger in British football, Hulme had previously played for York and Blackburn and eventually won nine England caps, a lot for a winger at the time (it was always one of the obvious, more detached, positions that the selectors liked to change time and again). Hulme was not only the joker of the team, he was also a very good cricketer. The most famous story concerning him was when he was batting for Middlesex against the very fast West Indian bowler Learie Constantine. Hulme had completely missed three consecutive bumpers and, on the fourth, the umpire called: 'No ball.' 'So that's what's happening — I knew something was wrong,' shouted Hulme. He had happier cricketing days — in 1934 he set up a record sixth wicket stand for Middlesex of 212 with Gubby Allen.

All in all, 1925–26 proved to be a successful first season for Chapman. The results were not spectacular, but kept going the right way and Arsenal finished with 52 points, which took them to second place in the League. They never really challenged Huddersfield though, who took their third consecutive Championship and the first ever hat-trick, later to be matched by the Gunners and Liverpool. It would no doubt have surprised their fans and directors to be told, at the moment of their greatest triumph, that Huddersfield would never again win a major prize. Arsenal's 52 points was the most they had ever achieved in the First Division (eight more than in 1920–21) and the greatest number ever achieved by a London club. Second place was also the highest ever reached by a club from the capital, equalling Spurs' performance of 1922.

But if anyone at Highbury thought that here was the brave new world, then they were wrong. Chapman said it would take five years to win a trophy and he was right, though quite why he was right remains elusive despite the speculations about the gathering legal storm clouds over Norris and his manager. The next four years in the League were almost a definition of mediocre — 11th, 10th, 9th and 14th. Perhaps it was because the team was always in a state of flux as

Chapman added to it, or tried to incorporate the skills of a Jack or a James. Certainly it was to continue to be a period of team building.

The next significant purchase was Tom Parker, Southampton's right back. Relatively slow but very good positionally, Chapman particularly wanted him as a steadying, intelligent captain. He played 155 consecutive League games and was easy to pick out (there were no numbers in the League until 1939) because of his bald head. Chapman always had a perchant for miners, not surprisingly given his own mining background, and there were over a dozen on the staff during his regime. One of the most popular was the ungainly but highly effective Jack Lambert, acquired as an inside forward for £2,000 from Doncaster Rovers. Chapman was always trying to find the perfect centre forward and constantly seemed to be buying, or trying to buy, Lambert's replacement. But he always returned to the big fellow and the quest for the ideal was not actually satisfied until after the manager's death, with the arrival of Ted Drake. Lambert stayed with the club after his playing career had finished, going down to Margate to manage Arsenal's nursery club in that town (they played in the Southern League from 1933, winning their sections in 1936 and 1937). Tragically the big centre forward was to be killed in a road accident at the start of the Second World War.

For the other side of the field from Hulme, Chapman originally bought Welsh international Charlie Jones from Nottingham Forest. Jones was a very intelligent, worrying type of player, but an odd choice in the long term for outside left as he lacked speed. Chapman later moved him to right half, where he became a permanent fixture in the great team of the early 1930s. Jack Butler, on the other hand, failed to adapt to his new stopper centre half role, all too often venturing upfield and being caught out of position. In December 1926 Chapman somehow found a tall 21-year-old redhead playing for Oswestry on the Welsh borders and bought him for just £200. Roberts became such a feature of Arsenal's success that he has remained identified forever as the basic mould for the stopper, policeman, centre half. Rarely moving upfield, he performed his central defensive role consistently and effectively season after season.

Roberts was never a particularly skilful player, but he became an essential part of the tactical formation. As Cliff Bastin said: 'As an all-round player he may have had his failings, but he fitted in perfectly with the Arsenal scheme of things. Seldom was it that he wasted a ball. . . Alex James picked up ball after ball from him in midfield.' Roberts rarely scored a goal, though he won the 1932 FA Cup quarter-final at Huddersfield with a totally unexpected header from a corner right at the start of the match. He is also remembered for scoring two identical own goals in the same game for Derby at Highbury. His case is an interesting one for, by everyone's admission, not only was he not a skilful player, he was a relatively poor kicker of the ball.

Whittaker said that: 'Roberts' genius came from his intelligence and, even more important, that he did what he was told.' His orders were to stay in the centre of the defence, to intercept all the balls down the middle and either head them clear or pass them short to a team-mate. 'Because he carried out his orders,' said Whittaker, 'his inability to kick a ball hard or far was camouflaged.'

While 1926–27 was not a notable year in the League, it did end on a high note. After forty years, Arsenal made their first appearance in an FA Cup final. It was, incidentally, Chapman who at this time insisted on changing the common name from The Arsenal to plain Arsenal, arguing that it would mean the club always came first in any alphabetical list — a point which remained valid only until 1932, when Aldershot joined the Third Division South.

In forty years the club had only gone beyond the second round/fourth round stage (i.e. last 32) on four occasions, frankly a dreadful record for a first-class club, so the Wembley appearance was certainly something to celebrate. The run to the final was a tough one. Sheffield United were beaten 3–2 at Bramall Lane, then Port Vale 1–0 in a replay. Liverpool were beaten 2–0 at Highbury in the fifth round (the old first round or last 64 had become the third round in 1925–26) with both goals coming from headers at free-kicks. Wolves also came to Highbury for the quarter-final. Arsenal won the game 2–1, the winning goal being a remarkable one. A Joe Hulme centre was headed straight into the net from around 25 yards by centre half Jack Butler, who was yet to be replaced by Roberts. Arsenal were in the semis for the first time in 20 years and were lucky enough not to have to leave London as they were drawn against Southampton, then in the middle of the Second Division, and the game was played at Stamford Bridge. The Gunners were even luckier to win on a blustery, wet day. Southampton pressed for much of the match but could only score once, late in the match, through their centre forward Rawlings, who had played for England while Southampton were still a Third Division side. By that time Hulme and Buchan had made the game safe.

The final is remembered for three things. One is the very first Cup final radio commentary, the second is Cardiff City taking the Cup out of England for the only time. The third is the tragic goal, the only one of the match, that, in truth, lost it for Arsenal rather than won it for Cardiff. Keeper Dan Lewis, a Welshman himself, had only come into the side for the third round tie at Sheffield. He replaced Bill Harper, who immediately set off for the States in search of fame and fortune (and returned to the club slightly disillusioned four years later). Lewis was also to find fame in the final, but not the kind he would have sought.

It had not been a very good game, played on a greasy pitch with much commitment but little skill. Arsenal had been the better side, winning all of the game's eight corners.

At Stamford Bridge on 26 March 1927, forty years after their foundation, Arsenal finally won a semi-final. Their opponents were Southampton and the goals in a 2-1 success were scored by Joe Hulme and Charlie Buchan. Hulme's goal (*above* – he is out of picture) was the first and is being celebrated by Arsenal players (left to right) Billy Blyth, Jimmy Brain and Syd Hoar.

With just 16 minutes left, Cardiff skipper Fred Keenor took a throw and found his Scots centre forward Hugh Ferguson around 25 yards out. Ferguson advanced and tried a half-hearted, weak ground shot which should have given Lewis no trouble. The keeper did indeed stop the ball but, turning away slightly to avoid the oncoming Ferguson, it slid out of his grasp and under his left arm. Even now the situation was not lost but, in an attempt to gather the ball up again, Lewis turned and simply knocked it with his elbow so that it trickled gently over the line. The film of the incident is appalling to behold — the whole thing happens in slow motion, as if the projector was running at half speed.

Even then the game was not over, for Arsenal were soon to be offered the best chance of the match. Sid Hoar put in a long, high centre. Cardiff keeper Tom Farquharson misjudged the flight, it bounced once and passed over his head. Brain and Buchan both rushed in to nod the ball into the empty net. But as Buchan then describes it: '. . . at the last moment Jimmy left it to me; I unfortunately left it to him.' The ball bounced harmlessly away past a post and, with it, Arsenal's remaining hopes.

After the presentations, Lewis threw his losers' medal to the turf, from where it was retrieved by fellow Welshman Bob John. 'Never mind, you'll have another chance,' said John,

Above: **A delightful picture of the Arsenal** first team taken behind Highbury's southern terracing two days before the 1927 FA Cup final. Left to right: Billy Blyth, Bob John, Horace Cope, Andy Kennedy, Tom Parker, Dan Lewis, Bill Seddon, Jack Butler, Alf Baker, Joe Hulme, Jimmy Brain, Syd Hoar and Charlie Buchan. Horace Cope had been injured two weeks before the final at Huddersfield and was replaced at full back by Kennedy. Though only 5ft 9in, Cope weighed over 13 stone and when he arrived at Highbury from Notts County special shorts had to be made for him as the club had none that would fit. Alf Baker remains unique among all the men who have played for the club in 100 years, for he is the only one ever to have appeared in all eleven positions in first-class games.

Left: **An Arsenal corner** during the 1927 FA Cup final against Cardiff City. The attackers are Buchan, Blyth and, challenging keeper Farquharson, Jimmy Brain. Arsenal won all eight corners awarded in the game, evidence of their dominance in every department except goals.

but he was wrong and Lewis was to be injured just before the 1930 final. The Arsenal team in 1927 was Lewis, Parker, Andy Kennedy, Baker, Butler, John, Hulme, Buchan, Brain, Billy Blyth and Sid Hoar. Grease on Lewis' new jersey was partly blamed for the disaster, and when Arsenal reached the 1930 final Tom Whittaker told Charlie Preedy to wear an old, unwashed jersey rather than a new one. The ritual was observed in all the subsequent finals through the Chapman, Allison and Whittaker eras.

Chapman was not discouraged. He had lost important matches before. The team building continued. The left full back position was something of a weakness, the current incumbents being Horace Cope and Andy Kennedy. To fill the slot, Chapman showed another of his strengths, that of finding rare talents in unlikely places. He had shown this with Roberts and was to show it again with Bastin. Eddie (actually Edris Albert) Hapgood was particularly special because he had played only 12 games for non-League Kettering and in no way looked the part. A 19-year-old milkman who had not been signed at the crucial moment by his home town club, Bristol Rovers, he weighed only 9 stone 6 pounds. Although he was, and remained, a physical

Above and right: **The moment that was to haunt** keeper Dan Lewis for the rest of his life. He had stopped a weak, speculative shot from Cardiff forward Hugh Ferguson in the 1927 final but, somehow, the ball slipped from his grasp and gently rolled towards the line. Turning to gather it, he caught the ball with his elbow and knocked it over the line. The time the virtually slow motion incident took can be judged from the positions of Tom Parker in the two pictures. The Cardiff forward is not Ferguson, but winger Len Davies. It was the only goal of the game and the only occasion the Cup has ever left England. Lewis was himself a Welshman and lost his chance of retrieving his reputation when he played right through to the semi-final stage in 1930 but was injured before the final. Grease on his jersey was blamed for the error, but the belief that Arsenal always wash new jerseys before a final is not accurate. What Tom Whittaker insisted afterwards was that the keeper should wear an *unwashed* (and hence ungreasy) shirt.

fitness fanatic, he was relatively weak and was often literally knocked out when heading the wet, heavy, leather ball of the period. Arsenal invested heavily in their £750 signing, Tom Whittaker forcing the ex-vegetarian to eat steaks and build up both his strength and weight. A few years later, after an accident in which Hapgood had been burned quite badly, Tom Whittaker built a special leather harness for his body so that he could play without the burns rubbing the whole time, proof of Hapgood's remarkable physical courage and unswerving commitment to the game and to the club.

It was sad that Hapgood eventually became rather estranged from the game. His relations with Allison were never as good as with Chapman, and between him and Whittaker strains gradually developed as they appeared rivals for future senior roles at the club. This was a great pity, as Hapgood had written in 1944 (before Whittaker took over from Allison as manager) that: 'Tom Whittaker has, perhaps of all the people who helped me at Highbury, been my closest friend.' Hapgood was later manager at Blackburn, Watford and Bath but, after losing the Bath job in 1956, he asked Arsenal for a retrospective benefit and was very upset when the club was unable to agree. In his commitment and obsession

Left: **Joe Hulme cuts in to score** from the right wing past Sheffield United full back Green on 3 September 1927. Note that the letters have been removed from the stand. Arsenal won the game 6-1, but lost the return four months later 4-6. Hulme was the fastest winger in the game in the 1920s and it was the use Chapman made of his two outstanding wingers (Bastin was the other) which was really the key to Arsenal's unstoppable style in the early 1930s. Apart from his speed, sense of humour and cricketing ability (he played for Middlesex), Hulme was noted for his trick of flicking the ball back over his shoulder and then immediately backheeling it forwards again for him to run onto.

with physical fitness there was a boyish naivety which was best illustrated on his very first trip to Highbury after Chapman had signed him from Kettering. On the train journey he lost his whole signing on fee (£10) to a gang playing the three-card trick. In some ways, it was a lesson he never entirely benefitted from.

Whatever else he now had, by 1927 Chapman clearly felt he lacked the great names and, with the exception of perhaps Buchan and Hulme, the great players. His two great transfer coups were still to come — David Jack and Alex James. The David Jack story has been told so often that it has become part of soccer folklore, but no doubt it bears repetition.

By 1928 David Jack was one of the great names of English football. A cultured, stylish (he used to turn up at the ground in spats) inside forward, he was one of those rare animals, an automatic choice for England. He had scored the first ever goal at Wembley, in the 1923 Cup final, and won winners' medals with Bolton in that year and again in 1926. Bolton were one of the handful of top teams at the time, but in the close-season of 1928 informed other clubs that they would consider offers for any player, excepting only David Jack. Chapman and George Allison went to Bolton to see their board, initially meeting a blank refusal. Eventually, however, the question was asked: 'How much would we have to offer for you to change your minds?' Bolton, probably to get Chapman and Allison to go away, said £13,000 — almost double the existing record.

Allison and Chapman returned to the Midland Hotel in Manchester for dinner, eventually invited the Bolton chairman and secretary to join them and haggled until the small hours. In the

end an offer of £11,500 plus the accrued benefit to be paid to Jack was accepted (players then received a benefit after five years, but if they left a club after, say, three years, they could be given a sum to represent three fifths of what they might have expected to receive). Oddly, the fee is usually quoted as £10,670 or £10,890, but all the parties agree in their memoirs that it was £11,500. David Jack was roused from his bed and belatedly asked his opinion. After talking to his father (then the Plymouth manager) he was amenable and agreed to come to London the following day to sign.

That day was coincidentally the first time Bob Wall had ever been involved in a transfer. He had just been taken on as secretary/assistant to Herbert Chapman. Wall takes up the story as he and Chapman headed off for the Euston Hotel to meet the Bolton party off the Manchester train: 'We arrived at the hotel half-an-hour early. Chapman immediately went into the lounge bar. He called the waiter, placed two pound notes in his hand and said: "George, this is Mr Wall, my assistant. He will drink whisky and dry ginger. I will drink gin and tonic. We shall be joined by guests. They will drink whatever they like. See that our guests are given double of everything but Mr Wall's whisky and dry ginger will contain no whisky and my gin and tonic will contain no gin".' According to Bob Wall, their guests were in a cheerful mood by the time the deal was finalised and were not inclined to question anything further.

Charlie Buchan had by now retired, his last game being the famous 3–3 draw at Everton on 5 May 1928 when Dixie Dean got a hat-trick and broke the League scoring record with 60 goals in a single season. Without Buchan, Chapman

Above: **The classic Arsenal golfing party** of the great years – Tom Parker, David Jack, Herbert Chapman and Alex James. The picture was taken at Hatch End on 14 November 1929. It was not a good period for the club – they were to win only three of their next 16 League games but had still, by season's end, won a first major trophy and laid the foundations for the decade that was to follow.

lacked a commander on the field. There was actually no obvious candidate whom Chapman could pay the earth for. David Jack was Buchan's counterpart in goalscoring ability, but not as a leader, the intelligence on the pitch. As Bernard Joy rightly pointed out, the way the Arsenal system had developed, the key man had become the foraging inside forward, the centre of the W, the man who picks up clearances from the defenders and sends the forwards away. Clem Stephenson had done a similar job for Chapman at Huddersfield, but there were very few players in the game with either the technical or strategic skills, never mind both.

One player who did have the vision was Alex James, the creator behind the Scots Wembley Wizards of 1928, infamous 5–1 humiliators of England. He had gone from Raith to Preston, where he was less a schemer than an attacking inside forward. In four years there (admittedly in the Second Division) he had scored 60 goals and he was known to have often commented along the lines of: 'I'm never going to chase an opponent in possession.' In June 1929 Preston, surprisingly, put him up for sale. Maybe they decided that being known as 'Alex James and the other ten' was not good for the club in the long run. Chapman beat most of the big clubs — including Villa, Liverpool and Manchester City — for his signature.

George Allison said of James: 'No one like him ever kicked a ball. He had a most uncanny and wonderful control, but because this was allied to a split second thinking apparatus, he simply left the opposition looking on his departing figure with amazement.' The small size of the transfer fee (£8,750) was such a surprise that the Football League held an inquiry before

Arsenal were allowed to register James. With so many clubs interested it had naturally been assumed that the fee would break the David Jack record, and the Lancashire clubs, possibly with the recent Norris case in mind, were muttering about inducements. The inquiry showed Arsenal were completely clean — all they had done was to help find James a job in Selfridge's, the London store. But even the inquiry had more to it than met the eye. Chapman knew he would face rumours about the impending transfer (he had already secretly obtained James' signature) and it was actually the manager himself who quietly asked the League to set up the inquiry. He then publicly insisted he would not sign James (something of a deceit) until *after* such an investigation.

It could not be said that James was the perfect club man. It took a season for him to settle in to his new role, after which he virtually gave up scoring goals. Chapman always treated him slightly differently from the other players (he was allowed to stay in bed until noon on matchdays, for instance). Alex was the key, that was the message; and it is certainly true that the side did not win anything before James arrived but started winning everything soon afterwards.

Chapman's patience was, nonetheless, sorely tested. In the summer of 1931 James refused to re-sign, presumably looking for some sort of extra inducements. In August the club sent him on holiday, then Chapman called him back saying the club had decided to despatch him on a cruise instead. He hurried back to London Docks, only to find that Chapman had booked him a berth on a banana and general cargo boat. John Peters, the assistant secretary, somehow persuaded James to go on board and he was finally released in Bordeaux. He always claimed to have quite enjoyed it. James eventually signed the week before the season began. When the team, who were training, heard the news they raided the Arsenal band room and serenaded James into the ground by murdering 'See the Conquering Hero Comes.' More serious was James' failure to turn up at the celebration banquet after the Championship success of 1933. He had refused to go to Belfast to play Cliftonville in the last week of the season and was dropped. As club captain he should have received the trophy from League President John McKenna (the same man who had done so much to help put Arsenal where they were 14 years before). James' place was left empty and Charlie Jones accepted the award as vice-captain.

James is probably one of the ten or so greatest players in British football history — ranking alongside the likes of Matthews, Greaves, Charlton, Bloomer, Morton, Best, Blanchflower and Goodall. It is always necessary to ask whether such players would be as great in another age. The philosopher Hegel, in a rather profound answer to the question, said: 'The great man of his age is the one who can put into words or actions the will of his age, tell his age what its will is, and accomplish it. What he does is the heart and essence of his age.' Hegel was speaking of the great statesman, but on the narrower canvas of a football field Alex James *was* the heart and essence of his age. Arsenal were the team of the era, and James was the heart of the team, the definition of football success. Without him the style, the system and the successes would probably never have been achieved. Whether James would have done as much in another era is an interesting point. Some of the greats would arguably not have achieved as much at a different time — Matthews in the 1970s, for instance — but James was probably a player for any age and every era.

All of this is probably rather peripheral to the essential truth about Alex James — that at the critical time he was the hub of the whole team. He foraged so far back that he was no longer an inside forward, and Bastin therefore had no one inside him for most of the time. For many teams this would have caused problems, but for Arsenal it was an encouragement to develop different moves. The classic was the James/ Hulme/Bastin triangle. James, often facing his own goal, would hit a long pass up the right wing. Hulme would race past the defence, and hit his centre way over to the left for Bastin either to shoot or dribble in on goal. Up the middle would steam Lambert, looking for any crumbs that might fall from the table. In 1932–33 Bastin and Hulme scored 53 goals between them, perfect evidence that Arsenal did play the game very differently from their con-temporaries, who tended to continue to rely on the wingers *making* goals for the centre forward, rather than scoring themselves. By playing the wingers this way, Chapman was able to have one more man in midfield, and thus control the supply of the ball, primarily through James. But it was only possible because both wingers were exceptional footballers — Hulme because of his speed and Bastin because of his tactical brain and coolness. Bastin's calm was legendary. Tom Whittaker said of him in 1950: 'Coupled with his sincerity and his loyalty to all his bosses, he had a trait few of us are blessed with — that is, he had an ice-cold temperament.'

Boy Bastin was the very last of the major signings, coming a couple of weeks after James. Bastin is very amusing on his first meeting with the Scotsman. James was already a star, while Bastin was hoping just to play for the reserves. James came up and introduced himself to Bastin in an accent which, Bastin says: 'I have never heard rivalled, before or since. I must confess,' Bastin goes on, 'that my chief reaction, apart from feeling rather more at home than I had a few moments earlier, was of trying to understand just what Alex was saying. Alex and I may have developed a well-nigh perfect understanding on the field, but off it I always found him a trifle incomprehensible.' Bastin knew him well of course, and had enormous admiration for the man, particularly for his self-confidence. 'Nobody had greater faith in the qualities of Alex James than Alex James himself — not even

Herbert Chapman, and that is saying something. Alex needed all his self-confidence during his first few months at Highbury, for he was very slow to settle down.'

As part of the settling down process, James further established his own trademark — the baggy shorts. They were apparently not his idea at all. Cartoonist Tom Webster drew him playing for Preston in the *Daily Mail* one Monday with rather long shorts, possibly to emphasize James' small stature. James liked the idea, and insisted on going out to buy a pair to fit the cartoon. They also kept his knees warm, he would tell admirers.

By 1930 James was indeed beginning to fit, but there must have been frustration in the boardroom as well as on the terraces. In five years under Chapman, Arsenal had spent a fortune but the world remembered them only for an excruciating goal in the 1927 Cup final and a chairman permanently banned from the game.

It is interesting to speculate what would have happened if Chapman had died exactly four years earlier, in January 1930. Certainly his own reputation would have been dramatically lessened, his days at Huddersfield perhaps questioned as a peculiar fluke or the work of Clem Stephenson (just as Jimmy Seed was, at that very moment, receiving the credit for Sheffield Wednesday's Championships of 1929 and 1930).

But would the team have gone on to greatness in the 1930s? Who can say, but in the last month of the 1920s no one would have predicted anything very much for the club, Chapman or not. The season had begun so badly that relegation looked the only sort of news Arsenal were likely to make. The forward line (now temporarily including David Halliday from Sunderland for £6,000) had cost £34,000, by a mile the most expensive in football history, and yet it couldn't score goals. But perhaps there was something magic in that new decade, in the rather less than celebrated (away from Highbury at least) 1930s. For it was the turn of the year, the passing of the 'gay twenties', that was the turning point for Arsenal. In the League they achieved no more than respectability (finishing 14th), but in the Cup they truly achieved glory.

The second week of the new decade saw the third round of the FA Cup. Arsenal drew Chelsea at Highbury, never an easy game. Chapman made a courageous decision, possibly the most difficult in his career, and dropped James. If the team wasn't scoring with the class of forward they had, then it had to be the provider who was at fault. Halliday was also dropped, in came John, Thompson and Lambert. Arsenal won 2–0 in a rainstorm. Two weeks later Chapman simply ordered James to bed. The Scotsman had always suffered from a form of rheumatism in the ankles, which made it difficult for him to play golf, and Chapman felt James needed a complete rest. In the fourth round Birmingham (who reached the final the following year) came to Highbury and went

away with a 2–2 draw. Leslie Knighton was now their manager and Chapman knew the replay would be a tough one. If Arsenal lost it, then the whole season would have gone and Chapman's judgment on his big signings could only come into serious question.

Bernard Joy, who was with the team in the 1930s and whose opinion has always been highly respected, argued in 1952 that Chapman's decision after the first Birmingham game that Saturday night, 25 January 1930, was the turning point in the modern history of the club. Thirty-three years after Joy, one has not only to agree but to go further; it was, with the semi-final a few weeks later, probably the most critical moment in the whole hundred years.

Chapman had to win the replay at St Andrew's the following Wednesday. On the Sunday morning he went round to Alex James' home, got him out of bed and took him off to Highbury for training. Chapman gambled that James would react to the crisis, to the obvious placing of responsibility on his shoulders. It worked, not spectacularly, but it worked. Alf Baker scored from the penalty spot, the only goal of a hard game. The fifth and six rounds were no easier — a 2–0 win away at Ayresome Park and a convincing 3–0 win at West Ham, banishing memories of the pep-pill farce of five years before. The semi-final looked easy — Hull City at Elland Road. Hull were at the bottom of the Second Division and were relegated to the Third a month later. It was also their first semi-final. Quite what they were doing there was anyone's guess, but most knowing observers put it down to the wily management of Bill McCracken, the full back who had perfected the offside game ten years before. All the interest was in the other semi-final between the two Yorkshire giants, Huddersfield and League Champions Wednesday (between them they had won five of the seven most recent championships). This was indeed to

be a famous match; with Huddersfield leading 2–1 a Wednesday shot entered the net just as the whistle blew for full time. The referee disallowed the goal but many of the crowd went home not knowing whether there would be a replay or not.

Back at the supposedly less interesting semi-final at Elland Road, shocks were in store. After 15 minutes keeper Dan Lewis cleared a ball from the edge of his area. It was a poor kick, travelling only 30 yards or so, and it went straight to the Hull inside left Howieson. He lobbed it straight back on the volley and it flew over Lewis' head into the net from a full 45 yards out. After 30 minutes Eddie Hapgood sliced a Duncan shot into his own net and Arsenal were 2–0 down at half-time. In the second half, the goals just wouldn't come. And it was not until twenty minutes from the end that whichever gods control football ended their little joke. Those last few minutes are among the most important in the club's history, and they bear a remarkable similarity to the last minutes of the 1971 semi-final against Stoke at Hillsborough, when the Gunners also came back from a 2–0 deficit with two Peter Storey goals and went on to perform the Double. In both 1930 and 1971, the semi-final result was vital to the history of the club, just as vital as the finals themselves.

Firstly Alf Baker got Joe Hulme away on the wing, he crossed and David Jack finally defeated McCracken's offside trap and converted the centre. Twelve minutes later Cliff Bastin picked up a ball from Alex James, took on the defenders in a solo run and hit the ball into the top right-hand corner. Arsenal were unlucky not to get a third, but the teams met again for a midweek replay at Villa Park. Hull seemed bitter about being robbed so late in the first game and the tackling was fierce. So much so that, in the second half, the Hull centre half Arthur Childs became the first (and for another 50 years the only) man to be sent off in a semi-final. He was despatched for taking a kick at Jack Lambert. That was the end for Hull. Soon afterwards Joey Williams (taking the place of the injured Hulme) hared off down the right wing, pulled the ball back from the goal-line and David Jack connected with a right-foot volley to score the game's only goal. Arsenal were at Wembley for the second time in four years, Huddersfield were there for the fourth time in a decade.

The defeat of Hull seemed to lift a great weight from the Arsenal attack. Two weeks before the Cup final the Gunners ran up their biggest First Division win to date, 8–1 over Sheffied United (they were to equal this margin against the very same team three years later). And five days before the final they set yet another record when, having been 3–1 down at half-time, they eventually drew 6–6 at Leicester. It remains the highest scoring draw in any English first-class game, having only been equalled by Charlton v Middlesbrough in 1960. Oddly Lambert's deputy, David Halliday, had an excellent game at Leicester, scoring four times to justify his remarkable record at Sunderland, where he had recorded 155 goals in 167 matches. But the centre forward spot was firmly Jack Lambert's by now, a decision that was to be fully justified five days later at Wembley.

The final against Huddersfield (for all the details of the game see the first chapter of this book) was formally the start of the great decade, but it was the following year that has always been known as the great season. 1930–31 saw the establishment of the record points total for a Championship side (66 — later to be surpassed by Leeds United under the now defunct two-point system), and the remarkable total of 127 goals scored would have then been, and remained for all time, a First Division record had Aston Villa not, incredibly, scored 128 the same year. In London, Birmingham and elsewhere it was a wonderful season for spectators.

The season was a massive success for the Gunners from start to finish. The first two games were away, at Blackpool and Bolton. They were both won 4–1. Arsenal were not defeated until their tenth game, at the Baseball Ground against one of the consistently best sides of the 1930s, Derby County. Despite Arsenal's tremendous performance through the whole season, strangely they were never clear of challengers and were not sure of the trophy until two weeks before the end of the contest, when Liverpool went down 3–1. Villa were, of course, the biggest threat, countering a 5–2 defeat by the Gunners at Highbury with a 5–1 win at Villa Park and the friendly rivalry between the clubs was marked by Villa's attendance at the season's end celebration banquet. Villa were also the first opponents in the Cup, and went 2–0 up at Highbury before Lambert and Jack forced a draw. Arsenal played well to win the replay 3–1 but surprisingly went out 2–1 at Stamford Bridge. It certainly was a surprise — Arsenal had beaten Chelsea there 5–1 in the League in November. Though a disappointment, it did not upset the team. Four days later they beat Grimsby 9–1 at Highbury, still their biggest ever First Division win (they also beat Sheffield United 9–2 in 1932–33) and, a week later, won 7–2 at Leicester, to make it

The 1930 semi-final against Hull at Elland Road on 22 March was to be a traumatic day. Two down at half-time, Arsenal pressed for the whole of the last 45 minutes against a packed Second Division defence which denied (*bottom left*) Jack Lambert's header and (*bottom right*) Cliff Bastin's shot. David Jack eventually broke the deadlock by converting a Joe Hulme cross but it was not until eight minutes from time that the draw was safe. Cliff Bastin, the scorer, tells the story: 'I hadn't even touched the ball for 20 minutes and it was agony standing on that wing when we needed a goal so badly. Then Alex James gave me the ball. I took it past Mills, the Hull right half, and cracked it into the top right hand corner of the net.' The last few minutes of that game were among the most important ever played by the club. The similarity they bear to the dying moments of the semi-final against Stoke at nearby Hillsborough in 1971, and their comparable importance, is uncanny.

13 goals in consecutive appearances at Filbert Street.

The Gunners lost only four games in all, and their home and away records were identical — 14 wins, 5 draws and 2 defeats. The team for the final game of the season is probably the one that is best remembered as the great team of the whole era — Ted Harper in goal, Tom Parker and Eddie Hapgood at full back, Herbie Roberts at centre half, Charlie Jones and Bob John at half back, Joe Hulme and Cliff Bastin on the wings, Alex James, as the provider, David Jack and Jack Lambert up front.

Harper had just returned from his four year sojourn in the United States, and was re-signed. He replaced Dutchman Gerry Keyser, a wholesale fruiterer who was an amateur with both Arsenal and Charlton. Cliff Bastin described Keyser as mildly crazy: '. . . Gerry was utterly reckless, whether between the posts or crouched behind the wheel of one of the huge American cars which were his heart's delight.'

Jack Lambert was now reasonably established as Chapman's first choice, and the manager let David Halliday go to Manchester City in November. The first of the two meetings between Arsenal and Villa at Villa Park in the 1930–31 season was the celebrated occasion when the Midlanders' magnificent England international centre forward Pongo Waring cheerfully taunted Chapman with his obsession for buying centre forwards: 'I bet you'd like to get me Herbert, wouldn't you?' said Waring. And Chapman would have, for Waring was the best in the country until Drake came along, but

he was also one of the few players Chapman could never manage to get his hands on. Underrated Jack Lambert actually set up an Arsenal record in 1930–31 with his 38 League goals, though this was soon to be beaten by Drake.

Those eleven names for the last game of 1930–31 would certainly have to be supplemented by one or two others to complete the real first-class roll of honour for the era. The three obvious omissions are George Male, Wilf Copping and Frank Moss. Male became Hapgood's full-back partner late in 1932 before Tom Parker went to Norwich as manager. Male actually played in the 1932 Cup final in his normal position, left half, but with Parker ready to retire Chapman needed a replacement and selected Male, who already had a reputation for all-round skill, strength and steadiness. Male told how Chapman called him into his office and astonished him by explaining how Male was about to become a right back. Chapman was so convincing about Male's skills that, said Male: 'I wasn't only convinced I was a right back, I knew I was the best right back in the country!' And so it proved, Male eventually taking over the England captaincy from Hapgood. He played his first game at right back on 15 October 1932 and within months he had been chosen for an international trial. Bernard Joy argued that the success of the Male/Hapgood combination was a matter of contrasts: 'Hapgood was enthusiastic, volatile and poised, the born captain. Male was determined, rugged and fast in recovery; as a person quiet, retiring and modest, the ideal first mate.' Not only did they both captain England,

Arguably the most important goal in the history of Arsenal Football Club. The only goal of the game, it was scored by David Jack in the second half of the semi-final replay against Hull at Villa Park on Wednesday 26 March 1930. Joey Williams, deputizing for Joe Hulme, ran the ball down the right wing right to the touchline and crossed for Jack (centre) to volley right-footed into the left-hand corner of the net past keeper Gibson. Williams had overrun the goalline and is out of the picture to the left. On the right, arms aloft, is centre forward Jack Lambert. A few minutes earlier, Hull centre half Arthur Childs had aimed a kick at Lambert and been sent off for his pains. Childs thus acquired the sorry distinction of being the only player ever sent off during an FA Cup semi-final or final in the first 100 years of that competition. The goal took Arsenal to the 1930 final, their first major success, and onto the decade that became theirs. The story of Arsenal remains essentially a story of the 1930s and the tie against Hull was, in retrospect, the moment of truth at the beginning of that decade. Had they fallen at this hurdle, 2-0 down at Elland Road, then it is entirely credible to argue that the whole history of the club would have been very different. The importance of David Jack's volley, of Joey Williams' brief appearance on centre stage, can never to minimised.

SPORTS GUARDIAN

16

FA CUP COMMENTARY: David Lacey

Arsenal: Nation mourns

JUST before teatime on Saturday the news spread rapidly through the press boxes, press rooms and those dingy corners of football grounds where men with notebooks await the pleasure of men with words to fill them.

Even the strong-minded struggled to hide their emotions. There was a trembling of lower lips and a hasty simulation of coughs. Some gave up altogether and turned away, shoulders heaving. But sooner or later the fact had to be faced : Arsenal were out of the FA Cup.

Unluckily too by all accounts, their predictable goalless draw at Goodison Park

because of who they are and what they are, and following their easy dismissal of Altrincham their position will only be affected if they are given a difficult away tie in today's fourth round draw.

Visits to Southampton and West Bromwich Albion would fall into this category and Manchester City's form is such that even they might be able to sake off their perennial of Liverpool su them a h Saturday United in thi have at the hapless

ing football of such high quality that it appears they have just invented the sport and are introducing it to natives who are allowed only the occasional glimpse of a strange, white, round object that appears to be controlled by invisible wires.

Often, however, this period of supremacy is noth

Shaw to Withe, who promptly collided with the 6ft 4in defender and laid him out. On being revived Butcher had to change his ripped shirt and in doing so bared to the audience two ugly weals on the back which suggested that he had either offended the seventh Earl of Cardigan or been

several years the cover was identical with no mention of the participants) and Newcastle again in 1952 (*bottom right*) were all controversial defeats.

The 1936 success against Sheffield United (*right*) was a happier moment. The Gunners also appeared in two lesser known Wartime Cup finals at Wembley. In 1941 they played Preston in front of 60,000 people and drew 1-1 (Denis Compton

scored the goal) though the replay was lost 1-2 at Blackburn. In 1943 75,000 turned out to see Arsenal crush Charlton 7-1 in the Southern Cup final. Reg Lewis scored four, Ted Drake two and Compton got the other. They lost the play-off to Northern champions Blackpool 4-2.

***Top left:* After another FA Cup defeat,** in the third round against Everton on

3 January 1981, *The Guardian*'s David Lacey beautifully encapsulated half a century of 'Lucky Arsenal'. In just one headline and two paragraphs, Lacey summed up the provincial attitudes which were born in the 1930s and have never entirely died. Arsenal had reached the previous three FA Cup finals, the first club this century to achieve such a hat-trick.

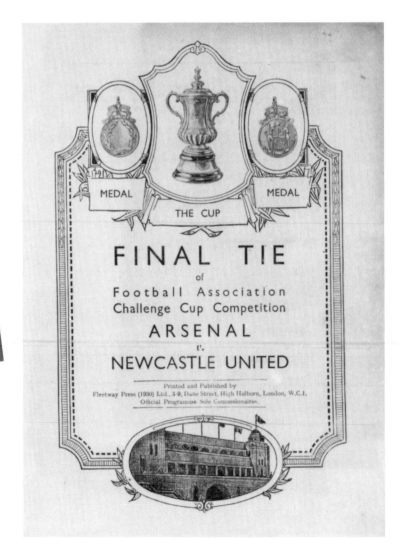

A selection of some of the programmes from Cup finals which featured Arsenal. By 1986, the Gunners had appeared in 15 major finals (eleven FA Cup, two League Cup, two European) but had won just six of them. It is interesting

to compare this record with that of Spurs, who have won far fewer Championships but succeeded in twelve out of fourteen Cup finals. The games against Cardiff in 1927 (*bottom left*), Newcastle in 1932 (*right*, the inside page as for

FINAL TIE

OF THE
FOOTBALL
ASSOCIATION
CHALLENGE CUP
COMPETITION

AT THE

Empire Stadium Wembley

SATURDAY, APRIL 25th, 1936

ARSENAL
v.
SHEFFIELD UNITED

Kick-off 3 p.m.

OFFICIAL PROGRAMME SIXPENCE

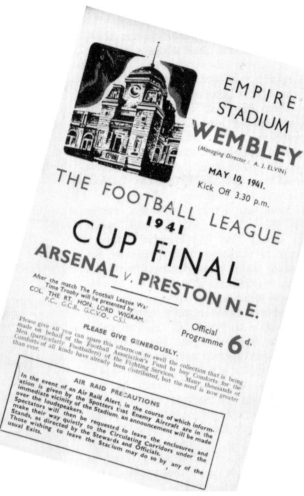

EMPIRE
STADIUM
WEMBLEY

(Managing Director : A. J. ELVIN)

MAY 10, 1941.
Kick Off 3.30 p.m.

THE FOOTBALL LEAGUE
1941
CUP FINAL
ARSENAL v. PRESTON N.E.

After the match The Football League War
Time Trophy will be presented by
COL. THE RT. HON. LORD WIGRAM.
P.C. G.C.B. G.C.V.O. C.S.I.

Official
Programme 6d.

PLEASE GIVE GENEROUSLY.

Please give all you can spare this afternoon to swell the collection that is being
made on behalf of the Football Association's Fund to buy Comforts for the
Men (particularly Footballers) of the Fighting Services. Many thousands of
Comforts of all kinds have already been distributed, but the need is now greater
than ever.

AIR RAID PRECAUTIONS

In the event of an Air Raid Alert, in the course of which information is given by the Spotters that Enemy Aircraft are in the
immediate vicinity of the Stadium, an announcement will be made
over the loudspeakers. Spectators will then be requested to leave the enclosures and
make their way quietly to the Circulating Corridors under the
Stands, as directed by the Stewards and Officials.
Those wishing to leave the Stadium may do so by any of the
usual Exits.

EMPIRE
STADIUM
WEMBLEY

Managing Director : A. J. ELVIN

SATURDAY, MAY 1st, 1943
Kick-off 3.0 p.m.

FOOTBALL LEAGUE (SOUTH)
WAR CUP FINAL
ARSENAL
v.
CHARLTON
ATHLETIC

OFFICIAL PROGRAMME SIXPENCE

AIR RAID PRECAUTIONS

In the event of an Air Raid Alert, in the course of which information is given by the Spotters
that Enemy Aircraft are in the immediate vicinity of the Stadium, an announcement will be
made over the loudspeakers. Spectators will then be requested to leave the enclosures and
make their way quietly to the Circulating Corridors under the Stands, as directed by the
Stewards and Officials. Those wishing to leave the Stadium may do so by any of the usual Exits.

THE FOOTBALL ASSOCIATION CHALLENGE CUP COMPETITION
FINAL TIE
ARSENAL v NEWCASTLE UNITED
SATURDAY, MAY 3rd, 1952 KICK OFF 3pm

EMPIRE STADIUM
WEMBLEY
OFFICIAL PROGRAMME · ONE SHILLING

they also played together for their country 14 times. They are, in all probability, the finest club full back pair that their country has ever fielded.

Wilf Copping was already an international when he came from Leeds in 1934, he and Jack Crayston (from Bradford) effectively replacing Charlie Jones and Bob John. Copping is probably best remembered for his remarkable display in the 'Battle of Highbury' against Italy on 14 November 1934 when Arsenal provided seven of the England team and the World Cup holders were beaten, in a bitter game, 3–2.

Frank Moss was actually only the reserve keeper at Second Division Oldham when Chapman signed him. Apparently Chapman pretended to be pursuing the first team keeper Jack Hacking and, when Oldham wouldn't release him, switched his interest to the reserve as an apparent afterthought (this story has been told about several of Chapman's signings). He was another agile keeper, totally fearless and a natural for the England jersey. His career was sadly cut short because of a recurrent shoulder injury. His last effective game for the club was at Everton on 16 March 1935, when he was injured, dislocating his troubled shoulder early on and playing the rest of the match on the wing. He was always a very good forward (for a time he hoped to continue in the game as an outfield player) and scored an excellent goal, cutting in past his defender and shooting into the corner for a peculiarly unfitting end to a goalkeeper's career. He did try to come back for a few games the next season, but the shoulder and collarbone were continually causing problems and he was forced to give up the game completely.

The team that brought the League Championship to the South of England for the very first time in 1931 was hardly anonymous, but it was unusual in that its back up was far more sophisticated than at any other club of the period. The cornerstone was Tom Whittaker, who eventually became manager after George Allison in 1947. It is almost impossible to do full justice to Whittaker either as coach, physiotherapist or inspiration. The stories about him are legion, almost invariably extremely complimentary. Bernard Joy said that: 'Chapman's success would have been impossible without Whittaker,' but George Allison reaches the essential Whittaker more succinctly. Allison was once asked: 'Is it true, what Tom Whittaker says?' 'Of course it is,' was Allison's reply. 'What did Tom say?'

Cliff Bastin was as effusive: 'I can never thank him enough for the care and expert treatment he lavished on me whilst I was at Highbury. Perhaps 'expert' is a badly chosen word, for Tom was something more than an expert. There was about him a touch of genius.' Bastin explained how men who would have remained on the injured list for three or four weeks at another club would be fit at Highbury within three or four days. Bastin, on one occasion, scalded his foot in a boiling hot bath and

Top left: **A flying George Male,** Arsenal and England right-back, fails to intercept a centre by Preston's O'Donnell on 11 December 1937. Arsenal won the game 2-0, Milne and Bastin getting the goals, and went on to take the League title for the fifth time in the decade. Preston had the consolation of winning the FA Cup, though they nearly pipped Arsenal and stole the Double. Male, whom Chapman had converted from a left half role, went on to make 316 first-class appearances in an 18-year playing career before joining the coaching staff. He never scored a goal for the senior side.

Bottom left: **Male's club and country** full back partner was Eddie Hapgood, seen here in 1936 defending in front of keeper Alex Wilson and the new East Stand. Hapgood made 440 first team appearances in 15 years and became a fixture as England captain.

Top right: **A flying Cliff Bastin** on the attack against West Brom on 31 August 1932. Arsenal lost 1-2, Stockill scoring their only goal. In the background is St John's College of Divinity, from which Henry Norris bought the ground to build Highbury. In 1913 it was just a cricket pitch and tennis courts used by students at the college. St John's burned down at the end of the Second World War and the present flats were later built on the site.

Bottom right: **Tom Whittaker examines Cliff Bastin's** notorious left knee. Bastin had a cartilage which would regularly slip out of place during matches, and Whittaker became expert at manipulating it back in again. When it eventually had to come out permanently (the scar is clearly visible), Whittaker assisted in the operation and the offending piece of gristle was so mis-shapen that it was put on permanent display in the Royal College of Surgeons.

couldn't stand on it. The foot was agony, but Whittaker built a special soft cast inside Bastin's boot so that the winger felt no pain. His only sensation when he ran, as he explained, was the water inside the blister running up and down his foot. Whittaker also used to snap Bastin's cartilage back into place on the field, doing this on at least a dozen occasions, and when Bastin eventually had to have an operation, Whittaker attended and assisted. The cartilage itself, having been removed, was apparently so unusually deformed that it has become a permanent exhibit at the Royal College of Surgeons.

Tom Whittaker was born in Aldershot in 1898. His father was a sergeant-major and Tom also had a military career, studying as a marine engineer and joining the Royal Artillery as, very appropriately, an ordnance engineer. It was while he was playing for the Army (he later transferred to the Navy to exploit his marine engineering) that Arsenal spotted him and brought him to Highbury, where he played as a wing half and later full back until his injury in Australia in 1925. His arrival at Highbury, on 11 November 1919, has a touch of the times about it — Leslie Knighton, newly installed as

manager, met him off the tube!

The surgeon who told Whittaker he would never play again in 1925, Sir Robert Jones, was so impressed by the player that he arranged a year's course in anatomy, massage and electrical treatment of injuries, particularly associated with muscles. Whittaker returned to Highbury after that injury unsure about his future. Arsenal had apparently been intending to let him go in 1925, but he was retained so that he could go on the FA tour (players without clubs were not allowed to represent the FA). Because he had been injured in a representative game, the FA was paying his wages. For six months Whittaker was unable to train and helped in the treatment room. Officially, he was just a player under treatment. One day in February 1926, Chapman called Whittaker up to the top of the stand. For a few moments there was silence, says Whittaker, then Chapman turned and, with his arm stretched out towards the pitch and emphasising every word, said: 'I am going to make this the greatest club ground in the world, and I am going to make you the greatest trainer in the game. What do you say to that?'

Whittaker later built the most modern treatment room in football, and possibly in the country, at Highbury. It was full of sunlamps, heating and electrical apparatus and attracted all sorts of sportsmen who had no association with Highbury. Whittaker was, for instance, also the official trainer for Britain's highly successful Davis Cup tennis team in the 1930s, as well as the regular England soccer team trainer.

He worked seven days a week and would treat anything short of a broken limb. His ability to get players back quickly, and hence help Chapman keep as settled a team as possible, was a crucial element in the club's consistent pattern of success between 1930 and 1936. The other great contribution Whittaker made to Chapman's personal success was relieving the manager of day to day control of the players. This was vitally important for it allowed Chapman time to watch new players, negotiate transfers and consider other essential matters for the club like trying to get the name of the tube station changed.

Whittaker actually became first-team trainer in February 1927. George Hardy, who had held the job since before the First World War, shouted a tactical switch to the players from the bench during a Cup match against Port Vale on 2 February 1927. Chapman said he wouldn't tolerate the trainer influencing tactics and relegated Hardy to the reserves, giving the 29-year-old Whittaker the job. Straight after that Port Vale game Chapman marched into the dressing room and, in front of everyone, told Whittaker to take over the first team immediately. Whittaker, who lodged with Hardy, was shocked, but he and Hardy remained friends, even after the latter left Highbury and went to White Hart Lane. Chapman's action was only an excuse. Hardy was of the old school, Whittaker was obviously the man Chapman wanted and,

more to the point, needed. The shout from the dugout, if it really happened, was merely the trigger.

Whittaker remained as trainer, apart from a spell during the Second World War, for twenty years. He finally took over as manager from Allison in 1947. Almost his first act that year was to call back Joe Shaw from Stamford Bridge as assistant manager. Shaw, the longest serving man on the staff, was the crucial third member of the management team in the 1930s. The fourth was John Peters, the second assistant manager who actually performed much of the secretary's role through to his death in 1952.

Before the 1931-32 season began the talk was of the chances of the Double, not performed since Aston Villa in 1896-97 and not to be performed again for another three decades. After a month the talk was what happened to the League Champions? Arsenal lost their opener at home to West Bromwich and didn't take both points until their fifth match. They never made up the gap that had already opened up and, although it was a good season, eventually finishing second was something of an anti-climax. Everton were champions, two points ahead. Bernard Joy says the team was over confident, pushing forward too eagerly, leaving too many holes for the counter-attack. It was a lesson that was learned for subsequent seasons.

The Cup should have provided compensation, but failed to do so after the most controversial goal in British domestic football (only the third England goal in the 1966 World Cup final possibly ranks above it.)

The run to the 1932 final was straightforward but hard work, and there were to be no replays. Lancashire Combination side Darwen (they had been in the League as recently as 1899) provided an 11-1 walkover in the third round, then Plymouth, with Ted Harper in goal, were removed 4-2. After a 2-0 away win against gradually improving Portsmouth (they reached the final in 1929 and 1934) the quarter-final brought Arsenal back to old adversaries Huddersfield at Leeds Road. After only two minutes Hulme won a corner; the winger held the ball until Herbie Roberts came up on a rare (but obviously pre-planned) foray, placed it right on Roberts' forehead and Arsenal had scored the only goal of the game.

The semi-final at St Andrew's also saw just one goal, this time at the end of the game rather than the beginning. The opponents were Manchester City, who were to reach the next two finals as compensation. The 1932 semi-final was already in time added on, with City frantically attacking, believing that they had to win there and then and would not do so well in a replay. But they left their defence relatively under-manned and as a final clearance came out from the Arsenal penalty area Bastin picked it up and hopefully knocked it towards the right-hand corner. The defender let the ball go, thinking it would go over the line, but Lambert suddenly appeared, hooked it back and there

This page: **The opening of the two new stands** (the West on 10 December 1932 and the East on 24 October 1936) was football's equivalent of the unveiling of the Taj Mahal. There was nothing like them anywhere in the country and it says much for the club and its architects that they remain as comfortable and efficient today, having served the club for more than half its life. One oddity of the club programme through the 1930s was that the cover remained identical, with only the reference to the season being changed. There was a supplement for the West Stand opening (*bottom left*) which highlighted another of Chapman's great public relations coups – persuading the Prince of Wales to perform the ceremony. Royalty was, apart from the Cup final, rarely associated with football at the time. The game was against Chelsea and the Prince met the players before the match. Hughie Gallacher, the opposing captain, is seen (*centre picture*) in a less than respectful pose with his arm round the future King Edward VIII. Herbert Chapman, to Gallacher's left, seems unsure of the protocol relating to Gallacher's behaviour. Many of the players signed this picture – Alex James top left, Hughie Gallacher centre (programmes by courtesy of John Motson).

ARSENAL · FOOTBALL · CLUB · LTD..

COLOURS:
RED SHIRTS WITH WHITE COLLARS AND SLEEVES
WHITE KNICKERS

Secretary-Manager:
GEORGE F. ALLISON

DIRECTORS:
THE RT. HON. THE EARL OF LONSDALE, K.G., G.C.V.O., D.L. (Chairman).
J. J. EDWARDS, Esq. (Vice-Chairman).
THE RT. HON. THE EARL OF WESTMORLAND.
THE RT. HON. THE EARL OF GRANARD, P.C., K.P., G.C.V.O.
COL. SIR MATHEW WILSON, Bart., C.B.I., D.S.O.
MAJOR SIR SAMUEL HILL-WOOD, Bart., D.L., J.P.
SIR FREDERICK WALL.
MAJOR-GENERAL J. H. McLAREN, M.P., C.M.G., D.S.O.
H. E. VANDERPANT, Esq.

Telegraphic Address:
"GUNNERETIC,
FINSPARK LONDON."

ARSENAL STADIUM,
HIGHBURY, N.5.

Vol. XXV.   No. 12.   Saturday, October 24th, 1936   Two-pence

The Inauguration of The East Stand.

This afternoon the new East Stand, which we have seen gradually developing before our eyes for the last two months, is inaugurated and takes its part as a portion of the Arsenal Stadium. Its predecessor, demolished last Spring, witnessed many a sternly-contested game and looked down through the years on many a brave player toiling and battling in the service of his club. Now it has gone, yielding place to a successor which in its turn will view the fortunes of the club as it passes down the years.

The East Stand is a noble thing, a building of wonder and unparalleled in football. Together with its slightly older companion on the West side, it will for many a day bear testimony to the craft of those who wrought it and to the skill and vision of the architects who dreamed it and then brought it to reality. Claude Ferrier, who brought the West Stand into being, is unhappily no longer with us, but to him also, as well as to William Binnie, the Stand inaugurated to-day stands as a monument of great work nobly achieved.

But we would err if we regarded the new Stand merely as an isolated structure, however wonderful. It is the completion of a labour of ground-improvement which has been spread over ten years. Although we recall it, we can only with difficulty visualise once more the Arsenal ground of 1926. A world of difference lies between that and the Arsenal Stadium of 1936. Step by step a new thing has been raised up for our use and this afternoon we have reached the culminating point. Yet there is a wider significance in the East Stand. It crowns not only the last ten years. In the autumn of 1886 a tiny football gathering first met in Dial Square at Woolwich Arsenal. The fifty years which separate us from them contain a varied history of mingled triumphs and falls of the club which started on that far-off day. Half a century of honourable struggle stands behind the edifice which starts upon its history to-day.

Above: **An unusually shy Alex James** poses for the camera before a reserve team game at Highbury on 13 April 1932. His fitness was being tested before the Cup final, then ten days away. A week later one final tackle by Tom Whittaker, in a practice game to please a photographer who had arrived late, caused James' knee to break down again and he left the field in tears, unable to play at Wembley. In the background the foundations of the new West Stand are well advanced.

was Bastin to touch it home with the last kick of the match. It was an interesting illustration of Chapman's belief that a team can attack for too long.

The final was to be against Newcastle. The preparations were dominated by whether or not Alex James would be fit. He had damaged knee ligaments against West Ham a couple of weeks earlier, being rushed back to Highbury by Tom Whittaker before the game at Upton Park was even over.

Three days before the Cup final Chapman announced his team — James and Hulme were not fit enough so in came George Male and Pat Beasley. The news was a surprise, and L. V. Manning, sports editor of the *Daily Sketch,* got James and Hulme to jog around the Highbury pitch and published a picture captioned: 'The two fittest men in football.' Chapman was furious, and ordered the pair down to Brighton, where the team were staying. Tom Whittaker gave them both a tough try-out the following morning on the Brighton ground, in front of 40 or so photographers. Both came through and were reinstated in the team for Saturday's final. Then, as everyone was making their way back to the dressing room, another photographer, whose car had broken down, came rushing into the ground to plead with Whittaker for a final shot. Whittaker agreed, tackled James once more and, suddenly, James fell to the ground clutching his

knee. He was carried to the dressing-room where, says Whittaker: '. . . almost crying with pain and disappointment, he would not let the doctor touch him and shouted at me to get everyone out of the room. Even Chapman had to go.' George Male, signed from the London amateur side Clapton earlier that season, had been in, out, and back in a Cup final side within the space of an hour. Male played left half, and it was on that side that the critical moment was to occur.

It was almost half-time (with Arsenal 1–0 up after Bob John had headed the ball home when United had made a hash of a clearance) when Newcastle centre half Davison over-hit a long pass up the right wing for inside forward Jimmy Richardson to chase. The ball appeared to cross the goal-line and the Arsenal defenders relaxed, but Richardson carried on and hooked the ball into the centre. Eddie Hapgood could probably have intercepted it, but didn't bother. Centre forward Jack Allen did bother, flicking it neatly into the net. Referee Bill Harper gave a goal, the Arsenal players were incredulous but did not argue. L. V. Manning said in the *Sunday Graphic* the next day: 'One cannot praise too highly the restraint of the Arsenal players when the first Newcastle goal was scored. Every man must have known what was so clear to the onlookers — that the ball had crossed the line — but there was not the slightest attempt at a demonstration

or protest.' Tom Parker got their minds back on the game but the timing was perfect for New-castle, who came out for the second half a different team and Allen scored again for United to win 2–1. Arsenal had thus finished runners-up in both major competitions, only the second time this had ever happened, the first being Huddersfield's misfortune in 1928.

Though it has always been claimed that the ball was over the line, in fairness it must be said that no convincing photograph exists (unlike the 1966 goal, where the evidence clearly shows that England's third goal should not have been allowed) and the angle of the most reproduced photograph is not necessarily a good one. The *whole* of the ball must be over the line, which means that it is perfectly possible for a bouncing ball to seem to be beyond the line in even a slightly angled picture, but not actually 100 per cent beyond in reality. Newcastle were the first team to win the final at Wembley after being behind in the match, and the first to come from behind in any final since they did the same thing themselves in 1910.

The disappointment of 1932 was only short-lived. For many years afterwards regret was expressed that, despite their dominance of the decade, the Arsenal of the 1930s never performed the Double. 1931–32 was to be the nearest they came for, like Liverpool in the 1970s and 1980s, they did not seem to be able to con-centrate on the FA Cup when they were lead-ing the League. And for the next three seasons Arsenal were to do exactly that, equalling Huddersfield's hat-trick with an impeccable period of dominance covering 1932–33, 1933–34 and 1934–35.

Above: **The first of the Cup final records,** half a century before they became tedious. The Arsenal team were photographed in the Columbia recording studios a month before the 1932 final. Captain Tom Parker is closest to the microphone. Arsenal recorded one side, Newcastle the other: there is no trace of its commercial success, as there were no record charts for another 20 years.

Left: **The shield which hangs** outside the boardroom at Highbury commemorating the hat-trick of Championships between 1932 and 1935. Huddersfield and Liverpool have almost identical trophies. The bust is of Denis Hill-Wood.

Most clubs which have such a successful spell do so with a very settled side. Indeed, it is almost a truism of the game that a great side lasts for no more than three good seasons. The Arsenal of the first half of the 1930s were almost exactly the opposite. By 1935 no more than three of the regulars of 1932 were still in the team — Hapgood, Roberts and Bastin. Most of the missing had simply succumbed to age, though Frank Moss was an exception. Much more significantly, Herbert Chapman was dead and had been replaced by George Allison. Yet the period was one of remarkably consistent results, with only 24 League games lost and a points average of 58. By Championship standards, none of the three seasons was particularly outstanding, certainly not to be compared with the record breaking 1930–31, and their number of defeats (9, 8 and 7 in the three seasons) was no better than average for a Championship side. On the other hand, the pattern of consistency during a period of team rebuilding was most certainly outstanding; against that, while there were other good sides around such as Sheffield Wednesday, Manchester City, Sunderland and Derby none of them managed to put together a settled team for long enough in the early 1930s. If this sounds like grudging praise, it is only so in the context of the heady two years which followed the 1930 Cup win.

Many of the individual replacements proved to be the match of their predecessors. George Male was already a Highbury stalwart when he replaced Parker in 1932, Eddie Coleman and an ageing Jimmy Dunne appeared in Lambert's shirt, though neither truly became a fixture, and the great David Jack played only 14 games

in 1933–34 and then went to Southend as manager. He was replaced by Ray Bowden, who arrived from Plymouth in March 1933. Bastin was still a youngster, though he suffered from periods of injury and his deafness was beginning to be a worry, but Joe Hulme proved very difficult to duplicate.

The Arsenal wingers had performed very different jobs compared with men in the number 7 and 11 shirts at other clubs and it was not easy to slot new men into Arsenal's unique system. They had not only to be very fast in the conventional sense, but also significant goalscorers as well. Only Alex James was allowed the liberty of not appearing on the scoresheet. As has been said before, it was the role of Hulme and Bastin, more than any other aspect of their style, which marked the Arsenal of the early 1930s apart from their competitors. That meant the club's wingers could, and would, often also double up as inside forwards. Pat Beasley, who arrived from Stourbridge, would play in either Bastin or Hulme's place if they were injured, or act as Bastin's inside forward. He would have played in the 1932 Cup final if Hulme had not recovered from that injury but, ironically, he and Hulme then played on opposite wings for Huddersfield in the 1938 Cup final. Ralph Birkett, who later won an England cap while with Middlesbrough, was bought from Torquay specifically to take over from Hulme, but was never an adequate replacement, and by 1935 Alf Kirchen from Norwich was on the right wing.

The midfield men were more easily replaced, Jack Crayston from Bradford and Wilf Copping from Leeds coming in for Charlie Jones and Bob John with remarkably little disruption in the summer of 1934. When Alex James was unavailable the remarkable Peter Dougall would take his place. By all accounts he was an even cleverer player, but could never consistently harness his fabulous ball skills to the team effort, but then it was perhaps unfair to expect anyone to replace the hub of the wheel. In goal Alex Wilson replaced Moss in a quiet, competent way. He had come from Morton in May 1933. When Moss was injured at Goodison in March 1935, however, Wilson was also hurt and George Allison had no other first-class keeper. That day also happened to be the transfer deadline, so he asked Everton if Arsenal could sign their reserve keeper George Bradshaw there and then. Bradshaw was a little bemused by this sudden turn of events, but eventually agreed and came to Highbury for a number of years.

The first year of the hat-trick, 1932–33, did not start particularly well. Charlie Jones was injured and, in their first home match, Arsenal lost to West Brom for the second consecutive year. But this season was to be different, with 32 of the next 36 points finding their way back to Highbury. Yet again, though, Villa managed to score five goals in Birmingham and the 5–3 defeat was Arsenal's only setback in that 18-game run. The final match in the sequence was the Christmas Eve 9–2 thrashing of Sheffield United at Highbury. Jack Lambert scored five, his best ever for the club, in what was virtually his valedictory performance. That particular game is often recalled as the height of Arsenal's powers in the whole inter-war period, though, oddly, two days later they went down 1–2 at home to Leeds. Villa and Wednesday continued to press until April when, though Arsenal were ahead, both their challengers had games in hand. By chance both came to Highbury in April, where Arsenal finished things off in fine style. Villa went down 5–0 and ended four points behind, Wednesday lost 4–2 and were eventually three points further back. The month saw five wins in a row and the last, 3–1 versus Chelsea at Stamford Bridge, confirmed the Gunners' second title in three years. The forwards had been magnificent all season, and the total of 118 goals was the club's second highest ever and included one 9, two 8s and one 7. Cliff Bastin's 33 goals still remain a Football League record for a winger.

The next season, 1933–34, was a strangely subdued one compared with those before and after. It was marred, of course, by Herbert Chapman's death, but, though it saw one more point won (59 rather than 58) the goalscoring record was completely different. Only 75 were scored compared with 118 the season before and 115 the season after. One major reason was Alex James' injury against Birmingham in the first match of the season. He was out for half of the campaign, as was Joe Hulme. However, Arsenal quickly went to the head of the table, putting together a spell of 27 points out of a possible 32. Derby and Huddersfield both took the lead briefly, but they had to play the Gunners in

consecutive matches in Easter week. Arsenal beat Derby 4–2 at the Baseball Ground and followed up with a 3–1 defeat of Huddersfield at Highbury. In the end only Huddersfield kept up the challenge, eventually finishing three points in arrears. Spurs finished third.

It was actually one of those strangely quiet seasons when not a lot seems to happen and no team can really impose its authority. Both Villa and Wednesday had lost their sparkle, finishing mid-table, and Arsenal, despite the loss of Chapman, were able to hold their ground by virtue of their established patterns of play and their consistency. Even so, they had to survive a number of poor results — home defeats by Everton and Spurs within the space of four days, a 4–1 crushing at Leicester and a 3–0 defeat at Sunderland — and were perhaps lucky that their crisis season coincided with a corporate lethargy among their competitors.

The third year of the hat-trick saw a genuine new star in the making. He was Ted Drake, George Allison's first signing (from Southampton) in March 1934. Drake was to score a record 42 goals with the Gunners in this, his first season. That total included four matches in which he scored four goals and three in which he notched mere hat-tricks. The newcomer almost carried the team. There were numerous major injuries — Dunne, Copping and Bastin all had cartilage operations and even the two trainers, Tom Whittaker and Billy Milne, both had to be hospitalized during the season. Most of the reserves had fair spells in the first team, but still went on to win the Football Combination for the seventh time in nine seasons. Had Chapman lived, he would have seen it as the perfect validation of his insistence that the reserves play to the same patterns and tactics as their seniors.

The 1934–35 season had started well with an 8–1 crushing of Liverpool (how Highbury would applaud such a result today) and the first four home games produced 21 Arsenal goals. Away matters did not give rise for similar congratulations, with only a single victory prior to the New Year. But none of their regular challengers could put together anything like a convincing set of results and Arsenal headed the table until March when Sunderland, inspired by the young Raich Carter, went a point ahead. Arsenal had games in hand, however, and though Sunderland held them to a goalless draw at Highbury, Arsenal made Sunderland's task almost impossible with a 2–0 win at Everton on 16 March 1935. This was the game in which Frank Moss scored Arsenal's second, magnificent goal as a highly inappropriate finale to his mainstream goalkeeping career. Sunderland ended the season four points behind with Sheffield Wednesday, perhaps Arsenal's most dogged challengers in the Chapman era, another five adrift.

Chapman was always surprised, and perhaps a little distressed, that Huddersfield could not get to a Cup final during their hat-trick years. The Yorkshiremen were there in 1920 and 1922, and

The planning department:
Bob John, Herbert
Chapman and Alex James
discuss the forthcoming
FA Cup final against
Newcastle early in
April 1932.

again in 1928 and 1930, but in the middle years, 1924 to 1926, when they should by rights have made it, they were nowhere to be seen. Arsenal had a peculiarly similar record. They reached the final in 1930, 1932 and 1936, but missed out in 1933, 1934 and 1935. Oddly, they never even reached a semi-final in those seasons. In 1934 Villa played well to win 2–1 at Highbury in the quarter-final. It is odd that the paths of Villa and Arsenal seemed to be constantly crossing, and that Villa appear to leap from the pages of history as the Gunners most prestigious and difficult rivals. Odd, because Villa did not win a single prize between 1920 and 1957. It was Wednesday, the other major challengers, who knocked Arsenal out in 1935, also 2–1 but this time at Hillsborough.

We have skirted around what happened on 14 January 1933. It is not usual in the history of a great club, when there is so much to tell, to dwell for very long on a game that was lost, particularly in the third round of the Cup, but this one is an exception. Fifty years later, when Walsall came to Highbury, still as a Third Division side, and surprisingly won again (this time in the Milk Cup) no one tried to make any

serious comparison between the two matches. There was no way they could. Walsall's 2–0 defeat of Arsenal in 1933 remains, very simply, the greatest act of giant-killing in English club history. This is vaguely peculiar. There have been giant killers whose performances have seemed far more praiseworthy since, there have been non-League clubs knocking out First Division sides, but whenever a giant-killer arises, the comparison is automatically made, above all other games, with Walsall 2 Arsenal 0.

We need to stand back a little to judge the real significance of this result. Arsenal, it should be remembered, had just gone through a run obtaining 32 points from 18 matches. Three weeks before meeting Walsall, they had crushed Sheffield United 9–2. They were well clear at the head of the First Division and were, in a sense, at their very peak, for they had no obvious rivals. It is difficult to find comparisons, because there are none, but perhaps Liverpool in 1983 come closest. In the three previous seasons Arsenal had won the Cup, then the League, then been runners-up in both. The Double in 1932–33 seemed a very strong possibility.

77

The game must also be put in a social and economic context. This was the height of the depression. Three million were out of work, a far higher percentage of the work force then than 50 years later, and benefits were far less generous where they existed at all. As in the 1980s, there was very real resentment in the provinces against London, Westminster, 'them' as opposed to 'us'. Walsall may not have corresponded with Lancashire or Tyneside today, but it was a moderate sized provincial town with problems enough of its own. Arsenal, in its way, was a very visible representative of London, a symbol of the richness of life there compared with the provinces. The fact that this was unfair, that most of the players were from the north and many had been miners, was not the point. What mattered were the symbols, what people wanted to believe was true.

It is also realistic (and it should not be ignored) to point out that Arsenal were not a popular club outside London, compared with, say, the Spurs side of the early 1960s. This was a difficult attitude to analyse, for it was a feeling abroad without any rational base, rather than a justifiable dislike. In part it was due to the 'Bank of England' reputation, Chapman's and later Allison's apparent desire to buy success at almost any price, though many clubs had gone the same route and failed dismally. In part it was also the tactical style; the holding back, occupying midfield space, the numerous goals which came from quick breaks from James to Bastin and Hulme, rather than the constant attacking pressure which was the traditional approach of the day. Spectators, having come to expect fast dribbling wingers crossing from the goal-line for thundering centre forwards in the Dixie Dean or Pongo Waring mould, found Arsenal's style odd and, therefore, somehow 'lucky'.

Fans had yet to realise the simplest of all football truths, that the winning team is, by definition, the one which scores most goals. Eighty-five minutes of unrewarded but naive pressure may somehow seem more valuable than a single breakaway goal, but that isn't what the laws of the game say. Actually, such perceptions as they related to Arsenal were not only extremely unfair but, very simply, wrong — Arsenal scored 127 League goals in 1931, 118 in 1933 and 115 in 1935, overall considerably more than any of their competitors, and, to repeat the obvious, they couldn't all have come from lucky breakaways. What is true is that, like all teams, Arsenal tended to play differently away from Highbury than at home. Equally, other sides would attack them more on their own grounds, forcing Arsenal towards the use of their 'smash and grab' style. It is very difficult for the generation of fans born after the Second World War to imagine how little exposure pre-war crowds had to the big clubs. North London fans could watch Arsenal every other week but a Liverpudlian or a Mancunian was only able to see this dominating force once or twice a year —

thus his views about the sort of team they were, and the way they played, could only be based on very limited evidence. He had no opportunity of seeing Arsenal 20 or 25 times a year on television (as he certainly would in the early 1980s) and thus building a more balanced view. Arsenal at Villa, Hillsborough or Roker would always face a hard game, would always be forced to defend, and would probably rely on Hulme and Bastin for a winning goal. It was the fact that they succeeded so often which bred the resentment.

In any event, the key to the Walsall result, the way it was greeted and the reason it has remained the giant-killing feat *par excellence*, lies as much in the times as in the football. Walsall were the small, underprivileged, provincial David overthrowing the rich, lucky London-based Goliath and the Midland side's success was feted far and wide, often by people who probably had not the slightest idea where Walsall was.

Vol. XII.   No. 426.

Our Red Letter Day.

WHEN the history of our club comes to be written, there can be little doubt that January 14, 1933, will be given prominence in it as a Red Letter Day.

The glorious uncertainty of the F.A. Cup competition has brought some well-known clubs to Walsall in the past—West Bromwich Albion, Burnley, Bury, Bradford City, T... ...thians, Middlesbrough and...

Left and right: **The cover and first page** of the programme for the greatest giant-killing feat in English club history. Arsenal came to Walsall on top of the First Division, having reached two of the three previous finals. The guns and reproduction of James confronting the teddy bear are a delight for a Third Division programme of half a century ago. The programme editor could not possibly have realised how right he was when he wrote: 'When the history of our club comes to be written, there is little doubt that January 14, 1933 will be a . . . Red Letter Day.' Even now, whenever the name Walsall is mentioned, the instant thought is of that one afternoon long ago. What the editor could not have realised, however, was just how largely this day would feature in the history of Arsenal as well.

Chapman has been accused of underestimating Walsall, but there is little evidence to support this contention. Walsall had been watched, and, though their last four matches comprised three draws and a 5–0 defeat, Chapman was under no illusions as to the kind of game he was facing. His real problem had been influenza, earlier claiming Bob John, Jack Lambert and Tim Coleman. Eddie Hapgood and Joe Hulme had also been injured and Chapman therefore had to decide whether to play recently unavailable men or some of his well-prepared reserves. He chose the reserves — it would be a hard match but here would be a good opportunity for the second-teamers to push their claims for a first team place. In many respects, they were less likely than the internationals to be upset by rough Third Division tackling. So in came Scot

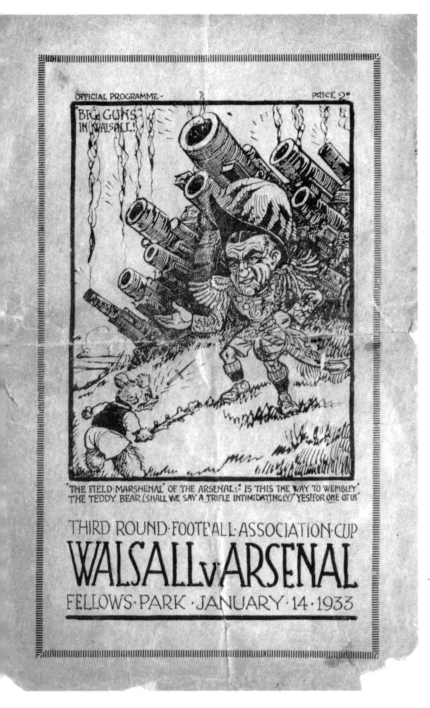

'BIG GUNS IN WALSALL!'

'THE FIELD MARSHENAL' OF THE ARSENAL: IS THIS THE WAY TO WEMBLEY' THE TEDDY BEAR (SHALL WE SAY A TRIFLE INTIMIDATINGLY) 'YES! FOR ONE OF US'

THIRD ROUND · FOOTB'ALL · ASSOCIATION · CUP

WALSALL v ARSENAL

FELLOWS · PARK · JANUARY · 14 · 1933

'Arsenal, the Rich, the Confident, the League leaders, the £30,000 aristocrats, against the little Third Division team that cost £69 all-in. Arsenal train on ozone, brine-baths, champagne, gold and electrical massage in an atmosphere of prima donna preciousness. They own £87 worth of football boots. Walsall men eat fish and chips and drink beer, and the entire running expenses of the club this season have been £75.'

The players didn't quite see it like that. One or two of the reserves were particularly edgy. Just before leaving the dressing-room Chapman came over to Charlie Walsh: 'I'm expecting a lot of you today, son, we're relying on you to show us your best.' Walsh, who had been nagging Chapman for a first team chance for months, replied: 'OK Mr Chapman, I'm ready to play the game of my life.' Chapman answered: 'Good lad, you'll do,' and then, just as he was turning away, paused: 'Oh, and by the way, you'd better put your stockings on or the crowd will laugh at you.' Walsh was so nervous he had put on his boots before his socks. Walsh's apprehensions were more justified than his team-mates would have guessed. Walsall employed classic cup-tie tactics. Their enthusiasm was overwhelming, their tackling, especially on James, could only be described as grim. Arsenal failed to settle throughout the match, but should still have won it. Walsh, now complete with socks, made a complete hash of the easiest chance of the first-half when he missed a simple Bastin centre and the ball came off his shoulder. In the second the centre forward's intervention was even more disastrous when he took the ball off David Jack's toe just as Jack seemed certain to score.

As Arsenal failed to score, Walsall became more confident, the inches of mud which covered the pitch being much more to their liking. After 60 minutes Gilbert Alsop, the home side's centre forward, headed home a Lee corner-kick to put Walsall a goal up. Fifty years later Alsop, still marking out pitches at 73, remembered: 'We had a corner and their full back (Black) was marking me. He didn't get up. The ball was just a big plum pudding that day and I headed it off my forehead straight into the corner of the net. I'd been watching Dixie Dean play for England.' Alsop also remembered the foul which, five minutes later, sealed the game for Walsall. He could still point to a scar on his knee which, he claimed, was caused by Tommy Black's violent tackle after 65 minutes. It was in the penalty area and, as a result, Billy Sheppard scored from the spot.

The Arsenal players had been getting more and more irritated by the Walsall tactics. 'They could not have complained if five of their men had been sent off in the first quarter of an hour,' said Bastin afterwards, 'We had ten free-kicks in the first ten minutes.' Black had become particularly irate, the more so after failing to prevent Alsop's goal, and Arsenal paid the penalty.

The Gunners could do nothing to retrieve the two-goal deficit in the last 25 minutes and the packed 11,000 crowd chaired the Walsall players

Tommy Black at left back, Norman Sidey at left half, Billy Warnes at outside right and Charlie Walsh at centre forward. The last two had both been recruited from local amateur clubs. Too much has been made of the side's inexperience — it still contained Moss, Male, Roberts, Jack, James and Bastin. Tom Whittaker later dismissed the suggestion that the first-teamers were unavailable, though, afterwards, Chapman seems to have encouraged this belief. Everyone travelled to Walsall says Whittaker, in the team's own railway coach the day before. During the journey Chapman announced the team to, in Whittaker's own words: '. . . murmurs of amazement.'

The newspapers, always loving a David versus Goliath, gave the game the usual build-up and their angles were predictable enough. Said one:

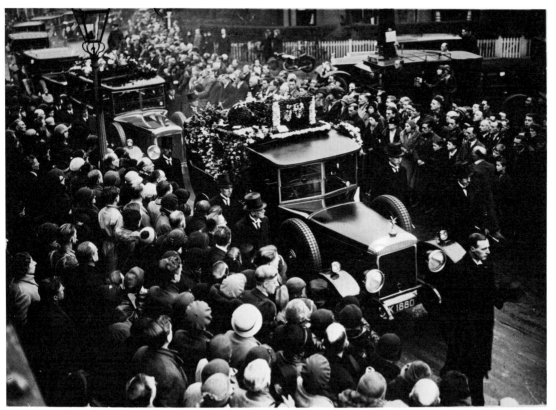

Left: **10 January, 1934; the saddest day** of the glorious 1930s. The cortege carrying Herbert Chapman's body moves slowly through the streets of Hendon, where he was buried in the churchyard of what was then still a quiet village. The pallbearers were numbered among the great names of British football history – David Jack, Eddie Hapgood, Joe Hulme, Jack Lambert, Cliff Bastin, Alex James. The decade was not yet half way through. The hat-trick of Championships was only one third complete.

off at the end. For the Arsenal team, retribution was swift. Chapman was apoplectic. He refused to let Black return to Highbury and had transferred him to Plymouth within a week. Whether this was because of Chapman's anger at Black's tackle on Alsop, or because of his all-round performance in the match, was never absolutely clear, though Chapman certainly said the former. Walsh, whose display was almost as wretched as Black's, was sold to Brentford by the end of January, having, despite his ambitions, played just that one first-team match for Arsenal. Warnes went to Norwich at the end of the season. Only Sidey remained in the reserves, a competent back-up for Roberts.

For Walsall the game was something of an inspiration. Though they were knocked out by eventual finalists Manchester City in the next round, they managed to finish the season third in the Third Division North. For Arsenal it was a hiccup, though one that was to echo down the years as, in all probability, the most famous Cup tie the club have ever contested. Exactly fifty years later the fact that it was Walsall, rather than any other Third Division club, who knocked the Gunners out of the Milk Cup at Highbury must have made some small contribution to Terry Neill's departure from the manager's office.

Walsall was the last FA Cup defeat Herbert Chapman ever suffered. By the time Villa defeated the Gunners in the quarter-final of 1934 Chapman was dead. It was so sudden, so unexpected, that it was almost prosaic. There is somehow very little than can be said about it. On Saturday 30 December 1933 Arsenal had drawn 0–0 at Birmingham. They were a comfortable four points clear at the top of the League. It was

to be a typical, perhaps slightly busy, week for Chapman. On the Monday, New Year's Day, he went to see Bury play Notts County, who had someone in whom he was interested. He then crossed the Pennines to watch Sheffield Wednesday play Birmingham on the Tuesday. Wednesday were the visitors at Highbury the following Saturday and were Chapman's greatest fear for the title. By the Wednesday he had clearly developed a heavy cold but ignored the advice of Dr Guy Pepper, the club doctor, and went down to Guildford to see the third team. 'I don't get a chance to see the lads very often,' he commented. On returning home to Hendon he was much worse and went to bed. By Friday, 36 hours later, he seemed rather better but the pneumonia, as it presumably was, suddenly worsened and he died at 3 am on the Saturday morning.

The news came as a complete shock. The players arrived at Highbury a few hours later to discover suddenly that the Boss, who was perfectly healthy when they had last seen him in Birmingham, was dead. Bastin told of the terrible blow the players felt: 'As I approached the ground, the newspaper-sellers were shouting out the news of Chapman's death. It seemed just too bad to be true. In the dressing-room, nobody had anything to say, yet each of us knew what (the others) were thinking. Herbert Chapman had been loved by us all.' George Male was walking past a tube station when he saw the newspaper board: 'Herbert Chapman Dead.' . . . 'That was the first I knew about it. I couldn't believe it.' Arsenal and Wednesday stood to attention before the game. 'I suppose Arsenal gave quite a good display that day, considering that to the players the game was

The most famous of all Arsenal pictures: Alex James leaves a trail of Manchester City defenders behind him during a game at Highbury on 13 October, 1934. The left-hand member of the trio is Matt Busby. The view is towards the North Bank, then graced by the famous clock. The FA had recently told the club to change it from a 45-minute timer to a proper clock. It was eventually moved to the southern end when the North Bank stand was built. Arsenal won on this particular game against City 3-0 and ended the season as Champions for the third consecutive time (picture by courtesy of *The Sunday Times*).

just an unimportant incident,' said Bastin. 'Even the crowd was practically silent throughout the ninety minutes of a game which seemed to go on for ninety years.' Arsenal and Wednesday drew 1–1, but the team collapsed afterwards and lost three consecutive games, including two home matches against Spurs and Everton.

Herbert Chapman was buried at Hendon, the church he had attended regularly, four days later. The pall-bearers were among the greatest names in the game's history — David Jack, Eddie Hapgood, Joe Hulme, Jack Lambert, Cliff Bastin and Alex James. The crowds were huge and the Reverend A Hunt Cooke, a close friend of Chapman's at St Mary's, recalled that the scenes were a little shocking: 'There were

people climbing all over the graves with cameras. Mr Chapman would not have approved.'

Bob Wall, then Chapman's secretary, said that, for several years afterwards, he regularly heard Chapman's measured footsteps in the Highbury corridors late in the evening, along the upper landing, through the boardroom and cocktail bar, into the Press Room and on into the stand. He, and other members of the staff, often looked down the corridors to see if anyone was there — but no one ever was. If there are such things as ghosts, then Chapman's at Highbury would be perfect. In every sense, he has continued to live on in the club and the ground that he raised, just as he promised Tom Whittaker, to the very heights of football.

· CHAPTER 6 ·
Allison's Arsenal

Chapman's death was so unexpected that there was no obvious successor. The players probably favoured Joe Shaw, who was deservedly popular and fully versed in Arsenal's ways. Shaw, apparently, was not particularly keen on the glare of publicity that was now an essential part of the job as manager at Highbury and stayed behind the scenes. Whether George Allison, the director in charge, actually formally offered him the job is unclear. The choice of a successor was an almost impossible one for the board — to follow Chapman was the hardest task in football. As it turned out, the problems were not as intractable as the board probably imagined. The club was run on a day to day basis by Joe Shaw, Tom Whittaker and John Peters, all of them highly competent, and the fact that between Chapman's death and the outbreak of war Arsenal won three Championships and the FA Cup (more trophies, interestingly, than when he was alive) is largely due to them. It was also true, of course, that the players were much more responsible now than they had been earlier, or, indeed, were probably to be later, and the club had established a style and approach to the game that could survive even the passing of a Herbert Chapman.

The solution that the board came up with, while unlikely, proved in the end to be rather clever. George Allison, who had been involved with the club since its Woolwich days and became a director in the early 1920s, moved from the board room to the manager's office. For some months after Chapman's death, Allison had been acting as Managing Director/Secretary. He did not actually become manager until the end of the 1933–34 season. It was a clever move because it avoided any great disruption, it allowed Shaw and Whittaker to continue to manage the team, the training and the tactics, it saved the club from facing any new broom that an outsider would probably want to bring, even to so successful a club as the Gunners, and it allowed the team to continue playing exactly as before. And the proof of the pudding has to be in the eating — the results showed that it worked.

Technically Joe Shaw had become team manager, John Peters secretary and Tom Whittaker trainer. The 'official' job of secretary-manager was not actually advertised, but there

Left upper: George Allison ponders the future at Highbury soon after the death of Herbert Chapman in 1934. Allison did not succeed Chapman immediately, taking the title of Managing Director until the end of the year. Joe Shaw was team manager for most of 1934, until Allison resigned as a director and officially became secretary-manager. At the time directors could not be paid employees of the club.

Left lower: Allison (left) puts on his broadcasting gear before a radio commentary. His assistant is Derek McCulloch, later better known as Uncle Mac on BBC's Children's Hour. McCulloch's job was to call out the position of the ball on the field and the listener matched this to a numbered grid published in the *Radio Times*. Allison first came to public prominence as the commentator on FA Cup finals, and handled both the 1927 and 1930 finals despite being an Arsenal director. The first game on which there had ever been a live commentary was from Highbury on 22 January 1927, though the commentator on this occasion was H. B. T. Wakelam. The match was a 1-1 draw between Arsenal and Sheffield United and it fell to Charlie Buchan to score the first goal ever broadcast live. Highbury was always chosen for experimental radio and television broadcasts, not because of the club's importance but because it was so close to the BBC studios at Alexandra Palace.

were hundreds of applications anyway, to which Allison had to reply. One from Wales claimed the ability to run 14 miles in an hour, a mile in 3½ minutes and '. . . to have developed a private system of team control on the field by verbal orders that will break any defence or attack that does not use my methods. . .' Allison was asked to reply promptly to this application, stating what he would offer for '. . . serving as (a) manager, (b) trainer, (c) recruiter and (d) player, as I am considering taking up heavily paid posts overseas for opulent salaries. . .' As Allison said, presumably tongue in cheek, being the only one who saw the applications gave him ample opportunity to put examples like that to one

assistant was Derek McCulloch, who went on to become the BBC's premier 1940s and 1950s children's broadcaster under the name Uncle Mac.

Bernard Joy, who played for Allison, described him as: '. . . tactful, friendly and good-hearted. But he fell short in his handling of footballers and lacked the professional's deep knowledge of the game. (Allison) wisely left dressing-room discipline in Tom Whittaker's hands and it was Whittaker and Joe Shaw who took the brunt of the strained relations which occasionally developed between management and players. The two of them were loyalty itself to Allison — they had to be or the club would have fallen

Right: **The months after Chapman's death** saw a great outflowing of emotion in North London. Gates were closed for game after game despite the fact that the club suffered an inevitable reaction to events and a slump in form. The picture was taken from the North Bank a full hour before the kick-off against Spurs on 31 January 1934. Spurs won 1-3, Bastin getting the only home goal. The Gunners didn't win a First Division game that tragic January.

side, lest they endanger his prospects.

Allison was actually three years older than the Arsenal, having been born in Darlington in 1883. He had built a reasonable reputation for himself as a journalist, and had for a time been the manager's assistant at Middlesbrough, but his name came to national attention when he was chosen to be Britain's first ever radio sports commentator. The very first major event to be broadcast live was to be the 1927 Cup final, played on 23 April between Arsenal and Cardiff City. In actual fact there was a trial broadcast earlier of an Arsenal game versus Sheffield United on 22 January 1927 but this had a very small audience (Highbury was always used for pre-war radio and television trials because of its proximity to the studios at Alexandra Palace, not because of Arsenal's reputation). Oddly, no one seemed to think it unreasonable that the commentator for the Cup final should also be a director of one of the teams playing. Allison's

apart.' Cliff Bastin, who also played for the next five years under Allison, clearly agreed with Joy, but there is a slight edge to comments in his autobiography. Having pointed out that Joe Shaw was unhappy with the glare of publicity, Bastin comments: 'The man who did take over the position was one to whom the limelight was far from unwelcome. . . he was not, however, a successor shaped in the Chapman mould. Indeed, relations between him and Mr Chapman had not always been of the happiest. . . He (Allison) had the name of Arsenal splashed across the front pages of the press, but he lacked Herbert Chapman's gift of getting the best out of his players.'

These were commonly held views when Allison took over, and were to be heard often enough through the rest of the decade. But others were prepared to look at the results and accept what was plain to see; few men, if any, could have taken over from Herbert Chapman, and there were still plenty of trophies on the board room sideboard. Frank Carruthers, one of the leading journalists of the period, wrote in 1937: 'The continuance of Arsenal's power is a wonderful tribute to Mr George Allison, who has borne his office through a period of extreme difficulty which would have taxed the ingenuity of a Herbert Chapman to surmount.' And to sum up his views about George Allison's success he said, simply: 'Well, we have all been wrong.' The public image of Allison was never to change. The publicity blurb for his autobiography declared: 'Famous director and manager of Arsenal FC, broadcaster and journalist, for 40 years a pioneer in the success of one of the greatest teams ever to take the field; the friend of Kings and statesmen, the confidant of players, the brain behind a hundred transfers, George Allison has now written his story.'

For the season and a half after Chapman's death things went as well as they could have done for anyone. No other man has come into a manager's seat and won the Championship in his first two seasons. But while Arsenal clearly remained the team to beat through the rest of the 1930s (as, say, Manchester United were in the 1960s) they were no longer unquestionably the best. In the last four seasons prior to the outbreak of war in 1939 their record was a creditable sixth, third, first and fifth, though the Championship of 1938 was won with a mere 52 points, the lowest ever in a full 42-match season. The Cup was again highly creditable, but arguably not outstanding compared with the impossibly high standards set by Chapman between 1930 and 1934. There were, nonetheless, three quarter-finals and the 1936 final victory over Sheffield United.

When Allison's third season in charge began in August 1935 success had become a habit. It was seven seasons since Arsenal had not won or threatened to win one or both trophies. In 1930 there was the FA Cup, in 1931 the League, in 1932 the runners-up slot in both, in 1933, 1934 and 1935 the Championship. Could they do it again? After seven matches and only two wins it didn't look likely.

All great teams come to the end of their eras. Some settle slowly, as Arsenal did, some rapidly, as Manchester City did after their Championship of 1937. For Arsenal, as we have seen, nearly all of the major players had already gone. Alex James and Herbie Roberts were approaching the end of their careers, Frank Moss' shoulder injury recurred in a Cup tie against Blackburn and his career was finally over, reserve centre forward Ronnie Westcott, of whom great things were expected, injured a knee in only his second League match and never played again.

Allison later wrote that, just before the manager's death, Chapman had told him: 'The team's played out Mr Allison, we must rebuild.' At the time the club was top of the First Division and half way through the hat-trick. In many ways the quote rings untrue. Perhaps it was just Chapman's way of loosening up a

director for yet more major expenditures, or perhaps it was a throw-away line after a single poor game. Nonetheless, the team was rebuilt, and not so much because of Allison's desire to buy new players as the ageing of the first-team squad. Allison's first signing was Ted Drake, the reluctant gas inspector from Southampton, in March 1934. And the highlight of the 1935–36 season was to be one game involving the same Ted Drake.

The date was 14 December 1935 and the match was one of the standard classics of the decade — Aston Villa versus Arsenal at Villa Park. About 70,000 were packed inside the ground to see another instalment in a rivalry which provided a series of highly memorable encounters since 1930. They were not to be disappointed though, for once, neither Arsenal nor Villa were heading the League. The Gunners were already eight points behind Sunderland while Villa, having conceded 52 goals in 18 games were bottom. Founder members of the

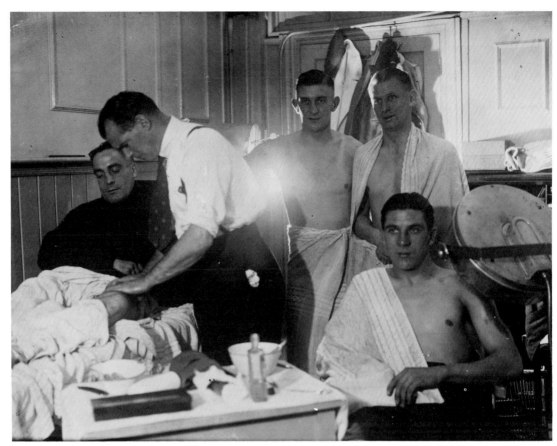

League in 1888, Villa had never been relegated and, in an attempt to stave off that ignominy, had recently spent so heavily that Chapman's and Allison's earlier behaviour looked like that of paupers by comparison. Between November 1935 and January 1936 Villa were actually to spend £35,000 on five players, more than the cost of Arsenal's famous 'Bank of England' forward-line. Villa were fielding six internationals, Arsenal were without James and Hulme. Centre forward Ted Drake had been in the reserves and was carrying a knee injury, which was heavily strapped for the first time.

For the first quarter hour Villa were the better team, but at half-time they went in 3–0 down and Drake had a hat-trick. All the goals were classic Arsenal — a long-ball from Pat Beasley for Drake to run on to, a long pass from Bastin which Drake picked up and ran with to the edge of the area before scoring, and a rebound from a Pat Beasley shot from the wing. At the end of an hour Drake had a double hat-trick and Arsenal were 6–0 up. This time the goals came from a mistake by Villa centre half Tommy Griffiths, who assumed a ball was going over the goal line only to see it rebound off the post for Drake, another pass from Bastin to Drake and an instant return from a bad goalkeeping clearance.

Drake was controlling the ball perfectly, beating defenders at will and shooting so accurately that the Villa keeper, Merton, had no chance. It was the exhibition of a complete centre forward. By this stage the entire Villa half back line was marking Drake, but it made little difference for his seventh shot actually hit the bar and bounced down to be cleared. It was one of only two goal attempts of the whole afternoon which missed its mark (the other was saved). Villa did score once, but Drake had the last word in the final minute with yet another goal from a Bastin cross-field pass; seven goals away from home with just nine shots.

One reason it was the season's highlight for Drake was that he was injured for much of it. As the 1936 Cup final approached, in which Arsenal were to play Sheffield United, Allison needed to test Drake's fitness after a cartilage operation. The game before the final was against Villa at Highbury. Ted Drake scored the winning goal and it was the final nail in Villa's relegation coffin.

Drake's seven goals in Birmingham were a League record, equalling Jimmy Ross Junior's alleged total for Preston against Stoke set way back in 1888 (and since found to be incorrect). By one of those peculiar statistical coincidences, however, Drake's was to remain the record for just 12 days, when Bunny Bell of Tranmere scored nine against Oldham in the Third Division North, though Drake's record remains for the First Division. Drake's goals made little difference to the title race — Sunderland beat the Gunners 5–4 in an exciting game at Roker and went on to win the Championship easily. Arsenal finished sixth, their worst position since 1930, with Derby, Huddersfield, Stoke and Brentford also in front of them.

The Cup was to be a different story. Bristol Rovers were defeated 5–1 at Eastville, then Liverpool 2–0 at Anfield. 'Recorder' in the Arsenal programme was particularly effusive about that display: 'It will go down in Arsenal history as one of the most glorious performances. The form of our team . . . was superb and would probably have accounted for any team in the land.' The next game was again away (the seventh consecutive away draw) at Newcastle, whom Arsenal had never beaten in the Cup and who had, of course, beaten them in the 1932 final. Moss, Roberts and Drake were all out injured, and the Gunners did well to draw 3–3. The replay at Highbury was easier, a 3–0 win including two Bastin penalties. The sixth round finally saw a home draw and a 4–1 defeat of Barnsley. The semi-final was at Huddersfield against highly unfashionable Grimsby (but then a First Division club) and there were some concerns that this might be another struggle like the one against the other Humberside team, Hull, in the semi-final six years before. It was certainly a hard game, Bastin's goal being the only one of the match and taking Arsenal to Wembley for the fourth time in ten years. Bastin had a habit of scoring the critical goal in semi-finals and in this case, he shot past Grimsby's centre half Hodgson whom Alex James had spotted (while on a scouting mission for Allison) was rather weak on his right side. Bowden and

A Smart Alec!

By TOM WEBSTER

THE ARSENAL PERFORMER – SAT IN HIS CORNER EATING HIS APRIL PIE HE PUT IN HIS THUMB – AND PULLED OUT A PLUM AND SAID "WHAT A GOOD BOY AM I."

[Daily Mail Copyright.]

THE YOUNGER GENERATION—By Cumberworth

THERE IS KEEN RIVALRY BETWEEN ALEX JAMES AND HIS SON AGED NINE YEARS. RECENTLY THE LATTER ARRIVED HOME AND SHOOK THE PATERNAL PRESTIGE BY ANNOUNCING THAT HE HAD SCORED 7 GOALS. TO RECOVER

BAGGED THREE GOALS TODAY!

SEZ YOU!

HIS POSITION IN THE HOUSEHOLD PA JAMES MADE HIS DESPERATE EFFORT OF LAST SATURDAY.

TOMORROW, ALL FATHERS WILL HOPE THAT ALEX DOES NOT SLIP BACK TO HIS OLD NON SCORING GAME.

IF HE DOES WE SUGGEST THAT HE WAITS ON THE DOORSTEP TILL HIS OFFSPRING HAS BEEN PACKED OFF TO BED.

Left: **A cartoon commemorating** the famous game against Sheffield Wednesday on 2 February 1935, in which Alex James scored a hat-trick in 20 minutes. That morning James' nine-year-old son had come home to tell his father that he had scored seven goals in a school game and wanting to know why his father never scored anymore. James produced his only Arsenal hat-trick that afternoon, also provoked by finding out that Wednesday manager Billy Walker had told his defenders not to bother with James near to goal as:'. . . he never scores these days . . .' Cliff Bastin wrote to Harry Homer, the programme editor, a week later saying: 'Alex surprised us all by scoring a hat-trick, much to the amusement of the crowd.' James soon slipped back into his old ways and by December that year Trevor Wignall was writing of him in the *Daily Express*: 'Alex James was, as usual, magical and marvellous, but if he had to depend for a living on finding the net he would starve to

Bastin practised playing on this weakness at Highbury the day before the semi-final, with Bowden working on how to draw Hodgson to the right, going past on the outside and slipping the ball back inside for Bastin coming into the gap. Bowden tried the move exactly as practised in the 40th minute; it worked just as planned and Arsenal won the game 1–0.

With no chance of winning the League, Allsion had been resting his injured players (such as Roberts and Drake) between Cup ties. This did not please the League, who fined Arsenal £250 in a show of displeasure which became almost an annual ritual directed at some club or other between the wars. When the final came round Drake, Roberts, James and Hapgood were all unwell. Drake was barely recovered from a cartilage operation and had only played his comeback game one week before. Allison decided he had to risk the centre forward and reshuffled his attack — putting Ray Bowden at inside forward and moving Bastin back to the left wing (he had been playing inside). The

upshot was that Pat Beasley, who had been in Bastin's spot for much of the season, was dropped before the final, just as he had been hours before the 1932 game. The FA again refused to mint an extra medal for him. The team that therefore took the field was Wilson, Male, Hapgood, Crayston, Roberts, Copping, Hulme, Bowden, Drake, James, Bastin.

Their opponents were Second Division Sheffield United, who had beaten Burnley, Preston, Leeds, Spurs and finally Fulham to get to Wembley. For most of the game United were on top, almost going ahead in the first minute when Alex Wilson dropped the ball in the 6-yard box, and later unluckily hitting the bar with a Jock Dodds header after half an hour. There were no goals until the 74th minute, when Bastin picked up a clearance and passed the ball through the middle to Ted Drake. Drake side-stepped past United captain Tom Johnson and hit the ball hard, left-footed, past keeper Smith. United attacked for the rest of the match and suffered further wretched luck when Dodds hit the death. The corner flags were, as usual, more in danger of being struck than the goal-posts . . .'

Above left: **Another James cartoon,** this time by Tom Webster, who was responsible not only for prompting James' long shorts but also the design of Arsenal's shirts. This cartoon was published on 22 April 1935, two days after a 1-0 Highbury win had guaranteed Arsenal their third consecutive League title. Pat Beasley had scored the goal and it was highly appropriate that the opponents had been Huddersfield, the only other team to perform such a hat-trick and also, of course, under Chapman's management.

Top right: **James, dressed in unlikely garb,** watches the Barnsley keeper Ellis during an FA Cup quarter-final tie at Highbury on Leap Year's Day, 1936. Arsenal won 4-1 with goals from Bastin, Bowden and Beasley (2).

Bottom right: **More Yorkshire connections** at Kings Cross three weeks later on 21 March 1936, as the fans gather to catch the special trains to Huddersfield for the semi-final against Grimsby. They were rewarded by a single goal from Ray Bowden and a trip to Wembley.

Left: **The 1936 FA Cup final** against Sheffield United was not to prove the most glittering moment in the club's history, but the demand for tickets never faltered. The Monday after those fans had set off for Huddersfield (previous page) the Highbury staff faced this postbag of requests for Cup final tickets. Some things never change. The post obviously worked well in those days – particularly the Sunday collections. 1936 did have a particular significance for the club, of course; it was the 50th anniversary of their foundation and, hence, the mid-point in this history.

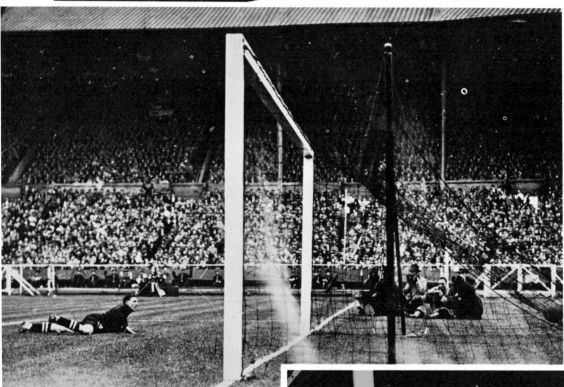

Above. **The only goal of the 1936 FA Cup final:** Drake picked up a pass from Bastin, side-stepped the Sheffield captain Tom Johnson and hit the ball hard, left-footed past keeper Smith. Drake, strapped and barely recovered from a cartilage operation, had struggled for much of the game and could not get up after the goal. He took no further part in the game. The moment, *right*, is often described as the goal but was actually a very similar incident earlier in the match when Drake's shot went just wide of Smith's post.

Right: **Celebrations at the end of the 1936 final.**
From left to right the players are Hapgood (who had been told that James would replace him as captain only that morning), James, Hulme and manager Allison. It was only Arsenal's second Cup success.

Below: **The evening was spent** at the Café Royal, where the club always had their celebration dinners. A cheerful crowd includes George Male (complete with obligatory cigarette – how times change), Alex James and, at the far right, Mrs James.

Below right: **The victorious team.** Back row: George Male, Jack Crayston, Alex Wilson, Herbie Roberts, Ted Drake, Eddie Hapgood;

centre: George Allison, Joe Hulme, Ray Bowden, Alex James, Cliff Bastin, Tom Whittaker; bottom: Pat Beasley and Wilf Copping. Beasley had been dropped days before the Cup final for the second time (1932 was the first). The club asked permission to mint a special medal for him, but the FA refused. Beasley was eventually to play in a final in 1938, when he was on the opposite wing to Joe Hulme in the losing Huddersfield team against Preston. If it was a first for Beasley, for Hulme it was a last. It was Hulme's fifth Wembley FA Cup final, a record equalled but not surpassed, and he never played in another first-class game.

woodwork a second time. Drake, who had been uncomfortable for the whole game, said afterwards that when he got the ball from Bastin he knew it was now or never. After he had scored James and Bastin were the first to reach him, but he was on his hands and knees in the grass, unable to get up because of the pain in his injured knee. Drake stayed on the field for the rest of the game, but took no further part. It was the only goal of the game and Alex James took the trophy. Hapgood had not realised he wouldn't be captain until he read the morning papers, a communication slip by Allison which appears to have rankled with Hapgood afterwards.

The captain and the manager never had a particularly close relationship, Hapgood being another who has described Allison as lucky to take over when he did and not possessing the football knowledge of Chapman (but then who could have compared, one is forced to ask?) Later Hapgood was particularly hurt that Allison was prepared to let him go to Luton at the start of the 1943–44 season, when the player wanted a final year with the Gunners. But the full back tells a good story about Allison in his autobiography, admitting that the manager was also very amused by it. Shortly after taking over, Allison was running a team talk preparing for the following day's match: 'The danger man for Wednesday is Charlie Napier,' he told Jack Crayston, 'and you have the job of marking him and not letting him have the ball.' Crayston tried to interrupt but Allison stopped him: 'Wait a moment, let me finish and then give me your views.' When Allison had finished he asked what Crayston wanted to say. 'Napier does play well for Wednesday, Mr Allison,' the half back commented, 'but we're playing Blackpool tomorrow.'

Having been largely outplayed by a Second Division side in the 1936 final, Arsenal were forced to face the realities of their new position. They were no longer *the* outstanding side. Others, having watched what Chapman had achieved, had begun to copy many of his methods. Arsenal's tactical game was no longer a surprise, particularly when Bastin, Hulme and James became older, slower and less effective. Individual players retired, others were injured. The strain of a decade with every game played like a Cup tie was taking its toll.

And yet there was still no single club ready to take over the mantle — Sunderland were always in at the kill, Preston often looked good, Huddersfield kept popping up, Wolves and Derby threatened to win everything and eventually won nothing. So, at the end of the day, Arsenal still maintained a better overall record than any other club — it is just that we are tempted to judge them by the standards not of the Chapman era as a whole, but solely against the 1930–34 period. None of the other sides really approached Arsenal for more than a single season; it was Arsenal's decade from beginning to end.

The realities of Arsenal's slightly diminished status were clear in the first few games of 1936–37. The Gunners won only two of their initial nine matches and, by the end of October, were 17th. In a now familiar story, though, the side fought back until, by mid-March, they were on top and seemed to be on the way to a seventh trophy in eight years. But, in true fairy story tradition, Manchester City came with an astonishing run of 36 points out of 40 from the New Year onwards. The crucial game was at Maine Road on 10 April 1937, when the Gunners went down 2–0 and left City clear to take the title. The following season City scored the highest number of goals in the First Division (80) and somehow managed to get themselves relegated, the only time the Champions have gone straight back down. For Arsenal, the season's most significant event was probably Alex James' retirement. His last League game was against Bolton on 1 May 1937 and was hardly the send off he or the club might have wished. Bernard Joy, now in the team in place of the injured Herbie Roberts, called the Mayday goalless draw 'dismal'. James' final match was actually played at Feijenoord on a summer tour a month later.

It is impossible to underestimate James' contribution to the successful Arsenal side of the 1930s. He was simply the key man. Before he arrived, as has often been repeated, they had won nothing, despite the big signings. In the six years after his arrival they won four Championships and reached three FA Cup finals. 'You might have suspected,' said Don Davies in an obituary in the *Manchester Guardian*, 'when you saw him shuffle onto the field for the first time that there was one who might lay claim to genius. Some held that James' slovenly appearance was natural, others said it was a pose. But it was in sharp contrast to one of the tidiest minds

Alex Wilson and Herbie Roberts combine to stop Everton's Dixie Dean during a League match on 29 August 1936. Hapgood, Bowden and James scored in a 3-2 victory. Roberts became the definitive 'policeman' stopper centre half, serving Arsenal in that position for a decade, though he was acknowledged to be a player with weaknesses. Whittaker said of him: 'Herbie's genius came from his intelligence and, even more important, that he did as he was told. His orders were to stay in the centre, intercept balls down the middle and head them clear or pass them short. His inability to kick a ball hard or far was thus camouflaged.' The picture also shows the revised strip with red shirts, white sleeves and red and white socks (previously the socks had been blue because the club couldn't find a red that matched and wouldn't run). Cartoonist Tom Webster, who inspired Alex James' shorts, was also responsible for the new shirts. Webster had turned up for a game of golf with the Chelsea chairman wearing a blue sleeveless sweater over a white shirt. The chairman, whose team wore blue shirts and white shorts at the time, liked this original combination and wanted to introduce it at Stamford

Bridge. Dave Calderhead, then the Chelsea manager, disagreed and refused to allow it. When Webster told the story to Chapman, he picked up the idea instantly and sent out his team in the distinctive style which has lasted to this day – Arsenal happily ignoring the almost annual cosmetics that too many clubs indulge in nowadays. The new shirts were first worn on 4 March 1933 at Highbury against Liverpool and could not be said to have had exactly a talismanic effect. Liverpool won 0-1 and Arsenal, though they won the Championship, did not enjoy a single success that March. That the change came so soon after Walsall may not be entirely coincidental.

in football. James hated waste, particularly wasted effort. To him it was the surest mark of inadequate technique. "Let the ball do the work" was his motto.' After he had begun to heed Chapman's advice to: '. . . . . cut out the circus tricks until we're winning 3–0,' James was at the centre of everything. That was why he was always treated slightly differently from the rest. Chapman would not have put up with his antics, his disappearances in the night and his lying in bed until noon from any other player. When he finished playing he took up a job with one of the pools companies. As a result, he was banned from playing or managing for a while, including a petty objection to his turning out for Northampton in wartime games. He later became a Sunday paper reporter and eventually returned to Highbury as a coach. He was to live only until 1953, aged 51, one of several of the great names of the 1930s to die tragically young.

James proved almost impossible to replace, though Allison tried. He bought Bobby Davidson from St Johnstone, but he was not to be the playmaker Arsenal needed. Nor, in the end, was Cliff Bastin, who featured for most of the 1936–37 season where he had started out, at inside forward. Allison searched further afield, buying Leslie Jones from Coventry (already a Welsh international) and George Drury from Sheffield United to fill the gap, but they didn't work either. In the end, he made the move which was, to a large extent, to become the albatross around the neck of his reputation — the purchase of Bryn Jones from Wolves.

Bob John retired on the same day as Alex James, Herbie Roberts never came back from his injury and a bloodclot complication and Joe Hulme was out for virtually a year and a half after injuring his back when he ran into a concrete wall at one end of the Huddersfield pitch. Oddly, it was back there to Leeds Road that Hulme eventually went in January 1938, and within three months he was playing outside right in the famous FA Cup final against Preston, won by the latter with a last minute George Mutch penalty. Hulme was the first man to play in five Wembley FA Cup finals, a record later to be equalled by Pat Rice. The 1938 Cup final was actually Joe Hulme's last ever first-class match, a wonderful way to end any career. Denis Compton almost did the same in 1950 (and got a winner's medal into the bargain) but he eventually played one more League match, against Portsmouth, after the Wembley finale.

Herbie Roberts had a less happy sequel to his Arsenal career, which ended after that bad injury on 30 October 1937 versus Middlesbrough. He became part of the backroom staff, moving down to train the nursery club at Margate. After only a brief time there, shortly after the outbreak of the war, he was to die of erysipelas, a rare bacterial infection of the skin which penicillin can cure relatively easy today. He was a great loss to Arsenal and to football and was the second (after Jack Lambert) of the great team to die soon after moving to Margate.

The nursery club idea had been another of Chapman's brainwaves. It was much better to have your youngsters competing in a real League than against other juniors, he reasoned. His first move was to try to take over Clapton (later Leyton) Orient, then a Third Division South club, who were threatened with expulsion by the FA in 1931 unless they paid off their debts. Chapman effectively took over the club late that year and all of the players were registered with Arsenal. It was a nice, if short-lived, irony as, 20 years before, Orient had been one of the main objectors to the move to Highbury. Needless to say, the League objected strongly and ordered Chapman to desist (they had clearly had enough of Arsenal bosses running two clubs twenty years earlier). The upshot was that Jimmy Seed, Orient manager since April 1931, found himself just a few weeks from the start of the 1932–33 season with no team, no directors and no registered players.

It was not Chapman, but Allison, who later turned to the Southern League, which was not concerned about the two clubs idea, and Arsenal acquired Margate instead. Seed was to have his own revenge on Arsenal — between 1934 and 1936 he took Charlton from the Third Division to the First and in 1936–37 he squeezed into second place between Manchester City and the Gunners.

So, having finished third in 1936–37 and been knocked out of the Cup in the quarter-finals at the Hawthorns, it did appear that Arsenal were in decline. All the more surprising, then, was their Championship in 1937–38, the fifth in eight years. Their record was almost identical to that of 1936–37, with exactly the same number of points, 52. They lost as many as 11 games (their highest number of defeats in any season in the 1930s to date, with the sole exception of 1935–36 when they lost 12) and scored only 77 goals, their lowest total since 1929–30 apart from the 75 in 1933–34, that peculiarly quiet season containing Chapman's death.

The side was not in any sense a settled one and the season was tough and inconsistent. At the end the Gunners were to just squeeze past Wolves and Brentford, who were performing the surprise Charlton role one season later. George Hunt had been bought from Spurs (one of the rare transfers between these two clubs at that time) to partner Drake up front and did so well that it was a surprise when Allison transferred him to Bolton at the end of the season. Joy had replaced Roberts and Bastin and Male were now the only survivors from the great days, making another Championship both more surprising and impressive. By February, Arsenal and Wolves were favourites for both major competitions and found themselves drawn together in the Cup one week after meeting in the League. Wolves won the League game 3–1 to go ahead of Arsenal in the table, though both were then several points behind Brentford. In the Cup the roles were reversed, Arsenal winning a very tough game 2–1 with goals from Drake and Kirchen in what Bernard Joy called the most exciting tie he ever played in. It must have exhausted them, for they went out 1–0 to eventual winners Preston in the next round at Highbury.

Brentford, despite having been seven points ahead of Arsenal at one stage, were like many other clubs who have risen through the divisions quickly. The elements of unfamiliarity and surprise carry them so far for so long, but the lack of strength in depth tends to tell in the end. Brentford walked the tightrope for a long time, but when they fell they fell heavily. In eight games Brentford took only two points and were out of contention.

At Highbury new names were making their mark — Mel Griffiths at outside right, Eddie Carr, a successful centre forward when Drake was injured, as he so often was. A long run of success put Arsenal three points clear of Wolves, at Easter, but then came disaster. Over the holiday period the Gunners could only draw 0–0 at Birmingham and then lost both games against Brentford. The matches against their London rivals, who were back in form now that their chance had virtually gone, were particularly inept, notable for Ted Drake's injury at Griffin Park, where he was knocked out and then came back on the field despite having blood pouring down his face from a head wound. That was the Drake of Arsenal inter-war legend. He ended this particular game being carried off the field half-conscious hung over Tom Whittaker's shoulder.

The Easter debacle put Wolves back on top and the contest went to the last match. Preston had made a late run from behind and were being tipped for the Double. Arsenal were perhaps fortunate to go to Deepdale a week before the Cup final (in which Preston defeated Huddersfield) and, with the Preston players no doubt tense and afraid of injury, as teams always are at that point, the Gunners won 3–1 when, on form, the game should have seen the end of their title hopes. On the very last day Wolves were away to Sunderland. If Wolves won, they were champions no matter what the opposition did, but if they drew, and Arsenal beat Bolton at Highbury, then Arsenal would be champions again. It was one of those odd moments when all the hopes and all the fears of perhaps years of effort come together in a single match.

The Bolton game was easy for a committed Arsenal, who won 5–0. But, though Sunderland had nothing to play for, they threw themselves into their game with Wolves with a vengeance. So determined were they that one of their defenders was sent off and they still won 1–0. Wolves, who had come so close, were thus to win absolutely nothing in the 1930s. The game at Roker had kicked off 15 minutes before that at Highbury, and when the result came through on the scoreboards and the crowd started cheering Bernard Joy called to Eddie Hapgood: 'They've lost Eddie.' Hapgood, typically, was so embroiled in the game, though Arsenal were already 4–0 up, that he simply didn't understand what Joy was talking about.

The final season before the Second World War proved to be notable for little but the purchase of Bryn Jones. This was really the

Bottom left: Demolition work begins on the old Main (East) Stand at Highbury on 21 April 1936. It had stood since 1913 and its replacement was complete the following October.

Top right: Television comes to Highbury; the first match shown live anywhere in the world was played at Highbury on Thursday 16 September 1937. Excerpts were shown on the BBC from a practice game between the first team and the reserves.

Bottom right: George Allison demonstrates on the famous tactical table during a midweek session in September 1938. The picture was taken in the boardroom, which retains the identical features to this day, down to the hat-rack. By this time Allison was not only manager but also the club's second largest shareholder (with 566 shares – J. J. Edwards had 752). Out of 470 shareholders, over 400 held just one share. The cost of the two new stands had put enormous financial pressure on the club and by August 1939 they were in debt to the tune of £22,960 and had only £3 18s 6d in the bank (£3.92). As in 1914-15, they found themselves going into a world war in a precarious financial state.

during the six seasons 1933–39, the total profit amounted to £136,000, a massive sum for any football club or moderate sized company of the period. In 1934–35 the club became the first ever to have gate receipts of over £100,000, and made a profit of £35,000. Of the other clubs only Portsmouth, with £14,961, even got into double figures. The financial reserves were then £60,000 and even programme sales brought in nearly £2,500.

Financially more debatable, as it happened, was the building of the stands. The West Stand cost £45,000 and was opened by the Prince of Wales (later the Duke of Windsor) on 10 December 1932. It had actually been first used on 12 November for a game against Chelsea (Arsenal won 1–0) and was, by a large margin, the grandest and most expensive structure on any League ground at the time. It incorporated three flats, an electric lift, and had 4,100 seats and the lower level, which was originally all standing, could theoretically hold another 20,000. Work had actually begun on redeveloping the ground in 1931, when the club started building up the banking on all four sides. Local inhabitants were encouraged to bring in their rubbish to help the process and, as Simon Inglis mentions in his invaluable *The Football Grounds of England and Wales*, one coal merchant backed up too close to a hole in the North Bank and saw his horse and cart disappear into the cavity. The animal was so badly injured that it had to be destroyed and it is buried where it fell, in the middle of the North Bank terracing.

The North Bank roof was originally built in 1935 (the clock then being moved to the South Bank) but was destroyed by bombs in the war. The new East, or Main, Stand was not planned to be built until 1941, but the original stand was deteriorating so fast, and the finances appeared to be so favourable, that the decision was made to rebuild in 1935 (it was first used for the game v Grimsby on 24 October 1936).

point at which Allison was accused of taking over Chapman's 'money bags' reputation with a vengeance. Interestingly such criticisms were a source of unusual irritation to Allison, who usually took disagreements and press comment in his stride. He was very quick to point out that, between 1925 and 1934, Chapman spent £101,000 in fees and received £40,000 for those he sold — a balance of around £7,000 per annum. Between Allison taking over and the war, Arsenal spent £81,000 and received £51,000, a net expenditure of £30,000. This was certainly more than manageable when,

As the club had already borrowed quite heavily to erect the other stands, by early 1937 Arsenal had debts of £200,000 and needed average crowds of 40,000 simply to pay the running expenses and finance the debt. The Main Stand, though planned to be identical to the West Stand, finally cost far more (£130,000 to be precise) and when the war came in 1939 the club found themselves in a similar position to that of Henry Norris in 1914. The war years clearly left the problem unsolved but, with the enormous boom in attendances between 1945 and 1952, and some intelligent management, the problem happily, and perhaps a little fortuitously, solved itself. One reason why the East Stand cost more than the West was that it had an expensive public frontage — the West is built entirely behind a row of houses and is effectively invisible from that side.

When George Allison finally decided he had to buy Bryn Jones in August 1938, the record fee was still the £11,500 he and Chapman had paid out for David Jack ten years before. Eventually

This page: **Left, right and out.** The magnificent Ted Drake was probably the greatest of all Arsenal centre forwards. His 42 goals in 1934-35 have never been surpassed, nor have his seven goals for the club at Villa Park on 14 December 1935, the most ever scored by a single player in any First Division game. The top picture shows Brentford keeper Crozier deflecting a shot from Drake at Griffin Park on 8 September 1938. Brentford defeated the Champions 1-0. The middle picture was taken a year earlier, against Sunderland at Highbury on 18 September 1937 and shows Drake's goal in a 4-1 win (Hulme, Davidson and Milne got the others). The lower picture is a classic, also taken at Brentford but on 18 April 1938, when the home side won 3-0. Arsenal lost twice to Brentford in the space of three days but still just squeezed in to win the League by a point, their total of 52 being the lowest which has ever headed the Championship in a 42-match season. Drake was injured three times in the match, was twice carried off, finished with two broken bones in his wrist, nine stitches in his head and was eventually (pictured) carried off unconscious over Tom Whittaker's shoulder. It was an extreme performance even by the tough and brave standards of Ted Drake. A young Denis Compton looks concerned on the left, Cliff Bastin on the right. Players were (as can be seen) still unidentified but shirt numbering was introduced for all games the following year.

Wolves forced Allison up to £14,000, and Jones was left to carry the very distracting tag of 'most expensive player'. Many players before and since have found this difficult, not least Bryn's own nephew Cliff Jones when he came to Spurs for £35,000 two decades later. Bryn started well enough though, scoring in his first game, against Portsmouth, and getting two more in the next three matches. But he never really settled that season, not enjoying the limelight as much as an Alex James and feeling the crowd and club's expectations weighing very heavily on his light shoulders.

It was the sort of pressure he could never escape from at Highbury — when he and Allison agreed that a run in the relative calm of the reserves might improve his form, 33,000 turned up to see his second team debut. As they had nearly all come to see Jones, this was even worse than being in the first team and the experiment was never repeated. Allison was understandably unrepentant about his purchase, pointing out that: '. . . he was not a prolific goalscorer (though he had scored 52 goals in 163 games for Wolves) just like Alex James, because his chief asset was the holding together of the line and the making of openings for the more vigorous of his team-mates.'

Allison said that Jones often asked to be saved from the ever-present, ever-insistent limelight, and believed that, given time to settle down, he would have made the grade: 'My faith never failed and I have never for a moment considered him a bad buy. Please don't think I'm going to say that I've never had bad buys. I have, but Bryn was not one of them.' Allison's point seems a fair one. It took Alex James a season to settle down and there was no reason to expect Jones, just as important a buy, to adapt any faster. He played exceptionally well on the team's close-season tour of 1939 but never really had another chance except in the very different atmosphere of wartime football. Like many great players, notably Stan Cullis of Wolves, his best years were inevitably lost to the war.

Interestingly, other members of the club did not share Allison's optimism. Cliff Bastin, in his autobiography, said: 'I thought at the time this was a bad transfer, and subsequent events did nothing to alter my views. . . I had played against Bryn in club and international matches and had ample opportunity to size him up. To my mind, he was essentially an attacking player, who was successful at Wolverhampton largely because the rest of the team was playing well.'

Bastin argued that James had a first-class footballing brain and that Jones, while being a first-class footballer, did not. James, whom

Below: **Leslie Jones** (second left) scores for Arsenal against Grimsby on 19 March 1938. Jones was a regular Welsh international but should not be confused with his compatriot and namesake Bryn Jones, whose arrival in August of the same year was to be the most controversial of all the major transfers in the inter-war period. Arsenal beat Grimsby easily 5-1, with the other goals coming in pairs from Griffiths and Bastin.

Bastin of course called one of the most self-confident people he had ever met, was able to weather the bad patch of the transition, while Jones, quiet, modest and self-effacing, was not. Bastin was the wing partner of them both, of course, so his judgement is possibly the most reliable available. Sadly, his conclusion is rather dismissive: 'It was his (Jones) natural instinct to play as far upfield as I. Arsenal's attempt to curb that instinct failed. . . (He) would have been much happier if he had never left Wolverhampton.'

Apart from Jones, the goalkeepers were also in the news in the last season before the war. George Marks, hailing from the non-footballing town of Salisbury, became the first-team keeper and was England's first choice for much of the war, losing his place only after a bad head injury sustained against Wales towards the end of hostilities. Much more serious was the tragedy that befell the reserve keeper David Ford. Aged only 18, he had played well in a Combination game for the second team against Portsmouth at Highbury. On the way home, he collapsed in the tube station, was rushed to hospital and found to have a duodenal ulcer, the pain of which he had foolishly kept quiet. He never recovered and died the following Saturday. More were to die in the hostilities that followed — of the 42 players on the staff in 1938–39, nine were dead by the end of the war. Nearly all the players joined the forces (Whittaker had served in the First World War and Bastin's deafness disqualified him so the two of them manned the Air Raid post on top of the main stand). The ground was bombed several times — Eddie Hapgood recalled one occasion when the incendiaries missed the stands but somehow managed to set fire to both sets of goalposts. Soon afterwards a barrage balloon arrived and was moored on the practice pitch. This did not prevent a 1,000-pound bomb hitting the same pitch, nor various other aerial objects destroying both the North Stand and some of the terracing. If this seems like bad luck, Birmingham were much worse off — St Andrew's was hit no less than 18 times! Arsenal and Spurs shared an undamaged White Hart Lane for most of the war and Arsenal won

the London League in 1941–42, the League South in 1942–43 and the League South Cup in 1942–43.

Arsenal were to conclude their inter-war glories with a flourish in 1939. Though they had never been in the hunt for the League title (Everton won it easily) the Gunners did win five of their last six games to finish, as in 1914–15, fifth. By this time Hitler had already invaded Czechoslovakia and the normality of football already seemed a little unreal. Although three games were played at the start of the aborted 1939–40 season, it was fitting that the last official pre-Second World War match should have been as peculiar, in its own way, as the last game in 1914–15. That was at Highbury on 6 May 1939, against bogey team Brentford, and was used to film the playing sequences for a thriller called *The Arsenal Stadium Mystery* by one Leonard Gribble. Brentford wore white shirts and black shorts instead of their usual change strip (to provide contrast for the black and white cameras) and played the part of the mythical Trojans. Several Arsenal players, as well as George Allison, enlivened the plot. Whether the script called for a 2–0 home win is not clear, but that's the way the game ended. It was Arsenal's last official first-class match for over six years.

Above: **The last League game before the Second World War** was as peculiar, in its own way, as its equivalent before the break for the First World War. It was against Brentford on 6 May 1939 and Arsenal won 2-0 with goals from Alf Kirchen and Ted Drake, but it was more notable for the fact that it was used to make the film 'The Arsenal Stadium Mystery'. Brentford, in unusual change strip, played the fictional part of 'The Trojans' and several Arsenal personalities took part in the film, including Cliff Bastin, Tom Whittaker and, seen being made up, George Allison.

Below: **One of Ted Drake's two goals** in the 1943 League South Wartime Cup final on 1 May 1943. Arsenal won 7-1, the highest victory recorded in a first-class Wembley final. Blackpool then beat Arsenal 4-2 in a North-South play-off at Stamford Bridge. The war was to prove a tragic time for a heavily bombed Highbury. No less than nine of the 42 professionals on the books in 1939 failed to survive it, the highest loss of any club. The nine were Henry Cook, Bobby Daniel, William Dean, Hugh Glass, Leslie Lack, William Parr, Sidney Pugh, Herbie Roberts and Cyril Tooze.

Above: **Charlton on the attack** against Arsenal at White Hart Lane during a Regional Wartime League South match on 2 November 1940. The game was drawn 2-2 with Arsenal ending the season fourth in the League (Crystal Palace won the League that season). Arsenal shared White Hart Lane with Spurs throughout the War. Highbury was used as an air-raid lookout post (largely because of the marshalling yards nearby) and was also bombed on several occasions. Among the damage was the total destruction of the original North Stand.

Dennis Compton, like most of the Arsenal players, joined the forces, becoming (appropriately) a gunner in the army.

Arsenal captain George Male shakes hands with his Charlton counterpart, Don Welsh, before the Football League South Cup final on 1 May 1943. Arsenal won the game 7-1, completing a hat-trick having previously won the Football League (South) and the League Cup (South).

· CHAPTER 7 ·
Whittaker's Arsenal

Forty-two of Arsenal's 44 professionals in September 1939 had gone into the services. The administrators at Highbury followed, and the ground itself played a part in the war effort — Arsenal Stadium was transformed into a stronghold for ARP (Air Raid Precautions). The club was temporarily based at White Hart Lane, though for a time George Allison converted the referees' room at Highbury into a small flat. Amid the confusion of wartime competitions and the difficulties of finding who was able to play when and where, Arsenal's success nonetheless continued.

In 1939–40 the South 'A' League was won, and in the following season the club reached another Wembley final in the Football League War Cup. With young Laurie Scott partnering Hapgood at full back and Bernard Joy at centre half, the attack was led by Les Compton, who at Wembley against Preston North End missed a penalty. Brother Denis' goal earned a replay, but with Drake now replacing the elder Compton Arsenal lost the replay at Blackburn 2–1.

The football honours, such as they were in such austere circumstances, continued: Champions of the London League in 1941–42 and the Football League South the following season, when there was also a successful return to Wembley, this time in the Football League South Cup final. Reg Lewis, who was to make his mark at the Empire Stadium in more illustrious peace-time circumstances, contributed four goals in a 7–1 thrashing of Charlton Athletic. The gifted forward whose casual approach and happy knack of scoring was to make him such a popular figure at Highbury in the early post-war years 'finished the 1942–43 season with a remarkable tally of 53 goals, which were partly responsible for the high total attendance of 670,000 at Arsenal's 39 games.

Two seasons later Lewis was not available and Arsenal's scoring honours were shared by Drake and Stan Mortensen from Blackpool, one of many guest players. Stanley Matthews was another in one wartime league game — he scored. For Ted Drake, though, a slipped disc proved to be one injury that even that gallant forward could not overcome, and his dramatic career ended.

The effort of continuing football in the war years proved extremely costly. Pre-war debts of some £150,000 were a millstone when the 1945–46 season began with regional Leagues retained and the return of the FA Cup the major concession to normality. White Hart Lane was still the home venue for the most remarkable match of that confused season. Late in 1945 Moscow Dynamo arrived on an unprecedented tour. With regular European football still more than a decade away, the visit was greeted with a sense of mystery mingled with anticipation. The Russians themselves were singularly suspicious of their hosts. The drama of the plot was heightened by the prevailing weather for much of their stay, a London pea-souper fog.

George Allison's own account of the events surrounding the match tell of the scurrying around to find a team worthy of the illustrious pre-war standards that Moscow Dynamo would expect and the opposition's misunderstanding of these efforts.

The manager's dealings finally produced six 'guests': goalkeeper Bill Griffiths from Cardiff, left back Joe Bacuzzi from Fulham, left half Reg Halton from Bury and three illustrious forwards — Matthews, Mortensen and Ronnie Rooke, whom Allison would sign from Fulham the following season. George Drury, now 31, and Horace Cumner, both survivors from the Arsenal pre-war scene, were the other two forwards, while Joy was at centre half, 33-year-old Cliff Bastin at right half and Scott at right back.

The crowd of 54,620 had only sporadic views of the proceedings as the fog occasionally lifted. So did the referee, a Russian, and his two linesmen who used the Soviet system of controlling the match with both linesmen on the same side of the field and the senior official operating from the other side.

Moscow Dynamo scored in their first attack, through Bobrov, but Rooke equalised and then the ebullient Mortensen struck twice. At half-time it was 3–2 but sinister whisperings reached the ears of George Allison that the referee would abandon the match if Dynamo fell further behind. On the other hand, if they were to recapture the lead the match would be played to a finish, however thick the fog.

The Russians did score twice in the second half, and the match did run its allotted span; the suggestion of subterfuge could not disguise the flair and discipline glimpsed through the fog.

George Male retired as a player in 1948. His very last first-class game was a perfect ending to a great career; it was on 1 May 1948 at home to Grimsby and Arsenal won 8-0, confirming their status as League Champions. Though Male played two more games on tour that summer, the Grimsby match was the last formal appearance of any of the players from the Chapman era. Like many of his colleagues, Male then went onto the coaching staff and became a tough task-master.

Conventional League fare resumed in August 1946, and for the first match at Highbury, a Football Combination fixture against Clapton Orient, the programme notes had a poignant ring:

'Our last programme was published on the second of September 1939 and not one of us will want to be reminded of what happened on the third. We beat Sunderland that day and Ted Drake scored a hat-trick. And it happened almost seven years ago. Where have we all been since then and what have we not seen. . . .'

First Division football returned to Arsenal Stadium on 4 September against Blackburn Rovers and Marksman summed up the mood of joy, without forgetting 'You who talked Arsenal with me over a campfire in Assam and the chap with the Italy Star on the train in India who informed me of Herbert Roberts passing on, the fellow in the Skymaster on the long hop from Ceylon to the Cocos Islands who told me about our Cup Final win and all those who played with or against Tom Whittaker's Arsenal Arps in the very early days of ARP. And the older ones who

stuck to the job in London through bomb and fire and rocket yet still made the long trek up to White Hart Lane to give the boys a cheer. We're home again now!'

On the field the resumption was inauspicious. It began with a defeat at Wolves where six goals and one of Bernard Joy's eyeteeth were lost. Reg Lewis, after scoring, ended up in goal, but at least his eleven goals in the first ten matches papered over some of the cracks. But others ran deep with little young talent immediately available; the move to White Hart Lane had temporarily ended the production line at Highbury. Icelander Albert Gudmundsson, an amateur, was one of 31 players used in the League. The charismatic Doctor Kevin O'Flanagan, an international at football and rugby, on one occasion on successive weekends, was another. Walley Barnes made his debut early in November, but it was two signings in the subsequent weeks which lifted Arsenal from the bottom of the First Division.

Joe Mercer, who had been in the England team as an attacking wing half at the outbreak of war, was in dispute with Everton. At 32 he had virtually decided to retire from football to concentrate on a grocery business in Wallasey. Surprise interest from Arsenal reawakened his ambition. He signed on one condition, that he could live and train in Liverpool. Allison and Tom Whittaker were not worried about his ageing, bandy legs. They had purchased a football brain, and by converting Mercer to a defensive half back they got full return for an investment of £7,000. Mercer also gave value to his team-mates off the field; it was not unknown for him to arrive in London on a match day with some extra provisions acquired through his grocery connections; in times of severe rationing such generosity made the genial Merseysider even more popular.

Two weeks after Mercer Arsenal added another bargain. At 35 Ronnie Rooke looked an even more unlikely buy, but the short-term need for goals was critical. Rooke struck 21 in 24 League games and the details of his transfer — a fee of £1,000 plus two players moving from Highbury to Fulham — emphasised again the shrewdness of the Arsenal management. Rooke did not finish top scorer. That honour fell to Lewis with a splendid 29 in 28 First Division matches. From the foot of the table the two lifted Arsenal to the respectability of mid-table; in thirteenth place they still finished top of the London pecking order, although in the third match of a five-hour FA Cup third round saga Chelsea finally triumphed on 'neutral' soil at White Hart Lane with two goals from Tommy Lawton.

For two tremendous servants, however, the road had come to an end. Cliff Bastin had been restricted to just six League matches, and he needed a major operation on his middle ear in April 1947. The dreadful winter led to an extension of the season into June. It was too much for an already wearied George Allison who, after an intimate association with the club of four decades, announced his resignation: 'Now I feel the need for a less strenuous life and I leave the future of Arsenal in other hands.'

Those hands had already cared for so many Arsenal players and other sportsmen of great renown. Tom Whittaker, the master-trainer, had modestly stayed in the background, vastly influential on the football side of the club while Allison had shown his considerable talents in the business and publicity departments. Now, for all his personal reluctance to step into the limelight, the time was right for him to accept the demanding post of secretary-manager.

Bob Wall always recalled Whittaker at work in shirt-sleeves with a pot of tea never far away. A gentle, kindly man, he had spent the war in the RAF. As a qualified engineer he had repaired aircraft, sending them out to battle again with the painstaking detail which had aided the recovery of so many Arsenal footballers. Having fought in the First World War, he was awarded the MBE for secret work in connection with the D-Day landings in the Second.

Joe Shaw returned from Chelsea, where he had been assistant manager, to become Tom Whittaker's right-hand man. The 1947–48 season began with a temporary captain. Les Compton still had cricket responsibilities for Middlesex, so Joe Mercer led out Arsenal for the opening League game at home to Sunderland. The pitch had been reseeded, the running track around it re-surfaced. There was optimism in the air and it was to be well-founded.

The playing strength was augmented by two more signings. Archie Macaulay from Brentford had starred for Scotland at Wembley the previous April and also represented Great Britain against the Rest of Europe. The cultured, red-haired wing half had much of the spirit of the Scottish terriers depicted on the lucky charm he carried with him all the time.

After much persuading — Whittaker made eleven trips to see him before the deal was done — forward Don Roper arrived from Southampton and a football family. His grandfather played for Chesterfield, his father for Huddersfield Town and Royal Marines, with whom he won an Amateur Cup medal. Rejection by Hampshire County Cricket Club after trials during the summer of 1947 had sharpened Roper's appetite to make a career in football.

What was to become a historic season began on 23 August with a 3.30 kick-off at Highbury against Sunderland. Three goals, from Ian McPherson, Jimmy Logie and Rooke, all in the opening 15 minutes of the second half, produced a 3–1 victory. Four days later Charlton were swept aside 4–2 at The Valley, with McPherson running riot against the FA Cup holders, scoring one and laying on the other three for Roper, Lewis and Logie. The Scottish winger had returned to football with impressive war-time credentials as an RAF pilot, his bravery winning him the DFC and bar. Though naturally an

outside right, his early contributions to Whittaker's bright start to the season were on the opposite flank.

A third successive victory came at Bramall Lane, Rooke levelling the score before Roper's 35-yarder was fumbled by the home goalkeeper Smith with only three minutes remaining. Reg Lewis then took centre stage with four goals — Rooke claimed the other two — in a 6–0 demolition of Charlton in the return match at Highbury; the visitors were handicapped by an eighth-minute injury to defender Peter Croker who went off with knee ligaments damaged trying to curb McPherson.

The buoyant mood at Highbury was maintained by news from Hastings that Denis Compton had struck the 17th century of his golden summer representing the South of England against the touring South Africans — and by the prospect of Manchester United's forthcoming visit to challenge the 100 per cent record that had lifted Arsenal to the top of the First Division. Ten thousand fans were still outside when the gates were closed and they missed another victory, by 2–1 with goals from the forceful pairing of Rooke and Lewis. The sense of expectation at the club was highlighted even more by the decision of Bryn Jones to turn down a move to Newport County. 'I'll stay until they chase me away, first team or not,' was the retort of the skilful Welsh international for whom the advent of war had forever rendered theoretical the question of whether his record transfer fee was justified.

For the first time Arsenal extended a sequence of wins at the start of a season to six — Bolton Wanderers, the next victims, were defeated 2–0 at Highbury. McPherson and a Rooke penalty contributed the goals in a match which Arsenal finished with only seven fit men. Lewis, recently watched by England selectors, pulled a thigh muscle after ten minutes. Before half-time Alf Fields strained tendons leaping over his own goalkeeper, George Swindin. Rooke and McPherson were also limping at the end of the match. Tom Whittaker sensed the need for the return of Les Compton, who had been given permission to continue his cricket with Middlesex.

The tall wicket-keeper was back in the Arsenal dressing room at Deepdale for match number seven and, as club captain, was given a ball by Whittaker to lead out the team. Modestly Compton passed it to Mercer saying: 'If you don't mind Tom, I think Joe should have this. He's not done too badly with the job so far.' Thus Mercer retained the captaincy which was to bring more than a touch of romance to the twilight days of his career. Without Lewis at the sharp end of the attack the first point was dropped at Preston in a goalless draw, but the following week Stoke City were on the receiving end of a three-goal first-half performance, with Bryn Jones enjoying a rare first-team appearance.

Lewis was back but Mercer missing because of food poisoning for a tough trip to Burnley, which brought a hard-fought success, with Barnes making one desperate clearance off the line. The winning goal from Lewis came against the balance of play. With two reserves, Paddy Sloan and the loyal George Male, as wing halves, Arsenal could only draw the next match at home to Portsmouth, but victory had been there for the taking when Rooke's 39th-minute penalty was brilliantly saved by Butler.

Goals remained hard to come by throughout October, a time when the flair of Denis Compton might have added an extra spice to Whittaker's recipe for success. But Britain's most glamorous sports star was confined to a hospital bed for the removal of some floating body from a troublesome knee. Aston Villa's visit to Highbury drew a 61,000 capacity crowd and a 1–0 win, but the goal was disputed with Rooke getting away with a push on centre half Moss before racing clear to score. A thumping penalty from Rooke brought a share of the points at Molineux — Roper fouled by Shorthouse — after Jesse Pye had given Wolves the lead right on half-time. It was a penalty against Arsenal, conceded by Leslie Compton and converted by Eddie Wainwright, that cost a point in the next match against Everton at Highbury. The brilliance of visiting goalkeeper Ted Sagar had restricted Arsenal to a solitary score from Lewis in the 65th minute.

With football such an attraction after the sacrifices of war, Arsenal, as First Division leaders, had already become the major draw. Stamford Bridge played host to a crowd of 67,277 for Chelsea's clash with the Gunners on 1 November. Astonishingly some 27,000 also watched the reserve game between the two clubs at Highbury on the same afternoon; the appearance of Tommy Lawton in the Chelsea second string heightened the appeal of the fixture.

In the senior match Arsenal came away with a goalless draw, the unbeaten record still intact. It remained so seven days later when Blackpool, with Mortensen and Matthews, were beaten 2–1 at Highbury through another Rooke penalty and a goal for Don Roper. That week — in November 1947 — the Football Association had written to all clubs with warnings about hooliganism! Before the Blackpool match Tom Whittaker addressed the Highbury crowd with a request to 'Keep up your reputation for sportsmanship. Don't barrack the referee.'

Arsenal's colours were lowered 4–3 by the Racing Club in Paris, when the traditional meeting reached unprecedented heights of excitement — but the League record still had two more matches to run. A splendidly struck 25-yard drive from Rooke brought back both points from Blackburn Rovers, then Rooke was also a scorer along with the diminutive Logie in a 2–0 Highbury triumph over Huddersfield Town.

With more than a third of the season gone Arsenal stood proudly six points clear of Burnley at the top of the tree, with a record of: Played 17, Won 12, Drawn 5, Lost 0, goals for 31, against 8. Yet the tag of 'lucky' was still being pinned on the team. Public opinion held the view that progress had come from efficient organisation and defensive discipline rather than football of a higher level than the opposition.

Thus the inevitable first defeat, on 29 November at Derby County, did not come as shattering news. The Baseball Ground was packed to the rafters to see the pursuit of a record (22 games unbeaten from the start of a season) held by Preston and Sheffield United collapse to a goal in the 32nd minute. Steel and Morris both had shots blocked but finally the loose ball was despatched past Swindin by winger Reg Harrison.

A goal in the same minute a week later, by Black of Manchester City at Highbury, threatened another defeat, but five minutes from time Les McDowall, who was later to manage the Maine Road club, was penalised for hand-ball. Rooke sent his penalty unerringly past Frank Swift, and there was no disputing that, on this occasion, Arsenal were fortunate.

In such circumstances a visit to bottom club, Grimsby Town, could only be viewed as a welcome opportunity to return to the groove of earlier in the season. The Blundell Park club had conceded three goals per match on average over the first half of the seaon; Arsenal managed four through the reliable Rooke 2, Logie and Roper.

The Saturday before Christmas has now been accepted an an attendance low spot with the demands of shopping for the festivities ahead. It was not so in 1947 when more than 58,000 flocked to Roker Park to watch Arsenal in the flesh. The vast majority of them almost had an early holiday treat when Davis sent Sunderland into the lead with only ten minutes remaining, but five minutes later the limping Barnes, a passenger at centre forward, helped create an equaliser. Bryn Jones was to play only seven times in the Championship season but his Roker Park equaliser, his solitary goal of the campaign, held great significance; a second defeat with the congested holiday fixture list ahead might have badly disturbed the Arsenal momentum.

Instead the two Christmas matches produced typically contrary results. The Football League in pre-computer days, with scant regard for the family life of footballers, paired Arsenal home and away with Liverpool! Only Mercer with his Merseyside base could have relished the Christmas morning start at Anfield, but the team responded to the challenge with two goals from Rooke and another from Roper which ended Liverpool's unbeaten home record. Two days later though, revenge was claimed. Albert Stubbins and Billy Liddell struck to stop Arsenal's invincible run at Highbury; Lewis replied too late to salvage a draw from a match for which touts did a roaring trade, with reports of tickets valued at 7s. 6d. (37p) changing hands at more than four times that price!

On New Year's Day, Arsenal, 1–0 winners at Bolton, stood five points clear at the top. Thirty-seven-year-old George Male was pressed into service at Burnden Park and gave a sound performance. Bolton claimed that they had equalised a 32nd minute goal from Lewis in a late scramble when the ball appeared to have crossed the line before Swindin pulled it clear. The crowd was allowed in only half an hour before an early start on a pitch flooded by melted snow and the referee dispensed with the half-time interval.

Arsenal's quest for football honour continued with a 3–2 victory over Sheffield United in the last game of the holiday programme. United were down to ten men when Rooke grabbed an important second goal; the player off the field was Alex Forbes, the flame-haired wing half shortly to return to Highbury as part of Whittaker's team strengthening. Forbes had been concussed and remembered nothing of his return to the pitch, during which time United scored twice in the last five minutes to give the scoreline a rather flattering look.

With the FA Cup providing a new challenge and a break to the slog for the Championship, Tom Whittaker was not the sort of man to underestimate a kindly draw, a home tie with Second Division Bradford Park Avenue. Consequently, he took his players to Brighton (shades of pre-war delights) for a few days' preparation in the bracing sea air. It did not have the desired effect. In Billy Elliott, the Yorkshire club possessed a locally born left winger who would later play for England after a transfer to Burnley; the 22-year-old Elliott knocked in a first-half goal. Bradford also included a centre half whose involvement in post-war football would span almost 40 years, many at a very high level of influence. Ron Greenwood became the cornerstone of Bradford's rearguard action in that third round tie at Highbury, and Arsenal's FA Cup ambitions perished.

There was little time for despondency. The next two First Division opponents also had their eyes on the League title, Manchester United and Preston. United still played their home matches at Maine Road, because of war damage at Old Trafford, and the interest in the visit of the leaders was massive. More than 80,000 crammed into the ground for a game that finished level after Lewis had drawn first blood and Jack Rowley equalised. The attendance remains the highest ever recorded for a Football League fixture, to be precise, 83,260.

Lewis was now operating at inside right and he retained the position for the tussle with Preston, striking two more valuable goals. Rooke was also on target, while Don Roper enjoyed an inspired afternoon. With those three important points in the bag since the Cup disappointment, Arsenal continued to set a blistering pace at the top of the League. In February Stoke City took the unusual step of making their home match all-ticket against the leaders, but the 41,000 ticket-holders did not witness a goal, largely due to a succession of saves from Swindin.

For the Valentine's Day fixture against Burnley, the Arsenal team appropriately contained a touch of romance. Denis Compton, who had turned out in only one post-war League match, was called into the senior side in place of the injured McPherson. For such a charismatic performer it was a perfect opportunity against a side which came to Highbury needing a win to close the gap at the top. Compton's return captured the imagination of the paying public; 20,000 arrived too late to get into the packed ground and with shades of Wembley 1923 a policeman mounted on a white horse strove to maintain order in the streets around Highbury.

It took Compton only fourteen minutes to play his part. His lob was punched by goalkeeper Strong straight to Roper who drove the ball into the Burnley net. Rooke added two more, with Compton also involved in the move that led to Arsenal's third goal. With 13 matches still to play, the Gunners now held an eight-point advantage over their closest challengers.

Meanwhile, Tom Whittaker had not grown complacent about the depth of talent at the club. Because of the immediate post-war circumstances Arsenal were fielding one of the oldest sides ever to win the Championship, with Rooke, now 36, Les Compton 35 and Mercer 33 holding three of the key roles. Quietly, Whittaker was adding to his staff. Cliff Holton, an amateur from Oxford City, was signed in November 1947. Peter Goring, eternally to be dubbed as the butcher's boy, gave up his part-time football with Cheltenham Town to join the Arsenal staff the following January, and the next month a senior player arrived in the shape of Alex Forbes, whose swashbuckling performances for Sheffield United had often caught the eye of the Highbury crowd.

Forbes' debut was delayed until after the third defeat of the League campaign, at Aston Villa on 28 February, which should really not have happened at all. An own goal by Moss and another from Rooke gave Arsenal a 2–1 lead when Denis Compton was tripped in the Villa penalty area. Rooke put his penalty wide, and Villa revelled in the second chance they had been given. Les Compton had been injured in training and played with one leg strapped from ankle to knee. In Trevor Ford, the fiery Welsh international, the home side had the perfect forward to capitalise on a weak link. Ford roasted his marker, and scored twice as Villa raced home 4–2.

Alex Forbes was chosen at inside left for his debut, with Wolves the opposition on a foggy Highbury afternoon. Many of the crowd were still settling down when Hancocks caught Arsenal cold with a goal after 80 seconds, but Forbes immediately began to justify his £12,000 transfer fee. His equaliser in the eighth minute delighted his new supporters and his dance back to the centre won him a place in their hearts. It was a tremendous start for a player who had once turned his back on football in favour of ice hockey. Whittaker had sent Macaulay to persuade him come to Highbury when Forbes was in hospital recovering from appendicitis.

The Compton brothers, mainstays of the team in the 1940s. Leslie Compton was the regular centre half from the war to 1951 and is seen here (left) tackling Jimmy Mullen of Wolves on 25 September 1948. Champions Arsenal won 3-1 with two goals from Reg Lewis and the third from Denis Compton. Denis, his cricketing obligations being a major restriction, was much less of a regular than Leslie, though he would have been if available. Though forever associated with the era, Denis actually played only 60 first-class matches in an Arsenal career lasting from 1935 to 1950, while Leslie wore the colours 273 times. But Denis was there when it mattered, specifically during the 1950 FA Cup run. The shot (below right) ended as Arsenal's second goal in the 1950 fifth round tie against Burnley on 11 February. Reg Lewis scored the other for a 2-0 win. Both the Comptons won Cup winners' medals that season, the final against Liverpool on 29 April almost being Denis Compton's last first-class game. He did, however, appear against Portsmouth in the League four days later before hanging up his football (but not cricket) boots for good. Note that there was no stand on the North Bank in 1948.

Wolves led again but with Denis Compton in irrepressible form in the second half Arsenal bounced back to win 5–2. A week later at Goodison Park the cricketing footballer did even better, scoring his first two post-war League goals in a 2–0 triumph over Everton.

After only three defeats in 32 games, it came as a surprise that two more followed in the next three matches. The first came at Highbury where Chelsea chalked up a 2–0 victory. John Harris did a magnificent job containing Rooke and Chelsea carried enough venom in their attack to strike through Bobby Campbell and Roy Bentley. The other loss was sustained at Blackpool, where two goals from Stan Mortensen took him to the top of the First Division scorers list, with one more than the 27 of Rooke, who had to observe at close quarters his tally being overtaken.

A week earlier fate had not been kind to Bob Anderson, whose misfortune it was to make his League debut in the Middlesbrough goal against Arsenal at Highbury. Smarting from the home defeat by Chelsea, Arsenal confronted the untried keeper in a mean mood. Among the seven goals that flashed past Anderson were two more from Denis Compton, and a hat-trick from Rooke, which was completed when he headed a tentative clearance from the goalkeeper straight back past him. So one-sided was the match that newspaper reports at the time make reference to several thousand supporters leaving at half-time. Poor Bob Anderson, for whom Good Friday in 1948 hardly lived up to that billing; he never played again in the First Division, although he did reappear in League football in the 1950s with Crystal Palace, Bristol Rovers and Bristol City. Goodfellow, the regular keeper that season, had returned on the Easter Monday when Arsenal made the long journey to Ayresome Park. Rooke had to settle this time for just one goal and Middlesbrough recovered some dignity in a 1–1 draw.

With fewer and fewer fixtures available for the chasing pack to close on their prey, Arsenal moved a step nearer to safety by completing the double over Blackburn Rovers at Highbury, Logie's sixth goal of the season and Rooke's 29th providing a margin of sufficient comfort; on 10 April Arsenal took the field at Huddersfield nine points clear with just five matches left. A win at Leeds Road would see Whittaker's men breasting the tape. The conclusion, however, was not so decisive.

A goal from Don Roper brought only one point, and the players had to bath and change so quickly to catch the London train that they could not discover the day's other results. It was Denis Compton who broke the glad tidings. At Doncaster he ran for a paper which reported defeats for Manchester United, Burnley and Derby County. Arsenal were Champions, and had led from start to finish. George Male, the last of the great pre-war side, played at Huddersfield, and as ever turned in a highly polished performance.

Inevitably anti-climax followed, with Derby winning at Highbury the following Saturday, and two successive goalless draws at Portsmouth and Manchester City. There was, however, a celebration on 1 May, though only 35,000, the smallest home gate of the season, were there to see it. Yorkshire-born Lionel Smith was given his League baptism at centre half, but it was the attack which made the headlines. Arsenal ripped into Grimsby to the tune of 8–0, and four goals for Rooke confirmed him, with 33, as the Football League's leading scorer — and this at the age of 36! Grimsby were scuppered into the Second Division and are still waiting to return.

George Swindin had conceded only 32 goals in the full League programme and added a second Championship medal to that gained in 1938. Rooke was the only other ever-present, though Macaulay, Mercer and Roper missed just two matches and Logie and Laurie Scott three. Les Compton collected a League winners' medal to go with his memento of cricket championship success the previous September (a rare double). So too did brother Denis, though he had to wait until October to receive his because of doubts as to whether his 14 appearances were sufficient qualification (hereafter 14 was regarded as the acceptable minimum).

Undoubtedly the tremendous consistency of the big-hearted Rooke proved to be a marvellous attribute throughout the season, but much of Arsenal's success came from the reliability of their defensive method. Joe Mercer labelled it as the 'retreating' defence. The prevailing style of the day was to try to win the ball in midfield with an attempted tackle on the opponent in possession. If that tackle was lost then there was little sophisticated covering. Mercer, with Macaulay as a shrewd ally, preferred Arsenal to leave the ball with the opposition and back off, packing the centre of the defence. Arsenal's captain had noted the success of such manoeuvres in basketball during the war, when he'd played service games with Americans. The crowd did not always like the tactic, newspaper comment denounced it as negative, but the rest of the First Division, with the exception of Derby County, who beat Arsenal twice, could not fathom out a solution. The seven-point margin at the end of the season was ample testimony to Arsenal's worth as champions. It was no more than an extension of everything Chapman had taught the club.

The players presented Tom Whittaker with a silver cigarette box inscribed 'To Tom/In Appreciation/From The Boys'. The manager, however, was already aware that the side had not been built to last. Before the end of May 1948 he had acquired the potential of Doug Lishman, a regular scorer for Walsall in the Third Division South. Nevertheless, the 1948–49 season began with the air still full of anti-climax. It took a run of wins in the autumn to lift the club from the bottom half of the table to fifth place, where Arsenal stayed. Derby County again proved to be a bogey team, taking three of the four League points and knocking Whittaker's side out of the FA Cup at the Baseball Ground in the fourth round.

One match did stand out, an extravagant 4–3 victory in the Charity Shield against the Cup holders Manchester United at Highbury. Incredibly Arsenal led 3–0 after just five minutes — Jones, Lewis and Rooke — but United's resolve stood the test. Lewis scored again for Arsenal, a splendid solo goal, but the destiny of the Charity Shield was not finally settled until the last blast of the referee's whistle.

Rooke's magnificent contribution to the history of Arsenal Football Club ended in June 1949. Sixty-eight goals in 88 First Division games were ample evidence of his contribution. At 37 he refused to contemplate retirement, and moved as player-manager to Cystal Palace, his pre-war club, where he paid his way in goals for two more seasons. A man of iron who never flinched from the physical contact of those who tried to stop him, he left Highbury with the satisfaction of having more than answered the call of George Allison: 'Ronnie, we're in trouble. We've got to get goals, by hook or by Rooke.'

The other half of the duo who turned the tide at Highbury in 1946 remained at the club. Joe Mercer passed his 35th birthday during pre-season training prior to the 1949–50 season, and if one target drove him to continue playing it was a search for the honour which had eluded him, an FA Cup winners' medal. Mercer had been a young reserve at Everton when they had won the most romantic of the game's trophies in 1933. The following day a kindly Albert Geldard, who had played in that final, was cleaning his boots beside Mercer at Goodison Park and offered the youthful Mercer a piece of Wembley turf. 'No thanks, I'll get some myself one day,' was the confident reply. It seemed that those words would haunt him.

Four defeats in the opening five matches may well have concentrated the players' minds on the FA Cup; the only win during that dismal start had come at Chelsea where Peter Goring scored on his debut and Swindin captained the side in the absence of Mercer and Les Compton. Brother Denis had ended speculation that he had played his last for Arsenal by signing for the new season on the eve of the third Test against New Zealand, thus becoming one of 54 professionals on the staff.

League performances improved sufficiently to achieve a respectable sixth place at the end of the season but it was the Cup which cheered all at Highbury. A run began which contained all the superstitions and omens which somehow surround the competition. For example, it began on an anniversary. Sheffield Wednesday came to north London on 7 January 1950, sixteen years virtually to the day when they had been the opposition for an Arsenal devastated by the loss of Herbert Chapman. In 1950, that was an anniversary remembered as if it were yesterday.

Now, in the FA Cup third round, they were in-form opponents, unbeaten for three months.

Their team-work almost came to their rescue in spite of losing right back Vince Kenny, injured in the tie. Reg Lewis finally made the breakthrough with 13 seconds left on the referee's watch. Oddly the crowd was ten thousand less than capacity because publicity suggesting a huge attendance had deterred many from what they believed would be a wasted journey.

The signs remained good in the draw for the fourth round, another home game against Swansea Town, who were labouring in the lower half of the Second Division. On a frosty pitch the underdogs performed gallantly while Arsenal again looked anything but potential winners of the competition. The decisive goal in a fortunate 2–1 win came ironically from a Welshman. Keane handled and Walley Barnes, whose career had been rescued from persistent knee trouble by little more than his own strength of will, slotted the penalty past the left hand of goalkeeper Jack Parry.

George Swindin, the dry Yorkshireman who had been signed from Bradford City in 1936, had added the role of prophet to his more usual occupation of goalkeeper. Before each round so far he had foretold that Arsenal would be given a home tie. Again his words rang true when Burnley came out of the hat to visit Highbury in round five. In a small way the visitors had contributed to the Cup aspirations of the team they now faced, because on the opening day of the season it had been Burnley who had beaten Arsenal in the capital and thus set the Highbury League campaign off on a flat note.

The lure of the Cup, not for the first or last time, produced an indulgence in preparation. There was no seaside training in the traditional manner; instead the Arsenal squad were treated to sessions under sunray equipment to tone them up. Goals from Lewis and Denis Compton did the trick, though Mercer remembers getting away with hand-ball in his own goalmouth.

Swindin forecast another home draw with the added prediction that Leeds United would be the opposition. Incredibly it came true, and it looked as though, in football parlance, Arsenal's 'name was on the FA Cup'. Leeds also languished in the Second Division, but their reaction to a first Cup tie at Highbury produced a creditable display. Lewis, who was to finish behind Goring in the League charts, added to his catalogue of significant Cup goals by darting between two defenders to score. Arsenal were into the semi-finals and they had not been forced to leave Highbury to get there.

A semi-final pairing with Chelsea meant that they still did not have to leave North London, and the saga of the tie remains as memorable as the final itself. At White Hart Lane Chelsea brought back the former England international Len Goulden; at 37 he had been out of favour for six months. When Chelsea sprinted into a 2–0 lead after 25 minutes, both goals from Bentley, Goulden must have been dreaming of a fairytale visit to Wembley. Arsenal had other ideas, although it needed an outright stroke of good fortune to help put those ideas into effect.

Outside right Freddie Cox knew White Hart Lane well; he had been signed from Spurs in September 1949 in an attempt to halt the slide at the start of the season. The best years of his footballing life had been sacrificed in wartime when he had flown Dakotas in Transport Command. His interest in aerial subjects extended to birds; Freddie was a keen ornithologist. In the semi-final he took a corner, the aerodynamics of which must have surprised even him.

In the dying seconds of the first half Cox struck this corner with the outside of his foot. The ball veered in towards the Chelsea goal and was over the line before Harry Medhurst, the goalkeeper, made a vain attempt to keep it out. Cox, who died in 1973 after a career in League management, never claimed any deliberate intent, but Arsenal gratefully accepted the touch of luck, and came out for the second half in determined vein.

Yet with a quarter of an hour remaining they were still trailing. Another corner, this time from the left wing, came to the rescue. Again the goal had a story behind it. As Denis Compton prepared to take the flag kick he waved forward brother Leslie. Joe Mercer countered by telling the centre half to stay back, but blood being thicker than water and the need for an equaliser pressing, Compton the elder ignored his captain's instructions. The fraternal pair emphatically won the argument when Denis' corner found the forehead of Les and the ball sped into the Chelsea net. On balance of play Arsenal had been fortunate to earn a replay, but this had been Chelsea's chance and it had gone.

Arsenal's form was much improved in the replay, which also took place at Tottenham, the following Wednesday. George Swindin's ability to predict the future passed, it seemed, to Eileen, the wife of Freddie Cox. On the Tuesday night she dreamed that her husband would score

the goal that took Arsenal to Wembley. And so he did, but not until the 14th minute of extra time, with his weaker left foot.

The journey to the Empire Stadium, therefore, became the longest Arsenal had had to make in the entire Cup run. By an odd coincidence Liverpool had reached the final without leaving Lancashire, beating Blackburn at Anfield, after a replay, winning home ties against Exeter, Stockport and Blackpool, then a semi-final success, of extra satisfaction, over Everton at Maine Road, Manchester. Bob Paisley, later to become the most successful of all Liverpool managers, had scored the vital goal against Everton, but he was left out of the team for the final. His only memento was to be in the Wembley match programme, in which he was listed as left half.

That job in the Arsenal team went of course to Mercer, with most of the country's neutrals hoping that one of the game's most-loved characters would at last complete his collection of medals. Yet unwittingly Arsenal's captain found himself in the midst of a potentially embarrassing situation. He had continued to train in the north-west — with Liverpool! Understandably he was asked not to join the Liverpool first team at Anfield for fear that he would find out too much about their Wembley battleplan. He was not banned from the ground, but his access was restricted to afternoon sessions, often with Jimmy Melia, who was then on the Liverpool groundstaff.

Liverpool were managed by George Kay, West Ham's captain in the first Wembley final in 1923. Kay had nurtured a team the majority of whom had come through the ranks, notably the Scottish international forward Billy Liddell. Liddell, reckoned the Arsenal players, was the most likely barrier to their winning the Cup. Moreover, Liverpool held an important psychological advantage. They had won both League meetings with Arsenal, 2–1 at Highbury in

The goals that brought the Cup back to Highbury in 1950, both scored by inside left Reg Lewis. Both the first (top right) and second (bottom right) were sharp breaks which left Liverpool keeper Cyril Sidlow with little chance. It had been a good Cup year for Arsenal; they were drawn at home throughout, played both semis against Chelsea at White Hart Lane and thus never left London. Twenty-one years later, when they again met Liverpool in the final, they were drawn away in every round and compounded this by again reaching the final the following year without a single home draw (photographs by courtesy of The Sunday Times).

George Swindin saves at the near post from Liverpool right-winger Jimmy Payne's diving header during the 1950 FA Cup final. It was the closest Liverpool came, Arsenal winning the match 2-0 for their third success in the competition. The defenders are Joe Mercer and Leslie Compton, wearing the unfamiliar orange or old gold (the dye was somewhere between the two) change strip that, unusually, Arsenal adopted for the final.

September, 2–0 at Anfield on New Year's Eve.

On the eve of the final itself Mercer was hailed Footballer of the Year by the Football Writers' Association. Tom Whittaker had already decided upon his team. Lishman, McPherson, Macaulay and Roper had their merits considered but were passed over; Goring kept his place, the Wembley setting being a perfect ending to his first season at senior level, and his mother, father and seven of his eleven brothers and sisters travelled up from the West Country to see the match.

Rain fell heavily on 29 April 1950. Wembley was bursting at the seams, though the ticket allocation for each club ran to only 11,500 (4,500 seats, 7,000 standing) of the 100,000 capacity stadium. Arsenal assembled in the North dressing-room where a telephone link enabled the betting members of the team, of whom there were several, to settle their nerves with calls to their bookmakers about that afternoon's racing.

Both teams had to change from their usual red shirts; Liverpool opted for white with black shorts, Arsenal took the field in shirts of old gold with white shorts. Two pre-match decisions

The victorious 1950 Cup winning team; from left to right: Reg Lewis (scorer of the two goals), Freddie Cox, Peter Goring, Walley Barnes, Denis Compton, George Swindin, Joe Mercer (with the Cup), Laurie Scott, Alex Forbes, Leslie Compton and Jimmy Logie.

A mood of grey austerity presides over the Highbury of 1950 as Leslie Compton, Joe Mercer and the Cup depart for a triumphal tour of North London (photograph by courtesy of *The Sunday Times*).

helped turn the tide of the battle towards the north London club. Forbes had been given the task of subduing the threat of Liddell, and after some early alarms the forceful wing half, who had been recalled by Scotland two weeks before the final, coped splendidly.

An even more significant decision had been to keep faith with the 30-year-old Reg Lewis. It had not been taken lightly. Lewis undoubtedly scored goals, but at times he could look lazy and lethargic. His skill had not been in question from the moment he had begun his League career with a debut goal against Everton on New Year's Day 1938. Yet Whittaker often dropped him, and Mercer's voice among others was heard in defence of Lewis before his place was finally confirmed.

At Wembley he became the match-winner, collecting both goals, coincidentally for a father of twins, at identical times in each half. The first, after 17 minutes, came when Goring moved away, distracting the attention of Liverpool defenders. Jimmy Logie had the ball at his feet; the tiny inside right, who weighed little more than nine stone but was a giant in this match, immediately slotted a pass through a square defence for Lewis to chase.

It was a knife into the heart of Liverpool. Lewis comprehensively beat their Welsh international goalkeeper Cyril Sidlow. Seventeen minutes into the second half it was Lewis again, this time with assistance from Cox, and from then on there was little doubt that Joe Mercer would at last lay his hands on the FA Cup.

The medal to go with it almost escaped Arsenal's captain. His Majesty King George VI presented the trophy, and the personal memento came from the Queen. Joe was just about to go down the Royal Box steps with a *loser's* medal when the error was spotted.

One Arsenal player did retire a few days later but it was not Joe Mercer. Approaching his 32nd birthday Denis Compton realised that the combination of international cricket, top-flight football and a knee that was protesting more and more about wear and tear was no longer viable. He had already decided to abdicate from football before the Cup final, a fact used to Arsenal's advantage by Tom Whittaker at half-time at Wembley.

Compton's first-half contribution had been less than memorable. 'Now,' said the Arsenal manager, weighing each word carefully, 'you've got 45 minutes left of your soccer career. I want you to go out there and give it every ounce you possibly can.' Denis Compton rarely lacked confidence, but this time he needed fortification. A glass of whisky was produced, and Arsenal's outside left played a full part in a strong second half performance. Nor was it quite his football finale. The following week Portsmouth came to Highbury needing points to win the Championship. Compton gave a brilliant performance; Goring scored twice in a 2–0 victory, though Pompey eventually took the title.

While Denis Compton, after knee surgery, turned his thoughts towards representing England's cricketers in Australia in 1950–51 (a tour which incidentally also robbed Arsenal of the services of an aspiring inside forward, Brian Close, who had been signed from Leeds United) football's international selectors sought the services of Les Compton. On 15 November 1950 at the astonishing age of 38 Arsenal's veteran centre half represented his country for the first time, England's oldest international debutant. England beat Wales 4–2 at Sunderland with Lionel Smith also winning his first cap and Ray Daniel, Compton's club deputy, called up for Wales. Compton retained his place a week later when Yugoslavia forced a 2–2 draw at Highbury, but the next international was five months later so a short but remarkable international career was over.

Arsenal led the First Division at the half-way mark of the 1950–51 season, but two injuries on Christmas Day against Stoke City turned a Championship sprint into a stumble. Lishman broke a leg, thus robbing the team of its leading scorer; four of his 16 goals had come in one match against Sunderland in November. Swindin was also hurt, allowing Ted Platt an extended run in goal. Although Whittaker turned again to Lewis — who typically responded with a sequence of four games in each of which he scored twice — and for the first time to the raw Holton, the team unit did not function as smoothly in the second half of the season. Arsenal finished fifth in the League, which was won for the first time by Spurs, and lost their grip on the FA Cup to a Stan Pearson goal for Manchester United in the fifth round.

Arsenal's Double of 1970–71 is of course well documented in this history and elsewhere. Less easily recalled are the events of the 1951–52 season when the Gunners stood three games away from what would have been the first Double of modern times. Had those three games been won instead of lost the season would have been legendary. Instead it was a marvellously bold attempt which foundered in the final analysis on injuries.

Swindin had shrugged aside his injury from the previous year and played a full season in goal, Barnes was absent for just one League game though the fallibility of his knee became a major factor in the last chapter of the story. Mercer, Forbes, Logie and Roper added further threads of continuity. By now Daniel had superseded Compton at centre half, and the goalscoring department lay at the feet and heads of Lishman and Holton. The cricket connection had not entirely disappeared with the Comptons; Arthur Milton, the Gloucestershire batsman, operated on the right wing on a semi-regular basis. Indeed after just 13 League appearances he played for England against Austria, and though his football career did not develop to the heights promised he opened the innings for his country, joining the distinguished list of double internationals.

Progress in the First Division was steady,

always in the challenging bunch of clubs, occasionally on top. Lishman enjoyed a golden spell of hat-tricks in three consecutive home games; Fulham, West Bromwich Albion and Bolton were his victims. The League matches were punctuated by occasional prestige friendlies, with floodlights installed at the ground, treating the Highbury faithful to the new experience of watching evening matches. The ground also enclosed the biggest post-war attendance at the club; the visit of Spurs luring 72,164 to see whether the Champions could be toppled.

The FA Cup run began at Carrow Road, where Norwich City could not rise up above their Third Division South status. Barnsley in round four provided no more testing opposition; Lewis, now a weapon to be used only occasionally, added to his personal store of Cup-tie memories with a first-half hat-trick. Lishman claimed the other in another confident triumph.

On paper the fifth round draw brought a more testing problem. Leyton Orient in the lower reaches of the Third Division South were on the giant-killing trail. The homely East London club had beaten two high-flying Second Division outfits, Birmingham City and Everton, both slain on their own territory. Now the 'O's' were at home and the prospect of a meeting with Arsenal attracted massive interest.

Whittaker's side, however, did not capitulate, although Lewis was injured scoring the first goal and limped through more than half the match; averaging a goal a game in the League at the time plus his four in the FA Cup, he might have forced his way into another Cup final team until this misfortune. Arsenal, however, coped easily with the handicap at Brisbane Road, and Lishman hit two more to kill off the giant-killers.

Arsenal had to travel again in the sixth round, again not very far and the draw against Second Division Luton Town meant that the top clubs were again avoided. After only nine minutes Luton became the first side to put the ball past Swindin in the 1952 FA Cup. Moore headed in a corner taken by Mitchell. Without Jimmy Logie to orchestrate their midfield play, Arsenal were still trailing at the interval, during which Whittaker reshuffled his forward line.

Freddie Cox was switched to the left wing and lived up to his billing as a Cup tie specialist. Arthur Milton came back to his sparkling best. Cox equalised from a very acute angle and with Luton handicapped by injuries to Davies and Owen the match tilted away from them. Three goals inside five minutes completed the scoring with Cox cutting in again to find the back of the net from an oblique position and then crossing for Milton to collect Arsenal's third. A penalty

The crowd rather than the players is the focus of this unusual shot taken on 16 September 1950. Peter Goring (number 9) is seen completing his hat-trick in a 6-2 thrashing of traditional rivals Huddersfield. Jimmy Logie and Doug Lishman got the others.

from Mitchell was Luton's last reply in a rivetting match.

What Mrs Cox dreamed before the semi-final has not been recorded but the match certainly produced a case of *deja vu* for her husband. Again Chelsea provided the opposition. Again White Hart Lane was the venue. And again the first match, postponed this time by snow from its original date, finished in a draw. In truth it rarely held the imagination of the crowd; no corners in the first hour during which Arsenal scored in the 35th minute. Almost inevitably Cox was the marksman, served with a touch of subtlety by Logie. Chelsea equalised 27 minutes from the final whistle through Billy Gray.

Forty-eight hours later the teams reassembled at Tottenham, and, as two years earlier, Arsenal won through, this time 3–0. The Cox-Logie combination eased the tensions by conjuring an early goal, and Cox broke the back of the Chelsea resistance with his second 20 minutes from time. Roper, operating at outside left, took his only corner in either game and the diminutive Cox found space to head home. Lishman made sure of Arsenal's return to Wembley with another header.

The final itself offered a showdown between the competition's two most recent superpowers, the holders Newcastle United against the winners from the previous year. It was a match which had statisticians trotting out comparisons with 20 years earlier. Then Arsenal had been beaten in the 'over the line' match in which Newcastle had become the first side to concede the opening goal in a Wembley final and come from behind to win.

In 1932 Arsenal had also sought the Double, only to fall between the two stools of cliché. They also had to meet Newcastle at home in the League between the semi-final and final just as they had to do in the fixture-congested April of 1952 (drawing 1–1 with Milton, who did not play at Wembley, Arsenal's goalscorer). By then injuries were beginning to damage hopes of bringing the League title to Highbury.

On Good Friday, 11 April, Ray Daniel broke his arm in a goalless draw at Blackpool. The next day Lionel Smith wrenched a knee at Bolton; Arsenal lost 2–1. Leslie Compton stepped out of the shadows to help out in the crisis.

Three home games brought a fine return of five points, but at the cost of wearying key players. Mercer felt the strain so keenly that Whittaker persuaded his captain to stand down from the crucial visit to West Bromwich Albion, the clubs eighth game in 17 days. Understandably the flesh was weak, even if the spirit was strong. Albion won 3–1 with Arsenal giving Scottish forward Jimmy W. Robertson his only First Division outing.

That defeat effectively ended the League challenge; only a seven-goal victory at Old Trafford on the Saturday before the Cup Final would take the title from Manchester United. Reg Lewis turned out for his last senior appearance; Lionel Smith proved his recovery from injury; but United celebrated their title with a runaway 6–1 victory. Nor did Arsenal escape unscathed physically. Arthur Shaw, who might have pipped Daniel for the centre half spot in the Wembley line-up, suffered a fractured wrist, a similar injury to his rival. Nevertheless, had the Gunners won those two last games, against West Bromwich and United, they would have been champions.

Newcastle United's passage over the run-in to the final had been as smooth as Arsenal's had been choppy. Moreover, the holders were able to relax at the seaside while Tom Whittaker and his medical team were checking the casualty list at Highbury. Daniel had not played for more than three weeks, but with a plaster supervised by the manager so that it would pass the scrutiny of the referee the Welsh international was chosen for the fray. So too was Logie, who had been hospitalised earlier in the week leading up to the final.

Lishman, the ex-commando, who had just missed selection two years earlier, tried quickly to make up for lost time with a hooked shot that passed just wide of Newcastle's goal. Arsenal settled quickly and were looking good when fate took a hand, as so often happened in FA Cup finals during the 1950s. Barnes twisted a knee so painfully that though he returned with the joint bandaged, he could not continue. Arsenal faced the prospect of surviving for the last 55 minutes with ten men.

Roper, strong and robust, was immediately switched from outside left to right back; his heroic display typified Arsenal's tenacity. Smith had to clear a Milburn effort off the line when for once the supreme Swindin was beaten, but the depleted team did not just settle for survival. Cox forayed infield and Forbes added to his usual labour with many attempts to support the undermanned attack. Eleven minutes from the end Lishman rose to meet a corner from Cox but the ball skimmed the bar.

Five minutes later the gallant stand ended. Of the ten Arsenal players remaining Holton and Roper both went down, in urgent need of the trainer's attention. Daniel's arm was aching; Logie's damaged thigh could no longer be concealed. Mercer yelled at referee Arthur Ellis to stop the game to allow treatment for Holton and Roper. The ball was still in play and Mitchell was allowed to cross into the middle where George Robledo climbed above Smith to send in a header which dropped in off the post. Roper, still on the ground, could only sit and watch it happen. There was still time for Forbes to hit the bar, but Newcastle became the first club in the twentieth century to win the FA Cup in consecutive seasons.

Mercer made sure his team left the pitch together to tremendous appreciation from the crowd. Later that night he addressed the guests at the traditional banquet, speaking with great emotion: 'I thought football's greatest honour was to captain England. I was wrong. It was to captain Arsenal today.'

The only goal of the 1952 FA Cup final; Chilean George Robledo beats Lionel Smith to a Mitchell centre and squeezes the ball off the post past George Swindin to give Newcastle a 1–0 victory and allow them to become the first club to retain the FA Cup in the twentieth century. Number 9 is the great Jackie Milburn. Smith made 181 first-class appearances for the club at both centre half and left back and, though he never became an automatic club choice at full back, won six England caps in that position.

Perhaps some of the resolution forged over those 90 minutes at Wembley brought the players even closer. Certainly those who represented the club in the following 1952–53 First Division campaign proved to be too good for their rivals. The title came to Highbury for the seventh time, setting a new record, but it was to be mighty close.

Barnes was missing for the entire season, though Joe Wade and John Chenhall made light of his absence. Others made meaningful contributions, like Don Oakes, who marked his League debut on the opening day of the season at Aston Villa by scoring the winning goal. A tall inside forward from Rhyl, Oakes had waited almost seven years for his chance. He kept his place of course for the following match but suffered injury helping in another winning cause at home to Manchester United. Such are the vagaries of football that he did not reappear at first-team level until the last nine matches of the 1954–55 season, when he operated at wing half. With a regular place beckoning at long last, he contracted a serious illness on tour in the summer of 1955. After protracted treatment, he had to accept medical advice to retire.

With two victories in those first two matches, Arsenal failed to build on such an optimistic start, winning only once in their next six outings. Sunderland and Charlton both plundered two points on visits to Highbury. Only the return of Milton with almost 2,000 runs banked for Gloucestershire in a prolific season of batsmanship inspired a victory in this dismal spell; the cricketer-winger struck the bigger ball cleanly with one of the goals in a 3–1 home success against Portsmouth. The return match, however, encapsulated the uncertainties at that time. Holton struck twice before half-time only for Arsenal to allow Pompey to fight back for a draw.

In November the spotlight turned on Jimmy Logie. His impish genius was recognised at last by Scotland's selectors. The Alex James of his generation, Logie wore the blue jersey against Austria at Hampden Park. In the same month as his 33rd birthday the honour came too late for him to make an impact for his country. It was his only cap, but at least it conferred much deserved international status on a man whose talents put him alongside many players from Arsenal, or anywhere else, who won more caps.

Ten days after Logie's international, Arsenal put on a display of their own from the very top drawer, demolishing Liverpool 5–1 at Anfield. Ben Marden, one of many professionals at the club who might have earned a regular berth away from Highbury, struck twice in his first senior match of the season and Holton weighed in with a hat-trick.

The last match of 1952 deserves special mention, not just because it brought the bonus of an away victory. On Christmas morning the Arsenal players were again a long way from their families, at Burnden Park, Bolton. The first half was above average but not exceptional. Willie Moir sent the home side into the lead but by the interval Milton had equalised and Holton, whose power of shot was formidable, had edged the visitors ahead.

In the second half those who might have had their minds on their Christmas dinners were first able to gorge themselves on a glut of goals. Within the opening five minutes of the half

Logie and Roper had increased the Arsenal advantage to 4–1. Then it was Moir making it 4–2 before a Daniel penalty restored the lead to three goals. The action of the final eight minutes was even more frantic. Bolton's defensive generosities extended to the conceding of another goal to Holton, before Nat Lofthouse ended the year in which he had been tagged The Lion of Vienna for his England heroics with two late replies for Bolton. Believe it or not there was still time for Bolton to earn a penalty, which could have made it 6–5, but Kelsey, facing a spot kick for the first time in League football, saved Langton's attempt. Sadly the action of a marvellous match was never captured; all the local photographers preferred Christmas at home!

1952-53 was not to be one of the great Championship seasons – it is rightly more remembered for the FA Cup final. Arsenal eventually finished with 54 points, one of the lowest ever for a title-winning team, they lost nine games in all and did not win any of six games between 2 March and 3 April. The excitement was in the finish with Arsenal and Preston neck-and-neck and the fixture list taking the Gunners to Deepdale on the last Saturday of the season.

The points situation meant the Gunners' title ambitions could survive a defeat but not a heavy beating. Preston won 2–0 with goals from their two most revered forwards, Tom Finney and Charlie Wayman. Both clubs now had one match left but not on the same day.

Preston were first into action on the Wednesday before the Cup final. Away to bottom club Derby County, they won 1–0 and left for an end of season tour not knowing their fate. Arsenal's finale was staged before a packed Highbury two days later on Cup final eve; only a win would be enough. Burnley, the opposition, were in the top six of the table. It took only three minutes for the drama to take its first twist.

Roy Stephenson, Burnley's outside right, who was to win a Championship medal nine years later with Ipswich Town, drove in a crisp, low, centre. Confident of his own touch on the ball but not yet in tune with the pace of the match, Mercer tried to cut out the danger. He succeeded only in diverting the ball into his own net. At that moment the title looked bound for Deepdale.

It was no time for patience. Arsenal threw caution to the winds in a display of forceful attacking football which brought goals for Forbes, in one of his most passionate performances for the club, Lishman and Logie. Burnley then cut the deficit in the second half, and the all-out policy gave way to the tactics of entrenchment, and what they had Arsenal held. When the sums were done Tom Whittaker's team had won the League on goal average – by less than one-tenth of a goal.

The summer of 1953 was to bring the shock of the premature death, at 51, of Alex James from cancer. It was perhaps a portent

Arsenal's attempt to defend their title began dreadfully. Six of the first eight matches were lost, the other two drawn. The club's predicament reached a crisis point at Sunderland in what turned out to be Swindin's last League match. Lishman had given Arsenal the boost of a goal before the veteran goalkeeper was hurt in a collision with Trevor Ford, with Sunderland by then leading 2–1. Swindin was, in all, beaten seven times, and the match must have been relished by Daniel, who had been sold to Roker Park in the close season, complaining that he did not like the style Arsenal expected of their centre half.

Dodgin had accepted the tactics more readily, and Barnes, who had not played since his Wembley injury, battled back to sufficient fitness to earn a recall though his problems were to persist. To strengthen his hand in attack Tom Whittaker sought a short-term solution. Tommy Lawton, the nation's pin-up centre forward throughout the 1940s, was struggling as player-manager of Brentford. At 34 his best years were behind him, but Ronnie Rooke had more than risen to the challenge of a late call to Highbury. Could Lawton do the same?

The deal was done in secret and Lawton was unveiled to the Highbury public on 19 September 1953, against Manchester City. He could not, however, in his two and a half seasons with the club, sustain a regular place; it was almost seven months before his first League goal against Aston Villa. Yet Lawton loved the glamour attached to being an Arsenal player and recalled that his biggest mistake in football had been in not signing for the club when George Allison wanted him from Burnley in 1936 (he chose Everton instead).

The years that followed were a bleak period for the club that had, by 1953, become the most celebrated in the world. They were to win nothing again until the Fairs Cup all of 17 years later. And between 1954 and 1969 they

Jimmy Logie scores the all important third goal against Burnley on 1 May 1953. It was the goal that won the Championship, for with it Arsenal overcame Burnley 3–2 on the day and pipped Preston on goal average for the title. The other goals were scored by Forbes and Lishman. On 25 April, a week before, Arsenal had lost 2–0 at Preston to give the Lancastrians hope of the title. A win in the final game of the season was thus vital for the Gunners, and they got it with nothing to spare to take the Championship by a goal average of 1.516 against Preston's 1.417. Had Preston won 5–0 rather than 2–0 a week earlier they, and not Arsenal, would have taken the title.

Anxious faces at Highbury in 1951 for manager Tom Whittaker (right) and his assistant Jack Crayston. Whittaker had been awarded the MBE for his wartime service as a Squadron Leader in the RAF, notable also because he had thus seen service through both wars in all three of the armed forces. He formally became manager in 1947 when Allison stepped down. He remained as manager until his death in 1956, departing, like Chapman, in harness. His managership had been no less successful than that of his mentor. Both were in full charge for nine years, both won two Championships, both reached two FA Cup finals, both won the first and lost the second two years later. The coincidences are, to say the least, interesting. Crayston succeeded Whittaker as manager, though he lasted only two years before George Swindin took over.

finished only once above 5th. Between 1930 and 1953 they had finished worse than 5th on only three occasions. Cup performances were, if anything, even worse – including terrible defeats by such lowly sides as Northampton (3-1) in 1958, Rotherham (2-0 after two draws) in 1960, and Peterborough (2-1) in 1965. Tom Whittaker was not there to witness the decline.

Tom Whittaker died on Wednesday 24 October 1956 in University College Hospital, where he had undergone an operation the previous Easter. Like his great mentor Herbert Chapman he passed away in harness, as he would have wished; and like Chapman he had sacrificed his health in the cause of a club which meant more to him than his own life.

Both had died tragically young (neither reached 60); both in differing ways had been the very heartbeat of Highbury. Tom Whittaker perhaps had a premonition that he would not outlive his job, once admitting: 'Someone has to drive himself too hard for Arsenal. Herbert Chapman worked himself to death for the club, and if it is to be my fate I am happy to accept it.'

Joe Mercer had been lured back into football as manager of Sheffield United; his moving tribute to the guardian angel who had extended his career at Highbury to such glorious heights appeared in the *Daily Express*:

'Meeting Tom Whittaker was the best thing that ever happened to me; he was the greatest man I ever met.

As the news of his death goes around the world thousands, perhaps millions, of people will say the same thing. And how so very deeply they will mean it. Arsenal was his kingdom but in every soccer-playing country in the world he was acknowledged as a prince of the game. There never has been a greater man in football. It is a game full of hard knocks. But Tom never hit anybody. He never shirked making a hard decision, like sacking or dropping a player, or any of the other things that can hurt deeply. But the way Tom did it, it never did.

Tom made bad sportsmen into good sportsmen. He made good footballers into great footballers.

Tom was responsible for none of the bad things in football. Cynics may smile and say "I wonder". But I know.

I know that he never did a bad thing. All problems had only one solution; the one done with kindness.

After Newcastle beat us in the 1952 final, Tom came into the dressing-room, looking as happy as we had ever seen him. He said: "I am really proud of you chaps. You played great football. I am as proud of Arsenal today as ever I have been." Damn it, he made us feel we had won the Cup.

The last time I saw Tom was a couple of months ago. He looked very ill, but he had already started a new phase in Arsenal history. He realised the days of big buying were over. His plans only included youngsters. And every youngster who ever went to Highbury quickly learned one thing. The only thing that mattered was the club.

Tom Whittaker never thought of the chairman, a player or anyone individually when he

Finally getting to play football after the long legal wrangle which led to the abolition of the 'retain and transfer' system, George Eastham scores for Arsenal versus Manchester United on 21 October 1961. The other goals in a 5–1 win came from Gerry Ward, John Barnwell and Alan Skirton (right). When Newcastle would not transfer Eastham to Arsenal a year earlier, the player refused to turn out for the Magpies again and, with Jimmy Hill of the PFA advising him, effectively sued the football authorities for restraint of trade. He was to win the case and Arsenal were to get their man.

made a decision. If it was good for the club then it was right .

Others wrote of his 'simple charm', his 'tolerance' and his 'sense of fairness'. Denis Compton recalled that he had never seen him lose his temper, 'although there were often occasions when he would have been justified in doing so. He took infinite trouble with everyone whom he considered to be his responsibility. In my early days at Highbury I often saw him there till eight, nine or ten o'clock at night, personally working to get players fit for the following Saturday. He'd do the work himself and wouldn't delegate it to anyone else. He had a kind of genius for it, I think.

The late Bob Wall remembered a genial side to his nature, and his huge physical strength. On one playful occasion he lifted the Compton brothers '. . . one under each arm as if they were babies, over a wall and dropped them into the team bath. He was a big man in many ways.'

Tom Whittaker's reputation had spread way beyond the confines of English football. When Arsenal took on the role of ambassadors on expeditions around the globe, the secretary-manager was the perfect head of the delegation. In 1949, for example, the summer tour took the club to Brazil where in Sao Paulo many supporters of the local team were of Italian extraction; Italy and the rest of the football world had just been stunned by the Superga aircrash which wiped out the brilliant Torino team. Whittaker's sensitivity recognised the need for a tribute to the dead and before the match, at his suggestion, the two teams and the crowd stood, heads bowed, to the music of Ave Maria.

Yet his kindness never became weakness.

Centre half Bill Dodgin returned from the 7–1 humiliation at Sunderland in that dreadful opening to the 1953–54 season feeling that he had let down the side – Arsenal, remember, had collected only two points from eight matches. Dodgin wanted to be left out of the team, and went to see Whittaker: 'I left his office quicker than I entered it. He told me very firmly that if there was any dropping to be done, he would do it.'

In February 1956, Arsenal tried to lighten the load on Tom Whittaker by appointing Leyton Orient manager Alec Stock as his assistant. Unfortunately, Stock lasted less than two months before returning to Orient and there was no sign of Whittaker taking any less of the responsibilities.

The obvious stress of the dual role of secretary-manager persuaded the Arsenal board to split the two jobs. Bob Wall was promoted to secretary. Jack Crayston, a member of two League Championship teams and the 1936 FA Cup winning side, took over as manager. Crayston had been an assistant to Tom Whittaker, his man 'downstairs at Highbury' helping particularly with the scouting and at times, because he had received some training as an accountant, with book-keeping.

Crayston had also won eight England caps before the war. Famed for his long throws he was a strapping wing half, over six feet tall, weighing 13 stones and needing specially constructed boots for his size 12 feet.

An even longer servant, Joe Shaw, finally retired. He had been signed as a player in 1907 from Accrington Stanley, hanging up his boots in 1923. Following a short spell with London rivals Chelsea he had resumed his Arsenal connection under the title of Head Coach and

Cliff Holton rises above Jimmy Scoular and the Newcastle defence to score in a First Division game on 30 November 1957. It was a poor season for the Gunners and this game was no better than many, Newcastle winning 3–2. Danny Clapton (whose brother Dennis, though playing only four games for the club, served to confuse statisticians for years) scored the other. Holton was also to find statistical fame when, playing for Watford three years later, he scored hat-tricks in consecutive matches on consecutive days.

Chief Representative, in effect Whittaker's number two.

On 13 March 1957, George Allison passed away; he had lived with indifferent health over the ten years since he had resigned from his football career at Highbury. 'George Arsenal', as he had been widely known, had risen from his humble start in the club ranks as the writer of the match programme to Secretary-Manager. His knowledge of the game might never have been deep, but he was clever enough to realise his limitations, not frightened to consult the opinions of others. Yet as a front person for the prestigious Arsenal organisation he had been perfect. His rapport with the media would have been a strength in any era.

The following day another death was recorded, that of J. W. Julian, club captain back in 1890 and the first to lead a professional side at Woolwich. He had been an enthusiastic and regular spectator at matches at Highbury right up to the time of his demise.

Jack Crayston's appointment was confirmed in December 1956. How can one tell whether he felt the shudders of history at that time? He was part of the lineage being put to rest with the deaths of Julian, Whittaker and Allison. Matters did not improve in Crayston's two years in charge.

Jack Crayston was not blind to the shortcomings of his team. He regularly asked the board for money to strengthen his hand, but it was not forthcoming. Cliff Jones was just one of a number of players he pursued, but Swansea realised the value of their winger, who was to play 59 times for Wales, and were determined not to sell him cheaply. When he finally became available it was Spurs who struck the deal, and Jones became part of the 1960–61 Double side whose rampaging success made

Arsenal's lack of progress at that time more difficult to bear.

The match programme outlined the Arsenal philosophy at the time: '. . . a policy not to bid for a player's transfer. We always ask the fee required, and having been told make up our mind whether the player is worth that fee.' Yet with increasing pressure for success in a market which was naturally declining after the post-war boom, the ethics of football business were to change for ever.

Crayston believed that the club did have the money to invest in the transfer market. At a board meeting at the end of the season clearly the frustrations became too much. 'Gentleman Jack' Crayston resigned, severing a tie with the club that had lasted almost 25 years. He moved back to Yorkshire for a spell as secretary-manager to Doncaster Rovers, before using his accountancy skills in a business career and finally retiring to live in the West Midlands. In 1985 he looked back on the changes in football with a twinkle in his eye: 'In my time players had short hair, wore long shorts and played in hob-nailed boots. Now they have long hair, short shorts and play in slippers.'

Although Joe Mercer was clearly the favourite to succeed, it was an Arsenal teammate, George Swindin, who was actually offered the job. He had brought Peterborough to national prominence with their giant-killing acts (they would later gain a League place as a result of these) and had therefore won his spurs. He was in charge for four seasons but while Arsenal were never relegation candidates, the history of the past 30 years meant that it was trophies or nothing. When Danny Clapton was chosen for England in 1959 he was the first Arsenal player for five years to be capped – an excellent cameo of the decline on

Billy Wright, then England and the world's most capped player, took over the manager's chair from George Swindin (who had held it for four years) in 1962. He, in his turn, was to last another four, by which time directors and fans were becoming restless as the club had not finished higher than seventh since the turn of the 1960s. Wright was the only one of the eight managers after Herbert Chapman not to have previously strong links with Highbury. This may have worked against him, as would putting the paper into the typewriter the wrong way round.

the field since the last Championship. Swindin also had to cope with the horrors of Nicholson, Blanchflower and the Tottenham Double of 1960-61 – so much sweeter for White Hart Lane as Arsenal had never achieved it in the 1930s. In that season Arsenal were to lose twice (2-3 at home and 2-4 away) to their neighbours but at least they had the satisfaction of seeing their rivals only match their own record points total of 66 (established 30 years earlier) and not exceed it.

More significant in the long run was the Eastham case. George Eastham was England's most skilful creative player. He wanted to leave Newcastle United to join Arsenal, but the Geordies would not let him go. Under the rules of the League at that time (called the 'retain and transfer' system) a player's current club could stop him moving anywhere, and no club could pay any player, from the best to the worst, more than £20 per week. Eastham challenged the system in court and, after a legal battle that began in 1960 and ended in July 1963, he won. By then he had moved to Arsenal for £47,500. Of that fee he got just £20.

George Swindin remained until March 1962 and Arsenal broke with tradition by appointing an outsider – the first since Chapman himself nearly 40 years earlier.

The club's choice had won more caps than any player in the world (105) and held the then

record for the most consecutive international appearances (70). He had captained Wolves to three League Championships and one FA Cup. But great players do not necessarily make great football managers. Despite the goalscoring heroics of Geoff Strong and Joe Baker (each scored 31 League and Cup goals in 1963-64) the defence was, surprisingly given Wright's pedigree, the weakness. The same year they conceded 82 goals, worse than one relegated club and the sort of number not seen at Highbury since the late 1920s. Even Leicester beat them 7-2!

Geoff Strong was to move to Liverpool and, despite the arrival of a then rather raw Frank McLintock from Leicester, the terrible 2-1 defeat to Third Division Peterborough in 1965 was to be the symbol of the period.

Season 1965–66 was the last in first-class football for the genial, kindly Billy Wright, whose playing days had been almost devoid of failure, but whose management days were as short on success. Maybe the writing was on the wall the previous summer with the decision to change the club colours to all-red shirts, with the only white being on the collar and the cuffs; white shorts with red seams and red stockings completed the design, which was seen as a return to the style of Nottingham Forest. The change was soon reversed and, to Arsenal's credit, they have been the only major club to ignore the money-chasing detail changes of recent years.

As most of football awaited the 1966 World Cup with an increasing sense of anticipation, Arsenal's and Wright's fortunes reached unprecedented depths. A home fixture against Leeds United was misguidedly rearranged for Thursday 5 May 1966, the same evening Liverpool contested the European Cup Winners Cup final against Borussia Dortmund at Hampden Park, shown live on television. That attraction, combined with Arsenal's dismal form, resulted in the Gunners attracting what remained the lowest First Division crowd since the First World War – 4,544 against the second placed club in the League! And they lost 3–0. Only a win over Leicester two days later elevated the club to 14th, their lowest place since 1930.

At the end of the season Billy Wright took a holiday; apart from his responsibilities at Highbury he had also been contracted by BBC Television to take part in their coverage of the World Cup finals. While he was away the board decided that recent results 'justified a change in management'. Denis Hill-Wood broke the news to him on his return. Outwardly it was accepted with the gentlemanly nature with which Wright, the player, had wooed the hearts of the football world. Inwardly it hurt bitterly: 'It was heartbreaking for me. Maybe I was too nice, but that is the way I am. But I wanted so much to make Arsenal great again, and I did feel that with the young players we were moving along the right lines.'

· CHAPTER 8 ·
Arsenal's Double

Many decisions were involved in the construction of the Double-winning side, which took Arsenal Football Club to the highest of all domestic achievements. Yet surely the most inspired was taken by the board of directors in the summer of 1966. While the media indulged in fruitless speculation about which of the game's big names would be appointed to succeed Billy Wright, the Highbury decision-makers were recognising a quality of leadership within the fold.

Bertie Mee was offered the manager's job at a private meeting with Denis Hill-Wood. The choice of the physiotherapist caught Fleet Street off their guard (though Whittaker was a precedent of course). It had the majority of the playing staff believing that it could only be a stop-gap appointment, and even surprised the recipient of the offer: 'It was a surprise, but a very pleasant one. I had not planned to become a football club manager. I was very happy in the career of my special interest, and I was enjoying a great deal of job satisfaction from it. But I was used to positions of responsibility. I had run organisations of various types. So my response was that if that's what the board would like, then I would give it a go.'

With two successful careers already behind him – in the military and medical spheres – Bertie Mee was the right man at the right time for a club which needed an urgent injection of authority. Yet though Bertie Mee was by no means a household name, he was very well known inside the game. He had been running the treatment of injuries courses for the Football Association for almost 20 years. At establishments such as Lilleshall he had lectured to all football's leading managers and coaches, and he had their respect. Such experiences had given the new Arsenal manager a sound working knowledge of the highways and byways of the Football League.

Bertie Mee also brought to the job an immediate insight into what was wrong inside the dressing-room. After all, it had been his area of operation for six years. The players also knew that he stood for no nonsense in the discipline of recovering fitness. Most significant of all, he was not overawed at what he had been chosen to do, but with a characteristic and sensible touch of caution he did make sure that an exit

was available should it be required: 'I asked the chairman if I could initially take the job for twelve months, and that if it didn't work out, I could revert to my previous position. He was most agreeable. So I began by approaching the task in terms of management, from purely a management point of view. It was my belief that there was nothing radically wrong, but the club had to be more professional from all angles. We needed a general tightening-up. The players were a good crowd, but I felt that they could be more dedicated to the job, and certainly could care more about Arsenal. The danger was that mediocrity was being perpetuated.'

With Les Shannon also leaving the club following the change of management, Mee required a new coach, and successfully sought the services of an old friend, Dave Sexton, then with Fulham. Frank McLintock, in his 1969 autobiography *That's The Way The Ball Bounces* summed up the players' response to Sexton: 'I haven't come across many people in the game who has his ability to get through to players without shouting the odds and screaming at them. I don't know what it is that Dave has, maybe it's a gift of leadership. That is perhaps simplifying his effect, all I know is that he could have persuaded us to do anything. He thinks deeply about football and pointed out things I wouldn't have dreamed of – and before he came I thought I knew most of it.'

At first, relatively little seemed to have changed. Mee's first two seasons saw the side finish 7th and 9th, the only trophy being BBC's Quizball, a panel game won for the club by Terry Neill and the astonishing intellectual skills of Scots international Ian Ure. Arsenal had not entered the League Cup until 1966-67 but 1968 was to see them reach their first final for 16 years. Coventry, Reading, Blackburn and Burnley were the victims on the way, with Huddersfield going down 6-3 on aggregate in the two-legged semi-final. The opponents were Leeds, then still a club without a single trophy in their history. The game was not a classic, rather a forerunner of the titanic games that we were to see between the clubs in the next five years. Eddie Gray's corner, a perfect inswinger in front of Jim Furnell, was headed out by George Graham, but only to Terry Cooper who scored the only goal of the game.

Not everything was wine and roses... the great years of 1968–72 were to see no less than five major cup finals, one in each season. The memories are firmly of 1971, but three of the five were lost by tight margins. The 1968 Football League Cup final was decided by a single goal (opposite above) from Leeds United full back Terry Cooper (hidden in picture) after a corner. A year later Arsenal were back at Wembley for the final of the same competition and this time hot favourites to defeat Third Division Swindon Town, with nine of the previous year's twelve appearing again. The result was a shock 3–1 win by the underdogs, Don Rogers, with two, and Roger Smart scoring their goals. The only Arsenal response was from Bobby Gould, who left the field in tears (opposite centre) comforted by John Radford. Gould, a popular player with colleagues and crowd alike, made 83 first-team appearances in a four-year career with the club and scored 23 goals. Sadly, he was never to obtain that winner's medal.

Left: **In 1972 Arsenal came back** to Wembley looking to retain the FA Cup, a feat performed this century only by Newcastle and Spurs. They again failed by one goal, again to a Leeds United then at the height of their powers. The goal was a header from Allan Clarke which gave Geoff Barnett no chance. Barnett was deputising for Bob Wilson, who had been injured in one of those interminable semi-finals against Stoke.

Frank McLintock was disappointed at yet another losers' medal, but the team was gaining recognition with both Bob McNab and John Radford capped by Alf Ramsey.

The solidity that was binding Arsenal together did not always please the neutrals, but Mee had already established his first priority; his team was never likely to capitulate. Wilson was making great strides as a goalkeeper, his strength of character growing in the face of regular teasing from his team-mates about his background as a schoolteacher. He was an ever-present in the 1968–69 League campaign. So too was the cold-eyed Storey and the resident chatterbox, McNab. Court, who was to be sold to Luton on the eve of the Double, missed only two matches in midfield. Simpson was emerging as a more complete central defender than either Ure or Neill. The options in midfield were increased by experimenting in that area with Graham, who was blessed with a sure touch and sharp football brain, but whose lack of explosive pace was making life up front increasingly difficult for him.

The interest in the FA Cup ended once more in the fifth round, but hardly in disgrace, a 1–0 defeat away to West Bromwich Albion, fellow First Division rivals. Against a background of such consistency it is unfortunate that the season will ultimately only be recalled for another Wembley defeat in the League Cup final.

Unlike the Leeds experience the players could not walk off this time with heads held high. This time it was a shaming experience.

The two-leg semi-final with Spurs had produced more evidence of the competitive nature of Mee's team. In front of a full house of 55,000 at Highbury, Spurs were only seconds away from a goalless draw when Radford popped up with what turned out to be a crucial goal. Tottenham pinned their hopes of turning the tables at White Hart Lane on the mercurial Jimmy Greaves, who scored in a tough, and at times brutal, encounter, but so did Radford and Arsenal won 2–1 on aggregate.

The final was still three months away, and Mee and his players had to wait a fortnight to learn whom their opponents would be. When the news came, any thoughts that the hard part had been done by eliminating Tottenham could have been forgiven. Third Division Swindon Town had battled their way to Wembley by beating Burnley over three games.

As expected Arsenal carried the fight to Swindon from the outset, a series of attacks that in treacherous conditions took more energy to mount than to defend against. With eight of the side still touched by the after-effects of a flu virus which had caused the postponement of a League match the week before, such energy spent was not easily recouped. For some it was not recouped at all. At this point in

The 1970 Fairs Cup final against Anderlecht was a happier occasion. Arsenal lost the first leg 3–1 in Brussels and were left with a lot to do in the return. No team had ever come back from a two-goal deficit to win a two-legged European final, nor from a three-goal deficit at any point in a final. Nor has any team done either since, a tribute to the Gunners' outstanding achievement in a match which is often overlooked because of the drama which followed a season later. The goals in the second leg at Highbury were scored by Kelly, Radford and Sammels and John Radford is seen celebrating his with the help of Charlie George.

their League programme Arsenal had let in just 18 goals in 30 matches, all of them chiselled out of the granite of their organisation. Thirty-four minutes into the League Cup final they allowed Swindon to take the lead with a mix-up between Ure and Wilson which presented Smart with the most open of open goals.

Swindon kept the lead until four minutes from time. Then goalkeeper Downsbrough, a superman on the day, ventured out of his area in an attempt to kick the ball to safety, away from the on-rushing Gould. Instead, the ball rebounded off the Arsenal forward, who reacted quickly and headed it into the unguarded net. With extra time beckoning, relieved Arsenal fans believed that their team now had a psychological advantage.

Down at pitch level Don Howe was not so sure. He wanted extra time to be abandoned by referee Bill Handley to spare the players the slog in the cloying mud. He recognised the weariness in his own players, aggravated by their recent illnesses. McLintock, usually a natural athlete, had cramp in both legs. McNab was also in distress. Graham had already replaced the weary Simpson.

For a team of Swindon's humble status it would have been forgivable if they had not seized their opportunity. It was a measure of their quality that they grasped it firmly. After 15 minutes of extra time, Don Rogers poked the ball home from a corner, though McNab on the line almost prevented the ball crossing it. Rogers had been peripheral for much of the match, and is pictured in a strip unsullied by dirt surrounded by defenders covered in mud when he put Swindon into the lead. In the second period he etched his trademark onto a Wembley final, running half the length of the pitch for a memorable solo goal. It was like sticking a knife into a dying body.

Stan Harland went up the Wembley steps to collect the League Cup from Princess Margaret. McLintock – now a four-time loser – was stunned. He had not contemplated defeat this time. A good-luck telegram from Don Revie wishing that he could 'be first up the steps this time' had an ironic touch. The Leeds United manager had forgotten that the League Cup final's formalities have the losers collecting their mementoes first.

Mee and Howe began the arduous task of reviving morale which had once been so high. Only the strong would swim and not sink after such a distressing experience. Among them was Bob Wilson, whose fierce pride was aroused by the humiliation. Sixteen years later he put the desolation of defeat into perspective: 'I truly believe that the rise of the Double side stemmed from that afternoon at Wembley. We came home to headlines about the "Shame of Arsenal", and a lot of us were determined that it would never happen again. We craved success with even more intensity because of it.'

The one consolation was that fourth place in the League brought them a place in the European Fairs Cup, albeit because Swindon were denied their's by virtue of being a Third Division side. Arsenal's progress was convincing against Glentoran, Sporting Portugal, Rouen, Dinamo Bacau and Ajax in the semi-final. In retrospect Arsenal's 3-0 win over Ajax at Highbury looks a lot better than it did at the time. Within a couple of years their opponents won a hat-trick of European Cups and at Highbury fielded Cruyff, Krol, Suurbier, Keizer and the elder Muhren. One week later Arsenal were back in the Low Countries facing Anderlecht. The Belgians chose to play in their away strip in Brussels so that their fans could see the famous red and white shirts. It did not damage Anderlecht's performance – they were ahead 3–0 in the first leg with Jan Mulder scoring twice. It looked as though Frank McLintock was sure to collect his fifth losers medal. Late in the game Kennedy, still a raw youngster, headed one back and the Gunners returned to Highbury 1–3 in arrears.

Bob Wilson vividly recalled: 'Even with the late goal we were all downcast. It looked as though we could be foiled yet again in our efforts to bring the club a trophy. Initially Frank McLintock felt it the most keenly, and he was cursing about being in another losing final. But Frank was always impulsive. If he saw you in a suit he liked he had to get one like it straight away. If you'd been to a great restaurant he'd have to go there the next night. But just as suddenly the mood would change. In Brussels his initial despair turned straight into optimism. He came out of the bath yelling that we were going to win. He lifted everybody, and by the time we left the ground, nobody had their heads down. You could say that the second leg was won at that point.'

McLintock, by his own admission, finds specific matches hard to remember, but his attitude that night remained in his memory: 'Anderlecht were good. Mulder and van Himst were special players. But defensively they had looked vulnerable when we had been able to attack. Their centre half looked poor in the air. I believed we could do it, and I wanted to make sure the rest of the lads did.'

McLintock's captaincy was based on such strength of purpose. Others would have been broken by the succession of disappointments. Though he had thought seriously about seeking fresh pastures after the League Cup final defeat by Leeds, he had eventually withdrawn his transfer request. His hunger for honours was about to be satisfied.

The second leg of the Fairs Cup final took place at Highbury on Tuesday 28 April 1970. In the match programme Bertie Mee paid tribute to McLintock's new role at centre half, which earlier in the month had earned him a recall by Scotland after three years out of the international limelight. The manager also wrote of the crop that was being harvested from the youth policy which had been tended by Billy Wright and himself after George

Swindin had sown the seeds. George, Kennedy and Kelly were singled out for special mention.

Eddie Kelly repaid the compliment. A stunning early shot brought Anderlecht within reach. Arsenal tore into their opponents with such frantic commitment that McLintock was asked afterwards by one of the Belgians if Mee's players had taken drugs. But the stimulus was not artificial; it was the desire for achievement. In the dressing-room the talk about Arsenal's past glories had become more than wearisome.

The weakness in the air spotted by McLintock was exploited in the second half, and the muscular Radford found space to head Arsenal's second. Thanks to Kennedy's 'away' goal, Arsenal now led, but were in no position to relax as Mulder hit a post. The complexities of the two-legged scoring system kept the 51,000 crowd anxious to the very last. Sammels, who was to lose his regular place during the Double year, ensured a deserved place on the roll of honour by adding a third. Had Anderlecht managed just one in reply they would have been level on aggregate. Even Bertie Mee's considerable ability to detach himself from the emotion of match action was tested to the limit.

When the final whistle eventually sounded, the floodgates opened. Delirious supporters surged on to the pitch. George for one had his shirt pulled from his back by souvenir hunters. Sir Stanley Rous, then FIFA's President, presented the Fairs Cup, which stayed in England for the third successive year following the victories of Leeds United and Newcastle United. For Arsenal it was the end of 17 barren years. McLintock had his hands on a trophy at last and there they stayed as he was carried shoulder-high around the pitch. Oddly, despite its significance, it was not a much-heralded victory at the time and it is not particularly well remembered now. There were two good reasons. One was that the season had been shortened because of the World Cup and England's defence of that trophy was claiming everyone's attention. The other reason was not clear for a year – the glow from the Double was eventually to dull everything around it.

The Arsenal Board had never made any secret of the fact that the League was the main priority. It had been nearly 20 years since Highbury had held the prize that once seemed theirs by right. But no one ever mentioned the Double – achieved just once in the twentieth century and only three times in more than 80 years.

If you were looking for a team on which to stake a few pounds to accomplish such a feat, Arsenal would not have been among the favourites. Twelfth in 1969–70, averaging just one point per game with 51 goals scored and 49 conceded, was hardly the foundation to suggest such glories. A much better bet would have been Leeds United, runners-up in both competitions in the previous season, or perhaps Chelsea, FA Cup winners and third in the League, or even Everton, the 1970 League Champions.

The season that was eventually to become the most celebrated in even Arsenal's famous history, 1970–71, began quietly. The first four games saw two draws and two wins. The fifth game was at Stamford Bridge, where Arsenal suffered their first defeat at the hands of Cup holders Chelsea, 2–1. 54,000 people saw Mulligan and Hollins score for Chelsea and Eddie Kelly respond for the Gunners. They also saw Frank McLintock and Peter Osgood in argumentative mood. This was the game about which Mario Zagalo, manager of the victorious Brazilian World Cup team, later commented that if it was typical of the Football League then it was no wonder that the English game produced no Peles.

running strongly and at oblique angles, began to lose Kendall and before the half-hour he had scored twice. After 14 minutes Graham, rising by the near post flicked on Armstrong's corner and Kennedy nodded the ball squarely past Rankin. Six minutes later, as Rice's free kick came over from the right, Graham ran forward, Everton followed him and Kennedy was left with time and space to head the second The third goal came in the sixty-sixth minute when Radford's throw was nodded down by Graham for Kelly to score with an excellent half-volley, though the course of the shot was diverted by Keith Newton's knee. With two Newtons in the side Everton might be expected to deal better with round objects falling from the sky.

David Lacey's cryptic comment after the 4–0 defeat of Everton at Highbury on 17 October. The goals were scored by Kelly, Storey and Kennedy and all basically came from high balls pumped into the penalty area. Everton had just purchased Henry Newton and thus had two Newtons in the back four. It was the start of a run of 12 games during which just two points were dropped – the foundation stones of the Double. The game's other significance was that well-beaten Everton were the reigning Champions.

With a touch of irony, the Double year began at the home of the defending champions. On paper it could hardly have been a tougher start, but Bertie Mee's policies of stabilising Arsenal into a side that did not readily concede defeat had already paid dividends. From the outset of his management every goal let in had been put under an analytical microscope. Those days of capitulation away from home which had marred the early 1960s were long gone.

With the benefit of hindsight the events at Goodison Park on Saturday 15 August 1970 said much about the qualities which were to provide the basis for such an historic campaign, the resilience which was to shine through so many battles in the months ahead.

The manager's selection had already been affected by pre-season injuries. Peter Simpson required a knee operation. Jon Sammels had a leg in plaster. John Roberts, the strong-man from Wales known as Garth, came into the defence alongside McLintock. The strength of Everton's midfield trio of Howard Kendall, Colin Harvey and Alan Ball was recognised in the role given to Peter Storey, who marked Ball throughout; Storey's job at right back went to Pat Rice, who had played just 13 League games in the previous three seasons.

Royle and Ball were to score for Everton, with Charlie George cracking two bones to provide one equaliser and Graham the second with a floater. It was only a draw, but it was away at the home of the Champions and, as Frank McLintock said afterwards: 'This is the best Arsenal side in my six years with the club.'

On 1 September 1970 Arsenal had the honour of ending Leeds' perfect record so far that season. Geoffrey Green in *The Times* encapsulated the tone of the night in the pithy intro-

duction to his match report: 'There were no goals and no broken legs at Highbury last night, and there might well have been one or two of both. Most of the plaudits of heroism went to the home side. Referee Iowerth Jones from Treharris, Glamorgan, quite properly sent off Kelly for kicking Billy Bremner; that senseless episode after 28 minutes seemed to have condemned Arsenal to defeat. The ten men, however, resisted manfully with the raw Rice, in particular, responding to the challenge. Leeds were not allowed to make use of their advantage. Bertie Mee was never given to exaggeration, so his after-match comment deserves recording: "This was the best performance I have ever seen by an Arsenal team against a side of the calibre of Leeds. I am tremendously proud of all of them, and if we can live through an occasion like this we can live through anything."'

It was never going to be an easy season for Arsenal, but the toughest evening proved to be in far away Rome, where the Gunners were defending their Fairs Cup. The game was a 2–2 draw but there were no feuds simmering when the two sides attended an after match dinner together. At some point in the evening Ray Kennedy was set upon by a Lazio player and the meal turned into a full scale brawl. UEFA sided with Arsenal and fined the Italians, Arsenal winning the second leg 2–0. Europe rather proved a distraction during the season – victories against Sturm Graz and Beveren Waas leading only to departure on the away goals rule to FC Koln of Germany. There were rather more historic fish to fry. A few days after their Lazio game Arsenal went to Stoke and were hammered 5–0. Stoke were to recur time and time again in the next two seasons, but never with this script. Bob Wilson was criticised for talking about the goals on television (Bertie Mee felt he was betraying inside information) and the nature of the defeat remains a mystery. It could have had a dramatic effect –but it didn't and the defence only let its shield down once more during the remainder of the season – and that was for another 45 minutes against Stoke. The defeat preceded the run which really laid the foundations for the Championship. After Stoke, Arsenal went 14 games without defeat, drawing just three, until a sticky patch in January when they lost against Huddersfield and Liverpool. Nonetheless, they were still not taken seriously as contenders – the League was clearly there for Leeds to lose rather than anyone else to win, and Leeds were to eventually oblige in dramatic fashion against West Bromwich.

In the Cup, wins against Yeovil and Portsmouth were to take Arsenal to the fifth round at Maine Road against a team which was then one of England's best.

At the same time the 'high-morale' battle between Leeds United and Liverpool at Elland Road was going in Liverpool's favour – and Arsenal's. The gap was reduced to three

points. Charlie George caught the eye of Brian Glanville, *The Sunday Times* correspondent at the match: 'He must surely resemble the late Charlie Buchan; his height, his powerful physique, the delicacy of touch so astonishing in one so large. To see him receive a ball amidst a ruck of defenders and escape them with the skill of a Houdini is delightful.'

They were prophetic words. George was to settle the fifth round FA Cup tie against Manchester City ten days later. The match was put back from the Saturday to the following Wednesday because the Maine Road pitch was flooded, and it remained very heavy. Two goals from George, now operating as a raider from midfield in place of Graham, confirmed Arsenal's superiority in a deserved victory.

The exact date is not important, but it was around this time, in February 1971, that Bertie Mee addressed his players. To a nation which believed that the twentieth-century Double could only be achieved by a team with the swagger of the Spurs 1961 side, Arsenal were not contenders. There was speculation about whether they could win the League. The pursuit of Leeds United was becoming one of the season's most fascinating features. But there were no public suggestions that Arsenal could emulate Tottenham and clear all the hurdles.

Inside Highbury it was a different matter. Mee saw the possibilities and had for some time: 'I told the players we could expect two matches a week for the rest of the season: "As this is the case now is the time for you to be really ambitious and to aim for the success

which may never be possible for you as players again in your lifetimes." The point was forcibly expressed that all three trophies should be aimed for. Extra discipline and a dedication beyond that which even the most reliable modern professional soccer player is expected to give. They owed it to themselves and their colleagues to accept the challenge of the next three months.' They also owed it to the fans and to the tradition that was Highbury.

Although Leeds were clear favourites, Arsenal just kept winning. Between 6 February and 20 April they played 12 League games and won 11 of them, losing only at Derby (0–2). At the end of that run they had just four League games left to play, and had worked their way through to their first FA Cup final since 1952.

Arsenal were in the semi-finals for the first time for 19 years, though Leicester City in the quarter-final replay had once more proved to be a tough nut to crack. The match attracted Highbury's biggest crowd of the season, more than 57,000, and they witnessed a match that became the tale of two headers.

The first by Fern after 13 minutes was disallowed by referee Jim Finney on the evidence of his linesman. The Leicester forward was adjudged to have pushed Rice as he moved in to connect with Farrington's centre; it was a very close call. Then, with Mr Finney counting the seconds towards half-time, George rose perfectly to meet Armstrong's corner.

Such a blow right on the interval did not diminish Leicester's efforts. An absorbing contest continued to the very last kick, and only

Anxious moments for (left to right) Don Howe, trainer and physio George Wright and Bertie Mee during the 2–0 defeat of Liverpool on 28 November 1970.

then were Arsenal sure of their place in the last four. McLintock locked out his old club in the end, and Leicester, gallant in defeat, certainly had a boost to their self-belief which helped in their run-in to the Second Division title.

The semi-final draw had paired together Everton and Liverpool for a special derby, while Arsenal were drawn against Stoke City, on League form the weakest of the four survivors.

The matching of the underdogs and the Arsenal machine produced a riveting contest at Hillsborough. Forty-one years earlier an FA Cup semi-final triumph in Yorkshire in dramatic circumstances provided the impetus to a decade of success; without that recovery against Hull City the glories of the 1930s might never have happened. Now, in the frantic pace of a semi-final in the 1970s, the club wrote the most relevant page in the entire story of the Double season.

Quite simply Arsenal looked as though they had stumbled irretrievably at the penultimate hurdle. Stoke might have been nervously caught up in a desire to reach a first major final, or as the less fancied outfit they might have been the more relaxed team. Certainly Arsenal were at times tentative to the point of distraction in the first half, and their players left the field after 45 minutes trailing by 2–0.

Semi-finals by nature are cautious, inhibited affairs; the price of defeat is so high that few risks are taken; winning is all-important, the means scarcely matter. Arsenal began the match in that vein, with a greater share of possession in the first 20 minutes but no end product to show for it.

The cautious approach, though, had to be thrown out of the window after a most unusual goal which lifted this semi-final out of the rut. Wilson properly conceded a corner by pushing behind a teasing cross from Greenhoff. Arsenal did not deal conclusively with the corner kick, and as Storey booted the ball away, it struck Denis Smith and flew into the Arsenal net.

In the very next attack the flame-haired Conroy played a very effective one-two with

Peter Storey, scourge of a generation of First Division attackers and whose contribution to the Double is impossible to overestimate. He was, apart from the Irish full backs, the only member of the squad to become an established international. Despite the well-documented personal problems that later beset him, Storey was known at Highbury as the quiet member of the team. Bertie Mee regularly gave him lifts from Cockfosters to the London Colney training ground and once said that he never heard Storey speak more than half-a-dozen words on a journey.

Mahoney only to put his shot inches wide. Banks twice put his stamp on the game with sharp saves, foiling Kennedy on both occasions, before Stoke, fortified by their goalkeeper, were boosted further in the 29th minute. It was a gift from George. With time to spare the 20-year-old, stricken perhaps with butterflies in this most draining of matches, sent a dreadfully underhit back pass in the direction of Wilson. Ritchie pounced with the predatory instincts of a marksman playing for his moment of glory and reached the ball just before the Arsenal goalkeeper, took it past him and planted it in the yawning goal. It would have been a disaster for any Sunday morning team, let alone one which was pursuing the elusive dream of a League and Cup Double. Stoke should have gone 3–0 ahead when Greenhoff broke clear a few minutes later. Running through from the centre circle he bore down on

Wilson carrying many decades of hope from the Potteries and all the fears of North London. But, at a vital moment for both himself and his club, he lost his nerve and shot high, wide and anything but handsome. Just like Elland Road in 1930, the tide had turned.

Early in the second half Mahoney charged clear yet again through the constantly square defence. Wilson this time was able to reach the ball. It was a good piece of goalkeeping from a splendid technician, but it carried greater import as Arsenal swept upfield. What might have been 3–0 suddenly became 2–1. Armstrong fed Kennedy, whose chip into the middle caused confusion in the Stoke ranks. Storey unleashed an instinctive drive from 20 yards and even Banks could do nothing.

Yet it was Stoke who reacted more positively to the goal. Arsenal were not allowed to dictate the play in their quest for an equaliser, largely

Charlie George scores the all important first goal of the fifth round FA Cup tie against Manchester City at Maine Road on 17 February 1971. A free-kick had been given after Joe Corrigan handled the ball outside his area in the eighteenth minute. George simply shot past the City wall of George Heslop, Mike Doyle, Colin Bell, Tommy Booth and Tony Book. George scored another in the second half and one response from Colin Bell wasn't enough, the Gunners winning 2–1. It had been two weeks earlier, on 6 February, that Bertie Mee made his celebrated speech in the Highbury dressing room after Arsenal had defeated

Mahoney prevented a goal. Referee Partridge was perfectly placed to award the penalty. The Arsenal players began to leap in jubilation.

The thousands of supporters who had made the journey north to Sheffield roared. One Gunner was less than thrilled, however. Peter Storey had made the penalty job his own with a succession of nervelessly executed kicks. Even in the heat of the toughest battle he now realised the enormity of his task: 'The rest of the lads were all hugging each other as though we'd scored. But I was the one who had to stick it in. And past Gordon Banks too!'

At the other end of the ground Wilson dropped to his knees in prayer. The bedlam gave way to hush. It was one of those moments when the world stops. Had Storey missed, his name, like Bonetti's or perhaps Rix's, would have been engraved forever on the hearts of thousands. But Peter Storey was the man for Arsenal's hour of need. He repaid the faith of colleagues whose celebrations had looked so premature to the penalty taker. As Storey ran up, England's goalkeeper switched his weight on to his right foot and started to move in that direction. Storey sent his shot low, placed with the inside of his right foot, to Banks' left. Stoke City 2 Arsenal 2, the rescue was complete.

If, from the whole season, we are to choose just one moment in which the Double was won but might have been lost, then it was Jimmy Greenhoff's miss in the first half. In a remarkable display of touch football, Greenhoff had been a giant that day ('You could have fired a cannonball at him, and he'd just have nodded it down to John Ritchie's feet,' said one report), but, at the vital moment, he had failed and Arsenal were saved. At 3–0 they must have been out. John Mahoney could have given Stoke the game as well, but he was neither a forward nor the star of the day, and Wilson was more than equal to the Welshman's abilities.

There can be no doubt that the semi-final was the moment of truth. A League match can be lost (even 1–0 at Elland Road, as we shall see) and the Double still won. But every Cup tie has to end positively. All Cup-winning teams have one match where luck plays its part, when they come through a game they could or even should have lost. This was Arsenal's.

Psychologically, after Hillsborough Arsenal were now in the ascendant. Deep down, for all their boasts that they would finish the job at Villa Park, the Stoke squad knew that they had missed their chance. Bertie Mee's players realised that their escape came almost from the pages of schoolboy fiction. There was another omen too. Liverpool had beaten Everton in the other semi-final, and would be waiting at Wembley just as they had been 21 years earlier, the last time Arsenal had won the FA Cup.

Both managers announced unchanged teams, George having recovered from his bruised ankle and spirits, but the match had a very different flavour. Arsenal assumed control from the start and maintained it.

the same City side 1–0 in the League. He told the team that he thought they had a chance of winning all three trophies (they were still in the Fairs Cup) but it would mean two hard matches a week from there onwards. And the appeal did not lack emotion, as Mee later wrote: 'I told them: "Now is the time for you to be really ambitious and to aim for the success which may never be possible for you as players again in your lifetimes." '

because Greenhoff, in a supreme individual performance which contrasted with his finishing earlier, kept two and even three defenders constantly occupied. Twice on another day he might have brought Stoke the insurance of a third goal. Arsenal's momentum was also interrupted by an injury to George, which brought Sammels on for the last 15 minutes. The resultant injury time proved a blessing in disguise.

It was in the two minutes that Pat Partridge, the referee, added on, that the salvation came to keep alive Arsenal's appointment with history. Banks was pressed into conceding a corner, angrily protesting after the match that he had been fouled and that the decision should have been a Stoke free-kick. Armstrong took the corner from the Arsenal right, and this time Banks was nowhere. McLintock, a rescuing figure yet again, steered his header towards the left-hand post, where only the hands of John

Arsenal's skill at set pieces had kept their tally of goals ticking along for most of the season. In Armstrong the team possessed a master craftsman at corners. Radford, Kennedy, Graham, McLintock and George all relished attacking his accurate crosses. So, in the 13th minute of the FA Cup semi-final replay, Armstrong's service was again a work of precision and Graham's header was so powerful that it completely beat Banks from fully 15 yards.

After the interval Arsenal quickly reaffirmed their grip with a second goal, which held special significance for the provider and the scorer. In terms of scoring the partnership of Radford and Kennedy was undergoing its most fruitless spell of the season. Neither had scored in the previous seven matches. But two minutes into the second half Radford darted down the left and as his cross slithered across the goalmouth Kennedy was in exactly the right place to turn the ball into goal. The two danced a jig of relief and triumph. It was the end of the scoring.

McLintock emerged from the dressing-room, his own positive nature sharpened by the experience: 'We are going for the Double! There is real character in this Arsenal side, and now we are going to show we can win League and Cup. This will be my fifth time at Wembley and after being on the losing side in four finals the law of averages says I must have a great chance of a winners' medal this year. The way we are playing we can certainly do it.' Bertie Mee sat for the photographers in the dressing-room posed between the two goalscorers, a bottle of champagne in hand. It was a night to enjoy, but the manager soon had to restore the concentration. There were ten League games to be fitted in before the Cup

final. What happened in those would determine whether Arsenal were going to Wembley simply for the Cup or for the Double.

While the dramas were unfolding at Hillsborough, Leeds United had been losing at Chelsea. Now they had 54 points from 35 games; Arsenal were on 48 points from three fewer matches. If they won them all, they would be level. Any projected forecasts about the outcome of the race had to take into account that Arsenal had to visit Elland Road.

It brought the set of matches for the clubs on 17 April into even sharper focus. By twenty to five that afternoon the lead had changed. Arsenal, seemingly always the more likely losers in the title race, suddenly found themselves topping the table.

The circumstances were very much in keeping with the story of the season for each contender. Leeds lost at home to West Bromwich Albion in a blaze of controversy. Arsenal beat Newcastle at Highbury with a display which did not easily bring poetic description to mind, but nonetheless brought them two points.

To deal with the events in North London first the two precious points were gathered courtesy of a superb goal from George 19 minutes from the end of a mediocre match. Newcastle had drawn goalless at Highbury in each of the three previous seasons, and were intent on adding to that sequence. The first half contained more flare than flair, particularly when George reacted so angrily to a foul by Keith Dyson that the Arsenal man was booked. The other side of his nature appeared just when a goal was beginning to look beyond the home side. A packed penalty area ahead was not a daunting proposition when the ball

A timely interception for ex-schoolmaster Bob Wilson at Filbert Street during the FA Cup quarter-final tie against Leicester on 6 March 1971. The game ended scoreless and Arsenal won the replay 1–0. It was Arsenal's fourth consecutive away draw in the competition. Wilson and Armstrong played in all 56 games during the Double season.

dropped to George. He made sufficient inroads to disrupt the massed defence before turning sharply to drive a scorching left-footed shot past McFaul. For the rest of the action George Armstrong provided the perfect postscript: 'I don't suppose anybody will remember the game, but they'll all remember the result.'

Conversely, at Elland Road everybody will remember one particular incident. The turning point of the match concerned a decision by referee Ray Tinkler. He allowed Albion's Tony Brown to burst forward with the ball from just inside the Leeds half on the West Bromwich right. In a more central position his team-mate Colin Suggett was clearly in an offside position, but not, ruled the referee, interfering with play. Brown ran on with the Leeds defence expecting the whistle, drew goalkeeper Gary Sprake out to meet him, and passed across the goal for Jeff Astle (also in an offside position) to score at will. The crowd invaded the pitch. Chaos ensued.

The Leeds protests carried such venom that the Football Association subsequently fined the club £750 and ordered them to play their opening four home games the following season away from Elland Road. Albion, who had not

won away for 16 months, and were to finish the season sixth from bottom, eventually triumphed 2–1. For the Leeds morale it was a devastating blow, made worse by repeated television showings of the crucial episode which increased their sense of grievance. It is an interesting point for debate as to whether Arsenal would have more readily shrugged aside their disappointment. Leeds were to win their last three League matches and the Fairs Cup, but will always feel that the title was taken from them on a piece of refereeing interpretation.

This dramatic match, in a sense the perfect symbol of that whole period when Leeds dominated English football, was to continue to have repercussions 12 months on. The 1971–72 season ended with Leeds missing that Championship by just one point from Derby County. Of the four League matches the West Brom riot had caused them to play away from home, Leeds won two and drew two. It is perfectly reasonable to assume that they would have picked up that one point had those games been played at Elland Road (where they dropped only two points from their remaining 17 games). Hence it is still argued in Yorkshire today that Ray Tinkler's decision cost Leeds not one League title, but two.

If it was a piece of good fortune then Arsenal readily accepted it. Three days later another one-goal victory at Highbury condemned Burnley to the Second Division. With Storey and McNab on international duty for England against Greece in the European Championship, Kelly returned to midfield, and Roberts was given his only League outing over the second half of the season in defence. The absence of Storey in one other respect was covered by George because it was he, in the 26th minute, who accepted the responsibility of taking and scoring the match-winning penalty. The victory was less in doubt than some of Arsenal's one-goal successes during the season, and Wilson's only moment of real anxiety resulted from a careless back pass by Kelly. Paul Fletcher became the latest victim of the bravado of Arsenal's goalkeeper as he sped off his line to take the ball from the toes of the Burnley number nine. From 2 March to 20 April Arsenal had won all their nine League matches; the 18 points were captured with only 16 goals, but in those 13½ hours of First Division hurly-burly the defence was penetrated only once, at Southampton.

It was at The Dell where Leeds returned to winning ways on Saturday 24 April, the day that the Gunners' run of victories was halted, ironically by West Bromwich Albion, at the Hawthorns. In some ways it was an unusual match, not least because Asa Hartford scored for both sides. His goal at the right end was the first of the four. For once Wilson's charge off his line could not rescue a square defence.

Albion held their lead for only four minutes. Yet again an Armstrong corner unsettled those defending against it, particularly goalkeeper

'Charlie is their darling' screamed the predictably unoriginal headlines, but it was certainly true that this was George's golden era. This glorious header, executed while hanging four feet off the ground, was the only goal of the FA Cup quarter-final replay against Leicester on 15 March 1971. George scored in the fourth, fifth and sixth rounds, then saved his finale for the perfect moment. The goalkeeper, all those years ago, is Peter Shilton.

Jim Cumbes. The ball dropped for George, who was denied a goal himself by a block on the line. McLintock, however, was first to the rebound to notch his third goal in five games, this one at the right time to celebrate the announcement that he had been chosen as the Footballer of the Year.

Arsenal lost Rice at half-time, the legacy of a twisted ankle. Storey moved to right back but was still prepared to charge forward in the 55th minute in pursuit of a chipped pass from George. Hartford eagerly ran back, aware of the danger, only to increase it with a back pass. Cumbes was caught coming off his line and the ball rolled into goal with a simplicity which would have driven wild any Leeds United fans present. Five minutes from the end, however, Tony Brown, the scourge of the Elland Road supporters a week earlier, earned their gratitude with a thumping equaliser. Arsenal now had 61 points from 39 matches, Leeds were on 60 from 40 games.

Before leaving the Hawthorns, McLintock reflected on the impending clash of the Titans the following Monday: 'It's obviously going to be tough at Leeds, but the odds are still in our favour. I'm sure Leeds would be happy to swap positions with us. Our run of nine League wins had to end sometime. And Brown did it with a great goal. He hit the ball perfectly.'

Leeds had just reached the Fairs Cup final and a match with Juventus; against Arsenal they needed nothing less than victory for their Championship dreams to survive. A draw would be very much to Arsenal's liking, and for most of the game it looked the most likely outcome. The Gunners' sense of discipline and tactical organisation, a cornerstone of the season, served them well. Leeds, with Mick Bates deputising for Peter Lorimer, were kept at arm's length throughout a first half in which

The moment of truth in the Double year. Just as the last minutes of the 1930 semi-final against Hull at Elland Road clearly altered the history of the club, so the last 60 seconds of the semi-final against Stoke at Hillsborough on 27 March 1971 were ultimately the key to the Double. How remarkably similar the last minutes of these two games were – even down to their Yorkshire location, their final score, the venue of the replay, the eventual reckoning. In the history of all great clubs, there are such moments. The seconds were ticking away at Hillsborough with Stoke hanging on to their 2–1 lead. Arsenal won a corner on the right. George Armstrong took it. Up went McLintock (top) at the single most important moment of his career with the club. He beat Denis Smith (5) to the ball, directed it towards the left-hand corner and saw Stoke's John Mahoney palm it off the line. Referee Pat Patridge (centre left) saw the same thing, as did the Arsenal players and the Stoke defence. The Staffordshire men (bottom left), the collapse of whose world can be seen in their expressions and postures, are, left to right, Jimmy Greenhoff, Mickey Bernard, Eric Skeels, Alan Bloor and John Ritchie, scorer of the first goal. But the most interesting thing about this picture is the clock on top of the Hillsborough stand. 4.44pm it reads, four minutes beyond the normal final whistle. Of all the moments, of all the moves, of all the minutes, of all the matches that went to make up the 1970–71 season,

this was the one which won the Double.

For one man, however, the shouting was anything but over. That was Peter Storey, who said afterwards that: 'It was all very well them (his team-mates) jumping about and going mad, but I had to stick the ball in the net. And against Gordon Banks (then the England keeper).' He did so easily (top), dummying Banks to move right while the ball sped to his left. The celebrations followed, particularly from Radford, Kennedy and Armstrong (above left). Alan Bloor (6) and John Ritchie (9) seem less enamoured, their dreams shattered. They surely knew their chance had gone. So did the Arsenal supporters, who knew who was the hero of the hour (above right).

Peter Storey had scored both the goals, one of them among the two or three most important in the club's history. Bertie Mee said after the game that: 'I shall never forget the two matches against Stoke – the 5–0 thrashing and this success after being 2–0 down. After the 5–0 beating at Stoke we promised ourselves never again to enter a match with the casual feeling that it was half won before the kick-off.'

both teams were kept under excellent control by Norman Burtenshaw from Great Yarmouth, a late replacement for the elected referee Jim Finney, who had been hurt in a car crash.

Wilson's main task in the opening 45 minutes was to gather in a succession of crosses, but the pattern altered in the second half. The home side redoubled their efforts; Arsenal partly by design, partly because of Leeds' extra determination, opted to see out the siege rather than attack. And for all the creativity of Bremner and Johnny Giles, the best pair of midfield operators in the land at the time, Leeds were continually frustrated by a massed defence. It remained a stern, unrelenting battle, and though the prize

was so great the conduct of the players was more orderly than in other meetings of the period between these two rivals.

It all changed in the dying moments. The ubiquitous Paul Madeley triggered off another Leeds foray. Bremner, who had never ceased in his quest for an opening, played his part, and suddenly the ball broke for Jack Charlton all alone in front of Wilson's goal. England's World Cup centre half of 1966 directed the ball past the Arsenal goalkeeper as other defenders stood frozen, arms raised in a uniform appeal for offside. Even then the gods, for once, favoured Leeds because the ball struck a post and rebounded out, only for a long Charlton leg to reach it before McNab. Instantly Norman Burtenshaw confirmed the goal.

Arsenal's protests were long in time and short in temper. George booted the ball into the stand and was rightly booked. Wilson and McLintock led the pursuit of the referee, and it was fully five minutes before he could restart the game. The linesman whose flag had stayed down was also turned upon by aggrieved visiting players.

There was still time for Graham to send a back header inches over Gary Sprake's crossbar, before more furious words were directed at the referee when he blew the final whistle.

Many off the pitch queried the goal at the time, though Bertie Mee confined himself to commenting that 'never was a defeat less deserved. Arsenal were fantastic, tremendous.' However, subsequent television re-runs convinced a number of the most bitter Arsenal players at the time that referee and linesman had been absolutely right. McNab, it seemed, had been too slow moving out. Mr Burtenshaw was able to look forward to his next Arsenal match with confidence; he had been appointed the FA Cup final referee.

Whatever the merits of the decision it meant that Leeds were back on top of the First Division, but William Hill, the bookmakers, still made Arsenal, who had a game in hand, favourites for the Champion-ship at 4–5; Leeds were quoted as even-money.

May Day brought victories for both candidates in the race to be named Champions. Leeds struck twice in the first half at Elland Road, through Bremner and Lorimer, to make sure that their League season ended with a win over Nottingham Forest. Arsenal had to wait longer before gaining a win against their semi-final victims Stoke.

It was the type of game which had become the norm at Highbury towards the end of the season. Stoke, like other visitors, were not brimming with ambition. The cautious approach of five midfield players and a solitary attacker, Greenhoff, was unlikely to gain revenge for an FA Cup semi-final defeat.

Arsenal began as though their boots were weighted down with tension. No opportunity was created until three minutes before half-time. George's forward pass caught the Stoke defence in a line, and Radford bore down on the Stoke goal and its guardian, Gordon Banks. He dallied so long that Smith was able to rush back and prevent the shot. It looked a significant miss and Radford later explained: 'Initially I stopped because I thought I was offside. Then I realised I wasn't and tried to lob the ball over Banks. But he started back-pedalling so I had to hold the ball. One of their blokes came in and I've the gash to prove it.'

Early in the second half Arsenal suffered again; Storey limped off with a groin strain and Kelly entered the congested midfield area. It was the start of a memorable week for the 20-year-old Scot. He had been on the field 12 minutes when he spotted the potential of a long ball into the goalmouth from Armstrong. Graham flicked it on to Radford who skilfully manipulated it into Kelly's path. The substitute blasted in the decisive goal.

Arsenal knew exactly what they had to do to win the League for the first time for 18 years. Leeds had finished their League programme: Played 42, Won 27, Drawn 10, Lost 5, Goals For 72, Against 30, Points 64. Arsenal's record

read: Played 41, Won 28, Drawn 7, Lost 6, For 70, Against 29, Points 63.

With a wonderful sense of occasion the last fixture was against Tottenham Hotspur, at White Hart Lane. The game had been originally scheduled for the day of the FA Cup semi-finals and was now rearranged for the Monday night of Cup final week. Spurs needed three points from the meeting with Arsenal and a trip to Stoke to be sure of qualifying for the next European campaign. Bonuses of £400 per man could depend on beating Arsenal.

The mathematical permutations were even more remarkable. A win would give the title to Arsenal, a defeat would send the trophy to Elland Road. But a goalless draw would mean success for Arsenal while (because of the peculiarities of the goal average system then in force) any scoring draw (even 1–1) would conclude matters in Leeds' favour. The mathematics meant it was more important for Arsenal not to concede a goal than to score one.

Arsenal's players had only reached this situation through a deep yearning for success. The prospect of crossing another minefield did not alarm them. Frank McLintock rarely lost his sense of optimism: 'I'm sure we can make it. We always give good performances at White Hart Lane.' George Armstrong was equally confident: 'We're playing better away from home because we are not under the same tension, and it's in our favour that Spurs are not a defensive side.'

Alan Mullery, Tottenham's captain, reinforced the belief that it would be a mighty clash: 'Arsenal have got as much chance of being handed the title by Spurs as I have of being given the Crown Jewels. They are the last people we want winning the Championship. Everybody is on about the great season Arsenal are having. Well, we're not doing too badly. We have won the League Cup and reached the sixth round of the FA Cup. Now we mean to round off our season by beating Arsenal – and that will put us third in the table. That can't be bad.'

Manager Bill Nicholson recognised that the League title could be the prelude to the Double to which he had guided Spurs ten years earlier: 'We are tremendously proud of our Double achievement. I suppose some other club has got to do it again sometime but we will be doing our best to see that it isn't Arsenal. My instructions to the Tottenham players will be to go out to try to win.'

Don Revie was glad to hear such words. The Leeds manager declared: 'We have done all we can and now we are helpless. My players have been magnificent all season. I would hate to see them pipped on the post again. We have got 64 points and there have never been runners-up with a collection as big as that. ' Revie was right – whichever side lost, they would have amassed the biggest runners-up points total ever.

The Arsenal players rested on the Sunday as usual, but for Storey there was not enough time for recovery. When the players reported for

The two goals which won the semi-final replay against Stoke on 31 March 1971. The first (top) came from George Graham (out of the picture) and the second (bottom picture) from Ray Kennedy (far right). Stoke could not respond, their moment of hope had dissolved four days before. Kennedy's arrival in the team had been as successful as it was swift. He had played only four League games in 1969–70 and came on as substitute twice in the Fairs Cup. In part he owed his early introduction in 1970–71 to a spate of injuries, but he took his chance perfectly.

light training on the morning of the match it was clear that Kelly would be in the team from the start. Sammels was chosen as substitute.

The players lunched at their own homes before reconvening at the South Herts Golf Club, the regular pre-match meeting place, at 4.30pm. Already the football fans of North London were on the march towards White Hart Lane. The gates were locked more than an hour before kick-off with 51,192 spectators inside. Twice that number were on the outside.

The volume of traffic even surprised the police. The Arsenal team coach crawled along.

Bertie Mee recalled: 'We gave ourselves an hour for a drive which normally takes 20 minutes. But even then it was a very difficult journey. I have never seen scenes like it. But there was never the pressure that we were going to be late, and seeing those thronging crowds increased the sense of occasion for us. There was no way we were going to be beaten.'

The referee, Kevin Howley, had to abandon his car a mile away to fight his way on foot through the crowds. It was the last League match in a distinguished career, a great occasion on which to bow out. Making his whistle heard in the din which echoed around the ground from start to finish became a problem. The vociferous McLintock bellowed orders to his team-mates which passed largely unheard.

McLintock had his hands full coping with the powerful Martin Chivers. The wise Alan Gilzean continually sought to steal a yard on Simpson. Jimmy Neighbour probed ceaselessly down Tottenham's left and stretched Rice to the full, and all the while Martin Peters hovered menacingly in the Spurs midfield, always likely to time a late run into a scoring position. For all the attacking intent clear-cut chances were few. Peters flicked the top of the Arsenal bar with a swerving shot, and almost scored with a header. Joe Kinnear forced a courageous and painful dive from Wilson at his feet. Gilzean all but connected as the ball flashed across the Arsenal goalmouth.

At the other end George brought an athletic save from Pat Jennings in the opening minute. McLintock saw his goalbound shot bounce clear off the body of Collins. Graham's header curved on to the top of the Spurs goal. Radford and Kennedy hassled at Peter Collins and Phil Beal. Armstrong was everywhere.

For all the energy imparted into the match by both teams, whose conduct had been first class, a goalless draw beckoned. But three minutes from time, Kinnear tried to dribble clear of trouble inside his own penalty area. George recaptured the ball from the Spurs right back, and twisted instantly to conjure a cross from an angle which would have defeated most players. Even then it seemed as though Arsenal had been denied. Jennings made the save of the night as Radford met the ball provided so cleverly by George.

Tottenham stopped to a man, perhaps in admiration of their goalkeeper, but also because they expected the ball to run behind for a corner. Armstrong had barely stood still all season, and was not going to break the habit now. Rescuing it from near the line his chip back across goal was met by Kennedy's header. The ball sped high to Jennings' left, above the leap of Cyril Knowles behind him. It clipped the underside of the bar and was over the line.

The goal was greeted by instant exhilaration from every Arsenal player. But almost as quickly misgivings followed, particularly from the scorer. In one respect, the goal was irrelevant. A Tottenham goal would still give the Championship to Leeds and there was still time for it. 'That was the longest three minutes I have ever known,' recalled Kennedy. 'I remember thinking to myself as Tottenham came back at us that perhaps it might have been better had my header not gone into the net.'

Spurs hurled themselves forward as the seconds ticked away. One last corner could still have deprived the Gunners, but Wilson's last act in an almost faultless series of performances throughout the 42-game First Division programme was to grasp the ball as though the lives of he and his team-mates depended upon

Frank McLintock throws himself in front of Southampton's Jimmy Gabriel to score a vital goal at The Dell on 10 April 1971. Arsenal won the match 2–1, part of a sequence of nine consecutive League wins with only one goal (that by Terry Paine for Southampton) conceded. John Radford scored the other goal, his last of the season and the only one he recorded in the last seventeen matches of the Double year. Don Howe, then coach and number two to Bertie Mee, was unstinting in his praise of McLintock around this time: 'They talk of Dave Mackay and Bobby Moore as great captains, but Frank is more inspiring than either. I'm beginning to feel obsolete in the dressing-room. Frank is doing as much talking as I am, and working wonders with his words.'

it. As he fell to the ground he was surrounded by other players, half of them hoping for a fumble, the other half protecting their goalkeeper. For a few seconds it seemed that the match would end in acrimony, but Kevin Howley stepped in firmly.

Moments later he blew a whistle in League football for the last time. The title belonged to Arsenal for a record eighth time. It had been won by a clear point at the last gasp of a marathon that had never been less than compelling. Leeds deserved sympathy for coming so close, but none could deny the magnificence of Arsenal's victory. Like a dog with a bone they had refused to let go right to the end.

Bedlam reigned on the pitch. George, close to the touchline, leapt into the arms of Don Howe. As thousands of fans raced to congratulate their heroes Bob Wilson found himself marooned. Unable to contain his joy he hugged the only participant he could reach – referee Howley! McLintock found a Leeds United scarf wrapped around his neck as he was chaired off shoulder high.

The celebrations became so protracted that Don Howe found his own joy giving way to anxiety: 'My thoughts turned straight to the Cup final and I was worried that the crowd might injure our players. They were ripping at their shirts. Some wanted their boots, which of course they had to wear on Saturday. I was frightened that they would tread on somebody's foot and keep him out of the final.'

Twenty minutes after the end of the match some of the players still had not made it back to the sanctuary of the dressing-room. Arsenal officials turned to the police for a rescue party, but with the footballers unable to get off the pitch the constables were unable to make their way on to it. Eventually all were rounded up minus only a few shirts.

Bertie Mee lost his club tie as he returned to the directors' box to acknowledge the crowd's appreciation. Tottenham for their part were most magnanimous in defeat, which the Arsenal manager remembers with great affection: 'We were given champagne in the dressing-room by Bill Nicholson. The club could not have done more to help us celebrate our great night. There had been a lot of petty rivalries between the two clubs in past years but in my time we did a lot of work to improve relationships. They must have been very disappointed that they had lost but they didn't let that spoil our evening.'

The party spirit continued long into the night. The team moved on to the White Hart in Southgate. There were no curfews posted or restrictions made. Tuesday, which had already begun by the time everyone reached home, would be a day for recharging batteries. Wednesday was the time really to begin the concentration on the FA Cup final.

Much of that day was given over to the needs of the media, but not for long. Bertie Mee's medical background gave him strong views about Wembley finals: 'Over the years so much had been said about the problems of playing there, particularly the victims of cramp. Now cramp is really an emotional problem. It does of course have physical symptoms, but they can often be a result of pressure. I wanted to protect the team from emotional stress, so there was no involvement with the press or television after Thursday.'

Don Howe concentrated on the physical preparation. Amidst the lush acres of the London Colney training ground, the players did their training on a pitch marked to the exact specifications of Wembley. The grass had been allowed to grow to cultivate the feel of the Empire Stadium turf. Two recent League Cup final defeats had raised doubts about the team's ability to win at Wembley. No stone was left unturned in an attempt to create the right atmosphere this time.

For George Wright, the physiotherapist, it was becoming a race against the clock. Peter Storey's presence in midfield was vital to the construction of the side; his injury was responding to intensive treatment, but only slowly. On Friday night he joined up with the other players at the Grosvenor Hotel in Park Lane. The hall porter reminded them that it had been a lucky venue for West Bromwich Albion three years earlier when they had brought the Cup back for their post-match banquet.

Bertie Mee had one major decision to make, and Storey was chosen to start the game. It was a risk but one that was calculated; the converted full back had become a fearsome opponent in midfield. Liverpool would not relish the bite in his tackles even if he was less than one hundred per cent fit.

There were psychological battles to be won. No one knew that better than Bill Shankly, Liverpool's manager, to whom the old cliche applied: 'a legend in his own life-time.' Shankly had surprisingly appeared by the side of the pitch the day before the final when Arsenal were taking a preparatory stroll to acclimatise to the Wembley environment. There was rain about, and Bob Wilson was greeted by one of the masters of gamesmanship and kidology with the comment: 'Bob, it'll be a nightmare for goalkeepers out here tomorrow.' Directed at a character with less perception than Wilson, it might have induced a sleepless night.

In fact 8 May 1971 was a stifling day. The Arsenal ritual did not include the usual lie-in of most Cup final teams. By ten o'clock the players were on the road to familiar surroundings. At the South Herts Golf Club they took their pre-match lunch with words of encouragement from Dai Rees, the resident professional.

The opportunity to gain a spot of revenge on Shankly came 15 minutes before the kick-off. Arsenal had recent memories of the formalities of Wembley finals. Officials are keen to have the teams standing in the tunnel ready to walk out at the appropriate minute. Often the wait is so protracted that the nervous begin to suffer.

Debating time at Leeds on 26 April 1971. Bob Wilson is injured, Charlie George seems cheerful enough, but Frank McLintock is engaged in a heated discussion with his Leeds counterpart, Billy Bremner (partly hidden behind Bob McNab). Leeds won the game (Arsenal's fortieth – only two more to go) 1–0 with a Jack Charlton disputed goal, the Arsenal defence claiming offside. Even at this stage, Arsenal did not really seem likely Double winners. Leeds continued to do well in the League, Arsenal had to win their last two games to be sure, and there was still the hurdle of Liverpool at Wembley. Of all the differences between the Spurs Double of 1961 and the Arsenal Double of 1971 this is the most striking. In 1960–61 the Press and their fans were talking excitedly of a Spurs' Double from January onwards, if not well before. Ten years later, it hardly seemed worthy of speculation until after Arsenal had beaten Spurs in the final League game. The mere possibility only crept up on the football public literally in the last two weeks of the season.

So at 2.45pm Bertie Mee politely told the FA representative that he was finishing his team talk and his players would be out in a moment. A few minutes later the call came again. This time he replied: 'A couple of the players are just tying their boots, we won't be a minute.'

It was only at the third time of asking that Arsenal appeared. Liverpool had come out at the first request and been kept waiting. Shankly scowled, realising that for once he had been outfoxed. There was no delay for Arsenal; immediately they were led out into the sunlight and the wall of sound that was waiting beyond the end of the tunnel.

It had been six weeks since Liverpool had qualified for Wembley. While Arsenal's attentions had been very much elsewhere, at Anfield there had been no escape from the publicity machine. It had been one long round of interviews and discussions about the match in the weeks leading up to the great day itself. Arsenal's worries were whether the rigours of the League campaign would now begin to take their toll, and those unhappy memories of League Cup defeats. They were playing their fourth major final in five years under Mee.

Liverpool's early promise brought no reward, only the bruises of battle as Storey came in high and late on Heighway. Toshack was then misused by Rice and McLintock. It took a telling pass from George to switch the balance of the opening minutes. Kennedy's running was never speedy, and recovering defenders forced him away from the goal and the danger evaporated.

Indeed it was not to be Kennedy's day, and six minutes into the second half he failed with another opportunity much closer to goal. In contrast Radford recaptured the form which had been elusive towards the end of the League season. No one contributed more to Arsenal's

Eddie Kelly gets the late, all important winner against Stoke on 1 May 1971. The Stoke defender is Mickey Bernard, the goalkeeper, of course, Gordon Banks. Stoke were still smarting from their semi-final defeat of a month earlier and it was a hard game. Kelly's goal, though less heralded, was as important as Kennedy's at Tottenham two days later. Stoke had some cause for their bitterness. In the two seasons 1970–71 and 1971–72, they played Arsenal no less than eight times. In those eight games, Stoke scored ten goals to Arsenal's eight. But Arsenal won three and Stoke only won two, including the 5–0 thrashing on 26 September 1970, the only time in the Double year that any team scored more than twice against Arsenal. Stoke's problem was that Arsenal won the two that mattered – the semi-final replays.

While both halves of the Double were won in London, neither was secured at Highbury. On 3 May 1971 Arsenal went to White Hart Lane needing a win or a goalless draw to pip Leeds for the title. A scoring draw would have given the title to Leeds. Their fate rested on their near neighbours and rivals, the only other team to win the Double this century, the team they had displaced from the First Division half a century before. The crowd was enormous. Steve Perryman only just made the kick-off, taking an hour to travel 600 yards. The police estimated a crowd of around 150,000 tried to see the match; even the Spurs directors called it the biggest turn-out in the club's history. Those lucky enough to get inside saw just one goal (top left), a Ray Kennedy (out of the picture) header minutes from time. The desperate defenders are Knowles, Jennings and Kinnear. Statistically the goal made little difference – Arsenal still needed to *prevent* Spurs scoring. The Championship would have been theirs whether they had scored or not, just as long as Spurs didn't. At the final whistle the fans were to celebrate Arsenal's eighth Championship on the pitch (centre) while (top right) Armstrong, Kennedy and Radford preferred the champagne in the dressing-room.

eventual victory than the muscular Yorkshireman in the number nine shirt. Though he did not score himself he was the provider of both opportunities which were taken; throughout the match he used the Gunners' possession to excellent effect.

Armstrong was another who could not quite capture his normal excellence, though once, arriving at the far post, he almost beat Clemence for a goal which would surely have spared the players extra time. Graham, however, strutted through the match with an arrogance that set him apart and he was awarded the Man of the Match prize. Twelve minutes from time he climbed characteristically to direct Radford's long throw beyond Clemence, but it came off the bar. Smith hooked the rebound for a corner which Armstrong planted once more on Graham's head. This time left back Alec Lindsay cleared off the line.

Both sides used their substitutes. Storey, as expected, gave way to Kelly midway through the second half. Four minutes later Peter Thompson who, along with Chris Lawler, Tommy Smith and Ian Callaghan, was a survivor from the 1965 Cup-winning team, was brought on in an attempt to inject more thrust into Liverpool's performance; the ineffective Alun Evans was replaced. Nevertheless, neither team could break the mould of the match in normal time. It had been a highly technical 90 minutes, with both sides cautious in their attempts to seek an advantage. The uncommitted neutrals, however, were seeking a more cavalier approach in the extra 30 minutes.

They had to wait only two minutes. Steve Heighway had rarely freed himself from the shackles imposed on the Arsenal right, but suddenly he slipped past Rice and Armstrong and from a tight angle cut in from the left. Wilson automatically took up position covering his near post. With his usually accurate sense of anticipation already predicting that Heighway should cut the ball back for Toshack arriving in the middle, the goalkeeper slightly overcompensated for the cross. Heighway was nothing

And so to Wembley; Bertie Mee leads out his men for their tryst with destiny. More than one team had come to Wembley needing just one more victory to achieve the Double, and so far only Spurs had achieved it. In that sense the odds were firmly against Arsenal, as Manchester United found in 1957, as Liverpool were to discover in 1977 and as Everton were to regret in 1985.

Early on, the game was a tense one; referee Norman Birkenshaw and tattooed John Radford are pictured suggesting to Charlie George that he keeps his thoughts to himself. Radford was both a popular and an under-rated player, says Terry Neill: 'Very intelligent, very astute. When the tackle from behind was commonplace, he was the first footballer I knew to put shin pads down the back of his legs.' One of Radford's particular skills, the long throw into the goalmouth, became a trademark. So much so that using it as a decoy secured the only Arsenal goal of the first 1972 semi-final, again versus Stoke. Radford shaped to take a long throw, the whole Stoke defence retreated, Radford threw it short to an unmarked colleague instead and was himself still unmarked long enough to receive the return and set up the goal.

Goalmouth incidents in the first ninety minutes of the 1971 FA Cup final were not exactly numerous. One of Liverpool's closest shaves came when George Armstrong beat Tommy Smith to a close-range header and Ray Clemence pushed the ball upwards (despite the keeper's apparent position in this picture) and caught it as it came down. Liverpool, though they finished only fifth, had an excellent defence that season. They scored only 42 goals but conceded just 24, then a First Division record.

There was no score in the 1971 FA Cup final until the first minute of extra time. Then Steve Heighway, a recent, rather unpredictable newcomer to the Liverpool first team from non-League football, broke down the left wing (left), slipped George Armstrong and shot for the near post before Pat Rice could cover. Bob Wilson had left just too much room (bottom picture) and the ball ended in the back of the net. Liverpool 1 Arsenal 0. Only four teams since the Second World War had won the Cup after conceding the first goal and only six others have done so since 1971. Which means, if the half century since the Second World War can be said to be typical, that the side that scores the first goal in the Cup final wins four times out of five.

if not unorthodox and his shot fizzed into the gap that Wilson had left to his right. Only the beaten goalkeeper heard the nick as the ball glanced the post on its way in; it was no fluke, Heighway had scored from a similar angle in a Merseyside derby earlier that season.

Wilson had little time for self-recrimination. Within moments he had saved Arsenal from certain defeat, plunging to keep out a close-range shot from Hall. On the bench Don Howe was sending George Wright to the touchline with a vital message: 'My first reaction was here we go again, losing at Wembley, but anyway we'd had a tremendous season. But my next thought was that we'd got to change something to pull that goal back. I told George to get to the touchline and tell George Graham to go forward. Charlie George was nearly out on his feet because of the heat and was struggling to make any runs forward, so he was told to drop back into midfield.'

There were four minutes left in the first period of extra time when the move paid divi-dends. Radford hooked the ball over his shoulder into a crowded Liverpool penalty area, where the congestion was perhaps too great for Clemence to risk an intervention. Larry Lloyd, Emlyn Hughes, Smith and Lawler were all between the Liverpool goalkeeper and the ball, which fell for Kelly simply to touch it forward. It certainly could never be called a serious shot.

Yet on it rolled between a tangle of legs as Graham swept in to view. He swung a leg at the ball and Clemence, now very much the last line of defence, could do nothing to prevent its progress into the net. Graham wheeled away in celebration of the goal that everyone in the ground believed to be his. But football had entered a television age. The BBC and ITV were competing on the sporting front and the Cup final was the showpiece for each channel to show off its technical and editorial skills. New camera angles were one area of that competition, and the day after the final the London Weekend Television look-back at the match included a 'revelation', from a camera behind

Arsenal came back quickly. A seemingly hopeful ball into the crowded centre was pushed forward by Eddie Kelly (left in picture opposite). George Graham slipped between Tommy Smith and Emlyn Hughes and seemed to flick it past Ray Clemence. As he wheeled away in triumph (picture above) the goal was obviously credited to Graham. Liverpool 1 Arsenal 1. Later television replays encouraged an interesting, arguably unique, debate. Had George Graham actually touched the ball? In the end the goal was credited to Eddie Kelly, who was the first substitute to score in an FA Cup final. Graham was naturally distressed that anyone should think he would try to steal a colleague's goal, and remains convinced he touched the ball. Further viewing of the film tends to support his case, or at least leave the matter unresolved. What probably happened is that he did get a slight touch to the ball, but the direction and speed were not varied at all. This was to prove vital. Ray Clemence's advance had been made with an allowance for a Graham touch to change the direction of the ball. Had he done so, Clemence might well have saved.

the goal, that Graham had not touched the ball. The last certain touch came from Kelly, declared Brian Moore and Jimmy Hill.

Thus the club credited the scoring of the equalising goal to Eddie Kelly. Fifteen years after the event George Graham still believes he made contact with the ball, and is understandably embarrassed at being recalled from time to time as the man who claimed a vital goal which apparently was not his. BBC Television's Barry Davies was stationed that afternoon among the photographers close to Ray Clemence's net. Watching with the eyes of a trained observer, he still believes that the goal should be Graham's. Ray Clemence, who ought to have been in the best position to judge, could throw no light on the subject. A recent study of the television pictures supports the Kelly theory, but camera angles can be deceptive. It is certainly true that the ball did not change direction whether Graham touched it or not, so Graham's swing might at least have worked like a good dummy on Clemence.

The debate matters now only in the search for accuracy. At the time it did not matter in the slightest whose goal it was. Arsenal, yet again in this astonishing season, had refused to accept second place. But back on the bench the search for victory was not quite so immediate for Don Howe: 'Once we had equalised I settled for the draw. It hadn't really been our day overall, and I felt it would be better to steady ourselves and start out afresh for the replay. I decided to get George Graham back into midfield just to make sure he got behind the ball. Charlie still looked exhausted so I wanted him back up front. Out of the way really. He found his way forward because we were trying to protect our position for the draw.'

No one had explained the finer points of this theory to George himself. With the replay nine minutes away he interpassed with the magnificent Radford before letting fly from 20 yards with a right-footed shot which belied his weary appearance. The force in the drive would surely have beaten Clemence even if it had not

The *coup de grâce,* that final dramatic moment towards which the whole of Arsenal's season had seemed to be building. And who else to supply it but the ex-North Bank supporter himself, Charlie George. With just nine minutes of extra time remaining, George picked up the ball around 25 yards out. He moved a few paces and, despite the exhaustion

which had dulled his game for the last half-hour, hit a crisp right-foot shot (top left). The ball took a tiny upward deflection off the top of Larry Lloyd's outstretched right boot and moved too quickly for a flying Ray Clemence (top right) to reach. Clemence just had time to turn in mid-air and see it hit the back of the net.

The game won, George (number 11 in bottom picture) turned and fell to the floor in the gesture for which he will always be remembered. McLintock and Radford ran to greet him. The Liverpool defenders are Peter Thompson and Tommy Smith. Note that the scoreboard gives the first goal to George Graham, who was to be voted Man of the Match.

taken a slight upward deflection off the lunging Lloyd. George marked the moment with a novel salute; his arms were outraised as in more conventional celebration, but he was lying flat on his back at the time! It remains the outstanding image of this unusual character.

How appropriate that Arsenal's Double was sealed by one of North London's own. Charlie George, born in Islington, a product of Holloway School, used to stand on Highbury's North Bank. With his flowing hair and his obvious mocking of convention he acted out the dreams of so many young Arsenal followers. At 20 years old he had earned himself and his team-mates an extra £12,000 a man with that winning goal. The money mattered, but the glory was priceless.

Frank McLintock became a Wembley victor at long last, at the fifth time of asking. Bill Shankly, generous in defeat, was quick to shake his hand. George did handsprings of jubilation. Kennedy embraced Lloyd in consolation. Wilson assured Clemence, a loser on his first Wembley visit, that he would be back.

Bob Wilson later admitted that on a baking afternoon he had gone cold all over at the instant George had struck his momentous goal; such was the feeling of salvation after his earlier slip. His recollections at the final whistle are also sharp: 'Frank was in so much of a hurry to go up and grab the Cup that I pulled him back. He'd waited so long. I shouted at him that it might never happen again and that he should savour every moment. Not to rush it.' Wilson was right, of course – it never did happen again for McLintock.

Wilson followed McLintock up to the Royal Box, where the second leg of the Double was presented to Arsenal's captain by the Duke of Kent. On the way back to ground level the

The 1970-71 Double winning Arsenal squad. Back row, left to right: Pat Rice, Sammy Nelson, Peter Marinello. Centre: Bob McNab, Peter Simpson, Charlie George, Geoff Barnett, Bob Wilson, John Roberts, Ray Kennedy, Peter Story. Seated: George Wright (trainer and physiotherapist), George Armstrong, Eddie Kelly, John Radford, Bertie Mee (manager), Frank McLintock, George Graham, Jon Sammels, Don Howe. Of the players, only Geoff Barnett did not make any first-team appearances during the Double season.

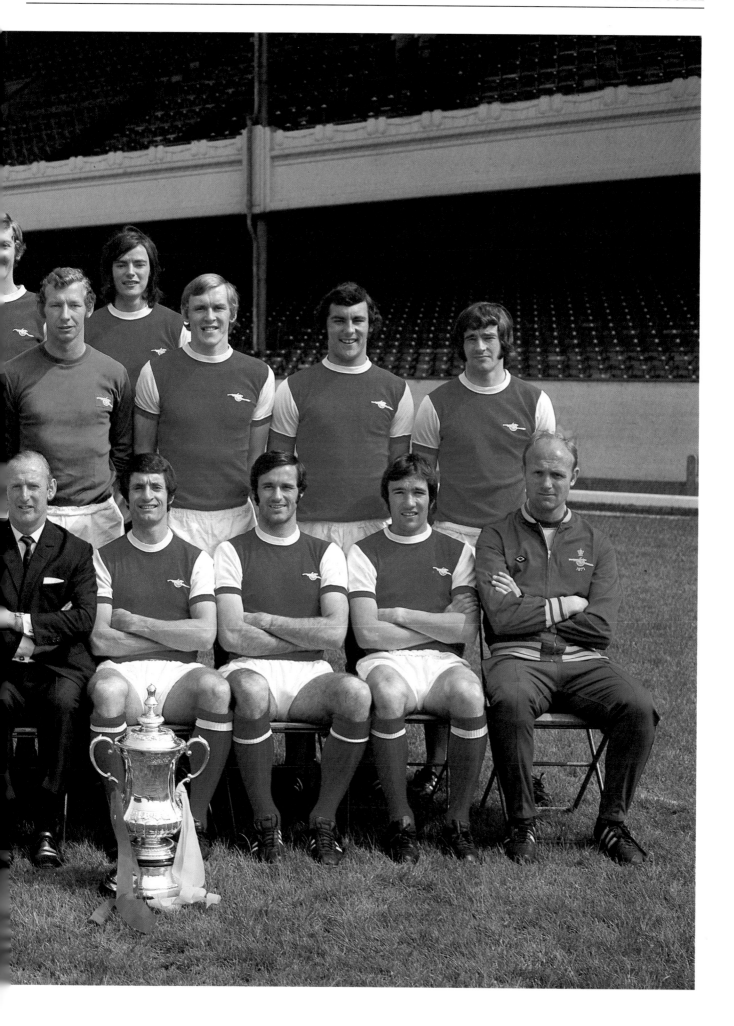

goalkeeper, by complete coincidence, spotted his older brother Hugh, who had been a great mentor in younger days. For the Wilsons it was a special moment on a special day.

For some it was too much to take. McLintock relished the ending of his Wembley hoodoo, but years later he confessed that he had no emotion left: 'It may seem strange but I've never been able to feel that supreme thrill of winning the Double. Our Fairs Cup win the year before meant so much. And winning the League was terrific. Maybe I was just too drained at the end of it all.'

A quarter of a million people still had the energy to line the route from Highbury to Islington Town Hall the following day. Both trophies were displayed by the team from an open-top bus, along with the FA Youth Cup, the product of more success for the club's prospective stars. Bertie Mee had guided the club to a year of unprecedented achievement. It had taken 51 matches to win the Double, a longer road than that of any of the three previous holders of that accolade. 'I wanted the boys to win the Cup for Frank McLintock. The League Championship was for my chairman Denis Hill-Wood. For myself? I wouldn't mind the European Cup next season. I know we have done the Double, but at the moment it is too much to take in.'

In any walk of life achieving success is only half the battle. Living with the difficulties it can create is another matter altogether. A month after the Double was won, North London was alive with rumours of the first split in the camp.

No member of the Highbury staff was fuelled with more ambition than Don Howe. It was understandable that other clubs looking to fill managerial positions should be attracted by his credentials. None of them knew him better than his old club, West Bromwich Albion and on 8 July Bertie Mee had to respond to the news that Albion had attracted Howe to the Hawthorns: 'There is little need for me to repeat how highly I value Don as a coach – and how sorry I am to see him leaving.'

The popular view at the time was that Don Howe had left because he wanted to step into Mee's shoes. Ten years later he strongly refuted those rumours: 'I did want to manage in my own right. That was only natural. But I wasn't in a hurry. Being manager of Arsenal was still my ambition but I would have been prepared to wait four, five, ten years if necessary. All it would have taken to keep me at Highbury would have been a promise that when Bertie decided to finish I would have been given a go as manager for a year or two. But nobody said that.'

He was speaking then as a Highbury employee, the right-hand man to Terry Neill. Later, when Neill was dismissed, Don Howe finally fulfilled his ambition. After an initial spell as caretaker-manager he was appointed almost 13 years after his departure for West Bromwich Albion. Back in 1971, what would

have been a simple sense of loss became more acrimonious when Albion also signed George Wright and youth coach Brian Whitehouse. Denis Hill-Wood was angry enough to go into print. 'Loyalty is a dirty word, these days,' said the Chairman. 'There is nothing I can do about what West Bromwich have done in raiding our staff except just to ignore them.'

There is always the issue of what comes next. It is a truism that great football sides usually last three years. It seems to have been true of the Arsenal of 1970 to 1972. Somehow the magic goes, other sides watch and learn and the unexpected is now expected. It is no secret that the 1971–72 season, started as Double winners, was eventually to be a disappointment. The first priority was obviously the European Cup. Of English clubs only Manchester United had ever succeeded, and the competition was still redolent of Real Madrid, of Benfica, of impossibly long journeys across the steppes of Eastern Europe. The first two rounds brought easy draws – against Stroemsgodset of Norway and Grasshoppers of Europe. But the real thing came next in the quarter-finals. Ajax of Amsterdam were European Champions, and formed the heart of the Dutch side that should have won the World Cup two years later. In Amsterdam Gerrit Muhren scored twice although Kennedy got one back with a header. At Highbury one goal would have been enough, and Arsenal scored it. Unfortunately it was at the wrong end and Graham's own-goal ended Arsenal's best chance of winning the world's premier club trophy.

The League was not to prove much kinder, despite the arrival of Alan Ball for a record £220,000. Three losses in a week in August were both a shock and too much to recover from. In the end Arsenal finished fifth, and in a season which did not produce an outstanding team and one which went to the wire between Derby, Leeds and Liverpool. None of their totals came near Arsenal's the season before.

Alan Ball's influence was most sharply felt in an FA Cup run which with a suitable touch of irony started at Swindon. Eight of the Swindon side which had inflicted so much agony on their First Division opponents at Wembley almost three years earlier took part in the match, as did a revered opponent, Dave Mackay, who in his last season as a player at 37 was also managing the Wiltshire club.

Ball was not ravaged by memories of the gloomy day at Wembley, and while the pundits waited for Arsenal to be toppled, the recent signing started to repay some of his transfer fee. He set up the game's first goal for Armstrong before opening his own account.

There was a scare in the fourth round, at Reading of the Fourth Division. Arsenal muddled through 2–1, courtesy of an own goal and Pat Rice bursting forward to strike Arsenal's winner, which was deflected.

The fifth round brought three skirmishes

with Derby County. At the Baseball Ground Charlie George netted twice, as in the fifth round a year earlier, but Derby matched his two efforts with an Alan Hinton penalty and a goal from Alan Durban. Neither side could break through in the replay, which went to extra time in front of a packed Highbury crowd of 63,077. Because of Arsenal's European commitments the third match was two weeks later, only five days before the quarter-final. On neutral soil at Leicester, Kennedy produced the crucial goal.

Away again in the sixth round, for the 18th time in the last 21 draws, Arsenal only had to travel a few miles. Orient were struggling to avoid relegation to the Third Division, but they had knocked out high-flying Chelsea at Brisbane Road in the last round.

East London was out in force to see whether Arsenal would go the way of Chelsea. With the League title now looking less likely, the Gunners had their hearts set on retaining the Cup. Orient thus met sterner opposition and shortly after half-time Ball, resplendent in the white boots which were briefly in fashion, ended Orient's dreams.

By a strange coincidence Arsenal's semi-final opponents were once again Stoke City. Again the venue was Villa Park, where the thrilling saga had ended a year earlier. Arsenal's side showed only one change from the previous semi-final. Ball's inclusion meant Kennedy dropping down to substitute. George wore the number nine shirt, and Radford, recently freed from suspension, partnered him. Storey had briefly been the player to stand down to accommodate Ball, but since March had reclaimed his place in midfield.

Stoke included three players who had not been involved in the 1971 semi-final, all veterans: Alex Elder, Peter Dobing and George Eastham, whose return from South Africa into the First Division had given the season a certain romantic flavour.

Unlike at Hillsborough a year earlier it was Arsenal who received the boost of scoring first. Armstrong received a clearance just outside the penalty area, took the pace off the ball, and drove it past Banks.

That might have been the end of the matter but for an injury to Wilson, which left the goalkeeper hobbling in agony. He tore a cartilage, but the decision was made to keep him on the pitch. It made reasonable sense. Wilson's courage was unquestioned. Better him on one leg than any fit outfield player.

That judgement, however, was faulty. Defenders suddenly tried to take too much care of the wounded Wilson. In the end Simpson aimed to cut out a cross he would normally have left for the goalkeeper, who moved out to try to gather it but not at sufficient speed. The end product was that Simpson nudged the ball into his own goal. With more than 15 minutes remaining it was time for a re-think. Wilson was pulled off and

Kennedy brought into the action. The call for an emergency keeper was answered by Radford, a stern enough character to cope with the task of helping his team stay in the Cup in such an unfamiliar role. He was sufficiently aware of Arsenal's tradition to begin by joking about the famous jersey which was blamed for the slip by Dan Lewis in the 1927 final. Radford coped admirably with the shots that Stoke managed; the stand-in gave every impression of hugely enjoying the experience. Stoke once again seemed unable to believe their good luck.

The replay was at Goodison Park – the perfect setting for Geoff Barnett's return to first team action after more than two years patience in reserve. Arsenal's other ex-Evertonian, Alan Ball, was invited to lead out the team on his return to the pitch he had graced so often. Ball had been a semi-final loser in Everton's colours a year earlier. Then Liverpool had come from behind. Now it was Arsenal's turn.

The first two goals were penalties: Greenhoff for Stoke, George for Arsenal, with Storey not required this time. It was fitting that Arsenal's winner fell to Radford; he had earned it with his goalkeeping stint at Villa Park. The goal was controversial, however, George breaking away from a seemingly offside position.

Leeds had already confirmed their place at Wembley with a one-sided 3–0 triumph over Birmingham City at Hillsborough. Arsenal's quest in the final had a double edge, not just to retain the FA Cup but to end Leeds' strong challenge for the Double, which could take some of the glitter from the glories of 1970–71.

The League insisted that both clubs fulfil an outstanding League fixture on the Monday before the Cup final. It was not an unreasonable request although neither manager looked kindly upon it. Arsenal would still be left with two games after the final, Leeds with one.

At Coventry on Monday, 1 May, Arsenal fielded the side which booked their Wembley places by winning 1–0, McLintock being the scorer with his first goal since August. Barnett would keep goal at Wembley, with the unfortunate Wilson needing surgery. His involvement was restricted to organising the players pool for the perks of the occasion, for which he was the unanimous choice of his team-mates. Kennedy could not force his way back into the attack and was named as substitute.

The bookmakers made Don Revie's team 4–7 to lift the Cup. Arsenal were the underdogs at 6–4. The news that Eddie Gray, who had given a virtuoso Wembley performance in the 1970 Cup final, was fit to play did nothing to shorten the odds against the Gunners.

It was the centenary year of the competition and the Queen and Prince Philip marked the occasion with their presence. Half an hour before the kick-off a parade representing the winning clubs over the 100 years increased the anticipation of spectators.

This year both clubs were able to wear their

traditional colours. Both Arsenal's post-war triumphs in the FA Cup had been won in a change strip. Neither team was new to Wembley, but sadly this did little to raise the tone of the contest.

Referee David Smith from Stonehouse had barely started the game when he was reaching for his notebook. McNab, who had made a splendid return to the senior side for the semi-final after a long absence, cut down Lorimer. From this undistinguished beginning the contest rarely improved. The kindest interpretation of the drab 90 minutes would be to point to the respect that each team clearly felt for the other. Had it been a boxing match the referee would have called for more action.

The only abiding memory is of a winning goal of high quality which mercifully spared the frustrated crowd an extra 30 minutes. It did not come from Arsenal, whose attack rarely got out of second gear, even when Kennedy replaced Radford. Eight minutes into the second half the two Leeds central strikers pieced together a move which deserved to win the match. The foraging Mick Jones tricked McNab on the Leeds right. Allan Clarke met the driven cross with a diving header, stooping to conquer. Barnett and Wilson together would have had difficulty in keeping it out.

For Clarke it was a third time lucky affair. He had been voted Man of the Match as a loser for Leicester in 1969; the following year he had been beaten playing for Leeds against Chelsea. Now he had the decisive goal and another Man of the Match trophy. Jones deserved better than to collect his winners' medal in pain after

dislocating an elbow in the dying minutes.

It was a costly injury. With the first leg of the Double in their pockets, Leeds needed only a point from their trip to Wolves two days after Wembley. But they badly needed Jones to respond to a very competitive performance from a team with nothing to play for. Leeds were beaten 2–1, lamenting that they should have had two penalties. It was a surprising result, and meant that for the second consecutive season Leeds missed the title by a point.

So Arsenal had lost the Cup and the League but happily not to the same club. The Gunners also had their say in the destiny of the Championship because, had Liverpool won at Highbury the night Leeds were losing at Molineux, Bill Shankly's men would have been Champions. The game, however, finished goalless, and to their astonishment Derby County, on a plane bound for an end-of-season holiday, heard that the League Championship was theirs. Derby finished with 58 points, one more than Leeds, Liverpool and Manchester City. Arsenal had to be content with fifth place with 52 points.

In many ways it had been a satisfactory season, though the placing in the League was not high enough to qualify for a spot in the UEFA Cup. But the standards had been set a year earlier and deep down the players who had discovered capacities for success beyond their wildest dreams knew that they had missed a great opportunity. It would not have taken too much more for the players to have really challenged for a second successive League and Cup combination.

The final chapter of the Arsenal-Stoke semi-final story was played out at Goodison on Wedenesday 19 April 1972. Arsenal won 2–1 after a seemingly offside Charlie George put John Radford through for one goal and George scored the other. The key incident was, however, at the other end when a Denis Smith (third left) header was cleared by Bob McNab. Stoke claimed the ball had crossed the line and the photographic evidence seems to support them. Geoff Barnett was in goal after Wilson's injury in the first game at Villa Park. After four semi-final matches against the Gunners and not a single victory, this was to be Stoke's last hurrah. They have yet to progress so far or have such a successful (if disappointing) spell again.

CHAPTER 9

And so to Anfield...

Liam Brady easily outpaces Wolves' Peter Daniel in 1979. In an Arsenal career which lasted from 1973 to 1980, Brady made 307 first-class appearances and scored a creditable 59 goals for a midfielder. His departure for Italy was, with Frank Stapleton's defection to Old Trafford, one of the two insurmountable blows Terry Neill had to counter at the beginning of the 1980s. He was never to find effective replacements, probably because, in reality, none was available.

At the beginning of 1973 Arsenal had reached five Cup finals in five seasons but Bertie Mee felt the sands of time running out. In what he later described as his greatest mistake, he bought Jeff Blockley from Coventry to clearly be the replacement for Frank McLintock. The mood was turning and, although Arsenal finished the League second to Liverpool, perhaps the final game of the season, a 6-1 defeat against Leeds at Elland Road, was to be the more symbolic. McLintock had been at the core of the Double team but Don Howe's departure had never adequately been dealt with and by the beginning of the 1973-74 season Howe's successor, Steve Burtenshaw, was to be replaced by Bobby Campbell. Thirteen years later Burtenshaw was to briefly become Arsenal's caretaker manager when he again followed a Howe resignation.

Gradually the Double side drifted away. Ray Kennedy went to greater and unexpected glories at Anfield, Charlie George became an unexpected failure at Derby County. Despite his central role in the Arsenal history, George had played just 169 games for the Gunners. McLintock and Kelly moved, with some success, to QPR while Alan Ball, though not part of the Double team, suffered two broken legs, failed to carry the team to similar glories, and eventually went to Southampton.

By 1976 Bertie Mee, influenced by the retirement of his friend Bill Nicholson two years earlier, decided that the time had come for him to bow out. It had been a poor season, the club's 17th place the worst since Chapman's arrival in 1925. It showed yet again how fragile success on a football field can be.

Mee's replacement was a surprise, although he followed the tradition of being an Arsenal man. Terry Neill, previously captain of Northern Ireland and manager of Hull, had managed Spurs with no great success for the past two years and became the youngest ever manager at Highbury.

What was to be Neill's most memorable step came almost instantly – the signature of Malcolm Macdonald for £333,333 from Newcastle. Whatever good it did Neill, it effectively ended Gordon Lee's time as manager at St James's, so popular was Supermac in Newcastle. He arrived saying he would get 30 goals in his first season and he ended just one short. He also gave a boost to the careers of the then youngsters Liam Brady, David O'Leary and Frank Stapleton (an Irish contingent to keep their manager company). Eventually even John Radford, driest and perhaps the sharpest of the Double team, moved on – after 379 League games and 111 goals – to West Ham. Now only Rice, Nelson and Armstrong remained. Additions came with Alan Hudson from Stoke – never to fulfil his early promise at Chelsea – Pat Jennings came from Spurs to replace Jimmy Rimmer (who went on to win a second European Cup winner's medal and Championship medal with Villa) and, most important of all, the return of the prodigal Don Howe. The scene was now set for the highlight of the 20 year gap between the Championships of 1971 and 1989 – the hat-trick of Cup finals of 1978, 1979 and 1980. The Gunners contrived to win the one they were expected to lose and to lose the two they were expected to win, but that is typical of Wembley.

The 1978 game was to be a 0-1 defeat by Ipswich, the 1979 game was to be the "five minute final" concluding in the 3-2 victory over Manchester United, and the 1980 final was to be the 0-1 defeat by Second Division West Ham. Arsenal became the first club to reach three successive Wembley FA Cup finals and only the third ever to achieve a hat-trick of finals. Perhaps surprisingly, both Everton and Manchester United have achieved it since. Oddly Arsenal failed by just two months to be the very first club to reach three successive Wembley finals – Forest having reached the League Cup final in the same three years.

The 1978 FA Cup rounds were to see an impressive progression – five successive wins (Sheffield United, Wolves, Walsall, Wrexham and Orient) with 17 goals scored, seven from Macdonald who scored in every game except the final. That being said, it was not the toughest test a finalist has faced, and the Wembley confrontation was to be an unhappy experience. Brady was not fit and had to be substituted, Macdonald was to end with a third loser's medal and never to have another chance – three days later he went into hospital for the first of many knee operations that ended his career at the age of 29. Roger Osborne scored the only goal for Ipswich to win the contest.

1979 was more fulfilling for the Gunners, and rather more interesting for everyone. The Third Round should have been easy – against a Sheffield Wednesday then in the Third Division. It took five games and 540 minutes for Arsenal to triumph. Immediately afterwards Neill acquired Brian Talbot for

£400,000 from Ipswich, after Talbot's fine display in the 1978 Cup final. Talbot was, as a result, to become only the second player to win Cup winner's medals with different clubs in successive seasons. Notts County were the next victims, then came the key game in the Cup run. Arsenal were drawn at the City Ground, where League Champions Forest had not lost in 52 matches. Stapleton scored the only goal with a fine header and, after that, Southampton and Wolves were relatively easy meat. The final brought Manchester United back to London as favourites after their defeat of new Champions Liverpool in the semi-final.

It was to be a hot, stifling day. Talbot was the star again, running his heart out, but Brady and Stapleton looked world-class. In the first 85 minutes there were two goals. The first was unique at Wembley – Sunderland and Talbot arriving simultaneously for the scoring shot, although Talbot later claimed it – and the second was a fine header from Stapleton. Then, in the last five minutes McQueen and McIlroy scored for United and extra-time seemed a certainty. But Graham Rix set off down the left, swung the ball over for Alan Sunderland and he pushed it past Gary Bailey to make it 3-2 with no time left.

The following year was memorable for the semi-final – a four game marathon against Liverpool which was finally won by a gal from Brian Talbot. It was a series which set up a string of records. It was the longest ever semi-final at 420 minutes, a record now unlikely ever to be beaten with automatic penalties after the second match, it was the only semi-final to be played at Coventry, Alan Sunderland scored the fastest ever semi-final goal after 13 seconds in the third game, and 169,163 people saw the series, excluding finals the most ever to witness a British Cup tie.

Unfortunately Arsenal had only nine days between the semi and the final, against Second Division West Ham, and they still had two League matches in those nine days. The final itself was unmemorable apart from Willie Young's terrible foul on Paul Allen with just three minutes left, and Trevor Brooking's stooping header which won the game for West Ham. It was one of only three headed goals that Brooking ever scored.

Just four days later an exhausted Arsenal had to travel to Brussels for their second ever European final – the Cup Winners Cup against Valencia, the reward for the 3-2 win against Manchester United a year before. The progress in a quiet year had been against Fenerbahce, Magdeburg, IFK Gothenburg and Juventus. The Turin semi-final, after a 1-1 draw at Highbury, is probably Arsenal's greatest performance in Europe. No British club had ever won there, and Juventus had not lost a European game there in ten years. Paul Vaessen, in his one moment of glory, scored the only goal two minutes from time and two minutes from elimination. Within two years his playing career was cut short by a serious injury.

The final in Brussels was, like Wembley against West Ham, a poor game and scoreless. It went to a penalty shoot out with the great Mario Kempas and Liam Brady missing the first two attempts. No one else missed until Graham Rix's shot was guessed right by Valencia keeper Pereira and this exhausting season ended without a trophy. Arsenal ended having played 15 games in 45 days, and 70 in all – the most ever played by a British club in a single season.

Just as the 1970-72 great period had lasted just three years, so had the four cup final team of 1978-80. The decline from here on was as dramatic as in the early 1970s. Apart from a curiously symmetrical pair of semi-finals in both cup competitions against Manchester United in 1983 (Arsenal lost all three games), the news was rarely good. Defeats in cup games by Middlesbrough and York City were bad enough, but the real moment of truth was the 1-2 home defeat by legendary Walsall in the League Cup on 29 November 1983.

Defeats by Third Division sides were not that uncommon, but Terry Neill was already under pressure and unlucky that it was Walsall of all clubs and that it was exactly 50 years since

1933. Little else was going right. Charlie Nicholas, who had cost £650,000 in the summer, had scored in just one game and had yet to score in front of his own fans. Neill was phlegmatic under pressure: "They don't seem to know what it is to hunger for goals and glory. On (some) days I think they just want to pick up their money and go home. But I'll tell you now; we'll finish in the top six again this season. Whether or not I'll be around to see it is another matter." They did finish sixth, and Neill was not around to see it.

Arsenal have (to date) had only 13 managers and hardly any have ever been sacked. But Walsall was to be the bullet that struck the heart and Don Howe, after 14 years as coach (seven under Mee, seven under Neill), finally became manager. It was not to be a happy two and a half years for Howe. Attendances fell dramatically – falling regularly to below 20,000 for the first time since Chapman's days. On 22 March 1986, after a 3-0 win against Coventry (the fourth win in a row) Don Howe resigned – hurt by constant speculation that the club were keen to bring Terry Venables back from Barcelona.

And it was to the Double team that the club were to turn for Howe's successor – not just to the Double team, but to the player who was voted Man of the Match at the moment of ultimate triumph – George Graham, 'Stroller'.

Graham's managerial experience to date had been limited. He had done a good job at troubled Millwall, not letting crowd problems deflect from a competent young team. But he was hardly a proven quantity. Nonetheless, twelve months on, the choice seemed no less than inspired. He knew Highbury, he had the confidence of the players, the board, the public (he had always had a good image as a skilful, intelligent player) and even the sponsors, JVC, who had been totally loyal to the club since the first days of real football commercialism, saw him as the right man at the right time.

On the pitch the season was nothing less than a revelation. Firstly Graham did not spend, saying he needed time to assess the staff and he wasn't going to buy anyone unless he was sure he was good enough. Indeed, it wasn't until season's end that he purchased Alan Smith from Leicester. So he relied on what he had – rehabilitating the impetuous Steve Williams, trusting the imperfect Niall Quinn and showing faith in young Tony Adams at centre-back with David O'Leary. Even Charlie Nicholas was not guaranteed a place in the team, having to fight his way in from a relatively small back-up squad after a September injury.

The side settled to a steady, if unspectacular, pattern. The rock was, in Arsenal tradition, the defence. By season's end three of the back four (Anderson, Sansom and Adams) were England regulars and O'Leary, of course, had been Eire's mainstay for years. After 27 September 1986, when they lost 1-0 at League leaders Forest, the defence locked and defeat was not

Tottenham captain Steve Perryman is no match for a determined combination of Stewart Robson and Brian Talbot (left). Talbot had the distinction of being in the winning side in succesive FA Cup finals for different teams – first for Ipswich *against* Arsenal and second *for* Arsenal.

151

Early season training for Alan Sunderland and Terry Neill in September 1979. Sunderland appears not to be taking matters too seriously, something which occasionally worried Neill. The manager said later of the player: 'He was the most sarcastic of all the players. Sundy's wit was frequently bitter. He was intelligent and sharp but his comments could hurt. In the end he was not a particularly popular player around the club.' Sunderland, after scoring 92 goals in 281 first-class appearances, left for Ipswich in 1984.

to be an issue until 24 January 1987, after another 22 games, a club record for Arsenal. In that period they won 17 and drew 5, scoring 47 and conceding just 11. It was a great effort, not least because little credibility was given to Arsenal's chances at the start of the season.

Graham was adamant from the beginning of the run: Arsenal were not good enough to win the title, he insisted, and it was not said simply to generate good press copy. When the side did lose, the disappointment was, nonetheless, intense. The match was at Old Trafford, where United had been struggling all season.

By the time of the defeat by United Arsenal were well ahead of the League and going strongly in both Cups. It had been a glorious winter, capped on 27 December 1986 by a wonderful celebration of the actual centenary, which had been two days earlier, on Christmas Day itself. An enormous crowd turned out for the game against Southampton (won 1–0) and so did a great array of stars past and present. Most notable of many notables were, perhaps, Joe Mercer, Ted Drake and, above all others, George Male, the only man present to have played under Herbert Chapman (though flying wingers Bastin and Hulme were both still alive). Male played no less than 316 first-class matches for the club and never scored a goal. Though his career was sadly cut short by the war (without it he would probably have played 600 first-class matches) his very last game was in 1948 and Arsenal ended a Championship-winning season with a stunning 8–0 victory over Grimsby. A great way to go out. And 40

years on, that Boxing Day, he was there to hear the whole crowd, North Bank and all, cheering the men who had made Arsenal what it is today even more loudly than they cheered Niall Quinn's winning goal. And they had much to cheer: how appropriate that Arsenal were top of Division I that centenary day, how appropriate that Bob Wilson should be the master of ceremonies, how appropriate that the crowd was large, well behaved and appreciative; and, some might say, how appropriate that the defence did not concede a goal against Southampton. It was almost as if a fairy god-mother had decided to shine on this great club's celebration.

And so it may have appeared three months later as the Gunners approached the series of games for which the centenary year will surely always be remembered. Having disposed of Huddersfield, Manchester City, Charlton and Forest in the League (now renamed Littlewoods) Cup, Arsenal were drawn to play, and defeated, a newly confident Spurs in the semi-final. Both clubs were also in the FA Cup quarter-finals. Heady days in North London.

Frank McLintock, captain of the Double team, watched the match with his coach that year, Don Howe: 'Like us in the 1970s, they've got players who hate to be beaten. I don't remember us losing when we were a goal up.' Spurs arguably didn't remember winning when they were a goal up against Arsenal.

McLintock went on to talk about Graham: 'He was an unusual player for Arsenal. We were a hard-driving team whereas George was

***Below right*: A year** after winning the Cup with IpswichTalbot was back at Wembley, just as determined but this time in Arsenal colours (again, oddly, yellow shirts for the third time in an FA Cup final in the 1970s). Here he (numbered 4) and Alan Sunderland collide in the scoring of Arsenal's first goal in the 1979 FA Cup final against Manchester United. Though the two appeared to strike the ball almost simultaneously, the goal was later credited to Talbot. Talbot was only the second man to appear in consecutive FA Cup winning teams for different sides. The first was Lord Arthur Kinnaird for Wanderers and Old Ftonians in 1878 and 1879, exactly one hundred years before. Malcolm Macdonald's appearance in the 1978 final (right top) had prompted one of the funniest, but probably

played seven matches in 21 days, Graham's and physio Theo Foley's view on their League chances was clearly realistic. Liverpool came to Highbury in the League. Rush scored and that was that. Was it to be a portent? Dalglish had done a job, but Graham's young lions had contributed to the evening. At least, one no longer felt as one had in the early 1980s that the problem was not the fact that Arsenal did not win anything, but that they did not seem likely to win anything. The game against Liverpool clearly showed that Graham, as he had said, did not have the resources in depth that he really needed to run Liverpool and Everton close over a full season. But, Highbury hoped, that would come. A quarter-final defeat (3–1) by Watford at Highbury ended the team's interest in the FA Cup and all that was left to think about was Wembley and Liverpool.

No matter how good they appeared in day-to-day terms, this was not the great Liverpool side of the early 1980s. They were eventually to win nothing in 1987; shades of 1985 when they

unfairest, *bon mots* of the era when a Mr Lebor wrote to *The Guardian* saying: 'In answer to the question (in your football quiz) "What is always brought to the cup final but never used?" (the ribbons in the colours of the losing team) the answer should surely be Malcolm Macdonald".' Macdonald had certainly had unfortunate experiences of finals in the previous few years – in 1974 he played in the Newcastle side which lost the FA Cup 3–0 to Liverpool, in 1976 Newcastle lost the League Cup final 2–1 to Manchester City, and in 1978 he had a frankly poor game for Arsenal. On the other hand, he had scored in every round except the final in 1978, getting seven goals in all, as Arsenal romped through without a replay and aggregating 17 goals to 4 in their five games. Hence the essential unfairness of the joke.

a bit laconic. He scored some great goals but sometimes he couldn't keep up the momentum for the whole 90 minutes. But he added that bit of class, that touch of the unexpected and we needed that at times.' McLintock also sympathised with Don Howe's position: 'I couldn't help feeling a bit sorry for him sitting there. George rightly deserves the credit, but Don encouraged a lot of this success and it's all been forgotten so quickly. He wasn't that far away. The players were all his. George hasn't bought anyone.'

Arsenal had drawn the Littlewoods final card no one wanted – Liverpool. After this point any pretensions in the League disappeared completely. Players who might find themselves suspended for the final were rested and, having

not only suffered the Heysel tragedy but (it is easily forgotten) won none of the six trophies they contested. Arsenal were not short of ability. They had their defence, which remained outstanding. Tony Adams was to become Young Player of the Year and a major asset. 'If we had that boy,' said another First Division manager, 'we'd conquer the world.' And there was always the joker, Charlie Nicholas.

Arsenal won the toss for colours and, interestingly, chose to play in their own red shirts. Twice before they had met Liverpool at Wembley. In 1950 they had played in gold shirts, in 1971 in yellow shirts and blue shorts. They had won both times but this time they reverted to the familiar. It was the first time in five finals Arsenal had gone out on the pitch wearing red and only the fifth time (1951, 1968, 1970, 1972 were the others) in 12 post-war finals that they had worn their own colours.

The game was on 5 April. The press unfailingly chose Liverpool, who had already won the trophy on four consecutive occasions in the 1980s. Liverpool had, of course, won 1–0 at Highbury a month before. It was to be Ian Rush's last appearance at Wembley before his move to Juventus, perhaps his last ever. Liverpool had even set a record with a 10–0 defeat of Fulham on their way to the final. But this was, perhaps, all a little misleading. Arsenal had lacked Anderson, Rocastle and Williams when they lost 1–0 four weeks before.

After 23 minutes Craig Johnston put Ian Rush through to open the scoring. Tediously the football world told itself, yet again, that Liverpool had never lost any of the games (almost 150) in which Ian Rush had scored. But even the oldest records have to go eventually (he scored against Norwich in the League a week later, and Liverpool lost again) and it was to be the enigmatic Charlie Nicholas who did the damage. The Gunners seemed remarkably unaffected by Rush's goal and took control for the remaining three-quarters of the match. Nicholas poked the ball home after a scramble on the stroke of half-time and it was Liverpool under pressure in the second half.

Seven minutes from the end Perry Groves, on as a substitute, roared in from the left, depositing a trail of defenders behind him, and pushed the ball to Nicholas. The golden boy shot rather weakly, but the ball took a peculiarly spinning deflection and left Grobbelaar stranded as it meandered into the net. It was really Perry Groves' goal, but Charlie got credit for them both and that was that.

The Times offered promise: 'Arsenal had no need to win the Littlewoods Cup at Wembley. Their season has already been lined with enough golden memories. To add a touch of silver as well is not only highly lucrative but it is an unexpected bonus that no one could realistically have foreseen when their centenary season began seven months ago.'

But after that unexpected bonus to conclude their first 100 years, Arsenal and George Graham were quickly brought back to a shuddering start to the second one hundred. The very first game of Graham's second season in charge was at home to Liverpool on 15 August. A crowd of 55,000 saw the Gunners lose 2–1 and suffer a goalless draw at Old Trafford four days later. These were to be the sides which finished first and second in the League and which the Gunners only occasionally looked like emulating. A week later Arsenal were 19th in the First Division.

Charlie Nicholas played just the first three games of the 1987–88 season and then fell into the reserves. He was later sold to Aberdeen in January 1988 and disappeared into relative obscurity – a classic case of unfulfilled promise.

Graham kept looking for another forward to complement Smith, but made only one serious bid – £2 million for Tony Cottee at the end of the 1987–88 season. Cottee chose to go to Everton, which was perhaps an interesting comment on the perceptions of Arsenal at that time. If Cottee had come to Highbury, his transfer would at last have superseded the nine-year-old club record of £1,250,000 for the non-playing Clive Allen. Graham, perhaps more by necessity than choice, encouraged Paul Merson at the end of the 1987–88 season, partly because the previous year's leading scorer, Martin Hayes, had slipped into a surprising obscurity. It was very odd to find Hayes (who scored 19 goals in 35 League games and another four in the Cup competitions in 1986–87) scoring just once in 27 League appearances a season later. As it happened, Hayes also scored a sub's goal against Luton at Wembley, in the Littlewoods Cup final.

Sunday 24 April 1988 was a delightfully bright, sunny day and an unexpectedly pleasing conclusion to a season that was otherwise disappointing. Back at Wembley for the Littlewoods Cup final, Arsenal were faced with a very different proposition from 1987, when they had defeated hot favourites Liverpool to take the trophy for the first time. In 1988 the positions were firmly reversed. Arsenal's opponents this time were Luton Town, who had never won a trophy in their 102-year history and who arrived at Wembley with morale, injury and selection problems.

Arsenal won all their seven games on the way

Pat Jennings clears from Manchester United's Joe Jordan in the 1979 FA Cup final. This was the game which was to become known as 'the five-minute final'. Arsenal were leading 2–0 in the 85th minute. United then scored twice, and Arsenal also got the winner, all in the next five minutes. Jennings, having been transferred by Keith Burkinshaw from Spurs when his career seemed near to an end, went on to play no less than 308 first-class games for his new club. He reached his 1,000th first-class game versus WBA on 26 February 1983 and, by the time he set off for the Mexico World Cup in mid-1986, had made a home countries record 115 international appearances as well.

Another view of Brian Talbot's goal which gave Arsenal the lead in the 1979 FA Cup final against Manchester United. Arsenal were at the mid point of the first twentieth-century hat-trick of FA Cup final appearances. The only teams to have done this before, all in the nineteenth century, were Wanderers, Old Etonians, Blackburn Rovers and West Bromwich Albion. Oddly Arsenal just missed by two months becoming the first team to achieve a hat-trick of first-class Wembley appearances. Nottingham Forest appeared in three League Cup finals in the same years (1978, 1979, 1980) and the League Cup final of 1980 was played two months before the FA Cup final.

Frank Stapleton scores Arsenal's second goal, a classic centre forward's header, against Manchester United in the 1979 final. Stapleton was to claim his own place in the record books when he scored *for* Manchester United against Brighton in the 1983 FA Cup final. He thus became the first man to score in an FA Cup final for two different teams (excluding own goals). His appearance in the 1985 final for Manchester United was his fifth, which equalled the record for Wembley FA Cup final appearances. This record is currently held by three Arsenal players (Pat Rice, Joe Hulme, Frank Stapleton) and Leeds United's Johnny Giles.

The third Arsenal goal of 1979 came in the dying seconds of the match with Alan Sunderland meeting a Rix centre at the far post and beating an astonished Gary Bailey. The sentiments of the United team, who had come back from 2–0 to 2–2 in the previous five minutes, are easy to read on Bailey's face.

to the final, scoring 15 goals and conceding only one. Their opponents had been Doncaster, Bournemouth, Stoke, Sheffield Wednesday and Everton and the highlight was clearly the first leg of the semi-final at Goodison Park. Perry Groves had scored the only goal to give the Gunners a comfortable lead, which was built on with a pleasing 3–1 win in the second leg at Highbury.

Luton had experienced a considerably more traumatic season. A few weeks before the final all had seemed to be going so well. Luton had reached the final of the Simod Cup, the semi-final of the FA Cup and were in the Mercantile Classic Centenary celebration to be played among 16 clubs at Wembley on 17 April. Luton were, therefore, looking to play an unprecedented four times at Wembley in the space of six weeks. It all went horribly wrong. They lost the FA Cup semi-final 2–1 to Wimbledon when they really should have done much better. Even worse, they somehow contrived to lose the Simod Cup final 4–1 to lowly Reading, who spent the rest of the season failing to avoid relegation from the Second Division. Luton were then knocked out in their first game in the 16-team Mercantile tournament and came back to Wembley for the Littlewoods Cup shell-shocked.

As it happened, it was the Arsenal defence which was shell-shocked after a quarter of an hour at Wembley. After Harford had very nearly put Luton ahead with a powerful header, Foster put Brian Stein neatly through to score well and make it Luton 1 Arsenal 0. Luton scored first against Reading, thought the Gunners fans, and look what happened next.

Arsenal's first half was no better than poor and Luton started the second half the way they did the first. After just two minutes a superb save by Lukic from a Brian Stein header saved the day and was one of the moments of the season.

Smith, Rocastle and Groves were conspicuous by their near absence from proceedings and, indeed, after an hour Groves was replaced by Martin Hayes. This proved an excellent substitution. Hayes gave width and pace and, with a quarter of an hour left, scored after a scramble. Five minutes later Paul Davis put the ball wide to Alan Smith, who shot just between keeper Andy Dibble and the post. It was an excellent goal and, for Smith, only his second in ten games.

Only two minutes later Smith headed against the bar and Martin Hayes contrived to hit the post with the rebound from literally a yard out. Arsenal, after stuttering for an hour, were suddenly totally in charge, surging forward through a tired Luton midfield. Smith went through twice, only to see Dibble save well. Then with eight minutes left Rocastle fell in the area, the referee harshly said he was tripped and Nigel Winterburn, who had scored only once before for Arsenal, took the penalty. The shot went to Dibble's left, but the Luton reserve keeper dived beautifully and tipped it

round the post. It was only the second penalty ever missed in a major Wembley final, Clive Walker's for Sunderland v Norwich in the 1985 League Cup final being the other (John Aldridge was to add a third against Wimbledon in the FA Cup final later in the season).

Winterburn and Arsenal were made to pay within seconds. Caesar stumbled and lost the ball in the penalty area. A chaos of bodies ensued, ending with Danny Wilson making it 2–2 with just five minutes left.

That wasn't the end, for with virtually the last move of the match Ashley Grimes came round the back of Arsenal's left side, hammered the ball with his left foot to Brian Stein and into the net it went: 3–2 to Luton.

Nonetheless, Graham was not short of talent. He had inherited Tony Adams, David Rocastle, Paul Davis and Michael Thomas. All were coming to their peak and all would attract England's attention. The full-back slots had been a problem with the decline of Kenny Sansom and the failure of Gus Caesar to replace Viv Anderson, who headed off to Old Trafford. Graham solved the problem by replacing Sansom (who went, unhappily, to Newcastle) with Nigel Winterburn (who cost £400,000) and buying Lee Dixon from Stoke for the same modest £400,000. Winterburn, still then best known for his Wembley penalty miss, had been apprehensive about replacing Sansom: 'I was worried about being compared with Kenny – after all, he's won more caps than any other England left-back. Then I realised that the comparisons would be made anyway, so I just concentrated on my own game. Highbury's a bit like Wimbledon really. When I was there we were always being criticised, but we drew strength from these attacks. The mood's the same in the Arsenal dressing-room. We scored more goals than any other team in 1988–89, yet as soon as we experiment with a sweeper we're called negative.'

Graham's other signings before the Championship season of 1988–89 were equally modest — Brian Marwood from Sheffield Wednesday for £600,000, third centre-back Steve Bould from Stoke for £390,000 and Kevin Richardson for £200,000 from Watford. It was to be a memorable year for Richardson, who became one of the few players to win a Champions' medal with two different clubs — he also has one from Everton in 1985.

Graham fitted his new players to the existing structure and covered up well where he had deficiencies. This led, towards the end of the season, to the three centre-back sweeper system after the offside trap had been battered at Highbury by both Forest and Charlton.

Like the Double side of 1971 the team depended on perspiration rather than inspiration and, in David Lacey's words, was: '... fast, fit and pragmatic. They play the long ball towards the head of Smith and depend on the breakdown of opposition movements as a springboard for counter-attack.'

The Arsenal of 1989 were not as resilient as their predecessors of 1971. They lost and drew games the Double team would have won. Radford, Kennedy, Storey, Simpson and McLintock would force results in games where the team played badly. The 1989 team were not as dependable, particularly at Highbury, where, on occasions, they looked frighteningly frail. Again, the Double team had two clear creative talents – Charlie George and George Graham – who had no real equivalents in 1989. David Rocastle came closest, winning the Barclays 'Young Eagle of the Year' Award, but there was no pretension to the pure skill of a Liam Brady or the sheer unexpected explosiveness of George at his best. To an extent, though, this was a reflection of a changing game as much as a changed Arsenal.

Middlesbrough manager Bruce Rioch said of Arsenal early in the 1988–89 season: 'They work extremely hard to take possession. If you can't stop service into the penalty area, you're in trouble. They have massive midfield strength. Once they get the ball in your half they keep it there. They pressure you on the ball so you make mistakes. It's not easy playing them, and not very pretty either.' Arsenal were no strangers to the long-ball game, and it was when employing this style that their dependence on the brilliance and consistency of Alan Smith became clear. As the season progressed, he played better and better, ending it as the First Division's top scorer and gaining an international place. His performance at Liverpool in the final game was quite outstanding. 'You could have fired a cannonball at him that day and he'd have controlled it and laid it off to one of the midfielders without a second thought,'

The FA Cup tie against Liverpool in 1980 was eventually to become the longest semi-final in FA Cup history. There were four games in all, stretching from a goalless 12 April at Hillsborough through two 1–1 draws at Villa Park and finally reaching a conclusion at Coventry on 1 May 1980, just nine days before the FA Cup final. In the third game, on 28 April 1980, Alan Sunderland scored this goal (top picture) in just 13 seconds, the fastest semi-final goal ever. The tie was finally settled in the 12th minute of the fourth game by (bottom picture) a Brian Talbot header which left defenders Neal, Clemence and McDermott helpless. The tie lasted 420 minutes in all and would have been decided on penalties had there not been a result at Coventry. Arsenal now faced two League games in the nine days leading up to the final (they won one and drew the other) as well as two more after it, plus the Cup Winners Cup final.

said one of the Liverpool defenders afterwards.

The Championship season was, in truth, a patchy one. The Gunners did not reach the top of the League until Boxing Day, and then lost the lead to Liverpool with just 13 days left. They won more games away from home than at home (12 versus 10), which was very odd indeed for a Championship side. Far more peculiar was that the sides which finished second (Liverpool), third (Forest) and fourth (Norwich) did the same, all having better away than home records. All the top four lost at least three home games during the season.

There were four highlights in the season – and three of these games were outstanding away wins (at Everton, Forest and Anfield) and only one at home (against Norwich).

To some extent Arsenal's League ambitions were helped by early exits in the Cups. Liverpool won a League (Littlewoods) Cup third round tie after two replays while West Ham caused a great surprise in winning an FA Cup third-round replay 1–0 at Highbury. Arsenal had managed only to draw 2–2 at Upton Park, despite West Ham's dreadful League form, which eventually led to relegation. Arsenal had some minor consolation in the winning of the Mercantile Credit Trophy, another rather peculiar event which was part of the League's ill-fated centenary celebrations. The final was against Manchester United at Old Trafford and Michael Thomas and Paul Davis goals led to a 2–1 victory.

The League season had begun with a 5–1 victory away at FA Cup holders Wimbledon with Alan Smith scoring a very welcome hat-trick to provide a perfect foretaste of what the season was to hold for him. It was the only hat-trick that the club recorded all season – unusual for a Championship side with a good goal-scoring record (73 in the League alone). Unfortunately this was immediately followed by a 3–2 home defeat by Villa and a 2–1 reverse at Sheffield Wednesday.

Nonetheless, other results were steady and, with mediocre starts by other contenders (Liverpool, Forest and Everton particularly), Arsenal found themselves in second place early in November without having had to perform particularly well to get there.

On 6 November they had an outstanding televised win at the City Ground, totally outplaying Forest in a 4–1 crushing which, for the first time, made the press take Arsenal's season seriously. The goal scorers were Bould, Adams, Smith and Marwood and, although Arsenal were now second behind Norwich, the almost universal view was still that it was a matter of waiting for Liverpool to come good.

The situation, however, seemed to have changed completely by the second of Arsenal's memorable four performances. This was at Goodison on 14 January and, by the time that match was over, the Gunners had overtaken Norwich and were firmly at the top of the table five points clear. This was surprising statistically as, between Forest and Everton, Arsenal played 13 first-class games of which they drew four, lost three and won only six. This was not exactly Championship form, but in an open season, it was enough to put them in front.

They were also, it must be said, playing very well when it mattered. After the 3–1 win at Goodison, Peter Ball said in *The Times*: 'In the best superstitious footballing tradition, George Graham is refusing to count the Championship until it is hatched. No one else at Goodison Park on Saturday harboured any doubts about its destination as Arsenal demolished Everton with a massively authoritative performance.' Obviously Mr Dalglish had not been at Goodison that Saturday and, indeed, Liverpool were now no fewer than 11 points behind. The gap at one time between Arsenal and Liverpool was as great as 19 points, which Liverpool clawed back between January and the ultimate denouement on 26 May. That was an astonishing achievement by Liverpool, but not unprecedented – at Christmas time 1986 Arsenal were seven points clear at the top of the League and by the end of March 1987 Liverpool were nine points ahead – a gain of 16 points in three months. So Liverpool's ability to catch up was not in doubt – it was just that this year it seemed so unlikely that they would, so vulnerable did they look (they had just lost 3–1 at Old Trafford).

But, above all else, it was Arsenal's performance at Goodison on 14 January which was particularly impressive. Kevin Richardson, who scored one of Arsenal's three goals for his first of the season, was exceptionally enthusiastic. 'It's like history repeating itself,' he said after the game. 'The pattern, team balance and tactics are all very similar to the way Everton played in 1984–85 and that is why I find it so easy to fit in.' Richardson, who won a Championship medal with that Everton team in 1984–85, continued: 'The manager has laid down the same kind of requirements on closing down opponents, denying space and putting quality balls into the box. The Arsenal players are far more experienced now, having had two seasons when they've led the League for a while, and now we have the insurance of a five-point lead. If we don't win it now, it will be the fault of the players and nobody else.'

At Goodison Arsenal brought their impressive away record to eight wins and 29 away goals, true Championship form. This was particularly good as they were troubled by injury at the centre of defence, where O'Leary and Caesar were both only second-choice options, even when available. It was David Rocastle, though, who proved Everton's downfall. The first goal was the result of a fierce cross from the right which Merson finished off with the relish of a forward enjoying his sixth goal in seven games. Just seven minutes later Rocastle went past Sheedy to the by-line, hammered over a cross and Alan Smith flung himself at the ball for goal number two. Richardson

The month of May 1980 was to see Arsenal play seven first-class games, lose two finals and set up two records unlikely ever to be beaten. The first was that they finished the season having played no less than 70 first-class games, the most ever completed by an English side in a single year. The second was even odder; Arsenal failed to win the Cup Winners Cup having reached the final and not lost a single game in the tournament. Having passed Fenerbahce, Magdeburg, Gothenburg and Juventus (via Paul Vaessen's away winner seconds from time), they were to manage only a draw with Valencia in the Heysel Stadium, in Brussels, on 14 May 1980. Penalties were used to decide the match, for the first time in European club finals, and Valencia triumphed 5–4. From the Arsenal point of view, the culprits who missed were the two most surprising of their penalty takers – Liam Brady (seen walking away afterwards, bottom left) and Graham Rix. Valencia keeper Pereira moved early to Rix's shot (shown on the right), the final one in the tournament, and the Arsenal number 11 left the field wondering what might have been (bottom right) while Pereira was mobbed by his colleagues.

scored a clever third against his old club after a neat one-two with the outstanding Smith.

One of the few advantages of Liverpool's dominance of the 1980s was that no one else was expected to win anything, which took the pressure off them. It was only after the Everton game that Arsenal became Championship favourites and it is an interesting comment on what happened in the next four months that the bookmakers gradually changed their quotes from odds–on at the end of January to no less than 7–1 against on 26 May.

As soon as Arsenal became favourites, the pressure was on. Instead of a steady, if not triumphal, progress towards their rightful prize, the campaign became one of slow attrition, with Liverpool gradually creeping up point by point, week by week, and most people thinking that Liverpool were bound, in the end, to win it as they had done so often. Between the start of the year and that dramatic evening of 26 May Liverpool, in fact, played 24 games undefeated. In a sense, that was irrelevant to Arsenal. All the Gunners had to do was keep

winning and the title would be theirs. It was not like that, as we all know. Of the 17 games between Goodison and Anfield, Arsenal lost three (two at home) and drew five. Those 19 points dropped could have been, and indeed seemed, crucial as Liverpool closed a gap that had been precisely that size.

A 0–1 stutter at Coventry on 21 February was perhaps excusable, but the crisis really struck when Forest destroyed the leaders at Highbury on 11 March. This was the game that everyone attended knowing Arsenal had to win, but Forest scored three times in the first half and made the defence look ponderous, unintelligent and porous. In particular, the speed of Franz Carr and the intelligence of Nigel Clough turned the supposedly well-rehearsed offside-trap into a shambles. This was the third time Forest had won at Highbury in two seasons and suddenly the Gunners, though still leading the League, looked anything but Champions. Ten days later lowly Charlton, perennial relegation candidates, drew 2–2 at Highbury and George Graham made a critical move with the change that probably secured the Championship.

Deciding his rearguard was too vulnerable and with three experienced centre-backs now free from injury, he decided to change the pattern. Switching from the traditional four-across-the-back that Forest had so exposed, he switched to the very rare (in England) sweeper system with a third centre-back. By having David O'Leary sweep behind Bould and Adams, Graham reduced the likelihood of fast breaks cutting through a square back four. In addition, and as important, Graham perceived that, as few opponents played more than two men up front against Arsenal, the sweeper would allow the full-backs Dixon and Winterburn to push upfield to support David Rocastle and Kevin Richardson. This, in turn, released Rocastle from defensive duties and allowed him to go forward. In attack it worked perfectly – the full-backs scored three critical goals in the games that followed and midfielders Thomas and Rocastle two each. As a system it was seen at its best against Liverpool at Anfield, when the full-backs were key elements in the intense system of constant pressure that Arsenal applied to the home club and which, in the end, won them the game and the title.

It was rare for a club leading the League to change its tactics so late in the season but, as Graham said: 'I've always been a good learner and I'm prepared to apply the things I've learned. It's up to me to come up with solutions to the problems that present themselves. The players were no problem at all. I only told them about it a week before we put it into effect (against Manchester United on 2 April), but they were very willing to try it.' Tony Adams agreed: 'In my six years with the club we've always played with four across the back, but when the boss asked us to try it, we just got on with it. Good players adapt. Our usual

4–4–2 was becoming a bit stereotyped. We were all pushing up and getting caught on the break – like we did against Forest. But we've had to go for three points each time and this way we can use three attackers instead of two and the full-backs can push forward. We still have a solid base in defence.'

The Manchester United game was not the happiest for Adams, for he conceded an unlucky late own-goal This drew a peculiar response from what we must assume was an anti-Arsenal tabloid press, the *Mirror* in particular attacked Adams in the most puerile and unimaginative way. Happily for Arsenal, the effect was that it bonded the team closer than ever and led to Adams' most productive spell of the season. Indeed, the time between the 2–2 draw with Charlton on 21 March and the game against Derby on 13 May was really the period when Arsenal won the Championship. It was their best spell of the season, with five wins and the unlucky draw against United. Coming directly after a run of five matches in which they picked up only four points, it restored belief and set up the most remarkeable of pulsating finishes.

On 8 April Arsenal were finally overtaken by Liverpool and lost first place, if only for four hours. Liverpool kicked off at Anfield in the morning that day (because the Grand National was in the afternoon) and so went to the top of the table. Arsenal took the lead back again after a hard-fought win over Everton (Lee Dixon scoring from 25 yards for the first goal and Niall Quinn getting the second in his first game of the season), but the signs were ominous. The game was hardly a classic, but chairman Peter Hill-Wood was not downhearted: 'My feeling is that whether we win the League or not, I see no reason why we shouldn't go on to have a great deal of success with this team. I've never been so hopeful about the future.'

A dull 1–0 win over Newcastle on 15 April was totally overshadowed by what happened 200 miles further north, at Hillsborough. Liverpool's sudden surge from 19 points behind, their dramatic unbeaten run since the New Year and the prospect of another Double had generated an astonishing amount of interest in the FA Cup semi-final against Forest. These were the two in form clubs – having lost just two of 44 fixtures between them in 1989. The crowds at Hillsborough were massive, including thousands without tickets. The consequences are too well known to need repeating here, but the deaths of 95 fans were to cast long, long shadows over the English game for many years.

After the disaster there was considerable confusion as to what would happen next. Liverpool naturally suspended their fixtures, including the vital game against Arsenal at Anfield. Highbury refused the League's thoughtless request to continue as normal and cancelled their next game. Arsenal did not take the football field again for another 16 days.

The highlight of the Centenary Season, 1986-87, was a three part League Cup semi-final tie against Spurs. Arsenal never went ahead in the 300 minute long tie until two minutes from the end. The key moment was this last gasp equaliser from Viv Anderson in the second of the three games, although Spurs fans were quick to point out that Clive Allen scored in all three games against the club that had paid a record fee for him and then never given him a game.

When they did, on May Day, it was for a fixture which had been expected, several months before, to determine the Championship. Norwich had led the League up to Christmas and had maintained their challenge until the past few weeks. Then their collapse had been far more comprehensive than Arsenal's and this was their last chance to struggle back into the race. The Gunners, however, chose this day for their best display of the season to date (the very best was yet to come). As Stuart Jones said in *The Times*: 'Arsenal withdrew the hand of friendship and sympathy which had been so generously extended to Liverpool. The First Division leaders, whose reaction to Hillsborough was so honourable and dignified, confirmed that now they will show no mercy to opponents or to Merseyside.'

Norwich were completely overrun. Their manager, Dave Stringer, said afterwards: 'We were outclassed and outplayed. It was a hammering. We finished as also-rans. On that performance, Arsenal will walk away with the title.' George Graham was more guarded: 'Even if we finish first, it will be inevitably recorded by some as meaningless and empty. But there is a time for mourning and a time when you have to go back to work.'

The display was electric, despite the fact that a key figure in winger Brian Marwood was injured and would be out for the remainder of the season. Dixon and Winterburn pushed up and filled the wide areas. Smith was supported

everywhere and played superbly. Norwich were as vulnerable on the wings as in the centre. Winterburn, roaring through, scored the first, Smith a spectacular volleyed second just before the interval. In the second half Thomas got the third and then Smith and Rocastle provided a gala finish. It was Arsenal's biggest win of the season and it seemed to guarantee that the League race would go all the way to the end of the season, a date at this stage still unknown because of Liverpool's fixture pile-up.

There were now just four matches left for Arsenal. The next was rather more pedestrian – away at Middlesbrough, who were fighting to stay in the First Division.

There was just one goal, the result of what appeared to be an inspired substitution by George Graham. Martin Hayes, who had not scored all season, came on in place of Paul Merson in the 67th minute, was immediately fouled by Parkinson, got up and promptly scored. Lukic hammered the ball up-field, Smith headed it on and Hayes just managed to squeeze it in. The rest of the game is perhaps best forgotten, though it certainly bears comparison with the hard, taut game against Stoke at the end of the Double season, when substitute Eddie Kelly scored an absolutely essential goal.

After Middlesbrough came the stumble. All Arsenal needed to do by then was keep their heads up through the next two matches – at home to Derby and Wimbledon – and then the

most they would need was a draw at Anfield in the last game of the season, even assuming Liverpool won all their remaining matches. But the team seemed to crack. On Saturday 13 May Derby came to Highbury and went away with a 2–1 win. As George Graham said afterwards: 'We didn't take our chances and Peter Shilton was in superb form. If anything we were too keen. We hit too many long balls when we needed to build from the back. It's easy to demand patience from the players but it's hard for them to keep showing it when there is so much at stake. We've got to bounce back. We've been written off so many times before that it would be silly to write us off just yet.' But in his programme notes Graham sounded less confident, as if he was going through the motions, saying the right things, that not even he could really believe Liverpool would be beaten now. He declared that he had derived great satisfaction from the developments of the past three seasons and that he wanted Arsenal to take over from Liverpool as the yardstick by which football was measured.

In the still small hours it was hard for anyone really to believe that they could now do it. It was statistically possible, but no longer very likely. Liverpool were back on top. There were two games left. The penultimate match was at home against Wimbledon on Wednesday 17 May. The Dons were never easy opponents, although Arsenal had destroyed them 5–1 at Plough Lane on the opening day of the season.

That was easily Wimbledon's worst defeat of the season and they came looking for revenge. They achieved it of sorts, with a 2–2 draw that seemed to spell the end of any lingering hope for the Gunners. It was a tragedy to the hordes pouring away from Highbury that night; their favourites seemed to have thrown it away by failing to win two home fixtures at the end of the season. Surely these games were the acid tests of Champions? Surely these were the games you won if you were to add your name to the panoply of greats? To take one point out of six when the Championship beckoned – it was as much as flesh and blood could bear.

Liverpool tidied up an emotional but rather stunted occasion by beating Everton 3–2 in yet another Merseyside Cup final. When Liverpool won the Double in 1986 they had also beaten Everton in the FA Cup final. Here they had done it again. One game left and all Liverpool had to do was avoid defeat by two goals. A 0–1 or 1–2 defeat wouldn't be pretty, but the Double would be theirs.

Arsenal were out of it – that was their great strength. The big bookmakers quoted them at 7–1 against, but you could have got 20–1 and better on any street corner. George Graham seemed relaxed when he was asked about the pressure a few days before: 'I hope we get this sort of pressure every year. Pressure is something the media like to talk about, but I'll tell you what real pressure is – it's being bottom of the Third Division. This is enjoyable pressure.'

Left: **Charlie Nicholas** finally repays some of that £650,000 with Arsenal's first goal in the 1986 League Cup final – a slow sidefoot past Liverpool's Grobbelaar. Nicholas scored the second as well in a 2-1 win.

Below: **But two years later** the same venue was to be far less lucky for Arsenal against Luton, with Arsenal already 2-1 ahead, the Gunners are awarded a penalty in the 1988 League Cup Final. Andy Dibble makes a superb save from Nigel Winterburn's spot kick and the game is turned on its head, with Luton coming through for a 3-2 win. It was only the second penalty missed in a Wembley final.

When asked whether Arsenal would still win the Championship he was more guarded. 'I don't know whether we will win. I know that we can win. Any team can win one game, particularly with an away record like we've got.'

In many respects Graham was right. Arsenal's two advantages were that no-one expected them to win and, that all the top four sides had played better away than at home. This was not just a statistical freak. It was a reflection of the times and worthy of a diversion.

Everyone now tried to build a side which could absorb pressure in defence and then score on the break. The counter-attacking game with two, or at most three, very good front players was the order of the day. Liverpool had been playing this way for some time – though with Rush, Aldridge, Barnes and Beardsley their front runners were not exactly understaffed. Forest was perhaps best at it – as Arsenal had found out to their cost – but Graham had developed along these lines with great success during the season to the point where, as a counter-attacking force, Arsenal were perhaps comparable with the James/Bastin/Hulme triangle of the early 1930s. Alan Smith was critical, his growing ability to act as a target man and control long balls forward, as well as score goals, being one of the cornerstones of the season. Brian Marwood was a key supplier, and it was fortunate that Arsenal survived his late injury so well. David Rocastle was the joker, the one man who could provide the trickery and the unexpected on the right, Michael Thomas and

Kevin Richardson were the workers in midfield. Paul Merson, who filled the slot that would have been Tony Cottee's, had had a satisfactory season but ultimately did not score as many goals as he would have liked. Hence Perry Groves and Martin Hayes were always on hand as subs ready to slot into Merson's role and Graham played a 13-man team for the whole season.

To put their task in perspective, consider the following. Only twice since the 1971 Double year had Arsenal won at Anfield – the last time in November 1974. On only nine occasions since Arsenal's Double nearly 20 years before had Liverpool lost at home by two goals, the last time to Everton in 1986. The portents were a very long way from being encouraging.

Did it seem likely that Arsenal could perform such an unlikely feat at such an emotional moment? The game was an historian's goldmine. It was only the third time in 101 years of the Football League that the two leading clubs had met on the last day of the season with the fate of the Championship resting on the result. On one other occasion the Championship had gone to the final match in slightly similar circumstances when the last game of the season had been the only match that day. Surprisingly, all three occasions had involved either Liverpool or Arsenal.

The first had been on 29 April 1899, when Aston Villa and Liverpool met at Villa Park, each with 43 points. Villa, with a much better goal average, needed only to draw, but beat Liverpool 5–0 anyway. The second occasion

was a real oddity. The 1946–47 season was the most delayed ever because of an appalling winter. The final match in the First Division was not played until 14 June and it was the only game that day. It was at Bramall Lane between Sheffield United and Stoke City and Stoke needed to win to take the Championship for the only time in their history. They lost 2–1, and Liverpool became Champions.

The third occasion involved Arsenal on the last day of the 1951–52 season. They travelled to Old Trafford, where Manchester United had 55 points and Arsenal 53. Arsenal's chances were only theoretical. They needed to win 7–0 (beating their best ever away win, the 7–1 Drake's game at Villa) to be Champions. Needless to say, they didn't – United won 6–1 and Arsenal finished in third position.

And so to Anfield. The scene was set for a tumultuous end to a deeply emotional season. There were no fences – they had been taken down after Hillsborough and the astonishing sea of scarves and flowers. There would soon be no more Kop, because Liverpool were to install seating throughout the ground. The police appealed to the crowd before the game: 'Many millions are watching. Please do not come onto the pitch at any time. If we can achieve that you will see the presentation.' The crowd obeyed. They did see the presentation, but not the one they expected.

It is impossible to re-create the atmosphere. Perhaps only United's first game after Munich or Liverpool's replayed semi-final against Forest, both played at Old Trafford, bear comparison. As David Miller said in *The Times*: 'The public came out of Merseyside's mean streets and bleak apartment blocks as the sun disappeared and poured into Anfield for the last game of the season: to share that beautiful illusion which exists inside the stadium, to enjoy the aura of reflected glory which lifts them out of the ordinariness of everyday life … and the illusion was broken.'

The kick-off was delayed as so many Arsenal fans had been caught in traffic jams on the way to the ground. The tension was palpable, touchable. When Arsenal came out they presented a cheque for £30,000 to the Hillsborough disaster fund. All the players carried bouquets, which were taken to the supporters around the ground. It was an exceptionally thoughtful gesture, though the kindness ended here. Here was the crunch, the moment of truth, a time which these players would almost certainly never experience again in their professional lives. Liverpool had gone 24 games undefeated. It did not seem much to suppose that they would at least draw.

But Arsenal fought; fought harder than perhaps any side representing this famous club has ever fought in its history. They battled, even kicked, Liverpool out of their majestic stride. It was pressure, pressure, pressure. Dixon forced Barnes back towards his own half. Bould prevented Aldridge from controlling the ball in the

way he had done all season. Richardson, Thomas and Rocastle fought and harried in midfield and gradually overwhelmed their illustrious opponents. Were Liverpool tired, or did Arsenal just make them seem tired? They were leaden, they couldn't push forward, they couldn't compete with the fury of Arsenal's fight. It seemed to be sheer willpower which kept driving Arsenal forward. Their supporters seemed to be sucking the ball towards the Liverpool goal. Yet, for all this, Liverpool only had to survive. They didn't have to score themselves, they simply had to stop Arsenal scoring twice. And at half time it was still goalless. There had only been one real chance. Thomas, outpacing the aggressive McMahon, whose spirit had personified Liverpool since Hillsborough, put over a beautiful cross from the right. Grobbelaar missed it but Bould rose beautifully. Somehow, Nicol got to the header and deflected it over the bar.

In retrospect 0–0 at half time was a good thing. If Arsenal had scored in the first half it would have given Liverpool time to regroup and to come back, to score an equaliser and make the Gunners' task impossible. The ideal scenario had always been two late goals, preferably late enough to stop Liverpool replying or allowing the Arsenal players to relax for a moment.

The second half was as frenetic as the first. Said Patrick Barclay in *The Independent*: 'The tackling was ferocious. Seldom can English football have been played with such intensity.' The first goal came after 52 minutes. Nicol was punished for a foul on the edge of the Liverpool area. Winterburn went over to take the free kick. The ball drifted across the goal to the far post, where Alan Smith suddenly appeared, unmarked, to deflect it off the side of his head into the corner of the net. The Liverpool players surrounded the referee, David Hutchinson. The linesman had briefly flagged. Why? Some Liverpool players claimed a foul, others that Smith had not touched the ball from that indirect free-kick. Hutchinson consulted the linesman. Ten million watching caught them in close-up, as their conversation happened in front of the touchline camera. The destination of the Championship rested on that minute. The officials finally agreed: no foul, no reason to disallow the goal. Television replays showed they were right. Liverpool panicked. Rush had gone off in the first half after a distant shot (the best of the night from the home side) had caused him a leg injury. Beardsley was on in Rush's place, but Liverpool could not string their passes together. Everything foundered on the rock of the sweeper and Arsenal's determination and commitment. Never can a football team have expended so much energy in 90 minutes.

But while Liverpool were panicked, Arsenal were sitting on a depreciating asset – time. The minutes ticked by and it became harder to create a clear chance anywhere. Only one good

Below: **On 13 May,** the season having been delayed after Hillsborough, Arsenal had three remaining fixtures. Two were at home and should have been relatively straightforward. But, on that day, Derby came to Highbury and won 1-2. Peter Shilton was in excellent form, seen here punching away from Tony Adams and David Rocastle.

one was to appear in normal time. After 74 minutes a pass from Richardson found Thomas with an instant to spare on the penalty spot. He shot quickly, but not hard enough and too predictably and Grobbelaar saved easily going slightly to his right. Grobbelaar had not appeared on the losing side in 28 appearances so far this season. As long as it stayed 1–0, he wouldn't mind losing this one.

The sands of time were running out. It was to be the nearest close miss in history. The Kop breathed a sigh of relief as Arsenal seemed to have beaten themselves out pounding on the rock of Liverpool, a rock that seemed to be saying: 'Forget tonight, history is ours. This is the season of Hillsborough and the Double. This is what was meant to be.' With the minutes ticking by, there came a lull. Kevin Richardson was injured. Liverpool had stopped pressing completely. They had hardly had an effective attack all night. It was easy to say afterwards that they were unlucky knowing that even a one-goal defeat was enough. If they had to win, maybe they would have played differently. Perhaps. But when the referee correctly added two minutes on for Richardson's injury, Liverpool had just five minutes left to hold out.

The game completed its allotted 90 minutes.

The Kop whistled frantically for the finish, not just to the match, but to a season and to its place in the history books. The seconds ticked by as Arsenal pressed forward again. Surely one last time. A clearance from Lukic was controlled by Dixon, who pushed a long ball through to the magnificent Alan Smith, 30 yards from goal. Michael Thomas ran into the inside-right slot inside Smith. The centre-forward lobbed the ball on, straight into Thomas's path. The clock said 91 minutes and 26 seconds, 86 seconds overtime. Would there even be time for Thomas to finish the move? Steve Nicol came across to tackle. The ball bounced off the defender, onto Thomas and forward. Thomas was clear. He surged into the penalty area. Nicol and Houghton flung themselves at him in desperation. Grobbelaar, everything at stake, came out and spread himself. Thomas waited, then flicked the ball over Grobbelaar's body into the right-hand corner of the net. 2–0. There was a stunned silence and then, from the Arsenal fans, euphoria. The Double was gone; the Championship surely snatched from the jaws of certain Arsenal failure. Thomas, scorer now of the most famous goal in Arsenal history, ran at the Gunners' fans and took off in a somersault. It was a gesture of astonishment rather than excitement. For the millions watching it was beyond belief. 'Re-run the video, it can't have happened. We've strayed into a film script. Seasons just *don't* end like this.' It was many minutes before anyone believed it really had happened.

There were a few seconds left. Long enough for hero Thomas to intercept a Liverpool attack in his own penalty area and put the ball calmly back to Lukic. The whistle went. The most dramatic domestic season in living memory, probably ever, was at an end. Arsenal were Champions. For the first time the League Championship trophy was presented as if it were the FA Cup. And how ironic that Arsenal received it at Anfield. The Kop applauded them; the dream for Liverpool was over.

The memories were inevitably of another late goal, of another Double. But that goal, from a yellow-and-blue shirted Charlie George against a similarly red-shirted Liverpool had won a Double, whereas Michael Thomas's had prevented one. George lay down, a never to be forgotten gesture, Thomas took off in his somersault, another never to be forgotten moment.

George Graham was understandably euphoric: 'We have laid a foundation of belief at Highbury. If you lose hope, or lose belief, you may as well get out of football. Tonight was the fairy-tale, the unpredictable that makes us all love football. There is no doubt that we had a mountain to climb. A lot of people thought we would get carried away and try to play gung-ho football but in fact we were very controlled and content to be 0–0 at half time.' Graham gave the credit to his players, particularly Tony Adams: 'He has suffered a lot of stick which has been very undignified and done little for football. But he has proved his strength and character, and we all did that tonight. At the end of the day it is the players who go on and do it on the pitch, and we're delighted for them. It was nice to see Michael Thomas get the winner. In the first half of the season he was the most effective midfield player in the country. He has had a lapse, but exceptional players don't go bad overnight and he has soldiered on, staying in the side because of Paul Davis's injury. He's had his reward.'

The commentators found analysis almost impossible in the shadow of such unexpected and unlikely events. Rob Hughes probably got closer than anyone else: 'Arsenal looked like nervous wrecks in surrendering home points to Derby and Wimbledon. They were lions at Anfield. The reason, I believe, is that they are better chasing a cause than protecting one. If the roles had been reversed, and if Arsenal had been three points ahead with the final game at Highbury, what then would have been the result?' What indeed, but it is difficult enough to explain what happened without speculating on what might have been. What did happen is that Arsenal won the League Championship in circumstances which no fiction writer would have dared to create. It truly was the most remarkable end to a League season ever.

But as Arsenal had seen before, winning the Championship and retaining it were different propositions. In 108 years it had happened on just 19 occasions, two of them by Arsenal in 1934 and 1935. In the season 1989-90 a final position of fourth was no disgrace, but it was 17 points behind Liverpool and there was no joy in the Cups.

Graham went out to buy, in particular paying a record for a goalkeeper to acquire David Seaman from QPR. John Lukic, a stalwart in the Championship team, went back to Leeds. Like Jimmy Rimmer a decade before, he was to be rejected by Arsenal only to win a Championship medal quickly with his new club. Anders Limpar provided variety on the wings, and Andy Linighan came from Norwich to compete in an already crowded defence.

The next season, 1990-91, was to be something of a fairy tale, with Limpar buzzing like a bluebottle, Seaman keeping 29 clean sheets in 50 matches and the season starting with 17 games undefeated. It came to an end in an astonishing game at Highbury when Manchester United won a League Cup tie 6-2. Young Lee Sharpe scored a hat-trick in what will probably be the game of his career. Seaman had only conceded six goals in the season's previous 17 games.

Four days later Champions Liverpool were convincingly despatched 2-0 by Merson and Dixon but the Gunners had other worries. An undistinguished fight on the pitch at Old Trafford six weeks before – involving almost all 22 players – had generated an FA Commission, with Arsenal particularly concerned because they had been fined £20,000 for a similar scrap

with unlikely Norwich City the previous season.

On November 13, a five-man FA commission deliberated for three-and-a-half hours on the Old Trafford skirmish and deducted two League points from Arsenal – precisely the punishment the directors' swift censure of their players and manager had sought to avoid. In addition, United were docked one point and both clubs were fined £50,000. To the Gunners, this was a drop in the ocean compared to the potential loss of revenue if they were pipped to the title by one or two points. Of the previous 30 Championships, as many as nine had been won by such a margin. Vice-chairman David Dein estimated the commercial benefits of that glorious night at Anfield as at least £2 million to the club in sponsorship, advertising revenue and prize money.

The two-point deduction left Liverpool eight points clear at the top. The Arsenal players privately conceded that the commission's verdict was tantamount to handing the Championship to Kenny Dalglish with less than a third of the season gone. But, on the pitch, they showed no signs of a side who believed they were chasing a lost cause. Four days after the FA hearing, Southampton were trounced 4–0 at Highbury and three impressive wins over the Christmas holiday period brought the Gunners back to Liverpool's shoulder. This, in itself, was triumph over adversity after another bodyblow to Graham in the week before Christmas. Tony Adams, convicted at Southend Crown Court of reckless and drunk driving, was sentenced to four months' imprisonment.

The timing of the England defender's incarceration could scarcely have been less propitious. A first-team fixture since 1986, he had just regained his international place after losing out to Des Walker and Mark Wright for Italia '90. And, for Graham, who regarded Adams as the bedrock of his back line, there was no disguising the disappointment of his captain's extended leave. 'He is my eyes and ears in the dressing-room and my sergeant-major on the pitch,' said the manager.

Arsenal stood four-square behind their captain who, one suspects, was something of a victim of the judiciary's modern approach: making an example of a celebrity. Managing director Ken Friar pledged: 'The player has made a mistake and has been punished for it. As far as the club are concerned, he will continue to be an Arsenal player and will receive our full support.' It is to Adams' credit that he maintained a remarkable level of physical fitness; and his unequivocal refusal to sell his story of 'life on the inside' to national newspapers who were ready to wield six-figure cheques in his direction – allowed him to resume his career with dignity.

Adams was restored to his beloved No. 6 shirt in the FA Cup fifth round at Shrewsbury Town's Gay Meadow, where cigar-smoking John Bond's underdogs had already seen off 1988 winners Wimbledon in the previous

17 May 1989 was the final home game of the season. A win would still make Arsenal favourites to take the title, but opponents Wimbledon managed to hold them for a 2-2 draw and the chance appeared to have gone forever. Paul Merson scored one of Arsenal's goals, here volleying past Scales, and Nigel Winterburn the other. All that now remained was for Arsenal to go to Anfield on the last day of the season, Friday 26 May, and to win by at least two clear goals. Even a one goal win would not be enough as the title, and the Double, would then go to Liverpool.

round. In total, Tony Adams missed 13 games.

Four of them comprised the fourth round FA Cup marathon with Leeds, in which Highbury witnessed two goalless draws and Elland Road most of the excitement. Limpar, with a brilliant solo goal, earned the second replay and Seaman's spectacular diversion of Gary McAllister's shot, destined for the top corner, took the sides back up the M1 for a third encore. Finally, and to the relief of both sides (who must have been sick of the sight of each other), Dixon and Paul Merson settled the issue. By this time, however, Arsenal had sacrificed the unbeaten League run of which they were justifiably proud.

The FA Cup arm-wrestle with Leeds was clearly draining the Gunners of sharpness and stamina when, on 2 February 1991, their record perished after 23 games at Stamford Bridge. Chelsea were already 2–0 up and worthy winners by the time Smith snatched a late consolation. Dixon said: 'That defeat hurt. A couple of years earlier, Liverpool had threatened to go unbeaten in the League all season until they came unstuck in the local derby with Everton. I suppose it was inevitable that we would lose our record in a local derby as well. With so many London clubs in the First Division, and all those Cup replays with Leeds, the players sometimes felt as if they were playing in a Cup final every other week. Even so, we were disappointed with the result at Chelsea. We were beginning to believe that we really could go right through the season unbeaten in the League, even though we knew that was being unrealistic.'

It had been 103 years since a First Division team had concluded a season undefeated,

Preston having not lost any of the 22 games they played in the first ever Football League.

That setback at Stamford Bridge was to be Arsenal's last of an astonishing First Division season. They had coped so well defensively in Adams' absence that it was almost a surprise when he was recalled at Shrewsbury; less startling was the hero's reception he was afforded by the travelling fans from London, and Michael Thomas made the skipper's return a happy one with the decisive goal.

The following week, the Gunners returned to Anfield for what was becoming the annual title decider. Nothing would be cut and dried with 13 games remaining, whatever the result of this proverbial six-pointer, but Merson gave Arsenal a huge psychological advantage with the winner in a thrilling match happily spared the attrition of normal top-of-the-table dogfights. Suddenly the talk around Highbury – though certainly not in George Graham's office – was of another Double.

The FA Cup quarter-final with Third Division Cambridge, before a season's best crowd of 42,960 at Highbury, took them a step nearer the dream. It also capped Adams' rehabilitation after his prison ordeal. Kevin Campbell put the Gunners in front with a typical opportunist effort before Cambridge, whose direct, primitive style had been described by one columnist as that of 'Wimbledon without the frills', hit back through Dion Dublin. The visitors had been galvanised into a stirring Cup run by manager John Beck's innovative methods of motivation, not least of which was pouring buckets of ice-cold water over his players before kick-off. Now, briefly, they threatened Arsenal's passage to the semi-finals before Adams, rising like a jump-jet at the far post, shattered the ambitions of Beck's would-be giant-killers.

Before the small matter of a North London semi-final with Tottenham at Wembley, the Gunners cemented their Championship challenge by taking 15 points from a possible 21, conceding just two goals in the process. Among those seven games was yet another meeting with Leeds; Campbell's double strike preserved the Gunners' unbeaten record against them and condemned Howard Wilkinson to his sixth match without a win in his exhausting personal test series with Graham.

All eyes then focused on Wembley. Twelve months previously 95 supporters had died in the disaster at Hillsborough during the Liverpool–Forest semi-final. Up to this point, the FA had never allowed a tie, other than the final, to be played at Wembley, for fear of devaluing the ultimate moment. But, apart from Wembley, no football stadium in the land, and certainly no neutral venue in the south, could have coped with ticket demands on a day critical to both Arsenal and Spurs.

'Common sense prevailed,' said Graham. 'After Hillsborough, staging the tie at Wembley was the only acceptable solution. I don't think it devalues the glamour or pomp of the Cup final just because we're playing the semi-final there as well.' Moreover, Wembley's lush turf was a welcome change from some of the bare, heavily-sanded surfaces to which semi-finalists had been exposed in previous seasons.

For both clubs, the match was not only an historic departure from tradition but a watershed. For Arsenal, the equation was simple: lose, and another Double was gone. But for Tottenham, whose financial plight had recently come to prominence – they were reported to be more than £10 million in the red – defeat threatened their very existence. Gascoigne's express recovery from a hernia operation gave them hope of eclipsing their North London rivals, installed by bookmakers as red-hot favourites … and although his contribution to the game lasted barely an hour, it was ultimately critical. The dramatic denouement was set to be played out with Alan Sugar and Terry Venables buying the club and it was already clear that Spurs really were in desperate straits. While we cannot play 'what might have been', it did seem that an FA Cup win and the revenue it would provide might just be the difference between survival and disappearance.

Less than five minutes of the semi-final had elapsed when Gascoigne's amazing 30-yard free-kick was too venomous for David Seaman's fingertips to alter its path towards the top left-hand corner. And when, 15 minutes later, Gary Lineker's predatory instincts finished a move inspired by Gascoigne's impudent back-heel, Arsenal's visions of another Double must have seemed like a cruel mirage to a desert explorer. Alan Smith briefly brought the dream back into view with a far-post header, but Lineker restored Spurs' two-goal

In the electric atmosphere of the Championship decider at Anfield, the inevitable Alan Smith helps Arsenal's cause by giving them the lead with a neat deflection from the side of his head after Adams had missed the cross. There was an extraordinary hushed delay before the goal was allowed because a nervous linesman had momentarily raised his flag.

cushion midway through the second half. Afterwards, there were tears in the Arsenal dressing-room. With just five League games left, the title was still there for the taking; but the FA Cup, which had beckoned Arsenal through seven ties, was suddenly gone. It was no consolation, but Gascoigne's goal has remained one of the most startling images of a football generation. Rarely has its like been seen at such a crucial moment.

'There was nothing to choose between the sides after the first 20 minutes. That's where the match was won and lost,' reflected Graham. 'In fact, we probably shaded it from that point onwards – but the damage had been done by then. You can't give a highly motivated team a two-goal start in Cup semi-finals because they're going to fight tooth and nail to protect it. It was a bitterly disappointing experience for my players, but the true test of their character is whether they can bounce back from these things.'

Spurs went on to win an even more remarkable final – 2–1 against Forest – during which Gascoigne committed two awful fouls, injuring himself so badly that he was out of the game for a season, and Lineker missed a penalty.

Arsenal had little time to lick their wounds. Three days later, Manchester City came to Highbury and exposed the frailty of their hosts' confidence. Paul Merson and Campbell hit the target, but a 2–2 draw was by no means the tonic Graham had in mind. Liverpool, despite showing their own symptoms of fallibility, were clinging to the Gunners' shirt-tails. On the same weekend as Arsenal's Wembley heartbreak, the Mersey men – now under the management of Graeme Souness following Dalglish's shock decision to take an extended holiday on the golf course – waltzed to a 4–0

Arguably the most memorable League goal ever scored. *Above:* Michael Thomas has just clipped the ball in the final minute of the final match of the season at Anfield, and the ball is on its way past Grobbelaar into the Liverpool net. It was the goal that made Arsenal, rather than Liverpool, the Champions.

Right: **A split second later** and Michael Thomas knows that he has scored the most dramatic goal in the whole history of the Football League – a climax to a season that can only happen once in 100 years.

half-time lead at Leeds. That they required a fifth goal after the break to sneak home 5–4 substantiated the views of those who claimed Dalglish had baled out of a club in decline. The Liverpool of old would surely have put up the shutters and sauntered past the post instead of requiring a desperate dive at the tape.

Graham, with three of the campaign's last four games at home, knew there was no margin for error. Three points separated the sides. Arsenal had held the initiative since late February, the weekend Dalglish quit Anfield, when they thrashed Crystal Palace 4–0 at Highbury and Liverpool's internal disarray was laid bare by an unexpected 3–0 defeat at lowly Luton. Now the Gunners couldn't lose the title – they could only throw it away. Graham felt his task was to ensure that any tension he sensed went undetected among his squad.

Graham told pressmen that his antidote to the despair which forced Dalglish to quit was gardening. 'A bunch of pansies never won the League,' said the *Today* newspaper, 'so green-fingered George grows one in his back garden to escape the managerial pressure trap. Often portrayed as a man obsessed with matching Liverpool's thirst for honours, Graham is using flower power to switch off away from the glare of publicity which claimed Dalglish.'

Nigel Winterburn, ever-present during the season and curiously overlooked by England, recalls: 'We could easily have gone unbeaten in the League all the way to February for nothing. Nobody would have remembered us for coming second in the table and going out in the FA Cup semi-finals. Or, at least, they wouldn't have remembered us for the right reasons. If we'd blown the last few games, we'd never have lived it down. People would simply have thought we'd bottled it at Wembley and bottled it on the League run-in, and we deserved better than that for our contribution to the season.'

On April 23, with four games to go, Arsenal's lead could still have been wiped out at a stroke as Queen's Park Rangers came to Highbury. Liverpool had, on paper at least, a comfortable home game against Crystal Palace the same evening. More than 42,000 fans came armed with smelling salts and transistor radios to Highbury for 90 minutes of ritual nail-biting. This, said Graham, was the final countdown. True to Don Howe's word, QPR were obstinate opponents and the match was hardly a classic. But as news filtered through of Liverpool's 3–0 canter against Palace, the Gunners dug deep. Merson scored for the second successive match and Dixon converted his fourth spot-kick of the season to keep the heat on Souness. Three games to go, no change in the cushion: three points.

It is not always easy to pinpoint the moment when Championships are won and lost, but Liverpool will always mourn the events of the May Day Bank Holiday weekend in 1991. Scotland team-mate Archie Gemmill once said of Souness: 'If he was a chocolate drop, he'd

David O'Leary acknowledges the crowd's tributes during his testimonial match in May 1993. He now holds Arsenal's all-time appearance record and ended his career on a remarkable high – playing in the winning team at Wembley in the FA Cup final replay victory of 1993, as Arsenal beat Sheffield Wednesday 2–1.

eat himself' – a reference to his self-possession – but these 48 hours must have aged the Liverpool manager more than any others. The demands of live television, becoming increasingly intrusive on the fixture calendar, twice fragmented the First Division programme, on each occasion leaving Arsenal to kick-off knowing the result of their closest rivals. On the Saturday, the Gunners were required to commence battle with Sunderland at Roker Park at the curious hour of 5.30pm – 45 minutes after the final whistle at Stamford Bridge, where Chelsea were entertaining Liverpool.

As the only team to get the better of Arsenal in 38 League games, it was perhaps appropriate that Chelsea should repay the debt by supplying their London neighbours with a giant helping hand towards the winning post. Liverpool's 4–2 demise at the Bridge left the Gunners safe in the knowledge that their leadership would be immune to any Roker revival on Wearside. As it transpired, Sunderland had neither the guile nor the firepower to breach Arsenal's dogged rearguard; Graham was far happier with a dour 0–0 draw than opposite number Denis Smith, for whom the result spelled almost certain relegation.

Monday 6 May was, in many ways, an average Bank Holiday. Twenty-mile traffic jams along coast roads caused by day trippers who wouldn't normally venture into their back gardens in such unspecial weather; the obligatory air traffic control dispute over mainland Europe; and in the pop world, Cher was No. 1 with the Shoop Shoop Song. Arsenal's home game with Manchester United, the only team

Right: **The brawl at Old Trafford** on 20 October 1990 which set the scene for the record breaking 1990-91 season. An FA Commission deducted two points from Arsenal and one from Manchester United. With Liverpool already six points clear, this appeared to have handed the League to the Merseysiders. A similar scuffle at Highbury on 4 November 1989, against a team not noted as one of the League's hard outfits, Norwich City, had earlier led to a £20,000 fine.

to have beaten them on home soil in 13 months, did not kick off until 8pm, yet the players congregated at the ground from lunchtime to watch Liverpool's game with Nottingham Forest.

With Arsenal now four points to the good and only 180 minutes of the season left, the algebra was elementary: if Liverpool lost, the title returned to Highbury; a draw gave them only the tiniest mathematical hope of keeping it in the Anfield boardroom. It was the ultimate irony in their season of disruption that Liverpool's flickering hopes were finally snuffed out by a 23-year-old unknown who used to cheer them on from the Kop. Ian Woan's 64th-minute winner at the City Ground made wonderful viewing for Graham's players after Nigel Clough and Jan Molby had exchanged penalties.

The result made Arsenal's fortunes against United academic. For ITV executives, who could not have foreseen Liverpool emerging pointless from their two holiday games, it was an anti-climax. But for the Highbury faithful, it turned a night of potentially unbearable nerve-jangling into a knees-up. No sooner had the Championship been clinched than the order was issued to open up the turnstiles and let 42,229 guests join the party.

Graham, returned to the boardroom from a TV interview in one of the Clock End boxes commandeered by a camera crew, found himself the recipient of a bear-hug and kiss from an East Stand season-ticket holder as he marched up the touchline, his face betraying barely a flicker of emotion. One by one the players emerged for the pre-match kick-in to thunderous acclaim. David Seaman, Lee Dixon and Michael Thomas entered the party spirit by donning a variety of headgear never previously

sanctioned on match-days by Graham. North Bank fans, who filled the terrace to bursting point with more than an hour to kick-off, persuaded the players to abandon the normal practice of plying the 'keeper with shots and crosses; even Seaman happily bludgeoned 25-yarders into the arms of supporters going through their repertoire of victorious refrains.

Dixon conducted the singing, Anders Limpar his own personal side-show – which might have been entitled 'Twenty Things You Never Knew You Could Do With A Football'. But such was the professionalism Graham had instilled in his side that, despite all the pre-match euphoria, there was a manifest determination not to let the party fall flat. As the sun sank reluctantly behind the North Bank, Arsenal set about United as if their medals depended on it. Champions or not, they were in no mood to show their illustrious visitors – soon to defeat mighty Barcelona and lift the European Cup Winners Cup – any clemency.

Alan Smith put the Gunners in front after 19 minutes with an accomplished finish to Dixon's right-wing cross and three minutes before the break he confirmed their swaggering superiority. Kevin Campbell's pass exposed United's back line and Smith applied another uncomplicated execution to the move from 18 yards. His night was complete when referee Bob Nixon penalised Steve Bruce for handball and regular penalty-taker Dixon stepped aside for Smith to complete his hat-trick from the spot. Perhaps the only blot on Arsenal's copybook – an eminently forgettable one – was the last-minute consolation Bruce claimed for United, which robbed Seaman of his 30th clean sheet of an outstanding term.

Graham, serenaded by the sarcastic and now ritual chants of 'Boring, Boring Arsenal' from his players in the dressing-room, modestly stayed in the tunnel while Tony Adams hoisted the trophy and led the team on a lap of honour. 'I didn't think it was important for me to join in...the players are the ones who have done it. I can enjoy all the reflective glory because of their efforts, but they deserve all the credit and limelight. The fans pay their money every week to watch them play football, not to watch me sit in the dugout. I felt it was appropriate for me to stay in the background this time.' He had, after all, done it all before.

Arsenal were finally in the European Cup. In 1989 they had not entered because of the post Heysel ban on English clubs. The competition's new format, with seeded teams kept apart in the first two rounds then thrown together in two round-robin groups of four, was thought to favour Arsenal's propensity for durability and compactness. And their chances did not seem unduly diminished by an indifferent start in the League – just three wins from their opening eight games. Graham, ostensibly satisfied with his squad depth, had surprisingly declined to increase it during the close season – a repeat of his apparent inertia after the Championship triumph of 1989.

There seemed little to concern Graham about his team's quality in a European context in the first round match with Austria Vienna, though. Drawn at home in the first leg, the Gunners secured an abyss between the sides, and 24,424 fans saluted their 6–1 rout. Liverpool trounced Finland's Kuusysi by the same score on the night and, like Arsenal, had their own hero. Colin Gibson of the *Daily Telegraph* wrote: 'Alan Smith emulated Liverpool's Dean Saunders with the four goals that must establish Arsenal as one of the most feared sides in this season's European Cup. Smith's goals, his first in Europe, but bringing his total to 20 in the last 20 games, demolished the Austrian challenge. His contribution in 14 remarkable second-half minutes was merely the cutting edge to a performance of the highest calibre by Arsenal, returning to their best form. Although Austrian football is at a low ebb, Vienna were not the worst side to have graced the competition by a long chalk. That was the frightening aspect for Arsenal's rivals.'

The Gunners could even afford the luxury of Dixon's penalty miss as Andy Linighan and Limpar completed the scoring. Vienna's 1–0 victory in the return was hollow, indeed, and by then Graham had left his domestic rivals behind with the crucial record £2.5 million outlay on Crystal Palace striker Ian Wright. Although he was ineligible for the early stages of the European Cup, Wright – capped by England seven months earlier – gave Graham an embarrassment of riches in attack.

Wright wasted little time in making an impact, scoring in the 1–1 League Cup draw at Leicester and then, spectacularly, a hat-trick in his first League game for the Gunners, at Southampton. But he had to sit out the next

continental expedition, which took Arsenal to Benfica's famous Stadium of Light in Lisbon.

In front of 84,000 devoted Portuguese, Arsenal acquitted themselves admirably – especially Paul Davis, whose attentive marking job on Brazilian midfield player Isaias clamped the biggest single threat to the Gunners' hopes of progress. The inclusion of Isaias had raised more than a few eyebrows in the Arsenal camp in the first place, particularly when he lined up beside two Soviet internationals and two Swedish imports, an apparent contravention of UEFA's ceiling of four foreigners per team. Dissection of UEFA's smallprint revealed that Isaias qualified for Portuguese citizenship through marriage, but Arsenal had every right to express their concern: only England's cricket team offers more qualification loopholes, though playing for the Republic of Ireland can be as obscure.

In the event, the sting was in the tail. Thanks to a disciplined rearguard action and Kevin Campbell's polished equaliser, the teams came to Highbury at 1–1, with the match well balanced. However, Isaias, so well shadowed in the Stadium of Light, found a new sphere of influence in the second leg. Arsenal's barnstorming start yielded an early goal from Colin Pates, making only his tenth appearance in 18 months, a disallowed 'goal' from Merson and Campbell's shot against an upright. But the early optimism among expectant home supporters was to be snuffed out ruthlessly by Isaias. The Brazilian possessed that elusive ability to change the course of a match. Now, he graduated to the ability to turn the course of an entire season – Arsenal's season, that is – with one stunning swing of his boot. The 30-yard volley with which he restored parity in the tie brought all Arsenal's worst fears to the surface: they now had to chase the winner knowing that, if Benfica caught them cold at the back, the European Cup would be wrenched irrevocably from their reach. In extra time, that is exactly what happened.

The Soviet, Kulkov, and then – inevitably – Isaias left the Gunners to count the cost of failing to reach the mini-league section of the competition. Conservative estimates put the loss of revenue at £1.5 million. Worse still, another potentially lucrative avenue had been sealed off to Graham between the two games with Benfica. Following the 1–0 League Cup defeat at Coventry, he had said the result 'may yet prove a blessing in disguise' because the club's fixture commitments were already 'frightening'. But elimination from two cup competitions in the space of eight days, sandwiched by a home defeat against struggling West Ham, suddenly limited the scope of Arsenal's ambitions.

Wright's form continued to be irresistible – he scored all four goals in the 4–2 home win against Everton, for example – but Arsenal's, collectively, was erratic. Graham, sensing that his team was off the pace in the First Division, made the FA Cup 'a major priority'. A disastrous Christmas, in which the point gleaned from a 1–1 draw with Wimbledon was their only return from three games, increased the Gunners' sense of urgency in the Cup. The third round draw handed them a trip to Fourth Division Wrexham. It was one of those heads-you-win, tails-I-lose ties that top players hate.

Deprived of the suspended Wright, Graham looked to Smith – just two goals between September 21 and the New Year – for increased productivity, and after 43 minutes of embarrassing superiority the penny finally dropped. Merson burrowed his way to the by-line and presented Smith with the kind of opportunity for which all strikers in a lean spell pray. Arsenal preserved their lead without undue alarm until the 82nd minute, when Mickey Thomas, a nomad with 37 years on the clock and 11 previous employers, equalised with a thunderous free-kick. Thomas had barely emerged from the scrummage of delirium when Steve Watkin hooked Gordon Davies' right-wing cross past Seaman for a barely plausible winner. The media predictably feasted on the biggest Cup upset since non-League Sutton's eclipse of Coventry in 1989.

Rob Hughes wrote in the *Sunday Times* 'Oh, what lovely pandemonium, what delightful illogicality the Cup still provides! Who will believe that Arsenal, prime movers of the Premier League (and hustling) through to kill 108 years of League tradition, should fall in a theatre principally of their own making. Arsenal should have won the game by half-time ... but this was hardly the mastery of Super Leaguers.'

Graham admitted bluntly the calamitous defeat in North Wales was 'the lowest point of my career'. Arsenal had become accustomed to adversity under his management and they were hardened against prejudice. Kicked when they were down, damned with faint praise when they won, Graham found himself yearning for the minor irritants of jealous epithets such as

'Boring Arsenal'. Widely regarded as one of the country's brightest and most perceptive managers, he suddenly assumed a jaundiced outlook. Out of the running for the cups, his team were also stranded in no-man's land in the Championship they had won so vibrantly seven months earlier. It seemed a re-run of 1990.

But the next season was to bring a more dramatic change – the end of the old First Division and the start of the Premier League. The Premier League's conception owed much to a handful of visionaries, including Gunners' vice-chairman David Dein, one of the first modern administrators to realise that aggressive marketing increased clubs' income and, in turn, provided a springboard for extra investment on facilities and players. History will judge the commercial orientation of Arsenal overseen by Dein, and the new, all-seater North Bank will perhaps come to be remembered as his personal monument to the club. A less visible driving force at the time was the Taylor Report, which obliged the top 40 clubs to incur the cost of all-seater stadia by 1994.

When the bulldozers moved in to replace the North Bank with a 12,500-seater edifice, brickbats flew over the methods chosen by Arsenal to finance the ground's biggest development in more than half a century. Bond schemes to pay for new facilities were pioneered successfully in the United States, and Glasgow Rangers' Ibrox Stadium was transformed without a murmur of dissent by way of a similar venture. In the face of a fierce recession, borrowing or flotation – the alternatives to a bond scheme – could have been monstrous burdens on Arsenal's finances. The board were very aware of two successive Spurs' boards being deposed as a result of the cost of new stands at White Hart Lane.

The reaction to the rebuilding programme at Highbury was perhaps a reflection of English football's parlous state in the summer of 1992. Graham Taylor's national side belly-flopped alarmingly in the European Championship finals in Sweden and the Premier League kicked off in funereal mood. One of the European Championship's stars, Danish midfielder John Jensen, impressed Graham so much he spent £1 million to bring him to Highbury, while Rocastle's love affair with Arsenal resulted in an amicable divorce. He joined new Champions Leeds United for £2 million, but failed to impress at Elland Road and became another of the 1989 Championship stars who seemed to have faded since the glorious night at Anfield.

Jensen, a bustling, no-nonsense player, had scored Denmark's first goal against Germany in their unexpected European Championship triumph after the Danes were called in as last-minute replacements for Yugoslavia, excluded as part of a United Nations sanctions package. His arrival reaffirmed Graham's determination to atone for the previous campaign's disappointments. In the 1992–93 Championship, however, they simply never got going.

Below: **2 February 1991, Dennis Wise celebrates** one of the unlikeliest goals and unexpected results of the season: Chelsea's 2–1 victory over Arsenal. It was Arsenal's only League defeat of the 38-game season. Arsenal's was the best record of the twentieth century. The only occasions that a team had done better in Football League history were in 1888–89, when Preston did not lose any of their 22 games, and in 1893–94, when Liverpool were undefeated in 29 Second Division games (including a play-off). No other team has ever finished a League season with just one defeat.

Arsenal's performances at Highbury were generally as incomplete as their North Bank. In an effort to camouflage the jungle of cranes and scaffolding, the club spent large sums of money commissioning and erecting an enormous mural, 75 yards wide and 18 yards high, to hang from corner to corner behind the North Bank goal. Thousands of painted faces peered out across Highbury in a commendable initiative to retain some of the atmosphere within the stadium (not to mention its qualities as a safety net which prevented wayward shots sailing into the building site). It was fun and an unusually creative motif at a football ground.

The mural received much good-humoured criticism and became a vehicle for political point-scoring when it came to light that none of its faces was black, an oversight quickly rectified. With ground capacity temporarily reduced to 29,000, home games were virtually sold out every week. To be frank, few provided great entertainment in the Premier League; one exception was the seven-goal thriller against Southampton. But this was to be a season in which Arsenal discovered a 'home from home', a venue at which they remained unbeaten in four games ... Wembley.

Prospects of the Gunners winning the League Cup (now sponsored by Coca-Cola as the latest of many, the names of whom are sensibly ignored by most writers and fans) looked anything but rosy when they trailed 1–0 to Millwall at Highbury in the second round, first leg; Kevin Campbell's late introduction spared Arsenal's blushes, and he worked the oracle again at The Den a fortnight later before the Gunners scraped through on penalties with the tie deadlocked at 2–2. With Millwall moving at

season's end, Arsenal were never to play again at their original 'local derby' location.

Arsenal needed two bites at the cherry to see off Derby in the next round (Campbell again scoring in both games) and two trips to the seaside before disposing of little Scarborough. The first was a wasted journey because of wintry weather, and conditions were far from ideal when Nigel Winterburn's winner earned the Gunners a quarter-final tie with Nottingham Forest. Six days and two Wright goals later, Arsenal were in the semi-finals.

By now, every other game in Arsenal's tiring schedule was a cup-tie, and Graham was almost prepared to forgive his team for an 11-week barren spell without a League win. Wright scored from the spot against his old club and the resurgent Smith netted twice at Selhurst Park in the first leg as Crystal Palace's bid to throw the Gunners off their inexorable collision course with Wembley was sunk almost before it had begun. The return at Highbury smacked of going through the motions as Wright, inevitably, and the increasingly assured Andy Linighan cemented the first half of Arsenal's unique cup double bid and completed a 5–1 aggregate rout of Palace.

Their opponents in the League Cup final were to become frequent imposters on Graham's path to glory this season. Sheffield Wednesday, conquerors of big-spending Blackburn Rovers, arrived at Wembley with a reputation for flowing – if defensively flawed – football, and the teams treated their fans to an enthralling afternoon. Without the injured Smith, the suspended Dixon and the cup-tied Martin Keown – repatriated from Everton for £2 million, ten times the figure Arsenal

Paul Merson teases a bedraggled Standard Liège in the second leg, second round Cup Winners Cup tie in Belgium on 3 November 1993. After winning the first leg 3–0, Arsenal achieved one of their biggest ever away wins with a 7–0 crushing of the Belgian side. Merson scored in both legs.

received when he was sold to Aston Villa in 1986 – the Gunners were forced to shuffle their pack. Paul Davis was recalled, to unanimous amazement, after just one comeback match in the reserves following hamstring trouble. And Northern Ireland defender Stephen Morrow, so often restricted to little more than walk-on parts in previous Arsenal productions, was pressed into service beside Davis in midfield, where he was to command centre stage.

England manager Taylor, under fire from all quarters for his refusal to restore Wednesday's former Tottenham winger Chris Waddle to the international boards, will have drawn some minor, though valueless, comfort from Waddle's familiar retreat towards anonymity after a promising start. He looked worthy of all Fleet Street's platitudes about his enduring skill as the Owls snatched an early lead through American John Harkes (the first American to score in a soccer game at Wembley). But Waddle was to be upstaged by Paul Merson, not least because of the 20th-minute equaliser which sparked an Arsenal revival.

Rob Hughes said in *The Times*: 'Like Wednesday's goal, Merson's goal came from a free-kick and finished, like Wednesday's, with a right-foot finish of class. When the ball was headed down to Merson just outside the penalty area, he hit across it to induce a kind of swerve that is sometimes mistakenly regarded in this country as the preserve of Brazilians. The ball obeyed his instruction and beat the diving Woods inside his left-hand post.'

Merson wasn't finished by any means, though. After 68 minutes, with Arsenal's vigour now firmly in the ascendancy, he fashioned the winner. Thrusting deep into Wednesday territory, his low cross from the left flank caught Carlton Palmer off balance and Morrow had the simple but joyous task of thrashing it past Woods – his first senior goal for the club. For Merson, it was the perfect climax to an emotional week in which he had become a father for the second time; but for Morrow, there was to be a painful sting in the tail. On the final whistle, Tony Adams hoisted his match-winner shoulder-high by way of playful celebration, only for Morrow to come crashing to earth and break his arm, ruling him out of action for the last month of the season. Adams was so upset that assistant manager Stewart Houston had to persuade him to climb Wembley's famous steps to accept the trophy.

Poor Morrow required oxygen and was carted out of Wembley by ambulancemen instead of on the shoulders of adoring supporters. He was unable to collect his winner's medal, and Graham said: 'It was silly, really, a freak accident. But you can't tell players not to celebrate when they've just won a major cup competition. It did, however, remove just a little of the gloss from our victory for me – you couldn't help feeling desperately sorry for the boy.' For the press the story was obvious: 'How did you break your arm?' 'I fell off a donkey ...', the donkey being the tabloids' less than friendly nickname for Tony Adams.

For Arsenal, the job was only half-done. They had another opportunity to test their cup-tie expertise against Wednesday in the FA Cup final. Never has the perverse nature of cup football been so ably demonstrated as in Arsenal's fortunes in successive seasons. After Wrexham, you wouldn't have backed them to knock out a pigeon with a tranquilliser gun; now they were the name everybody wanted to avoid when the numbered balls came out of the bag.

Not that the 1993 FA Cup started out that way. When the Gunners were required to tackle non-League Yeovil on their own patch at The Huish, the Press descended on the West Country ready to bury Graham again. But Ian Wright's hat-trick, and the League Cup win at Scarborough four days later, forced them to dispense with the obituaries and instead hail Arsenal's professionalism on two thankless missions. 'Sorry you've had two wasted journeys,' Graham taunted the media corps.

Trailing 2–0 to Leeds at Highbury in the fourth round, Arsenal demonstrated their newfound belief by bouncing back to force a replay through Ray Parlour's persistence and a 25-yard Merson special. In the Elland Road encore, the Gunners again had to force the issue when they found themselves 2–1 down with eight minutes left. Smith's first goal for three months was already a symptom of Arsenal's resurgent morale before Wright, returning from suspension to spectacular effect, struck twice to sink Leeds in extra time. The significance of that comeback was not lost on Graham. Smith's previous goal, against Coventry on November 7, had helped shoot the Gunners to the Premier League's summit for the first – and last – time that season.

Now Arsenal were through to the quarter-finals. Already in the Coca-Cola Cup final, they were 180 minutes from another medal for the mantelpiece. Ipswich, whose defensive blanket had smothered the life out of Arsenal's Boxing Day party, were more enterprising hosts at Portman Road. Much of the build-up had focused on the gash sustained by Tony Adams in a fall during a night out with friends, which forced him out of two games. More wisecracks at the captain's expense inevitably followed. Brian Woolnough sniggered in *The Sun*: 'Adams needed more stitches in his forehead than Arsenal have League points.' Typically, however, Adams had the last laugh. His return served only to inspire those around him and Ipswich were stitched up 4–2. Adams contributed to the scoring spree, which was an overdue statement of the Gunners' attacking resources. The previous 14 League games had yielded only four goals.

The semi-final draw was, in itself, a mandate for civil strife in Sheffield and North London: Wednesday v United and Arsenal v Tottenham. Mouth-watering prospects, but powder kegs to boot. Falling at the final hurdle

STAND. SIGN FOR THE ARSENAL. THE ARSENAL BOND. 0345-198991   **LOOKING TO**

During the rebuilding of the North Bank, Arsenal broke new ground with the now famous Highbury mural. It was intended to represent a crowd and ensure that balls were returned to the keeper quickly. After the new stand was completed, Arsenal offered the whole mural for sale at a knockdown five-figure sum. The game shown is against Sheffield Wednesday on 29 August 1992, Merson and Parlour scoring in a 2–1 victory.

before the Cup final is still the most soul-destroying experience in football. Add local pride to the equation and the stakes become even greater. Adams greeted the pairing with Spurs in a cautious, circumspect manner. 'It's one for the fans to get excited about and it obviously gives us a chance to gain revenge for our semi-final defeat in 1991,' he said. 'But semis aren't about revenge or settling old scores – they're all about getting through to the final, and we mustn't lose sight of that.'

Adams' apprehension was entirely justified. Arsenal's League match at White Hart Lane four months earlier had been pock-marked by a series of niggles and unpleasantness. Spurs' 1–0 win was a travesty and their coach, Doug Livermore, was evidently carried away by euphoria when he declared it 'a great day for football'. In truth, it was nothing of the sort. Referee Alf Buksh seemed to lose his grip as early as the second minute, when Dean Austin's palpably illegal tackle on Ray Parlour warranted a penalty.

Buksh's failure to intervene became a licence for misbehaviour. Graham complained to him in the tunnel at half-time that the game was almost out of control – which later earned him a £500 rebuke from the FA. Wright was not among the five names Buksh scribbled in his notebook, but TV cameras caught him aiming a rabbit-punch at Tottenham's David Howells and he was later suspended for three matches.

Spurs defender Justin Edinburgh admitted later that he had 'wound up' Adams by using 'the D-word' (a reference to the terrace insult aimed at Arsenal's captain by opposition fans and now so familiar that it has almost become a compliment) and warned of no truce in the Cup semi-final. For the Gunners, the ominous promise of more trench warfare was not necessarily as worrying as it was for Spurs. In the end

the game was a great anti-climax, not remotely comparable with Gazza's game two years earlier. The only goal was a far post Tony Adams header from a Paul Merson free-kick.

By the time the big day arrived, fatigue was clearly going to be a major factor. Arsenal were playing their 48th competitive match of the campaign and their 12th in six weeks. Graham preferred Jensen to Selley in midfield, while Morrow – looking perky on his return to the venue which treated him to glory and black comedy within minutes of each other – collected his League Cup winner's medal before kick-off. He was the only man to enjoy the privilege on a desperately disappointing day.

In the *Sunday Times*, Brough Scott mourned: 'Exhaustion won. Long before the end this great clawing hand had gripped the legs and minds of everyone on the pitch. Two teams had played themselves to a standstill. We went into the 15th round and beyond. The two old prize-fighters had met each other so many times that they knew each other's every move. A catastrophic mistake or knockout blow was needed.'

If the rise and fall of Morrow whetted the appetite, the sequel was barely palatable viewing. Chris Waddle threatened briefly to ruffle Arsenal's feathers but, after one rasping free-kick was diverted by Seaman, he became more and more anonymous.

Wright, playing with a broken toe, struggled for 90 minutes before Graham granted him sanctuary on the bench. But he did at least make the most of his only clear-cut opportunity. After 21 minutes, Paul Davis flighted a right-wing free-kick on to Linighan's head and the big centre-half nodded it across the six-yard box. Wright, lurking with Paul Warhurst on the far post, outjumped his marker to head firmly beyond Chris Woods. Arsenal were one

176

up, and the familiar chorus of 'Ian Wright-Wright-Wright' rang round Wembley. As the lovely Emily Bell of *The Observer*, perhaps something of a fan, said: 'Wright is the yeast in the bread, the coke in the cola, the buck in the fizz, the Pardoner in Chaucer's Tales. Without him, there is a void, an impenetrable black hole of uncertain future … ' Wednesday's renowned artistry never surfaced, but they summoned enough strength to conjure David Hirst's 68th-minute equaliser. That only hastened the onset of stalemate and neutrals agreed unanimously that parity was the only fair result.

Forty-eight hours later, Arsenal put out a full-strength side at Highbury against Manchester United in a testimonial for David O'Leary, granted a free transfer after 20 years' service. O'Leary thought the Cup final would be his last competitive appearance for the Gunners and was hoping all three major domestic trophies would be on display at his benefit game – Arsenal parading the two cups and United the Premier League trophy they had won with such panache. It turned out to be the sandwich filling between the Cup final and its replay, although 24,000 fans paid their respects to him.

O'Leary admitted: 'To be honest, I didn't want my time at Arsenal to end. But I was thrilled to be able to complete 20 full years of service with them. I would have hated to be shown the door after 19. The 20-year landmark kept me going. When I realised it was all over, that I had worn the red shirt for the last time, there was a tear or two in my eye. But I wouldn't have missed it for the world. And one day, if the club ever decide they want me back, I'd love to return to Highbury as a coach or manager. That would be the ideal happy ending to the fairy-tale.' And if you're going to go out, an FA Cup final is the ideal setting.

Thursday came round and Arsenal found Wednesday waiting for them again. The FA Cup final replay attracted only 62,367 spectators, the lowest crowd ever for the fixture at Wembley and the lowest FA Cup final attendance for 71 years. But at least they saw a climax as dramatic as Anfield '89. This was in contrast with the early portents, it must be said. With the kick-off delayed by 30 minutes and Wednesday fans jamming the BBC switchboard with pleas for more time to reach Wembley after a crash caused tail-backs on the M1, the game started in heavy rain. Maybe, as Rob Hughes put it: 'The heavens were weeping at the prospect of the renewal of Saturday's dire game.' The consensus was that this had become the least interesting final in living memory.

But if the quality of the original tie left much to be desired, it was preferable to the brutality which scarred the opening stages of its successor. Adams (on Hirst) and Jensen (on Waddle) were given the benefit of the doubt by referee Keren Barratt for challenges which looked worse than the damage they inflicted. But Mark Bright's aerial confrontation with Linighan after 19 minutes was clearly unacceptable even to the most lenient officials. Bright appeared to use his right elbow maliciously as he jumped and the yellow card scarcely seemed sufficient punishment for an offence which left Linighan with a broken nose, although he carried on playing.

Once football was restored to the top of the agenda, Wright deservedly put the Gunners ahead after 33 minutes. It was his 30th goal of a fragmented season, his 56th in 79 Arsenal appearances and his fourth FA Cup final goal in four Cup final appearances. Two of the goals came as a late substitute for Crystal Palace in 1990. It put him close to the list of final scorers – only Ian Rush, with five goals, has scored more. Smith, restored to the starting line-up, provided a judicious through ball and Wright, galloping clear, belied his excitable nature to chip Woods from 12 yards . Waddle, booed for some apparent play-acting when he hit the ground as if pole-axed by Winterburn, claimed Wednesday's equaliser after 66 minutes with a deflected volley. Now, at last, tired legs were no longer able to compress space so readily and the chances came thick and fast at either end. Mark Bright spurned the best of the lot, shaving the outside of an upright from ten yards, but perhaps this

Ian Wright is robbed by Gary Mabbutt during Arsenal's 1–0 win at White Hart Lane on 16 August 1993. Wright scored the goal, which is not surprising given that he claimed 21 of the 40 goals Arsenal scored in all competitions from the start of the season to the year end. The previous season, Wright had scored no fewer than 30 of the Gunners' 73 first-class goals, indicating the club's dependence upon his mercurial talent.

was divine retribution for his earlier offence.

The excitement even stirred Mr Barratt, who chose to show yellow cards to Davis and – for the first time in his career – Smith for fouls innocuous compared to those which he allowed to disfigure the first half. Merson, struggling to live up to the high standard of his League Cup heroics, suffered from the same profligacy which afflicted Bright, and the tie was doomed to more extra-time torture when Woods recovered a Merson shot which had squirted under his body inches from the line.

Punch-drunk and dreading the prospect of a penalty shoot-out, the teams traded shots and tackles until, right on time, Arsenal won a left-wing corner. Merson dragged his weary legs across the sodden turf as Mr Barratt checked his watch. Would there be time to take it? Adams and Linighan ventured forward for one last fling. On the bench, Graham was apoplectic. What if Wednesday hoiked the ball clear and raced upfield to score? Who would take the penalties? Had they practised them enough?

O'Leary, who had again been brought on for Wright, must have let his mind wander, back to Genoa with the Republic of Ireland and to the 1980 Cup Winners Cup nightmare against Valencia, when Rix and Brady had missed. Please, God. Not penalties.

Merson's corner swung in invitingly. Woods stayed rooted to his line and Wednesday's defence followed his lead fatally. Linighan, who had spent years as a million-pound spare part in the reserves, who had heard his name greeted with groans when it was announced on the Highbury tannoy, sensed Wednesday's collective inertia. He rose like a phoenix above Bright, whose elbows this time remained firmly by his sides, and connected with a thumping header. Its power carried it through the grasp of Woods, arching back on his line, and Nigel Worthington's attempt to hack it clear only confirmed initial impressions: it had crossed the line, Worthington's clearance hit the roof of the net and raised the roof at Arsenal's end of the stadium.

Linighan was engulfed by a tide of red-and-white delirium. Just 18 months earlier, he had asked for a transfer because he could not gain regular first-team football. Now he will be remembered as the man who scored the latest FA Cup goal of all time. The Cup has traditionally bestowed greatness on lesser lights – who, for example, remembers Roger Osborne for anything but the Ipswich goal at Wembley in 1978 or Mike Trebilcock for anything but his two goals for Everton in 1966?

The significance of Linighan's goal was not lost on Graham, the first man to win all three major domestic trophies as both a player and manager. He said: 'Andy's goal is strange because, like Stephen Morrow, he's scored the winner in a cup final and has finished with broken bones. But I'm delighted that our heroes on both occasions have been players who would not normally command such attention.

They are not really the people you think of in these situations. I never thought of taking him off just because he had a broken nose. I tried to get one throughout my career because it adds some character to your face!'

History will judge Arsenal's record-breakers. It will also be kinder to the Gunners than the Press, who curtailed the fanfares for Graham by harking back to his shortcomings in the League. There is no persecution complex at Highbury. But if any other club in the land had lifted two cups in one season, they would likely have been fêted as heroes and celebrities.

Graham's men were, one must admit, largely ignored for their unique double. To the uncommitted, they are not Cup football experts or knockout kings. Just Arsenal. Boring Arsenal. Lucky Arsenal. But two League titles and two cups in four years can't all be down to luck. Think of Arsenal and you think of greatness. The club's very strength is in its name. But it had been an odd season. The denouement had gone on too long. Arsenal and Wednesday had come to Wembley too often. To think that there were 18,000 empty seats at a Cup final with two such prominent teams playing is a remarkable comment on the season's end. Despite Manchester United finally winning the League, the new Premier title had seemed to create uncertainty. More attention was paid to Clough and Forest's decline than to Villa's or Norwich's challenge for the title. As for Arsenal, it is hard to escape the conclusion that they owed it all to Wright. In the League the Gunners scored just 40 goals in 42 games, while in the two Cup competitions they managed 33 in 17 games. To score only 40 League goals and still end the season with two major trophies is an unlikely achievement. Of the season's 73 goals in all, no fewer than 30 were scored by Wright. No other player even reached double figures in all competitions, Campbell scoring just nine in all and Smith a depressing six, despite appearing in much of the Cup campaign and in no fewer than 31 League matches.

With Manchester United running away with the League, 1993-94 was to be about the Cup Winners Cup. After Odense and Standard Liege came Torino in the quarter finals. The first leg against Arsenal was no consolation for the Italians. Arsenal were well on top, played a tight formation, and went back to Highbury with a 0–0 draw. It was not a great night for the fans and it hardly set the pulse racing, but this was Arsenal's last real chance of a trophy in 1994 and caution was the only credible watchword. A 1–0 win, with another goal scored by Tony Adams, was an appropriate reward for a very tight and conservative approach.

Interestingly, George Graham chose to play Campbell rather than Wright. Campbell had been the butt of intense jeering from Arsenal fans after a 3-1 defeat at Highbury by Bolton. Certainly Campbell missed a number of chances, but the current Arsenal game remained directed towards Ian Wright, and Campbell had to fill the roll of foil throughout his career. As Chris Lightbown pointed out in the *Sunday Times*, Arsenal were a team that tended to run deep from defence or knock the ball over the top for Wright to run on to. They have never been a pure, instinctive passing team in the style of Liverpool or Spurs and the Highbury crowd has had a tendency to impatience with a side which doesn't show the tenacity and grit to grind out results. The passing game was probably an essential for success in Europe – here sweepers are much more capable of plucking off the long through balls that Wright thrives on. Only Merson and Limpar of the contemporary players really exhibited the skills that can turn a game despite its tactical pattern and Limpar continued to be in and out of the team with Merson continuing to look uneasy on the left. Indeed, by the end

of March, George Graham had sold Limpar to struggling Everton and, despite a good 1–0 defeat of Liverpool, it was clear that only the Cup Winners Cup counted.

On Thursday 29 March the team travelled to Paris for the semi-finals to play the French League leaders, Paris St Germain, who were unbeaten in 35 first-class matches. For perhaps the first time realistic memories of that shoot-out with Valencia 14 years before entered the head. Graham surprised everyone by picking Ian Wright and the striker had another outstanding game, leading the line and tirelessly running off the ball to create room for Merson and Smith. Wright had just come off an excellent away hat-trick at Ipswich and was playing as well as he ever had. In the 35th minute Graham's decision paid off, with Wright beating his marker to a Paul Davis free-kick and heading just inside the far post.

Right: Steve Morrow celebrates his goal in the Coca-Cola Cup final on 18 April 1993. He and Merson secured a 2–1 win and a psychological advantage over the team they were to meet in the FA Cup final: Sheffield Wednesday. It was the first time that the same clubs had contested the two domestic Cup finals, and the first time the same club had won both. *Below Left:* After falling off Tony Adams' back, Morrow suffers a broken arm at the end of the game. He eventually received his winner's medal before the FA Cup final.

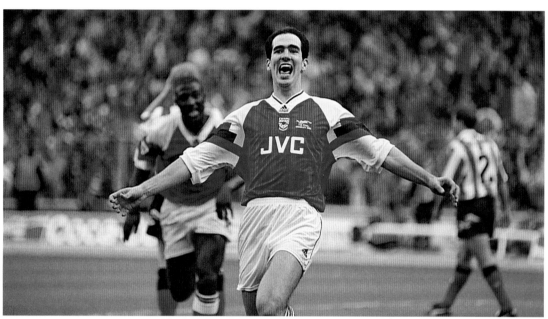

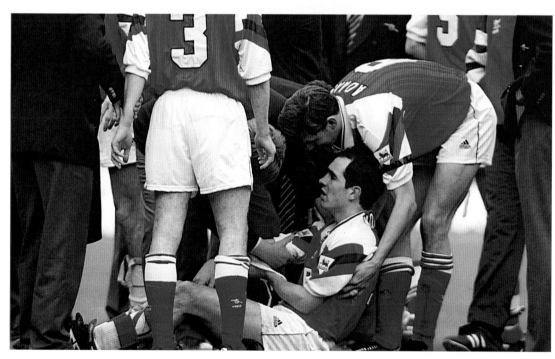

After 50 minutes St Germain equalised from a corner, but Arsenal's organisation was outstanding. At 1–1, with a precious away goal, everything was set up for the game in London.

This task proved not particularly difficult by Arsenal's high standards. One goal, early on in the game from the previously abused Campbell, proved more than adequate and Arsenal held their ground in reasonable comfort. Paris St Germain were impressed. Said their manager: 'The quality of Arsenal's play surprised us. We knew they would be strong in defence but did not expect quite so much creativity upfront or in midfield.' But there were negatives, in particular a second yellow card for the irreplaceable Ian Wright. George Graham was pleased to have concluded an inconsistent season with a cup final, the first in Europe for so long. In an interview with Joe Lovejoy he praised Manchester United: 'Everyone's getting out of their prams right now about United, and rightly so, but it took them 25 years to get it right. They've got more gifted individuals than us, but they've not got a Chippy Brady or Glenn Hoddle... The difference between them and us is that their midfield players are better than ours. I still think that Cantona will let you down at the very highest level... If Limpar (before he was sold) or Merson would work harder, that would improve our midfield. I'm not saying it would make it right, but it would help. What I really need is a young Peter Reid to be the boss there.'

Graham agrees that, if Manchester United wish to be personified by Cantona, then Tony Adams is the heart of Arsenal. 'We have always been strong defensively,' says Graham, 'and what's wrong with that? What I won't have is all this talk about us being a long-ball team. Sometimes we do bypass the midfield, but not all the time. Without Alan Smith (who was

having an excellent end to the season) we don't hit it as long. We play better football... I don't know anyone who wants to be successful without playing attractive football, and I'm no different from anyone else in that respect.'

On the all too familiar subject of boring Arsenal, Graham is direct. 'We won two Championships playing super football. We played great football with a team that had great individuals. We went to Liverpool and won it in the best Championship finale there has ever been. Then we won a second title and lost one game in the whole season. That's the first time anyone's done that in a hundred years. But I agree there was some pretty ropy stuff last season (1992–93) and in the early part of this (1993–94). We were terrible in the League last year, but we still won two cups. I know we're not right at the moment because I know what it takes to win Championships. We've got a defence as good as any in the country, but we definitely need more quality in midfield, although we've got good forwards.'

Like managers from time immemorial, Graham believes Arsenal are criticised unfairly, and he's right in seeing the prevailing attitude towards Arsenal nowadays as a cultural stereotype – almost impossible to eradicate. People who've never seen a football match in their lives seem to know that Arsenal are supposed to be boring. 'Generally, we're criticised unfairly. Who else from the south has won a Championship recently? We'll have a go. We'll go up north and take them on. Who else will?'

A fair point, and Arsenal also proved to be the only English club for three years to have progressed to the final stages of a European competition. As they flew to Copenhagen for the 1994 Cup Winners Cup final against Parma on 4 May their worries revolved around a squad hit by injury and suspension – Wright,

Captain Tony Adams scores the only goal of the FA Cup semi-final against Spurs at Wembley on 4 April 1993, gaining revenge for the defeat at the same stage two years earlier.

May 1993 and yet another trip to Wembley, Arsenal's third of the season. This time it was the FA Cup final, in which Ian Wright played with a broken toe but maintained his remarkable goalscoring record for the season, striking with his only clear-cut opportunity. After 21 minutes Wright outjumped Paul Warhurst to give Arsenal the lead after Andy Linighan headed on a Paul Davis free-kick. The match was a repeat of the Coca-Cola Cup final, and after David Hirst equalised in the 68th minute the teams had to face each other for a third time at Wembley, in a replay.

Jensen, Hillier and Keown would all be missing. Parma were the reigning Cup Winners Cup holders, having beaten Royal Antwerp 3–1 in the final a year before. Parma were not a grand club, but they had a rich benefactor and the Swede Brolin's outstanding skills playing just behind the front two, Asprilla and Zola.

The absentees meant George Graham had to change the 4–3–3 formation he had introduced after the Cup defeat by Bolton. The traditional 4–4–2 had begun to go stale with too much being expected of Ian Wright, and the switch to Wright, Smith and Campbell upfront allowed Wright more freedom on the flanks to rove around. It was a system that depended on Alan Smith's ability to hold the ball and it was to be Alan Smith who shocked Parma in the 21st minute of the final with a stunning left-foot volley from 20 yards. Dixon took a throw 40 yards out and Minotti, one of Italy's best sweepers, attempted an unnecessary overhead clearance. The ball fell to Alan Smith, who chested it down and struck it on the volley to perfection. The shot flew off the post into the net with keeper Bucci just beaten and Arsenal were 1–0 up in front of a crowded Copenhagen stadium. Just six minutes before, an excellent shot from Brolin had hit Seaman's right-hand post and bounced back from the inside along the line. Parma were at this stage much the better team, with the relatively inexperienced Selley and Morrow (who seemed to save his appearance for Cup finals) holding the midfield line for Arsenal.

But that, in a sense, was that. Parma had 80 per cent of the game, Brolin was outstanding, but they could not score. Adams and, in particular, Bould were excellent and both were called up to the England squad a week later. They defended superbly while Alan Smith held the ball up front and frustrated Parma. George Graham said later: 'Once we went a goal in front I knew we had a chance because our strength is keeping clean sheets. We had a team of heroes tonight and none more so than Alan Smith, who worked tirelessly up front.' In the end Brolin's shot against the post was the closest Parma came and Arsenal had won their first European title in 24 years. Steve Bould won the Man of the Match plaudits and, given their injury problems, it had been a remarkable evening for the Gunners.

Graham was rightly effusive in his praise of Parma after the match: 'They were fitter than us, they were sharper than us. Their forwards, particularly Brolin, were outstanding and it was a marvellous defensive performance by Arsenal. We're a club with marvellous team spirit and everyone – including the guys who couldn't play – was completely involved. You have to remember that around ten of the Parma squad will be in the World Cup in a month's time and, at the end of a long, hard season, they were a very tough proposition for us.'

Parma had passed the ball around well and played the game prettily. But Arsenal, as Joe Lovejoy said, had marked and chased assiduously and kept their cleverer opponents at bay. Few teams do it better than Arsenal when it comes to defending a lead, said Lovejoy, and

they slipped comfortably into the familiar 'what we have, we hold' mode. Nevio Scala, the Parma manager, also praised Arsenal: 'Tactically and technically we did not function. This was because Arsenal were a better team.'

The season that followed was to be all about Europe, but it was not to be until the arrival of Sampdoria in the semi-final that Arsenal faced the real test of their strength in the renewed European campaign of 1994–95. The manager of the team from Genoa was Sven Göran Eriksson, one of Europe's most successful chiefs of the past two decades. He had already won the Swedish title with Gothenburg, three Portuguese titles with Benfica and taken Roma to a European final. Sampdoria were no slouches, having been Italian Champions as recently as 1991. The last time Eriksson had been at Highbury, his Benfica team had thoroughly embarrassed Arsenal in the European Cup of 1992.

Perhaps the most surprising pre-match statistic was that Arsenal had now played 24 consecutive European Cup Winners Cup matches undefeated – easily a record for the competition. The run covered a 'Who's Who' of European names – Fenerbahce, Magdeburg, IFK Gothenburg, Juventus, Valencia, Odense, Standard Liège, Torino, Paris St Germain, Parma, Omonia, Brondby and Auxerre. Of the 24 games, 13 had been won and 11 drawn. It hardly needs to be added that Arsenal didn't actually win the Cup Winners' Cup of 1980.

Sampdoria were without David Platt and Ruud Gullit at Highbury but most certainly did not come to defend. With a magnificent recent record, they were one of Europe's experienced teams. No fewer than seven of the starting eleven were over 30. The first half was full of excitement. After 28 minutes Bould flicked on a corner and Tony Adams got a touch to put it into the corner of the net. The goal was disallowed because the referee believed that Wright had jumped into goalkeeper Walter Zenga. It was a sign of things to come.

After 35 minutes an excellent swerving shot from Lee Dixon was brilliantly tipped away by Zenga. From the resulting corner David Hillier shot from the edge of the area, Zenga saved well but the ball fell to Steve Bould, who carefully steered the ball home with the delicacy of an Ian Wright. It was Bould's first goal of the season. It took him just two minutes to double his total. Yet another corner from Stefan Schwarz was met by Bould at the near post. The ball looped backwards, Adams and Wright jumped at the near post but the only touch was a slight one by Walter Zenga and the ball was in the net. Steve Bould had scored again.

Fifteen minutes into the second half Sampdoria pulled one back through the Yugoslav Jugovic. But with 20 minutes left, Paul Merson drove a beautiful ball from the centre circle for Ian Wright to run onto. There were two defenders around him and Zenga came out fractionally too early, giving Wright the opportunity to flick the ball into the right-hand corner of the net. At 3–1 it all seemed set for Arsenal to reach their second consecutive final, but just eight minutes later Jugovic was

Above: **Andy Linighan scores** one of the most celebrated of all Arsenal goals – the winner in the 2–1 defeat of Sheffield Wednesday in the 1993 FA Cup final replay. The goal, from a Merson corner, came in the 120th minute and is the latest ever to have won the final. Another few seconds and Wembley would have seen the first FA Cup final to be decided by penalties. It was Arsenal's fourth trip to Wembley in 1993, and this fact was reflected by the 18,000 empty seats and the lowest ever attendance at a Wembley FA Cup final.

again left free in the penalty area and the score was a very different 3–2. Not only that, but Sampdoria were clearly much the more creative side in the second half.

It was Arsenal's 25th game undefeated in the Cup Winners Cup, but Sampdoria ended it the happier team.

Back on the domestic front, Arsenal were in the unfamiliar throes of a relegation struggle. With four teams to go down at the end of the 1994–95 season, there was an undignified scramble at the bottom of the Premier League. At Easter, only five points separated nine clubs in danger for the final two places (with Ipswich and Leicester already relegated). Arsenal were one of those nine, but two excellent wins (4–1 against Ipswich and 4–0 at Villa Park) made the flight to Genoa more comfortable than it would otherwise have been.

Arsenal were facing a much stronger Sampdoria team than at Highbury, with Martin Keown given a marking job on Jugovic, who had scored the two goals in the first leg. After 13 minutes Mancini broke away with the Arsenal back four appealing for offside. He lobbed the ball over a Seaman stranded in no-man's land and it was 1–0 to Sampdoria. In many ways Arsenal were fortunate that the goal came so early. But it took until the 62nd minute for the Gunners to respond. One of numerous corners from Merson was headed on by Hartson and the ball bounced off Wright's legs into the net; 1–1 and Arsenal were ahead again on aggregate. The game was surprisingly open, if a little aggressive, and Arsenal were openly adventurous with Wright a continual threat until he went off, battered and bruised, with 10 minutes left. He had so far scored in every game. Just as Wright went off, Sampdoria won a free-kick 30 yards out. It was hit against the wall, but the return fortuitously reached substitute Bellucci, who deflected it into the net. Within a minute Lombardo broke away and, with Arsenal concentrating on attack, Bellucci was on hand to slot a third past Seaman. With just six minutes to go Sampdoria were 3–1 up and 5–4 ahead on aggregate. It had to be all over. But on 87 minutes Stefan Schwarz took a free-kick from fully 35 yards out. He hit it low and not exceptionally hard but somehow it travelled through the wall and into the corner of Zenga's net off the keeper's left hand; 3–2 to Sampdoria, an impossibly unlikely 5–5 on aggregate at 90 minutes. It was the first time Sampdoria had ever played an English side in European competition and they were not likely to quickly forget a 5–5 result.

Sampdoria had much the best of extra time but could not score the all important sixth goal. The Arsenal attack, in the unlikely shape of Kiwomya, Hartson and McGoldrick (hardly the classic Arsenal line-up of recent years) made little headway against the Italian defence.

And so to penalties. After 26 games undefeated in Cup Winners Cup matches, it was all down to David Seaman in the Arsenal goal. The keeper, despite conceding three goals, had had a very good night indeed.

Lee Dixon went first and scored easily. Seaman saved from Michaelovic going to his left. McGoldrick put his shot way over the bar. Seaman then saved from Jugovic low to his right. After four shots, it was 1–0 to Arsenal. Hartson made it 2–0. Aspero scored for Sampdoria; 2–1. Tony Adams made it 3–1 to the Gunners. Then Sampdoria scored; 3–2. So it was left to Merson to score and finish things. He didn't, Zenga saving. But Seaman made his third save out of five to deny Lombardo and Arsenal were through to their third Cup Winners Cup final. Real Zaragoza had gone through 4–3 on aggregate against Chelsea (17 goals in the two semi-finals was something of a surprise), so the final was to be in Paris. Had Chelsea won, the game would have been at Wembley. Arsenal were seeking to become the first team for 35 years to retain the European Cup Winners Cup on May 10.

David Lacey was, as ever, the man who summed it up perfectly in *The Guardian*: 'Arsenal are back in the final of the Cup Winners Cup because, in the home of Christopher Columbus, Sampdoria were ultimately thwarted by an able Seaman.'

A glorious end to an era rather than a new era in itself was Ian Ridley's assessment on 1994–95 for Arsenal. It was a season completely dominated by three events of significance matched only by their unlikelihood. One was the dramatic departure of George Graham – winner of more trophies than even the incomparable Chapman – and the second was an unimaginable 5–5 draw with Sampdoria in the European Cup Winners Cup semi-final. The latter match was even more astonishing because it was the result of three goals in the last ten minutes, extra time and a glorious penalty shoot out. The third event was to come at the very end. Of the rest of the season, there is arguably little to say. The Gunners scored in only one of their first five League matches, fell immediately to mid-table mediocrity and stayed there through the season.

The news that Arsenal had fired George Graham finally came on 21 February, but circumstances had been moving towards that conclusion for some time. In some regards, the whole affair was the result of a shower of sheer bad luck. In the second leg of the European Cup Winners Cup Arsenal were drawn to play Brondby of Denmark. Arsenal won the tie 4–3 on aggregate in October and November 1994. It was from Brondby that Arsenal had bought the scorer of the winning goal in the 1992 European Championship, John Jensen.

Hamburg, who had transferred Jensen to Brondby, were due 20 per cent of the fee and had recently approached Arsenal for confirmation of the amount involved. Presumably the answers they were getting from Brondby were not entirely satisfactory. Arsenal did not

answer Hamburg's enquiry, but it was one reason why David Dein, Arsenal's vice-chairman, asked Brondby to confirm what they had received for Jensen when the two clubs met in Denmark. Both sides knew there was an agent, Rune Hauge, involved, and certainly expected him to have taken a cut. But as Peter Hill-Wood told Mihir Bose of the *Daily Telegraph*: 'The Brondby chairman said they had kept £900,000, which did surprise us.' It meant simply that some £676,000 must have gone somewhere else.

Not all the details are clear, and may never be so, but it was established that George Graham had declared to the Inland Revenue that he had received £425,000 as an unsolicited gift or gifts from Rune Hauge. Eventually Graham paid this money back to Arsenal. This happened some time before his eventual departure, and Hillwood later told Bose that Graham had also asked to leave Highbury with two years of his contract left. He felt he could not motivate the players and he and Hill-Wood agreed he could leave at the end of the 1994–95 season.

But on 17 February Peter Hill-Wood and Ken Friar were asked to meet the Premier League's investigation committee. Rick Parry, Robert Reid, Steve Coppell and John Quinton, the League's chairman, went through their findings of an investigation into transfers of foreign players in detail. They revealed that there had been a similar situation over the transfer of Pal Lydersen from the Norwegian club IK Start. Although Graham had paid back everything, which he described as unsolicited gifts, and had asked for an open hearing on the

whole affair, the Arsenal board felt justified in dismissing him on 21 February.

Despite the fact that many had expected it, the mood was one of intense shock. This was after all Arsenal, the most upright of all English clubs, the bearer of the historical banner for the English game. It was inevitable that many should say that Graham was unlucky and that the allegations were only the tip of the iceberg, and a reflection of a season of similar behaviour elsewhere in the game. It had been a season of many such allegations – not least against Spurs, Brian Clough and later against Bruce Grobbelaar and other players. There was certainly a great deal of money sloshing about in the game since the arrival of the Premier League and the Sky television deal. Very modest players were receiving signing-on fees which made the wages of the greatest stars of George Graham's day seem like a pittance.

Stewart Houston was to be the new George Allison – taking over from the most successful manager, in terms of silverware won, in the club's history. But Houston inherited a team past its best and one steeped in Graham's trademarks – defensive orientation, the grinding out of results, 1–0 to Arsenal, the acquisition of numerous central defenders but only two forwards, Wright and Smith (before Hartson and Kiwomya in the 1994–95 season).

George Graham was always aware of the attitudes taken towards Arsenal, and clearly cared deeply about them. He was presumably aware of criticisms about the lack of creativity – the lack of a new Liam Brady or (from another era) even Alex James. At the start of the 1993–94

Tony Adams became an increasingly consistent and valuable goal scorer in vital matches during the 1990s. This is Arsenal's third goal in the 7–0 demolition of Standard Liège in the Cup Winners' Cup, 3 November 1993.

season he had said: 'The fans keep on at me about a midfield player. They're telling me nothing I don't already know. Every paper, every radio station, every TV station is saying "George needs to buy a midfield player." In fact I actually had a T-shirt made up which said "I AM TRYING TO BUY A MIDFIELD PLAYER". I was thinking of wearing it at a press conference after a game, but eventually thought better of it …'

Graham appeared to eschew the star system somewhat. He has often commented on the importance of hunger in his teams and he has put that into practice by regularly buying from the lower divisions rather than acquiring established stars. This has led to an integrated dressing-room with an 'all for one, one for all' attitude in recent years, evidenced perhaps in Arsenal winning trophies for which their individual qualities did not seem to fit them.

Graham's system changed in his nine years with the club. To begin with, Graham played Brian Marwood wide and his contribution to the 1989 Championship was enormous. And despite a lengthy flirtation with the massively popular Limpar, Marwood was never really replaced and Arsenal changed to a straightforward four-man midfield, with Wright up front partnered by Smith, Campbell and, more recently, Hartson. This has made life harder for the second-choice forwards. As Alan Smith says: 'We don't have a crosser anymore. If Paul Merson or Kevin Campbell play wide, they're not exactly wingers, are they? As a result, we play in straight lines. I'm flicking it on, which means I'm out of the game and someone else has to score.'

Dependence upon him is hardly Ian Wright's fault and it has become a truism of the modern game that without a recognised goalscorer no team achieves anything. The 1994–95 Premier League season was as good an example as any. Newcastle fell away dramatically when they lost their supply of goals in the form of Andy Cole. Blackburn won the Championship because of two sources – Shearer and Sutton. Their third forward, Stuart Ripley, went the whole season without a single goal. Forest came from nowhere because of Stan Collymore and Liverpool lived off Robbie Fowler.

Graham had not solved this problem by the time he left. He had created a team and a system which was very much his. As Lee Dixon says: 'The keys to the success have been the manager and the team spirit within the club. If you look at the Anfield team of '89, there is still that nucleus of players who are at the club. We've done it all. It is something George Graham can take the credit for, he's bought new players but based it around that core – built around defence. And the defence that won the League in '89 and '91 went on to Copenhagen and Paris four years later.'

'George wants to be remembered as someone who has been successful,' says Brian Marwood, 'and that's definitely how people

will view him. They will say he was successful but not a great character. The man (ran) a high-pressure football club and he's won two Championships, two League Cups, an FA Cup and the European Cup Winners Cup. That's good going. Practically something every year… as time passes he will become a greater and greater figure in Arsenal's history. People's views are always kinder with history. He'll be a terribly hard act to follow. I wouldn't like to think I was taking over from him.'

Dixon had insights into Graham's total coaching method. 'On the coach to away games, we'll always have the opposition's last game on the video. But you think "I only played against him a few months ago", plus there's so much football on television that you're seeing the opposition every week. The boss might get very excited watching the video and say: "Look lads, come and watch this", and we'd say: "Right, boss, and just carry on playing cards."'

The striker of strikers was, of course, Ian Wright. No successful Arsenal team had ever been so dependent on one man. Through a season beset with poor form, scandals and crises, Wright had kept scoring. By the time he ran out in the Parc des Princes on 10 May 1995, he had already scored 30 precious goals in the season. He had now scored more than one hundred for Arsenal and had already become the club's highest ever scorer in Europe. In November 1994 he scored in 12 successive matches, a record for Arsenal.

But there were other records which needed to be achieved. No club had ever retained the Cup Winners Cup and Arsenal were to become no less than the seventh holders to be defeated in the following season's final.

There was a full house of 48,000 at the Parc des Princes, and all of them would leave with one abiding memory. The game went to extra time, Esnaider scoring for Real Zaragoza to become the first man to score in every round of a European competition, and Hartson equalising for Arsenal. With just 25 seconds left of the 120 minutes, and everyone in the ground convinced it was to be penalties yet again, the truly remarkable happened – a moment which comes rarely in a lifetime of watching football. It was to be the perfect goal, not only in its execution, but also in its total unexpectedness.

Nayim, usually the Zaragoza playmaker, had been policed constantly since the game began – first by Keown, then by Hillier. But everyone had become tired after 120 minutes of chasing back and closing down space and there was now just a little more room on the park.

Nayim picked up a loose ball out on the right. He was fifteen yards from the centre line and five yards in from the touch-line. Unusually, Hillier was not in attendance, and Nayim had time to look up and see if anyone was making a forward run. There was no apparent danger – no one in the penalty area. Nayim had played five years for Spurs, and, in

Alan Smith turns away after scoring a stunning volley against Parma in the Cup Winners Cup final on 4 May 1994 in Copenhagen. It proved to be the only goal of the game as Arsenal practised their 'we hold what we have' approach, so familiar to English fans down the years post-Herbert Chapman. It was yet another trophy, the fourth in four years, and it leaves the Gunners needing only the European Cup to complete a full set of European and domestic trophies.

Gascoigne's shadow, the skills which Terry Venables recognised in Barcelona had not been much appreciated in North London. But it was to be the nightmare of the 1991 FA Cup semi-final relived as Nayim, again in white shirt and blue shorts, took aim. With no other long option available, and with time running out, Nayim lofted the ball towards the Zaragoza fans. It looped off his foot in a delicate parabola, dropping finally towards Seaman's goal like a baseball pitcher's slider for a third strike. It seemed to take forever to fall, the whole ground appeared to stop breathing, and from nothing suddenly there was drama.

Seaman, who had been correctly positioned around ten yards out, started back-pedalling at speed. But the ball, by design or pure chance, was perfectly positioned. Another ten centimetres further back and it would have struck the crossbar. Another ten centimetres further forward and Seaman's hands would have pushed it over the bar. As it was the goalkeeper, hero in Genoa, could only help it into the roof of the net. There was silence, and then the sigh that accompanies news of a great disaster from the Arsenal end. Very few had any idea who had scored, or even how.

Had the shot gone over, it would have been the game's last moment. By the time Seaman had taken a goal-kick, the referee would have blown to bring on the penalty shoot-out.

The Zaragoza players and officials rolled around on the ground, completely obscuring Nayim. His shot, carefully judged, had been from all of 50 yards. Seaman later blamed himself, but he was wrong. The goal was neither a freak nor a fluke, but there are always some percentages on a football pitch that no goal-

Ian Wright scores
Arsenal's first goal in the second leg of the Cup Winners Cup semi-final against Sampdoria on 20 April 1995. A Merson corner was headed on by Hartson and the ball virtually bounced off Wright's legs into the far corner. It meant that he had scored in every game of the tournament so far, and if he did so in the final, he would become the first player to score in every game or round of any European competition. In the end, of course, Zaragoza's Esnaider scored in the final and became the record breaker, but the Paris final could have seen two players achieve this scoring feat. Early on in the season, Wright had scored in 12 consecutive games for the club – a new record – and he finished the season with 30 goals. In truth, the team was too dependent on his scoring abilities which had, perhaps, compensated for other areas of weakness.

Stewart Houston took over when George Graham left the club so dramatically on 21 February 1995. There is no precedent in the club's history for such an elevation – the nearest was probably George Allison's promotion on Herbert Chapman's death. Allison, however, had the advantage of being a director and one of the club's largest shareholders. Houston had no such defence and, despite winning his first two games in charge, he always seemed to be a stop-gap. Had the team won the final in Paris, the board's position might have been more difficult, but in June they announced the arrival of Bruce Rioch from Bolton.

keeper can weigh the odds for. As for Nayim, he had written his epitaph. He will always be remembered for this moment. The *Sun* was astonishingly eloquent: 'In one beautiful moment, he changes the way he will be remembered in Britain for ever more. He will no longer be Nayim the playactor, Nayim the diver, Nayim the fake, the nuisance. He will be Nayim who scored probably the greatest goal ever in any European final.' The English papers showed a remarkable grasp of Arabic, none of them failing to comment that Nayim means lucky in that language. In Spanish, Ali Amar Mohamed, alias Lucky Nayim, gave an account which suggested little was down to luck. 'It was the last minute and the last chance. I didn't have any option but to try, really. I saw Esnaider was offside. I saw the goalkeeper was a bit forward from his line and I tried. I was quite clear in what I was trying and I was really concentrating.' Terry Venables confirmed Nayim's own account: 'I've seen

him try the same thing in training and in a match. He and Gazza were always trying to outdo each other in training. If he had just lobbed it, Seaman would probably have got back, but he really whacked it and put a whip on it, and that's what beat David.'

And so it was over. Zaragoza were the better team and deserved to win. Arsenal had now played a total of 27 games in the European Cup Winners Cup, had reached the final every time they competed, had lost only the last two of their 27 matches, and had still failed in two of their three finals. The crowd may have sung 'We'll win 'cos we're Arsenal' but it was ultimately as empty as it was unimaginative and for years Spurs fans would sing 'Nayim from the halfway line'. A more imaginative banner read 'One life, one game, one club, one nil' and that perhaps summed up the mood of Highbury in the last two seasons. Where Spurs had *The Glory Game* as their contribution to football literature, Arsenal had the very personal, anguished Nick Hornby and *Fever Pitch*. It was as good an epitaph to the Graham era as anyone was likely to produce.

A year of transition began on June 15. Ex-Bolton manager Bruce Rioch was named as Arsenal's new boss. Stewart Houston reverted to first team coach.

Rioch's arrival promised a positive approach after the dourness of the previous three years. The day after he was appointed, Rioch spent six hours with the coaching staff, dissecting the Gunners squad.

"They told me we probably had only one 20 goals-a-season man, Ian Wright," remembers Rioch. He moved quickly to boost Arsenal's firepower. The Dutchman, Dennis Bergkamp, arrived from Internazionale for a club record £7.5million, swiftly followed by England captain David Platt from Sampdoria for £4.75million. Those signings signalled a radical change of policy for a club hitherto reluctant to spend huge sums in transfer fees or wages.

Meanwhile, Kevin Campbell left for Nottingham Forest at the end of his contract – and Arsenal soon lost two more experienced players. Stefan Schwarz was one of 1994-95 successes. But the Swedish midfielder and his family never settled in England. On he moved, to Fiorentina in Italy.

Then Rioch's plans took another knock when Alan Smith confirmed that a prolonged cartilage injury had ended his career.

Highbury fans saw a new-look team, in style as well as personnel. After the gloom of the months before, smiles were back in fashion. "We go into training every morning and feel relaxed," said Tony Adams.

"Take care of the ball and it will take care of you; that's the message I preach," said Rioch. The Gunners took to the passing game. By the end of the season, senior pros were admitting, they'd been through a learning process. Arsenal had gained a UEFA Cup place too, though it was a close run thing. With eight minutes of the final Premiership Sunday left, Rioch's team were 0–1 down to relegated Bolton at Highbury. A repeat of the fixture at Burnden Park in October – when Arsenal tore Wanderers apart, but lost 0–1 – looked on the cards. Then Platt popped up with the equaliser. Two minutes later Bergkamp drilled home the winner, and another full house crowd celebrated; in relief as much as triumph.

"That's what I bought them for!" smiled Rioch.

The two new signings' fortunes contrasted sharply. After Bergkamp had scored – two corkers in the 4–2 win over Southampton - he settled down to become the fulcrum of the attack. The actor and Arsenal fanatic Tom Watt summed up his impact: "He's made the season for me. I'd pay to watch him train, he's got that much ability."

Injury wrecked Platt's season. He volleyed a brilliant goal in the fourth game, a 1–1 draw against Forest – then went into hospital for a cartilage operation that kept him out until November. More time on the sidelines followed early in the new year. As Rioch said: "It was a stop-start campaign for him."

Injuries and suspensions caused the manager all sorts of problems after an impressive start. Ligament injuries ruled out Ray Parlour for two spells. Steve Bould missed the last four months because of a groin problem. Adams was out for nearly as long after a cartilage operation. Suspensions forced Rioch to make changes too. Wright was the most high profile victim. The manager wanted his topscorer on the pitch, not banned. In March, Wright asked for a transfer, which the club refused.

With his skipper and Bould ('the colossus')

injured, Rioch switched to a 3-5-2 formation. Martin Keown, Andy Linighan and Scott Marshall formed the back line – and the Gunners conceded only seven goals in 12 matches.

Keown had an outstanding year, ending as captain in Adams' absence. It was a remarkable turn-round for the versatile defender, who'd admitted he was concerned about his future after not playing in the pre-season friendlies.

Marshall was one of several young players who came into contention. So did lively, fellow Scot Paul Dickov, left winger Adrian Clarke and midfielder Paul Shaw. There were encouraging signs that the youth policy was producing again. Matthew Rose, Stephen Hughes and Gavin McGowan all came through from Pat Rice's 1994 Youth Cup winners to play in the first team.

High points of the season? The 3–0 win at Leeds, when Wright netted an unbelievable chip. Beating Manchetser United 1–0 at Highbury. Premiership and Coca Cola wins (both 2–0) over Newcastle.

David Seaman, Lee Dixon and a rejuvenated Paul Merson were ever-present. Merson finished the season with a bumper benefit match against an International Select, with the 1971 'Double' squad in attendance.

The low points? Disappointing league form in December and January when knocks and bans began to hurt; third round FA Cup disaster in a replay at Endsleigh League Sheffield United – and the Coca Cola semi-final against Aston Villa. Bergkamp played superbly against the competition's eventual winners, poaching two memorable goals to put Arsenal 2–0 up in the first leg. Defensive lapses

This page: **The semi-final of the Cup Winners Cup** in 1995, between Arsenal and Sampdoria, ended in a highly unlikely 5-5 draw and went to penalties. David Seaman saved three of them, the last from Lombardo, to put his team through to the final. As he said afterwards: 'Well, I let in five in normal time, so I had to save a few didn't I? Anyway, I'd much rather be saving them than taking them. '

Top right: **John Hartson stabs home Paul Merson's pass** to equalise for Arsenal in the final of the 1995 Cup Winners Cup in Paris. Earlier Esnaider had put Real Zaragoza ahead and the game went to extra time.

Bottom right:**The denouement of denouements.** There are just 25 seconds left in the 1995 Cup Winners Cup final. Everyone is preparing for penalties, not least David Seaman. Nayim lobs the ball 50 yards and the ball spins under the crossbar as Seaman grabs at air. The picture reflects what happens superbly - although the shot was parabolic and not a rocket, there is no defender or attacker anywhere near the goal. So Arsenal lost just 2 of the 27 games they have played in the Cup Winners Cup, reached the final all three times they entered, and still won it just once.

enabled Dwight Yorke to strike twice in reply. The second leg at Villa Park stayed goalless despite extra time, meaning Arsenal were knocked out on the away goal rule. Aston Villa went on to beat Leeds in the final.

So 1995–96 turned out to be a season of 'what might have been'. But it certainly wasn't unsuccessful. A cup semi-final appearance, fifth in the Premiership and a place in Europe for 1996–97 would have been something the fans would gladly have settled for during the turbulence taking place before Bruch Rioch's arrival.

There seemed little to worry about when Arsenal eased into their 1996–97 pre-season friendlies with a trip to St Albans on 19 July and a comfortable 6–0 run-around of St Albans City. But as it happened that was the only win in their eight warm-up matches. A strong Arsenal side were beaten 1–0 at Birmingham City.

A crowd of 47,300 turned out at Parkhead to see Arsenal take a half-time lead over Celtic, courtesy of Lee Dixon's third goal in three matches, but Celtic replied twice after the interval for a 2–1 win. Glasgow-born Paul Dickov came on as a substitute and thus realised a life-long ambition to play on Celtic's turf. He was to leave when the season started for Manchester City. Three days later it was

the turn of 41,245 Rangers fans to see what the Gunners could do. In this match the old Arsenal favourite, goalkeeper John Lukic, signed in the summer on a free transfer from Leeds as backup for David Seaman, reappeared behind his old buddies Dixon, Winterburn and Bould. It must have seemed as if the clock had turned back several years. Unfortunately he had to pick the ball out of the net three times as Rangers beat Arsenal 3–0.

It was off to Italy next for the Gunners, where they played in a strange triangular practice in Florence, playing 45-minute matches on the same day with the hosts Fiorentina and the other visitors, Benfica of Portugal. Arsenal lost both matches, 2–0 and 3–1 respectively. Sub John Hartson got the goal.

Back in England Arsenal's poor pre-season form continued. Ipswich held them to a 1–1 draw and Northampton Town beat them 3–1. Arsenal shared with Northampton sadness over the death in the summer of Cliff Holton, former club captain and centre-forward in the 1952 Cup Final side. Cliff later played for Northampton and set their season's goal-scoring record with 36 League goals in 1961–62.

Five days before the Premiership season started, Arsenal parted company with Bruce

Above: **The new order at Highbury:** Manager Bruce Rioch, who took over in June 1995, flanked by his expensive signings from the Italian League, England skipper David Platt (left) who was acquired from Sampdoria, and Dutch international forward Dennis Bergkamp (right), who became Arsenal's most expensive player when bought from Internazionale for £7.5 million. Bergkamp's subtle brilliance, and the explosive accuracy of his finishing, brought a new dimension to Arsenal's football.

Rioch. A statement from Peter Hill-Wood, the Arsenal chairman, announced that the board had decided that it was in the best interest of the club that Bruce Rioch should leave and that accordingly the club had released him from his position as manager. Rioch's 14-month reign was the shortest of any Arsenal manager this century.

Mr Hill-Wood announced that the club had a successor in mind but that it was not possible at that stage to identify him. It did not take long for Fleet Street to name the new manager-in-waiting as a Frenchman, Arsene Wenger, who was managing Nagoya Grampus Eight in Japan, with whom he had a contract which would keep him there until January 1997. Wenger had been thinking over an offer to become the FA's technical director. An intelligent man, he appeared to be a typical Arsenal type, knowledgeable and authoritative without being flamboyant.

While waiting to announce the new appoint-

ment, Stewart Houston, assisted by first team coach Pat Rice, were responsible for team affairs. It was the second time that Houston had stepped into the shoes of manager, as he had ably filled the gap between the departure of Graham and arrival of Rioch. Two new appointments for the season were old Arsenal men Tom Walley, the new youth team coach, and Liam Brady, head of youth development. Brady, of course, was one of Arsenal's greatest players and since then had experienced big-time management at Celtic.

On the playing side, John Jensen had returned to Brondby in Denmark and two newcomers arrived just in time for the new season. Both had French international honours. Patrick Vieira, a tall midfielder, was an Under-21 international, having been born in Senegal. He had begun his career with Cannes in France and had been made captain at just 19 years of age. He'd been snapped up by AC

Below: **Nigel Winterburn races for the ball** on the opening day of the 1996-97 season at Highbury. Arsenal got the campaign off to a great start with a 2–0 victory.

Milan to whom Arsenal paid just over £3 million for him. A strong and fast player, although still only 20, he was regarded throughout France as a star of the future. The second newcomer, Remi Garde, a midfielder/sweeper, was 30, and had played for Lyon and Strasbourg, from whom Arsenal engaged him under the Bosman ruling, his contract having expired. He had made his international debut in 1990, and had won six French caps.

So Arsenal at the last minute had signed two top players from the continent. The Bosman ruling in the European courts had denied the right of clubs to claim transfer fees on players whose contracts had expired, thus giving players a new freedom of movement. This, together with the Premiership's new wealth, arising out of Sky Television contracts, had led to the import into England of a number of top continental players. Chelsea set the pace for the season with the acquisition of the Italians Zola, Vialli and Di Matteo, plus Frenchman Leboeuf, while Middlesbrough engaged Ravanelli from Italy and acquired two Brazilians, Juninho and Emerson. Arsenal could not to be left behind.

Neither of Arsenal's imports appeared in the opening match of the season. Captain Tony Adams was also missing from the line-up although, along with Seaman, Platt and Bergkamp, he had played in the biggest football event in England for 30 years – Euro 96, the European championships. He had played, with Bruce Rioch's blessing, despite not having fully recovered from a knee operation in January. He had another operation afterwards and did not return until well into September. Ian Wright, too, was not fully fit and was to be a substitute in the first four League games of the season, during which he still scored twice.

Arsenal got off to a good start by beating West Ham 2–0 at Highbury. Hartson and Bergkamp, with a penalty, scored the goals. It was the reverse story at Liverpool, where the Gunners lost 2–0, but an away win at Leicester, again 2–0, had them third in the table already. There was then an exciting game with Chelsea at Highbury, in which Chelsea led 2–0, but Arsenal came back to lead 3–2, only for a last-minute goal from Chelsea's Dennis Wise to restrict the Gunners to a draw. Another 2–2

Lee Dixon outpaces Gary Kelly as the Gunners romped to a 3–0 win at home to Leeds. Dixon went on to score in this match with Bergkamp and Wright bagging a goal apiece.

Above: **Goalkeeper John Lukic** was Bruce Rioch's last signing as Arsenal manager. It turned out to be an astute move, as the veteran keeper was called upon to make 15 League appearances in 1996–97.

Right: Martin Keown enjoyed an excellent first season under Arsene Wenger. By the end of the campaign the stylish defender had impressed the new England manager, Glenn Hoddle, enough to be included in the national squad for a busy summer schedule.

draw at Villa was a good result and, with Bergkamp, Wright and Merson already on the scorer's chart with two apiece, things looked very promising for the first leg of the UEFA Cup, which was a home tie against the German Bundesliga giants Borussia Monchengladbach.

Arsenal's display was disappointing, hampered as it was by Dennis Bergkamp having to go off early in the match with a hamstring injury. Arsenal were 2–0 down soon after half-time, staged a rally but finished 3–2 down. It left a big task ahead for the second leg.

Three days later (Friday the 13th) Stewart Houston resigned. He had been offered a post as assistant to George Graham who, after being banned from football management for a year, had taken over at Leeds. However Houston, who said it was clear to him he would never get the no. 1 job at Highbury, stated that he was not interested in being no. 2 any more. Houston's move was to facilitate him taking over the managership at First Division Queen's Park Rangers. He gave the Loftus Road side a distinct ex-Arsenal look when he appointed Bruce Rioch to be his assistant.

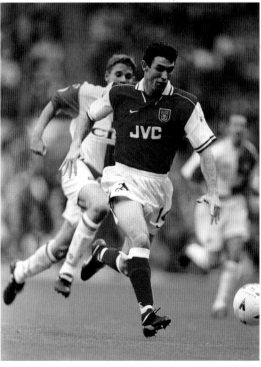

Euro joy: the Arsenal bench, which included Arsene Wenger for the first time, celebrates an away goal against UEFA Cup opponents Borussia Monchengladbach. Unfortunately it was not enough to overturn a first leg deficit.

With what appeared to be crisis looming at Highbury, chairman Peter Hill-Wood revealed he had been in contact with Japan and expected Arsene Wenger to be released from his contract with Grampus Eight and to be able to take over earlier than expected. Meanwhile Pat Rice was the new caretaker manager at Highbury, and in his first programme notes he confessed that what he wanted for Arsenal was to get back to some 'boring' 1–0 wins again, the way to win trophies in his view.

Ian Wright emphasised Arsenal's buoyant outlook in the next game by scoring a hat-trick in a 4–1 home win over Sheffield Wednesday and he got another goal in a 2–0 win at Middlesbrough, where Adams returned as a substitute, before Arsenal went to Monchengladbach to try to win by two goals and keep themselves in Europe. Arsene Wenger flew in to join Arsenal for his first match, although for the time being Pat Rice remained in control. Wenger was encouraged by what he saw. After going one behind, Arsenal equalised just before half time through Wright and went ahead just afterwards through Merson. One more might have led to them winning on aggregate but, after Monchengladbach scored again in the 64th minute, Arsenal's pressing need was for a goal to force parity over the two legs, and in pressing they conceded another in injury time to lose the tie 6–4.

Wenger had flown in to take over before Arsenal's next match, and saw good wins over Sunderland and Blackburn to lift Arsenal to second in the table. Two draws with midlands teams followed, at home to Coventry and away at Stoke, the second being in the third round of the Coca-Cola Cup – Arsenal, in keeping with some other top clubs, had been given a bye to this stage. Before Arsenal could beat their First Division opponents Stoke in the replay 5–2, George Graham returned to Highbury in charge of Leeds United. Former Arsenal favourite David O'Leary was with Graham as his no. 2 at Leeds. The Gunners won 3–0.

Arsenal's interest in the Coca-Cola Cup ended in the fourth round on 27 November when they were well beaten 4–2 at Anfield, the two coming from Ian Wright penalties. However, three days later it was a different story in a remarkable match at Newcastle against the Premiership leaders. A minute after a 12th-minute goal by Dixon had been replied to by a 21st-minute Shearer equaliser, Tony Adams brought down Shearer when he was through on goal and was sent off. It seemed all over for the Gunners, but they withstood the Newcastle siege and, in the 60th minute, an Ian Wright breakaway goal put Arsenal top of the table. 'There is something special about this team', said Wenger. 'They have a good camaraderie because they have been playing together for a long time'.

Right: **Arsenal supporters had been demanding a stylish midfielder** since Liam Brady departed in 1980. Wenger's arrival at Highbury coincided with the signing of just such a player: Patrick Vieira. The 20-year-old Frenchman proved to be not only skilful, but also strong and could pass, shoot, head and tackle. The supporters were rightly satisfied.

Below: **Lee Dixon celebrates** his goal against Newcastle at St James'. The long-serving full-back seemed to find a new enthusiasm for the game in 1996–97 and his energetic displays were widely acclaimed.

Arsenal's table-topping didn't last long and a surprise 2–1 defeat at relegation strugglers Nottingham Forest plus a couple of draws began a mini-slide that dropped them to third. In January Arsenal negotiated the third round of the FA Cup by winning a replay 2–0 at Sunderland, this otherwise frenetic encounter was illuminated by an exquisite goal from Dennis Bergkamp. On 4 February at home to Leeds in the fourth round, they crashed 1–0 to a 12th minute goal by Rod Wallace and inspired goalkeeping by Nigel Martyn. Apart from the UEFA Cup defeat, it was Arsenal's first defeat of the season at home, and the first time Leeds had beaten Arsenal in the Cup in ten encounters since the Cup final of 1972.

So their ejection from their third Cup competition left Arsenal with just the Premiership to fight for, or at worst a place in Europe, in either the Champions' Cup (the runners-up were to qualify this season) or the UEFA Cup. But the next home defeat, which quickly followed on 19 February, was a blow. Two first-half goals by leaders Manchester United, only one of which Bergkamp pulled back in the second half, left Arsenal trailing five points behind in third place, and with more games played than their rivals. After this match Wenger wrote off Arsenal's title chances, and when a 1–0 defeat by Wimbledon in Arsenal's next match, also at Highbury, dropped the club to a distant fourth, everybody seemed to agree with him.

In March Wenger completed the signing of Nicolas Anelka, a talented French striker days

195

short of his 18th birthday, from Paris St Germain. The tall, slim youngster delighted with appearances as a sub in Arsenal's run-in.

Strangely, because Arsenal strung together some good wins and other title contenders faltered, their mathematical hopes of taking the title continued nearly to the end of the season, and their prospects of a Champions' League place right to the last day. The title hopes disappeared with another home defeat – a vital one to rivals Liverpool. Arsenal's 2–1 defeat was overshadowed by a controversial penalty decision against them. Robbie Fowler stumbled over David Seaman and immediately jumped up, waving his arms to indicate that he did not think a penalty should be awarded. Referee Gerald Ashby had already pointed to the spot, and wasn't inclined to change his mind. Although the referee thought Fowler had been tripped by Seaman he did not send the keeper off. Seaman blocked Fowler's weak spot kick, but Jason McAteer slammed in the rebound for the vital goal.

On the second-to-last day of the season Arsenal entertained close rivals Newcastle United in another vital home match. And again they lost, 1–0. Wenger noted they had lost at home to all their immediate rivals: Manchester United, Liverpool and Newcastle.

Unfortunately, these late-season defeats were to cost them dear.

With Manchester United already champions, Liverpool, Newcastle and Arsenal could all finish second in the Premiership and gain a Champions' League place on the last day of the season, with Arsenal and Newcastle on identical points and goal differences.

Arsenal played Derby County at the last match to be played at the Baseball Ground, and things looked black after 11 minutes with Adams sent off and Arsenal a goal down, but they rallied to win 3–1. It was in vain as Newcastle won 5–0. Arsenal's third place ensured a UEFA Cup place – but it could have been so much better…

During a season in which Arsenal's charismatic ex-player Denis Compton died to worldwide tributes, Arsenal had found young players likely to uphold the reputation of the club for quality in the future. Patrick Vieira had been a great success in his first season, 20-year-old Stephen Hughes, picked for England's Under-21 side, had impressed in a late run in the team and Nicolas Anelka's promise was obvious. The 'old-stagers' were also showing no signs of slipping – Nigel Winterburn had a deserved benefit match in a 3–3 draw with Rangers on 13 May. With Arsene Wenger in charge, things looked bright for Arsenal.

Nicolas Anelka was the third French player to arrive at Arsenal in 1996–97. The tall young striker was given just four substitute appearances, but showed enough enterprise and ability to suggest that he had a bright future in the English game.

· CHAPTER 10 ·

Wenger's Double

As the final whistle was blown at the Baseball Ground to bring a trophyless 1996-97 campaign to a close, Arsene Wenger was already plotting how to improve his team for his first full season in charge at Highbury. The summer break would be far from a time of rest for the Frenchman. While Martin Keown, Ian Wright, David Seaman and Tony Adams travelled to Wenger's homeland to represent England in Le Tournoi, the Arsenal coach was also heading to the continent as he sought to strengthen his side.

There was an abundance of European talent available to Premiership managers – particularly those based in the capital city – during the summer of 1997. The Bosman ruling and the increased profile of English football, not to mention high wages, had made the Premiership the desired choice of a multitude of European-based players. The Arsenal coach had identified his targets and wasted no time in moving to clinch their signatures.

The first name on Wenger's wanted list was the electric-paced Dutchman Marc Overmars. Some critics had expressed doubts about the fitness of the Ajax winger after a knee injury had kept him out of the game for eight months. The good news for Wenger was that these doubts had left just two clubs – Arsenal and Real Betis – willing to match the Amsterdam club's £5m valuation. Wenger was confident that the Dutchman was fit and mentally prepared for the exertions of the Premiership and later remarked: 'When I did my homework on him I discovered he was upset at the rumours he was not fit and that he could never play to his true ability again. That was a good sign for me, a hurt player. He had something to prove.' Overmars opted to move to Highbury, leaving the Spaniards to look elsewhere for attacking talent.

Arsenal fans were no doubt excited about the prospect of seeing Overmars – a player whose pace had destroyed England (and, inparticular, Des Walker) in a World Cup qualifier in 1993 – line up in the famous red and white shirt. However, the anticipation of a new hero was tempered by disappointment at the departure of a current crowd-pleaser. Paul Merson had moved to First Division Middlesbrough after more than 10 years at Highbury.

Two other experienced players arrived at Arsenal over the summer, both from Wenger's former club Monaco. Gilles Grimandi and Emmanuel Petit crossed the channel to arrive in North London in time for pre-season training and reports suggested that they were intended as ready-made replacements for members of Arsenal's veteran-filled defence. Petit was a player who Wenger knew well, having handed him his debut as an 18-year-old at Monaco. For much of his career, he had operated as a defender – usually on the left side of the backline – but Wenger had a different assignment in mind for him at Highbury. The Arsenal coach planned to pair Petit with Patrick Vieira, who had proved a major success in his first year of English football. Grimandi, meanwhile, was exactly what he appeared: a 27-year-old defender who would provide cover right across the back four.

Having added experience to his squad, Wenger was also keen to inject youth into his first team pool. With this in mind, two young strikers – Christopher Wreh and Luis Boa Morte – and 23-year-old midfielder, Alberto Mendez, arrived to join 18-year-old defender Matthew Upson, who had made the short trip from Luton Town in May. All would play some part in first-team

Right: Emmanuel Petit, along with Gilles Grimandi, arrived from Wenger's old club Monaco during summer 1997. After a slow start he made himself an invaluable presence in midfield forging a formidable partnership with Patrick Vieira. Both players would be rewarded by call ups to the French national squad for the 1998 World Cup.

affairs during a season that would see Arsenal play 54 matches in all competitions.

With the World Cup on the horizon, the domestic season kicked-off a week earlier than usual and Arsenal began their Premiership campaign with a difficult away fixture at Leeds United. Predictably it was Ian Wright who grabbed the Gunners' first goal of the season to earn a share of the points. Wright was again on the scoresheet two days later when Coventry City visited Highbury. His double-strike gave Arsenal a comfortable victory and edged him to within a single goal of Cliff Bastin's 81-year-old Gunners scoring record. Wright's pursuit of the record would dominate the back-page headlines for the next month, but on the field it was the breathtaking form of Dennis Bergkamp that demanded attention.

The game against a dogged Southampton side at the Dell brought the best out of Bergkamp. With an hour played and the scores at 1–1 the Dutchman made his mark. He picked up the ball in midfield and carried it into the Saints' penalty area and, with the almost apologetic home defence fearfully backing-off, drove a precise shot past Paul Jones. Twenty minutes later, the Saints' defence opted for a different approach when finding Bergkamp in possession. In an effort to restrain the Arsenal striker, Francis Benali gripped hold of Bergkamp's shirt, but his crude challenge was in vain. Shrugging the defender aside, the Dutchman moved forward before unleashing an unstoppable shot into the Saints' goal.

Two draws followed Bergkamp's virtuoso performance at the Dell. First there was a trip to Filbert Street to take on Martin O'Neill's Leicester City. In a match full of hard work, enterprise and far too many defensive errors,

Bergkamp provided a faultless display of forward play. The Dutchman's three goals were of the highest quality and included the winner of the BBC *Match of the Day* Goal of the Season. With the deftest of touches Bergkamp used his left foot to control a cross from the right, moving the ball onto his right foot before calmly despatching it past the on-rushing Leicester keeper. A home draw against Spurs three days later, left Arsenal sitting in fifth place, four points behind leaders Blackburn Rovers and Manchester United at the end of August.

Bergkamp's domination of Arsenal's scoring had left Ian Wright marooned on 177 goals since the second game of the season as he pursued Bastin's record. Fortunately for Wright his strike partner was in generous mood as newly promoted Bolton Wanderers came to Highbury in September. In the 20th minute, a Bergkamp through-ball gave Wright a sight of goal and the striker made no mistake, sliding the ball past Bolton keeper Keith Branagan. Wright had now equalled Bastin's total (although Bastin had scored all of his in just the Football League and the FA Cup). But the goal that would set a new record came just five minutes later and again Bergkamp was at the hub of things. The Dutchman stabbed a shot goalward, but was foiled by Branagan and the loose ball broke to Wright two yards out in front of an unguarded net. Beaming afterwards Wright joked: 'I was happy before I even put it in. I'll never score an easier one.' Ray Parlour added a third goal, but nobody could gatecrash Ian Wright's party and the record-holder completed his hat-trick in the second half. After the game, Wright was keen to make it clear that his work at Highbury was not yet done: 'I'm glad it's out of the way, but, at 33, there's so much I want to achieve. I want to help us win something.'

Wright barely had time to bask in the glory of his goalscoring achievements before he was on a plane heading for Greece and the first leg of Arsenal's UEFA Cup tie against PAOK Salonika. One player who would not be boarding the plane was Bergkamp. The Dutchman's much-publicised fear of flying forced Arsene Wenger to rejig his team. Despite the absence of Bergkamp, Wenger opted for an attacking line-up in Salonika, naming 19-year-old Nicolas Anelka alongside the experienced pair of Overmars and Wright.

On a frustrating night for the Gunners, Wenger's attacking approach failed to reap rewards. Several good chances had been squandered by the time Greek international Fratzeskos skipped into the area to put the ball past Seaman. It was little more than the home team deserved and after the game Wenger declared: 'PAOK were more consistent overall. We dropped our level in the second half. The atmosphere was not an excuse and nor was the absence of Dennis Bergkamp. Now we have to win by two goals, which will not be easy.' Wenger's concern was well-founded. Despite an early goal from Bergkamp, Arsenal failed to score a second and were eliminated from the competition when the Greeks snatched a decisive equaliser.

Between the games against Salonika, the Gunners had beaten Chelsea at Stamford Bridge – courtesy of a rare goal from Nigel Winterburn – had comfortably overcome West Ham at Highbury and had drawn away at Everton. By the end of September, Arsenal had reached the summit of the League table. Eight goals from nine games for Dennis Bergkamp had undoubtedly been the catalyst for the Gunners' storming run to pole position in the Championship race. The Dutchman was again on the scoresheet as Barnsley were sent back to Yorkshire after conceding five goals without reply at Highbury in October. Just as it seemed Bergkamp could do no wrong, he received a booking in Arsenal's next match, away at Crystal Palace. That yellow card triggered an automatic suspension that would keep the striker out of vital matches against Derby, Manchester United and Sheffield Wednesday.

The trip to Pride Park, Derby's new ground, brought Arsenal's first defeat of the season. It was the worst possible preparation for the visit of Manchester United, who were Arsenal's opponents at Highbury the following Sunday. Despite the absence of the suspended Petit and Bergkamp, Arsenal got off to a sensational start against the Champions, scoring twice in the first half hour. Bergkamp's replacement, Nicolas Anelka, struck first before fellow Frenchman Patrick Vieira sent a superbly angled shot past Peter Schmeichel on 27 minutes. United came back strongly and Teddy Sheringham grabbed two goals, but the efforts of the former Spur were in vain, David Platt, in the team for Petit, heading a late winner. The triumph against United provided the only addition to Arsenal's points tally in November and by the end of the month they had slipped to fifth place in the table.

The Coca-Cola Cup was Arsenal's only early season respite from League action. However, this competition had lost much of its appeal since UEFA had threatened to withdraw the place in Europe which the winners had previously received. Wenger had used Arsenal's first game in the competition to field younger members of his squad, but for the tie against Coventry in November he selected a strong

Right: **'179, Just Done It!'** Ian Wright finally breaks Cliff Bastin's club record of 178 goals against Bolton in September. Wright confessed that the record-breaking goal was one of his easiest (tapping into an empty net after Vieira had set him up), but it was typical of Wright to cap the feat by completing a hat-trick as the Gunners ran out 4–1 winners.

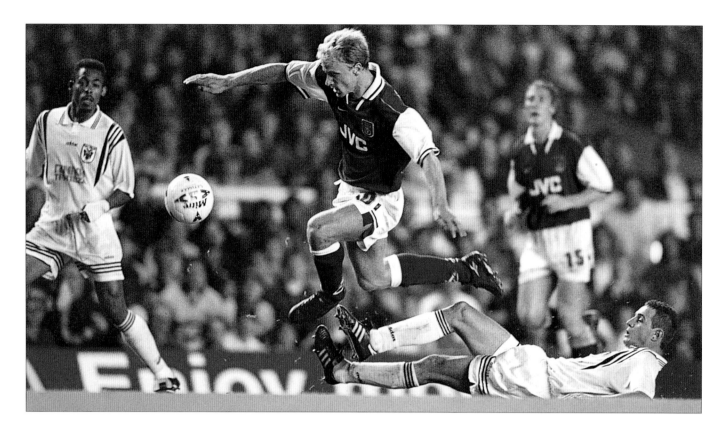

line-up that included Dennis Bergkamp. The Dutchman was eligible to play in the Coca-Cola Cup despite his League suspension and his extra-time goal decided the tie.

Arsenal's indifferent League form continued in December. The lowpoint of this frustrating period coming in a 3–1 reverse at home to Blackburn Rovers. A freak floodlight failure in the Gunners' next match, away at Wimbledon, denied Wenger's team the chance to get back on course in the title race. The match was abandoned with the score still at 0–0 after 46 minutes, it was scheduled be replayed in March, by which time Wenger hoped to have Arsenal running on full power again. The Christmas fixtures brought four points but little festive cheer for Gunners fans. A Steve Walsh own-goal was needed to decide the Boxing Day clash against Leicester at Highbury. Two days later a Ray Parlour strike secured a single point from the trip to struggling Spurs, but Arsenal's form was stuttering.

Arsenal were no longer playing the fluent, attacking football that had seen them waltz to the top of the table in the autumn. At the dawn of the New Year, Wenger's team were in sixth place, 12 points adrift of leaders Manchester United. Most pundits considered that Arsenal's chance had gone. Fortunately, the two domestic cup competitions gave a welcome distraction and a chance to get back to form in the early weeks of 1998.

The first Saturday in January brought with it the FA Cup third round, and for Arsenal a primed and armed booby trap in the shape of a home tie against First Division Port Vale. The 37,471 crowd watched in disbelief as Arsenal laboured to overcome a side that had not won

for two months. A 0–0 draw gave Wenger's team a second chance at Vale Park and for the replay they would be able to call upon record goalscorer Ian Wright.

Cup action continued the following Tuesday as Arsenal made the short trip around the North Circular to take on West Ham at Upton Park. The Hammers had a formidable home record, winning 12 of their 13 home games so far in all competitions. The game turned on an incident after just ten minutes. West Ham striker Paul Kitson darted into Seaman's penalty area, only to be met by the out-rushing keeper. The referee pointed to the spot and up stepped former Gunners striker John Hartson to take the kick. Hartson, the Premiership's top scorer v Seaman, England's top goalkeeper. It was a contest which had no doubt been played out during numerous Arsenal training sessions. The outcome was strangely inevitable. Seaman comfortably collected the striker's scuffed shot. Hartson bowed his head and Arsenal were buoyed. Goals from Overmars and Wright confirmed victory and put the Gunners into a two-legged semi-final against Ruud Gullit's Chelsea. The following week, Wenger's team navigated their passage to the FA Cup fourth round by overcoming Port Vale after a penalty shoot-out. In retrospect, it was perhaps the closest they came to missing the eventual Double – how strange that it was the other Potteries side, Stoke City, which was just a penalty away from destroying the 1971 Double.

In the League, a bad-tempered match against Coventry at Highfield Road saw Patrick Vieira sent off, but, more worryingly for Wenger, England custodian David Seaman suffered a finger injury which would keep him out for sev-

Above: **Bergkamp skips** over a challenge during the second leg of the UEFA Cup 1st round tie with PAOK Salonika. Despite Arsenal's domination of the game and another wonder goal from Bergkamp, Salonika snatched an equaliser three minutes from time to take them through 2–1 on aggregate.

eral weeks. The experienced keeper would be replaced by 20-year-old Austrian Alex Manninger. The blow of losing Seaman was slightly diminished by the return of skipper Tony Adams to first team duty. Adams had suffered a series of niggling injuries and had lost form in the first half of the season. Following the defeat against Blackburn in December he sought much needed rest and recuperation in the south of France. Adams celebrated his recall with his first goal of the season, heading home from a corner in a 3–0 win over Southampton.

Arsenal's football was beginning to rediscover the fluency and invention that had entertained the Highbury faithful so richly during early season. In the League, Wenger was forced to employ most of his squad members as the Gunners reeled in the chasing pack on their way up the table despite a growing list of injuries and suspensions. Wins over Crystal Palace and Chelsea had arrived courtesy of goals from two players, Gilles Grimandi and Stephen Hughes, who had been largely confined to the bench throughout the season. Despite this upturn in form, the pundits' view remained that Alex Ferguson's team had all but won the title and that the best Arsenal could achieve was runners-up spot and a place in the Champions League.

Wenger's squad continued to be stretched and the situation was not helped by increasing cup commitments. In the Coca-Cola Cup, the Gunners had taken a 2–1 lead to Stamford Bridge in the second leg of their semi-final. A narrow victory at Highbury had left Wenger reflecting on several missed chances: 'I think the right score tonight would have been 4–1, or maybe even 5–1, and I hope we won't regret it after the second game.' Arsenal's advantage

was not enough. The return in West London swung in Chelsea's favour when French midfielder Patrick Vieira was shown the red card just after half-time. A 3–1 victory gave Chelsea a 4–3 aggregate win.

Arsenal were left to focus their attention on the two trophies most coveted by the supporters: the Premiership title and the FA Cup. Wenger's team had little time to nurse their wounds after the bruising battle at Stamford Bridge. An FA Cup fourth round replay against Crystal Palace gave the Gunners the perfect opportunity to revive their Wembley ambitions. A striker shortage was, however, worrying Wenger before the trip to Selhurst. Ian Wright was struggling to recover from a hamstring injury, Marc Overmars had been on duty with the Dutch national team in America and was only due to arrive back in the UK on the morning of the game and Dennis Bergkamp had flu. Wenger need not have worried. First-half goals from Anelka and Bergkamp – who started the match but was replaced by Overmars in the second half – gave Arsenal a quarter-final tie against West Ham at Highbury. After the game, Wenger seemed satisfied with this team's performance: 'With so many injured players still out we have to consider it an excellent result and now we are through to a quarter-final. It is still a long way from winning the FA Cup but we are showing now that we can still be consistent even with players out.' Wenger was also quick to praise the commitment of the improving Marc Overmars: 'It was a big surprise that we could have him playing at all. Last night he was in America playing for Holland but he was able to catch a flight to Paris and was back in London this morning.'

Two London derbies against the Hammers followed. The first in the League was one of three games the Gunners' had in hand on leaders Manchester United as they attempted to close a 12-point gap. The clash at Upton Park saw the return from injury of French midfielder Manu Petit. After playing a key role in Arsenal's upturn in form, the former Monaco man was keen to keep the momentum going, declaring: 'I think it will be difficult for us because we have to continue our good run to put pressure on Manchester United and to leave the other clubs like Chelsea, Liverpool and Blackburn behind. We will lose some day. I just don't want it to be the next game.' A 0–0 draw was a good result given the Hammers form at Upton Park, but it was not enough. The champions' 11-point lead seemed unassailable and several bookmakers stopped taking bets on the Premiership title race. Wenger however would not concede that Arsenal's Championship bid was over: 'It's not over yet but, of course, it will be very difficult for us now. A point was a good result when you look at the tough match we faced at West Ham but in the context of the Championship now draws are not good enough for us. But we will just keep trying to win the matches we have left and not concern ourselves with what Manchester United do. We have no control over their situation apart

Below: **Stephen Hughes** scores his first goal of the season against Chelsea in the first leg of the Coca-Cola Cup semi-final. Marc Overmars netted for the fifth time in five matches, but Welshman Mark Hughes came off the bench to give Chelsea a lifeline. The Gunners were guilty of spurning a hatful of chances and they would pay a heavy price for their profligacy in the return fixture at Stamford Bridge.

from when we play them in two weeks' time.'

Arsenal's fixture backlog worsened six days later, when a Dennis Bergkamp penalty cancelled out an early West Ham goal and forced an FA Cup quarter-final replay at Upton Park. Before the game in East London, Arsenal faced two critical League matches. First there was a return to Selhurst for the aborted clash with Wimbledon, followed three days later by a summit meeting of the Premiership's top two at Old Trafford.

For both the Wimbledon and Manchester United games, Wenger decided to rotate his young strikers. Nicolas Anelka, whose form had been fitful in the early part of 1998 was replaced by Christopher Wreh. The young Liberian bubbled with confidence as he lined up for his first start of the season against the Dons. This jinxed fixture looked to be in jeopardy again when kick-off was held up by a bomb scare, but after a delay of half an hour the match got under way with all floodlights glowing. A crisp finish from Wreh on 22 minutes gave Arsenal a deserved lead at the interval. The second half saw Arsenal doggedly defend their lead in the face of growing Wimbledon pressure. If the first half had belonged to Wreh, then the second went to Manninger whose faultless display secured Arsenal all three points. The efforts of Arsenal's young stars prompted a glowing testimonial from Wenger after the game. He declared: 'I am very pleased for Chris Wreh. We have not had a chance to see the best of him yet and it has been a difficult year for him. Manninger was also very good and made some important saves. Unfortunately, he has taken a knock on his knee and there is a slight chance he could miss·the Manchester United match.'

Wenger needn't have worried about the fitness of his young keeper. The Austrian was in the midst of a 13-game run in the first team and was not prepared to relinquish his place. His performances while standing in for Seaman would earn him many plaudits and a place in the Austrian full international squad. Manninger also received the Carling Player of the Month award for March. By the end of the season, the young custodian was left in no doubt about his future at Highbury, with Wenger declaring: 'I see Alex as the future Arsenal goalkeeper. He is an excellent prospect and he is willing to learn and be patient.'

The win against Wimbledon had put a new complexion on the title race. As the Gunners were collecting maximum points at Selhurst, leaders Manchester United were settling for a single point at West Ham. The champions' lead was still significant – nine points – but Arsenal had three games in hand. The game at Old Trafford on 14 March, took on a new significance; if Arsenal could leave Manchester victorious, their fate would be in their own hands. Wenger made a vain effort to play down the billing of the match: 'There is a bit more pressure on United now, but not enough,' declared the Gunners coach. 'Even if we go there and win we will still have to win our

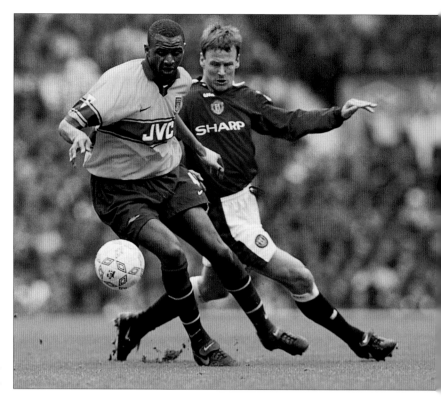

Above: **Patrick Vieira** produced a typically dominating performance at Old Trafford in March 1998. The tough-tackling Frenchman had an inspirational season that would take him back home to play in the World Cup for France.

games in hand to make it worthwhile. But I hear the bookmakers are taking bets again.'

It had seemed for so long that United would romp unchallenged to their third consecutive Premiership title, but as Arsenal closed the gap on the reigning champions, so interest returned to the battle brewing at the top of the table. The match at Old Trafford kicked-off at 11am and was screened live on Sky TV. Wenger had kept faith with Wreh after his scoring start at Selhurst, but after 67 minutes he withdrew the young Liberian and sent on the inhumanly quick Anelka to unsettle the United backline. The young Frenchman had been on the field for just 11 minutes when he rose to flick a header into the path of Marc Overmars. The Dutchman sprinted clear and dispatched the ball between Peter Schmeichel's legs. Thereafter, chances arrived for both teams but a combination of poor finishing and assured goalkeeping saw the score remain at 1–0 to Arsenal.

The leaders now looked decidedly catchable. Arsenal were in form and looked capable of converting their three games in hand into nine points and a place at the top of the table. Wenger remained circumspect: 'Manchester United have a small advantage because we have to take the points available from the games we have in hand and that won't be easy.'

Arsenal's punishing schedule continued with another Cup match against West Ham. Wenger, without Wright, Seaman, and Parlour, must have feared the worst when Dennis Bergkamp was shown the red card by referee Mike Reed after 32 minutes for elbowing Steve Lomas. The Gunners had controlled the game until the Dutchman's dismissal and, though they had been thwarted by French international goalkeeper Bernard Lama, an Arsenal goal seemed

Right: **The Direct wing play** of Marc Overmars was the difference between the Premiership's top two when they met at Old Trafford in March 1998. The Dutchman's goal meant that Arsenal moved to within six pionts of Manchester United with three games in hand.

inevitable. Bergkamp's dismissal visibly lifted the home side as they eagerly, almost desperately, strove forward, relieved that their chief tormentor had departed. The Hammers' security was ill-founded and deep into first-half injury time, Anelka pinched the ball from the boot of Vieira, took aim and curled an exquisite shot into the left-hand corner of Lama's goal.

The second half brought a faultless defensive display from Wenger's team in which both Manninger and Keown were outstanding. Keown's efforts in stopping former Gunners striker John Hartson were Herculean, but there was little the stopper could do as the Welshman bludgeoned his way into the penalty area to force a low drive inside Manninger's near post after 84 minutes. Extra time beckoned. With both teams flagging from an electric-paced 90 minutes, gaps began to appear at both ends, but amazingly the scores remained unaltered. For the second time in the competition, Arsenal faced a shoot-out at an away ground and this time they were without three recognised penalty takers – Ian Wright, Dennis Bergkamp and Lee Dixon. Manninger was once more the Gunners' hero, saving from Eyal Berkovic and watching as Hartson and Samassi Abou placed their kicks against the frame of his goal. For the second time in 1998, Arsenal could celebrate a quarter-final victory at Upton Park. Arsenal's opponents in the semi-final were to be First Division Wolverhampton Wanderers.

There were no Premiership fixtures for the weekend following the Gunners' Cup success in East London and for Dennis Bergkamp the break would be extended to two weeks. Following his clash with Lomas, the striker would miss two Premier League fixtures and the Cup semi-final. Before departing for his enforced absence, Bergkamp went some way to making amends for

his rash challenge by volleying a delicate winner from a Marc Overmars chip at home to Sheffield Wednesday. Arsenal would now visit struggling Bolton Wanderers on the last day of March, knowing that a win would take them to within three points of Manchester United with two games in hand. For Wenger, the urgent issue was his lack of striking options and the Frenchman stated: 'We will miss Dennis Bergkamp and the target for me is to find someone to replace him for Tuesday's game at Bolton.'

Once more Christopher Wreh stepped into the breach, playing alongside fellow rookie Nicolas Anelka. A fourth consecutive Premiership 1–0 win duly arrived courtesy of a sharply taken 20-yarder from the young Liberian on 47 minutes. Fifteen minutes after taking the lead, Martin Keown was dismissed for a second bookable offence and Steve Bould replaced Wreh, but Bolton rarely troubled the experienced Gunners rearguard. United's lead was now just three points, and the confidence of the Arsenal coach was growing. 'The message for Manchester is that we go from game to game and what is important is that we have another away victory. Now, like always, it is down to the most consistent team.' Arsenal's consistency was awesome.

The FA Cup semi-final brought a routine Gunners victory. An early Wreh goal, a tightly locked defence and another win. In truth, Arsenal had played well within themselves at Villa Park and though Wolves had tested them in the second half, the thought remained that if Wenger's team had conceded a rare goal – it would have been their first in five matches – they would merely have gone up the other end and restored their lead.

'We started well and I was only concerned for 20 minutes in the second half. It would not have been so tense had we taken our chances to

Left: **Most of Highbury** felt that David Seaman was irreplacable, but in Alex Manninger they had a more than adequate stand in. The 20-year-old Austrian international was the hero of the FA Cup quarter-final when 10-man Arsenal beat West Ham in a penalty shoot out.

score a second goal but we can't seem to do that at the moment. But, of course, I am happy with one-nil,' said the Arsenal coach after the game.

As spring arrived, Arsenal's run of impressive results continued. Newcastle United, who would provide the Gunner's Cup final opposition come May, arrived at Highbury when Premiership action resumed after a two-week break on 11 April. An Anelka brace and a 30-yard drive from Vieira broke a sequence of five 1–0 victories. A consolation goal for the Geordies represented the first goal conceded in League action since the end of January.

Arsenal were back to their fluent form of early season. The peak came on Easter Monday and the trip to Blackburn to face the last team to beat Arsenal in the League. With Bergkamp back in action the Gunners were untouchable and after 14 minutes the homeside were three goals down. Wave after wave of penetrating Arsenal attacks left the Rovers defence stunned as they chased shadows around Ewood. It took Bergkamp just 75 seconds to open the scoring as he burst onto an Anelka flick to fire home. Two more goals from the impressive Parlour and a clinical finish from Anelka gave Arsenal an unassailable lead. It was to be their best display of the whole season Arsenal were now favourites to win the League, but Wenger would not be coaxed into offering any sound bites that might inspire Alex Ferguson and his team. 'We didn't listen to anyone when people said we didn't have a chance and we won't listen now that we are favourites. The players were happy in the dressing room, but they were not going crazy,' explained the Arsenal coach to the Ewood Park press room.

The top of the Premiership now beckoned. If Manchester United failed to beat Newcastle United at home and Arsenal could defeat Wimbledon at Highbury, the Gunners would top the League for the first time since October. Nothing could stop Arsenal and the Dons were hit for five without reply. A draw at Old Trafford meant the Gunners were top and their single point lead was reinforced by two games

in hand. The win against the Dons saw Arsenal share the goals out amongst five scorers, but the loudest celebration greeted the fourth goal from Petit. The Frenchman had been an immense figure in the Arsenal midfield alongside Vieira and the Highbury faithful took immeasurable pleasure from the former Monaco star's first goal in an Arsenal shirt. The manner of Arsenal's rise to the top had the purists purring. Wenger himself was enjoying his side's expansive approach, declaring: 'Every manager's dream is to score lots of goals and concede none at the other end. So, obviously, I'm delighted. The real joy is to see my players playing at such pace and with so much quality in their passing.'

Another Petit strike, this time against Derby, was enough to leave Arsenal needing just one win from their final three fixtures to clinch the Championship. Between the Wimbledon and Derby games, the Gunners had condemned Barnsley to relegation with a 2–0 win at Oakwell Park courtesy of goals from Dutch duo, Overmars and Bergkamp. He had contributed 19 goals, and many more assists, in his 39 games but these impressive statistics fail to reveal the importance of his contribution. Bergkamp had quite simply been breathtaking. He had scored goals which left his opponents open-mouthed in disbelief, his passing was intuitive and his ball skills fast and faultless. Small wonder that both the football writers and Bergkamp's fellow pro-fessionals voted him their player of the season. The Gunners' achievements were appreciated throughout football. Petit followed up Mann-inger's Player of the Month award for March by taking the prize for April and Wenger, unsurprisingly, was named Manager of the Season.

Awards meant little, however, if the Gunners failed to deliver the major silverware that was in their grasp at the beginning of May. Arsenal's final two League games of the season were away, so if they were to celebrate with their home fans they would need to defeat relegation-threatened Everton. In a match which the visitors could ill afford to lose, Everton manager Howard Kendall named a defensive line-up – including Croatian defender Slaven Bilic in midfield. After just six minutes his plans were in tatters, as Bilic headed an own-goal to give Arsenal the lead. On 28 minutes Arsenal had a crucial second goal, Marc Overmars accelerating past three Everton defenders before sliding the ball underneath the advancing Thomas Myrhe. The only black spot in an Arsenal-dominated first half was an injury to Petit, who was forced out of the game after an ugly challenge from Don Hutchison. Overmars added a third goal, but the celebrations leapt into overdrive in the final minute when skipper Tony Adams latched onto a pass from Steve Bould to crash home his third goal of the season.

After seven years, the title had returned to the capital. The importance of the occasion was not lost on Wenger, who declared: 'This is my greatest ever achievement as a manager and I am proud for the club, my staff, the players

Above: **Captain Tony Adams** celebrates the goal that brings the title back to Highbury. His was the last in a 4–0 victory over Everton on 3 May that made the Gunners untouchable at the top of the table. Everton were never in the match as imperious Arsenal strode to the Championship through two goals from Overmars and a Slaven Bilic own goal. Arsenal's form during the second half of the season was formidable and the victory over Everton was their tenth successive League win.

before driving a shot into the corner of Given's goal. It may not have provided the drama of Charlie George's late winner against Liverpool in 1971, but Anelka's goal cued celebrations of similar proportions throughout North London.

After the game even the normally restrained Wenger was in animated mood. 'The Championship was our main aim,' said the Highbury boss, 'but it would have been terrible to have lost at Wembley because we really wanted the FA Cup too. In fact, we were trying to win more than the FA Cup – we were trying to win the Double. This club is over 100 years old but we have only won the Double once and that shows how remarkable this achievement has been.

'I would love to stay at Arsenal because I am happy in England and happy at Highbury. Yes, of course I will sign a new contract if I am offered one with the freedom I have at the club.

'The players are the important ones today though – who would have thought Wreh and Anelka would have been our strikers at Wembley when the season started? We have proved some people wrong, but that was not our aim – we just wanted to do our best and take the consequences of that, which have been very satisfying.'

Arsenal's second Double had arrived over 112 years after that Christmas Day in 1886 when 15 men met in the Royal Oak, next to Woolwich Arsenal Station, and decided that they should take their kickabouts seriously.

Memories that there ever was such a club south of the river have faded now. No more than a few can be left alive who remember standing on the long-gone terraces of Plumstead or the original Spion Kop at the Manor Ground, and who witnessed the woe-begone Woolwich Arsenal of that disastrous season in 1913. No brick or pillar of the ground remains, no film exists of those games. That sadness is perhaps what a history must also reflect. It is not all Wembley, champagne at the Café Royal and 'We're proud to say that name.'

When Highbury is still and the underground closed, it still echoes memories of the thousands of people who have walked up those dank, ill-lit Edwardian tunnels in the last eight decades. Perhaps 15,000 every match Saturday for seventy years? That's around 30 million, more than half the population of Great Britain. what dreams did they have, why did they come, what drew them to Gillespie Road, what did Arsenal mean to each and every one of them?

A quiet day is a good time to think of Bastin, of James, of Drake, of Jack, of Hapgood and Male; and, more recently, of a happier, demobbed and optimistic generation of 60,000 who would come every other week to see Reg Lewis and Ronnie Rooke, the immortal Joe Mercer and the golden 'Brylcreem Boy' Denis Compton, to live the two Championships and Cup finals of Tom Whittaker's tragically brief Highbury reign.

Think of the intensity, of the hopes and fears, imagine if you can the mood on 1 May 1971, the last home game of the Double season. The tension was unbearable, nothing but a win was

and the supporters. We have shown great spirit all season and our last goal typified that as Steve Bould sent Adams through. They have been great players for Arsenal. I am surprised but delighted that we have won the title so soon but this team can get better.'

Arsenal now had a glorious chance to complete their second League and FA Cup Double and emulate Bertie Mee's team of 1970–71. Before the Cup clash with Kenny Dalglish's Newcastle United, Wenger's team faced two away matches at Liverpool and Everton. Having won 10 consecutive League games to clinch the title, Arsenal could be forgiven for relaxing and recording two defeats. These games were no form guide for the showpiece final at Wembley on 16 May.

At Wembley, Wenger employed his tried and tested formula. A back four of Dixon, Winterburn, Adams and Keown was reinforced by the energetic presence of Petit and Vieira in midfield. The flanks were manned by Overmars and Parlour who were to supply the bulk of service to two strikers, on this occasion, Wreh and Anelka. Wenger's game plan got off to a stunning start with Overmars and Parlour both carving out good opportunities for Anelka, but each time the teenager spurned the chance. His moment would come, but before Anelka could redeem himself, Overmars acted. The Dutchman latched onto a Petit chip to race clear of the Newcastle defence and place the ball between Shay Given's legs and into the goal.

Newcastle responded and Seaman was forced into action by a Ketsbaia effort in the first half. After the interval the Magpies had their best chance of the match when Martin Keown's mistake, on 63 minutes, gave Alan Shearer a clear sight of goal. The England marksman struck a post and five minutes later Anelka collected a Parlour pass, and galloped forward

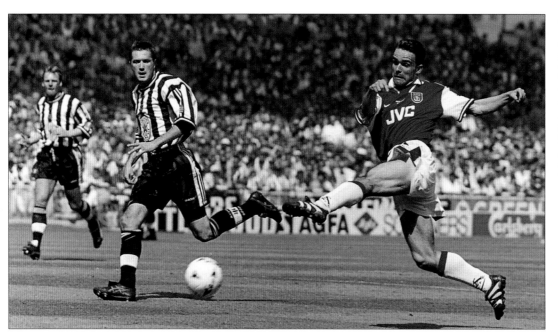

conceivable, and yet Arsenal's opponents, ironically, were to be Stoke City, just a month after the dramas of the Hillsborough semi-final. It would be easy to go on, but each generation has its own memories. The next will hopefully have its own, just as glorious. It is the great-grandchildren of the young men who cheered Jack Lambert and Joe Hulme who are already pinning pictures of Tony Adams and Ian Wright on their bedroom walls.

Arsenal are different from any other football club. Why? Because the history of English football can be told through their story, because they did dominate a crucial generation, historically a vital decade, because they are Herbert Chapman's legacy, because they did, if unexpectedly, win the Double that established their place in the élite.

So if you can spare the time to think of Highbury, still and stolid, a repository of memories rather than cheers on the quietest of days. Think of 24 April 1915, of that same Nottingham Forest who donated the red shirts a century ago, coming to Highbury to lose a Second Division game 7-0, the last match fifth-placed Arsenal ever played outside top company. Think of a new, shiny Wembley, almost exactly fifteen years to the day later, on 26 April 1930, the moment when the pendulum greatly swung from north to south, the day Arsenal first won the FA Cup in a game which still defines thirty years of English football, the day the Graf Zeppelin sat silently above the pitch. Think of forty years further on, of 27 March 1971 at far away Hillsborough, of a clock which read 4.44pm, of the dreams of a Double which paused an instant from consignment to the dustbin of football history. That was perhaps the most unforgettable moment of all, the perfect illustration that football can be, and should be, about the emotion such set-piece dramas can

evoke. Think what we would say now about the game had Frank McLintock's header hit the post rather than John Mahoney's hand, or if Gordon Banks had guessed right about Peter Storey's penalty. Think, at the end, of the glorious Double of 1997-98, when Arsenal won the Championship after being so far behind that the bookmakers had ceased betting on the result. Think about Michael Thomas and Bruce Grobbelaar. No matter how long we watch League football we will never live such a moment again.

It is one of the joys of the game that we can only wait and see. If the next hundred years can bring just moments like the last few seconds at Anfield in 1989, or the joy of achieving the second Double from such an impromising position in 1998, then we will all have much to justify our enthusiasm and anticipation.

Statistics: Pages 201 to 237 contain a complete record of every game played by Arsenal from 1886 to 1998, excluding the War years. From 1970–71 (the first Double season), to 1997–98, (the second), every game also includes a full team listing.

206

·CHAPTER 11·

The Arsenal Record Match by Match

SEASON 1886-1887
FRIENDLIES

11 Dec	Eastern W	A	W	6-0
8 Jan	Erith	H	W	6-1
15 Jan	Alexandria U	H	W	11-0
22 Jan	Eastern W	H	W	1-0
29 Jan	Erith	A	W	3-2
5 Feb	Millwall Rov	A	L	0-4
12 Feb	Alexandria U	A	W	6-0
26 Feb	2nd Rifle Brigade	H	D	0-0
12 Mar	Millwall Rov	H	W	3-0
26 Mar	2nd Rifle Brigade	A	L	0-1

	P	W	L	D	F:A
Arsenal	10	7	2	1	36:8

SEASON 1887-1888
FRIENDLIES

30 Sep	Alexandria U	H	W	5-1
15 Oct	Clapton Pilgrims		D	2-2
22 Oct	St Lukes			
5 Nov	Grange Institute		W	4-0
12 Nov	Iona Deptford		D	1-1
19 Nov	Tottenham H	A	L	1-2
26 Nov	Millwall Rov	A	L	0-3
2 Dec	Grange Park	H		
10 Dec	Brixton Rangers	H	L	1-2
16 Dec	Shrewsbury Park		W	4-0
31 Dec	Forest Gate Alliance	A	L	1-2
14 Jan	Iona Deptford	A	W	3-2
28 Jan	Champion Hill		W	6-0
3 Feb	Tottenham H	H	W	6-2
11 Feb	Millwall Rov	H	D	3-3
17 Feb	Erith		W	2-1
24 Feb	Forest Gate Alliance	H	D	1-1
2 Mar	Grange Institute		W	2-1
9 Mar	Brixton Ran		W	9-3
16 Mar	Ascham		W	5-0
30 Mar	Millwall Rov	H	W	3-0
6 Apr	Alexandria U	A	W	3-1

London Senior Cup

8 Oct	Grove House	H	W	3-1
29 Oct	Barnes		L	0-4

Junior Matches

19 Nov	Woolwich Pupils & Teachers	H	W	1-0
26 Nov	Erith	A	L	0-1
24 Feb	Thistle		L	1-2

	P	W	L	D	F:A
Arsenal	24	14	6	4	66:33

SEASON 1888-1889
FRIENDLIES

15 Sep	London Scottish		D	3-3
22 Sep	Tottenham H		L	0-1
29 Sep	Old St Pauls		W	7-3
6 Oct	Grove House		W	2-0
13 Oct	London Scottish		W	4-0
20 Oct	2nd Rifle Brigade		L	1-2
27 Oct	Brixton Ran		L	1-3
10 Nov	Millwall Rov			
17 Nov	St Lukes		D	1-1
1 Dec	Phoneix		D	0-0
22 Dec	St Brides			
5 Jan	Vulcan		D	1-1
12 Jan	Unity		D	0-0
26 Jan	St Lukes			
2 Feb	Ilford		L	1-2
16 Feb	Millwall Rov			
23 Feb	Ilford		L	0-1
2 Mar	London Caledonians		L	1-2
9 Mar	Tottenham H		W	1-0
16 Mar	South Eastern Ran		L	1-2
23 Mar	Royal Artillery		W	9-0
30 Mar	2nd Rifle Brigade		W	2-0
1 Apr	2nd Rifle Brigade		W	6-1
6 Apr	Old St Pauls		W	1-0
13 Apr	Millwall Rov		W	3-0
19 Apr	Boston T		L	1-4
20 Apr	Spartan Rov		W	6-0
23 Apr	Scots Guards		W	7-2
27 Apr	London Caledonians		L	0-1

London Association Cup

3 Nov	Phoneix		W	3-0
24 Nov	Dulwich		W	4-2
8 Dec	Old St Pauls		W	3-1
19 Jan	Clapton (Semi-Final)		L	0-2

Kent County Challenge Cup

10 Nov	Horton Kirby		W	6-2
29 Dec	Iona		W	5-1
9 Feb	Gravesend		D	3-3*

*Arsenal disqualified for refusing to play extra time.

	P	W	L	D	F:A
Arsenal	32	16	10	6	83:40

SEASON 1889-1890
FRIENDLIES

7 Sep	London Caledonians	H	D	2-2
14 Sep	Casuals	H	W	6-0
21 Sep	Tottenham H	H	W	10-1
28 Sep	Unity	H	W	8-0
19 Oct	St Old Marks College	A	W	2-1
30 Nov	Marlow	A	L	0-2
21 Dec	Ilford	A	W	2-0
25 Dec	Preston Hornets	H	W	5-0
26 Dec	Chatham	A	D	2-2
27 Dec	Reading T	H	W	5-1
4 Jan	Windsor Phoenix	H	W	3-1
18 Jan	Old Harrovians	H	W	2-1
25 Jan	Foxes	H	W	7-2
8 Feb	Chiswick Park	H	D	1-1
1 Mar	Birmingham St George	H	L	1-4
15 Mar	Ilford	A	W	4-1
28 Mar	Clapton	A	L	0-2
31 Mar	W. H. Loraine XI	H	W	3-1
7 Apr	1st Lincs. Regt.	H	W	2-1
12 Apr	Marlow	H	W	3-1
19 Apr	Chatham	H	W	1-0
26 Apr	Clapton	H	W	6-1
3 May	London Cal/Clapton Comb	H	W	3-2
10 May	Millwall Athletic	A	D	3-3

FA Cup

5 Oct	Lyndhurst (Q1)	H	W	11-0
26 Oct	Thorpe (Q2)	A	D	2-2*
16 Nov	Crusaders (Q3)	H	W	5-2
7 Dec	Swifts (Q4)	H	L	1-5

*Thorpe withdrew

London Cup

2 Nov	Unity	H	W	4-1
23 Nov	Foxes	H	W	4-1
14 Dec	St Martins Ath	H	W	6-0
11 Jan	London Caledonians	H	W	3-1
8 Mar	Old Westminster (Final)		L	0-1

London Charity Cup

1 Feb	Marlow	H	W	4-1
22 Feb	2nd Batt Scots Guards	H	W	3-0
5 Apr	Old Westminster (Final)	H	W	3-1

Kent Senior Cup

12 Oct	5th Northern Fusiliers	H	W	6-1
9 Nov	West Kent	H	W	10-1
14 Dec	Gravesend	H	W	7-2
15 Feb	Chatham	H	W	5-0
22 Mar	Thanet W (Final)		W	3-0

Six-a-Side Competition
Run by National Physical Recreation Society at Agricultural Hall

31 May	London Caledonians		W	15-7

	P	W	L	D	F:A
Arsenal	41	31	5	5	158:49

SEASON 1890-1891
FRIENDLIES

6 Sep	93rd Highlanders	H	D	1-1
13 Sep	Casuals	H	W	5-4
20 Sep	Ilford	H	W	6-0
27 Sep	London Caledonians	H	W	3-1
4 Oct	Chiswick Park	A	W	4-0
11 Oct	93rd Highlanders	H	W	4-1
18 Oct	Old St Marks	A	W	4-0
25 Oct	St Bartholomews Hospital	H	W	1-0
1 Nov	South Shore (Blackpool)	H	D	2-2
8 Nov	Ilford	A	W	3-0
15 Nov	Clapton	A	L	1-2
22 Nov	Gainsborough Trinity	H	W	2-1
1 Dec	Cambridge Univ	H	W	5-1
6 Dec	Casuals	H	D	0-0
24 Jan	Millwall Athletic	A	W	1-0
26 Jan	Everton	H	L	0-5
7 Feb	St Bartholomews Hospital	H	W	5-4
14 Mar	Old Harrovians	H	W	5-1
21 Mar	Sheffield U	H	D	1-1
27 Mar	Highland Light Infantry	H	W	3-1
28 Mar	Old Harrovians	H	W	5-0
30 Mar	Heart of Midlothians	H	L	1-5
31 Mar	Nottingham F	H	L	0-5
18 Apr	Clapton	H	W	3-1
25 Apr	Sunderland	H	L	1-3
30 Apr	London Caledonians	H	D	1-1
2 May	1st Highland Light Infantry	H	W	5-1
3 Jan	London Caledonians			(abandoned)

FA Cup

17 Jan	Derby Co (1)	H	L	1-2

London Cup

13 Dec	Old Westminster	A	W	4-1
31 Jan	Old Westminster	A	L	4-5
21 Feb	Casuals	H	W	3-2
28 Feb	Clapton	A	W	3-2
7 Mar	St Barts Hosp (Final)		W	6-0

London Charity Cup

14 Feb	Crusaders	H	W	1-0
4 Apr	Old Carthusians	A	D	1-1
8 Apr	Old Carthusians	A	D	2-2
11 Apr	Old Carthusians	A	L	1-2

	P	W	L	D	F:A
Arsenal	37	22	8	7	98:58

SEASON 1891-1892
FRIENDLIES

5 Sep	Sheffield U	H	L	0-2
12 Sep	Casuals	H	W	2-1
19 Sep	Gainsborough Trinity	H	L	1-4
26 Sep	W B A	H	D	1-1
3 Oct	St George Birmingham	H	L	1-5
8 Oct	Royal Engineers	H	W	8-0
10 Oct	Crusaders	H	W	4-1
17 Oct	Bootle	A	D	2-2
19 Oct	Sheffield Wed	H	L	1-8
24 Oct	Long Eaton Rangers	H	W	3-1
29 Oct	Royal Artillery	H	W	10-0
31 Oct	Clapton	A	W	7-0
5 Nov	Notts Co	A	L	3-4
7 Nov	London Caledonians	A	W	4-3
12 Nov	Erith	H	W	7-0
14 Nov	Cambridge University	H	W	5-1
19 Nov	Woolwich League	H	W	6-1
21 Nov	St Bartholomews Hospital	H	W	9-0
23 Nov	2nd Scots Guards	H	W	6-0
28 Nov	Canadians	H	D	1-1
30 Nov	Sheffield W	A	L	1-5
3 Dec	Canadians	H	W	4-0
5 Dec	Lincoln C	H	W	3-1
10 Dec	2nd Royal West Kent Reg	H	L	1-2
12 Dec	Chiswick Park	H	W	5-1
19 Dec	Preston N E	H	L	0-3
25 Dec	Sheffield U	A	D	3-3
26 Dec	1st Lincolnshire Reg	H	W	6-0
2 Jan	Cowlairs (Glasgow)	H	L	1-2
7 Jan	City Ramblers	H	W	3-0
9 Jan	Crusaders	H	W	4-1
21 Jan	Windsor Phoenix	H	W	3-1
23 Jan	Grimsby T	H	W	4-1
30 Jan	Burton W	H	W	3-1
4 Feb	Sheffield U	H	L	1-4
6 Feb	Cambridge University	H	W	2-1
13 Feb	Chatham	H	W	3-2
20 Feb	Burton Swifts	H	W	3-1
25 Feb	Windsor Phoenix	A	W	5-0
27 Feb	Derby Co	H	L	3-4
3 Mar	Borough Road College	H	W	5-1
5 Mar	Wolverhampton W	H	L	1-4
10 Mar	Casuals	H	W	3-1
12 Mar	Marlow	A	W	5-2
14 Mar	3rd Lanark Rovers	H	L	0-1
19 Mar	Highland Light Infantry	H	W	3-2
22 Mar	Preston N E	H	D	3-3
26 Mar	Everton	H	D	2-2
31 Mar	Notts Co	H	L	2-4
2 Apr	Chatham	H	W	5-3
9 Apr	South Shore Blackpool	H	D	1-1
15 Apr	Small Heath	H	L	1-2
16 Apr	Crewe Alexandra	H	W	2-1
18 Apr	Bootle	H	D	1-1
23 Apr	Clapton	H	W	4-1
26 Apr	Bolton W	H	W	3-2
30 Apr	Glasgow Ran	H	L	2-3

FA Cup

16 Jan	Small Heath (1)		L	1-5

	P	W	L	D	F:A
Arsenal	58	33	17	8	183:107

SEASON 1892-1893
FRIENDLIES

2 Sep	Highland Light Infantry		W	9-0
7 Sep	Gainsborough T		W	4-2
8 Sep	Scots Guards		W	5-1
10 Sep	Casuals		W	4-0
12 Sep	Sheffield U	A	L	0-1
16 Sep	Darlington		W	3-2
24 Sep	Crusaders		W	4-0
1 Oct	Marlow		W	4-0
6 Oct	3rd West Kent Rangers		W	3-0
8 Oct	Clapton		W	4-1
20 Oct	Sheffield U	H	W	1-0
22 Oct	Staffordshire Reg		W	1-0
27 Oct	Oxford University		L	0-4
5 Nov	Lincoln C	H	W	4-0
7 Nov	Fleetwood Rangers		L	1-2
12 Nov	Cambridge University		D	6-6
14 Nov	Sunderland	H	L	0-4
23 Nov	Ipswich T		W	5-0
25 Nov	Norfolk County		W	4-1
26 Nov	Clapton		W	5-0
3 Dec	W B A	H	W	3-1
12 Dec	Mr Armitage XI		W	3-1
17 Dec	Nottingham F	H	L	2-3
23 Dec	Leith Athletic	H	W	1-0
25 Dec	Burslem P V		L	1-3
26 Dec	Stockton		W	1-0
27 Dec	Blackpool	H	D	1-1
2 Jan	Glasgow Thistle	H	L	1-2
7 Jan	Middlesbrough		L	0-2
11 Jan	Sussex Martelos		W	2-0
12 Jan	Brighton		W	2-0
14 Jan	Wolverhampton W	H	L	1-3
25 Jan	Oxford University		L	0-1
28 Jan	Chatham		L	1-3
31 Jan	1st Batt Sherwood Foresters		W	3-0
3 Feb	Casuals		W	4-1
6 Feb	Royal Lancaster Regiment		W	2-0
9 Feb	Cambridge University		L	2-4
11 Feb	Small Heath	H	W	3-1
13 Feb	3rd Lanark	H	W	3-0
18 Feb	Millwall		W	5-0
25 Feb	Walsall Town Swifts	H	W	4-0
27 Feb	Notts Greenhalgh		L	1-3
3 Mar	Middlesbrough		L	0-2
11 Mar	Dumbarton	H	W	3-1
13 Mar	Aston Villa	H	L	0-1
18 Mar	Middlesbrough		W	4-2
25 Mar	Millwall		W	1-0
31 Mar	Middlesbrough		W	4-1
1 Apr	Accrington St	H	W	3-1
3 Apr	Grimsby T	H	L	3-5
8 Apr	Casuals		W	2-0
15 Apr	Crusaders		W	3-0
22 Apr	Derby Co	H	D	0-0
24 Apr	London Welsh		W	4-0
26 Apr	Sevenoaks		W	11-0
29 Apr	Stoke	H	L	0-1

FA Cup

15 Oct	Highland Light Infantry (Q1)	H	W	3-0
29 Oct	City Ramblers (Q2)	H	W	10-1
19 Nov	Millwall (Q3)	H	W	3-2
10 Dec	Clapton (Q4)	H	W	5-0
21 Jan	Sunderland (1)	A	L	0-6

	P	W	L	D	F:A
Arsenal	62	41	18	3	172:76

SEASON 1893-1894
FOOTBALL LEAGUE (DIVISION 2)

2 Sep	Newcastle U	H	D	2-2
9 Sep	Notts Co	A	L	2-3
11 Sep	Walsall	H	W	4-0
25 Sep	Grimsby T	H	W	3-1
30 Sep	Newcastle U	A	L	0-6
21 Oct	Small Heath	A	L	1-4
28 Oct	Liverpool	H	L	0-5
11 Nov	Aidwick	H	W	1-0
13 Nov	Rotherham	H	W	3-0
18 Nov	Burton Swifts	A	L	2-6
9 Dec	Northwick Victoria	A	D	2-2
25 Dec	Burslem	H	W	4-1
26 Dec	Grimsby T	A	L	1-3
30 Dec	Ardwick	A	W	1-0
1 Jan	Liverpool	A	L	0-2
6 Jan	Burslem	A	L	1-2
3 Feb	Lincoln C	A	L	0-3
6 Feb	Rotherham	A	D	1-1
10 Feb	Crewe Alexandra	H	W	3-2
12 Feb	Walsall	A	W	2-1
17 Feb	Lincoln C	H	W	4-0
24 Feb	Middlesbrough Ironopolis	A	W	6-3
3 Mar	Crewe Alexandra	A	D	0-0
10 Mar	Middlesbrough Ironopolis	H	W	1-0
23 Mar	Northwich Victoria	H	W	6-0
24 Mar	Notts Co	H	L	1-2
31 Mar	Small Heath	H	L	1-4
14 Apr	Burton Swifts	H	L	0-2

FA Cup

14 Oct	Ashford University (Q1)	H	W	12-0
4 Nov	Clapton (Q2)	H	W	6-2
25 Nov	Millwall (Q3)	H	W	2-0
16 Dec	2nd Scots Guards (Q4)	A	W	2-1
27 Jan	Sheffield W (1)	H	L	1-2

Friendlies

4 Sep	Doncaster Rov		W	4-1
16 Sep	Chatham		W	5-0
23 Sep	Middlesbrough	H	W	3-1
7 Oct	Casuals		W	5-1
9 Oct	Sunderland	H	L	1-4
12 Oct	London Caledonians		W	10-3
23 Oct	Mr Roston Bourkes XI		W	4-3
30 Oct	Wolverhampton W	H	W	1-0
30 Nov	London Caledonians		D	1-1
2 Dec	W B A	A	W	5-0
11 Dec	Preston N E		D	1-1
23 Dec	Crusaders		W	7-0
13 Jan	Accrington Stanley		W	2-0
15 Jan	Aston Villa	H	L	1-3
20 Jan	Chatham		W	4-0
29 Jan	Blackpool		W	5-2
1 Mar	London Caledonians		W	1-0
5 Mar	Luton T		W	2-0
12 Mar	Sheffield U	A	W	2-0
17 Mar	Millwall		D	2-2
26 Mar	St Mirren		L	1-3
2 Apr	Nottingham F	H	L	1-3
7 Apr	Millwall		W	4-1
9 Apr	Sheffield U	H	L	0-1
11 Apr	New Brompton		W	4-1
12 Apr	Westerham District XI		W	6-3
16 Apr	Luton T		D	3-3
21 Apr	Burnley	H	W	2-0
25 Apr	Corinthians	A	L	3-4
28 Apr	Stoke	H	D	3-3

Position in Football League Table

	P	W	L	D	F:A	Pts	
Liverpool	28	22	0	6	77:18	50	1st
Arsenal	28	12	12	4	52:55	28	9th

SEASON 1894-1895
FOOTBALL LEAGUE (DIVISION 2)

1 Sep	Lincoln C	A	L	2-5
10 Sep	Grimsby T	H	L	1-3
15 Sep	Burton Swifts	A	L	0-3
22 Sep	Bury	H	W	4-2
29 Sep	Manchester C	H	W	4-2
6 Oct	Lincoln C	H	W	5-2
13 Oct	Newton Heath	A	D	3-3
20 Oct	Rotherham	A	W	2-1
27 Oct	Notts Co	A	D	2-2
3 Nov	Notts Co	H	W	2-1
10 Nov	Walsall	A	L	1-4
24 Nov	Newcastle U	A	W	4-2
8 Dec	Darwen	H	W	4-0
15 Dec	Manchester C	A	L	1-4
25 Dec	Burslem Port Vale	H	W	7-0
26 Dec	Grimsby T	A	L	2-4
1 Jan	Darwen	A	L	1-3
7 Jan	Leicester Fosse	A	L	1-3
12 Jan	Newcastle U	H	W	3-2
19 Jan	Burslem P V	A	W	1-0
26 Jan	Burton Wanderers	H	D	1-1
9 Feb	Rotherham	H	D	1-1
23 Feb	Burton Swifts	H	W	3-0
2 Mar	Bury	A	L	0-2
9 Mar	Leicester Fosse	H	D	3-3
23 Mar	Crewe Alexandra	A	D	0-0
30 Mar	Newton Heath	H	W	3-2
6 Apr	Crewe Alexandra	H	W	7-0
12 Apr	Walsall	H	W	6-1
20 Apr	Burton W	A	L	1-2

FA Cup

2 Feb	Bolton W (1)	A	L	0-1

Friendlies

3 Sep	Nottingham F	H	W	3-2
8 Sep	Fleetwood Rovers		W	4-0
17 Sep	W B A		L	0-1
24 Sep	Renton		W	6-1
4 Oct	Casuals		W	8-0
15 Oct	Sunderland	H	W	2-1
29 Oct	Luton T		W	5-0
12 Nov	R. Bourkes XI		W	6-2
17 Nov	Casuals		W	4-1
21 Nov	Marlow		W	4-2
1 Dec	Stoke C	H	W	3-1
3 Dec	St Bernards	H	L	1-2
24 Dec	New Brompton		L	0-5
29 Dec	Dresden University		W	1-0
5 Jan	Sheppey University		W	6-1
11 Feb	Luton T		W	2-1
16 Feb	Chatham		W	6-0
25 Feb	Liverpool	H	W	4-3
6 Mar	Eastbourne		W	5-1
13 Mar	Bromley & District		W	4-1
16 Mar	Gainsborough Trinity	H	W	2-0
20 Mar	Home Park Plymouth		W	2-1
21 Mar	Weymouth		W	5-0
25 Mar	Millwall	H	D	1-1
1 Apr	Blackburn Rov	H	D	2-2
8 Apr	Millwall	A	D	0-0
13 Apr	Dumbarton		W	5-1
15 Apr	Small Heath	H	L	3-4
25 Apr	Royal Ordnance		L	0-1
27 Apr	Millwall	A	W	3-1
30 Apr	Grimsby T		L	0-2

Position in Football League Table

	P	W	L	D	F:A	Pts	
Bury	30	23	5	2	78:33	48	1st
Arsenal	30	14	10	6	75:58	34	8th

SEASON 1895-1896
FOOTBALL LEAGUE (DIVISION 2)

2 Sep	Grimsby T	H	W	3-1
7 Sep	Manchester C	H	L	0-1
14 Sep	Lincoln C	A	D	1-1
21 Sep	Lincoln C	H	W	4-0
28 Sep	Manchester C	A	L	0-1
5 Oct	Rotherham	H	W	5-0
12 Oct	Burton W	H	W	3-0
19 Oct	Burton Swifts	H	W	5-0
26 Oct	Rotherham	A	L	0-3
2 Nov	Notts Co	A	W	4-3
9 Nov	Newton Heath	H	W	2-1
16 Nov	Liverpool	H	L	0-2
30 Nov	Newton Heath	A	L	1-5
7 Dec	Leicester Fosse	H	D	1-1
14 Dec	Burton W	A	L	1-4
21 Dec	Burton Swifts	A	L	2-3
23 Dec	Crewe Alexandra	A	W	1-0
25 Dec	Burslem Port Vale	H	W	2-1
4 Jan	Loughborough	H	W	6-0
11 Jan	Liverpool	A	L	0-3
18 Jan	Newcastle U	A	L	1-3
25 Jan	Leicester Fosse	A	L	0-1
15 Feb	Burslem Port Vale	A	W	2-0
29 Feb	Loughborough	A	L	1-2
7 Mar	Notts Co	H	W	2-0
14 Mar	Darwen	A	D	1-1
21 Mar	Crewe Alexandra	H	W	7-0
4 Apr	Grimsby T	A	D	1-1
6 Apr	Newcastle U	H	W	2-1
18 Apr	Darwen	H	L	1-3

FA Cup

2 Feb	Burnley (1)	A	L	1-6

Friendlies

9 Sep	Millwall	A	W	3-1
23 Sep	Sheffield W	H	W	2-1
14 Oct	Everton	H	L	0-2
4 Nov	Royal Ordnance		W	3-1
21 Nov	Casuals		W	3-0
23 Nov	Barnsley St Peters		W	4-1
9 Dec	Sunderland	H	L	1-2
26 Dec	Cliftonville	H	W	10-1
28 Dec	Darlington		W	6-2
1 Jan	Hastings		W	12-0
20 Jan	Cambridge University	H	W	7-1
10 Feb	Royal Ordnance		W	6-0
22 Feb	Stirlingshire		W	5-0
24 Feb	Newton Heath	H	W	6-1
2 Mar	Casuals		W	4-1
16 Mar	Tottenham H		L	1-3
23 Mar	Sheffield U	H	W	3-1
26 Mar	Tottenham H		W	3-1
28 Mar	Millwall	A	W	3-1
2 Apr	Stockton		W	2-0
3 Apr	Dundee		W	3-1
7 Apr	Gravesend		W	4-0
11 Apr	Millwall	H	D	2-2

13 Apr	Everton	H	W	2-1
20 Apr	Whittaker XI		W	3-2
25 Apr	Luton T	H	W	5-2
27 Apr	Luton T	A	L	0-2
29 Apr	Chatham		W	1-0
30 Apr	Tottenham H		L	2-3

Position in Football League Table

	P	W	L	D	F:A	Pts	
Liverpool	30	22	6	2	106:32	46	1st
Arsenal	30	14	12	4	59:42	32	7th

SEASON 1896-1897
FOOTBALL LEAGUE (DIVISION 2)

5 Sep	Manchester C	A	D	1-1
12 Sep	Walsall	H	D	1-1
14 Sep	Burton Wanderers	A	W	3-0
19 Sep	Loughborough	H	W	2-0
26 Sep	Notts Co	H	L	2-3
12 Oct	Burton Wanderers	H	W	3-0
17 Oct	Walsall	A	L	3-5
24 Oct	Gainsborough	H	W	6-1
7 Nov	Notts Co	A	L	4-7
14 Nov	Small Heath	A	L	2-5
28 Nov	Grimsby T	H	W	4-2
5 Dec	Lincoln C	A	W	3-2
12 Dec	Loughborough	A	L	0-8
19 Dec,	Blackpool	H	W	4-2
25 Dec	Lincoln C	H	W	6-2
26 Dec	Gainsborough	A	L	1-4
1 Jan	Darwen	A	L	1-4
4 Jan	Blackpool	A	D	1-1
23 Jan	Newcastle U	A	L	0-2
13 Feb	Leicester Fosse	A	L	3-6
20 Feb	Burton Swifts	H	W	3-0
13 Mar	Burton Swifts	A	W	2-1
22 Mar	Newton Heath	A	D	1-1
29 Mar	Small Heath	H	L	2-3
3 Apr	Newton Heath	H	L	0-2
8 Apr	Grimsby T	A	L	1-3
16 Apr	Newcastle U	H	W	5-1
17 Apr	Leicester Fosse	H	W	2-1
19 Apr	Darwen	H	W	1-0
28 Apr	Manchester C	H	L	1-2

FA Cup

12 Dec	Leyton (Q)	H	W	5-2
2 Jan	Chatham (Q)	H	W	4-0
16 Jan	Millwall (Q)	A	L	2-4

United League

7 Sep	Rushden		W	3-2
3 Oct	Luton T		D	2-2
5 Oct	Rushden		L	3-5
19 Oct	Wellingborough		W	2-1
2 Nov	Kettering		D	1-1
9 Nov	Tottenham H		W	2-1
23 Nov	Kettering		W	1-0
30 Nov	Wellingborough		L	1-4
9 Jan	Loughborough		W	5-3
25 Feb	Tottenham H		D	2-2
27 Feb	Millwall		W	3-1
20 Mar	Luton T		L	2-5
7 Apr	Loughborough		L	0-4
24 Apr	Millwall		L	1-3

Friendlies

1 Sep	Rossendale		W	4-0
10 Sep	Millwall		W	2-1
10 Oct	Millwall		L	1-5
26 Oct	Luton		L	1-3
31 Oct	Clyde		L	2-3
21 Nov	Millwall		D	2-2
7 Dec	Aston Villa		L	1-3
30 Jan	Ilkeston		W	7-0
8 Feb	Luton		W	5-1
15 Feb	Celtic		L	4-5
1 Mar	Reading		W	6-2
6 Mar	Casuals		L	3-5
10 Mar	Reading		W	2-1
15 Mar	St Mary's, Southampton		W	2-1
27 Mar	Nottingham F		W	1-0
20 Apr	Norfolk		L	3-4
26 Apr	Sheffield U		D	1-1

Position in Football League Table

	P	W	L	D	F:A	Pts	
Notts Co	30	19	7	4	92:43	42	1st
Arsenal	30	13	13	4	68:70	30	10th

Position in United League Table

	P	W	L	D	F:A	Pts	
Millwall	14	11	2	1	43:22	23	1st
Arsenal	14	6	5	3	28:34	15	3rd

SEASON 1897-1898
FOOTBALL LEAGUE (DIVISION 2)

1 Sep	Grimsby T	H	W	4-1
4 Sep	Newcastle U	A	L	1-4
6 Sep	Burnley	A	L	0-5
1 Sep	Lincoln C	H	D	2-2
8 Sep	Gainsborough	H	W	4-0
5 Sep	Manchester C	A	L	1-4
2 Oct	Luton T	A	W	2-0
9 Oct	Luton T	H	W	3-0
6 Oct	Newcastle U	H	D	0-0
23 Oct	Leicester Fosse	H	L	0-3
6 Nov	Walsall	A	L	2-3
3 Nov	Walsall	H	W	4-0
7 Nov	Blackpool	H	W	2-1
4 Dec	Leicester Fosse	A	L	1-2
8 Dec	Loughborough	A	W	3-1
27 Dec	Lincoln C	A	W	3-2
1 Jan	Blackpool	A	D	3-3
8 Jan	Newton Heath	H	W	5-1
15 Jan	Burton Swifts	A	W	2-1
5 Feb	Manchester C	H	D	2-2
12 Feb	Grimsby T	A	W	4-1
26 Feb	Newton Heath	A	L	1-5
5 Mar	Small Heath	H	W	4-2
12 Mar	Darwen	A	W	4-1
19 Mar	Loughborough	H	W	4-0
26 Mar	Gainsborough	A	L	0-1
2 Apr	Burnley	H	D	1-1
9 Apr	Darwen	H	W	3-1
11 Apr	Burton Swifts	H	W	3-0
23 Apr	Small Heath	A	L	1-2

FA Cup

30 Oct	St Albans (Q)	H	W	9-0
20 Nov	Sheppey United (Q)	H	W	3-0
11 Dec	New Brompton (Q)	H	W	4-2
29 Jan	Burnley (Q)	A	L	1-3

United League

22 Sep	Loughborough	A	W	3-1
4 Oct	Kettering	H	W	4-0
11 Oct	Wellingborough	A	W	3-2
13 Dec	Rushden	H	W	3-1
20 Dec	Southampton	H	D	1-1
25 Dec	Tottenham H	H	L	2-3
10 Jan	Wellingborough	H	W	3-1
22 Jan	Millwall	A	D	2-2
19 Feb	Millwall	H	D	2-2
21 Feb	Luton T	H	D	2-2
28 Mar	Rushden	A	W	3-2
1 Apr	Loughborough	H	W	4-1
4 Apr	Kettering	A	W	2-1
8 Apr	Tottenham H	A	D	0-0
13 Apr	Southampton	A	L	0-3
16 Apr	Luton T	A	L	1-2

Friendlies

15 Sep	Gravesend	A	W	3-1
1 Nov	Reading	H	W	3-1
8 Nov	Blackburn Rov	H	W	3-0
15 Nov	Bristol C	A	L	2-4
9 Feb	Maidstone	A	W	3-0
21 Mar	Bristol C	H	W	3-1
26 Apr	Thames Iron Works	A	D	2-2
28 Apr	Tottenham H	H	W	5-0
30 Apr	Millwall	A	L	0-2

Position in Football League Table

	P	W	L	D	F:A	Pts	
Burnley	30	20	2	8	80:24	48	1st
Arsenal	30	16	9	5	69:49	37	5th

Position in United League Table

	P	W	L	D	F:A	Pts	
Luton	16	13	1	2	49:11	28	1st
Arsenal	16	8	3	5	35:24	21	3rd

SEASON 1898-1899
FOOTBALL LEAGUE (DIVISION 2)

3 Sep	Luton T	A	W	1-0
5 Sep	Burslem PV	A	L	0-3
10 Sep	Leicester Fosse	H	W	4-0
17 Sep	Darwen	A	W	4-1
24 Sep	Gainsborough	H	W	5-1
1 Oct	Manchester C	A	L	1-3
15 Oct	Walsall	A	L	1-4
22 Oct	Burton Swifts	H	W	2-1
5 Nov	Small Heath	H	W	2-0
12 Nov	Loughborough	A	D	0-0
26 Nov	Grimsby T	A	L	0-1
3 Dec	Newton Heath	H	W	5-1
10 Dec	New Brighton	A	L	1-3
17 Dec	Lincoln C	H	W	4-2
24 Dec	Barnsley	A	L	1-2
31 Dec	Luton T	H	W	6-2
7 Jan	Leicester Fosse	A	L	1-2
14 Jan	Darwen	H	W	6-0
21 Jan	Gainsborough	A	W	1-0
4 Feb	Glossop	A	L	0-2
11 Feb	Walsall	H	D	0-0
13 Feb	Glossop	H	W	3-0
18 Feb	Burton Swifts	A	W	2-1
25 Feb	Burslem PV	H	W	1-0
4 Mar	Small Heath	A	L	1-4
13 Mar	Loughborough	H	W	3-1
18 Mar	Blackpool	H	W	6-0
22 Mar	Blackpool	A	D	1-1
25 Mar	Grimsby T	H	D	1-1
1 Apr	Newton Heath	A	D	2-2
3 Apr	Manchester C	H	L	0-1
8 Apr	New Brighton	H	W	4-0
15 Apr	Lincoln C	A	L	0-2
22 Apr	Barnsley	H	W	3-0

FA Cup

28 Jan	Derby Co (1)	H	L	0-6

Chatham Charity Cup

18 Jan	Chatham	A	D	1-1
20 Feb	Chatham	H	D	3-3
6 Mar	Chatham	A	L	1-2

United League

14 Sep	Reading	A	D	1-1
3 Oct	Reading	H	W	2-0
8 Oct	Millwall	A	D	1-1
10 Oct	Luton T	H	W	3-2
17 Oct	Rushden	H	W	2-0
24 Oct	Kettering	A	L	1-2
29 Oct	Southampton	A	L	1-5
31 Oct	Brighton & HA	H	W	5-2
9 Nov	Bristol C	A	W	2-1
14 Nov	Wellingborough	A	L	0-3
19 Nov	Southampton	H	W	2-1
21 Nov	Rushden	A	W	6-0
12 Dec	Bristol C	H	L	1-3
26 Dec	Millwall	H	L	0-1
27 Dec	Luton T	A	D	1-1
4 Jan	Brighton & HA	A	D	1-1
6 Feb	Kettering	H	W	4-2
11 Mar	Tottenham H	H	W	2-1
31 Mar	Wellingborough	H	W	3-0
29 Apr	Tottenham H	A	L	2-3

Friendlies

1 Sep	Gravesend	H	L	0-1
19 Sep	Thames Iron Works	H	W	4-0
25 Oct	Gravesend		W	1-0
23 Nov	Corinthians	A	L	1-4
28 Nov	Chatham	A	L	1-3
8 Dec	Thames Iron Works	A	W	2-1
25 Jan	Sevenoaks	A	W	7-1
30 Jan	Millwall	H	L	2-4
15 Feb	Gravesend	A	L	2-3
23 Feb	Clapton	A	W	3-0
9 Mar	Casuals	A	W	3-1
23 Mar	Past XI *v* Present XI	Present won		3-1
4 Apr	Millwall	A	D	0-0
24 Apr	Notts Co	H	W	2-1
26 Apr	Woolwich Locals		W	3-0

Position in Football League Table

	P	W	L	D	F:A	Pts	
Manchester C	34	23	5	6	92:35	52	1st
Arsenal	34	18	11	5	72:41	41	7th

Position in United League Table

	P	W	L	D	F:A	Pts	
Millwall	20	14	3	3	42:19	31	1st
Arsenal	20	10	6	4	40:30	24	4th

SEASON 1899-1900
FOOTBALL LEAGUE (DIVISION 2)

2 Sep	Leicester Fosse	H	L	0-2
9 Sep	Luton T	A	W	2-1
16 Sep	Burslem PV	H	W	1-0
23 Sep	Walsall	A	L	0-2
30 Sep	Middlesbrough	H	W	3-0
7 Oct	Chesterfield	A	L	1-3
14 Oct	Gainsborough	H	W	2-1
21 Oct	Bolton W	A	L	0-1
4 Nov	Newton Heath	A	L	0-2
11 Nov	Sheffield Wed	H	L	1-2
25 Nov	Small Heath	H	W	3-0
2 Dec	New Brighton	A	W	2-0
16 Dec	Burton Swifts	H	D	1-1
25 Dec	Lincoln C	A	L	0-5
30 Dec	Leicester Fosse	A	D	0-0
6 Jan	Luton T	H	W	3-1
13 Jan	Burslem PV	A	D	1-1
20 Jan	Walsall	H	W	3-1
3 Feb	Middlesbrough	A	L	0-1
10 Feb	Chesterfield	H	W	2-0
17 Feb	Gainsborough	A	D	1-1
24 Feb	Bolton W	H	L	0-1
3 Mar	Loughborough	A	W	3-2
10 Mar	Newton Heath	H	W	2-1
12 Mar	Loughborough	H	W	12-0
17 Mar	Sheffield Wed	A	L	1-3
24 Mar	Lincoln C	H	W	2-1
31 Mar	Small Heath	A	L	1-3
7 Apr	New Brighton	H	W	5-0
14 Apr	Grimsby T	A	L	0-1
16 Apr	Grimsby T	H	W	2-0
21 Apr	Burton Swifts	A	L	0-2
23 Apr	Barnsley	A	L	2-3
28 Apr	Barnsley	H	W	5-1

FA Cup

28 Oct	New Brompton (Q)	H	D	1-1
1 Nov	New Brompton (QR)	A	D	0-0
6 Nov	New Brompton (QR)	A	D	2-2
8 Nov	New Brompton (QR)	A	D	1-1
14 Nov	New Brompton (QR)	A	L	0-1

Southern District Combination

11 Sep	Millwall		L	0-1
27 Sep	Reading		W	3-0
11 Oct	Southampton		L	0-3
23 Oct	Portsmouth		L	0-2
30 Oct	Bristol C		W	3-0
10 Jan	Bristol C		W	3-1
29 Jan	Chatham		W	4-0
7 Feb	Portsmouth		L	1-3
26 Feb	Chatham		W	2-1
5 Mar	Southampton		W	1-0
19 Mar	Q P R		W	5-1
26 Mar	Reading		D	1-1
2 Apr	Millwall		L	0-1
9 Apr	Q P R		L	0-3
17 Apr	Tottenham H		L	2-4
24 Apr	Tottenham H		W	2-1*

*unfinished

Friendlies

4 Sep	Stoke		W	5-3
2 Oct	Aston Villa		W	1-0
29 Nov	Eastbourne		W	2-1
9 Dec	Southampton		D	1-1
23 Dec	Swindon T		W	2-1
27 Jan	Bedminster		W	3-0
19 Feb	Derby Co		L	0-1
13 Apr	Burnley		W	2-0

Position in Football League Table

	P	W	L	D	F:A	Pts	
Sheffield Wed	34	25	5	4	84:22	54	1st
Arsenal	34	16	14	4	61:43	36	8th

Position in Southern District Combination League

	P	W	L	D	F:A	Pts	
Millwall	16	12	2	2	30:10	26	1st
Arsenal	15	7	7	1	25:21	15	4th

(Exclusive of match unfinished 24 April, against Tottenham H, Arsenal leading 2-1)

SEASON 1900-1901
FOOTBALL LEAGUE (DIVISION 2)

1 Sep	Gainsborough	H	W	2-1
8 Sep	Walsall	H	D	1-1
15 Sep	Burton Swifts	A	L	0-1
22 Sep	Barnsley	H	L	1-2
29 Sep	Chesterfield	H	W	1-0
6 Oct	Blackpool	A	D	1-1
13 Oct	Stockport Co	H	W	2-0
20 Oct	Small Heath	A	L	1-2
27 Oct	Grimsby	H	D	1-1
3 Nov	Leicester	H	W	2-1
10 Nov	Newton Heath	H	W	2-1
17 Nov	Glossop	A	W	1-0
24 Nov	Middlesbrough	H	W	1-0
1 Dec	Burnley	A	L	0-3
8 Dec	Burslem PV	H	W	3-0
15 Dec	Leicester	A	L	0-1
22 Dec	New Brighton	H	W	2-1
24 Dec	Walsall	A	L	0-1
29 Dec	Gainsborough	A	L	0-1
12 Jan	Burton Swifts	H	W	3-1
19 Jan	Barnsley	A	L	0-3
26 Jan	Lincoln C	A	D	3-3
16 Feb	Stockport Co	A	L	1-3
19 Feb	Chesterfield	A	W	1-0
2 Mar	Grimsby T	A	L	0-1
9 Mar	Lincoln C	H	D	0-0
16 Mar	Newton Heath	A	L	0-1
23 Mar	Glossop	H	W	2-0
30 Mar	Middlesbrough	A	D	1-1
6 Apr	Burnley	H	W	3-1
8 Apr	Blackpool	H	W	3-1
13 Apr	Burslem PV	A	L	0-1
22 Apr	Small Heath	H	W	1-0
27 Apr	New Brighton	A	L	0-1

FA Cup

5 Jan	Darwen (Q)	A	W	2-0
9 Feb	Blackburn Rov (1)	H	W	2-0
23 Feb	W B A (2)	H	L	0-1

Friendlies

1 Oct	Aston Villa	H	W	3-0
21 Nov	Southampton		L	1-4
25 Dec	West Ham U		W	1-0
26 Dec	Newcastle U	H	D	1-1
1 Jan	Newcastle U		L	1-5
4 Mar	Southern League XI		W	2-1
1 Apr	Millwall		D	1-1
5 Apr	Nottingham F	H	D	1-1
20 Apr	Notts Co	H	W	3-0
25 Apr	West Ham U		D	0-0

Position in Football League Table

	P	W	L	D	F:A	Pts	
Grimsby T	34	20	5	9	60:33	49	1st
Arsenal	34	15	13	6	39:35	36	7th

SEASON 1901-1902
FOOTBALL LEAGUE (DIVISION 2)

2 Sep	Barnsley	H	W	2-1
4 Sep	Leicester	H	W	2-0
14 Sep	Preston NE	A	L	0-2
21 Sep	Burnley	H	W	4-0
28 Sep	Burslem PV	A	L	0-1
5 Oct	Chesterfield	H	W	3-2
12 Oct	Gainsborough	A	D	2-2
19 Oct	Middlesbrough	H	L	0-3
26 Oct	Bristol C	A	W	3-0
9 Nov	Stockport Co	A	D	0-0
16 Nov	Newton Heath	H	W	2-0
23 Nov	Glossop	A	W	1-0
30 Nov	Doncaster Rov	H	W	1-0
7 Dec	Lincoln C	A	D	0-0
21 Dec	Burton Un	H	L	0-1
25 Dec	Blackpool	H	D	0-0
26 Dec	Burslem PV	H	W	3-1
28 Dec	Barnsley	A	L	0-2
4 Jan	Leicester	A	L	1-2
11 Jan	Preston NE	H	D	0-0
18 Jan	Burnley	A	D	0-0
1 Feb	Chesterfield	A	W	3-1
8 Feb	Gainsborough	H	W	5-0
15 Feb	Middlesbrough	A	L	0-1
22 Feb	Bristol C	H	W	2-0
1 Mar	Blackpool	A	W	3-1
8 Mar	Stockport Co	H	W	3-0
15 Mar	Newton Heath	A	W	1-0
22 Mar	Glossop	H	W	4-0
29 Mar	Doncaster Rov	A	L	0-1
31 Mar	W B A	H	W	2-1
5 Apr	Lincoln C	H	W	2-0
12 Apr	W B A	A	L	1-2
19 Apr	Burton Un	A	L	0-2

FA Cup

14 Dec	Luton T (Q)	H	D	1-1
18 Dec	Luton T (QR)	A	W	2-0
25 Jan	Newcastle U (1)	H	L	0-2

Southern Charity Cup

7 Apr	Portsmouth	A	W	2-1
23 Apr	Tottenham H (Semi Final)	H	D	0-0
29 Apr	Tottenham H (Semi Final)	A	L	1-2

London League

16 Sep	Tottenham H		L	0-2
30 Sep	Millwall		D	1-1
21 Oct	West Ham U		L	0-1
4 Nov	Tottenham H		L	0-5
3 Feb	Q P R		D	2-2
17 Feb	Q P R		W	3-0
24 Feb	Millwall		L	1-2
28 Mar	West Ham U		W	2-0

Friendlies

2 Nov	Reading	H	W	1-0
18 Nov	Southampton	H	L	0-1
1 Apr	Blackburn Rov	H	W	2-0
25 Apr	Plymouth Arg	A	W	4-1
26 Apr	W B A	H	L	0-1

Position in Football League Table

	P	W	L	D	F:A	Pts	
W B A	34	25	4	5	82:29	55	1st
Arsenal	34	18	10	6	50:26	42	4th

Position in London League Table

	P	W	L	D	F:A	Pts	
West Ham U	8	5	2	1	19: 9	11	1st
Arsenal	8	2	4	2	9:13	6	5th

SEASON 1902-1903
FOOTBALL LEAGUE (DIVISION 2)

6 Sep	Preston NE	A	D	2-2
13 Sep	Burslem PV	H	W	3-0
20 Sep	Barnsley	A	D	1-1
27 Sep	Gainsborough	H	W	6-1
4 Oct	Bristol C	A	L	0-1
11 Oct	Bristol C	H	W	2-1
18 Oct	Glossop NE	A	W	2-1
25 Oct	Manchester U	H	L	0-1
1 Nov	Manchester C	H	W	1-0
8 Nov	Blackpool	H	W	2-1
15 Nov	Burnley	A	W	3-0
22 Nov	Doncaster Rov	A	W	1-0
29 Nov	Lincoln C	H	W	2-1
6 Dec	Small Heath	A	L	0-2
20 Dec	Manchester C	A	L	1-4
25 Dec	Burton Un	A	L	1-2
27 Dec	Burnley	H	W	5-1
1 Jan	Stockport Co	A	W	1-0
3 Jan	Preston NE	H	W	3-1
10 Jan	Burslem PV	A	D	1-1
17 Jan	Barnsley	H	W	4-0
24 Jan	Gainsborough	A	W	1-0
31 Jan	Burton Un	H	W	3-0
14 Feb	Glossop NE	H	D	0-0
28 Feb	Stockport Co	H	W	3-1
7 Mar	Blackpool	A	D	0-0
9 Mar	Manchester U	A	L	0-3
14 Mar	Chesterfield	A	D	2-2
21 Mar	Doncaster Rov	H	W	3-0
28 Mar	Lincoln C	A	D	2-2
4 Apr	Small Heath	H	W	6-1
10 Apr	Chesterfield	H	W	3-0
11 Apr	Leicester	A	W	2-0
13 Apr	Leicester	H	D	0-0

FA Cup

13 Dec	Brentford (Q)	A	D	1-1
17 Dec	Brentford (QR)	H	W	5-0
7 Feb	Sheffield U (1)	H	L	1-3

Southern Charity Cup

9 Feb	Millwall	H	L	2-3

London League

1 Sep	West Ham U	A	W	3-1
15 Sep	Q P R	H	W	3-1
27 Oct	Q P R	A	W	3-0
10 Nov	Brentford	H	W	3-0
17 Nov	Tottenham H	H	W	2-1
1 Dec	Tottenham H	A	L	0-1
26 Dec	Millwall	A	L	0-3
21 Feb	West Ham U	H	L	0-1
23 Mar	Brentford	A	W	1-0
18 Apr	Millwall	H	L	0-2

Friendlies

8 Sep	New Brompton	A	W	3-2
18 Mar	Brighton & HA	A	W	3-1
14 Apr	Northampton T	A	D	1-1
20 Apr	Bristol C	A	W	2-1
25 Apr	Chesterfield	H	W	1-0

Position in Football League Table

	P	W	L	D	F:A	Pts	
Manchester C	34	25	5	4	95:29	54	1st
Arsenal	34	20	6	8	66:30	48	3rd

Position in London League Table

	P	W	L	D	F:A	Pts	
Tottenham H	10	7	2	1	19: 4	15	1st
Arsenal	10	6	4	0	14:10	12	3rd

SEASON 1903-1904
FOOTBALL LEAGUE (DIVISION 2)

5 Sep	Blackpool	H	W	3-0
12 Sep	Gainsborough	A	W	2-0
19 Sep	Burton Un	H	W	8-0
26 Sep	Bristol C	A	W	4-0
3 Oct	Manchester U	H	W	4-0
10 Oct	Glossop	A	W	3-1
24 Oct	Burslem PV	A	W	3-2
26 Oct	Leicester	H	W	8-0
31 Oct	Barnsley	A	L	1-2
7 Nov	Lincoln C	H	W	4-0
21 Nov	Chesterfield	H	W	6-0
28 Nov	Bolton W	A	L	1-2
19 Dec	Grimsby T	H	W	5-1
25 Dec	Bradford C	H	W	4-1
26 Dec	Leicester	A	D	0-0
1 Jan	Stockport Co	A	D	0-0
2 Jan	Blackpool	A	D	2-2
9 Jan	Gainsborough	H	W	6-0
16 Jan	Burton Un	A	L	1-3
30 Jan	Manchester U	A	L	0-1
27 Feb	Barnsley	H	W	3-0
29 Feb	Burnley	H	W	4-0
5 Mar	Lincoln C	A	W	2-0
12 Mar	Stockport Co	H	W	5-2
14 Mar	Bristol C	H	W	2-0
19 Mar	Chesterfield	A	L	0-1
26 Mar	Bolton W	H	W	3-0
1 Apr	Preston NE	A	D	0-0
2 Apr	Burnley	A	L	0-1
4 Apr	Glossop	H	W	2-1
9 Apr	Preston NE	H	D	0-0
16 Apr	Grimsby T	A	D	2-2
19 Apr	Bradford C	A	W	3-0
25 Apr	Burslem PV	H	D	0-0

FA Cup

12 Dec	Bristol Rov (Q)	A	D	1-1
15 Dec	Bristol Rov (QR)	H	D	1-1
21 Dec	Bristol Rov (QR)	A*	W	1-0
6 Feb	Fulham (1)	H	W	1-0
20 Feb	Manchester C (2)	H	L	0-2

*at Tottenham

Southern Charity Cup

12 Oct	West Ham U	W	1-0
18 Jan	Reading (Semi-Final)	W	3-1
28 Apr	Millwall (Final)	L	1-2

London League

1 Sep	Tottenham H	W	1-0
7 Sep	Fulham	W	2-0
14 Sep	West Ham U	W	4-1
14 Nov	Tottenham H	D	1-1
23 Nov	Brentford	D	1-1
7 Dec	Millwall	L	1-3
11 Jan	Q P R	W	6-2
8 Feb	Brentford	W	3-2
22 Feb	West Ham U	W	4-2
7 Mar	Millwall	L	0-3
21 Mar	Q P R	L	1-3
30 Apr	Fulham	L	0-1

Friendlies

17 Oct	Luton	D	2-2
30 Nov	Army	W	4-0

Position in Football League Table

	P	W	L	D	F:A	Pts	
Preston NE	34	20	4	10	62:24	50	1st
Arsenal	34	21	6	7	91:22	49	2nd

Position in London League Table

	P	W	L	D	F:A	Pts	
Millwall	12	11	0	1	38: 8	23	1st
Arsenal	12	6	4	2	24:19	14	3rd

SEASON 1904-1905
FOOTBALL LEAGUE (DIVISION 1)

3 Sep	Newcastle U	A	L	0-3
10 Sep	Preston NE	H	D	0-0
17 Sep	Middlesbrough	A	L	0-1
24 Sep	Wolverhampton W	H	W	2-0
1 Oct	Bury	A	D	1-1
8 Oct	Aston Villa	H	W	1-0
15 Oct	Blackburn Rov	A	D	1-1
22 Oct	Nottingham F	H	L	0-3
29 Oct	Sheffield Wed	A	W	3-0
5 Nov	Sunderland	H	D	0-0
12 Nov	Stoke	H	W	2-1
19 Nov	Derby Co	A	D	0-0
3 Dec	Small Heath	A	L	1-2
10 Dec	Manchester C	H	W	1-0
17 Dec	Notts Co	A	W	5-1
24 Dec	Sheffield U	H	W	1-0
26 Dec	Aston Villa	A	L	1-3
27 Dec	Nottingham F	A	W	3-0
28 Dec	Sheffield U	A	L	0-4
31 Dec	Newcastle U	H	L	0-2
7 Jan	Preston NE	A	L	0-3
14 Jan	Middlesbrough	H	D	1-1
21 Jan	Wolverhampton W	A	L	1-4
28 Jan	Bury	H	W	2-1
11 Feb	Blackburn Rov	H	W	2-0
25 Feb	Sheffield Wed	H	W	3-0
4 Mar	Sunderland	A	D	1-1
11 Mar	Stoke	A	L	0-2
18 Mar	Derby Co	H	D	0-0
1 Apr	Small Heath	H	D	1-1
5 Apr	Everton	A	L	0-1
8 Apr	Manchester C	A	L	0-1
15 Apr	Notts Co	H	L	1-2
22 Apr	Everton	H	W	2-1

FA Cup

4 Feb	Bristol C (1)	H	D	0-0
8 Feb	Bristol C (1R)	A	L	0-1

Southern Charity Cup

10 Oct	Tottenham H	H	L	1-3

Friendlies

1 Sep	Bristol C	H	W	3-2
12 Sep	West Ham U	A	D	1-1
31 Oct	Cambridge Univ	H	W	3-0
22 Nov	Cambridge Univ	A	W	4-3
5 Dec	French International Team	H	W	26-1
18 Feb	Corinthians	A	L	1-2
27 Feb	Queens Park (Glasgow)	H	W	6-1
25 Mar	Burnley	H	W	3-0
12 Apr	Southend U	A	W	2-0
21 Apr	New Brompton	H	W	3-1
24 Apr	Dundee	H	W	3-0
26 Apr	Ipswich T	A	W	3-1
27 Apr	Norwich C	A	L	1-2
29 Apr	Sheffield U	A	L	2-3

Position in Football League Table

	P	W	L	D	F:A	Pts	
Newcastle U	34	23	9	2	72:33	48	1st
Arsenal	34	12	13	9	36:40	33	10th

SEASON 1905-1906
FOOTBALL LEAGUE (DIVISION 1)

2 Sep	Liverpool	H	W	3-1
9 Sep	Sheffield U	A	L	1-3
16 Sep	Notts Co	H	D	1-1
18 Sep	Preston NE	H	D	2-2
23 Sep	Stoke	A	L	1-2
30 Sep	Bolton W	H	D	0-0
7 Oct	Wolverhampton W	A	W	2-0
14 Oct	Blackburn Rov	A	L	0-2
21 Oct	Sunderland	H	W	2-0
28 Oct	Birmingham	A	L	1-2
4 Nov	Everton	H	L	1-2
11 Nov	Derby Co	A	L	1-5
18 Nov	Sheffield Wed	H	L	0-2
25 Nov	Nottingham F	A	L	1-3
2 Dec	Manchester C	H	W	2-0
9 Dec	Bury	A	L	0-2
16 Dec	Middlesbrough	H	D	2-2
23 Dec	Preston NE	A	D	2-2
25 Dec	Newcastle U	H	W	4-3
27 Dec	Aston Villa	A	L	1-2
30 Dec	Liverpool	A	L	0-3
1 Jan	Bolton W	A	L	1-6
6 Jan	Sheffield U	H	W	5-1
20 Jan	Notts Co	A	L	0-1
27 Jan	Stoke	H	L	1-2
10 Feb	Wolverhampton W	H	W	2-1
17 Feb	Blackburn Rov	H	W	3-2
3 Mar	Birmingham	H	W	5-0
17 Mar	Derby Co	H	W	1-0
21 Mar	Everton	A	W	1-0
24 Mar	Sheffield Wed	A	L	2-4
2 Apr	Nottingham F	H	W	3-1
7 Apr	Manchester C	A	W	2-1
13 Apr	Aston Villa	H	W	2-1
14 Apr	Bury	H	W	4-0
16 Apr	Newcastle U	A	D	1-1
21 Apr	Middlesbrough	A	L	0-2
25 Apr	Sunderland	A	D	2-2

FA Cup

13 Jan	West Ham U (1)	H	D	1-1
18 Jan	West Ham U (1R)	A	W	3-2
3 Feb	Watford (2)	H	W	3-0
24 Feb	Sunderland (3)	H	W	5-0
10 Mar	Manchester U (4)	A	W	3-2
31 Mar	Newcastle U (Semi-Final)*		L	0-2

*at Stoke

Southern Charity Cup

9 Oct	West Ham U	H	W	3-2
9 Apr	Tottenham H	A	D	0-0
28 Apr	Tottenham H	H	W	5-0
30 Apr	Reading (Final)	A	W	1-0

Friendlies

21 Sep	Faversham Rangers	A	W	9-0
18 Oct	Corinthians	A	L	1-2
30 Oct	Oxford Univ	H	W	3-1
26 Dec	Corinthians	H	D	1-1
15 Jan	Cambridge Univ	H	W	4-2
22 Jan	Oxford Univ	A	W	4-0
18 Apr	West Hartlepool	A	W	4-0

Position in Football League Table

	P	W	L	D	F:A	Pts	
Liverpool	38	23	10	5	79:46	51	1st
Arsenal	38	15	16	7	62:64	37	12th

SEASON 1906-1907
FOOTBALL LEAGUE (DIVISION 1)

1 Sep	Manchester C	A	W	4-1
3 Sep	Bury	A	L	1-4
8 Sep	Middlesbrough	H	W	2-0
15 Sep	Preston NE	A	W	3-0
22 Sep	Newcastle U	H	W	2-0
29 Sep	Aston Villa	A	D	2-2
6 Oct	Liverpool	H	W	2-1
13 Oct	Bristol C	A	W	3-1
20 Oct	Notts Co	H	W	1-0
27 Oct	Sheffield U	A	L	2-4
3 Nov	Bolton W	H	D	2-2
10 Nov	Manchester U	A	L	0-1
17 Nov	Stoke	H	W	2-1
24 Nov	Blackburn Rov	A	W	3-2
1 Dec	Sunderland	H	L	0-1
8 Dec	Birmingham	A	L	1-5
15 Dec	Everton	H	W	3-1
22 Dec	Derby Co	A	D	0-0
26 Dec	Bury	H	W	3-1
29 Dec	Manchester C	H	W	4-1
1 Jan	Sheffield Wed	A	D	1-1
5 Jan	Middlesbrough	A	L	3-5
19 Jan	Preston NE	H	W	1-0
26 Jan	Newcastle U	A	L	0-1
9 Feb	Liverpool	A	L	0-4
16 Feb	Bristol City	H	L	1-2
2 Mar	Sheffield U	H	L	0-1
16 Mar	Manchester U	H	W	4-0
27 Mar	Bolton W	A	L	0-3
28 Mar	Sheffield Wed	H	W	1-0
30 Mar	Blackburn Rov	H	W	2-0
1 Apr	Aston Villa	H	W	3-1
6 Apr	Sunderland	A	W	3-2
10 Apr	Everton	A	L	1-2
13 Apr	Birmingham	H	W	2-1
15 Apr	Stoke	A	L	0-2
17 Apr	Notts Co	A	L	1-4
27 Apr	Derby	H	W	3-2

FA Cup

12 Jan	Grimsby T (1)	A	D	1-1
16 Jan	Grimsby T (1R)	H	W	3-0
2 Feb	Bristol C (2)	H	W	2-1
23 Feb	Bristol Rov (3)	H	W	1-0
9 Mar	Barnsley (4)	A	W	2-1
23 Mar	Sheffield Wed (Semi-Final)*		L	1-3

*at Birmingham

Southern Charity Cup

10 Dec	Millwall	H	L	1-2

Friendlies

12 Sep	Reading	A	W	1-0
19 Sep	West Norwood	A	W	1-0
5 Nov	Oxford Univ	H	W	7-1
19 Nov	Clapton Orient	A	W	3-1
3 Dec	Cambridge Univ	A	W	3-1
25 Dec	Celtic	H	L	0·2
14 Jan	Cambridge Univ	H	W	6-3

On Tour

5 May	Racing Club, Brussels	W	2-1
7 May	The Hague	W	6-3
9 May	BFC Pressen, Berlin	W	9-1
12 May	SP Sportorina, Prague	W	7-5
16 May	Klub Slavia, Prague	W	4-2
18 May	Combined Vienna Team	W	4-2
19 May	Magyaren Buda Pesth	W	9-0
20 May	Buda Pesth	D	2-2

Position in Football League Table

	P	W	L	D	F:A	Pts	
Newcastle U	38	22	9	7	74:46	51	1st
Arsenal	38	20	14	4	66:59	44	7th

SEASON 1907-1908
FOOTBALL LEAGUE (DIVISION 1)

2 Sep	Notts Co	H	D	1-1
7 Sep	Bristol C	H	L	0-4
9 Sep	Bury	A	L	2-3
14 Sep	Notts Co	A	L	0-2
21 Sep	Manchester C	H	W	2-1
28 Sep	Preston NE	A	L	0-3
5 Oct	Bury	H	D	0-0
12 Oct	Aston Villa	A	W	1-0
19 Oct	Liverpool	H	W	2-1
26 Oct	Middlesbrough	A	D	0-0
2 Nov	Sheffield U	H	W	5-1
9 Nov	Chelsea	A	L	1-2
16 Nov	Nottingham F	H	W	3-1
23 Nov	Manchester U	A	L	2-4
30 Nov	Blackburn Rov	H	W	2-0
7 Dec	Bolton W	A	L	1-3
14 Dec	Birmingham	H	D	1-1
21 Dec	Everton	A	D	1-1
25 Dec	Newcastle U	H	D	2-2
28 Dec	Sunderland	H	W	4-0
31 Dec	Sheffield Wed	A	L	0-6
1 Jan	Sunderland	A	L	2-5
4 Jan	Bristol C	A	W	2-1
18 Jan	Manchester C	A	L	0-4
25 Jan	Preston NE	H	D	1-1
8 Feb	Aston Villa	H	L	0-1
15 Feb	Liverpool	A	L	1-4
22 Feb	Middlesbrough	H	W	4-1
29 Feb	Sheffield U	A	D	2-2
7 Mar	Chelsea	H	D	0-0
14 Mar	Nottingham F	A	L	0-1
21 Mar	Manchester U	H	W	1-0
28 Mar	Blackburn Rov	A	D	1-1
4 Apr	Bolton W	H	D	1-1
11 Apr	Birmingham	A	W	2-1
17 Apr	Newcastle U	A	L	1-2
18 Apr	Everton	H	W	2-1
20 Apr	Sheffield Wed	H	D	1-1

FA Cup

11 Jan	Hull C (1)	H	D	0-0
16 Jan	Hull C (1R)	A	L	1-4

Southern Charity Cup

23 Sep	Reading	H	L	0-1

Friendlies

16 Sep	Barnsley	H	W	1-0
14 Oct	Rest of Kent	A	W	3-1
26 Dec	Liverpool	H	D	2-2
1 Feb	Tottenham H	A	W	1-0

On Tour

21 Apr	Hearts	L	1-3
22 Apr	Raith Rovers	L	0-1
23 Apr	Aberdeen	L	1-4
25 Apr	Dundee	L	1-2
27 Apr	Motherwell	D	1-1
28 Apr	Glasgow Rangers	D	1-1
29 Apr	Greenock Morton	L	0-1
30 Apr	Kilmarnock	W	2-1

Position in Football League Table

	P	W	L	D	F:A	Pts	
Manchester C	38	23	9	6	81:48	52	1st
Arsenal	38	12	14	12	51:63	36	15th

SEASON 1908-1909
FOOTBALL LEAGUE (DIVISION 1)

2 Sep	Everton	H	L	0-4
5 Sep	Notts Co	A	L	1-2
7 Sep	Everton	A	W	3-0
12 Sep	Newcastle U	H	L	1-2
19 Sep	Bristol C	A	L	1-2
26 Sep	Preston NE	H	W	1-0
3 Oct	Middlesbrough	A	D	1-1
10 Oct	Manchester C	H	W	3-0
17 Oct	Liverpool	A	D	2-2
24 Oct	Bury	H	W	4-0
28 Oct	Chelsea	A	W	2-1
31 Oct	Sheffield U	A	D	1-1
7 Nov	Aston Villa	H	L	0-1
14 Nov	Nottingham F	A	W	1-0
21 Nov	Sunderland	H	L	0-4
5 Dec	Blackburn Rov	H	L	0-1
12 Dec	Bradford C	A	L	1-4
19 Dec	Manchester U	H	L	0-1
25 Dec	Leicester	A	D	1-1
26 Dec	Leicester	H	W	2-1
28 Dec	Sheffield Wed	A	L	2-6
2 Jan	Notts Co	H	W	1-0
9 Jan	Newcastle U	H	L	1-3
23 Jan	Bristol C	H	D	1-1
30 Jan	Preston NE	A	D	0-0
13 Feb	Manchester C	A	D	2-2
20 Feb	Liverpool	H	W	5-0
27 Feb	Bury	A	D	1-1
13 Mar	Aston Villa	A	L	1-2
17 Mar	Middlesbrough	H	D	1-1
20 Mar	Nottingham F	H	L	1-2
27 Mar	Sunderland	A	L	0-1
1 Apr	Sheffield U	H	W	1-0
3 Apr	Chelsea	H	D	0-0
10 Apr	Blackburn Rov	A	W	3-1
12 Apr	Sheffield Wed	H	W	2-0
17 Apr	Bradford C	H	W	1-0
27 Apr	Manchester U	A	W	4-1

FA Cup

16 Jan	Croydon Common (1)*		D	1-1
20 Jan	Croydon Common (1R)	H	W	2-0
6 Feb	Millwall (2)	H	D	1-1
10 Feb	Millwall (2R)	A	L	0-1

*at Crystal Palace

London FA Challenge Cup

28 Sep	Fulham	A	W	1-0
9 Nov	Crystal Palace	A	W	2-1
22 Feb	Clapton Orient (Semi-Final)	A	L	1-2

London Professional Charity Fund

7 Dec	Chelsea	H	W	1-0

Friendlies

7 Oct	Rest of Kent	A	W	3-0
22 Oct	Ryde	A	W	2-0
10 Mar	Hastings	A	W	3-1
9 Apr	Exeter	A	L	2-3

Position in Football League Table

	P	W	L	D	F:A	Pts	
Newcastle U	38	24	9	5	65:41	53	1st
Arsenal	38	14	14	10	52:49	38	6th

SEASON 1909-1910
FOOTBALL LEAGUE (DIVISION 1)

1 Sep	Aston Villa	A	L	1-5
4 Sep	Sheffield U	H	D	0-0
11 Sep	Middlesbrough	A	L	2-5
18 Sep	Bolton W	A	L	0-3
25 Sep	Chelsea	H	W	3-2
2 Oct	Blackburn Rov	A	L	0-7
7 Oct	Notts Co	A	L	1-5
9 Oct	Nottingham F	H	L	0-1
16 Oct	Sunderland	A	L	2-6
23 Oct	Everton	H	W	1-0
30 Oct	Manchester U	A	L	0-1
6 Nov	Bradford C	H	L	0-1
13 Nov	Sheffield Wed	A	D	1-1
20 Nov	Bristol C	H	D	2-2
27 Nov	Bury	A	W	2-1
4 Dec	Tottenham H	H	W	1-0
11 Dec	Preston NE	A	W	4-3
18 Dec	Notts Co	H	L	1-2
25 Dec	Newcastle U	H	L	0-3
27 Dec	Liverpool	H	D	1-1
1 Jan	Liverpool	A	L	1-5
8 Jan	Sheffield U	A	L	0-2
22 Jan	Middlesbrough	H	W	3-0
29 Jan	Bolton W	H	W	2-0
12 Feb	Blackburn Rov	H	L	0-1
26 Feb	Sunderland	H	L	1-2
2 Mar	Nottingham F	A	D	1-1
7 Mar	Everton	A	L	0-1
12 Mar	Manchester U	H	D	0-0
19 Mar	Bradford C	A	W	1-0
25 Mar	Newcastle U	A	D	1-1
26 Mar	Sheffield Wed	H	L	0-1
28 Mar	Chelsea	A	W	1-0
2 Apr	Bristol C	A	D	0-0
9 Apr	Bury	H	D	0-0
11 Apr	Aston Villa	H	D	1-1
16 Apr	Tottenham H	A	D	1-1
23 Apr	Preston NE	H	L	1-3

FA Cup

15 Jan	Watford (1)	H	W	3-0
5 Feb	Everton (2)	A	L	0-5

London FA Challenge Cup

20 Sep	Bromley	H	W	4-0
11 Oct	West Ham U	H	L	0-1

London Professional Charity Fund

1 Nov	Tottenham H	A	L	0-3

Foord Flood Relief Fund

25 Nov	Shorncliffe Garrison and District XI (at Folkestone)	W	5-2

Friendlies

22 Sep	Rest of Kent	A	W	3-2
19 Feb	Fulham	H	D	2-2
5 Mar	Millwall	A	D	3-3
28 Apr	Colchester		W	3-2
30 Apr	Ilford		L	2-3

Position in Football League Table

	P	W	L	D	F:A	Pts	
Aston Villa	38	23	8	7	84:42	53	1st
Arsenal	38	11	18	9	37:67	31	18th

SEASON 1910-1911
FOOTBALL LEAGUE (DIVISION 1)

1 Sep	Manchester U	H	L	1-2
3 Sep	Bury	A	D	1-1
10 Sep	Sheffield U	H	D	0-0
17 Sep	Aston Villa	A	L	0-3
24 Sep	Sunderland	H	D	0-0
1 Oct	Oldham	H	D	0-0
8 Oct	Bradford C	A	L	0-3
15 Oct	Blackburn	H	W	4-1
22 Oct	Nottingham F	A	W	3-2
29 Oct	Manchester C	H	L	0-1
5 Nov	Everton	A	L	0-2
12 Nov	Sheffield W	H	W	1-0
19 Nov	Bristol C	A	W	1-0
26 Nov	Newcastle U	H	L	1-2
3 Dec	Tottenham H	A	L	1-3
10 Dec	Middlesbrough	H	L	0-2
17 Dec	Preston NE	A	L	1-4
24 Dec	Notts Co	H	W	2-1
26 Dec	Manchester U	A	L	0-5
31 Dec	Bury	H	W	3-2
7 Jan	Sheffield U	A	L	2-3
28 Jan	Sunderland	A	D	2-2
11 Feb	Bradford C	H	D	0-0
18 Feb	Blackburn Rov	A	L	0-1
25 Feb	Nottingham F	H	W	3-2
4 Mar	Manchester C	A	D	1-1
6 Mar	Oldham Ath	A	L	0-3
11 Mar	Everton	H	W	1-0
15 Mar	Aston Villa	H	D	1-1
18 Mar	Sheffield Wed	A	D	0-0
25 Mar	Bristol C	H	W	3-0
1 Apr	Newcastle U	A	W	1-0
8 Apr	Tottenham H	H	W	2-0
14 Apr	Liverpool	H	D	0-0
15 Apr	Middlesbrough	A	D	1-1
17 Apr	Liverpool	A	D	1-1
22 Apr	Preston NE	H	W	2-0
29 Apr	Notts Co	A	W	2-0

FA Cup

14 Jan	Clapton Orient (1)*			
16 Jan	Clapton Orient (1)	A	W	2-1
4 Feb	Swindon T (2)	A	L	0-1

*match abandoned, fog

London FA Challenge Cup

19 Sep	Q P R	H	W	3-0
10 Oct	Millwall	A	L	0-1

London Professional Charity Fund

26 Sep	Fulham	A	W	3-2

Position in Football League Table

	P	W	L	D	F:A	Pts	
Manchester U	38	22	8	8	72:40	52	1st
Arsenal	38	13	13	12	41:49	38	10th

SEASON 1911-1912
FOOTBALL LEAGUE (DIVISION 1)

2 Sep	Liverpool	H	D	2-2
9 Sep	Aston Villa	A	L	1-4
16 Sep	Newcastle U	H	W	2-0
23 Sep	Sheffield U	A	L	1-2
30 Sep	Oldham Ath	H	D	1-1
7 Oct	Bolton W	A	D	2-2
14 Oct	Bradford C	H	W	2-0
21 Oct	Preston NE	A	W	1-0
28 Oct	Manchester C	A	D	3-3
4 Nov	Everton	H	L	0-1
11 Nov	W B A	A	D	1-1
18 Nov	Sunderland	H	W	3-0
25 Nov	Blackburn Rov	A	L	0-4
2 Dec	Sheffield Wed	H	L	0-2
9 Dec	Bury	A	L	1-3
16 Dec	Middlesbrough	H	W	3-1
23 Dec	Notts Co	A	L	1-3
25 Dec	Tottenham H	A	L	0-5

26 Dec	Tottenham H	H	W	3-1
30Dec	Liverpool	A	L	1-4
1 Jan	Manchester U	A	L	0-2
6 Jan	Aston Villa	H	D	2-2
20 Jan	Newcastle U	A	W	2-1
27 Jan	Sheffield U	H	W	3-1
10 Feb	Bolton W	H	W	3-0
17 Feb	Bradford C	A	D	1-1
24 Feb	Middlesbrough	A	W	2-0
2 Mar	Manchester C	H	W	7-0
9 Mar	Oldham Ath	A	D	0-0
16 Mar	WBA	H	L	0-2
23 Mar	Sunderland	A	L	0-1
27 Mar	Everton	A	L	0-1
5 Apr	Manchester U	H	W	2-1
5 Apr	Sheffield Wed	A	L	0-3
6 Apr	Preston NE	H	W	4-1
8 Apr	Bury	H	W	1-0
22 Apr	Blackburn Rov	H	W	5-1
27 Apr	Notts Co	H	L	0-3

FA Cup

13 Jan	Bolton W (1)	A	L	0-1

London FA Challenge Cup

18 Sep	Q P R	A	W	2-0
16 Oct	Chelsea	H	L	2-3

London Professional Charity Fund

4 Sep	Chelsea	A	D	2-2
30 Oct	Chelsea	H	W	1-0

Charity Match Titanic Disaster

29 Apr	Tottennham	H	W	3-0

Friendlies

25 Mar	West Ham U	H	W	3-0
20 Apr	Glasgow Rangers	A	D	0-0

On Tour

17 May	Hertha Berlin		W	5-0
12 May	Viktoria Berliner		D	2-2
16 May	Prague Deutscher		W	4-1
19 May	Furth		W	6-0
22 May	Toma Graz		W	6–0
24 May	Tottenham Vienna		W	4-0
26 May	Vienna Rapide		W	8-2
27 May	Wiener Athletic		W	5-0
29 May	Budapest		W	2-1

Position in Football League Table

	P	W	L	D	F:A	Pts	
Blackburn Rov	38	20	9	9	60:43	49	1st
Arsenal	38	15	15	8	55:59	38	10th

SEASON 1912-1913
FOOTBALL LEAGUE (DIVISION 1)

2 Sep	Manchester U	H	D	0-0
7 Sep	Liverpool	A	L	0-3
14 Sep	Bolton W	H	L	1-2
16 Sep	Aston Villa	H	L	0-3
21 Sep	Sheflield U	A	W	3-1
28 Sep	Newcastle U	H	D	1-1
5 Oct	Oldham Ath	A	D	0-0
12 Oct	Chelsea	H	L	0-1
19 Oct	Sunderland	H	L	1-3
26 Oct	Bradtord PA	A	L	1-3
2 Nov	Manchester C	H	L	0-4
9 Nov	W B A	A	L	1-2
6 Nov	Everton	H	D	0-0
23 Nov	Sheffield Wed	A	L	0-2
30 Nov	Blackburn Rov	H	L	0-1
7 Dec	Derby Co	A	L	1-4
14 Dec	Tottenham H	L	H	0-3
21 Dec	Middlesbrough	A	L	0-2
25 Dec	Notts Co	H	D	0-0
26 Dec	Notts Co	A	L	l-2
28 Dec	Liverpool	H	D	1-1
1 Jan	Sunderland	A	L	1-4
4 Jan	Bolton W	A	L	1-5
18 Jan	Sheflield U	H	L	1-3
25 Jan	Newcastle U	A	L	1-3
8 Feb	Oldham Ath	H	D	0-0
15 Feb	Chelsea	A	D	1-1
1 Mar	Bradford PA	H	D	1-1
8 Mar	Manchester C	A	W	1-0
15 Mar	WBA	H	W	1-0
21 Mar	Manchester U	A	L	0-2
22 Mar	Everton	A	L	0-3
24 Mar	Aston Villa	A	L	1-4
29 Mar	Sheflield Wed	H	L	2-5
5 Apr	Blackburn	A	D	1-1
12 Apr	Derby Co	H	L	1-2
19 Apr	Tottenham H	A	D	1-1
26 Apr	Middlesbrough	H	D	1-1

FA Cup

11 Jan	Croydon Common (l)	A	D	0-0
15 Jan	Croydon Common (1R)	H	W	2-1
1 Feb	Liverpool (2)	H	L	1-4

London FA Challenge Cup

23 Sep	Clapton Orient	A	L	2-4

London Professional Charity Fund

30 Sep	Chelsea	A	W	3-1

Kent Senior Shield

16 Oct	Crystal Palace	A	L	0-1

Position in Football League Table

	P	W	L	D	F:A	Pts	
Sunderland	38	25	9	4	86:43	54	1st
Arsenal	36	3	23	12	26:74	18	20th

SEASON 1913-1914
FOOTBALL LEAGUE (DIVISION 2)

6 Sep	Leicester C	H	W	2-1
13 Sep	Wolverhampton W	A	W	2-1
15 Sep	Notts Co	H	W	3-0
27 Sep	Barnsley	A	L	0-1
4 Oct	Bury	H	L	0-1
11 Oct	Huddersfield	A	W	2-1
18 Oct	Lincoln C	H	W	3-0
25 Oct	Blackpool	A	D	1-1
1 Nov	Nottingham F	H	W	3-2
8 Nov	Fulham	A	L	1-6
15 Nov	Grimsby T	A	D	1-1
22 Nov	Birmingham	H	W	1-0
29 Nov	Bristol C	A	D	1-1
6 Dec	Leeds C	H	W	1-0
13 Dec	Clapton Orient	A	L	0-1
20 Dec	Glossop	H	W	2-0
25 Dec	Bradford PA	A	W	3-2
26 Dec	Bradtord PA	H	W	2-0
27 Dec	Leicester	A	W	2-1
1 Jan	Notts Co	A	L	0-1
3 Jan	Wolverhampton W	H	W	3-1
17 Jan	Hull C	A	W	2-1
24 Jan	Barnsley	H	W	1-0
7 Feb	Bury	A	D	1-1
14 Feb	Huddersfield T	H	L	0-1
21 Feb	Lincoln C	A	L	2-5
28 Mar	Blackpool	H	W	2-1
7 Mar	Nottingham F	A	D	0-0
14 Mar	Fulham	H	W	2-0
28 Mar	Birmingham	A	L	0-2
4 Apr	Bristol C	A	D	1-1
10 Apr	Stockport Co	H	W	4-0
M Apr	Leeds C	A	D	0-0
13 Apr	Stockport Co	H	W	4-0
18 Apr	Clapton Orient	H	D	2-2
23 Apr	Grimsby T	H	W	2-0
25 Apr	Glossop	A	W	2-0

FA Cup

10 Jan	Bradford PA (1)	A	L	0-2

London FA Challenge Cup

22 Sep	Q P R	H	D	1-1
29 Sep	Q P R	A	W	3-2
20 Oct	Chelsea	A	W	1-0
10 Nov	Tottenham H	A	L	1-2

London Professional Charity Fund

27 Oct	West Ham U	A	L	2-3

Friendly

31 Jan	Everton	H	L	1-2

Position in Football League Table

	P	W	L	D	F:A	Pts	
Notts Co	38	23	8	7	77:36	53	1st
Arsenal	38	20	9	9	54 38	49	3rd

SEASON 1914-1915
FOOTBALL LEAGUE (DIVISION 2)

1Sep	Glossop	H	W	3-0
5 Sep	Wolverhampton W	A	L	0-1
8Sep	Glossop	A	W	4-0
12 Sep	Fulham	H	W	3-0
19 Sep	Stockport Co	A	D	1-1
26 Sep	Hull C	H	W	2-1
3 Oct	Leeds C	A	D	2-2
10 Oct	Clapton Orient	H	W	2-1
17 Oct	Blackpool	H	W	2-0
24 Oct	Derby Co	A	L	0-4
31 Oct	Lincoln C	H	D	1-1
7 Nov	Birmingham	A	L	0-3
14 Nov	Grimsby T	H	W	6-0
18 Nov	Nottingham F	A	D	1-1
21 Nov	Hudderstield T	A	L	0-3
28 Nov	Bristol C	H	W	3-0
5 Dec	Bury	A	L	1-3
12 Dec	Preston NE	H	L	1-2
25 Dec	Leicester	A	W	4-1
26 Dec	Leicester	H	W	6-0
1 Jan	Barnsley	A	L	0-1
2 Jan	Wolverhampton W	H	W	5-1
16 Jan	Fulham	A	W	1-0
23 Jan	Stockport Co	H	W	3-1
6 Feb	Leeds C	H	W	2-0
13 Feb	Clapton Orient	A	L	0-1
20 Feb	Blackpool	A	W	2-0
27 Feb	Derby Co	H	L	1-2
6 Mar	Lincoln C	A	L	0-1
13 Mar	Birmingham	H	W	1-0
20 Mar	Grimsby T	A	L	0-1
27 Mar	Huddersfield T	H	L	0-3
2 Apr	Hull C	A	L	0-1
3 Apr	Bristol C	A	D	1-1
5 Apr	Barnsley	H	W	1-0
10 Apr	Bury	H	W	3-1
17 Apr	Preston NE	A	L	0-3
24 Apr	Nottingham F	H	W	7-0

FA Cup

9 Jan	Menthyr T (1)	H*	W	3-0
30 Jan	Chelsea (2)	A	L	0-1

by arrangement

London FA Challenge Cup

21 Sep	Tufnell Park	H	W	6-0
19 Oct	Q P R	H	W	2-1
9 Nov	Crystal Palace	A	W	2-0
7 Dec	Millwall (Final)	A	L	1-2

London Protessional Charity Fund

2 Nov	West Ham U	H	W	1-0

Friendly

19 Dec	Swindon T		L	1-2

Position in Football League Table

	P	W	L	D	F:A	Pts	
Derby Co	38	23	8	7	71:33	53	1st
Arsenal	38	19	14	5	69:41	48	5th

No League football was played throughout the First World War. Competitive football was played, by Arsenal, during the seasons 1915-16 through 1919-1920, in the form of the London Football Combination and other London based friendlies. Arsenal's highest placing in the London Football combination was 3rd for seasons 1915-16 and 1918-19. Arsenal was a Second Division club at the outbreak of the First World War, finishing fifth in the last pre-war season. After the war, the First Division was increased from 20 to 22 clubs, and Arsenal illogically and possibly corruptly, were elected to one of the new places. Since then they have remained a First Division club, and from now on the records are given in more detail.

SEASON 1919-1920
FOOTBALL LEAGUE (DIVISION 1)

30 Aug	Newcastle U	H	L	0-1
1 Sep	Liverpool	A	W	3-2
6 Sep	Newcastle U	A	L	1-3
8 Sep	Liverpool	H	W	1-0
13 Sep	Sunderland	A	D	1-1
20 Sep	Sunderland	H	W	3-2
27 Sep	Blackburn Rov	A	D	2-2
4 Oct	Blackburn Rov	H	L	0-1
11 Oct	Everton	A	W	3-2
18 Oct	Everton	H	D	1-1
25 Oct	Bradford C	H	L	1-2
1 Nov	Bradford C	A	D	1-1
8 Nov	Bolton W	H	D	2-2
15 Nov	Bolton W	A	D	2-2
22 Nov	Notts Co	H	W	3-1
29 Nov	Notts Co	A	D	2-2
6 Dec	Chelsea	H	D	1-1
13 Dec	Chelsea	A	L	1-3
20 Dec	Sheffield Wed	H	W	3-1
25 Dec	Derby Co	A	L	1-2
26 Dec	Derby Co	H	W	1-0
27 Dec	Sheffield Wed	A	W	2-1
3 Jan	Manchester C	H	D	2-2
17 Jan	Manchester C	A	L	1-4
24 Jan	Aston Villa	H	L	0-1
7 Feb	Oldham Ath	H	W	3-2
11 Feb	Aston Villa	A	L	1-2
14 Feb	Oldham Ath	A	L	0-3
21 Feb	Manchester U	H	L	0-3
28 Feb	Manchester U	A	W	1-0
6 Mar	Sheffield U	A	L	0-2
13 Mar	Sheffield U	H	W	3-0
20 Mar	Middlesbrough	A	L	0-1
27 Mar	Middlesbrough	H	W	2-1
3 Apr	Burnley	A	L	1-2
5 Apr	W B A	H	W	1-0
6 Apr	W B A	A	L	0-1
10 Apr	Burnley	H	W	2-0
17 Apr	Preston NE	A	D	1-1
24 Apr	Preston NE	H	D	0-0
28 Apr	Bradford PA	A	D	0-0
1 May	Bradford PA	H	W	3-0

FA Cup

10 Jan	Rochdale (1)	H	W	4-2
31 Jan	Bristol C (2)	A	L	0-1

Appearances (Goals)

Baker A 17 · Blyth W 29 (4) · Bradshaw F 33 (2) · Buckley C 23 (1) · Burgess D 7 (1) · Butler J 21 (1) · Coopland W 1 · Cownley F 4 · Dunn S 16 · Graham J 22 (5) · Greenaway D 3 · Groves F 29 (5) · Hardinge H 13 (3) · Hutchins A 18 · Lewis C 5 (1) · McKinnon A 41 · North F 4 1 · Pagnam F 25 (13) · Pattison G 1 · Peart J 5 · Rutherford J 36 (3) · Shaw J 33 · Toner J 15 (1) · Voysey C 5 · White H 29 (15) · Whittaker T 1 · Williamson E 26 · Total: 27 players (56)

Position in League Table

	P	W	L	D	F:A	Pts	
W B A	42	28	10	4	104:47	60	1st
Arsenal	42	15	15	12	56:58	42	10th

SEASON 1920-1921
FOOTBALL LEAGUE (DIVISION 1)

28 Aug	Aston Villa	A	L	0-5
30 Aug	Manchester U	H	W	2-0
4 Sep	Aston Villa	H	L	0-1
6 Sep	Manchester U	A	D	1-1
11 Sep	Manchester C	H	W	2-1
18 Sep	Manchester C	A	L	1-3
25 Sep	Middlesbrough	H	D	2-2
2 Oct	Middlesbrough	A	L	1-2
9 Oct	Bolton W	H	D	0-0
16 Oct	Bolton W	A	D	1-1
23 Oct	Derby County	A	D	1-1
30 Oct	Derby County	H	W	2-0
6 Nov	Blackburn R	A	D	2-2
13 Nov	Blackburn R	H	W	2-0
20 Nov	Huddersfield T	A	W	4-0
27 Nov	Huddersfield T	H	W	2-0
4 Dec	Chelsea	A	W	2-1
11 Dec	Chelsea	H	D	1-1
18 Dec	Bradford C	A	L	1-3
25 Dec	Everton	A	W	4-2
27 Dec	Everton	H	D	1-1
1 Jan	Bradford C	H	L	1-2
15 Jan	Tottenham	A	L	1-2
22 Jan	Tottenham	H	W	3-2
29 Jan	Sunderland	H	L	1-2
5 Feb	Sunderland	A	L	1-5
12 Feb	Oldham Ath	A	D	1-1
19 Feb	Oldham Ath	H	D	2-2
26 Feb	Preston N E	A	W	1-0
12 Mar	Burnley	A	L	0-1
19 Mar	Burnley	H	D	1-1
26 Mar	Sheffield U	H	L	2-6
28 Mar	W B A	H	W	2-1
29 Mar	W B A	A	W	4-3
2 Apr	Sheffield U	A	D	1-1
9 Apr	Bradford PA	H	W	2-1
16 Apr	Bradford PA	A	W	1-0
23 Apr	Newcastle U	H	D	1-1
25 Apr	Preston NE	H	W	2-1
30 Apr	Newcastle U	A	L	0-1
2 May	Liverpool	H	L	0-0
7 May	Liverpool	A	L	0-3

FA Cup

8 Jan	Q P R (1)	A	L	0-2

Appearances (Goals)

Baker A 37 (2) · Blyth W 39 (7) · Bradshaw F 21 · Buckley C 4 (1) · Burgess D 4 · Butler J 36 · Cownley F 1 · Dunn S 9 · Graham A 30 (5) · Groves G 13 (1) · Hopkins J 8 (2) · Hutchins A 39 · McKenzie A 5 (1) · McKinnon A 37 (2) · North E 8 2 · Pagnam F 25 (14) · Paterson Dr J 20 · Pattison G 6 · Peart J 1 · Rutherford J 32 (7) · Shaw J 28 · Smith J 10 (1) · Toner J 11 (3) · Walden H 2 (1) · White H 26 (10) · Whittaker T 5 · Willamson E 33 · Total: 27 players (59)

Position in League Table

	P	W	L	D	F:A	Pts	
Burnley	42	23	6	13	79:36	59	1st
Arsenal	42	15	13	14	59:63	44	9th

SEASON 1921-1922
FOOTBALL LEAGUE (DIVISION 1)

27 Aug	Sheffield U	H	L	1-2
29 Aug	Preston NE	A	L	2-3
3 Sep	Sheffield U	A	L	1-4
5 Sep	Preston NE	H	W	1-0
10 Sep	Manchester C	A	L	0-2
17 Sep	Manchester C	H	L	0-1
24 Sep	Everton	A	D	1-1
1 Oct	Everton	H	W	1-0
8 Oct	Sunderland	A	L	0-1
15 Oct	Sunderland	H	L	1-2
22 Oct	Huddersfield T	A	L	0-2
29 Oct	Huddersfield T	H	L	1-3
5 Nov	Birmingham	A	W	1-0
12 Nov	Birmingham	H	W	5-2
19 Nov	Bolton W	A	L	0-1
3 Dec	Blackburn Rov	A	W	1-0
10 Dec	Blackburn Rov	H	D	1-1
12 Dec	Bolton W	H	D	1-1
17 Dec	Oldham Ath	A	L	1-2
24 Dec	Oldham Ath	H	L	0-1
26 Dec	Cardiff C	H	D	0-0
27 Dec	Cardiff C	A	L	3-4
31 Dec	Chelsea	A	W	2-0
14 Jan	Chelsea	H	W	1-0
21 Jan	Burnley	H	D	0-0
4 Feb	Newcastle U	H	W	2-1
11 Feb	Newcastle U	A	L	1-3
20 Feb	Burnley	A	L	0-1
25 Feb	Liverpool	A	L	0-4
11 Mar	Manchester U	A	L	0-1
18 Mar	Aston Villa	A	L	0-2
22 Mar	Liverpool	H	W	1-0
25 Mar	Aston Villa	H	W	2-0
1 Apr	Middlesbrough	H	D	2-2
5 Apr	Manchester U	H	W	3-1
8 Apr	Middlesbrough	A	L	2-4
15 Apr	Tottenham H	A	L	0-2
17 Apr	W B A	A	W	3-0
18 Apr	W B A	H	D	2-2
22 Apr	Tottenham H	H	W	1-0
29 Apr	Bradford C	A	W	2-0
6 May	Bradford C	H	W	1-0

FA Cup

7 Jan	Q P R (1)	H	D	0-0
11 Jan	Q P R (1R)	A	W	2-1
28 Jan	Bradford C (2)	A	W	3-2
18 Feb	Leicester C (3)	H	W	3-0
4 Mar	Preston NE (4)	H	D	1-1
8 Mar	Preston NE (4R)	A	L	1-2

Appearances (Goals)

Baker A 32 (4) · Blyth W 25 (1) · Boreham R 22 (10) · Bradshaw F 32 (2) · Burgess D 2 · Butler J25 (2) · Cownley F 10 · Creegan W 5 · Dunn S 1 · Earle S 1 · Graham A 21 (3) · Henderson W 5 · Hutchins A 37 · Hopkins J 11 (3) · Maxwell T 1 · Milne W 4 · McKenzie A 3 · McKinnon A 17 · North F 11 (3) · Paterson Dr J 2 · Pattison G 2 · Rutherford J 36 · Shaw J 6 · Toner J 24 (1) · Turnbull R 5 · Voysey C 1 · Whittaker T 36 (1) · White H 35 (14) · Williamson E 41 · Young A 9 (2) · Total: 30 players (47)

Position in League Table

	P	W	L	D	F:A	Pts	
Liverpool	42	22	7	13	63:36	57	1st
Arsenal	42	15	20	7	47:56	37	17th

SEASON 1922-1923
FOOTBALL LEAGUE (DIVISION 1)

26 Aug	Liverpool	A	L	2-5
28 Aug	Burnley	H	D	1-1
2 Sep	Liverpool	H	W	1-0
4 Sep	Burnley	A	L	1-4
9 Sep	Cardiff C	A	L	1-4
16 Sep	Cardiff C	H	W	2-1
23 Sep	Tottenham H	A	W	2-1
30 Sept	Tottenham H	H	L	0-2
2 Oct	Sheffield U	A	L	1-2
7 Oct	W B A	H	W	3-1
14 Oct	W B A	A	L	0-7
21 Oct	Newcastle U	A	D	1-1
28 Oct	Newcastle U	H	L	1-2
4 Nov	Everton	A	L	0-1
11 Nov	Everton	H	L	1-2
18 Nov	Sunderland	A	D	3-3
25 Nov	Sunderland	H	L	2-3
2 Dec	Birmingham	A	L	2-3
9 Dec	Birmingham	H	W	1-0
16 Dec	Huddersfield T	H	D	1-1
23 Dec	Huddersfield T	A	L	0-4
25 Dec	Bolton W	A	L	1-4
26 Dec	Bolton W	H	W	5-0
30 Dec	Stoke C	H	W	3-0
1 Jan	Blackburn Rov	A	W	5-0
6 Jan	Stoke C	A	L	0-1
20 Jan	Manchester C	H	W	1-0
27 Jan	Manchester C	A	D	0-0
3 Feb	Nottingham F	A	L	1-2
10 Feb	Nottingham F	H	W	2-0
17 Feb	Chelsea	A	D	0-0
24 Feb	Chelsea	H	W	3-1
3 Mar	Middlesbrough	A	L	0-2
10 Mar	Middlesbrough	H	W	3-0
17 Mar	Oldham Ath	H	W	2-0
24 Mar	Oldham Ath	A	D	0-0
31 Mar	Aston Villa	H	W	2-0
2 Apr	Blackburn	H	D	1-1
7 Apr	Aston Villa	A	D	1-1
14 Apr	Preston NE	H	D	1-1
21 Apr	Preston NE	A	W	2-1
28 Apr	Sheffield U	H	W	2-0

FA Cup

13 Jan	Liverpool (1)	A	D	0-0
17 Jan	Liverpool (1R)	H	L	1-4

Appearances (Goals)

Baker A 29 (6) · Blyth W 31 (9) · Boreham R 27 (8) · Bradshaw F 17 · Butler J 18 · Clarke J 2 · Dunn S 17 · Earle S 1 (1) · Elvey J 1 · Graham A 17 (1) · Henderson W 2 · Hopkins J 2 (2) · Hutchins A 10 (1) · John R 24 · Kennedy A 24 · McKenzie A 7 (1) · Milne W 31 · Mackie J 23 · Paterson Dr J 27 · Robson J 20 · Roe A 4 (1) · Rutherford J 26 (1) · Toner J 7 · Townrow F 1 · Turnbull R 35 (20) · Voysey C 18 (4) · White H 11 (1) · Whittaker T 13 (1) · Willamson E 5 · Young A 13 (3) · Own goals 1 · Total: 30 players (61)

Position in League Table

	P	W	L	D	F:A	Pts	
Liverpool	42	26	8	8	70:31	60	1st
Arsenal	42	16	16	10	61:62	42	11th

SEASON 1923-1924
FOOTBALL LEAGUE (DIVISION 1)

25 Aug	Newcastle	H	L	1-4
27 Aug	West Ham U	A	L	0-1
1 Sep	Newcastle U	A	L	0-1
8 Sep	W B A	A	L	0-4
10 Sep	West Ham U	H	W	4-1
15 Sep	W B A	H	W	1-0
22 Sep	Birmingham	A	W	2-0
29 Sep	Birmingham	H	D	0-0
6 Oct	Manchester C	A	L	0-1
13 Oct	Manchester C	H	L	1-2
20 Oct	Bolton W	A	W	2-1
27 Oct	Bolton W	H	D	0-0

3 Nov	Middlesbrough	H	W 2-1
10 Nov	Middlesbrough	A	D 0-0
17 Nov	Tottenham H	H	D 1-1
24 Nov	Tottenham H	A	L 0-3
1 Dec	Blackburn Rov	H	D 2-2
8 Dec	Blackburn Rov	A	L 0-2
15 Dec	Huddersfield T	H	L 1-3
22 Dec	Huddersfield T	A	L 1-6
26 Dec	Notts Co	A	W 2-1
27 Dec	Notts Co	H	D 0-0
29 Dec	Chelsea	H	W 1-0
5 Jan	Chelsea	A	D 0-0
19 Jan	Cardiff C	H	L 1-2
26 Dec	Cardiff C	A	L 0-4
9 Feb	Sheffield U	A	L 1-3
16 Feb	Aston Villa	H	L 0-1
25 Feb	Sheffield U	H	L 1-3
1 Mar	Liverpool	H	W 3-1
12 Mar	Aston Villa	A	L 1-2
15 Mar	Nottingham F	A	L 1-2
22 Mar	Nottingham F	H	W 1-0
2 Apr	Liverpool	A	D 0-0
5 Apr	Burnley	H	W 2-0
12 Apr	Sunderland	H	W 2-0
18 Apr	Everton	A	L 1-3
19 Apr	Sunderland	A	D 1-1
21 Apr	Everton	H	L 0-1
26 Apr	Preston NE	A	W 2-0
28 Mar	Burnley	A	L 1-4
3 May	Preston NE	H	L 1-2

FA Cup

12 Jan	Luton (1)	H	W 4-1
2 Feb	Cardiff (2)	A	L 0-1

Appearances (Goals)

Baker A 21 (1) · Blyth W 27 (3) · Boreham R 2 · Butler J 24 · Clarke J 2 · Earle S 2 (2) · Graham A 25 (1) · Haden S 31 (3) · John R 15 · Jones F 2 · Kennedy A 29 Mackie J 31 · Milne W 36 (1) · Neil A 11 (2) · Paterson Dr J 21 · Ramsay J 11 (4) · Robson J 42 · Rutherford J 22 (2) · Toner J 3 · Townrow F 7 (2) · Turnbull R 18 (6) · Voysey C 10 (2) · Wallington E 1 · Whittaker T 8 · Woods H 36 (8) · Young A 25 (2) Own goals 1 · Total: 26 players (40)

Position in League Table

	P	W	L	D	F:A	Pts	
H.field T	42	23	8	11	60:33	57	1st
Arsenal	42	12	21	9	40:63	33	19th

SEASON 1924-1925
FOOTBALL LEAGUE (DIVISION 1)

30 Aug	Nottingham F	A	W 2-0
1 Sep	Manchester C	H	W 1-0
6 Sep	Liverpool	H	W 2-0
13 Sep	Newcastle U	A	D 2-2
17 Sep	Manchester C	A	L 0-2
20 Sep	Sheffield U	H	W 2-0
27 Sep	West Ham U	A	L 0-1
4 Oct	Blackburn Rov	H	W 1-0
11 Oct	Huddersfield T	A	L 0-4
13 Oct	Bury	H	L 0-1
18 Oct	Aston Villa	H	D 1-1
25 Oct	Tottenham H	H	W 1-0
1 Nov	Bolton W	A	L 1-4
8 Nov	Notts Co	H	L 0-1
15 Nov	Everton	A	W 3-2
22 Nov	Sunderland	H	D 0-0
29 Nov	Cardiff C	A	D 1-1
6 Dec	Preston NE	H	W 4-0
13 Dec	Burnley	A	L 0-1
20 Dec	Leeds U	H	W 6-1
25 Dec	Birmingham	A	L 1-2
26 Dec	Birmingham	H	L 0-1
27 Dec	Nottingham F	H	W 2-1
3 Jan	Liverpool	A	L 1-2
17 Jan	Newcastle U	H	L 0-2
24 Jan	Sheffield U	A	L 1-2
7 Feb	Blackburn Rov	A	L 0-1
14 Feb	Huddersfield T	H	L 0-5
28 Feb	Tottenham H	A	L 0-2
7 Mar	Bolton W	H	W 1-0
14 Mar	Notts Co	A	L 1-2
21 Mar	Everton	H	W 3-1
23 Mar	West Ham U	H	L 1-2
28 Mar	Sunderland	A	L 0-2
1 Apr	Aston Villa	A	L 0-4
4 Apr	Cardiff C	H	D 1-1
11 Apr	Preston NE	A	L 0-2
13 Apr	W B A	A	L 0-2
14 Apr	W B A	H	W 2-0
18 Apr	Burnley	H	W 5-0
25 Apr	Leeds U	A	L 0-1
2 May	Bury	A	L 0-2

FA Cup

14 Jan	West Ham U (1)	A	D 0-0
21 Jan	West Ham U (1R)	H	D 2-2
26 Jan	West Ham U (1R)	A	L 0-1

Appearances (Goals)

Baker A 32 (2) · Blyth W 17 (1) · Brain J 28 (12) · Butler J 39 (3) · Clarke J 2 · Cock D 2 · Haden S 15 (1) · Hoar S 19 · Hughes J 1 · John R 39 (2) · Kennedy A 40 · Lewis D 16 · Mackie J 19 · Milne W 32 · Neil A 16 (2) · Ramsey J 30 4 · Robson J 26 · Roe A 1 · Rutherford J 20 2 · Toner J 26 (2) · Turnbull R 1 · Whittaker T 1 · Woods H 32 (13) · Young A 8 (2) · Total: 24 players (46)

Position in League Table

	P	W	L	D	F:A	Pts	
H.field T	42	21	5	16	69:28	58	1st
Arsenal	42	14	23	5	46:58	33	20th

SEASON 1925-1926
FOOTBALL LEAGUE (DIVISION 1)

29 Aug	Tottenham H	H	L 0-1
31 Aug	Leicester	H	D 2-2
5 Sep	Manchester U	A	W 1-0
7 Sep	Leicester C	A	W 1-0
12 Sep	Liverpool	H	D 1-1
19 Sep	Burnley	A	D 2-2
21 Sep	West Ham U	H	W 3-2
26 Sep	Leeds U	H	W 4-1
3 Oct	Newcastle U	A	L 0-7
5 Oct	West Ham U	A	W 4-0
10 Oct	Bolton W	H	L 2-3
17 Oct	Cardiff C	H	W 5-0
24 Oct	Sheffield U	A	L 0-4
31 Oct	Everton	H	W 4-1
7 Nov	Manchester C	A	W 5-2
14 Nov	Bury	H	W 6-1
21 Nov	Blackburn Rov	A	W 3-2
28 Nov	Sunderland	H	W 2-0
5 Dec	Huddersfield T	A	D 2-2
12 Dec	W B A	H	W 1-0
19 Dec	Birmingham	A	L 0-1
25 Dec	Notts Co	H	W 3-0
26 Dec	Notts Co	A	L 1-4
1 Jan	Tottenham H	A	D 1-1
16 Jan	Manchester U	H	W 3-2
23 Jan	Liverpool	A	L 0-3
3 Feb	Burnley	H	L 1-2
6 Feb	Leeds U	A	L 2-4
13 Feb	Newcastle U	H	W 3-0
23 Feb	Cardiff C	A	D 0-0
13 Mar	Everton	A	W 3-2
17 Mar	Sheffield U	H	W 4-0
20 Mar	Manchester C	H	W 1-0
27 Mar	Bury	A	D 2-2
2 Apr	Aston Villa	A	L 0-3
3 Apr	Blackburn Rov	H	W 4-2
5 Apr	Aston Villa	H	W 2-0
10 Apt	Sunderland	A	L 1-2
17 Apt	Huddersfield T	H	W 3-1
24 Apr	W B A	A	L 1-2
28 Apr	Bolton W	A	D 1-1
1 May	Birmingham	H	W 3-0

FA Cup

9 Jan	Wolves (3)	A	D 1-1
13 Jan	Wolves (3R)	H	W 1-0
30 Jan	Blackburn R (4)	H	W 3-1
20 Feb	Aston Villa (5)	A	D 1-1
24 Feb	Aston Villa (5R)	H	W 2-0
6 Mar	Swansea (6)	A	L 1-2

Appearances (Goals)

Baker A 31 (6) · Blyth W 40 (7) · Brain J 41 (33) · Buchan C 39 (19) · Butler J 41 · Cock D 1 · Haden S 25 (2) · Harper W 19 · Hoar S 21 (3) · Hulme J 15 (2) · John R 29 · Kennedy A 16 · Lawson H 13 (2) · Lewis D 14 · Mackie J 35 · Milne W 5 · Neil A 27 (6) · Parker T 7 (3) · Paterson Dr J 1 (1) · Ramsey J 16 · Robson J 9 · Rutherford J 3 · Rutherford J J 1 · Seddon W 1 · Toner J 2 · Voysey C 1 · Woods H 2 · Young A 7 · Own goals 3 · Total: 28 players (87)

Position in League Table

	P	W	L	D	F:A	Pts	
H.field T	42	23	8	11	92:60	57	1st
Arsenal	42	22	12	8	87:63	52	2nd

SEASON 1926-1927
FOOTBALL LEAGUE (DIVISION 1)

28 Aug	Derby Co	H	W 2-1
1 Sep	Bolton W	H	W 2-1
4 Sep	Sheffield U	A	L 0-4
6 Sep	Bolton W	A	D 2-2
11 Sep	Leicester C	H	D 2-2
15 Sep	Manchester U	A	D 2-2
18 Sep	Liverpool	H	W 2-0
25 Sep	Leeds U	A	L 1-4
2 Oct	Newcastle U	H	D 2-2
9 Oct	Burnley	A	L 0-2
16 Oct	West Ham U	H	D 2-2
23 Oct	Sheffield Wed	H	W 6-2
30 Oct	Everton	A	L 1-3
6 Nov	Blackburn Rov	H	D 2-2
13 Nov	Huddersfield T	A	D 3-3
20 Nov	Sunderland	H	L 2-3
27 Nov	W B A	A	W 3-1
4 Dec	Bury	H	W 1-0
11 Dec	Birmingham	A	D 0-0
18 Dec	Tottenham H	H	L 2-4
27 Dec	Cardiff C	A	L 0-2
28 Dec	Manchester U	H	W 1-0
1 Jan	Cardiff C	H	W 3-2
15 Jan	Derby Co	A	W 2-0
22 Jan	Sheffield U	H	D 1-1
5 Feb	Liverpool	A	L 0-3
10 Feb	Leicester C	A	L 1-2
12 Feb	Leeds	H	W 1-0
26 Feb	Burnley	H	W 6-2
7 Mar	West Ham U	A	L 0-7
12 Mar	Sheffield Wed	A	L 2-4
19 Mar	Everton	H	L 1-2
2 Apr	Huddersfield T	H	L 0-2
6 Apr	Newcastle U	A	L 1-6
9 Apr	Sunderland	A	L 1-5
15 Apr	Aston Villa	H	W 2-1
16 Apr	W B A	H	W 4-1
18 Apr	Aston Villa	A	W 3-2
28 Apr	Blackburn Rov	A	W 2-1
30 Apr	Birmingham	H	W 3-0
4 May	Bury	A	L 2-3
7 May	Tottenham H	A	W 4-0

FA Cup

8 Jan	Sheffield U (3)	A	W 3-2
29 Jan	Port Vale (4)	A	D 2-2
2 Feb	Port Vale (4R)	H	W 1-0
19 Feb	Liverpool (5)	H	W 2-0
5 Mar	Wolves (6)	H	W 2-1
26 Mar	Southampton (SF) (at Chelsea)		W 2-1
23 Apr	Cardiff (F) (at Wembley)		L 0-1

Appearances (Goals)

Baker A 23 · Barley J 3 1 · Blyth W 33 3 · Bowen E 1 · Brain J 37 31 · Buchan C 33 14 · Butler J 31 · Cope H 11 · Haden S 17 4 · Harper W 23 · Hoar S 16 2 · Hulme J 37 8 · John R 41 3 · Kennedy A 11 · Lambert J 16 1 · Lee J 7 · Lewis D 17 · Milne W 6 · Moody J 2 · Parker T 42 4 · Peel H 9 · Ramsey J 12 2 · Roberts H 2 · Seddon C 17 · Shaw J 5 1 · Tricker R 4 3 · Young A 6 · Total: 27 players 77

Position in League Table

	P	W	L	D	F:A	Pts	
Newcastle U	42	25	11	6	96:58	56	1st
Arsenal	42	17	16	9	77:86	43	11th

SEASON 1927-1928
FOOTBALL LEAGUE (DIVISION 1)

27 Aug	Bury	A	L 1-5
31 Aug	Burnley	H	W 4-1
3 Sep	Sheffield U	H	W 6-1
5 Sep	Burnley	A	W 2-1
10 Sep	Aston Villa	A	D 2-2
17 Sep	Sunderland	H	W 2-1
24 Sep	Derby Co	A	L 0-4
1 Oct	West Ham U	H	D 2-2
8 Oct	Portsmouth	A	W 3-2
15 Oct	Leicester C	H	D 2-2
22 Oct	Sheffield Wed	A	D 1-1
29 Oct	Bolton W	H	L 1-2
5 Nov	Blackburn Rov	A	L 1-4
12 Nov	Middlesbrough	H	W 3-1
19 Nov	Birmingham	A	D 1-1
3 Dec	Huddersfield	A	L 1-2
10 Dec	Newcastle U	H	W 4-1
17 Dec	Manchester U	A	L 1-4
24 Dec	Everton	H	W 3-2
27 Dec	Liverpool	A	W 2-0
31 Dec	Bury	H	W 3-1
2 Jan	Tottenham H	H	D 1-1
7 Jan	Sheffield U	A	L 4-6
21 Jan	Aston Villa	H	L 0-3
4 Feb	Derby Co	H	L 3-4
11 Feb	West Ham U	A	D 2-2
25 Feb	Leicester C	A	L 2-3
7 Mar	Liverpool	H	W 6-3
10 Mar	Bolton W	A	D 1-1
14 Mar	Sunderland	A	L 1-5
17 Mar	Blackburn Rov	H	W 3-2
28 Mar	Portsmouth	H	L 0-2
31 Mar	Birmingham	H	D 2-2
6 Apr	Cardiff C	H	W 3-0
7 Apr	Tottenham H	A	L 0-2
9 Apr	Cardiff C	A	D 2-2
14 Apr	Huddersfield	H	D 0-0
18 Apr	Middlesbrough	A	D 2-2
21 Apr	Newcastle U	A	D 1-1
28 Apr	Manchester U	H	L 0-1
2 May	Sheffield Wed	H	D 1-1
5 May	Everton	A	D 3-3

FA Cup

14 Jan	W B A (3)	H	W 2-0
28 Jan	Everton (4)	H	W 4-3
18 Feb	Aston Villa (5)	H	W 4-1
3 Mar	Stoke C (6)	H	W 4-1
24 Mar	Blackburn R (SF) (at Leicester)		L 0-1

Appearances (Goals)

Baker A 36 (3) · Barley J 2 · Blyth W 39 (7) · Brain J 39 (25) · Buchan C 30 (16) · Butler J 39 · Clark A 1 · Cope H 24 · Hapgood E 3 · Hoar S 38 (9) · Hulme J 36 (8) · John R 39 (1) · Kennedy A 2 · Lambert J 16 (3) · Lewis D 33 · Moody J 4 · Parker T 42 (4) · Paterson W 5 · Peel H 13 · H 3 · Seddon C 4 · Shaw J 6 (3) · Thompson L 1 · Tricker R 7 (2) · Own goals 1 · Total: 24 players (82)

Position in League Table

	P	W	L	D	F:A	Pts	
Everton	42	20	9	13	102:66	53	1st
Arsenal	42	13	14	15	82:86	41	10th

SEASON 1928-1929
FOOTBALL LEAGUE (DIVISION 1)

25 Aug	Sheffield Wed	A	L 2-3
29 Aug	Derby Co	H	L 1-3
1 Sep	Bolton W	H	W 2-0
8 Sep	Portsmouth	A	L 0-2
15 Sep	Birmingham	H	D 0-0
22 Sep	Manchester C	A	L 1-4
26 Sep	Derby Co	A	D 0-0
29 Sep	Huddersfield	H	W 2-0
6 Oct	Everton	A	L 2-4
13 Oct	West Ham U	H	L 2-3
20 Oct	Newcastle U	A	W 3-0
27 Oct	Liverpool	H	D 4-4
3 Nov	Cardiff C	A	D 1-1
10 Nov	Sheffield U	H	W 2-0
17 Nov	Bury	A	L 0-1
24 Nov	Aston Villa	H	L 2-5
1 Dec	Leicester C	A	D 1-1
8 Dec	Manchester U	H	W 3-1
15 Dec	Leeds	A	D 1-1
22 Dec	Burnley	H	W 3-1
25 Dec	Blackburn Rov	A	L 2-5
26 Dec	Sunderland	H	D 1-1
29 Dec	Sheffield Wed	H	D 2-2
1 Jan	Sunderland	A	L 1-5
5 Jan	Bolter W	A	W 2-1
19 Jan	Portsmouth	H	W 4-0
2 Feb	Manchester C	H	D 0-0
9 Feb	Huddersfield	A	W 1-0
23 Feb	West Ham U	A	W 4-3
9 Mar	Liverpool	A	W 4-2
13 Mar	Birmingham	A	D 1-1
16 Mar	Cardiff C	H	W 2-1
23 Mar	Sheffield U	A	D 2-2
29 Mar	Blackburn Rov	H	W 1-0
30 Mar	Bury	H	W 7-1
2 Apr	Newcastle U	H	L 1-2
6 Apr	Aston Villa	A	L 2-4
13 Apr	Leicester C	H	D 1-1
20 Apr	Manchester U	A	L 1-4
22 Apr	Everton	H	W 2-0
27 Apr	Leeds U	H	W 1-0
4 May	Burnley	A	D 3-3

FA Cup

12 Jan	Stoke (3)	H	W 2-1
26 Jan	Mansfield T (4)	H	W 2-0
16 Feb	Swindon T (5)	A	D 0-0
20 Feb	Swindon T (5R)	H	W 1-0
2 Mar	Aston Villa (6)	A	L 0-1

Appearances (Goals)

Baker A 32 · Barley J 3 · Blyth W 20 (1) · Brain J37 19 · Butler J 22 · Cope H 23 · Hapgood E 17 · Hoar S 6 (1) · Hulme J 41 (6) · Jack D 31 25 · John R 34 (1) · Jones C 39 (6) · Lambert J 6 (1) · Lewis D 32 · Parker T 42 (3) · Parkin R 5 3 · Paterson W 10 · Peel H 24 (5) · Roberts H 20 · Thompson L 17 (5) · Tricker R 1 · Own goals 1 · Total: 21 players (77)

Position in League Table

	P	W	L	D	F:A	Pts	
Sheffield Wed	42	21	11	10	86:62	52	1st
Arsenal	42	16	13	13	77:72	45	9th

SEASON 1929-1930
FOOTBALL LEAGUE (DIVISION 1)

31 Aug	Leeds U	H	W 4-0
4 Sep	Manchester C	A	L 1-3
7 Sep	Sheffield Wed	A	W 2-0
11 Sep	Manchester C	H	W 3-2
14 Sep	Burnley	H	W 6-1
21 Sep	Sunderland	A	W 1-0
25 Sep	Aston Villa	H	L 2-5
28 Sep	Bolton W	H	L 1-2
5 Oct	Everton	A	D 1-1
12 Oct	Derby Co	H	D 1-1
19 Oct	Grimsby T	H	W 4-1
26 Oct	Manchester U	A	L 0-1
2 Nov	West Ham U	H	L 0-1
9 Nov	Birmingham	A	W 3-2
23 Nov	Blackburn Rov	A	D 1-1
27 Nov	Middlesbrough	H	L 1-2
30 Nov	Newcastle U	H	L 0-1
14 Dec	Huddersfield T	H	W 2-0
16 Dec	Sheffield U	A	L 1-4
21 Dec	Liverpool	A	L 0-1
25 Dec	Portsmouth	A	W 1-0
26 Dec	Portsmouth	H	L 1-2
28 Dec	Leeds U	A	L 0-2
4 Jan	Sheffield W	H	L 2-3
18 Jan	Burnley	A	D 2-2
1 Feb	Bolton W	A	D 0-0
8 Feb	Everton	H	W 4-0
19 Feb	Derby Co	A	L 1-4
22 Feb	Grimsby T	A	D 1-1
8 Mar	West Ham U	A	L 2-3
12 Mar	Manchester U	H	W 4-2
15 Mar	Birmingham	H	W 1-0
29 Mar	Blackburn Rov	H	W 4-0
2 Apr	Liverpool	H	L 0-1
5 Apr	Newcastle U	A	D 1-1
9 Apr	Middlesbrough	A	D 1-1
12 Apr	Sheffield U	H	W 8-1
18 Apr	Leicester	H	D 1-1
19 Apr	Huddersfield	A	D 2-2
21 Apr	Leicester C	A	D 6-6
28 Apr	Sunderland	H	L 0-1
3 May	Aston Villa	H	L 2-4

FA Cup

11 Jan	Chelsea (3)	H	W 2-0
25 Jan	Birmingham (4)	H	D 2-2
29 Jan	Birmingham (4R)	A	W 1-0
15 Feb	Middlesbrough (5)	A	W 2-0
1 Mar	West Ham U (6)	A	W 3-0
22 Mar	Hull C (SF) (at Leeds)		D 2-2
26 Mar	Hull C (SFR) (at Aston Villa)		W 1-0
26 Apr	Huddersfield T (F) (at Wembley)		W 2-0

Appearances (Goals)

Baker A 19 · Bastin C 21 (7) · Brain J 6 · Butler J 2 · Cope H 1 · Halliday D 15 (9) · Hapgood E 38 · Haynes A 13 · Hulme J 37 (14) · Humpish E3 · Jack D 33 (12) · James A 31 (5) · John R 34 · Johnstone W 7 (3) · Jones C 31 (2) Lambert J 20 (19) · Lewis D 30 · Parker T 41 (3) · Peel H 1 · Preedy C 12 · Roberts H 26 · Seddon C 24 · Thompson L 5 (1) · Williams J 12 (3) · Total: 24 players (78)

Position in League Table

	P	W	L	D	F:A	Pts	
Sheffield Wed	42	26	8	8	105:57	60	1st
Arsenal	42	14	17	11	78:66	39	14th

SEASON 1930-1931
FOOTBALL LEAGUE (DIVISION 1)

30 Aug	Blackpool	A	W 4-1
1 Sep	Bolton W	A	W 4-1
6 Sep	Leeds U	H	W 3-1
10 Sep	Blackburn Rov	H	W 3-2
13 Sep	Sunderland	A	W 4-1
15 Sep	Blackburn Rov	A	D 2-2
20 Sep	Leicester C	H	W 4-1
27 Sep	Birmingham	A	W 4-2
4 Oct	Sheffield U	H	D 1-1
11 Oct	Derby Co	A	L 2-4
18 Oct	Manchester U	A	W 2-1
25 Oct	West Ham U	H	D 1-1
1 Nov	Huddersfield T	A	D 1-1
8 Nov	Aston Villa	H	W 5-2
15 Nov	Sheffield Wed	A	W 2-1
22 Nov	Middlesbrough	H	W 5-3
29 Nov	Chelsea	A	W 5-1
13 Dec	Liverpool	A	D 1-1
20 Dec	Newcastle U	H	L 1-2
25 Dec	Manchester C	A	W 4-1
26 Dec	Manchester C	H	W 3-1
27 Dec	Blackpool	H	W 7-1
17 Jan	Sunderland	H	L 1-3
28 Jan	Grimsby T	H	W 9-1
31 Jan	Birmingham	H	D 1-1
5 Feb	Leicester	A	W 7-2
7 Feb	Sheffield U	A	D 1-1
14 Feb	Derby Co	H	W 6-3
21 Feb	Manchester U	H	W 4-1
28 Feb	West Ham U	A	W 4-2
7 Mar	Huddersfield T	H	D 0-0
11 Mar	Leeds U	A	W 2-1
14 Mar	Aston Villa	A	L 1-5
21 Mar	Sheffield W	H	W 2-0
28 Mar	Middlesbrough	A	W 5-2
3 Apr	Portsmouth	A	D 1-1
4 Apr	Chelsea	H	W 2-1
6 Apr	Portsmouth	H	D 1-1
11 Apr	Grimsby T	A	W 1-0
18 Apr	Liverpool	H	W 3-1
25 Apr	Newcastle U	A	W 3-1
2 May	Bolton W	H	W 5-0

FA Cup

10 Jan	Aston Villa (3)	H	D 2-2
14 Jan	Aston Villa (3R)	A	W 3-1
24 Jan	Chelsea (4)	A	L 1-2

FA Charity Shield

8 Oct	Sheffield Wed (at Chelsea)		W 2-1

Appearances (Goals)

Baker A 1 · Bastin C 42 (28) · Brain J 16 (4) · Cope H 1 · Hapgood E 38 · Harper W 19 · Haynes A 2 · Hulme J 32 (14) · Jack D 35 (31) · James A 40 (5) · John R 40 (2) · Johnstone W 2 (1) · Jones C 24 (1) · Keyser G 12 · Lambert J 34 (38) · Male G 3 · Parker T 41 · Preedy C 11 · Roberts H 40 (1) · Seddon C 18 · Thompson L 2 · Williams J 9 (2) · Total: 22 players (127)

Position in League Table

	P	W	L	D	F:A	Pts	
Arsenal	42	28	4	10	127:59	66	1st

SEASON 1931-1932
FOOTBALL LEAGUE (DIVISION 1)

29 Aug	W B A	H	L	0-1
31 Aug	Blackburn Rov	A	D	1-1
5 Sep	Birmingham	A	D	2-2
9 Sep	Portsmouth	H	D	3-3
12 Sep	Sunderland	H	W	2-0
16 Sep	Portsmouth	A	W	3-0
19 Sep	Manchester C	A	W	3-1
26 Sep	Everton	H	W	3-2
3 Oct	Grimsby T	A	L	1-3
10 Oct	Blackpool	A	W	5-1
17 Oct	Bolton W	H	D	1-1
24 Oct	Leicester C	A	W	2-1
31 Oct	Aston Villa	H	D	1-1
7 Nov	Newcastle U	A	L	2-3
14 Nov	West Ham W	H	W	4-1
21 Nov	Chelsea	A	L	1-2
28 Nov	Liverpool	H	W	6-0
5 Dec	Sheffield Wed	A	W	3-1
12 Dec	Huddersfield	H	D	1-1
19 Dec	Middlesbrough	A	W	5-2
25 Dec	Sheffield U	A	L	1-4
26 Dec	Sheffield U	H	L	0-2
2 Jan	W B A	A	L	0-1
16 Jan	Birmingham	H	W	3-0
30 Jan	Manchester C	H	W	4-0
6 Feb	Everton	A	W	3-1
17 Feb	Grimsby	H	W	2-0
20 Feb	Blackpool	H	W	2-0
2 Mar	Bolton W	A	L	0-1
5 Mar	Leicester C	H	W	2-1
19 Mar	Newcastle U	H	W	1-0
25 Mar	Derby Co	H	W	2-1
26 Mar	West Ham U	A	D	1-1
28 Mar	Derby C	A	D	1-1
3 Apr	Chelsea	H	D	1-1
6 Apr	Sunderland	A	L	0-2
9 Apr	Liverpool	A	L	1-2
16 Apr	Sheffield Wed	H	W	3-1
25 Apr	Aston Villa	A	D	1-1
27 Apr	Huddersfield	A	W	2-1
30 Apr	Middlesbrough	H	W	5-0
7 May	Blackburn Rov	H	W	4-0

FA Cup

9 Jan	Darwen (3)	H	W	11-1
23 Jan	Plymouth (4)	H	W	4-2
13 Feb	Portsmouth (5)	A	W	2-0
27 Feb	Huddersfield (6)	A	W	1-0
12 Mar	Manchester C (SF) (at Aston Villa)		W	1-0
23 Apr	Newcastle U (F) (at Wembley)		L	1-2

FA Charity Shield

7 Oct	W B A (at Aston Villa)		W	1-0

Appearances (Goals)

Bastin C 40 (15) · Beasley A 3 · Coleman E 6 (1) · Compton L 4 · Cope H 1 · Hapgood E 41 · Harper W 2 · Haynes A 7 · Hulme J 40 (14) · Jack D 34 (20) · James A 32 (2) · John R 38 (3) · Jones C 37 · Lambert J 36 (22) · Male G 9 · Moss F 27 · Parker T 38 · Parkin R 9 (7) · Preedy C 13 · Roberts H 35 · Seddon C 5 · Stockill R 3 (1) · Thompson L 1 · Williams J 1 · Own goals 5 · Total: 24 players (90)

Position in League Table

	P	W	L	D	F:A	Pts	
Everton	42	26	12	4	116:64	56	1st
Arsenal	42	22	10	10	90:48	54	2nd

SEASON 1932-1933
FOOTBALL LEAGUE (DIVISION 1)

27 Aug	Birmingham	A	W	1-0
31 Aug	W B A	H	L	1-2
3 Sep	Sunderland	H	W	6-1
10 Sep	Manchester C	A	W	3-2
14 Sep	W B A	A	D	1-1
17 Sep	Bolton W	H	W	3-2
24 Sep	Everton	H	W	2-1
1 Oct	Blackpool	A	W	2-1
8 Oct	Derby Co	H	D	3-3
15 Oct	Blackburn Rov	A	W	3-2
22 Oct	Liverpool	A	W	3-2
24 Oct	Leicester C	H	W	8-2
5 Nov	Wolverhampton W	A	W	7-1
12 Nov	Newcastle U	H	W	1-0
19 Nov	Aston Villa	A	L	3-5
26 Nov	Middlesbrough	H	W	4-2
3 Dec	Portsmouth	A	W	3-1
10 Dec	Chelsea	H	W	4-1
17 Dec	Huddersfield	A	W	1-0
24 Dec	Sheffield U	H	W	9-2
26 Dec	Leeds U	H	L	1-2
27 Dec	Leeds U	A	D	0-0
31 Dec	Birmingham	H	W	3-0
2 Jan	Sheffield W	A	L	2-3
7 Jan	Sunderland	A	L	2-3
21 Jan	Manchester C	H	W	2-1
1 Feb	Bolton W	A	W	4-0
4 Feb	Everton	A	D	1-1
11 Feb	Blackpool	H	D	1-1
22 Feb	Derby Co	A	D	2-2
25 Feb	Blackburn Rov	H	W	8-0
4 Mar	Liverpool	H	L	0-1
11 Mar	Leicester C	A	D	1-1
18 Mar	Wolverhampton W	H	L	1-2
25 Mar	Newcastle U	A	L	1-2
1 Apr	Aston Villa	H	W	5-0
8 Apr	Middlesbrough	A	W	4-3
14 Apr	Sheffield Wed	H	W	4-2
15 Apr	Portsmouth	H	W	2-0
22 Apr	Chelsea	A	W	3-1
29 Apr	Huddersfield	H	D	2-2
6 May	Sheffield U	A	L	1-3

FA Cup

14 Jan	Walsall (3)	A	L	0-2

Appearances (Goals)

Bastin C 42 33 · Bowden R 7 2 · Coleman E 27 24 · Compton L 4 · Cope H 4 · Hapgood E 38 · Haynes A 6 · Hill F 26 1 · Hulme J 40 20 · Jack D 34 18 · James A 40 3 · John R 37 · Jones C 16 · Lambert J 12 14 · Male · G Moss F 41 · Parker T 5 · Parkin R 5 · Preedy C 1 · Roberts H 36 · Sidey N 2 · Stockill R 4 3 · Total: 22 players 118

Position in League Table

	P	W	L	D	F:A	Pts	
Arsenal	42	25	9	8	118:61	58	1st

SEASON 1933-1934
FOOTBALL LEAGUE (DIVISION 1)

26 Aug	Birmingham	H	D	1-1
2 Sep	Sheffield W	A	W	2-1
6 Sep	W B A	H	W	3-1
9 Sep	Manchester C	H	D	1-1
13 Sep	W B A	A	L	0-1
16 Sep	Tottenham H	A	D	1-1
23 Sep	Everton	A	L	1-3
30 Sep	Middlesbrough	H	W	6-0
7 Oct	Blackburn Rov	A	D	2-2
14 Oct	Newcastle U	H	W	3-0
21 Oct	Leicester C	H	W	2-0
28 Oct	Aston Villa	A	W	3-2
4 Nov	Portsmouth	H	D	1-1
11 Nov	Wolverhampton W	A	W	1-0
18 Nov	Stoke C	H	W	3-0
25 Nov	Huddersfield T	A	W	1-0
2 Dec	Liverpool	H	W	2-1
9 Dec	Sunderland	A	L	0-3
16 Dec	Chelsea	H	W	2-1
23 Dec	Sheffield U	A	W	3-1
25 Dec	Leeds U	A	W	1-0
26 Dec	Leeds U	H	W	2-0
30 Dec	Birmingham	A	D	0-0
6 Jan	Sheffield W	H	D	1-1
20 Jan	Manchester C	A	L	1-2
31 Jan	Tottenham H	H	L	1-3
3 Feb	Everton	H	L	1-2
10 Feb	Middlesbrough	A	W	2-0
21 Feb	Blackburn	H	W	2-1
24 Feb	Newcastle U	A	W	1-0
8 Mar	Leicester C	A	L	1-4
10 Mar	Aston Villa	H	W	3-2
24 Mar	Wolverhampton W	H	W	3-2
30 Mar	Derby Co	H	W	1-0
31 Mar	Stoke C	A	D	1-1
2 Apr	Derby Co	A	W	4-2
7 Apr	Huddersfield	H	W	3-1
14 Apr	Liverpool	A	W	3-2
18 Apr	Portsmouth	A	L	0-1
21 Apr	Sunderland	H	W	2-1
28 Apr	Chelsea	A	D	2-2
5 May	Sheffield U	H	W	2-0

FA Cup

13 Jan	Luton (3)	A	W	1-0
27 Jan	Crystal Palace (4)	H	W	7-0
17 Feb	Derby Co (5)	H	W	1-0
3 Mar	Aston Villa (6)	H	L	1-2

FA Charity Shield

18 Oct	Everton	A	W	3-0

Appearances (Goals)

Bastin C 38 (13) · Beasley A 23 (10) · Birkett B 15 (5) · Bowden R 32 (13) · Coleman E 12 (1) · Cox G 2 · Dougall P 5 · Drake E 10 (7) · Dunne J 21 (9) · Hapgood E 40 · Haynes A 1 · Hill F 25 Hulme J 8 (5) · Jack D 14 (5) · James A 22 (3) John R 31 (1) · Jones C 29 · Lambert J 3 (1) · Male G 42 · Moss F 37 · Parkin R 5 · Roberts H 30 (1) · Sidey N 12 · Wilson A 5 · Own goals 1 · Total: 24 players (75)

Position in League Table

	P	W	L	D	F:A	Pts	
Arsenal	42	25	8	9	75:47	59	1st

SEASON 1934-1935
FOOTBALL LEAGUE (DIVISION 1)

25 Aug	Portsmouth	A	D	3-3
1 Sep	Liverpool	H	W	8-1
5 Sep	Blackburn Rov	H	W	4-0
8 Sep	Leeds U	A	D	1-1
15 Sep	W B A	H	W	4-3
17 Sep	Blackburn Rov	A	L	0-2
22 Sep	Sheffield Wed	H	D	0-0
29 Sep	Birmingham	H	W	5-1
6 Oct	Stoke C	A	D	2-2
13 Oct	Manchester C	H	W	3-0
20 Oct	Tottenham H	H	W	5-1
27 Oct	Sunderland	A	L	1-2
3 Nov	Everton	H	W	2-0
10 Nov	Grimsby T	A	D	2-2
17 Nov	Aston Villa	H	L	1-2
24 Nov	Chelsea	A	W	5-2
1 Dec	Wolverhampton W	H	W	7-0
8 Dec	Huddersfield T	A	D	1-1
15 Dec	Leicester C	H	W	8-0
22 Dec	Derby Co	A	L	1-3
25 Dec	Preston NE	H	W	5-3
26 Dec	Preston NE	A	L	1-2
29 Dec	Portsmouth	H	D	1-1
5 Jan	Liverpool	A	W	2-0
19 Jan	Leeds U	H	W	3-0
30 Jan	W B A	A	W	3-0
2 Feb	Sheffield W	H	W	4-1
9 Feb	Birmingham	A	L	0-3
20 Feb	Stoke C	H	W	2-0
23 Feb	Manchester C	A	D	1-1
6 Mar	Tottenham H	A	W	6-0
9 Mar	Sunderland	H	D	0-0
16 Mar	Everton	A	W	2-0
23 Mar	Grimsby T	H	D	1-1
30 Mar	Aston Villa	A	W	3-1
6 Apr	Chelsea	H	D	2-2
13 Apr	Wolverhampton W	A	D	1-1
19 Apr	Middlesbrough	H	W	8-0
20 Apr	Huddersfield T	H	W	1-0
22 Apr	Middlesbrough	A	W	1-0
27 Apr	Leicester C	A	W	5-3
4 May	Derby Co	H	L	0-1

FA Cup

12 Jan	Brighton & HA (2)	A	W	2-0
26 Jan	Leicester C (3)	A	W	1-0
16 Feb	Reading (4)	A	W	1-0
2 Mar	Sheffield W (5)	A	L	1-2

FA Charity Shield

28 Nov	Man City	H	W	4-0

Appearances (Goals)

Bastin C 36 (20) · Beasley A 20 (6) · Birkett R 4 (2) · Bowden E 24 (14) · Compton L 5 (1) · Copping W 31 · Crayston J 37 (3) · Davidson R 11 (2) · Dougall P 8 (1) · Drake E 41 (42) · Dunne J 1 · Hapgood E 34 (1) · Hill F 15 (3) · Hulme J 16 (8) · James A 30 (4) · John R 9 · Kirchen A 7 (2) · Male C 39 · Marshall Drj 4 · Moss F 33 (1) · Roberts L 36 · Rogers L 5 (2) · Sidey N 6 · Trim R 1 · Wilson A 9 · Own goals 3 Total: 25 players (115)

Position in League Table

	P	W	L	D	F:A	Pts	
Arsenal	42	23	7	12	115:46	58	1st

SEASON 1935-1936
FOOTBALL LEAGUE (DIVISION 1)

31 Aug	Sunderland	H	W	3-1
3 Sep	Grimsby T	A	L	0-1
7 Sep	Birmingham	A	D	1-1
11 Sep	Grimsby T	H	W	6-0
14 Sep	Sheffield Wed	H	D	2-2
18 Sep	Leeds U	A	D	1-1
21 Sep	Manchester C	H	L	2-3
28 Sep	Stoke C	A	W	3-0
5 Oct	Blackburn Rov	H	W	5-1
12 Oct	Chelsea	A	D	1-1
19 Oct	Portsmouth	A	L	1-2
26 Oct	Preston NE	H	W	2-1
2 Nov	Brentford	A	L	1-2
9 Nov	Derby Co	H	D	1-1
16 Nov	Everton	A	W	2-0
23 Nov	Wolverhampton W	H	W	4-0
30 Nov	Huddersfield T	A	D	0-0
9 Dec	Middlesbrough	H	W	2-0
14 Dec	Aston Villa	A	W	7-1
25 Dec	Liverpool	A	W	1-0
26 Dec	Liverpool	H	L	1-2
28 Dec	Sunderland	A	L	4-5
4 Jan	Birmingham	H	D	1-1
18 Jan	Sheffield Wed	A	L	2-3
1 Feb	Stoke C	H	W	1-0
8 Feb	Blackburn Rov	A	W	1-0
22 Feb	Portsmouth	H	L	2-3
4 Mar	Derby Co	A	W	4-0
7 Mar	Huddersfield T	H	D	1-1
11 Mar	Manchester City	A	L	0-1
14 Mar	Preston NE	A	L	0-1
25 Mar	Everton	H	D	1-1
28 Mar	Wolverhampton W	A	D	2-2
1 Apr	Bolton W	H	D	1-1
4 Apr	Brentford	H	D	1-1
10 Apr	W B A	H	W	4-0
11 Apr	Middlesbrough	A	D	2-2
13 Apr	W B A	A	L	0-1
18 Apr	Aston Villa	H	W	1-0
27 Apr	Chelsea	H	D	1-1
29 Apr	Bolton W	A	L	1-2
2 May	Leeds U	H	D	2-2

FA Cup

11 Jan	Bristol Rov (3)	A	W	5-1
25 Jan	Liverpool (4)	A	W	2-0
15 Feb	Newcastle (5)	A	D	3-3
19 Feb	Newcastle (5R)	H	W	3-0
29 Feb	Barnsley (6)	H	W	4-1
21 Mar	Grimsby T (SF) (at Huddersfield)		W	1-0
25 Apr	Sheffield U (F) (at Wembley)		W	1-0

FA Charity Shield

23 Oct	Sheffield Wed	H	L	0-1

Appearances (Goals)

Bastin C 31 (11) · Beasley A 26 (2) · Bowden R 22 (6) · Cartwright S 5 · Compton L 12 (1) · Copping W 33 · Cox G 5 (1) · Crayston J 36 (5) · Davidson R 13 · Dougall R 8 (3) · Drake E 26 (24) · Dunne J 6 (1) · Hapgood E 33 · Hill F 10 · Hulme J 21 (6) · James A 17 (2) · John R 6 · Joy B 2 · Kirchen A 6 (3) · Male G 35 · Milne J 14 (6) · Moss F 5 · Parkin R 1 (1) · Roberts H 26 (1) · Rogers E 11 (3) · Sidey N 11 · Tuckett E 2 · Westcott R 2 (1) · Wilson A 37 · Own goals 1 · Total: 29 players (78)

Position in League Table

	P	W	L	D	F:A	Pts	
Sunderland	42	25	11	6	109:74	56	1st
Arsenal	42	15	12	15	78:48	45	6th

SEASON 1936-1937
FOOTBALL LEAGUE (DIVISION 1)

29 Aug	Everton	H	W	3-2
3 Sep	Brentford	A	L	0-2
5 Sep	Huddersfield T	A	D	0-0
9 Sep	Brentford	H	D	1-1
12 Sep	Sunderland	H	W	4-1
19 Sep	Wolverhampton W	A	L	2-4
26 Sep	Derby Co	H	D	2-2
3 Oct	Manchester U	A	L	0-2
10 Oct	Sheffield Wed	H	D	1-1
17 Oct	Charlton Ath	A	W	2-0
24 Oct	Grimsby T	H	D	0-0
31 Oct	Liverpool	A	L	1-2
7 Nov	Leeds U	H	W	4-1
14 Nov	Birmingham	A	W	3-1
21 Nov	Middlesbrough	H	W	5-3
28 Nov	W B A	A	W	4-2
5 Dec	Manchester City	H	L	1-3
12 Dec	Portsmouth	A	W	5-1
19 Dec	Chelsea	H	W	4-1
25 Dec	Preston NE	H	W	4-1
26 Dec	Everton	A	D	1-1
28 Dec	Preston NE	A	W	3-1
1 Jan	Bolton W	A	W	5-0
2 Jan	Huddersfield T	H	D	1-1
9 Jan	Sunderland	A	D	1-1
23 Jan	Wolverhampton W	H	W	2-1
3 Feb	Derby Co	A	L	4-5
6 Feb	Manchester U	H	D	1-1
13 Feb	Sheffield Wed	A	D	0-0
24 Feb	Charlton Ath	H	D	1-1
27 Feb	Grimsby T	A	W	3-1
10 Mar	Liverpool	H	W	1-0
13 Mar	Leeds U	A	W	4-3
20 Mar	Birmingham	H	D	1-1
26 Mar	Stoke C	H	D	0-0
27 Mar	Middlesbrough	A	D	1-1
29 Mar	Stoke C	A	D	0-0
3 Apr	W B A	H	W	2-0
10 Apr	Manchester City	A	L	0-2
17 Apr	Portsmouth	H	W	4-0
24 Apr	Chelsea	A	L	0-2
1 May	Bolton W	H	D	0-0

FA Cup

16 Jan	Chesterfield (3)	A	W	5-1
30 Jan	Manchester U (4)	H	W	5-0
20 Feb	Burnley (5)	A	W	7-1
6 Mar	W B A (6)	A	L	1-3

FA Charity Shield

28 Oct	Sunderland	A	L	1-2

Appearances (Goals)

Bastin C 33 (5) · Beasley A 7 (1) · Biggs A 1 · Boulton F 21 · Bowden R 28 (6) · Cartwright S 2 · Compton D 14 (4) · Compton L 15 · Copping W 38 · Crayston J 30 (1) · Davidson R 28 (9) · Drake E 26 (20) · Hapgood E 32 (1) · Hulme J 3 James A 19 (1) · John R 5 · Joy B 6 · Kirchen A 33 (18) · Male G 37 · Milne J 19 (9) · Nelson D 8 (3) · Roberts H 30 (1) · Sidey N 6 Swindin G 19 · Wilson A 2 · Own goals 1 · Total: 25 players (80)

Position in League Table

	P	W	L	D	F:A	Pts	
Manchester C	42	22	7	13	107:61	57	1st
Arsenal	42	18	8	16	80:49	52	3rd

SEASON 1937-1938
FOOTBALL LEAGUE (DIVISION 1)

28 Aug	Everton	A	W	4-1
1 Sep	Huddersfield T	H	W	3-1
4 Sep	Wolverhampton W	H	W	5-0
8 Sep	Huddersfield T	A	L	1-2
11 Sep	Leicester C	A	D	1-1
15 Sep	Bolton W	A	L	0-1
18 Sep	Sunderland	H	W	4-1
25 Sep	Derby Co	A	L	0-2
2 Oct	Manchester C	H	W	2-1
9 Oct	Chelsea	A	D	2-2
16 Oct	Portsmouth	H	D	1-1
23 Oct	Stoke C	A	D	1-1
30 Oct	Middlesbrough	H	L	1-2
6 Nov	Grimsby T	A	L	1-2
13 Nov	W B A	H	D	1-1
20 Nov	Charlton Ath	A	W	3-0
27 Nov	Leeds U	H	W	4-1
4 Dec	Birmingham	A	W	2-1
11 Dec	Preston NE	H	W	2-0
18 Dec	Liverpool	A	L	0-2
25 Dec	Blackpool	A	L	1-2
27 Dec	Blackpool	H	W	2-1
1 Jan	Everton	H	W	2-1
15 Jan	Wolverhampton W	A	L	1-3
29 Jan	Sunderland	A	D	1-1
2 Feb	Leicester C	H	W	3-1
5 Feb	Derby Co	H	W	3-0
16 Feb	Manchester C	A	W	2-1
19 Feb	Chelsea	H	W	2-0
26 Feb	Portsmouth	A	D	0-0
5 Mar	Stoke C	H	W	4-0
12 Mar	Middlesbrough	A	L	1-2
19 Mar	Grimsby	H	W	5-1
26 Mar	W B A	A	D	0-0
2 Apr	Charlton Ath	H	D	2-2
9 Apr	Leeds U	A	W	1-0
15 Apr	Brentford	H	L	0-2
16 Apr	Birmingham	H	D	0-0
18 Apr	Brentford	A	L	0-3
23 Apr	Preston NE	A	W	3-1
30 Apr	Liverpool	H	W	1-0
7 May	Bolton W	H	W	5-0

FA Cup

8 Jan	Bolton W (3)	H	W	3-1
22 Jan	Wolves (4)	A	W	2-1
12 Feb	Preston NE (5)	H	L	0-1

Appearances (Goals)

Bastin C 38 (15) · Biggs A 2 · Boulton F 15 · Bowden R 10 (1) · Bremner G 2 (1) · Carr E 11 7 · Cartwright S 6 (2) · Collett E 5 · Compton D 7 1 · Compton L 9 (1) · Copping W 38 Crayston J 31 (4) · Davidson R 5 (2) · Drake E 27 (17) · Drury G 11 · Griffiths W 9 (5) · Hapgood E 41 · Hulme J 7 (2) · Hunt G 18 (3) · Jones L 28 (3) · Joy B 26 · Kirchen A 19 (6) · Lewis R 4 (2) · Male G 34 · Milne J 16 (4) · Roberts H 13 · Sidey N 3 · Swindin G 17 · Wilson A 10 · Own goals 1 · Total: 29 players (77)

Position in League Table

	P	W	L	D	F:A	Pts	
Arsenal	42	21	11	10	77:44	52	1st

SEASON 1938-1939
FOOTBALL LEAGUE (DIVISION 1)

27 Aug	Portsmouth	H	W	2-0
3 Sep	Huddersfield T	A	D	1-1
8 Sep	Brentford	A	L	0-1
10 Sep	Everton	H	L	1-2
14 Sep	Derby Co	H	L	1-2
17 Sep	Wolverhampton W	A	W	1-0
24 Sep	Aston Villa	H	D	0-0
1 Oct	Sunderland	A	D	0-0
8 Oct	Grimsby T	H	W	2-0
15 Oct	Chelsea	A	L	2-4
22 Oct	Preston NE	H	W	1-0
29 Oct	Bolton W	A	D	1-1
5 Nov	Leeds U	H	L	2-3
12 Nov	Liverpool	A	D	2-2
19 Nov	Leicester C	H	D	0-0
26 Nov	Middlesbrough	A	D	1-1
3 Dec	Birmingham	H	W	3-1
10 Dec	Manchester U	A	L	0-1
17 Dec	Stoke C	H	W	4-1
24 Dec	Portsmouth	A	D	0-0
27 Dec	Charlton Ath	A	L	0-1
31 Dec	Huddersfield T	H	W	1-0
14 Jan	Everton	A	L	0-2
21 Jan	Charlton Ath	H	W	2-0
28 Jan	Aston Villa	A	W	3-1
1 Feb	Wolverhampton W	H	D	0-0
4 Feb	Sunderland	H	W	2-0
18 Feb	Chelsea	H	W	1-0
21 Feb	Grimsby T	A	L	1-2
25 Feb	Preston NE	A	L	1-2
4 Mar	Bolton W	H	W	3-1
11 Mar	Leeds U	A	L	2-4
18 Mar	Liverpool	H	W	2-0
25 Mar	Leicester C	A	W	2-0
1 Apr	Middlesbrough	H	L	1-2
7 Apr	Blackpool	A	L	0-1
8 Apr	Birmingham	A	W	2-1
10 Apr	Blackpool	H	W	2-1
15 Apr	Manchester U	H	W	2-1
22 Apr	Stoke C	A	L	0-1
29 Apr	Derby Co	A	W	2-1
6 May	Brentford	H	W	2-0

FA Cup

7 Jan	Chelsea (3)	A	L	1-2

FA Charity Shield

26 Sep	Preston	H	W	2-1

Appearances (Goals)

Bastin C 23 (3) · Bremner G 13 (3) · Carr E 1 · Cartwright S 3 · Collett R 9 · Compton D 1 · Compton L 18 (2) · Copping W 26 · Crayston J 34 (3) · Cumner R 12 (2) · Curtis G 2 · Drake E 38 (14) · Drury G 23 (3) · Farr A 2 (1) · Fields A 3 · Hapgood E 38 · Jones B 30 (4) · Jones B 30 4 · Jones L 18 · Joy B 39 · Kirchen A 27 (9) · Lewis R 15 (7) · Male G 28 · Marks G 2 · Nelson D 9 (1) · Pryde D 4 · Pugh S 1 · Swindin G 21 · Walsh W 3 · Wilson A 19 · Own goals 3 Total: 29 players (55)

Position in League Table

	P	W	L	D	F:A	Pts	
Everton	42	27	10	5	88:52	59	1st
Arsenal	42	19	14	9	55:41	47	5th

SEASON 1939-1940
FOOTBALL LEAGUE (DIVISION 1)

(Prior to outbreak of War)

26 Aug	Wolverhampton W 2 Arsenal 2
30 Aug	Arsenal 1 Blackburn Rov 0
2 Sep	Arsenal 5 Sunderland 2
21 Aug	Jubilee Match
	Arsenal 1 Tottenham H 1 (Drury)

Goal Scorers (Football League)

Drake	4
Bastin	1
Drury	1
Lewis	1
Kirchen	1

The Football League was again suspended during the Second World War, the 1939-1940 competition having been cut short after just four matches. During the seven seasons that followed the outbreak of the War, Arsenal played in a variety of competitions: the Regional League South, the London War Cup, the London League, the League Cup (South) and the Football League (South).

Arsenal won the Regional League South (A Division) in the season 1939-1940, won the London League in 1942 and retained the title the following year. They won the League Cup (South) in the season 1942-1943 and again in the season 1944 -1945.

Arsenal finished 11th in the League Table (South), in season 1944-1945 the full Football League was reinstated the following season.

SEASON 1946-1947
FOOTBALL LEAGUE (DIVISION 1)

31 Aug	Wolverhampton W	A	L	1-6
4 Sep	Blackburn Rov	H	L	1-3
7 Sep	Sunderland	A	D	2-2
11 Sep	Everton	A	L	2-3
14 Sep	Aston Villa	A	W	2-0
17 Sep	Blackburn Rov	A	W	2-1
21 Sep	Derby Co	H	L	0-1
28 Sep	Manchester U	A	L	2-5
5 Oct	Blackpool	A	L	1-2
12 Oct	Brentford	H	D	2-2
19 Oct	Stoke C	H	W	1-0
26 Oct	Chelsea	A	L	1-2
2 Nov	Sheffield U	H	L	2-3
9 Nov	Preston NE	A	L	0-2
16 Nov	Leeds U	H	W	4-2
23 Nov	Liverpool	A	L	2-4
30 Nov	Bolton W	H	D	2-2
7 Dec	Middlesbrough	A	L	0-2
14 Dec	Charlton Ath	H	W	1-0
21 Dec	Grimsby T	A	D	0-0
25 Dec	Portsmouth	H	W	2-1
26 Dec	Portsmouth	A	W	2-0
28 Dec	Wolverhampton W	H	D	1-1
4 Jan	Sunderland	A	W	4-1
18 Jan	Aston Villa	H	L	0-2
1 Feb	Manchester U	H	W	6-2
8 Feb	Blackpool	H	D	1-1
22 Feb	Stoke C	A	L	1-3
1 Mar	Chelsea	H	L	1-2
15 Mar	Preston NE	H	W	4-1
22 Mar	Leeds U	A	D	1-1
4 Apr	Huddersfield T	H	L	1-2
5 Apr	Bolton W	A	W	3-1
7 Apr	Huddersfield T	A	D	0-0
12 Apr	Middlesbrough	H	W	4-0
19 Apr	Charlton Ath	A	D	2-2
26 Apr	Grimsby T	H	W	5-3
10 May	Derby Co	A	W	1-0
24 May	Liverpool	H	L	1-2
26 May	Brentford	A	W	1-0
31 May	Everton	H	W	2-1
7 June	Sheffield U	A	L	1-2

FA Cup

11 Jan	Chelsea (3)	A	D	1-1
15 Jan	Chelsea (3R)	H	D	1-1
20 Jan	Chelsea (3R)		L	0-2
	(at Tottenham)			

Appearances (Goals)

Barnes W 26 · Bastin C 6 · Calverley A 11 · Collett E 6 · Compton D 1 1 · Compton L 36 · Curtis G 11 · Drury G 4 · Fields A 8 · Grant C 2 Gudmundsson A 2 · Hodges C 2 · Jones B 26 1 ·Joy B 13 · Lewis R 28 (29) · Logie J 35 (8) · Male G 15 · McPhersonl 37 (6) · Mercer J 25 · Morgan S 2 · Nelson D 10 · Dr O'Flanagan K 14 (3) · Platt T 4 · Rooke R 24 (21) · Rudkin T 5 2 · Scott L 28 · Sloan P 30 (1) · Smith A 3 · Swindin 38 · Wade J 2 · Waller H 8 · Total: 31 players (72)

Position in League Table

	P	W	L	D	F:A	Pts	
Liverpool	42	25	10	7	84:52	57	1st
Arsenal	42	16	17	9	72:70	41	13th

SEASON 1947-1948
FOOTBALL LEAGUE (DIVISION 1)

23 Aug	Sunderland	H	W	3-1
27 Aug	Charlton Ath	A	W	4-2
30 Aug	Sheffield U	A	W	2-1
3 Sep	Charlton Ath	H	W	6-0
6 Sep	Manchester U	H	W	2-1
10 Sep	Bolton W	A	W	2-0
13 Sep	Preston NE	A	D	0-0
20 Sep	Stoke C	H	W	3-0
27 Sep	Burnley	A	W	1-0
4 Oct	Portsmouth	H	D	0-0
11 Oct	Aston Villa	H	W	1-0
18 Oct	Wolverhampton W	A	D	1-1
25 Oct	Everton	H	D	1-1
1 Nov	Chelsea	A	D	0-0
8 Nov	Blackpool	H	W	2-1
15 Nov	Blackburn Rov	A	W	1-0
22 Nov	Huddersfield T	H	W	2-0
29 Nov	Derby Co	A	L	0-1
6 Dec	Manchester C	H	D	1-1
13 Dec	Grimsby T	A	W	4-0
20 Dec	Sunderland	A	D	1-1
25 Dec	Liverpool	A	W	3-1
27 Dec	Liverpool	H	L	1-2
1 Jan	Bolton W	A	W	1-0
3 Jan	Sheffield U	H	W	3-2
17 Jan	Manchester U	A	D	1-1
31 Jan	Preston NE	H	W	3-0
7 Feb	Stoke C	A	D	0-0
14 Feb	Burnley	H	W	3-0
28 Feb	Aston Villa	A	L	2-4
6 Mar	Wolverhampton W	H	W	5-2
13 Mar	Everton	A	W	2-0
20 Mar	Chelsea	H	L	0-2
26 Mar	Middlesbrough	H	W	7-0
27 Mar	Blackpool	A	L	0-3
29 Mar	Middlesbrough	A	D	1-1
3 Apr	Blackburn Rov	H	W	2-0
10 Apr	Huddersfield T	A	D	1-1
17 Apr	Derby Co	H	L	1-2
21 Apr	Portsmouth	A	D	0-0
24 Apr	Manchester C	A	D	0-0
1 May	Grimsby T	H	W	8-0

FA Cup

10 Jan	Bradford C (3)	H	L	0-1

Appearances (Goals)

Barnes W 35 · Compton D 14 (6) · Compton L 35 · Fields A 6 · Forbes A 11 (2) · Jones B 7 (1) Lewis R 28 (14) · Logie J 39 (8) · Macaulay A 40 · Male G 8 · McPhersonl 29 (5) · Mercer J 40 · Rooke R 42 (33) · Roper D 40 (10) · Scott L 39 · Sloan W 3 · Smith L 1 · Swindin G 42 · Wade J 3 · Own goals 2 · Total: 19 players (81)

Position in League Table

	P	W	L	D	F:A	Pts	
Arsenal	42	23	6	13	81:32	59	1st

SEASON 1948-1949
FOOTBALL LEAGUE (DIVISION 1)

21 Aug	Huddersfield T	A	D	1-1
25 Aug	Stoke C	H	W	3-0
28 Aug	Manchester U	H	L	0-1
30 Aug	Stoke C	A	L	0-1
4 Sep	Sheffield U	A	D	1-1
8 Sep	Liverpool	H	D	1-1
11 Sep	Aston Villa	H	W	3-1
15 Sep	Liverpool	A	W	1-0
18 Sep	Sunderland	A	D	1-1
25 Sep	Wolverhampton W	H	W	3-1
2 Oct	Bolton W	A	L	0-1
9 Oct	Burnley	H	W	3-1
16 Oct	Preston NE	A	D	1-1
23 Oct	Everton	H	W	5-0
30 Oct	Chelsea	A	W	1-0
6 Nov	Birmingham C	H	W	2-0
13 Nov	Middlesbrough	A	W	1-0
20 Nov	Newcastle U	H	L	0-1
27 Nov	Portsmouth	A	L	1-4
4 Dec	Manchester C	H	D	1-1
11 Dec	Charlton Ath	A	L	3-4
18 Dec	Huddersfield T	H	W	3-0
25 Dec	Derby Co	H	D	3-3
27 Dec	Derby Co	A	L	1-2
1 Jan	Manchester U	A	L	0-2
15 Jan	Sheffield U	H	W	5-3
22 Jan	Aston Villa	A	L	0-1
5 Feb	Sunderland	H	W	5-0
19 Feb	Wolverhampton W	A	W	3-1
26 Feb	Bolton W	H	W	5-0
5 Mar	Burnley	A	D	1-1
12 Mar	Preston NE	H	D	0-0
19 Mar	Newcastle U	A	L	2-3
2 Apr	Birmingham C	A	D	1-1
9 Apr	Middlesbrough	H	D	1-1
15 Apr	Blackpool	A	D	1-1
16 Apr	Everton	A	D	0-0
18 Apr	Blackpool	H	W	2-0
23 Apr	Chelsea	H	L	1-2
27 Apr	Manchester C	A	W	3-0
4 May	Portsmouth	H	W	3-2
7 May	Charlton Ath	H	W	2-0

FA Cup

8 Jan	Tottenham H (3)	H	W	3-0
29 Jan	Derby Co (4)	A	L	0-1

FA Charity Shield

6 Oct	Manchester U	H	W	4-3

Appearances (Goals)

Barnes W 40 · Compton D 6 (2) · Compton L 40 · Daniel R 1 · Fields A 1 · Forbes A 25 (4) · Jones B 8 1 · Lewis R 25 (16) · Lishman D 23 12 · Logie J 35 (11) · Macaulay A 39 (1) · McPhersonl 33 (5) · Mercer J 33 · Platt E 10 · Rooke R 22 (14) · Roper D 31 (5) · Scott L 12 · Smith L 32 · Swindin G 32 · Vallance T 14 (2) · Own goals 1 · Total: players 20 (74)

Position in League Table

	P	W	L	D	F:A	Pts	
Portsmouth	42	25	9	8	84:42	58	1st
Arsenal	42	18	11	13	74:44	49	5th

SEASON 1949-1950
FOOTBALL LEAGUE (DIVISION 1)

20 Aug	Burnley	H	L	0-1
24 Aug	Chelsea	A	W	2-1
27 Aug	Sunderland	A	L	2-4
31 Aug	Chelsea	H	L	2-3
3 Sep	Liverpool	H	L	1-2
7 Sep	W B A	A	W	2-1
10 Sep	Huddersfield T	A	D	2-2
14 Sep	W B A	H	W	4-1
17 Sep	Bolton W	A	D	2-2
24 Sep	Birmingham C	H	W	4-2
1 Oct	Derby Co	A	W	2-1
8 Oct	Everton	H	W	5-2
15 Oct	Middlesbrough	A	D	1-1
22 Oct	Blackpool	H	W	1-0
29 Oct	Newcastle U	A	W	3-0
5 Nov	Fulham	H	W	2-1
12 Nov	Manchester C	A	W	2-0
19 Nov	Charlton Ath	H	L	2-3
26 Nov	Aston Villa	A	D	1-1
3 Dec	Wolverhampton W	H	D	1-1
10 Dec	Portsmouth	A	L	1-2
17 Dec	Burnley	A	D	0-0
24 Dec	Sunderland	H	W	5-0
26 Dec	Manchester U	A	L	0-2
27 Dec	Manchester U	H	D	0-0
31 Dec	Liverpool	A	L	0-2
14 Jan	Huddersfield T	H	W	1-0
21 Jan	Bolton W	H	D	1-1
4 Feb	Birmingham C	A	L	1-2
18 Feb	Derby Co	H	W	1-0
25 Feb	Everton	A	W	1-0
8 Mar	Middlesbrough	H	D	1-1
11 Mar	Charlton Ath	A	D	1-1
25 Mar	Fulham	A	D	2-2
29 Mar	Aston Villa	H	L	1-3
1 Apr	Manchester C	H	W	4-1
8 Apr	Blackpool	A	L	1-2
10 Apr	Stoke C	H	W	6-0
15 Apr	Newcastle U	H	W	4-2
22 Apr	Wolverhampton W	A	L	0-3
3 May	Portsmouth	H	W	2-0
6 May	Stoke C	A	W	5-2

FA Cup

7 Jan	Sheffield W (3)	H	W	1-0
28 Jan	Swansea T (4)	H	W	2-1
11 Feb	Burnley (5)	H	W	2-0
4 Mar	Leeds U (6)	H	W	1-0
18 Mar	Chelsea (SF)		D	2-2
	(at White Hart Lane)			
22 Mar	Chelsea (SFR)		W	1-0
	(at White Hart Lane)			
29 Apr	Liverpool (F)		W	2-0
	(at Wembley)			

Appearances (Goals)

Barnes W 38 (5) · Compton D 11 (1) · Compton L 35 · Cox F 32 (3) · Daniel R 6 · Forbes A 23 (2) · Kelly N 1 · Lewis R 31 (19) · Lishman D 14 (9) · Logie J 34 (7) · Macaulay A 24 · McPherson 27 (3) · Mercer J 35 · Platt E 19 · Roper D 27 (7) · Scott L 15 · Shaw A 5 · Smith L 31 · Swindin G 23 · Vallance T 1 · Wade J 1 · Own goals 2 · Total: 22 players (79)

Position in League Table

	P	W	L	D	F:A	Pts	
Portsmouth	42	22	11	9	74:38	53	1st
Arsenal	42	19	12	11	79:55	49	6th

SEASON 1950-1951
FOOTBALL LEAGUE (DIVISION 1)

19 Aug	Burnley	A	W	1-0
23 Aug	Chelsea	H	D	0-0
26 Aug	Tottenham H	H	D	2-2
30 Aug	Chelsea	A	W	1-0
2 Sep	Sheffield W	H	W	3-0
6 Sep	Everton	H	W	2-1
9 Sep	Middlesbrough	A	L	1-2
13 Sep	Everton	A	D	1-1
16 Sep	Huddersfield T	H	W	6-2
23 Sep	Newcastle U	A	L	1-2
30 Sep	W B A	H	W	3-0
7 Oct	Charlton Ath	A	W	3-1
14 Oct	Manchester U	H	W	3-0
21 Oct	Aston Villa	A	D	1-1
28 Oct	Derby Co	H	W	3-1
4 Nov	Wolverhampton W	A	W	1-0
11 Nov	Sunderland	H	W	5-1
18 Nov	Liverpool	A	W	3-1
25 Nov	Fulham	H	W	5-1
2 Dec	Bolton W	A	L	0-3
9 Dec	Blackpool	H	D	4-4
16 Dec	Burnley	H	L	0-1
23 Dec	Tottenham H	A	L	0-1
25 Dec	Stoke C	H	L	0-3
26 Dec	Stoke C	A	L	0-1
30 Dec	Sheffield W	A	W	2-0
13 Jan	Middlesbrough	H	W	3-1
20 Jan	Huddersfield T	A	D	2-2
3 Feb	Newcastle U	H	D	0-0
17 Feb	W B A	A	L	0-2
24 Feb	Charlton Ath	H	L	2-5
3 Mar	Manchester U	A	L	1-3
10 Mar	Aston Villa	H	W	2-1
17 Mar	Derby Co	A	L	2-4
23 Mar	Portsmouth	H	L	0-1
24 Mar	Wolverhampton W	H	W	2-1
26 Mar	Portsmouth	A	D	1-1
31 Mar	Sunderland	A	W	2-0
7 Apr	Liverpool	H	L	1-2
14 Apr	Fulham	A	L	2-3
21 Apr	Bolton W	H	D	1-1
2 May	Blackpool	A	W	1-0

FA Cup

6 Jan	Carlisle U (3)	H	D	0-0
11 Jan	Carlisle U (3R)	A	W	4-1
27 Jan	Northampton (4)	H	W	3-2
10 Feb	Manchester U (5)	A	L	0-1

Appearances (Goals)

Barnes W 35 (3) · Bowen D 7 · Compton L 36 · Cox F 13 (2) · Daniel R 5 · Fields A 1 · Forbes A 32 (4) · Goring P 34 (15) · Holton C 10 (5) · Kelsey J 4 · Lewis R 14 (8) · Lishman D 26 (17) · Logie J 39 (9) · McPhersonl 26 · Marden B 11 (2) · Mercer J 31 · Milton A 1 · Platt E 17 Roper D 34 (7) · Scott L 17 · Shaw A 16 · Smith L 32 · Swindin G 21 · Own goals1 · Total: 23 players (73)

Position in League Table

	P	W	L	D	F:A	Pts	
Tottenham H	42	25	7	10	82:44	60	1st
Arsenal	42	19	14	9	73:56	47	5th

SEASON 1951-1952
FOOTBALL LEAGUE (DIVISION 1)

18 Aug	Huddersfield T	H	D	2-2
22 Aug	Chelsea	A	W	3-1
25 Aug	Wolverhampton W	A	L	1-2
29 Aug	Chelsea	H	W	2-1
1 Sep	Sunderland	H	W	3-0
5 Sep	Liverpool	H	D	0-0
8 Sep	Aston Villa	A	L	0-1
12 Sep	Liverpool	A	D	0-0
15 Sep	Derby Co	H	W	3-1
22 Sep	Manchester C	A	W	2-0
29 Sep	Tottenham H	H	D	1-1
6 Oct	Preston NE	A	L	0-2
13 Oct	Burnley	H	W	1-0
20 Oct	Charlton Ath	A	W	3-1
27 Oct	Fulham	H	W	4-3
3 Nov	Middlesbrough	A	W	3-0
10 Nov	W B A	H	W	6-3
17 Nov	Newcastle U	A	L	0-2
24 Nov	Bolton W	H	W	4-2
1 Dec	Stoke C	A	L	1-2
8 Dec	Manchester U	H	L	1-3
15 Dec	Huddersfield T	A	W	3-2
22 Dec	Wolverhampton W	H	D	2-2
25 Dec	Portsmouth	H	W	4-1
26 Dec	Portsmouth	A	D	1-1
29 Dec	Sunderland	A	L	1-4
5 Jan	Aston Villa	H	W	2-1
19 Jan	Derby Co	A	W	2-1
26 Jan	Manchester C	H	D	2-2
9 Feb	Tottenham H	A	W	2-1
16 Feb	Preston NE	H	D	3-3
1 Mar	Burnley	A	W	1-0
13 Mar	Charlton	H	W	2-1
15 Mar	Fulham	A	D	0-0
22 Mar	Middlesbrough	H	W	3-1
11 Apr	Blackpool	A	D	0-0
12 Apr	Bolton	A	L	1-2
14 Apr	Blackpool	H	W	4-1
16 Apr	Newcastle U	H	D	1-1
19 Apr	Stoke C	H	W	4-1
21 Apr	W B A	A	L	1-3
26 Apr	Manchester U	A	L	1-6

FA Cup

12 Jan	Norwich C (3)	A	W	5-0
2 Feb	Barnsley (4)	H	W	4-0
23 Feb	Leyton Orient (5)	A	W	3-0
8 Mar	Luton T (6)	A	W	3-2
5 Apr	Chelsea (SF)		D	1-1
	(at Tottenham)			
7 Apr	Chelsea (SFR)		W	3-0
	(at Tottenham)			
3 May	Newcastle (F)		L	0-1
	(at Wembley)			

Appearances (Goals)

Barnes W 41 (2) · Bowen D 8 · Chenhall J 3 · Compton L 4 · Cox F 25 (3) · Daniel R 34 · Forbes A 38 (2) · Goring P 16 (4) · Holton C 28 17 · Lewis R 9 (8) · Lishman D 38 (23) · Logie J 34 (4) · Marden R 7 2 · Mercer J 36 · Milton A 20 (5) · Robertson J 1 · Roper D 30 (9) · Scott L 4 · Shaw A 8 · Smith L 28 · Swindin G 42 · Wade J 8 · Own goals 1 · Total: 22 players (80)

Position in League Table

	P	W	L	D	F:A	Pts	
Manchester U	42	23	8	11	95:52	57	1st
Arsenal	42	21	10	11	80:61	53	3rd

SEASON 1952-1953
FOOTBALL LEAGUE (DIVISION 1)

23 Aug	Aston Villa	A	W	2-1
27 Aug	Manchester U	H	W	2-1
30 Aug	Sunderland	H	L	1-2
3 Sep	Manchester U	A	D	0-0
6 Sep	Wolverhampton W	A	D	1-1
10 Sep	Portsmouth	H	W	3-1
13 Sep	Charlton Ath	H	L	3-4
17 Sep	Portsmouth	A	D	2-2
20 Sep	Tottenham H	A	W	3-1
27 Sep	Derby Co	A	L	0-2
4 Oct	Blackpool	H	W	3-1
11 Oct	Sheffield W	H	D	2-2
25 Oct	Newcastle U	H	W	3-0
1 Nov	W B A	A	L	0-2
8 Nov	Middlesbrough	H	W	2-1
15 Nov	Liverpool	A	W	5-1
22 Nov	Manchester C	H	W	3-1
29 Nov	Stoke C	A	D	1-1
13 Dec	Burnley	A	D	1-1
20 Dec	Aston Villa	H	W	3-1
25 Dec	Bolton W	A	W	6-4
3 Jan	Sunderland	A	L	1-3
17 Jan	Wolverhampton W	H	W	5-3
24 Jan	Charlton Ath	A	D	2-2
7 Feb	Tottenham H	H	W	4-0
18 Feb	Derby Co	H	W	6-2
21 Feb	Blackpool	A	L	2-3
2 Mar	Sheffield W	A	W	4-1
7 Mar	Cardiff	H	L	0-1
14 Mar	Newcastle U	A	D	2-2
19 Mar	Preston NE	H	D	1-1
21 Mar	W B A	H	D	2-2
28 Mar	Middlesbrough	A	L	0-2
3 Apr	Chelsea	A	D	1-1
4 Apr	Liverpool	H	W	5-3
6 Apr	Chelsea	H	W	2-0
11 Apr	Manchester C	A	W	4-2
15 Apr	Bolton W	H	W	4-1
18 Apr	Stoke C	H	W	3-1
22 Apr	Cardiff	A	D	0-0
25 Apr	Preston NE	A	L	0-2
1 May	Burnley	H	W	3-2

FA Cup

10 Jan	Doncaster Rov (3)	H	W	4-0
31 Jan	Bury (4)	H	W	6-2
14 Feb	Burnley (5)	A	W	2-0
28 Feb	Blackpool (6)	H	L	1-2

Appearances (Goals)

Bowen D 2 · Chenhall J 13 · Cox F 9 (1) · Daniel R 41 (5) · Dodgin W 1 · Forbes A 33 (1) · Goring P 29 (10) · Holton C 21 (19) · Kelsey J 25 · Lishman D 39 (22) · Logie J 32 (10) · Marden R 8 (4) · Mercer J 28 (2) · Milton A 25 7 · Oakes D 2 (1) · Platt E 3 · Roper D 41 (14) · Shaw A 25 · Smith L 31 · Swindin G 14 · Wade J 40 · Own goals1 · Total: 21 players (97)

Position in League Table

	P	W	L	D	F:A	Pts	
Arsenal	42	21	9	12	97:64	54	1st

SEASON 1953-1954
FOOTBALL LEAGUE (DIVISION 1)

19 Aug	W B A	A	L	0-2
22 Aug	Huddersfield T	H	D	0-0
24 Aug	Sheffield U	A	L	0-1
29 Aug	Aston Villa	A	L	1-2
1 Sep	Sheffield U	H	D	1-1
5 Sep	Wolverhampton W	H	L	2-3
8 Sep	Chelsea	H	L	1-2
12 Sep	Sunderland	A	L	1-7
15 Sep	Chelsea	A	W	2-0
19 Sep	Manchester C	H	D	2-2
26 Sep	Cardiff	A	W	3-0
3 Oct	Preston NE	H	W	3-2
10 Oct	Tottenham H	A	W	4-1

17 Oct	Burnley	H	L	2-5
24 Oct	Charlton Ath	A	W	5-1
31 Oct	Sheffield W	H	W	4-1
7 Nov	Manchester U	A	D	2-2
14 Nov	Bolton W	H	W	4-3
21 Nov	Liverpool	A	W	2-1
28 Nov	Newcastle U	H	W	2-1
5 Dec	Middlesbrough	A	L	0-2
12 Dec	W B A	H	D	2-2
19 Dec	Huddersfield T	A	D	2-2
26 Dec	Blackpool	A	D	2-2
28 Dec	Blackpool	H	D	1-1
16 Jan	Wolverhampton W	A	W	2-0
23 Jan	Sunderland	H	L	1-4
6 Feb	Manchester C	A	D	0-0
13 Feb	Cardiff	H	D	1-1
24 Feb	Preston NE	A	W	1-0
27 Feb	Tottenham H	H	L	0-3
6 Mar	Burnley	A	L	1-2
13 Mar	Charlton Ath	H	D	3-3
20 Mar	Sheffield W	A	L	1-2
27 Mar	Manchester U	H	W	3-1
3 Apr	Bolton W	A	L	1-3
6 Apr	Aston Villa	H	D	1-1
10 Apr	Liverpool	H	W	3-0
16 Apr	Portsmouth	H	W	3-0
17 Apr	Newcastle U	A	L	2-5
19 Apr	Portsmouth	A	D	1-1
24 Apr	Middlesbrough	H	W	3-1

FA Cup

9 Jan	Aston Villa(3)	H	W	5-1
30 Jan	Norwich(4)	H	L	1-2

FA Charity Shield

12 Oct	Blackpool	H	W	3-1

Appearances (Goals)

Barnes W 19 (1) · Bowen D 10 · Dickson W 24 1 · Dodgin W 39 · Evans D 10 · Forbes A 30 (4) Goring P 9 · Holton C 32 (17) · Kelsey J 39 · Lawton T 9 (1) · Lishman D 39 (18) · Logie J 35 (8) · Marden R 9 (3) · Mercer J 19 · Milton A 21 (3) · Roper D 39 (12) · Shaw A 2 · Smith L 7 Sullivan C 1 · Swindin G 2 · Tapscott D 5 (5) · Tilley P 1 · Wade J 18 · Walsh B 10 · Ward G 3 Wills L 30 · Own goals 2 · Total: 26 players (75)

Position in League Table

	P	W	L	D	F:A	Pts	
Wolverhampton W	42	25	10	7	96:56	57	1st
Arsenal	42	15	14	13	75:73	43	12th

SEASON 1954-1955
FOOTBALL LEAGUE (DIVISION 1)

21 Aug	Newcastle U	H	L	1-3
25 Aug	Everton	A	L	0-1
28 Aug	W B A	A	L	1-3
31 Aug	Everton	H	W	2-0
4 Sep	Tottenham H	H	W	2-0
8 Sep	Manchester C	A	L	1-2
11 Sep	Sheffield U	H	W	4-0
14 Sep	Manchester C	H	L	2-3
18 Sep	Preston NE	A	L	1-3
25 Sep	Burnley	H	W	4-0
2 Oct	Leicester C	A	D	3-3
9 Oct	Sheffield W	A	W	2-1
16 Oct	Portsmouth	H	L	0-1
23 Oct	Aston Villa	A	L	1-2
30 Oct	Sunderland	H	L	1-3
6 Nov	Bolton W	A	D	2-2
13 Nov	Huddersfield T	H	L	3-5
20 Nov	Manchester U	A	L	1-2
27 Nov	Wolverhampton W	H	D	1-1
4 Dec	Blackpool	A	D	2-2
11 Dec	Charlton Ath	H	W	3-1
18 Dec	Newcastle U	A	L	1-5
25 Dec	Chelsea	H	W	1-0
27 Dec	Chelsea	A	D	1-1
1 Jan	W B A	H	D	2-2
15 Jan	Tottenham H	A	W	1-0
5 Feb	Preston NE	H	W	2-0
12 Feb	Burnley	A	L	0-3
19 Feb	Leicester C	H	D	1-1
26 Feb	Sheffield W	H	W	3-2
5 Mar	Charlton Ath	A	D	1-1
12 Mar	Aston Villa	H	W	2-0
19 Mar	Sunderland	A	W	1-0
26 Mar	Bolton W	H	W	3-0
2 Apr	Huddersfield T	A	W	1-0
8 Apr	Cardiff	H	W	2-0
9 Apr	Blackpool	H	W	3-0
11 Apr	Cardiff	A	W	2-1
16 Apr	Wolverhampton W	A	L	1-3
18 Apr	Sheffield U	A	D	1-1
23 Apr	Manchester U	H	L	2-3
30 Apr	Portsmouth	A	L	1-2

FA Cup

8 Jan	Cardiff (3)	H	W	1-0
29 Jan	Wolves (4)	A	L	0-1

Appearances (Goals)

Barnes W 25 · Bloomfield J 19 4 · Bowen D 21 Clapton Danny 16 · Dickson W 4 · Dodgin W 3 · Evans D 21 · Forbes A 20 1 Fotheringham J 27 Goring P 41 1 · Guthrie R 2 · Haverty J 6 · Herd D 3 1 · Holton C 8 Kelsey J 38 Lawton T 18 6 · Lishman D 32 19 · Logie J 13 3 · Marden R 7 · Milton A 8 3 · Oakes D 9 · Roper D 35 17 · Shaw A 1 · Sullivan C 2 · Swallow R 1 · Tapscott D 37 13 · Wade J 14 · Walsh J 6 · Wilkinson J 1 · Wills L 24 1 · Total: players 30 (69)

Position in League Table

	P	W	L	D	F:A	Pts	
Chelsea	42	20	10	12	81:57	52	1st
Arsenal	42	17	16	9	69:63	43	9th

SEASON 1955-1956
FOOTBALL LEAGUE (DIVISION 1)

20 Aug	Blackpool	A	L	1-3
23 Aug	Cardiff C	H	W	3-1
27 Aug	Chelsea	H	D	1-1
31 Aug	Manchester C	A	D	2-2
3 Sep	Bolton W	A	L	1-4
6 Sep	Manchester C	H	D	0-0
10 Sep	Tottenham H	A	L	1-3
17 Sep	Portsmouth	H	L	1-3
24 Sep	Sunderland	A	L	1-3
1 Oct	Aston Villa	H	W	1-0
8 Oct	Everton	A	D	1-1
15 Oct	Newcastle U	H	W	1-0
22 Oct	Luton T	A	D	0-0
29 Oct	Charlton Ath	H	L	2-4
5 Nov	Manchester U	A	D	1-1
12 Nov	Sheffield U	H	W	2-1
19 Nov	Preston NE	A	W	1-0
26 Nov	Burnley	H	L	0-1
3 Dec	Birmingham C	A	L	0-4
10 Dec	W B A	H	W	2-0
17 Dec	Blackpool	H	W	4-1
24 Dec	Chelsea	A	L	0-2
26 Dec	Wolverhampton W	A	D	3-3
27 Dec	Wolverhampton W	H	D	2-2
31 Dec	Bolton W	H	W	3-1
14 Jan	Tottenham H	H	L	0-1
21 Jan	Portsmouth	A	L	2-5
4 Feb	Sunderland	H	W	3-1
11 Feb	Aston Villa	A	D	1-1
21 Feb	Everton	H	W	3-2
25 Feb	Newcastle U	A	L	0-2
6 Mar	Preston NE	H	W	3-2
10 Mar	Charlton Ath	A	L	0-2
17 Mar	Manchester U	H	D	1-1
24 Mar	Sheffield U	A	W	2-0
31 Mar	Luton T	H	W	3-0
2 Apr	Huddersfield T	H	W	2-0
3 Apr	Huddersfield T	A	W	1-0
7 Apr	Burnley	A	W	1-0
14 Apr	Birmingham C	H	W	1-0
21 Apr	W B A	A	L	1-2
28 Apr	Cardiff C	A	W	2-1

FA Cup

7 Jan	Bedford Town (3)	H	D	2-2
12 Jan	Bedford Town (3R)	A	W	2-1
28 Jan	Aston Villa (4)	H	W	4-1
18 Feb	Charlton Ath (5)	A	W	2-0
3 Mar	Birmingham C (6)	H	L	1-3

Appearances (Goals)

Barnes W 8 · Bloomfield J 32 (3) · Bowen D 22 · Charlton S 19 · Clapton Danny 39 (2) · Dickson W 1 · Dodgin W 15 · Evans D 42 · Forbes A 5 · Fotheringham J 25 · Goring P 37 · Groves V 15 (8) · Haverty J 8 (2) · Herd D 5 (2) · Holton C 31 (8) · Kelsey J 32 · Lawton T 8 (6) · Lishman D 15 (5) · Nutt G 8 (1) · Roper D 16 (4) Sullivan C 10 · Swallow R 1 (1) · Tapscott D 31 (17) · Tiddy M 21 · Walsh B · 1 · Wills 15 · Own goals 1 · Total: 26 players (60)

Position in League Table

	P	W	L	D	F:A	Pts	
Manchester U	42	25	7	10	83:51	60	1st
Arsenal	42	18	14	10	60:61	46	5th

SEASON 1956-1957
FOOTBALL LEAGUE (DIVISION 1)

18 Aug	Cardiff C	H	D	0-0
21 Aug	Burnley	H	W	2-0
25 Aug	Birmingham C	A	L	2-4
28 Aug	Burnley	A	L	1-3
1 Sep	W B A	H	W	4-1
4 Sep	Preston NE	H	L	1-2
8 Sep	Portsmouth	A	W	3-2
10 Sep	Preston NE	A	L	0-3
15 Sep	Newcastle U	H	L	0-1
22 Sep	Sheffield W	A	W	4-2
29 Sep	Manchester U	H	L	1-2
6 Oct	Manchester C	H	W	7-3
13 Oct	Charlton Ath	A	W	3-1
20 Oct	Tottenham H	H	W	3-1
27 Oct	Everton	A	L	0-4
3 Nov	Aston Villa	H	W	2-1
10 Nov	Wolverhampton W	A	L	2-5
17 Nov	Bolton W	H	W	3-0
24 Nov	Leeds U	A	D	3-3
1 Dec	Sunderland	H	D	1-1
8 Dec	Luton T	A	W	2-1
15 Dec	Cardiff C	A	W	3-2
22 Dec	Birmingham C	H	W	4-0
25 Dec	Chelsea	A	D	1-1
26 Dec	Chelsea	H	W	2-0
29 Dec	W B A	A	W	2-0
12 Jan	Portsmouth	H	D	1-1
19 Jan	Newcastle U	A	L	1-3
2 Feb	Sheffield W	H	W	6-3
9 Feb	Manchester U	A	L	2-6
23 Feb	Everton	H	W	2-0
9 Mar	Luton T	H	L	1-3
13 Mar	Tottenham H	A	W	3-1
16 Mar	Aston Villa	A	D	0-0
20 Mar	Manchester C	A	W	3-2
23 Mar	Wolverhampton W	H	D	0-0
30 Mar	Bolton W	A	L	1-2
6 Apr	Leeds U	H	W	1-0
13 Apr	Sunderland	A	L	0-1
19 Apr	Blackpool	H	D	1-1
20 Apr	Charlton Ath	H	W	3-1
22 Apr	Blackpool	A	W	4-2

FA Cup

5 Jan	Stoke C (3)	H	W	4-2
26 Jan	Newport Co (4)	A	W	2-0
16 Feb	Preston NE (5)	A	D	3-3
19 Feb	Preston NE (5R)	H	W	2-1
2 Mar	W B A (6)	A	D	2-2
5 Mar	W B A (6R)	H	L	1-2

Appearances (Goals)

Barnwell J 1 · Bloomfield J 42 (10) · Bowen D 30 (2) · Charlton S 40 · Clapton Danny 39 (2) · Dodgin W · 41 · Evans D 40 (4) · Goring P 13 · Groves V 5 (2) · Haverty J 28 (8) · Herd D 22 (2) Holton C 39 (10) · Kelsey J 30 · Nutt G 1 · Roper D 4 (3) · Sullivan C 12 · Swallow R 4 · Tapscott D 38 (25) · Tiddy M 15 (6) · Wills L 18 Own goals 1 · Total: 20 players 85

Position in League Table

	P	W	L	D	F:A	Pts	
Manchester U	42	28	6	8	103:54	64	1st
Arsenal	42	21	13	8	85:69	50	5th

SEASON 1957-1958
FOOTBALL LEAGUE (DIVISION 1)

24 Aug	Sunderland	A	W	1-0
27 Aug	W B A	H	D	2-2
31 Aug	Luton T	H	W	2-0
4 Sep	W B A	A	W	2-1
7 Sep	Blackpool	A	L	0-1
10 Sep	Everton	H	L	2-3
14 Sep	Leicester C	H	W	3-1
21 Sep	Manchester U	A	L	2-4
28 Sep	Leeds U	H	W	2-1
2 Oct	Aston Villa	H	W	4-0
5 Oct	Bolton W	A	W	1-0
12 Oct	Tottenham H	A	L	1-3
16 Oct	Everton	A	D	2-2
19 Oct	Birmingham C	H	L	1-3
26 Oct	Chelsea	A	D	0-0
2 Nov	Manchester C	H	W	2-1
9 Nov	Nottingham F	A	L	0-4
16 Nov	Portsmouth	H	W	3-2
23 Nov	Sheffield W	A	L	0-2
30 Nov	Newcastle U	H	L	2-3
7 Dec	Burnley	A	L	1-2
14 Dec	Preston NE	H	W	4-2
21 Dec	Sunderland	H	W	3-0
26 Dec	Aston Villa	A	L	0-3
28 Dec	Luton T	A	L	0-4
11 Jan	Blackpool	H	L	2-3
18 Jan	Leicester C	A	W	1-0
1 Feb	Manchester U	H	L	4-5
18 Feb	Bolton W	H	L	1-2
22 Feb	Tottenham H	H	D	4-4
1 Mar	Birmingham C	A	L	1-4
8 Mar	Chelsea	H	W	5-4
15 Mar	Manchester C	A	W	4-2
19 Mar	Leeds U	A	L	0-2
22 Mar	Sheffield W	H	W	1-0
29 Mar	Portsmouth	A	L	4-5
7 Apr	Wolverhampton W	H	L	0-2
8 Apr	Wolverhampton W	A	W	2-1
12 Apr	Newcastle U	A	D	3-3
19 Apr	Burnley	H	D	0-0
21 Apr	Nottingham F	H	D	1-1
26 Apr	Preston NE	A	L	0-3

FA Cup

4 Jan	Northampton (3)	A	L	1-3

Appearances (Goals)

Biggs A 2 · Bloomfield J 40 (16) · Bowen D 30 · Charlton S 36 · Clapton Danny 28 (5) · Dodgin W23 · Evans D 32 · Fotheringham J 19 · Goring P10 · Groves V 30 (10) · Haverty J 15 · Herd D 39 (24) · Holton C 26 (4) · Kelsey J 38 · U Roux D 5 · Nutt G 21 (3) · Petts J 9 · Standen J 1 · Sullivan C 3 · Swallow R 7 (3) · Tapscott D 8 (2) · Tiddy M 12 (2) · Ward G 10 · Wills L 18 (1) Own goals 3 · Total: 24 players (73)

Position in League Table

	P	W	L	D	F:A	Pts	
Wolverhampton W	42	28	6	8	103:47	64	1st
Arsenal	42	16	19	7	73:85	39	12th

SEASON 1958-1959
FOOTBALL LEAGUE (DIVISION 1)

23 Aug	Preston NE	A	L	1-2
26 Aug	Burnley	H	W	3-0
30 Aug	Leicester C	H	W	5-1
2 Sep	Burnley	A	L	1-3
6 Sep	Everton	A	W	6-1
9 Sep	Bolton W	H	W	6-1
13 Sep	Tottenham H	H	W	3-1
17 Sep	Bolton W	A	L	1-2
20 Sep	Manchester C	H	W	4-1
27 Sep	Leeds U	A	L	1-2
4 Oct	W B A	H	W	4-3
11 Oct	Manchester U	A	D	1-1
18 Oct	Wolverhampton W	H	D	1-1
22 Oct	Aston Villa	A	W	2-1
25 Oct	Blackburn Rov	A	L	2-4
1 Nov	Newcastle U	H	W	3-2
8 Nov	West Ham U	A	D	0-0
15 Nov	Nottingham F	H	W	3-1
22 Nov	Chelsea	A	W	3-0
29 Nov	Blackpool	H	L	1-4
6 Dec	Portsmouth	A	W	1-0
13 Dec	Aston Villa	H	L	1-2
20 Dec	Preston NE	H	L	1-2
26 Dec	Luton T	A	L	3-6
27 Dec	Luton T	H	W	1-0
3 Jan	Leicester C	A	W	3-2
17 Jan	Everton	H	W	3-1
31 Jan	Tottenham	A	W	4-1
7 Feb	Manchester C	A	D	0-0
21 Feb	W B A	A	D	1-1
24 Feb	Leeds U	H	W	1-0
28 Feb	Manchester U	H	W	3-2
7 Mar	Wolverhampton W	A	L	1-6
14 Mar	Blackburn Rov	H	D	1-1
21 Mar	Newcastle U	A	L	0-1
28 Mar	West Ham U	H	L	1-2
4 Apr	Nottingham F	A	D	1-1
11 Apr	Chelsea	H	D	1-1
14 Apr	Birmingham C	A	L	1-4
18 Apr	Blackpool	A	W	2-1
25 Apr	Portsmouth	H	W	5-2
4 May	Birmingham C	H	W	2-1

FA Cup

10 Jan	Bury (3)	A	W	1-0
24 Jan	Colchester U (4)	A	D	2-2
28 Jan	Colchester U (4R)	H	W	4-0
14 Feb	Sheffield U (5)	H	D	2-2
18 Feb	Sheffield U (5R)	A	L	0-3

Appearances (Goals)

Barnwell J 10 (3) · Biggs A 2 (1) · Bloomfield J 29 (10) · Bowen D 16 · Charlton S 4 · Clapton Danny 39 (6) · Docherty T 38 (1) · Dodgin W 39 Evans D 37 (5) · Fotheringham J 1 · Goring P 2 Goulden R · 1 · Goy P 2 · Groves V 33 (10) · Haverty J 10 (3) · Henderson J 21 (12) · Herd D 26 (15) · Holton C 3 (3) · Julians L 10 (5) · Kelsey J 27 · McCullough W 10 · Nutt G 16 (6) Petts J 3 · Standen J 13 · Ward G 31 (4) · Wills L 33 (1) · Own goals 3 · Total:26 players (88)

Position in League Table

	P	W	L	D	F:A	Pts	
Wolverhampton W	42	28	9	5	110:49	61	1st
Arsenal	42	21	13	8	88:68	50	3rd

SEASON 1959-1960
FOOTBALL LEAGUE (DIVISION 1)

22 Aug	Sheffield W	H	L	0-1
26 Aug	Nottingham F	A	W	3-0
29 Aug	Wolverhampton W	A	D	3-3
1 Sep	Nottingham F	H	D	1-1
5 Sep	Tottenham H	H	D	1-1
9 Sep	Bolton W	A	W	1-0
12 Sep	Manchester C	H	W	3-1
15 Sep	Bolton W	H	W	2-1
19 Sep	Blackburn Rov	A	D	1-1
26 Sep	Blackpool	H	W	2-1
3 Oct	Everton	A	L	1-3
10 Oct	Manchester U	A	L	2-4
17 Oct	Preston NE	H	L	0-3
24 Oct	Leicester C	A	D	2-2
31 Oct	Birmingham C	H	W	3-0
7 Nov	Leeds U	A	L	2-3
14 Nov	West Ham U	H	L	1-3
21 Nov	Chelsea	A	W	3-1
28 Nov	W B A	H	L	2-4
5 Dec	Newcastle U	A	L	1-4
12 Dec	Burnley	H	L	2-4
19 Dec	Sheffield W	A	L	1-5
26 Dec	Luton T	H	L	0-3
28 Dec	Luton T	A	W	1-0
2 Jan	Wolverhampton W	H	D	4-4
16 Jan	Tottenham H	A	L	0-3
23 Jan	Manchester C	A	W	2-1
6 Feb	Blackburn Rov	H	W	5-2
13 Feb	Blackpool	A	L	1-2
20 Feb	Everton	H	W	2-1
27 Feb	Newcastle U	H	W	1-0
5 Mar	Preston NE	A	W	3-0
15 Mar	Leicester C	H	D	1-1
19 Mar	Burnley	A	L	2-3
26 Mar	Leeds U	H	D	1-1
2 Apr	West Ham U	A	D	0-0
9 Apr	Chelsea	H	L	1-4
15 Apr	Fulham	H	W	2-0
16 Apr	Birmingham C	A	L	0-3
18 Apr	Fulham	A	L	0-3
23 Apr	Manchester U	H	W	5-2
30 Apr	W B A	A	L	0-1

FA Cup

9 Jan	Rotherham U (3)	A	D	2-2
13 Jan	Rotherham U (3R)	H	D	1-1
18 Jan	Rotherham U (3R) (at Sheffield Wed)		L	0-2

Appearances (Goals)

Barnwell J 28 (7) · Bloomfield J 36 (10) · Charles M 20 (8) · Clapton D P (Denis) 3 · Clapton D R (Danny) 23 (7) · Docherty T 24 · Dodgin W 30 · Evans D 7 (1) · Everitt M 5 · Groves V 30 (1) · Haverty J 35 (8) · Henderson J 31 (7) · Herd D 31 (14) · Julians L 8 (2) · Kelsey J 22 · Magill E 17 · MCcullough W 33 · Nutt G 3 · Petts J 7 · Snedden J 1 · Standen J 20 · Ward G 15 1 · Wills L 33 (1) · Own goals 1 Total: 23 players (68)

Position in League Table

	P	W	L	D	F:A	Pts	
Burnley	42	24	11	7	85:61	55	1st
Arsenal	42	15	18	9	68:80	39	13th

SEASON 1960-1961
FOOTBALL LEAGUE (DIVISION 1)

20 Aug	Burnley	A	L	2-3
23 Aug	Preston NE	H	W	1-0
27 Aug	Nottingham F	H	W	3-0
30 Aug	Preston NE	A	L	0-2
3 Sep	Manchester C	A	D	0-0
6 Sep	Birmingham C	H	W	2-0
10 Sep	Tottenham H	H	L	2-3
14 Sep	Birmingham C	A	L	0-2
17 Sep	Newcastle U	H	W	5-0
24 Sep	Cardiff C	A	L	0-1
1 Oct	W B A	H	W	1-0
8 Oct	Leicester C	A	L	1-2
15 Oct	Aston Villa	H	W	2-1
22 Oct	Blackburn Rov	A	W	4-2
29 Oct	Manchester U	H	W	2-1
5 Nov	West Ham U	A	L	0-6
12 Nov	Chelsea	H	L	1-4
19 Nov	Blackpool	A	D	1-1
26 Nov	Everton	H	W	3-2
3 Dec	Wolverhampton W	A	L	3-5
10 Dec	Bolton W	H	W	5-1
17 Dec	Bumley	H	L	2-5
23 Dec	Sheffield W	A	D	1-1
26 Dec	Sheffield W	H	D	1-1
31 Dec	Nottingham F	A	W	5-3
14 Jan	Manchester C	H	W	5-4
21 Jan	Tottenham H	A	L	2-4
4 Feb	Newcastle U	A	D	3-3
11 Feb	Cardiff C	H	L	2-3
18 Feb	W B A	A	W	3-2
25 Feb	Leicester C	H	L	1-3
4 Mar	Aston Villa	A	D	2-2
11 Mar	Blackburn Rov	H	D	0-0
18 Mar	Manchester U	A	D	1-1
25 Mar	West Ham U	H	D	0-0
31 Mar	Fulham	A	D	2-2
1 Apr	Bolton W	A	D	1-1
3 Apr	Fulham	H	W	4-2
8 Apr	Blackpool	H	W	1-0
15 Apr	Chelsea	A	L	1-3
22 Apr	Wolverhampton W	H	L	1-5
29 Apr	Everton	A	L	1-4

FA Cup

7 Jan	Sunderland (3)	A	L	1-2

Appearances (Goals)

Bacuzzi D 13 · Barnwell J 26 (6) · Bloomfield J 12 (1) Charles M 19 3 · Clapton D R (Danny) 18 2 · Clapton D P (Denis) 1 · Docherty T 21 · Eastham G 19 5 · Everitt M 4 (1) · Griffiths A 1 · Groves V 32 · Haverty J 12 (4) · Henderson J 39 10 · Herd D 40 (29) · Kane P 4 (1) · Kelsey J 37 · Magill E 6 · McClelland J 4 · McCullough W 41 · Neill T 14 (1) · O'Neill F 2 · Petts J 1 · Skirton A 16 (3) · Snedden J 23 · Standen J 1 · Strong G 19 (10) · Ward G 9 (1) · Wills L 24 · Young D 4 · Total: 29 players (77)

Position in League Table

	P	W	L	D	F:A	Pts	
Tottenham H	42	31	7	4	115:55	66	1st
Arsenal	42	15	16	11	77:85	41	11th

SEASON 1961-1962
FOOTBALL LEAGUE (DIVISION 1)

19 Aug	Burnley	H	D	2-2
23 Aug	Leicester C	A	W	1-0
26 Aug	Tottenham H	A	L	3-4
29 Aug	Leicester C	H	D	4-4
2 Sep	Bolton W	A	L	1-2
9 Sep	Manchester C	H	W	3-0
16 Sep	W B A	A	L	0-4
20 Sep	Sheffield W	A	D	1-1
23 Sep	Birmingham C	H	D	1-1
30 Sep	Everton	A	L	1-4
7 Oct	Blackpool	H	W	3-0
14 Oct	Blackburn Rov	A	D	0-0
21 Oct	Manchester U	H	W	5-1

28 Oct	Cardiff C	A	D	1-1
4 Nov	Chelsea	H	L	0-3
11 Nov	Aston Villa	A	L	1-3
14 Nov	Sheffield W	H	W	1-0
18 Nov	Nottingham F	H	W	2-1
25 Nov	Wolverhampton W	A	W	3-2
2 Dec	West Ham U	H	D	2-2
9 Dec	Sheffield U	A	L	1-2
16 Dec	Burnley	A	W	2-0
23 Dec	Tottenham H	H	W	2-1
26 Dec	Fulham	H	W	1-0
13 Jan	Bolton W	H	L	1-2
20 Jan	Manchester C	A	L	2-3
3 Feb	W B A	H	L	0-1
10 Feb	Birmingham C	A	L	0-1
24 Feb	Blackpool	A	W	1-0
3 Mar	Blackburn	H	D	0-0
17 Mar	Cardiff C	H	D	1-1
24 Mar	Chelsea	A	W	3-2
31 Mar	Aston Villa	H	L	4-5
7 Apr	Nottingham F	A	L	2-5
11 Apr	Fulham	A	L	2-5
14 Apr	Wolverhampton W	H	W	3-1
16 Apr	Manchester U	A	W	3-2
20 Apr	Ipswich T	A	D	2-2
21 Apr	West Ham U	A	D	3-3
23 Apr	Ipswich T	H	L	0-3
28 Apr	Sheffield U	H	W	2-0
1 May	Everton	H	L	2-3

FA Cup

6 Jan	Bradford C (3)	H	W	3-0
31 Jan	Manchester U (4)	A	L	0-1

Appearances (Goals)

Armstrong G 4 (1) · Bacuzzi D 22 · Barnwell J 14 (3) · Brown L 41 · Charles M 21 (15) · Clamp L 18 · Clapton Danny 5 (1) · Clarke F 1 · Eastham G 38 (6) · Griffiths A 14 (2) · Groves V 16 · Henderson J 12 · Kelsey J 35 · McLeod J 37 (6) · Magill E 21 · McClelland J 4 · McCullough J 40 · Mckechnie 13 · Neill T 20 · Petts 12 · Skirton 38 (19) · Snedden 15 · Strong 20 (12) · Ward 11 · Own goals 2 · Total: 24 players (71)

Position in League Table

	P	W	L	D	F:A	Pts	
Ipswich T	42	24	10	8	93:67	56	1st
Arsenal	42	16	15	11	71:72	43	10th

SEASON 1962-1963
FOOTBALL LEAGUE (DIVISION 1)

18 Aug	Leyton Orient	A	W	2-1
21 Aug	Birmingham C	H	W	2-0
25 Aug	Manchester U	H	L	1-3
29 Aug	Birmingham C	A	D	2-2
1 Sep	Burnley	A	L	1-2
4 Sep	Aston Villa	H	L	1-2
8 Sep	Sheffield W	H	L	1-2
10 Sep	Aston Villa	A	L	1-3
15 Sep	Fulham	A	W	3-1
22 Sep	Leicester C	H	D	1-1
29 Sep	Bolton W	A	L	0-3
6 Oct	Tottenham H	A	D	4-4
13 Oct	West Ham U	H	D	1-1
27 Oct	Wolverhampton W	H	W	5-4
3 Nov	Blackburn Rov	A	D	5-5
10 Nov	Sheffield U	H	W	1-0
14 Nov	Liverpool	A	L	1-2
17 Nov	Nottingham F	A	L	0-3
24 Nov	Ipswich T	H	W	3-1
1 Dec	Manchester C	A	W	4-2
8 Dec	Blackpool	H	W	2-0
15 Dec	Leyton Orient	H	W	2-0
9 Feb	Leicester C	A	L	0-2
16 Feb	Bolton W	H	W	3-2
23 Feb	Tottenham H	H	L	2-3
2 Mar	West Ham U	A	W	4-0
9 Mar	Liverpool	H	D	2-2
23 Mar	Blackburn Rov	H	W	3-1
26 Mar	Everton	H	W	4-3
30 Mar	Ipswich T	A	D	1-1
6 Apr	Nottingham F	H	D	0-0
8 Apr	Wolverhampton W	A	L	0-1
12 Apr	W B A	H	W	3-2
13 Apr	Sheffield U	A	D	3-3
15 Apr	W B A	A	W	2-1
20 Apr	Manchester C	H	L	2-3
24 Apr	Everton	A	D	1-1
27 Apr	Blackpool	A	L	2-3
6 May	Manchester U	A	W	3-2
11 May	Burnley	H	L	2-3
14 May	Fulham	H	W	3-0
18 May	Sheffield W	A	W	3-2

FA Cup

30 Jan	Oxford U (3)	H	W	5-1
12 Mar	Sheffield W (4)	H	W	2-0
19 Mar	Liverpool (5)	H	L	1-2

Appearances (Goals)

Anderson T 5 (1) · Armstrong G 16 (2) · Bacuzzi D (6) · Baker J 39 (29) · Barnwell J 34 (2) · Brown L 38 (1) · Clamp E 4 (1) · Clarke F 5 · Court D 6 (3) · Eastham G 33 (4) · Groves V 9 · MacLeod J 33 (9) · Magill E 36 · McClelland J 33 · McCullough W42 3 · McKechnie I (9) · Neill T 17 · Sammels J 2 (1) · Skirton A 28 (10) · Smithson R 2 · Snedden J 27 · Strong G 36 (18) · Ward G 2 · Own goals 2 · Total: 23 players (86)

Position in League Table

	P	W	L	D	F:A	Pts	
Everton	42	25	6	11	84:42	61	1st
Arsenal	42	18	14	10	86:77	46	7th

SEASON 1963-1964
FOOTBALL LEAGUE (DIVISION 1)

24 Aug	Wolverhampton W	H	L	1-3
27 Aug	W B A	H	W	3-2
31 Aug	Leicester C	A	L	2-7
4 Sep	W B A	A	L	0-4
7 Sep	Bolton W	H	W	4-3
10 Sep	Aston Villa	H	W	3-0
14 Sep	Fulham	A	W	4-1
21 Sep	Manchester U	H	W	2-1
28 Sep	Burnley	A	W	3-0
2 Oct	Everton	A	L	1-2
5 Oct	Ipswich	H	W	6-0
9 Oct	Stoke C	A	W	2-1
15 Oct	Tottenham H	H	D	4-4
19 Oct	Aston Villa	A	L	1-2
26 Oct	Nottingham F	H	W	4-2
2 Nov	Sheffield U	A	D	2-2
5 Nov	Birmingham C	H	W	4-1
9 Nov	West Ham U	H	D	3-3
16 Nov	Chelsea	A	L	1-3
23 Nov	Blackpool	H	W	5-3
30 Nov	Blackburn Rov	A	L	1-4
7 Dec	Liverpool	H	D	1-1
10 Dec	Everton	H	W	6-0
14 Dec	Wolverhampton W	A	D	2-2
21 Dec	Leicester C	H	L	0-1
28 Dec	Birmingham C	A	W	4-1
11 Jan	Bolton W	A	D	1-1
18 Jan	Fulham	H	D	2-2
1 Feb	Manchester U	A	L	1-3
8 Feb	Burnley	H	W	3-2
18 Feb	Ipswich	A	W	2-1
22 Feb	Tottenham H	A	L	1-3
29 Feb	Stoke C	H	D	1-1
7 Mar	Nottingham F	A	L	0-2
14 Mar	Chelsea	H	L	2-4
21 Mar	West Ham U	A	D	1-1
24 Mar	Sheffield W	H	D	1-1
28 Mar	Sheffield U	H	L	1-3
30 Mar	Sheffield W	A	W	4-0
4 Apr	Blackpool	A	W	1-0
11 Apr	Blackburn Rov	H	D	0-0
18 Apr	Liverpool	A	L	0-5

FA Cup

4 Jan	Wolves (3)	H	W	2-1
25 Jan	W B A (4)	A	D	3-3
29 Jan	W B A (4R)	H	W	2-0
15 Feb	Liverpool (5)	H	L	0-1

Inter-Cities Fairs Cup

25 Sep	Staevnet (1)	A	W	7-1
22 Oct	Staevnet (1)	H	L	2-3
13 Nov	FC Liege (2)	H	D	1-1
18 Dec	FC Liege (2)	A	L	1-3

Appearances (Goals)

Anderson T 10 (3) · Armstrong G 28 (3) · Bacuzzi D 5 · Baker J 39 (26) · Barnwell J 19 2 Brown L 22 (1) · Clarke F 5 · Court D 8 1 · Eastham G 38 (10)· Furnell J 21 · Groves V 15 · MacLeod J 30 (7) · Magill E 35 · McClelland J 5 · McCullough W 40 (1) · McKechnie 11 (1) · Neill T 11 · Radford J 1 · Simpson P 6 · Skirton A 15 7 · Snedden J 14 · Strong G 38 (26) · Urel 41 (1) · Wilson R 5 · Own goals 1 · Total: 24 players (90)

Position in League Table

	P	W	L	D	F:A	Pts	
Liverpool	42	26	11	5	92:45	57	1st
Arsenal	42	17	14	11	90:82	45	8th

SEASON 1964-1965
FOOTBALL LEAGUE (DIVISION 1)

22 Aug	Liverpool	A	L	2-3
25 Aug	Sheffield W	H	D	1-1
29 Aug	Aston Villa	H	W	3-1
2 Sep	Sheffield W	A	L	1-2
5 Sep	Wolverhampton W	A	W	1-0
8 Sep	Blackburn Rov	H	D	1-1
12 Sep	Sunderland	H	W	3-1
16 Sep	Blackburn Rov	A	W	2-1
19 Sep	Leicester C	A	W	3-2
26 Sep	Chelsea	H	L	1-3
6 Oct	Nottingham F	H	L	0-3
10 Oct	Tottenham H	A	L	1-3
17 Oct	Burnley	H	W	3-2
24 Oct	Sheffield U	A	L	0-4
31 Oct	Everton	H	W	3-1
7 Nov	Birmingham C	A	W	3-2
11 Nov	Leeds U	A	L	1-3
14 Nov	West Ham U	H	L	0-3
21 Nov	W B A	A	D	0-0
28 Nov	Manchester U	H	L	2-3
5 Dec	Fulham	A	W	4-3
12 Dec	Liverpool	H	D	0-0
19 Dec	Aston Villa	A	L	1-3
26 Dec	Stoke C	H	W	3-2
28 Dec	Stoke C	A	L	1-4
2 Jan	Wolverhampton W	H	W	4-1
16 Jan	Sunderland	A	W	2-0
23 Jan	Leicester C	H	W	4-3
6 Feb	Chelsea	A	L	1-2
13 Feb	Leeds U	H	L	1-2
20 Feb	Fulham	H	W	2-0
23 Feb	Tottenham H	H	W	3-1
27 Feb	Burnley	A	L	1-2
6 Mar	Sheffield U	H	D	1-1
13 Mar	Nottingham F	A	L	0-3
27 Mar	West Ham U	A	L	1-2
3 Apr	W B A	H	D	1-1
6 Apr	Birmingham C	H	W	3-0
16 Apr	Blackpool	A	D	1-1
19 Apr	Blackpool	H	W	3-1
24 Apr	Everton	A	L	0-1
26 Apr	Manchester U	A	L	1-3

FA Cup

9 Jan	Darlington (3)	A	W	2-0
30 Jan	Peterborough (4)	A	L	1-2

Appearances (Goals)

Anderson T 10 (2) · Armstrong G 40 (4) · Baker J 42 (25) · Baldwin T 1 · Burns A 24 · Clarke F 15 · Court D 33 (3) · Eastham G 42 (10) · Ferry G 11 · Furnell J 18 · Howe D 40 · MacLeod J 1 · Magill E 1 · McCullough W 30 · McLintock F 25 (2) · Neill T 29 (1) · Radford J 13 (7) · Sammels J 17 (5) · Simpson P 6 (2) · Skirton A 22 (3) · Snedden J 3 · Strong G 12 (3) · Tawse B 5 · Urel 22 (1) · Total: 24 players (69)

Position in League Table

	P	W	L	D	F:A	Pts	
Manchester U	42	26	7	9	89:39	61	1st
Arsenal	42	17	18	7	69:75	41	13th

SEASON 1965-1966
FOOTBALL LEAGUE (DIVISION 1)

21 Aug	Stoke C	H	W	2-1
25 Aug	Northampton T	A	D	1-1
28 Aug	Burnley	A	D	2-2
4 Sep	Chelsea	H	L	1-3
7 Sep	Nottingham F	A	W	1-0
11 Sep	Tottenham H	A	D	2-2
14 Sep	Nottingham F	H	W	1-0
18 Sep	Everton	A	L	1-3
25 Sep	Manchester U	H	W	4-2
28 Sep	Northampton T	H	D	1-1
2 Oct	Newcastle U	A	W	1-0
9 Oct	Fulham	H	W	2-1
16 Oct	Blackpool	A	L	3-5
23 Oct	Blackburn Rov	H	D	2-2
30 Oct	Leicester C	A	L	1-3
6 Nov	Sheffield U	H	W	6-2
13 Nov	Leeds U	A	L	0-2
20 Nov	West Ham U	H	W	3-2
4 Dec	Aston Villa	H	D	3-3
11 Dec	Liverpool	A	L	2-4
27 Dec	Sheffield W	A	L	0-4
28 Dec	Sheffield W	H	W	5-2
1 Jan	Fulham	A	L	0-1
15 Jan	Blackburn Rov	A	L	1-2
29 Jan	Stoke C	A	W	3-1
5 Feb	Burnley	H	D	1-1
19 Feb	Chelsea	A	D	0-0
5 Mar	Blackpool	H	D	0-0
8 Mar	Tottenham H	H	D	1-1
12 Mar	Everton	H	L	0-1
19 Mar	Manchester U	A	L	1-2
26 Mar	Newcastle U	H	L	1-3
5 Apr	W B A	H	D	1-1
11 Apr	W B A	A	D	4-4
16 Apr	West Ham U	A	L	1-2
20 Apr	Sunderland	A	W	2-0
23 Apr	Sunderland	H	D	1-1
25 Apr	Sheffield U	A	L	0-3
30 Apr	Aston Villa	A	L	0-3
5 May	Leeds U	H	L	0-3
7 May	Leicester C	H	W	1-0

FA Cup

22 Jan	Blackburn (3)	A	L	0-3

Appearances (Goals)

Armstrong G 39 (6) · Baker J 24 (13) · Baldwin T 8 (5) · Burns A 7 · Court D 38 (1) · Eastham G 37 (0) · Furnell J 31 · Howe D 20 (1) · McCullough W 17 · McGill A 2 · McLintock F 36 (2) · Neill T 39 · Neilson G 2 · Pack R 1 · Radford J 32 (8) · Sammels J 32 (6) · Simpson P 8 · Skirton A 24 (9) · Storey P · 28 · Urel 21 · Walley J 9 (1) · Wilson R 4 · Own goals 4 · Total: 22 players (62)

Position in League Table

	P	W	L	D	F:A	Pts	
Liverpool	42	26	7	9	79:34	61	1st
Arsenal	42	12	17	13	62:75	37	14th

SEASON 1966-1967
FOOTBALL LEAGUE (DIVISION 1)

20 Aug	Sunderland	A	W	3-1
23 Aug	West Ham U	H	W	2-1
27 Aug	Aston Villa	H	W	1-0
29 Aug	West Ham U	A	D	2-2
3 Sep	Tottenham H	A	L	1-3
6 Sep	Sheffield W	H	D	1-1
10 Sep	Manchester C	A	D	1-1
17 Sep	Blackpool	H	D	1-1
24 Sep	Chelsea	A	L	1-3
1 Oct	Leicester C	H	L	2-4
8 Oct	Newcastle U	H	W	2-0
15 Oct	Leeds U	A	L	1-3
22 Oct	W B A	H	L	2-3
29 Oct	Manchester U	A	L	0-1
5 Nov	Leeds U	H	L	0-1
12 Nov	Everton	A	D	0-0
19 Nov	Fulham	H	W	1-0
26 Nov	Nottingham F	A	L	1-2
3 Dec	Burnley	H	D	0-0
10 Dec	Sheffield U	A	D	1-1
17 Dec	Sunderland	H	W	2-0
26 Dec	Southampton	H	W	4-1
27 Dec	Southampton	A	L	1-2
31 Dec	Aston Villa	A	W	1-0
7 Jan	Tottenham H	H	L	0-2
14 Jan	Manchester C	H	W	1-0
21 Jan	Blackpool	A	W	3-0
4 Feb	Chelsea	H	W	2-1
11 Feb	Leicester C	A	L	1-2
25 Feb	Newcastle U	A	L	1-2
3 Mar	Manchester U	H	D	1-1
18 Mar	W B A	A	W	1-0
25 Mar	Sheffield U	H	W	2-0
27 Mar	Liverpool	A	D	0-0
28 Mar	Liverpool	H	D	1-1
1 Apr	Stoke C	A	D	2-2
19 Apr	Fulham	A	D	0-0
22 Apr	Nottingham F	H	D	1-1
25 Apr	Everton	H	W	3-1
29 Apr	Burnley	A	W	4-1
6 May	Stoke C	H	W	3-1
13 May	Sheffield W	A	D	1-1

FA Cup

28 Jan	Bristol Rov (3)	A	W	3-0
18 Feb	Bolton W (4)	A	D	0-0
22 Feb	Bolton W (4R)	H	W	3-0
11 Mar	Birmingham C (5)	A	L	0-1

Football League Cup

13 Sep	Gillingham (2)	H	D	1-1
21 Sep	Gillingham (2R)	A	D	1-1
28 Sep	Gillingham (2R)	H	W	5-0
5 Oct	West Ham U (3)	H	L	1-3

Appearances (Goals)

Armstrong G 40 (7) · Addison C 17 (4) · Baldwin T 8 (2) · Boot M 4 (2) · Coakley T 9 (1) · Court D 13 · Furnell J 42 · Graham G 33 (11) · Howe D 1 · McNab R 26 · McGill J 8 · McLintock F 40 (9) · Neill T 34 · Neilson G 12 2 · Radford J 30 (4) · Sammels J 42 10 · Simpson P 36 (1) · Skirton A 2 2 · Storey P 34 (1) · Urel 37 · Walley J 4 · Woodward J 3 · Own Goals2 · Total: 22 players (58)

Position in League Table

	P	W	L	D	F:A	Pts	
Manchester U	42	24	6	12	84:45	60	1st
Arsenal	42	16	12	14	58:47	46	7th

SEASON 1967-1968
FOOTBALL LEAGUE (DIVISION 1)

19 Aug	Stoke C	H	W	2-0
22 Aug	Liverpool	A	L	0-2
26 Aug	Nottingham F	A	L	0-2
28 Aug	Liverpool	H	W	2-0
2 Sep	Coventry C	H	D	1-1
6 Sep	W B A	A	W	3-1
9 Sep	Sheffield U	A	W	4-2
16 Sep	Tottenham H	H	W	4-0
23 Sep	Manchester C	H	W	1-0
30 Sep	Newcastle U	A	L	1-2
7 Oct	Manchester U	A	L	0-1
14 Oct	Sunderland	H	W	2-1
23 Oct	Wolverhampton W	A	L	2-3
28 Oct	Fulham	H	W	5-3
4 Nov	Leeds U	A	L	1-3
11 Nov	Everton	H	D	2-2
18 Nov	Leicester C	A	D	2-2
25 Nov	West Ham U	H	D	0-0
2 Dec	Burnley	A	L	0-1
16 Dec	Stoke C	A	W	1-0
20 Dec	Nottingham F	H	W	3-0
26 Dec	Chelsea	A	L	1-2
30 Dec	Chelsea	H	D	1-1
6 Jan	Coventry C	A	D	1-1
13 Jan	Sheffield U	H	D	1-1
20 Jan	Tottenham H	A	L	0-1
3 Feb	Manchester C	A	D	1-1
10 Feb	Newcastle U	H	D	0-0
24 Feb	Manchester U	H	L	0-2
16 Mar	Wolverhampton W	H	L	0-2
23 Mar	Fulham	A	W	3-1
29 Mar	West Ham U	A	D	1-1
6 Apr	Everton	A	L	0-2
10 Apr	Southampton	A	L	0-2
13 Apr	Leicester C	H	W	2-1
15 Apr	Southampton	H	L	0-3
20 Apr	Sunderland	A	L	0-2
27 Apr	Burnley	H	W	2-0
30 Apr	Sheffield W	H	W	3-2
4 May	Sheffield W	A	W	2-1
7 May	Leeds U	H	W	4-3
11 May	W B A	H	W	2-1

FA Cup

27 Jan	Shrewsbury T (3)	A	D	1-1
30 Jan	Shrewsbury T (3R)	H	W	2-0
17 Feb	Swansea T (4)	A	W	1-0
9 Mar	Birmingham C (5)	H	D	1-1
12 Mar	Birmingham C (5R)	A	L	1-2

Football League Cup

12 Sep	Coventry C (2)	A	W	2-1
11 Oct	Reading T (3)	H	W	1-0
1 Nov	Blackburn Rov (4)	H	W	2-1
29 Nov	Burnley (5)	A	D	3-3
5 Dec	Burnley (5R)	H	W	2-1
17 Jan	Huddersfield (SF)	H	W	3-2
6 Feb	Huddersfield (SF)	A	W	3-1
2 Mar	Leeds U (F) (at Wembley)			L 0-1

Appearances (Goals)

Addison C 11 (5) · Armstrong G 42 (5) · Court D 16 (3) · Davidson R 1 · Furnell J 29 · Gould R 16 (6) · Graham G 38 (16) · Jenkins D 3 · Johnston G 18 (3) · McLintock F 38 (4) · McNab R 30 · Neill T 38 (2) · Radford J 39 (10) · Rice P 6 · Sammels J 35 (4) · Simpson P 40 · Storey P 39 · Urel 21 · Wilson R 13 · Own goals 2 · Total: 19 players (60)

Position in League Table

	P	W	L	D	F:A	Pts	
Manchester C	42	26	10	6	86:43	58	1st
Arsenal	42	17	15	10	60:56	44	9th

SEASON 1968-1969
FOOTBALL LEAGUE (DIVISION 1)

10 Aug	Tottenham H	A	W	2-1
13 Aug	Leicester C	H	W	3-0
17 Aug	Liverpool	H	D	1-1
21 Aug	Wolverhampton W	A	D	0-0
24 Aug	Ipswich T	A	W	2-1
27 Aug	Manchester C	H	W	4-1
31 Aug	Q P R	H	W	2-1
7 Sep	Southampton A	A	W	2-1
14 Sep	Stoke C	H	W	1-0
21 Sep	Leeds U	A	L	0-2
28 Sep	Sunderland	H	D	0-0
5 Oct	Manchester U	A	D	0-0
9 Oct	Manchester C	A	D	1-1
12 Oct	Coventry C	H	W	2-1
19 Oct	W B A	A	L	0-1
26 Oct	West Ham U	H	D	0-0
9 Nov	Newcastle U	H	D	0-0
16 Nov	Nottingham F	A	W	2-0
23 Nov	Chelsea	H	L	0-1
30 Nov	Burnley	A	W	1-0
7 Dec	Everton	H	W	3-1
14 Dec	Coventry	A	W	1-0
21 Dec	W B A	H	W	2-0
26 Dec	Manchester U	H	W	3-0
11 Jan	Sheffield W	H	W	2-0
18 Jan	Newcastle U	A	L	1-2
1 Feb	Nottingham F	H	D	1-1
15 Feb	Burnley	H	W	2-0
18 Feb	Ipswich T	H	L	0-2
1 Mar	Sheffield W	A	W	5-0
22 Mar	Q P R	A	W	1-0
24 Mar	Tottenham H	H	W	1-0
29 Mar	Southampton	H	D	0-0
31 Mar	Liverpool	A	D	1-1
5 Apr	Sunderland	A	D	0-0
7 Apr	Wolverhampton W	H	W	3-1
8 Apr	Leicester C	A	D	0-0
12 Apr	Leeds U	H	L	1-2
14 Apr	Chelsea	A	L	1-2
19 Apr	Stoke C	A	W	3-1
21 Apr	West Ham U	A	W	2-1
29 Apr	Everton	A	L	0-1

FA Cup

4 Jan	Cardiff (3)	A	D	0-0
7 Jan	Cardiff (3R)	H	W	2-0
25 Jan	Charlton Ath (4)	H	W	2-0
12 Feb	W B A (5)	A	D	0-1

Football League Cup

4 Sep	Sunderland (2)	H	W	1-0
25 Sep	Scunthorpe U (3)	A	W	6-1
15 Oct	Liverpool (4)	H	W	2-1
20 Oct	Blackpool (5)	H	W	5-1
20 Nov	Tottenham H (SF)	H	W	1-0
4 Dec	Tottenham H (SF)	A	D	1-1
15 Mar	Swindon T (F) (at Wembley)		L	1-3*

*aet, 1-1 at 90 mins

Appearances (Goals)

Armstrong G 29 (5) · Court D 40 (6) · Gould R 38 (10) · Graham G 25 (4) · Jenkins D · 14 · (3)· Johnston G 3 · McLintock F 37 (1) · McNab R 42 · Neill T 22 (2) · Radford J 34 (15) · Robertson J 19 (3) · Sammels J 36 (4) · Simpson P 34 · Storey P 42 · Urel 23 · Wilson R 42 · Own goals 3 · Total: 16 players (56)

Position in League Table

	P	W	L	D	F:A	Pts	
Leeds	42	27	2	13	66:26	67	1st
Arsenal	42	22	8	12	56:27	56	4th

SEASON 1969-1970
FOOTBALL LEAGUE (DIVISION 1)

Date	Opponent			
9 Aug	Everton	H	L	0-1
13 Aug	Leeds U	A	D	0-0
16 Aug	W B A	A	W	1-0
19 Aug	Leeds U	H	D	1-1
23 Aug	Nottingham F	H	W	2-1
25 Aug	West Ham U	A	D	1-1
30 Aug	Newcastle U	A	L	1-3
6 Sep	Sheffield W	H	D	0-0
13 Sep	Burnley	A	W	1-0
16 Sep	Tottenham H	H	L	2-3
20 Sep	Manchester U	H	D	2-2
27 Sep	Chelsea	A	L	0-3
4 Oct	Coventry C	H	L	0-1
7 Oct	W B A	H	D	1-1
11 Oct	Stoke C	H	D	0-0
18 Oct	Sunderland	A	D	1-1
25 Oct	Ipswich T	H	D	0-0
1 Nov	Crystal Palace	A	W	5-1
8 Nov	Derby Co	H	W	4-0
15 Nov	Wolverhampton W	A	L	0-2
22 Nov	Manchester C	H	D	1-1
29 Nov	Liverpool	A	W	1-0
6 Dec	Southampton	H	D	2-2
13 Dec	Burnley	H	W	3-2
20 Dec	Sheffield W	A	D	1-1
26 Dec	Nottingham F	A	D	1-1
27 Dec	Newcastle U	H	D	0-0
10 Jan	Manchester U	A	L	1-2
17 Jan	Chelsea	H	L	0-3
31 Jan	Coventry C	A	L	0-2
7 Feb	Stoke C	H	D	0-0
14 Feb	Everton	A	D	2-2
18 Feb	Manchester C	A	D	1-1
21 Feb	Derby Co	A	L	2-3
28 Feb	Sunderland	H	W	3-1
14 Mar	Liverpool	H	W	2-1
21 Mar	Southampton	A	W	2-0
28 Mar	Wolverhampton W	H	D	2-2
30 Mar	Crystal Palace	H	W	2-0
31 Mar	Ipswich T	A	L	1-2
4 Apr	West Ham U	H	W	2-1
2 May	Tottenham H	A	L	0-1

FA Cup

Date	Opponent			
3 Jan	Blackpool (3)	H	D	1-1
15 Jan	Blackpool (3R)	A	L	2-3

Football League Cup

Date	Opponent			
2 Sep	Southampton (2)	A	D	1-1
4 Sep	Southampton (2R)	H	W	2-0
24 Sep	Everton (3)	H	D	0-0
1 Oct	Everton (3R)	A	L	0-1

European Fairs Cup

9 Sep	Glentoran (1)	H	W	3-0
29 Sep	Glentoran (1)	A	L	0-1
20 Oct	Sp Cb de Port (2)	A	D	0-0
26 Nov	Sp Cb de Port (2)	H	W	3-0
17 Dec	Rouen (3)	A	D	0-0
13 Jan	Rouen (3)	H	W	1-0
11 Mar	Dinamo Bacau (4)	A	W	2-0
18 Mar	Dinamo Bacau (4)	H	W	7-1
8 Apr	Ajax (SF)	H	W	3-0
15 Apr	Ajax (SF)	A	L	0-1
22 Apr	Anderlecht (F)	A	L	1-3
28 Apr	Anderlecht (F)	H	W	3-0

Appearances (Goals)

Armstrong G 17 3 · Barnett G 11 · Court D 21 · George C 28 (6) · Gould R 11 · Graham G 36 (7) · Kelly E 16 · (2) · Kennedy R 4 (1) · Marinello P 14 (1) · McLintock F 30 · McNab R 37 (2) · Neill T 17 (1) · Nelson S 4 · Radford J 39 (12) · Rice P 7 (1) · Roberts J 11 (1) · Robertson J 27 (4) · Sammels J 36 (8) · Simpson P 39 Storey P 39 1 · Urel 3 · Webster M (3) · Wilson R 28 · Own goals 1 · Total: 23 players (51)

Position in League Table

	P	W	L	D	F:A	Pts	
Everton	42	29	5	8	72:34	66	1st
Arsenal	42	12	12	18	51:49	42	12th

The next 25 years of statistics are presented in greater detail and include a full team listing, with details of goalscorers. They begin with Arsenal's Double winning season 1970-71.

1970-71

SEASON 1970-1971 FOOTBALL LEAGUE (DIVISION 1)

Date	Opponent	V	R	Score	1	2	3	4	5	6	7	8	9	10	11	Notes
15 Aug	Everton	A	D	2-2	Wilson	Rice	McNab	Kelly	Roberts	McLintock	Armstrong	Storey	Radford	George[1]	Graham1	Marinello for George
17 Aug	West Ham U	A	D	0-0	..	Storey	..	..	McLintock	Roberts	..	..	Radford	Kennedy	Marinello	..
22 Aug	Manchester U	H	W	4-0	..	Rice	..	..	..	..	..	Storey	Radford[3]	Kennedy	..[1]	Marinello for Radford
25 Aug	Huddersfield T	H	W	1-0	..	..	..	..	..	..	..	..	..	..[1]	..	Nelson for Radford
29 Aug	Chelsea	A	L	1-2	..	..	..	..[1]	..	..	..	..	Nelson	..	..	
1 Sep	Leeds U	H	D	0-0	..	..	..	..	..	..	..	..	Radford	..	..	
5 Sep	Tottenham	H	W	2-0	..	..	..	..	..	..[2]	..	..	..	..	..	Nelson for McLintock
12 Sep	Burnley	A	W	2-1	..	..	..	..	..	..	..	..	..[1]	..[1]	..	
19 Sep	W B A	H	W	6-2	..	..	..	..	..	opponents	..[1]	..	..	..[2]	..[2]	
26 Sep	Stoke C	A	L	0-5	..	..	..	..	..	..	..	..	..	..	..	
3 Oct	Nottingham F	H	W	4-0	..	..	..	..	..	..[1]	..	..	..	..[3]	..	
10 Oct	Newcastle U	A	D	1-1	..	..	..	..[1]	..	..	..	..	..	..	..[1]	
17 Oct	Everton	H	W	4-0	..	..	..	..	..	..	..	..	..[1]	..[2]	..[1]	
24 Oct	Coventry C	A	W	3-1	..	..	..	..	..	..	..	..	..[1]	..[1]	..[1]	
31 Oct	Derby Co	H	W	2-0	..	..	..	..[1]	..	..	..	..	..[1]	..	..	
7 Nov	Blackpool	A	W	1-0	..	..	..	..	..	..	..	..	..[1]	..	..	
14 Nov	Crystal Palace	H	D	1-1	..	..	..	..	..	..	..	..	..[1]	..	..	
21 Nov	Ipswich T	A	W	1-0	..	..	..	..	..	Simpson	..[1]	..	..	..	Sammels	
28 Nov	Liverpool	H	W	2-0	..	..	..	..	..	..	..[1]	..	..	..[1]	..	Graham[1] for Kelly
5 Dec	Manchester C	A	W	2-0	..	..	..	Graham	..	..	..[1]	..	..	..[1]	..	
12 Dec	Wolverhampton W	H	W	2-1	..	..	..	Storey	..	..	..	Sammels	..[1]	..	Graham[1]	
19 Dec	Manchester U	A	W	3-1	..	..	..	..	..[1]	..	..	..	..	..[1]	..	
26 Dec	Southampton	H	D	0-0	..	..	..	..	..	..	..	..	..	..	..	
9 Jan	West Ham U	H	W	2-0	..	..	Nelson	..	..	..	..	..	..	..[1]	..[1]	
16 Jan	Huddersfield T	A	L	1-2	..	..	McNab	..	..	..	..	..	..	..[1]	..	
30 Jan	Liverpool	A	L	0-2	..	..	..	..	..	..	..	..	..	..	..	
6 Feb	Manchester C	H	W	1-0	..	..	..	..	..	..	..	..	..[1]	..	George	
20 Feb	Ipswich	H	W	3-2	..	..	..	..	..[1]	..	..	..	..[1]	..	..[1]	
27 Feb	Derby Co	A	L	0-2	..	..	..	..	..	..	..	..	..	..	..	Graham for Rice
2 Mar	Wolverhampton W	A	W	3-0	..	..	..	..	..	..	..	..[1]	..[1]	..	..	Sammels[1] for George
13 Mar	Crystal Palace	A	W	2-0	..	..	..	..	..	..	..	Graham1	..	..	..	
20 Mar	Blackpool	H	W	1-0	..	..	..	..[1]	..	..	..	..	..	..	..	
3 Apr	Chelsea	H	W	2-0	..	..	..	..	..	..	..	..	..	..[2]	..	Kelly for Armstrong
6 Apr	Coventry C	H	W	1-0	..	..	..	..	..	..	..	..	..	..[1]	..	
10 Apr	Southampton	A	W	2-1	..	..	..	..	..	..	..[1]	..	..[1]	..	..	
13 Apr	Nottingham F	A	W	3-0	..	..	..	..[1]	..	..	..	..	..	..	..[1]	
17 Apr	Newcastle U	H	W	1-0	..	..	..	..	..	..	..	..	..	..	..[1]	
20 Apr	Burnley	H	W	1-0	..	..	Roberts	Kelly	..	..	..	..	..	..	..[1]	
24 Apr	W B A	A	D	2-2	..	..	McNab	Storey	..[1]	opponents	..	..	..	..	..	Sammels for Rice
26 Apr	Leeds U	A	L	0-1	..	..	..	..	..	..	..	..	..	..	..	
1 May	Stoke C	H	W	1-0	..	..	..	..	..	..	..	..	..	..	..	Kelly[1] for Storey
3 May	Tottenham H	A	W	1-0	..	..	..	Kelly	..	..	..	..	..	..	..[1]	..

FA Cup

Date	Opponent	V	R	Score	1	2	3	4	5	6	7	8	9	10	11	Notes
6 Jan	Yeovll T (3)	A	W	3-0	Wilson	Rice	McNab	Storey	McLintock	Simpson	Armstrong	Sammels	Radford[2]	Kennedy[1]	Graham	Kelly for McNab
23 Jan	Portsmouth (4)	A	D	1-1	..	..	..	..[1]	..	..[1]	..	..	..	..	..	George for Rice
1 Feb	Portsmouth (4R)	H	W	3-2	..	..	..	..[1]	..	..[1]	..	..	..	..	George[1]	
17 Feb	Manchester C (5)	A	W	2-1	..	..	..	..	..	..	..	..	..	..	..[2]	
6 Mar	Leicester C (6)	A	D	0-0	..	..	..	..	..	..	..	..	..	..	..	
15 Mar	Leicester C (6R)	H	W	1-0	..	..	..	..	..	..	..	Graham	..	..	..[1]	
27 Mar	Stoke C (SF)		D	2-2	..	..	..	..	..[2]	..	..	..	..	..	..	Sammels for George
	(at Sheffield W)															
31 Mar	Stoke C (SFR)		W	2-0	..	..	..	..	..	..	..	..	..[1]	..	..[1]	
	(at Birmingham)															
8 May	Liverpool (F)		W	2-1*	..	..	..	..	..	..	..	..	..	..	..[1]	Kelly[1] for Storey
	(at Wembley)															
*aet, 0-0 at 90 mins																

Football League Cup

Date	Opponent	V	R	Score	1	2	3	4	5	6	7	8	9	10	11	Notes
8 Sep	Ipswich T (2)	A	D	0-0	Wilson	Rice	McNab	Kelly	McLintock	Roberts	Armstrong	Storey	Nelson	Kennedy	Graham	
28 Sep	Ipswich T (2R)	H	W	4-0	..	..	..	..	..	..[1]	..	..	Radford[1]	..[2]	..[1]	
6 Oct	Luton T (3)	A	W	1-0	..	..	..	..	..	..	..	..	..	..	..[1]	
28 Oct	Crystal Palace (4)	A	D	0-0	..	..	..	..	..	..	..	..	..	..	..	
9 Nov	Crystal Palace (4R)	H	L	0-2	..	..	..	..	..	..	..	..	..	..	..	

European Fairs Cup

Date	Opponent	V	R	Score	1	2	3	4	5	6	7	8	9	10	11	Notes
16 Sep	Lazio Roma (1)	A	D	2-2	Wilson	Rice	McNab	Kelly	McLintock	Roberts	Armstrong	Storey	Radford[2]	Kennedy	Graham	
23 Sep	Lazio Roma (1)	H	W	2-0	..	..	..	..	..[1]	..	..	..	..[1]	..	..	Nelson for Graham
21 Oct	Sturm Graz (2)	A	L	0-1	..	..	..	..	..	..	..	..	..	..	..	
4 Nov	Sturm Graz (2)	H	W	2-0	..	..	..	..	..	..	..	..	..[2]	..[1]	..	
2 Dec	Beveren Waas (3)	H	W	4-0	..	..	..	Sammels[1]	..	Simpson	..	..	..	..	..	
16 Dec	Beveren Waas (3)	A	D	0-0	..	..	..	Storey	Roberts	..	..	Sammels	..	..	..	Marinello for Armstrong, George for Radford
9 Mar	FC Koln (4)	H	W	2-1	..	..	..	..[1]	McLintock[1]	..	..	George	..	..	..	
23 Mar	FC Koln (4)	A	L	0-1	..	..	..	..	..	..	..	Graham	..	..	George	

217

Appearances (Goals)

Armstrong G 42 (7) · George C 17 (5) · Graham G 38 (11) · Kelly E 23 (4) · Kennedy R 41 (19) · Marinello P 3 · McLintock F 42 (5) · McNab R 40 · Nelson S 4 · Radford J 41 (15) · Rice P 41 · Roberts J 18 · Sammels J 15 (1) · Simpson P 25 · Storey P 40 (2) · Wilson R 42 · Own Goals 2 · Total: 16 players (71)

Position in League Table

	P	W	L	D	F:A	Pts	
Arsenal	42	29	6	7	71:29	65	1st

SEASON 1971-1972 FOOTBALL LEAGUE (DIVISION 1)

1971-72

14 Aug	Chelsea	H	W	3-0	Wilson	Rice	McNab	Storey	McLintock[1]	Simpson	Armstrong	Kelly	Radford[1]	Kennedy[1]	Graham	
17 Aug	Huddersfield T	A	W	1-0	..	..	..	..	..	..	..	..	..	..[1]	..	
20 Aug	Manchester U (Liverpool)	A	L	1-3	..	..	..	..	..[1]	..	..	..	..	..	..	
24 Aug	Sheffield U	H	L	0-1	..	..	..	..	..	..	..	..	..	..	..	
28 Aug	Stoke C	H	L	0-1	..	..	..	..	..	..	..	..	..	..	..	Roberts for Rice
4 Sep	W B A	A	W	1-0	..	..	..	..	..	Roberts[1]	..	..	..	..	..	
11 Sep	Leeds U	H	W	2-0	..	..	..	..[1]	..	..	..	Simpson	..	..	..[1]	
18 Sep	Everton	A	L	1-2	..	..	..	..	..	..	..	..	..	..[1]	..	Kelly for McLintock
25 Sep	Leicester C	H	W	3-0	..	..[1]	Nelson	..	Simpson	..	..	Kelly	..[2]	..	..	George for Storey
2 Oct	Southampton	A	W	1-0	..	..	..	McLintock	..[1]	..	..	..	..	..	..	
9 Oct	Newcastle U	H	W	4-2	..	..	..	..	..	George	..[1]	..[1]	..	..[1]	..[1]	Davis for Radford
16 Oct	Chelsea	A	W	2-1	..	..	..	..	Roberts	..	..	..	..	..[2]	..	Simpson for Kelly
23 Oct	Derby Co	A	L	1-2	..	..	..	..	..	..	..	..	..	..	..[1]	Simpson for Kelly
30 Oct	Ipswich T	H	W	2-1	..	..	..	Storey	..	McLintock	*opponents*	George[1]	..	..	..	
6 Nov	Liverpool	A	L	2-3	..	..	..	..	..	..	*opponents*	..	..	..[1]	..	
13 Nov	Manchester C	H	L	1-2	..	..	..[1]	..	..	..	..	..	..	..	..	
20 Nov	Wolverhampton W	A	L	1-5	..	..	..	..	..	..	..	..	..	..[1]	..	
24 Nov	Tottenham H	A	D	1-1	..	..	McNab	..	..	..	..	Kelly	..	..[1]	..	
27 Nov	Crystal Palace	H	W	2-1	..	..	..	..	..	..	..	..[1]	..[1]	..	..	
4 Dec	West Ham U	A	D	0-0	..	..	..	..	McLintock	Simpson	..	..	..	..	..	
11 Dec	Coventry C	H	W	2-0	..	..	..	..	..	..	..	..	..[2]	..	..	Marinello for Simpson
18 Dec	W B A	H	W	2-0	..	..	..	..	..	Roberts[2]	..	..	..	..	..	
27 Dec	Nottingham F	A	D	1-1	..	..	..	Kelly	..	Simpson	..	Ball	..	..	..[1]	
1 Jan	Everton	H	D	1-1	..	..	..	..	Roberts	..[1]	..	..	..	..	..	George for Armstrong
8 Jan	Stoke C	A	D	0-0	..	..	..	..	McLintock	..	..	..	..	..	..	
22 Jan	Huddersfield T	H	W	1-0	..	..	Nelson	..	..	..	..[1]	..	..	..	..	George for Ball
29 Jan	Sheffield U	A	W	5-0	..	..	..	Roberts	..	..[1]	..	..	George[2]	..[1]	..[1]	
12 Feb	Derby Co	H	W	2-0	..	..	..	Kelly	..	..	..	..	..[2]	..	..	
19 Feb	Ipswich T	A	W	1-0	..	..	..	..	..	..	..	..	..[1]	..	..	
4 Mar	Manchester C	A	L	0-2	..	..	..	Storey	..	..	..	..	..	Radford	..	
11 Mar	Newcastle U	A	L	0-2	..	..	..	..	Simpson	Graham	..	..	..	Kennedy	Radford	Batson for George
25 Mar	Leeds U	A	L	0-3	..	..	..	..	McLintock	Simpson	..	..	..	..	Roberts	Marinello for Roberts
28 Mar	Southampton	H	W	1-0	..	..	..	..	..	..	..	..	..	..	Marinello[1]	
1 Apr	Nottingham F	H	W	3-0	..	..	..	..	Roberts	..	..	..	..[1]	..[1]	..	Graham[1] for Kennedy
4 Apr	Leicester C	A	D	0-0	..	..	..	..	McLintock	..	..	..	..	Graham	..	
8 Apr	Wolverhampton W	H	W	2-1	..	..	..	..	..	..	Marinello	..	..	Kennedy	Graham[2]	Armstrong for Marinello
11 Apr	Crystal Palace	A	D	2-2	..	..	..	..	Roberts	..	Armstrong	..[1]	Radford[1]	George	..	
22 Apr	West Ham U	H	W	2-1	Barnett	..	McNab	..	McLintock	..	..	..[2]	..	..	..	Baston for McLintock
25 Apr	Manchester U	H	W	3-0	..	..	..	Roberts	..	..[1]	..	Nelson	..[1]	Kennedy[1]	..	Marinello for Graham
1 May	Coventry C	A	W	1-0	..	..	..	Storey	..[1]	..	..	Ball	..	George	..	
8 May	Liverpool	H	D	0-0	..	..	Nelson	..	..	..	..	..	..	Kennedy	..	Roberts for Rice
11 May	Tottenham H	H	L	0-2	..	..	McNab	Nelson	..	Roberts	..	Simpson	..	..	..	Marinello for Simpson

FA Cup

15 Jan	Swindon T (3)	A	W	2-0	Wilson	Rice	Nelson	Kelly	McLintock	Simpson	Armstrong[1]	Ball[1]	Radford	Kennedy	Graham	
5 Feb	Reading (4)	A	W	2-1	..	..[1]	..	..	..	*opponents*	..	..	George	..	..	
26 Feb	Derby Co (5)	A	D	2-2	..	..	..	..	..	..	..	..	..[2]	..	..	Storey for Kelly
29 Feb	Derby Co (5R)	H	D	0-0	..	..	..	Storey	..	..	..	..	..	..	..	Radford for Kennedy
13 Mar	Derby Co (5R) (at Leicester)		W	1-0	..	..	..	..	..	..	..	..	..	..[1]	..	
18 Mar	Orient (6)	A	W	1-0	..	..	..	..	..	..	..	..[1]	..	..	..	
15 Apr	Stoke C (SF) (at Villa Park)		D	1-1		Wilson injured Radford ingoal	..	McNab	..	..	..	..[1]	..	Radford	George	.. Kennedy for Wilson
19 Apr	Stoke C (SFR) (at Everton)		W	2-1	Barnett	..	..	..	..	..	..	..	..[1]	..[1]	..	
6 May	Leeds U (F) (at Wembley)		L	0-1	..	..	..	..	..	..	..	..	..	..	..	Kennedy for Radford

Football League Cup

8 Sep	Barnsley (2)	H	W	1-0	Wilson	Rice	McNab	Storey	McLintock	Roberts	Marinello	Kelly	Radford	Kennedy1	Graham	
6 Oct	Newcastle U (3)	H	W	4-0	..	..	Nelson	McLintock	Simpson	..	Armstrong	..	..[2]	..[1]	..[1]	
26 Oct	Sheffield U (4)	H	D	0-0	Barnett	..	..	Storey	Roberts	McLintock	..	George	..	..	..	
8 Nov	Sheffield U (4R)	A	L	0-2	Wilson	..	..	Kelly	..	..	..	..	..	..	..	McNab for McLintock

European Cup

15 Sep	St't Drammen (1)	A	W	3-1	Wilson	Rice	Simpson[1]	McLintock	McNab	Roberts	Kelly[1]	Marinello[1]	Graham	Radford	Kennedy	Davies for Marinello
29 Sep	St't Drammen (1)	H	W	4-0	..	..	Nelson	Kelly	Simpson	..	Armstrong[1]	George	Radford[2]	Kennedy[1]	Graham	
20 Oct	Gr'pers Zurich (2)	A	W	2-0	..	..	..	McLintock	Roberts	George	..	Kelly	..	..[1]	..[1]	
3 Nov	Gr'pers Zurich (2)	H	W	3-0	..	..	..	Storey	..	McLintock	..	George[1]	..[1]	..[1]	..	Simpson for Roberts, McNab for McLintock
8 Mar	Ajax Ams'dam (3)	A	L	1-2	..	..	..	..	McLintock	Simpson	..	..	..	..[1]	..	Roberts for Nelson
22 Mar	Ajax Ams'dam (3)	H	L	0-1	..	..	..	..	..	..	..	..	Marinello	..	..	Roberts for Nelson

Appearances (Goals)

Armstrong G 42 (2) · Ball A 18 (3) · Batson B 2 · Barnett G 5 · Davies P 1 · George C 23 (7) · Graham G 40 (8) · Kelly E 23 (2) · Kennedy R 37 (12) · McNab R 20 · McLintock F 37 (3) · Marinello P 8 1 · Nelson S 24 (1) · Radford J 34 (8) · Rice P 42 (1) · Roberts J 23 (3) · Simpson P 34 (4) · Storey P 29 (1) · Wilson R 37 · Own goals 2 · Total: 19 players (58)

Position in League Table

	P	W	L	D	F:A	Pts	
Derby Co	42	24	8	10	69:33	58	1st
Arsenal	42	22	12	8	58:40	52	5th

SEASON 1972-1973 FOOTBALL LEAGUE (DIVISION 1)

1972-73

12 Aug	Leicester C	A	W	1-0	Barnett	Rice	McNab	Storey	McLintock	Simpson	Armstrong	Ball[1]	Radford	Kennedy	Graham	
15 Aug	Wolverhampton W	H	W	5-2	..	..	..[1]	..	..	..[1]	..	..	..[2]	..[1]	..	Roberts for Simpson
19 Aug	Stoke C	H	W	2-0	..	..	..	..	..	Roberts	..	..	..	..[2]	..	
22 Aug	Coventry C	A	D	1-1	..	..[1]	..	..	..	Simpson	..	..	..	..	..	
26 Aug	Manchester U	A	D	0-0	..	..	..	..	..	..	..	..	George	..	..	
29 Aug	West Ham U	H	W	1-0	..	..	..	..	..	..	..	..[1]	Radford	..	..	George for Armstrong
2 Sep	Chelsea	H	D	1-1	..	..	..	..	..	*opponents*	..	..	..	..	..	George for Armstrong
9 Sep	Newcastle U	A	L	1-2	..	..	..	..	..	Roberts	Marinello	..	..	..[1]	..	
16 Sep	Liverpool	H	D	0-0	..	..	..	..	..	..	..	..	..	..	..	
23 Sep	Norwich C	A	L	2-3	..	..	..	..[1]	..	..	..	..	..[1]	..	..	
26 Sep	Birmingham C	H	W	2-0	..	..	..	..[1]	..	..	..	..	..	..	George[1]	
30 Sep	Southampton	H	W	1-0	..	..	..	..	..	..	..	..	..	..	..	Graham[1] for Kennedy
7 Oct	Sheffield U	A	L	0-1	..	..	..	..	..	Blockley	..	..	..	Graham	..	
14 Oct	Ipswich T	H	W	1-0	..	..	..	..	..	..	..	..	..	..[1]	..	
21 Oct	Crystal Palace	A	W	3-2	..	..[1]	..	..	..	..	..	Kelly	..[1]	..	..[1]	Nelson for Kelly
28 Oct	Manchester C	H	D	0-0	..	..	..	..	..	..	..	..	..	George	Graham	
4 Nov	Coventry C	H	L	0-2	..	..	..	..	..	..	..	Ball	..	..	Kelly	Graham for Kelly
17 Nov	Wolverhampton W	A	W	3-1	..	..	..	..	..	..	..[1]	..	..[2]	..	..	
18 Nov	Everton	H	W	1-0	..	..	..	..	Simpson	..	..	..	..[1]	..	..	

25 Nov	Derby Co	A	L	0-5	Wilson	..	..	..	McLintock	Simpson	..	..	..	..	..	Armstrong for Marinello
2 Dec	Leeds U	H	W	2-1					Blockley	..	Armstrong	..¹	..¹	Kennedy	..	
9 Dec	Tottenham H	A	W	2-1	..	..	..	..¹					..¹	..	..	McLintock for Simpson
16 Dec	W B A	H	W	2-1	Barnett	..	..	..	McLintock	opponents	..	..	..¹	..	..	George for Rice
23 Dec	Birmingham C	A	D	1-1	Wilson	Nelson	..	..	Blockley	..	..	..	..	..	..¹	
26 Dec	Norwich C	H	W	2-0	..	..	..	..	..	..	..	..¹	..¹	..	..	George for Nelson
30 Dec	Stoke C	A	D	0-0	..	Rice	..	..	..	..	..	..	..	..	..	
6 Jan	Manchester U	H	W	3-1	..	..	..	..	..	..	..¹	..¹	..	..¹	..	
20 Jan	Chelsea	A	W	1-0	..	..	..	..	..	..	..	..	..	..¹	..	McLintock for Kelly
27 Jan	Newcastle U	H	D	2-2	..	..	..	..	..	..	..	..¹	..	..¹	..	George for Armstrong
10 Feb	Liverpool	A	W	2-0	..	..	..	..	..	..	..	..¹	..¹	..	..	George for Radford
17 Feb	Leicester C	H	W	1-0	..	..	..	..	..	McLintock	opponents	..	..	..	..	George for Blockley
28 Feb	W B A	A	L	0-1	..	..	..	Batson	McLintock	George	..	..	..	..	..	
3 Mar	Sheffield U	H	W	3-2	..	..	..	George²	..	Batson	..	..¹	..	..	..	Nelson for Batson
10 Mar	Ipswich T	A	W	2-1	..	..	..	Storey	..	Simpson	..	..¹	..¹	..	..	
24 Mar	Manchester C	A	W	2-1	..	..	..	..	..	..	..	..	George¹	..¹	..	Nelson for Kelly
26 Mar	Crystal Palace	H	W	1-0	..	..	..	..	..	..	..	..¹	..	..	..	
31 Mar	Derby Co	H	L	0-1	..	..	..	..	..	..	..	..	..	..	..	Nelson for McLintock
14 Apr	Tottenham H	H	D	1-1	Wilson	Rice	McNab	Storey¹	Blockley	Simpson	Armstrong	Ball	Radford	Kennedy	Kelly	George for Kelly
21 Apr	Everton	A	D	0-0	..	..	..	..	..	..	..	..	..	..	..	George for Blockley
23 Apr	Southampton	A	D	2-2	..	..	..	..	Kelly	..	..	..	..¹	George¹	Kennedy	
28 Apr	West Ham U	A	W	2-1	..	..	..	..	..	..	..	..	..¹	Kennedy¹	George	
9 May	Leeds U	A	L	1-6	..	Batson	..	..	Blockley	..	..¹	..	..	..	Hornsby	Price for Hornsby

FA Cup

13 Jan	Leichester C (3)	H	D	2-2	Wilson	Rice	McNab	Storey	Blockley	Simpson	Armstrong¹	Ball	Radford	Kennedy¹	Kelly	
17 Jan	Leicester C (3R)	A	W	2-1	..	..	..	..	..	..	..	..	..¹	..	..¹	
3 Feb	Bradford C (4)	H	W	2-0	..	..	..	..	..	..	..	..¹	George¹	..	..	Marinello for George
24 Feb	Carlisle U (5)	A	W	2-1	Barnett	..	..	..	McLintock¹	..	..	..¹	Radford	..	..	Nelson for Storey
17 Mar	Chelsea (6)	A	D	2-2	Wilson	..	..	..	..	..	..	..¹	George¹	..	..	
20 Mar	Chelsea (6R)	H	W	2-1	..	..	..	..	..	..	..	..¹	..	..¹	..	
7 Apr	Sunderland (SF) (at Sheffield W)	A	L	1-2	..	..	..	..	Blockley	..	..	..	..¹	..	..	Radford for Blockley

Football League Cup

Sep	Everton (2)	H	W	1-0	Barnett	Rice	McNab	Storey¹	McLintock	Simpson	Marinello	Ball	Radford	Kennedy	Graham	
3 Oct	Rotherham U (3)	H	W	5-0	..	..	Nelson	..¹	..	Roberts	..¹	..	..²	Graham	George¹	
31 Oct	Sheffield U (4)	A	W	2-1	..	..	McNab	..	..	Simpson	..	Kelly	..¹	..	..¹	
21 Nov	Norwich C (5)	H	L	0-3	..	..	..	..	..	..	..	Ball	..	George	Kelly	

Appearances (Goals)

Armstrong G 30 (2) · Ball A 40 (10) · Barnett G 20 · Batson B 3 · Blockley J 20 · George C 27 (6) · Graham G 16 (2) · Hornsby B 1 · Kelly E 27 (1) · McLintock F 29 · McNab R 42 (1) · Marinello P 13 1 · Nelson S 6 · Price D 1 · Radford J 38 (15) · Rice P 39 (2) · Roberts J 7 · Simpson P 27 (1) · Storey P 40 (4) · Wilson R 22 · Own goals 3 · Total: 21 players (57)

Position in League Table

	P	W	L	D	F:A	Pts	
Liverpool	42	25	7	10	72:42	60	1st
Arsenal	42	23	8	11	57:43	57	2nd

SEASON 1973-1974 FOOTBALL LEAGUE (DIVISION 1)

25 Aug	Manchester U	H	W	3-0	Wilson	Rice	McNab	Price	Blockley	Simpson	Armstrong	Ball¹	Radford¹	Kennedy¹	George	Homsby for Radford
28 Aug	Leeds U	H	L	1-2	..	..	..	Storey	¹							Price for Simpson
1 Sep	Newcastle U	A	D	1-1	..	..	..	Price	..	Storey	..	..	Kelly	..	..¹	
4 Sep	Sheffield U	A	L	0-5	..	..	..	Batson	..	..	..	..	..	..	..	
8 Sep	Leicester C	H	L	0-2	..	..	..	Storey	..	Simpson	Kelly	..	Radford	..	..	Armstrong for Kelly
11 Sep	Sheffield U	H	W	1-0	..	..	..	..	..	..	Armstrong	..	..	..¹	Kelly	
15 Sep	Norwich C	A	W	4-0	..	..	..¹	..	..	George¹	..	..¹	..	..¹	..	
22 Sep	Stoke C	H	W	2-1	..	..	..	..	..	Simpson	..	..¹	..¹	..	George	Kelly for George
29 Sep	Everton	A	L	0-1	..	..	..	..	..	..	..	..	..	..	..	Kelly for George
6 Oct	Birmingham C	H	W	1-0	..	..	..	..	..	..	..	Chambers	..	..¹	Kelly	Brady for Blockley
13 Oct	Tottenham H	A	L	0-2	..	..	..	..	Simpson	Kelly	..	George	..	..	Brady	Batson for Radford
20 Oct	Ipswich T	H	D	1-1	..	..	..	..	..¹	..	..	..	Batson	..	Price	
27 Oct	Q P R	A	L	0-2	..	..	..	..	..	..	..	..	..	..	Powling	
3 Nov	Liverpool	H	L	0-2	..	..	..	..	..	Powling	..	..	Radford	..	Kelly	Batson for Kelly
10 Nov	Manchester C	A	W	2-1	..	..	..	..	..	Kelly¹	Ball	..	Homsby¹	..	Armstrong	
17 Nov	Chelsea	H	D	0-0	..	..	..	..	..	..	..	..²	..¹	..	..	
24 Nov	West Ham U	A	W	3-1	..	..	..	..	..	..	..	..²	..¹	..	..	Nelson¹ for Kelly
1 Dec	Coventry C	H	D	2-2	..	..	..	..	..	..	..	..	..¹	..	..	Hornsby¹ for George
4 Dec	Wolverhampton W	H	D	2-2	..	..	..	..	..	..	..	..¹	Radford	..	..	
8 Dec	Derby Co	A	D	1-1	..	..	..	..	opponents	..	Blockley	..	..	..	..	
15 Dec	Burnley	A	L	1-2	..	..	Nelson	..	..	Simpson	..	..	..	..	..	
22 Dec	Everton	H	W	1-0	..	..	McNab	..	Blockley	Simpson	Armstrong	Ball1	Homsby	..	Kelly	
26 Dec	Southampton	A	D	1-1	..	..	Nelson	..	..	..	..	..¹	Radford	..	..	Homsby for Kelly
29 Dec	Leicester C	A	L	0-2	..	..	..	..	..	..	..	..	..	..	Hornsby	
1 Jan	Newcastle U	H	L	0-1	..	..	..	..	..	..	..	..	..	..	Kelly	
12 Jan	Norwich C	H	W	2-0	..	..	Storey	Kelly	..	..	..	..²	..	..	Brady	
19 Jan	Manchester U	A	D	1-1	..	..	McNab	Storey	..	..	..	..	..	..¹	Kelly	
2 Feb	Burnley	H	D	1-1	..	..	Storey	Kelly	..	..	..	..¹	..	..	Brady	
5 Feb	Leeds U	A	L	1-3	..	..	Nelson	Storey	..	..	..	..¹	..	..	..	
16 Feb	Tottenham H	H	L	0-1	..	..	..	..	Simpson	Kelly	..	..	..	..	..	
23 Feb	Birmingham C	A	L	1-3	..	..	..	..	..	..	George	..	..	..¹	..	
2 Mar	Southampton	H	W	1-0	..	..	..	..	..	..	..	..¹	..	..	Armstrong	
16 Mar	Ipswich T	A	D	2-2	..	McNab	..	..	..¹	..	..	Brady	..²	..¹	..	
23 Mar	Manchester C	H	W	2-0	..	Rice	..	..	..	..	..	Ball	..²	..	..	
30 Mar	Stoke C	A	D	0-0	..	..	..	..	Blockley	..	Armstrong	..	..	..	George	Simpson for Kelly
6 Apr	West Ham U	H	D	0-0	..	..	..	..	..	..	..	..	..	..	..	
13 Apr	Chelsea	A	W	3-1	..	..	..	..	..	..	..	..	..¹	..²	..	Simpson for Kelly
15 Apr	Wolverhampton W	A	L	1-3	..	..	..	..	..	Simpson	..	..	..	..¹	..	Brady for Radford
20 Apr	Derby Co	H	W	2-0	..	..	..	..	..	Kelly	..	..¹	George¹	..	Brady	Simpson for George
24 Apr	Liverpool	A	W	1-0	Rimmer	..	..	..	..	..	..	..	Radford	..¹	..	Simpson for Blockley
27 Apr	Coventry	A	D	3-3	Wilson	..¹	..	..	Simpson	..	..	..	..¹	..¹	George	
30 Apr	Q P R	H	D	1-1	..	..	..	..	..	..	..	..	..	..	..	Brady¹ for Ball

FA Cup

5 Jan	Norwich C (3)	A	W	1-0	Wilson	Rice	McNab	Storey	Blockley	Simpson	Kelly¹	Ball	Radford	Kennedy	Armstrong	
26 Jan	Aston Villa (4)	H	D	1-1	..	..	..	..	..	..	Armstrong	..	..	..¹	Kelly	
30 Jan	Aston Villa (4R)	A	L	0-2	..	..	..	..	..	..	..	..	..	..	..	Brady for McNab

Football League Cup

2 Oct	Tranmere Rov (2)	H	L	0-1	Wilson	Rice	McNab	Storey	Blockley	Simpson	Armstrong	Ball	Radford	Kennedy	Kelly	Chambers for Ball

FA Cup (1972-73) Third Place Play-off

18 Aug	Wolverhampton	H	L	1-3	Wilson	Batson	McNab	Price	Blockley	Simpson	Chambers	Ball	Radford	Kennedy	Hornsby¹	

Appearances (Goals)

Armstrong G 41 · Ball A 36 (13) · Batson B 5 · Blockley J 26 (1) · Brady L 13 (1) · Chambers B 1 · George C 28 (5) · Hornsby B 9 (3) · Kelly E 37 (1) · Kennedy R 2 (12) · McNab R 23 (1) · Nelson S 19 (1) · Powling R 2 · Price D 4 · Radford J 32 (7) · Rice P 41 (1) · Rimmer J 1 · Simpson P 38 (2) · Storey P 41 · Wilson R 41 · Own goals 1 · Total: 20 players (49)

Position in League Table

	P	W	L	D	F:A	Pts	
Leeds U	42	24	4	14	66:31	62	1st
Arsenal	42	14	14	14	49:51	42	10th

SEASON 1974-1975 FOOTBALL LEAGUE (DIVISION 1) 1974-75

17 Aug	Leicester C	A	W	1-0	Rimmer	Matthews	Nelson	Storey	Simpson	Kelly	Armstrong	Brady	Radford	George	Kidd[1]	Price for Kelly
20 Aug	Ipswich T	H	L	0-1	..	Storey	..	Kelly	..	Matthews	..	Hornsby	..	Kidd	Brady	
24 Aug	Manchester C	H	W	4-0	..	Rice	..	..	..	Storey	Matthews	George	..[2]	..[2]	..	Armstrong for Simpson
27 Aug	Ipswich T	A	L	0-3	..	..	..	..	..	Matthews	Brady	..	..	..	Storey	
31 Aug	Everton	A	L	1-2	..	..	..	Storey	..	Kelly	Blockley	Brady	..	George	Kidd[1]	Powling for Kelly
7 Sep	Burnley	H	L	0-1	..	..	..	..	Blockley	Matthews	Armstrong	..	..	..	..	Simpson for Rice
14 Sep	Chelsea	A	D	0-0	..	Kelly	Simpson	..	..	..	..	George	..	Kidd	Brady	
21 Sep	Luton T	H	D	2-2	..	Simpson	Nelson	..	..	..	..	Kelly	..	..[2]	..	
28 Sep	Birmingham C	A	L	1-3	..	Storey	Simpson	Kelly	..	..	George1	Ball	..	..	..	
5 Oct	Leeds U	A	L	0-2	..	..	..	..	..	..	Armstrong	..	..	..	..	Powling for Blockley
12 Oct	Q P R	H	D	2-2	..	..	..	..	Powling	..	..	..	..[1]	..[1]	..	
16 Oct	Manchester C	A	L	1-2	..	..	..	Nelson	..	Kelly	Ball	Brady	..	..	Armstrong	
19 Oct	Tottenham H	A	L	0-2	..	..	Nelson	Kelly	..	Simpson	Armstrong	Ball	..	Brady	Kidd	
26 Oct	West Ham U	H	W	3-0	..	..	McNab	..	Mancini	..	Rice	..	..[1]	..[1]	..[1]	Armstrong for Rice
2 Nov	Wolverhampton W	H	D	0-0	..	..	..	..	..	..	Storey	..[2]	..	Kidd	Brady[1]	
9 Nov	Liverpool	A	W	3-1	..	Rice	..	..	..	..	..	..[2]	..	..[1]	..	
16 Nov	Derby Co	H	W	3-1	..	..	..	..	..	..	..	..[2]	..	..[1]	..	
23 Nov	Coventry C	A	L	0-3	..	..	..	..	Simpson	Powling	Armstrong	..	..	..	..	George for Brady
30 Nov	Middlesbrough	H	W	2-0	..	..	..	..	..	..	George	..[1]	..	..	..[1]	
7 Dec	Carlisle U	A	L	1-2	..	..	..	..	..	Mancini	Storey	..	..	..[1]	Cropley	
14 Dec	Leicester C	H	D	0-0	..	..	..	..	Mancini	Simpson	..	..	..	..	..	
21 Dec	Stoke C	A	W	2-0	..	..	..	..	..	..	..	..	..	..[2]	..	
26 Dec	Chelsea	H	L	1-2	..	..	..	..	..	..	..	..[1]	..	..	..	
28 Dec	Sheffield U	A	D	1-1	..	..	..	..	..	..	..	..	George[1]	..	..	Armstrong for Kelly
11 Jan	Carlisle U	H	W	2-1	..	..	..	..	..	..	Armstrong	..	Radford[1]	..	..[1]	
18 Jan	Middlesbrough	A	D	0-0	..	..	..	..	..	..	..	..	Storey	..	..	
1 Feb	Liverpool	H	W	2-0	..	..	..	Matthews	..	..	..	..[2]	Brady	..	Storey	Ross for Ball
8 Feb	Wolverhampton W	A	L	0-1	..	..	..	Ross	..	..	..	Brady	Radford	..	..	
22 Feb	Derby Co	A	L	1-2	..	..	..	Storey	..	..	..	Ball	..[1]	..	Brady	
1 Mar	Everton	H	L	0-2	..	..	..	..	..	..	..	..	..	..	..	
15 Mar	Birmingham C	H	D	1-1	..	..	Nelson	..	..	..	Matthews	..	..	..[1]	..	
18 Mar	Newcastle U	H	W	3-0	..	..	..	Rostron[1]	..	..	..	..	Hornsby	..[1]	..	
22 Mar	Burnley	A	D	3-3	..	..	..	Matthews	..	..	Rostron1	..	..[2]	..	..	Powling for Matthews
25 Mar	Luton T	A	L	0-2	..	..	..	Storey	..	..	..	Radford	..	..	Brady	
29 Mar	Stoke C	H	D	1-1	..	McNab	..	..	Kelly[1]	..	Matthews	..	Stapleton	Rostron	Hornsby	Brady for Stapleton
31 Mar	Sheffield U	H	W	1-0	..	..	Nelson	..	Mancini	..	..	Kelly	Hornsby	Kidd[1]	Armstrong	
8 Apr	Coventry C	H	W	2-0	..	..	..	..	..	..	..	..	..	..[2]	..	
12 Apr	Leeds U	H	L	1-2	..	..	..	..	..	..	Ball	..	..	..[1]	..	Brady for Nelson
19 Apr	Q P R	A	D	0-0	..	..	..	..	..	..	..	..	..	..	..	
23 Apr	Newcastle U	A	L	1-3	..	Matthews	..	..	..	Brady	..	..	..[1]	..	Rostron	Nelson for Kelly
26 Apr	Tottenham H	H	W	1-0	Barnett	..	Nelson	..	..	Simpson	..	Brady	..	..[1]	Armstrong	
28 Apr	West Ham U	A	L	0-1	..	Storey	..	Kelly	..	Matthews	..	..	..	..	Rostron	

FA Cup

4 Jan	York C (3)	H	D	1-1	Rimmer	Rice	McNab	Kelly[1]	Mancini	Powling	Storey	Ball	Armstrong	Kidd	Cropley	
7 Jan	York C (3R)	A	W	3-1	..	..	..	..	Simpson	Mancini	Armstrong	..	Radford	..[3]	..	
25 Jan	Coventry (4)	A	D	1-1	..	..	..	Storey	Mancini	Simpson	..	..[1]	..	..	George	Matthews for George
29 Jan	Coventry (4R)	H	W	3-0	..	..	..	Matthews[1]	..	..	..[2]	..	..	..	Storey	Brady for Radford
15 Feb	Leicester C (5)	H	D	0-0	..	..	..	Storey	..	..	..	..	..	..	Brady	
19 Feb	Leicester C (5R)	A	D	1-1	..	..	..	..	..	..	..	..	..[1]	..	Matthews	Brady for Matthews
24 Feb	Leicester C (5R)	A	W	1-0	..	..	..	..	..	..	..	..	..[1]	..	..	Brady for Matthews
8 Mar	West Ham (6)	H	L	0-2	..	..	..	..	..	..	Matthews	..	..	..	Brady	Armstrong for Radford

Football League Cup

10 Sep	Leicester C (2)	H	D	1-1	Rimmer	Kelly	Simpson	Storey	Blockley	Mathews	Armstrong	George	Radford	Kidd[1]	Brady	
18 Sep	Leicester C (2R)	A	L	1-2	..	Simpson	Nelson	..	..	..	..	Kelly	..	..	..[1]	

Appearances (Goals)

Armstrong G 24 · Ball A 30 (9) · Barnett G 2 · Blockley J 6 · Brady L 32 (3) · Cropley A 7 (1) · George C 10 (2) · Hornsby B 12 (3) · Kelly E 32 (1) · Kidd B 40 (19) · Mancini T 26 · McNab R 18 · Matthews J 20 · Nelson S 20 · Powling R 8 · Price D 1 · Radford J 29 (7) · Rice P 32 · Rimmer J 40 · Ross T 2 · Rostron W 6 2 · Simpson P 40 · Stapleton F 1 · Storey P 37 · Total: 24 players (47)

Position in League Table

	P	W	L	D	F:A	Pts	
Derby	42	21	10	11	67:49	53	1st
Arsenal	42	13	18	11	47:49	37	16th

SEASON 1975-1976 FOOTBALL LEAGUE (DIVISION 1) 1975-76

16 Aug	Burnley	A	D	0-0	Rimmer	Rice	Nelson	Kelly	Mancini	O'Leary	Armstrong	Cropley	Hornsby	Kidd	Brady	
19 Aug	Sheffield U	A	W	3-1	..	..[1]	..	..	..	..	..	..	..	..[1]	..[1]	
23 Aug	Stoke C	H	L	0-1	..	..	..	..	..	..	..	..	..	..	..	
26 Aug	Norwich C	H	W	2-1	..	..	Storey	..[1]	..	..	..	..	Ball[1]	..	..	
30 Aug	Wolverhampton W	A	D	0-0	..	..	Nelson	..	..	Ball	..	Radford	..	..	..	
6 Sep	Leicester C	H	D	1-1	..	..	..	..	..	..	..	..	Stapleton[1]	..	..	
13 Sep	Aston Villa	A	L	0-2	..	..	..	..	..	..	..	..	..	..	..	
20 Sep	Everton	H	D	2-2	..	..	..	..	..	..	..	..	..[1]	..[1]	..	
27 Sep	Tottenham H	A	D	0-0	..	..	..	..	..	..	..	..	..	Rostron	Brady for Rostron
4 Oct	Manchester C	H	L	2-3	..	..	..	..	Simpson	..	..[1]	..[1]	..	Brady	Rostron for Kelly
11 Oct	Coventry C	H	W	5-0	..	..	..	Powling	..	..	..[1]	..[2]	..	..[2]	Rostron for Cropley
18 Oct	Manchester U	A	L	1-3	..	..	..	Kelly[1]	O'Leary	Simpson	..	..[1]	..[1]	..	
25 Oct	Middlesbrough	H	W	2-1	..	..	..	..	..	..	..[1]	..[1]	..	..	Powling for Kelly
1 Nov	Newcastle U	A	L	0-2	..	..	..	..	..	..	Powling	..	..	..	
8 Nov	Derby Co	H	L	0-1	..	..	Storey	..	..	Powling	Cropley	Hornsby	Kidd	..	
15 Nov	Birmingham C	A	L	1-3	..	..	..	..	..	..[1]	..	..	Kidd	..	Matthews for Cropley
22 Nov	Manchester U	H	W	3-1	..	..	..	Nelson	..	opponents	..[1]	Armstrong[1]	..	..	
29 Nov	West Ham U	A	L	0-1	..	..	Nelson	Storey	..	..	..	..	..	..	
2 Dec	Liverpool	A	D	2-2	..	..	Storey	Nelson	..	..	..[1]	..	..	..[1]	
6 Dec	Leeds U	H	L	1-2	..	..	Nelson	Storey	..	Armstrong	Ball	..	..[1]	
13 Dec	Stoke C	A	L	1-2	Barnett	..	..	..	..	..[1]	..	..	..	Simpson for Nelson
20 Dec	Burnley	H	W	1-0	Rimmer	..	Simpson	Kelly	Mancini	..	..	Radford[1]	..	Stapleton for Brady
26 Dec	Ipswich	A	L	0-2	..	..	Kelly	Storey	O'Leary	..	..	..	..	
27 Dec	Q P R	H	W	2-0	..	..	Nelson	..	..	..	..[1]	Stapleton	..[1]	
10 Jan	Aston Villa	H	D	0-0	..	..	..	Powling	..	Mancini	..	..	
17 Jan	Leicester C	A	L	1-2	..	..	..	Ross[1]	..	..	..	..	
31 Jan	Sheffield U	H	W	1-0	..	..	..	..	Mancini	Powling	..	..	..[1]	Rostron for Nelson
7 Feb	Norwich C	A	L	1-3	..	..	Storey	..	..	Simpson	..	..[1]	
18 Feb	Derby Co	A	L	0-2	..	..	Nelson	..	..	Powling	..	Radford	
21 Feb	Birmingham C	H	W	1-0	..	..	..	..	..	..	..	..[3]	Simpson for Brady
24 Feb	Liverpool	H	W	1-0	..	..	..	..	..	..	..	..[1]	
28 Feb	Middlesbrough	A	W	1-0	..	..	..	..	..	..	..	..[1]	
13 Mar	Coventry C	A	D	1-1	..	..	..	..	..	..[1]	..	
16 Mar	Newcastle U	H	D	0-0	..	..	..	..	..	..	..	
20 Mar	West Ham U	H	W	6-1	..	..	..	..	..[1]	..[2]	..[3]	Stapleton for Rice

27 Mar	Leeds U	A L 0-3	..	..	..	..	..	..	..	..	..	..	..		
3 Apr	Tottenham H	H L 0-2	..	..	..	..	..	..	..	..	..	..	Cropley		
10 Apr	Everton	A D 0-0	..	..	..	..	..	..	..	..	..	..[1]			
13 Apr	Wolverhampton W	H W 2-1	..	..	..	..	..	..	..	..	..	..			
17 Apr	Ipswich T	H L 1-2	..	..	..	..	O'Leary	..	Rostron	..	Stapleton[1]	..			
19 Apr	Q P R	A L 1-2	..	..	..	..	..	..	Kidd[1]	..	Radford	..	..	Armstrong for Radford	
24 Apr	Manchester C	A L 1-3	..	..	..	..	Mancini	..	Armstrong[1]	..	Stapleton	..			

FA Cup

3 Jan	Wolves (3)	A L 0-3	Rimmer	Rice	Nelson	Storey	O'Leary	Powling	Armstrong	Ball	Stapleton	Kidd	Brady

Football League Cup

9 Sep	Everton (2)	A D 2-2	Rimmer	Rice	Nelson	Kelly	Mancini	O'Leary	Ball	Cropley[1]	Radford	Kidd	Brady	Stapleton[1] for Mancini
23 Sep	Everton (2R)	H L 0-1	..	..	..	..	..	..	..	..	Stapleton	..	Rostron	

Appearances (Goals)

Armstrong G 29 (4) · Ball A 39 (9) · Barnett J 1 · Brady L 42 (5) · Cropley A 20 (4) · Hornsby B 4 · Kelly E 17 (2) · Kidd B 37 (11) · Mancini T 26 (1) · Matthews J 1 · Nelson S 36 · O'Leary D 27 · Powling R 29 (1) · Radford J 15 (3) · Rice P 42 (1) · Rimmer J 41 · Ross T 17 (1) · Rostron W 5 · Simpson P 9 · Stapleton F 25 · 4Storey P 11 · Own goals 1 · Total: 21 players (47)

Position in League Table

	P	W	L	D	F:A	Pts	
Liverpool	42	23	5	14	66:31	60	1st
Arsenal	42	13	19	10	47:53	36	17th

1976-77

SEASON 1976-1977 FOOTBALL LEAGUE (DIVISION 1)

21 Aug	Bristol C	H L 0-1	Rimmer	Rice	Nelson	Ross	O'Leary	Simpson	Ball	Armstrong	Macdonald	Radford	Cropley	Storey for Cropley
25 Aug	Norwich C	A W 3-1	..	..	..[1]	..	..	..	..	..[1]	Stapleton1	Brady	..	
28 Aug	Sunderland	A D 2-2	..	..	..	..	..	..	..	..	..	..	..	
4 Sep	Manchester C	H D 0-0	..	..	..	..	..	..	..	Brady	..	..	Armstrong	Cropley for Stapleton
11 Sep	West Ham U	A W 2-0	..	..	..	..[1]	..	Howard	..	..[1]	Cropley	..	..	Storey for O'Leary
18 Sep	Everton	H W 3-1	..	..	..	..	Howard	Powling	..	..[1]	Macdonald[1]	..[1]	..	
25 Sep	Ipswich T	A L 1-3	..	..	..	..	O'Leary	Howard	opponents	..	..[1]	..	..	
2 Oct	Q P R	H W 3-2	..	..	..[1]	..	..	..	..	..[1]	..	..[1]	..	Storey for Nelson
16 Oct	Stoke C	H W 2-0	..	..	..[1]	Storey	..	..	..	..	..[1]	..	..	Radford for Stapleton
20 Oct	Aston Villa	A L 1-5	..	..	..	..	..	..	..[1]	..	..	..	..	
23 Oct	Leicester C	A L 1-4	..	..	..	..	Matthews	..	..	..	..	..[1]	..	
30 Oct	Leeds U	A L 1-2	..	..	Nelson	..	Simpson	..	Matthews[1]	..	..[1]	..	..	
6 Nov	Birmingham C	H W 4-0	..	..	..[1]	..[1]	O'Leary	Simpson	..	..	..[1]	..[1]	..	Storey for O'Leary
20 Nov	Liverpool	H D 1-1	..	..	..	..	..	..	Ball	..	..	..[1]	..[1]	
27 Nov	Coventry C	A W 2-1	..	..	..	..	..	..	..	..	..[1]	..[1]	..	
4 Dec	Newcastle U	H W 5-3	..	..	..	..[1]	..	Howard	..	..	..[3]	..[1]	..	Matthews for Rice
15 Dec	Derby Co	A D 0-0	..	..	..	..	..	Simpson	Storey	..	..	..	..	
18 Dec	Manchester U	H W 3-1	..	..	Powling	..	..	..	..	..[1]	..[2]	..	..	Rostron for Stapleton
27 Dec	Tottenham H	A D 2-2	..	..	..	..	..	..	..	..	..[2]	..	Rostron	
3 Jan	Leeds U	H D 1-1	..	..	..	..	..	..	Hudson	..	..[1]	..	Armstrong	
15 Jan	Norwich C	H W 1-0	..	..[1]	Nelson	..	..	..	..	..	..	..	..	
18 Jan	Birmingham C	A D 3-3	..	..	..	..	..	..	..	..	..[3]	..	..	
22 Jan	Bristol C	A L 0-2	..	..	..	Storey	..	..	..	..	..	..	Rostron	
5 Feb	Sunderland	H D 0-0	..	..	..	Ross	..	..	..	..	..	..	..	
12 Feb	Manchester C	A L 0-1	..	..	..	..	..	..	..	..	..	..	Howard	Matthews for O'Leary
15 Feb	Middlesbrough	A L 0-3	..	..	..	..	Howard	..	Matthews	Hudson	..	..	Rostron	Powling for Howard
19 Feb	West Ham U	H L 2-3	..	..	..	..	Powling	..	Hudson	Brady[1]	..	..[1]	Armstrong	
1 Mar	Everton	A L 1-2	..	..	..	..	Howard	Powling	Brady	Hudson	..[1]	..	..	
5 Mar	Ipswich T	H L 1-4	..	..	Young	..	..	..	..	Matthews	..[1]	..	..	Nelson for Matthews
8 Mar	W B A	H L 1-2	..	..	Nelson	Price	Young	Howard	..	Powling	..[1]	..	..	
12 Mar	Q P R	A L 1-2	..	..	..	Powling	..[1]	..	..	Hudson	..	..	..	Price for Hudson
23 Mar	Stoke C	A D 1-1	..	..	..	..	O'Leary	..	..	..	Price[1]	..	..	
2 Apr	Leicester C	H W 3-0	..	..	..	..	O'Leary[2]	Young	Rix[1]	Price	Stapleton	..	..	Matthews for Powling
9 Apr	W B A	A W 2-0	..	..	Matthews	Price	..	..	..	Hudson	..[1]	..[1]	..	
11 Apr	Tottenham H	H W 1-0	..	..	..	..	..	..	..	..	..[1]	..	..	Brady for Rix
16 Apr	Liverpool	A L 0-2	..	..	..	..	..	..	Brady	..	..	..	..	Rix for Ross
23 Apr	Coventry C	H W 2-0	..	..	..	Ross	..	..	..	..	..[1]	..[1]	..	Rix for Ross
25 Apr	Aston Villa	H W 3-0	..	..	Nelson[1]	Matthews	..	..	..	..	..[1]	..	..[1]	Howard for O'Leary
30 Apr	Newcastle U	A W 2-0	..	..	..	..[1]	..	..	..	..	..[1]	..	..	Rix for Young
3 May	Derby Co	H D 0-0	..	..	..	..	..	..	..	..	..	..	..	Price for Matthews
7 May	Middlesbrough	H D 1-1	..	..	..	..	..	..	..	Rix	..	..[1]	..	Rix for Young
14 May	Manchester U	A L 2-3	..	..	..	..	..	..	..[1]	Hudson	..	..[1]	..	

FA Cup

8 Jan	Notts Co (3)	A W 1-0	Rimmer	Rice	Nelson	Ross1	O'Leary	Simpson	Hudson	Brady	Macdonald	Stapleton	Armstrong	
29 Jan	Coventry C (4)	H W 3-1	..	..	..	..	..	..	..	..[2]	..[1]	..	Storey for Macdonald
26 Feb	Middlesbrough (5)	A L 1-4	..	..	..	..	..	..	Brady	Hudson	..[1]	..	Matthews for O'Leary

Football League Cup

31 Aug	Carlisle U (2)	H W 3-2	Rimmer	Rice	Nelson	Ross[2]	O'Leary	Simpson	Ball	Brady	Macdonald[1]	Stapleton	Armstrong	
21 Sep	Blackpool (3)	A D 1-1	..	..	..	..	Powling	Howard	..	..	..	..[1]	
28 Sep	Blackpool (3R)	H D 0-0	..	..	..	..	O'Leary	..	..	..	..	..	Storey for Nelson
5 Oct	Blackpool (3R)	H W 2-0	..	..	Storey	Matthews	..[1]	..	..	..	..[1]	..	
26 Oct	Chelsea (4)	H W 2-1	..	..	Nelson	Ross[1]	Simpson	..	..	..	..[1]	..	
1 Dec	Q P R (5)	A L 1-2	..	..	..	..	O'Leary	Simpson	..	..	..[1]	..	

Appearances (Goals)

Armstrong G 37 (2) · Ball A 14 (1) · Brady L 38 (5) · Cropley A 3 · Howard P 16 · Hudson A 19 · Macdonald M 41 (25) · Matthews J 17 (2) · Nelson S 32 (3) · O'Leary D 33 (2) · Powling R 12 · Price D 8 (1) · Radford J 2 · Rice P 42 (3) · Rimmer J 42 · Rix G 7 (1) · Ross T 29 (4) · Rostron W 5 · Simpson P 19 · Stapleton F 40 (13) · Storey P 11 · Young W 14 (1) · Own goals 1 · Total: 22 players (64)

Position in League Table

	P	W	L	D	F:A	Pts	
Liverpool	42	23	8	11	62:33	57	1st
Arsenal	42	16	15	11	64:59	43	8th

1977-78

SEASON 1977-1978 FOOTBALL LEAGUE (DIVISION 1)

20 Aug	Ipswich T	A L 0-1	Jennings	Rice	Nelson	Ross	Young	O'Leary	Powling	Brady	Macdonald	Stapleton	Rix	Price for Brady
23 Aug	Everton	H W 1-0	..	..	..	Powling[1]	O'Leary	Young	Brady	Ross	..	..	..	
27 Aug	Wolverhampton W	A D 1-1	..	..	..	..[1]	Young	O'Leary	Ross	Brady	..	Price	..	
3 Sep	Nottingham F	H W 3-0	..	..	..	..	O'Leary	Young	Brady[1]	Ross	..	Stapleton[2]	..	
10 Sep	Aston Villa	A L 0-1	..	..	..	Hudson	..	..	..	..	..	..	..	
17 Sep	Leicester C	H W 2-1	..	..	..	Price	..	..	..	..	..[1]	..[1]	..	
24 Sep	Norwich C	A L 0-1	..	..	..	..	..	Simpson	Matthew	..	..	..	..	Walford for Matthews
1 Oct	West Ham U	H W 3-0	..	..	..[1]	..	..	..	Brady[1]	..	..	..[1]	..	Matthews for Ross
4 Oct	Liverpool	H D 0-0	..	..	..	..	..	..	..	..	..	..	..	
8 Oct	Manchester C	A L 1-2	..	..	..	..	..	..	..	Matthews	..[1]	..	..	
15 Oct	Q P R	H W 1-0	..	..	..	..	..	Young	..	Hudson	..[1]	..	..	
22 Oct	Bristol C	A W 2-0	..	..	..	..	Young	Simpson	..	..	..[1]	..[1]	..	
29 Oct	Birmingham C	H D 1-1	..	..	..[1]	..	O'Leary	..	..	Ross	..	..	..	Heeley for Price
5 Nov	Manchester U	A W 2-1	..	..	..	..	..	Young	..	Sunderland	..[1]	..[1]	..	
12 Nov	Coventry C	H D 1-1	..	..	..	..	..	..	opponents	..	..	..[1]	..	
19 Nov	Newcastle U	A W 2-1	..	..	..	..	..	..	..[1]	..	Hudson	..[1]	..	
26 Nov	Derby Co	H L 1-3	..	..	..[1]	..	..	..	..	..	Macdonald	..	..	
3 Dec	Middlesbrough	A W 1-0	..	..	..	..	..	..	opponents	..	..	..	..	

10 Dec	Leeds U	H	D	1-1	..	..	..	..	..[1]	..	..	..[2]	..				
17 Dec	Coventry C	A	W	2-1	..	..	..	..	..	..	..	..[2]	..				
26 Dec	Chelsea	H	W	3-0	..	..	..[1]	..[1]	..	..	..	..	..[1]				Simpson for Stapleton
27 Dec	W B A	A	W	3-1	..	..	..	..	..[1]	..[1]	..[1]	..	..				
31 Dec	Everton	A	L	0-2	..	..	..	..	..	..	..	..	..				Simpson for Macdonald
2 Jan	Ipswich T	H	W	1-0	..	..	..[1]	..	..	..	..	..	Heeley				Simpson for Heeley
14 Jan	Wolverhampton W	H	W	3-1	..	..	..	..	..	..[1]	..	..	Stapleton[1]	..			
21 Jan	Nottingham F	A	L	0-2	..	..	..	..	..	..	..	..	..				
4 Feb	Aston Villa	H	L	0-1	..	..	..	..	..	..	..	..	Hudson				
11 Feb	Leicester C	A	D	1-1	..	..	..	..	..	..[1]	..	..	Stapleton	..			
25 Feb	West Ham U	A	D	2-2	..	..	..	..	..	..	..	..[2]	..				Walford for Rix
28 Feb	Norwich C	H	D	0-0	..	..	..	..	..	..	..	..	..	Hudson			Heeley for Macdonald
4 Mar	Manchester C	H	W	3-0	..	..	..[1]	..	..[1]	..	..[1]	Hudson	..	Heeley			Walford for Price
18 Mar	Bristol C	H	W	4-1	..	..	..[1]	..	..	..	..[1]	Macdonald	..[2]	Hudson			Rix for Sunderland
21 Mar	Birmingham C	A	D	1-1	..	..	..	..	..	..[1]	..	..	..				
25 Mar	W B A	H	W	4-0	..	..	..	..	..[1]	..	..	..[3]	..				Rix for Sunderland
27 Mar	Chelsea	A	D	0-0	..	..	..	..	..	..	Rix	..	..				
1 Apr	Manchester U	H	W	3-1	..	..	..	..	..	..	..	..[2]	..				
11 Apr	Q P R	A	L	1-2	..	..	..	..	..	..	Hudson	..	Rix				Matthews for Young
15 Apr	Newcastle U	H	W	2-1	..	..	..	..[1]	Walford	..[1]	Rix	..	Hudson				
22 Apr	Leeds U	A	W	3-1	..	Devine	..	..	Young	opponents	..	..[1]	..[1]	Matthews			
25 Apr	Liverpool	A	L	0-1	..	..	..	..	..	..	..	..	Hudson				Matthews for Brady
29 Apr	Middlesbrough	H	W	1-0	..	..	..	..	..	Sunderland	..	..[1]	..				
9 May	Derby Co	A	L	0-3	..	Price	Matthews	Harvey	..	Walford	Heeley	..	Sunderland	..			

FA Cup

7 Jan	Sheffield U (3)	A	W	5-0	Jennings	Rice	Nelson	Price	O'Leary[1]	Young	Brady	Sunderland	Macdonald[2]	Stapleton[2]	Rix
28 Jan	Wolves (4)	H	W	2-1	..	..	..	..	..	..	..	..[1]	..[1]	Hudson	..
18 Feb	Walsall (5)	H	W	4-1	..	..	..	..	..	..	..	..[1]	..[1]	Stapleton[2]	..
11 Mar	Wrexham (6)	A	W	3-2	..	..	..	..	..	..[1]	..	..	..[1]	..	Hudson
8 Apr	Orient (SF) (at Chelsea)	A	W	3-0	..	..	..	..	..	..	Rix[1]	..[2]	..	..	..
6 May	Ipswich (F) (at Wembley)	A	L	0-1	..	..	..	..	..	..	Sunderland	..	..	..	Rix for Brady

Football League Cup

30 Aug	Manchester U (2)	H	W	3-2	Jennings	Rice	Nelson	Powling	O'Leary	Young	Brady[1]	Ross	Macdonald[2]	Stapleton	Rix
25 Oct	Southampton (3)	H	W	2-0	..	..	..	Price	Young	Simpson	..[1]	Hudson	..	..[1]	..
29 Nov	Hull C (4)	H	W	5-1	..	..	..	..	O'Leary	Young	..[1]	Matthews[2]	..[1]	..	Simpson for O'Leary
18 Jan	Manchester C (5)	A	D	0-0	..	..	..	..	..	..	..	..	..	..	
24 Jan	Manchester C (5R)	H	W	1-0	..	..	..	..	..	..	..[1]	..	..	..	Hudson for Matthews
7 Feb	Liverpool (SF)	A	L	1-2	..	..	..	..	..	..	..	Hudson	..[1]	..	
14 Feb	Liverpool (SF)	H	D	0-0	..	..	..	..	..	..	..	..	..	..	

Appearances (Goals)

Brady L 39 (9) · Devine J 3 · Harvey J 1 · Heeley M 4 · Hudson A 17 · Jennings P 42 · Macdonald M 39 (15) · Matthews J 5 · Nelson S 41 (1) · O'Leary D 41 (1) · Powling R 4 2 · Price D 39 (5) · Rice P 38 (2) · Rix G 39 (2) · Ross T 10 · Simpson P 9 · Stapleton F 39 (13) · Sunderland A 23 (4) · Walford S 5 · Young W 35 (3) · Own goals 3 · Total: 20 players (60)

Position in League Table

	P	W	L	D	F:A	Pts	
Nottingham F	42	25	3	14	69:24	64	1st
Arsenal	42	21	11	10	60:37	52	5th

SEASON 1978-1979 FOOTBALL LEAGUE (DIVISION 1)

19 Aug	Leeds U	H	D	2-2	Jennings	Devine	Nelson	Price	O'Leary	Young	Brady[2]	Sunderland	Macdonald	Stapleton	Harvey	Kosmina for Price
22 Aug	Manchester C	A	D	1-1	Barron	Rice	..	..	..	..	Devine	..	..[1]	..	Walford	
26 Aug	Everton	A	L	0-1	..	..	..	..	..	..	Brady	..	..	..	Devine	Walford for Devine
2 Sep	Q P R	H	W	5-1	Jennings	..	..	..	..	..	..[1]	..	Walford	..[2]	Rix[2]	
9 Sep	Nottingham F	A	L	1-2	..	..	..	..	..	..	..[1]	..	..	..	..	Harvey for O'Leary
16 Sep	Bolton W	H	W	1-0	..	..	..	..	Walford	..	..	..	Stapleton[1]	Heeley	..	
23 Sep	Manchester U	H	D	1-1	..	..	..	..	O'Leary	..	..[1]	..	..	Walford	..	Heeley for Walford
30 Sep	Middlesbrough	A	W	3-2	..	..	..	..[1]	..	..	..[1]	..	..	Devine	..	Walford[1] for Devine
7 Oct	Aston Villa	H	D	1-1	..	..	..	..	..	..	..	..[1]	..	Walford	..	
14 Oct	Wolverhampton W	A	L	0-1	..	..	..	..	..	..	..	..	..	..	..	Stead for Sunderland
21 Oct	Southampton	H	W	1-0	..	..	..	Stead	Gatting	..	..	Heeley	..[1]	..	..	
28 Oct	Bristol C	A	W	3-1	..	..	..	Price	O'Leary	..	..[2]	Gatting	..[1]	Heeley	..	Walford for O'Leary
4 Nov	Ipswich T	H	W	4-1	..	..	..	..[1]	..	..	..	Sunderland	..[3]	Gatting	..	
11 Nov	Leeds U	A	W	1-0	..	..	..	..	..	..	..	..	..[1]	..	..	
18 Nov	Everton	H	D	2-2	..	..	..	..	..	..	..[2]	..	..	..	..	
25 Nov	Coventry C	A	D	1-1	..	..	..	..	..	..	..	..	..	Walford	..	Heeley for Price
2 Dec	Liverpool	H	W	1-0	..	..	..	..	..	..	..	..	..	Gatting	..	
9 Dec	Norwich C	A	D	0-0	..	..	..	..	..	..	..	..	..	..	..	Walford for Nelson
16 Dec	Derby Co	H	W	2-0	..	..	Walford	..[1]	..	..	..	..	..[1]	..	..	
23 Dec	Tottenham H	A	W	5-0	..	..	..	..	..	..	..[1]	..[3]	..[1]	..	..	
26 Dec	W B A	H	L	1-2	..	..	..	..	..	..	..[1]	..	..	..	..	
30 Dec	Birmingham C	H	W	3-1	..	..[1]	..	..	..	..	..[1]	..	..[1]	..	..	
13 Jan	Nottingham F	H	W	2-1	..	Walford	Nelson	Talbot	..	..	..	..	..[1]	Price[1]	..	
3 Feb	Manchester U	A	W	2-0	..	..	Rice	..	..	..	..	..[2]	..	..	..	
10 Feb	Middlesbrough	H	D	0-0	..	..	..	..	..	..	..	..	..	..	..	
13 Feb	Q P R	A	W	2-1	..	..	..	..	..	..	..[1]	..	..	..[1]	..	Walford for Young
24 Feb	Wolverhampton W	H	L	0-1	..	..	Gatting	..	..	Walford	..	..	..	..	..	Heeley for Gatting
3 Mar	Southampton	A	L	0-2	..	..	Nelson	..	..	..	..	Gatting	..	..	..	McDermott for Heeley
10 Mar	Bristol C	H	W	2-0	..	..	..	..	..	..	..	Heeley	..[1]	..	..[1]	Gatting for Price
17 Mar	Ipswich T	A	L	0-2	..	..	..	..	..	..	..	Sunderland	..	..	..	Gatting for Price
24 Mar	Manchester C	H	D	1-1	..	..	..	..	..	Young	Heeley	..[1]	..	..	..	McDermot for Young
26 Mar	Bolton W	A	L	2-4	..	..	..	..	..	Walford	Gatting	..	..	..[1]	..	Heeley[1] for Talbot
3 Apr	Coventry C	H	D	1-1	..	..	..[1]	..	..	Young	..	..	..	Heeley	..	Walford for Heeley
7 Apr	Liverpool	A	L	0-3	..	..	Walford	..	..	..	..	..	..	Price	..	Brignall for Stapleton
10 Apr	Tottenham H	H	W	1-0	..	..	..	..	..	..	Brady	..	..[1]	..	..	
14 Apr	W B A	A	D	1-1	..	..	Nelson	..	..	Walford	..	..	..	..	..	Gatting for Rix
16 Apr	Chelsea	H	W	5-2	..	..	..	..	..[1]	..	..[1]	..[2]	..[1]	..	..	
21 Apr	Derby Co	A	L	0-2	..	..	Walford	..	Gatting	Young	..	..	..	..	..	
25 Apr	Aston Villa	A	L	1-5	..	..	..	..	..	Devine	..	..	..	..	..	
28 Apr	Norwich C	H	D	1-1	..	Devine	Nelson	..	..	Walford[1]	..	..	..	..	..	
5 May	Birmingham C	A	D	0-0	Barron	Rice	..	..	O'Leary	Young	..	..	..	..	..	Walford for Barron- Price in goal
14 May	Chelsea	A	D	1-1	Jennings	..	..	..	..	..	..	Vaessen	Macdonald[1]	Devine	..	

FA Cup

6 Jan	Sheffield W (3)	A	D	1-1	Jennings	Rice	Walford	Price	O'Leary	Young	Brady	Sunderland[1]	Stapleton	Gatting	Rix
9 Jan	Sheffield W (3R)	H	D	1-1	..	..	Nelson	..	..	..	..[1]	..	..	..	..
15 Jan	Sheffield W (3R) (at Leicester)		D	2-2	..	..	..	..	..	..[1]	..	..[1]	..	..	..
17 Jan	Sheffield W (3R) (at Leicester)		D	3-3	Jennings	Rice	Nelson	Price	O'Leary	Young[1]	Brady	Sunderland	Stapleton[2]	Gatting	Rix
22 Jan	Sheffield W (3R) (at Leicester)		W	2-0	..	..	..	..	..	..	..	..[1]	..[1]	..	Walford for Nelson
27 Jan	Notts County (4)	H	W	2-0	..	..	..	Talbot[1]	..	..[1]	..	..	..	Price	..
26 Feb	Nottingham F (5)	A	W	1-0	..	..	..	..	Walford	..	..	..	..[1]	..	..
19 Mar	Southampton (6)	A	D	1-1	..	..	..	..	..	Young	..	..	..	..[1]	..	Walford for Price
21 Mar	Southampton (6R)	H	W	2-0	..	..	..	..	..	..	..	..	..[2]	..	..	Walford for Brady
31 Mar	Wolves (SF) (at Aston Villa)		W	2-0	..	..	..	..	..	..	Gatting	..	..[1]	..[1]	..

222

Date	Match	Ven	Res													Substitutes
12 May	Manchester U (F) (at Wembley)		W 3-2	..	..	..	..[1]	..	..	Brady	..[1]	..[1]	..	..		Walford for Price

Football League Cup

29 Aug	Rotherham U (2)	A L	1-3	Jennings	Rice	Nelson	Price	O'Leary	Young	Brady	Sunderland	Macdonald	Stapleton[1]	Rix	

UEFA Cup

13 Sep	L'motive Leipzig (1)	H W	3-0	Jennings	Rice	Nelson	Price	Walford	Young	Brady	Sunderland[1]	Stapleton[2]	Harvey	Rix		Gatting for Brady, Heeley for Harvey
27 Sep	L'motive Leipzig (1)	A W	4-1	..	..	..	..	O'Leary	..	..[1]	..[1]	..[2]	Devine	..		Vaessen for Price, Walford for Young
18 Oct	Hajduk Split (2)	A L	1-2	..	..	..	..	..	..	..[1]	Heeley	..	Kosmina	..	
1 Nov	Hajduk Split (2)	H W	1-0	..	..	..	..	..	..[1]	..	Gatting	..	Heeley	..		Kosmina for Heeley, Vaessen for Kosmina
22 Nov	Red Star B'grade (3)	A L	0-1	..	..	..	..	..	..	Heeley	Sunderland	..	Walford	..	
6 Dec	Red Star B'grade (3)	H D	1-1	..	..	..	..	..	..	..	..	..[1]	..	Gatting		Kosmina for Heeley, Macdonald for Rix

Appearances (Goals)

Barron P 3 · Brady L 37 (13) · Brignall S 1 · Devine J 7 · Gatting S 21 (1) · Harvey J 1 · Heeley M 10 (1) · Jennings P 39 · Kosmina A 1 · McDermott B 2 · Macdonald M 4 2 · Nelson S 33 (2) · O'Leary D 37 (2) · Price D 39 (8) · Rice P 39 (1) · Rix G 39 (3) · Stapleton F 41 (17) · Stead K 2 · Sunderland A 37 (9) · Talbot B 20 · Vaessen P 1 · Walford S 33 (2) · Young W 33 · Total: 23 players (61)

Position in League Table

	P	W	L	D	F:A	Pts	
Liverpool	42	30	4	8	85:16	68	1st
Arsenal	42	17	11	14	61:48	48	7th

1979-80

SEASON 1979-1980 FOOTBALL LEAGUE (DIVISION 1)

Date	Match	Ven	Res	Jennings	Rice	Nelson	Talbot	O'Leary	Young	Brady	Sunderland	Stapleton	Price	Rix	Substitutes
18 Aug	Brighton & HA	A W	4-0	Jennings	Rice	Nelson	Talbot	O'Leary	Young	Brady[1]	Sunderland[1]	Stapleton[1]	Price	Rix	Hollins for Brady
21 Aug	Ipswich T	H L	0-2	..	..	..	..	..	..	..	..	..	..	..	Hollins for Price
25 Aug	Manchester U	H D	0-0	..	..	..	..	..	..	Gatting	..	..	Hollins	..	Walford for Gatting
1 Sep	Leeds U	A D	1-1	..	..	..[1]	..	..	..	..	..	..	..	..	
8 Sep	Derby Co	A L	2-3	..	..	..	..	..	..	Brady	..[1]	..[1]	..	..	
15 Sep	Middlesbrough	H W	2-0	..	..	..	..	..	..	..	..[1]	..[1]	..	..	
22 Sep	Aston Villa	A D	0-0	Barron	..	..	..	..	..	..	..	..	..	..	
29 Sep	Wolverhampton W	H L	2-3	Jennings	..	..	..	Walford	..	..	..	..[1]	..[1]	..	Price for Talbot
6 Oct	Manchester C	H D	0-0	..	..	..	..	O'Leary	..	..	..	..	..	..	
9 Oct	Ipswich T	A W	2-1	..	Walford	..	..	..	..	..	..[1]	..[1]	..	..[1]	
13 Oct	Bolton W	A D	0-0	..	Rice	..	..	..	..	..	..	..	..	..	
20 Oct	Stoke C	H D	0-0	..	..	..	..	..	..	..	..	..	..	..	
27 Oct	Bristol C	A W	1-0	..	..	..	..	..	..	..	..[1]	..	..	..	
3 Nov	Brighton & HA	H W	3-0	..	Devine	..	..	..	..	..[1]	..[1]	..	..	..[1]	Gatting for Sunderland
10 Nov	Crystal Palace	A L	0-1	..	..	..	..	..	..	..	Gatting	..	Price	..	Walford for Devine
17 Nov	Everton	H W	2-0	..	..	..	..	..	..	..	Vaessen	..[2]	..	..	Gatting for Brady
24 Nov	Liverpool	H D	0-0	..	..	..	..	..	..	Gatting	Sunderland	..	..	..	
1 Dec	Nottingham F	A D	1-1	..	..	..	..	..	Walford	..	..	..[1]	..	..	
8 Dec	Coventry C	H W	3-1	..	..	..	..	..	..	Brady	..[1]	..[1]	Hollins	..	Gatting for Nelson
15 Dec	W B A	A D	2-2	..	..	..[1]	..	..	..	..	..	..[1]	..	..	
21 Dec	Norwich C	H D	1-1	..	..	..	..	..	..	..	..	..[1]	..	..	McDermott for Nelson
26 Dec	Tottenham H	H W	1-0	..	..	Rice	..	..	Young	..	..	..[1]	..	..	
29 Dec	Manchester U	A L	0-3	..	..	..	..	..	..	..	..	..	..	..	Walford for O'Leary
1 Jan	Southampton	A W	1-0	..	..	..	..	Walford	..[1]	Gatting	..	..	..	..	
12 Jan	Leeds U	H L	0-1	..	Rice	Nelson	..	..	..	Brady	..	..	..	..	
19 Jan	Derby Co	H W	2-0	..	..	..	..	..	..[1]	..[1]	..	..	Price	..	
9 Feb	Aston Villa	H W	3-1	..	..	..	..	O'Leary	..	..	..[2]	..	..	..[1]	
23 Feb	Bolton W	H W	2-0	..	..	..	..	..	..	..[1]	..[1]	..	..	..	Vaessen for Rice
1 Mar	Stoke C	A W	3-2	..	Devine	..	..	..	..	..[1]	..	..[1]	..[1]	..	
11 Mar	Bristol C	H D	0-0	..	..	..	..	..	..	..	Vaessen	..	..	..	
15 Mar	Manchester C	A W	3-0	..	..	..	..	..	..	..[2]	..[1]	..	..	..	Gatting for Stapleton
22 Mar	Crystal Palace	H L	1-1	..	..	..	..	..	..	..[1]	Sunderland	..	..	..	
28 Mar	Everton	A W	1-0	Barron	Rice	..	..	..	..	Gatting[1]	..	Vaessen	..	..	Vaessen for Nelson
2 Apr	Norwich C	A D	1-2	Jennings	Devine	..	..	..	..	Brady	..	Stapleton	..	..[1]	Vaessen for Price
5 Apr	Southampton	H D	1-1	..	..	..	Walford	..	..	..	..[1]	..	..	..	Vaessen for Stapleton
7 Apr	Tottenham H	A W	2-1	Barron	Rice	..	..	..	..	..	Devine	Vaessen[1]	Hollins	Davis	Sunderland[1] for Brady
19 Apr	Liverpool	A D	1-1	..	..	..	..	..	..	Gatting	Sunderland	Price	Hollins	..	Vaessen for Stapleton
26 Apr	W B A	H D	1-1	Barron	..	Devine	..	Walford	..	Brady	..	..[1]	Hollins	Vaessen	Gatting for Young
3 May	Coventry C	A W	1-0	..	..	Nelson	..	..	..	Gatting	..	Vaessen[1]	Price	Hollins	Davis for Price
5 May	Nottingham F	H D	0-0	Jennings	Devine	..	..	O'Leary	..	Brady	Vaessen	Stapleton	..	Rix	Hollins for Stapleton
16 May	Wolverhampton W	A W	2-1	..	Rice	..	..	Walford[1]	..	..	Sunderland	..	..	..	Vaessen for Price
19 May	Middlesbrough	A L	0-5	..	..	..	..	..	..	..	..	..	..	..	Vaessen for Walford

FA Cup

Date	Match	Ven	Res	Jennings	Rice	Nelson	Talbot	O'Leary	Young	Brady	Sunderland	Stapleton	Price	Rix	Substitutes
5 Jan	Cardiff C (3)	A D	0-0	Jennings	Rice	Devine	Talbot	Walford	Young	Gatting	Sunderland	Stapleton	Hollins	Rix	
8 Jan	Cardiff C (3R)	H W	2-1	..	..	Nelson	..	..	..	..	..[2]	..	..	..	
26 Jan	Brighton & HA (4)	H W	2-0	..	..	..[1]	..[1]	O'Leary	..	Brady	..	..	Price	..	
5 Feb	Bolton W (5)	A D	1-1	..	..	..	..	..	..	..	..	..[1]	..	..	
19 Feb	Bolton W (5R)	H W	3-0	..	..	..	..	..	..	..	..[2]	..[1]	..	..	
8 Mar	Watford (6)	A W	2-1	..	Devine	..	..	..	..	..	..[2]	..	..	..	Gatting for Sunderland
12 Apr	Liverpool (SF) (at Sheffield W)	D	0-0	..	Rice	..	..	..	..	..	..	..	..	..	Walford for Nelson
16 Apr	Liverpool (SFR) (at Aston Villa)	D	1-1	..	..	Walford	..	..	..	..	..[1]	..	..	..	
28 Apr	Liverpool (SFR) (at Aston Villa)	D	1-1	..	..	Devine	..	..	..	..	..[1]	..	..	..	
1 May	Liverpool (SFR) (at Coventry)	W	1-0	..	..	..	..[1]	..	..	..	..	..	..	..	
10 May	West Ham U (F) (at Wembley)	L	0-1	..	..	..	..	..	..	..	..	..	..	..	Nelson for Devine

Football League Cup

Date	Match	Ven	Res	Jennings	Rice	Nelson	Talbot	O'Leary	Young	Brady	Sunderland	Stapleton	Price	Rix	Substitutes
29 Aug	Leeds (2)	A D	1-1	Jennings	Rice	Nelson	Talbot	O'Leary	Young	Brady	Sunderland	Stapleton[1]	Hollins	Rix	
4 Sep	Leeds (2R)	H W	7-0	..	..	..[1]	..	..	..	..[2]	..[3]	..[1]	..	..	
25 Sep	Southampton (3)	H W	2-1	..	..	..	..	Walford	..	..[1]	..	..[1]	..	..	
30 Oct	Brighton & HA (4)	A D	0-0	..	..	..	..	O'Leary	..	..	..	..	..	..	Gatting for Rice
13 Nov	Brighton & HA (4R)	H W	4-0	..	Devine	..	..	..	..	..	Vaessen[2]	..[2]	Price	..	Hollins for Price
4 Dec	Swindon T (5)	H D	1-1	..	..	..	..	..	Walford	Gatting	Sunderland[1]	..	..	Hollins	
11 Dec	Swindon T (5R)	A L	3-4	..	..	Walford	..[1]	..	Young	Brady[2]	..	..	Hollins	..	

FA Charity Shield

Date	Match	Ven	Res	Jennings	Rice	Nelson	Talbot	O'Leary	Walford	Brady	Sunderland	Stapleton	Price	Rix	Substitutes
11 Aug	Liverpool (at Wembley)	L	1-3	Jennings	Rice	Nelson	Talbot	O'Leary	Walford	Brady	Sunderland[1]	Stapleton	Price	Rix	Young for Nelson, Hollins for Price

European Cup-Winners Cup

					Jennings	Rice	Nelson	Talbot	O'Leary	Young[1]	Brady	Sunderland[1]	Stapleton	Hollins	Rix	
19 Sep	Fenerbahce (1)	H	W	2-0	Jennings	Rice	Nelson	Talbot	O'Leary	Young[1]	Brady	Sunderland[1]	Stapleton	Hollins	Rix	
3 Oct	Fenerbahce (1)	A	D	0-0	..											
24 Oct	Magdeburg (2)	H	W	2-1	..					..[1]	..	..[1]	..	..	..	
7 Nov	Magdeburg (2)	A	D	2-2	..	Devine	..	..	..	..	..[1]	Gatting	..	..	..	Price[1] for Hollins, Walford for Nelson
5 Mar	IFK Gothenburg (3)	H	W	5-1	..	..	..	..	..	..[1]	..[1]	Sunderland[2] ..	Price[1]	..	..	Hollins for Brady, McDermott for Sunderland
19 Mar	IFK Gothenburg (3)	A	D	0-0	..	..	..	..	..	..	..	Vaessen ..	..	..	..	
9 Apr	Juventus (SF)	H	D	1-1	..	..	Walford	..	opponents	..	..	Sunderland ..	..	..	..	Vaessen for Devine, Rice for O'Leary
23 Apr	Juventus (SF)	A	W	1-0	..	Rice	Devine	..	..	..	..	..	..	..	..	Vaessen[1] for Price, Hollins for Talbot
14 May	Valencia (F) (at Brussels)		D	0-0*	..	..	Nelson	..	..	..	..	..	..	..	..	Hollins for Price

*lost 4-5 on penalties

Appearances (Goals)

Barron P 5 · Brady L 34 7 · Davis P 2 · Devine J 20 · Gatting S 14 1 · Hollins J 26 1 · Jennings P 37 · McDermott B 1 · Nelson S 35 2 · O'Leary D 34 1 · Price D 22 1 · Rice P 26 · Rix G 38 4 · Stapleton F 39 14 · Sunderland A 37 14 · Talbot B 42 1 · Vaessen P 14 2 · Walford S 19 1 · Young W 38 3 · Total: 19 players 52

Position in League Table

	P	W	L	D	F:A	Pts	
Liverpool	42	25	7	10	81:30	60	1st
Arsenal	42	18	8	16	52:36	52	4th

SEASON 1980-1981 FOOTBALL LEAGUE (DIVISION 1)

					Jennings	Devine	Sansom	Talbot	O'Leary	Young	Vaessen	Price	Stapleton[1]	Hollins	Rix	
16 Aug	W B A	A	W	1-0	Jennings	Devine	Sansom	Talbot	O'Leary	Young	Vaessen	Price	Stapleton[1]	Hollins	Rix	
19 Aug	Southampton	H	D	1-1	..	..	..	..	..	..	Hollins	Vaessen	Price	Stapleton[1]	..	McDermott for Talbot
23 Aug	Coventry C	A	L	1-3	..	..	..	..	..	..	..	Sunderland	Stapleton[1]	Price	..	Rice for Price
30 Aug	Tottenham H	H	W	2-0	..	..	..	..	..	..[1]	..	..	..[1]	..[1]	..	
6 Sep	Manchester C	A	D	1-1	..	..	..	..	..	..[1]	..	..	..	..	..	
13 Sep	Stoke C	H	W	2-0	..	..	..[1]	..	..	..	..	..	..	..	..[1]	
20 Sep	Middlesbrough	A	L	1-2	Wood	..	..	..	..	..	..	..	..	..	..[1]	
27 Sep	Nottingham F	H	W	1-0	..	..	..	..	..	..	..	..	..	Gatting	..[1]	
4 Oct	Leicester C	H	W	1-0	..	..	..	..	Walford	..	..	..	..[1]	..	..	
7 Oct	Birmingham C	A	L	1-3	..	..	..	..	..	..	..	..	..[1]	..	..	
11 Oct	Manchester U	A	D	0-0	..	..	..	..	..	..	..	..	..	..	..	
18 Oct	Sunderland	H	D	2-2	..	..	..	..	..	..[1]	..	..	..[1]	..	..	McDermott for Talbot
21 Oct	Norwich C	H	W	3-1	..	..	..[1]	..[1]	..	..	..	..	..	..	..	McDermott[1] for Hollins
25 Oct	Liverpool	A	D	1-1	..	..	..	..	..	..	..	..[1]	..	Price	..	Rice for Price
1 Nov	Brighton & HA	H	W	1-0	..	..	..	..	..	..	..	..	..	McDermott[1]	..[1]	
8 Nov	Leeds U	A	W	5-0	..	..	..	..[1]	..	..	..[2]	..[1]	Gatting[1]	..	..	
11 Nov	Southampton	A	L	1-3	..	..	..	..	..	..	..	..	McDermott	Gatting	..[1]	Price for Gatting
15 Nov	W B A	H	D	2-2	Jennings	..	..	..	O'Leary	..	opponents	..[1]	Stapleton	..	..	
22 Nov	Everton	H	W	2-1	..	..	..	..	..	Walford	..	..	McDermott[1]	..	..	Gatting for Sanson
29 Nov	Aston Villa	A	D	1-1	..	..	..	..[1]	Walford	Young	..	..	..	Gatting	..	
6 Dec	Wolverhampton W	H	D	1-1	..	..	..	..	..	..	..	McDermott	..[1]	..	..	Vaessen for Hollins
13 Dec	Sunderland	A	L	0-2	..	..	..	..	..	..	Price	..	..	..	Davis	Vaessen for Gatting
20 Dec	Manchester U	H	W	2-1	..	..	..	..	..	..	Vaessen[1]	..	..	..	Rix[1]	
26 Dec	Crystal Palace	A	D	2-2	..	..	..	..	..	..	Hollins	Vaessen	..[1]	McDermott[1]	..	
27 Dec	Ipswich T	H	D	1-1	..	..	..	..	..	..	..	Sunderland[1]	..	Gatting	..	
10 Jan	Everton	A	W	2-1	..	..	..	Davis	..	..	..	Vaessen[1]	..	..[1]	McDermott	Price for Hollins
17 Jan	Tottenham H	A	L	0-2	..	..	..	McDermott	..	..	..	Sunderland	..	..	Rix	
31 Jan	Coventry C	H	D	2-2	..	Hollins	..	Talbot1	..	..	McDermott	..	..[1]	..	..	
7 Feb	Stoke C	A	D	1-1	..	..	..	..	O'Leary	..	..	..	..[1]	..	..	
21 Feb	Nottingham F	A	L	1-3	..	..	..	..	..	..	..	..	..[1]	..	..	Devine for Gatting
24 Feb	Manchester C	H	W	2-0	..	Devine	..	..[1]	..	..	Hollins	..[1]	..[1]	..	..	
28 Feb	Middlesbrough	H	D	2-2	..	..	..	..	..	Walford	..[1]	..	..[1]	..	..	McDermott for Sunderland
7 Mar	Leicester C	A	L	0-1	..	..	..	..	..	Young	..	..	..	..	..	Price for Hollins
21 Mar	Norwich C	A	D	1-1	..	..	..	..[1]	..	..	Nicholas	..	..	McDermott	..	
28 Mar	Liverpool	H	W	1-0	..	..	..	..	..	..	Hollins	..[1]	..	Nicholas	..	Davis for Hollins
31 Mar	Birmingham C	H	W	2-1	..	..	..	..[1]	..	..	Davis	..	..[1]	..	..	McDermott for Devine
4 Apr	Brighton & HA	A	W	1-0	..	..	..	..	..	..	..	..	..	Hollins[1]	..	
11 Apr	Leeds U	H	D	0-0	..	..	..	..	..	..	Hollins	..	..	Nicholas	Davis	McDermott for Hollins
18 Apr	Ipswich T	A	W	2-0	..	..	..[1]	..	..	..	..	..	..	..[1]	..	
20 Apr	Crystal Palace	H	W	3-2	..	..	..	..[1]	..	..[1]	..	..	..	..	..[1]	McDermott for Sunderland
25 Apr	Wolverhampton W	A	W	2-1	..	..	..	..	..	..	opponents	McDermott	..[1]	..	..	
2 May	Aston Villa	H	W	2-0	..	Hollins	..	..	..	..[1]	McDermott1	Sunderland	..	..	..	Nelson for Talbot

FA Cup

					Jennings	Devine	Sansom	Talbot	O'Leary	Young	Hollins	Sunderland	Stapleton	Gatting	Rix	
3 Jan	Everton (3)	A	L	0-2	Jennings	Devine	Sansom	Talbot	O'Leary	Young	Hollins	Sunderland	Stapleton	Gatting	Rix	McDermott for Talbot

Football League Cup

					Jennings	Devine	Sansom	Talbot	O'Leary	Young	Hollins	Sunderland	Stapleton[1]	Price	Rix	
26 Aug	Swansea (2)	A	D	1-1	Jennings	Devine	Sansom	Talbot	O'Leary	Young	Hollins	Sunderland	Stapleton[1]	Price	Rix	
2 Sep	Swansea (2R)	H	W	3-1	..	..	..	..	Walford[1]	..	..[1]	..[1]	..	..	..	
22 Sep	Stockport Co (3)	A	W	3-1	Wood	..	..	..	O'Leary	..	..[1]	..[1]	..	..	..	

Appearances (Goals)

Davis P 10 (1) · Devine J 39 · Gatting S 23 (3) · Hollins J 38 (5) · Jennings P 31 · McDermott B 23 (5) · Nelson S 1 · Nicholas P 8 (1) · O'Leary D 24 (1) · Price D 12 (1) · Rice P 2 · Rix G 35 (5) · Sansom K 42 (3) · Stapleton F 40 (14) · Sunderland A 34 (7) · Talbot B 40 (7) · Vaessen P 7 (2) · Walford S 20 · Wood G 11 · Young W 40 (4) · Own goals 2 · Total: 20 players (61)

Position in League Table

	P	W	L	D	F:A	Pts	
Aston Villa	42	26	8	8	72:40	60	1st
Arsenal	42	19	8	15	61:45	53	3rd

SEASON 1981-1982 FOOTBALL LEAGUE (DIVISION 1)

					Jennings	Devine	Sansom	Talbot	O'Leary	Young	Davis	Sunderland	McDermott	Nicholas	Rix	
29 Aug	Stoke C	H	L	0-1	Jennings	Devine	Sansom	Talbot	O'Leary	Young	Davis	Sunderland	McDermott	Nicholas	Rix	Vaessen for Devine
2 Sep	W B A	A	W	2-0	..	..	..	..[1]	..	..	..	..[1]	..	..	..	
5 Sep	Liverpool	A	L	0-2	..	..	..	..	..	..	Hollins	..	..	..	..	Davis for Nicholas
12 Sep	Sunderland	H	D	1-1	..	Hollins	..	..	..	..	Davis	..[1]	..	..	..	
19 Sep	Leeds U	A	D	0-0	..	..	..	..	..	..	..	..	..	..	..	Devine for Nicholas
22 Sep	Birmingham C	H	W	1-0	..	Devine	..	..[1]	..	..	..	..	Hollins	..	..	
26 Sep	Manchester U	H	D	0-0	..	..	..	..	..	..	Hollins	..	Hawley	Nicholas	Davis	
3 Oct	Notts Co	A	L	1-2	..	Hollins	..	..	..	..	Davis	..	..[1]	..	Rix	McDermott for Hawley
10 Oct	Swansea C	A	L	0-2	..	Devine	..	..	..	..	..	..	..	..	Hollins	
17 Oct	Manchester C	H	W	1-0	..	Hollins	..	..	..	Whyte	..	..	Meade[1]	..	Rix	
24 Oct	Ipswich T	A	L	1-2	..	..	..	..	..	Young	Davis	..[1]	..	..	..	
31 Oct	Coventry C	H	W	1-0	..	..	..	..	opponents	Whyte	McDermott	Vaessen	Hawley	..	..	
7 Nov	Aston Villa	A	W	2-0	..	Devine	..	..	..	..	Hollins	Davis	..	..[1]	..	
21 Nov	Nottingham F	A	W	2-1	..	..	..	..[1]	..	..	..	Sunderland[1]	..	..	..	
28 Nov	Everton	H	W	1-0	..	..	..	..	..	..	..	..	..	..	..	McDermott[1] for Devine
5 Dec	West Ham U	A	W	2-1	..	Robson	..	..	..	..[1]	..[1]	..	..	..	..	
20 Jan	Stoke C	A	W	1-0	Wood	..	..	..	..	..	Hollins	..	..	..	..	
23 Jan	Southampton	A	L	1-3	..	..	..	..	..[1]	..	..	..	..	..	..	McDermott for O'Leary
26 Jan	Brighton & HA	H	D	0-0	..	..	..	..	Hollins	..	McDermott	..	..	..	..	Meade for Davis
30 Jan	Leeds U	H	W	1-0	..	Hollins	..	..	O'Leary	..	Vaessen[1]	..	..	..	..	

224

Date	Opponent	V	Res	Notes / Substitutions
2 Feb	Wolverhampton W	H	W 2-1	Hawley for Sunderland
6 Feb	Sunderland	A	D 0-0	
13 Feb	Notts Co	H	W 1-0	Meade¹ for Nicholas
16 Feb	Middlesbrough	H	W 1-0	Meade for Nicholas
20 Feb	Manchester U	A	D 0-0	Meade for Vaessen
27 Feb	Swansea C	H	L 0-2	Meade for Vaessen
6 Mar	Manchester C	A	D 0-0	(Gorman, Robson)
13 Mar	Ipswich T	H	W 1-0	
16 Mar	W B A	H	D 2-2	Meade¹ for Gorman
20 Mar	Coventry C	A	L 0-1	Devine · Meade for Gorman
27 Mar	Aston Villa	H	W 4-3	O'Leary · Meade¹
29 Mar	Tottenham H	A	D 2-2	Nicholas for Davis
3 Apr	Wolverhampton W	A	D 1-1	Hawley for Meade
10 Apr	Brighton & HA	A	L 1-2	Nicholas
12 Apr	Tottenham H	H	L 1-3	Hawley¹ · Nicholas · Rix · McDermott for Robson
17 Apr	Nottingham F	H	W 2-0	Davis
24 Apr	Everton	A	L 1-2	Hawley · Sunderland · Nicholas for Hollins
1 May	West Ham U	H	W 2-0	
4 May	Birmingham C	A	W 1-0	
8 May	Middlesbrough	A	W 3-1	Nicholas for Davis · Meade for Hawley
11 May	Liverpool	H	D 1-1	Nicholas · Hawley
15 May	Southampton	H	W 4-1	Davis²

Appearances (Goals)

Davis P 38 (4) · Devine J 11 · Gorman P 4 · Hawley J 14 (3) · Hollins J 40 (1) · Jennings P 16 · McDermott 13 (1) · Meade R 16 (4) · Nicholas P 31 · O'Leary D 40 (1) · Rix G 39 (9) · Robson S 20 (2) · Sansom K 42 · Sunderland A 38 (11) · Talbot B 42 (7) · Vaessen P 10 (2) · Whyte C 32 (2) · Wood G 26 · Young W 10 · Own goals 1 · Total: 19 players (48)

Position in League Table

	P	W	L	D	F:A	Pts	
Liverpool	42	26	9	7	80:32	87	1st
Arsenal	42	20	11	11	48:37	71	5th

1982-83

SEASON 1982-1983 FOOTBALL LEAGUE (DIVISION 1)

Date	Opponent	V	Res	1	2	3	4	5	6	7	8	9	10	11	Substitutions
28 Aug	Stoke C	A	L 1-2	Wood	Hollins	Sansom	Talbot	O'Leary	Whyte	Robson	Sunderland¹	Chapman	Woodcock	Rix	Davis for Sunderland
31 Aug	Norwich C	H	D 1-1	..	..	..	..	Davis	..	..	..	..	..¹	..	Devine for Sansom
4 Sep	Liverpool	H	L 0-2	..	..	Devine	..	O'Leary	..	..	Davis	..	..	..	
7 Sep	Brighton & HA	A	L 0-1	..	..	..	..	..	..	..	..	..	..	..	Hawley for Talbot
11 Sep	Coventry C	A	W 2-0	..	..	Sansom	..	..	..	Davis	Robson	..¹	..¹	..	
18 Sep	Notts Co	H	W 2-0	..	..¹	..	..	..	..	..	..	..	..	..¹	
25 Sep	Manchester U	A	D 0-0	..	..	..	..	..	..	..	..	..	..	..	
2 Oct	West Ham U	H	L 2-3	..	..	..	..	..¹	..	..¹	Sunderland	..	..	..	
9 Oct	Ipswich T	A	W 1-0	..	..	..	..	..	..	Robson	..¹	..¹	..	..	Hawley for Hollins
16 Oct	W B A	H	W 2-0	..	Devine	..	..	..	..	..	..	..	..	..	
23 Oct	Nottingham F	A	L 0-3	..	Hollins	..	..	..	..	..	..	..	..	..	Chapman for Robson
30 Oct	Birmingham C	H	D 0-0	..	O'Shea	..	..	..	..	..	..	..	..	..	Chapman for Woodcock
6 Nov	Luton T	A	D 2-2	..	..	..	..¹	..	..	..	..	..	..	..¹	
13 Nov	Everton	H	D 1-1	Jennings	..	..	..	..	..	..	..	Chapman	..	..	McDermott¹ for O'Leary
20 Nov	Swansea C	A	W 2-1	Wood	..	..	..	..	..	..	Sunderland	..	..¹	..	Chapman¹ for Woodcock
27 Nov	Watford	H	L 2-4	..	..	..	..¹	..	..	..	..	..	..¹	..	
4 Dec	Manchester C	A	L 1-2	..	..	..	..	..	..	..	..	Chapman	Robson	..	McDermott¹ for O'Shea
7 Dec	Aston Villa	H	W 2-1	..	Hollins	..	..	..	..¹	..	..	Robson	Woodcock¹	..	
18 Dec	Sunderland	A	L 0-3	Jennings	..	..	..	..	..	..	..	Chapman	..	..	Chapman for Davis
27 Dec	Tottenham H	H	W 2-0	..	..	..	..	..	Robson	..	..¹	Nicholas	..¹	..	
28 Dec	Southampton	A	D 2-2	..	..	..	..	..	..	..	..	..	..¹	..	Chapman¹ for Woodcock
1 Jan	Swansea C	H	W 2-1	..	..	..	..	..	..	..	..¹	Petrovic	..¹	..	Chapman for Sunderland
3 Jan	Liverpool	A	L 1-3	..	..	..	..	..¹	..	..	Nicholas	Chapman	..	..	Talbot for O'Leary
15 Jan	Stoke C	H	W 3-0	..	..¹	..	Whyte	..	Nicholas	Davis	Sunderland	..¹	..	..¹	Talbot for Davis
22 Jan	Notts Co	A	L 0-1	..	..	..	Robson	..	..	..	..	..	Davis	..	
5 Feb	Brighton & HA	H	W 3-1	..	..	..	..	..	..	Talbot	Meade²	..	Davis	..	Talbot for Rix
26 Feb	W B A	A	D 0-0	..	Key	..	..	Whyte	..	Devine	Davis	Meade	Woodcock	..	Meade for Sunderland
5 Mar	Nottingham F	H	D 0-0	..	Hollins	..	..	..	..	Talbot	..	Sunderland	..	..	Talbot for Petrovic
15 Mar	Birmingham C	A	L 1-2	..	..	..	..	..	..	Petrovic	..¹	..	..	..	Meade for O'Leary
19 Mar	Luton T	H	W 4-1	..	O'Leary	..	..	..	..	Talbot	..¹	..	..³	..	
22 Mar	Ipswich T	H	D 2-2	Wood	Hollins	..	Devine	..	..	..	..	..	..	..	
26 Mar	Everton	A	W 3-2	..	Robson¹	..	Whyte	O'Leary	..	..	..	..¹	..¹	..	
2 Apr	Southampton	H	D 0-0	..	Kay	..	..	..	..	..	..	..¹	..	..	Petrovic for Whyte
4 Apr	Tottenham H	A	L 0-5	..	Robson	..	..	..	..	..	..	Petrovic	..	..	Chapman for Nicholas
9 Apr	Coventry C	H	W 2-1	..	..	..	..	Kay	..	..	..	Petrovic	..¹	..¹	Hollins for Rix
20 Apr	Norwich C	A	L 1-3	..	Kay	..	Talbot	O'Leary	Whyte	McDermott	Hill	Davis¹	Chapman	..	Hawley for Woodcock
23 Apr	Manchester C	H	W 3-0	Jennings	..	..	..	Whyte	..	Nicholas	Talbot³	Davis	Woodcock	Hill	Petrovic for Hawley
30 Apr	Watford	A	L 1-2	..	..	..	..	..	..	..	..	..¹	Hawley	..	Petrovic for Hawley
2 May	Manchester U	H	W 3-0	..	Devine	..	..	..	..	..²	..	..	..	..	Hawley for Devine
7 May	Sunderland	H	L 0-1	..	..	..	..	..	..	..	..	Petrovic	McDermott	..	
10 May	West Ham U	A	W 3-1	..	Kay	..	..¹	..	..	..	..	..¹	..	..	
14 May	Aston Villa	A	L 1-2	..	Devine	..	..	..	..	..	..¹	McDermott	Petrovic	..	

FA Cup

Date	Opponent	V	Res	1	2	3	4	5	6	7	8	9	10	11	Substitutions
8 Jan	Bolton W (3)	H	W 2-1	Jennings	Hollins	Sansom	Talbot	O'Leary	Robson	Davis¹	Sunderland	Nicholas	Woodcock	Rix¹	
29 Jan	Leeds U (4)	H	D 1-1	..	..	..	Robson	..	Nicholas	Talbot	..¹	Petrovic	..	..	
2 Feb	Leeds U (4R)	A	D 1-1	..	..	..	..	..	..	..	..	..	..	..¹	Davis for Sunderland
9 Feb	Leeds U (4R)	H	W 2-1	..	..	..	..	..	..	..	Meade	..	..	..¹	
19 Feb	Middlesbrough (5)	A	D 1-1	..	..	..	Whyte	..	..	Davis	..	..	..¹		
28 Feb	Middlesbrough (5R)	H	W 3-2	..	..	..	..	..	..	..¹	Sunderland	..¹	..		
12 Mar	Aston Villa (6)	H	W 2-0	..	..	..	..	..	Petrovic¹	..	..	..	..		
16 Apr	Manchester U (SF) (at Aston Villa)		L 1-2	Wood	Robson	Hollins	Whyte	O'Leary	Hollins	Talbot	..	Petrovic	..¹	..	Chapman for Robson

Milk Cup

Date	Opponent	V	Res	1	2	3	4	5	6	7	8	9	10	11	Substitutions
5 Oct	Cardiff C (2)	H	W 2-1	Wood	Hollins¹	Sansom	Talbot	O'Leary	Whyte	Davis¹	Sunderland	Robson	Woodcock	Rix	
26 Oct	Cardiff C (2)	A	W 3-1	..	..	..	..	..	..	..¹	..¹	..	..¹	..	
9 Nov	Everton (3)	A	D 1-1	Jennings	O'Shea	..	..	..	..	..	..	..¹	..	..	Chapman for Sunderland
23 Nov	Everton (3R)	H	W 3-0	Wood	..	..	..	..	..	..³	..	..	..	..	Chapman for Sunderland
30 Nov	Huddersfield T (4)	H	W 1-0	..	..	..	..	..	..	..	..¹	..	..	..	
18 Jan	Sheffield W (5)	H	W 1-0	Jennings	Hollins	..	Nicholas	..	Robson	..	Petrovic	..¹	..		
15 Feb	Manchester U (SF)	H	L 2-4	..	..	..	Robson	..	Nicholas¹	Talbot	Meade	..¹	..		Davis for O'Leary
23 Feb	Manchester U (SF)	A	L 1-2	..	..	..	..	Whyte	..	..	..¹	..	..		Davis for Hollins

UEFA Cup

Date	Opponent	V	Res	1	2	3	4	5	6	7	8	9	10	11	Substitutions
14 Sep	Spartak Moscow (1)	A	L 2-3	Wood	Hollins	Sansom	Talbot	O'Leary	Whyte	Davis	Robson¹	Chapman¹	Woodcock	Rix	
29 Sep	Spartak Moscow (1)	H	L 2-5	..	..	..	..	opponents	..	..	..	..	..	..	Sunderland for Hollins, McDermott for Davis

Appearances (Goals)

Chapman L 19 (3) · Davis P 41 (4) · Devine J 9 · Hawley J 6 · Hill C 7 · Hollins J 23 (2) · Jennings P 19 · Kay J 7 · McDermott B 9 (4) · Meade R 4 2 · Nicholas P 21 · O'Leary D 36 (1) · O'Shea D 6 · Petrovic V 13 (2) · Rix G 36 (6) · Robson S 31 (2) · Sansom K 40 · Sunderland A 25 (6) · Talbot B 42 (9) · Whyte C 36 3 · Wood G 23 · Woodcock A 34 (14) · Total: 22 players (58)

Position in League Table

	P	W	L	D	F:A	Pts
Liverpool	42	24	8	10	87:37	82 1st
Arsenal	42	16	16	10	58:56	58 10th

SEASON 1983-1984 FOOTBALL LEAGUE (DIVISION 1)

27 Aug	Luton T	H	W	2-1	Jennings	Robson	Sansom	Talbot	O'Leary	Hill	McDermott[1]	Davis	Woodcock[1]	Nicholas	Rix	
29 Aug	Wolverhampton W	A	W	2-1	..	..	..	..	..	..	..	..	..	..[2]	..	
3 Sep	Southampton	A	L	0-1	..	..	..	..	..	..	..	..	..	..	..	Whyte for McDermott
6 Sep	Manchester U	H	L	2-3	..	..	..	..[1]	..	..	..	..	..[1]	..	..	Sunderland for McDermott
10 Sep	Liverpool	H	L	0-2	..	..	..	..	..	..	Sunderland	..	..	..	..	
17 Sep	Notts Co	A	W	4-0	..	..	..	Whyte	..	opponents	..	..	..[1]	..	..[1]	Talbot[1] for Nicholas
24 Sep	Norwich C	H	W	3-0	..	..	..	..	..	..	..[2]	..	Chapman[1]	..	..	McDermott for Nicholas
1 Oct	Q P R	A	L	0-2	..	..	..	..	..	..	..	..	..	..	..	
15 Oct	Coventry C	H	L	0-1	..	..	..	..	..	..	..	..	..	..	..	McDermott for Whyte
22 Oct	Nottingham F	H	W	4-1	..	..	..	..	..	..	..[1]	..[1]	Woodcock[2]	..	..	McDermott for Nicholas
29 Oct	Aston Villa	A	W	6-2	..	..	..	..	..	..	..	..	..[5]	..	..	McDermott for Robson
5 Nov	Sunderland	H	L	1-2	..	..	..	Adams	..	..	..	Talbot	..[1]	..	..	McDermott for Sunderland
12 Nov	Ipswich T	A	L	0-1	..	..	..	..	O'Leary	..	..	Davis	..	..	..	Gorman for Sunderland
19 Nov	Everton	H	W	2-1	..	..[1]	..	..	..	..	..[1]	Gorman	McDermott	..	..	Meade for Sunderland
26 Nov	Leicester C	A	L	0-3	..	..	..	..	..	Kay	..	Davis	Woodcock	..	..	Chapman for Rix
3 Dec	W B A	H	L	0-1	..	..	..	Caton	Adams	Hill	Madden	..	..	..	Allinson	Meade for Robson
10 Dec	West Ham U	A	L	1-3	..	Hill	..	Kay	Whyte[1]	Caton	..	..	..	..	..	Meade for Hill
17 Dec	Watford	H	W	3-1	..	..	..	Cork	..	..	Meade[3]	..	..	..	..	
26 Dec	Tottenham H	A	W	4-2	..	..	..	Robson	O'Leary	..	..[2]	..	..	..[2]	..	Cork for Robson
27 Dec	Birmingham C	H	D	1-1	..	..	..	Cork	Whyte	..	..	..	..	..[1]	..	McDermott for Caton
31 Dec	Southampton	H	D	2-2	..	..	..	..[1]	O'Leary	..	..	..	..[1]	..	..	
2 Jan	Norwich C	A	D	1-1	..	..	..	..	..	..	..	..	..[1]	..	..	
14 Jan	Luton T	A	W	2-1	..	Kay	..[1]	Talbot	..	..	..	..	..[1]	..	Rix	
21 Jan	Notts Co	H	D	1-1	..	..	..	..	Adams	..	..	..	..	..[1]	..	McDermott for Adams
28 Jan	Stoke C	A	L	0-1	..	..	..	..	O'Leary	..	McDermott	..	..	..	..	
4 Feb	Q P R	H	L	0-2	..	..	..	..	..	..	Meade	..	..	..	..	Cork for Meade
11 Feb	Liverpool	A	L	1-2	Jennings	Hill	Sansom	Talbot	O'Leary	Caton	Cork	Davis	Woodcock	Nicolas	Rix[1]	Allinson for Cork
18 Feb	Aston Villa	H	D	1-1	..	..	..	..	..	..	Davis	Nicholas	Mariner	Woodcock	..[1]	
25 Feb	Nottingham F	A	W	1-0	..	..	..	..	..	..	..	..[1]	..	..[1]	..	
3 Mar	Sunderland	A	D	2-2	..	..	..	..	..	..	..	..[2]	..	..[1]	..	Allinson for Rix
10 Mar	Ipswich T	H	W	4-1	..	..	..	..[1]	..	..	..	..	..	..[1]	..	
17 Mar	Manchester U	A	L	0-4	..	..	..	..	..	..	Robson	..	..	..	..	
24 Mar	Wolverhampton W	H	W	4-1	..	..	..	..	..	..	..	..[1]	..	..[1]	..[1]	
31 Mar	Coventry C	A	W	4-1	..	..	Sparrow	..[1]	..	Whyte[1]	..[1]	..	..[1]	..	..	Kay for Jennings
	(															Robson in goal)
7 Apr	Stoke C	H	W	3-1	Lukic	..	..	..	..	Caton	..	..[1]	..[1]	..[1]	..	Meade for Nicholas
9 Apr	Everton	A	D	0-0	..	..	Sansom	..	..	..	..	..	..	..	..	
21 Apr	Tottenham H	H	W	3-2	..	..	..	..	..	..	..	..[1]	..	..[1]	..	Davis for Rix
23 Apr	Birmingham C	A	D	1-1	..	..	..	..	..	..	..	..[1]	..	..[1]	..	Davis
28 Apr	Leicester C	H	W	2-1	Jennings	..	..	..	..	..	..	..	..	..[1]	Rix	Davis1 for Talbot
5 May	W B A	A	W	3-1	..	..	..	..[1]	..	..	..	..	..[1]	..	..	Davis for Robson
7 May	West Ham U	H	D	3-3	..	..	..	..[1]	..	..	..	..	..[1]	..[1]	..	Davis for Rix
12 May	Wartford	A	L	1-2	..	..	..	..	..	..	..[1]	Davis	..	Meade	..	

FA Cup

7 Jan	Middlesbrough (3)	A	L	2-3	Jennings	Hill	Sansom	Cork	O'Leary	Caton	Meade	Davis	Woodcock[1]	Nicholas[1]	Rix	Talbot for Cork

Milk Cup

4 Oct	Plymouth Arg (2)	A	D	1-1	Jennings	Robson	Sansom	Whyte	O'Leary	Hill	Sunderland	Davis	Woodcock	Nicholas	Rix[1]	Talbot for Woodcock
25 Oct	Plymouth Arg (2)	H	W	1-0	..	..	..	..	..	..	..[1]	..	..	..	..	
9 Nov	Tottenham H (3)	A	W	2-1	..	..	..	..	..	..	..	..	..[1]	..	..	
29 Nov	Walsall (4)	H	L	1-2	..	..[1]	..	..	..	..	..	..	..	..	Allinson	

Appearances (Goals)

Adams T 3 · Allinson I 9 · Caton T 26 · Chapman L 4 (1) · Cork D 7 (1) · Davis P 35 (1) · Gorman P 2 · Hill C 37 (1) · Jennings P 38 · Kay J 7 · Lukic J 4 · Madden D 2 · Mariner P 15 (7) · Meade R 13 (5) · McDermott B 13 (2) · Nicholas C 41 (11) · O'Leary D 36 · Rix G 34 (4) · Robson S 28 (6) · Sansom K 40 (1) · Sparrow B 2 · Sunderland A 12 (4) · Talbot B 27 (6) · Whyte C 15 (2) · Woodcock A 37 (21) · Own goals 1 · Total: 25 players (74)

Position in League Table

	P	W	L	D	F:A	Pts
Liverpool	42	22	6	14	73:32	80 1st
Arsenal	42	18	15	9	74:60	63 6th

SEASON 1984-1985 FOOTBALL LEAGUE (DIVISION 1)

25 Aug	Chelsea	H	D	1-1	Jennings	Anderson	Sansom	Talbot	O'Leary	Caton	Robson	Davis	Mariner[1]	Woodcock	Allinson	
29 Aug	Nottingham F	A	L	0-2	..	..	..	..	..	..	..	Nicholas	..	..	Davis	Allinson for Talbot
1 Sep	Watford	A	W	4-3	..	..	..	..[1]	..	..	..	Davis	..	..[1]	Nicholas[2]	
4 Sep	Newcastle U	H	W	2-0	..	..[1]	..	..[1]	..	..	..	..	..	..[1]	..	
8 Sep	Liverpool	H	W	3-1	..	..	..	..[2]	..	..	..	..	..	..[1]	..	
15 Sep	Ipswich T	A	L	1-2	..	..	..	..	..	..	..	Rix	..	..[2]	..[1]	
22 Sep	Stoke C	H	W	4-0	..	..	..	..[1]	..	..	..	..	..	..[1]	..	
29 Sep	Coventry C	A	W	2-1	..	..	..	..	..	..	..	..	..[1]	..[1]	..	Davis for Talbot
6 Oct	Everton	H	W	1-0	..	..	..	..	..	..	..	..	Allinson	..[1]	..	
13 Oct	Leicester C	A	W	4-1	..	..[1]	..	..[2]	..	..	..	..[1]	..	..	..	Davis for Woodcock
20 Oct	Sunderland	H	W	3-2	..	..	..	..[1]	..	..[1]	..	..	..	..[1]	..	
27 Oct	West Ham U	A	L	1-3	..	..	..	..	..	Hill	..	..	..	Davis	..	Adams for Rix
2 Nov	Manchester U	A	L	1-4	Lukic	..	..	..	..	Coton	Davis	Robson	Davis	Woodcock[1]	..	Allinson for Caton
10 Nov	Aston Villa	H	D	1-1	Jennings	..	..	..	..	..	Adams	..	Mariner[1]	..	..	Allinson for Caton
17 Nov	Q P R	H	W	1-0	..	..	..	..	..	..	..	..	Allinson	..	..	
25 Nov	Sheffield W	A	L	1-2	..	..	..	..	..	..	..	..	Mariner	..[1]	..	Allinson for O'Leary
1 Dec	Luton T	H	W	3-1	Lukic	..[1]	..	..	Adams	Caton	..	..	..	..[1]	Allinson[1]	Meade for Allinson
8 Dec	Southampton	A	L	0-1	..	..	..	..	O'Leary	Adams	..	..	..	..	..[2]	
15 Dec	W B A	H	W	4-0	..	..	..	..[1]	Adams	Caton	..	..[1]	..	..	..[1]	
22 Dec	Watford	H	D	1-1	..	O'Leary	Hill	..	..	..	Nicholas	..	..	..	..	Nicholas for Allinson
26 Dec	Norwich C	A	L	0-1	..	Anderson	Sansom	..	O'Leary	Adams	Caton	..	..	..	..	
29 Dec	Newcastle U	A	W	3-1	..	..	Caton	..[1]	..	..	Nicholas[2]	..	..	Nicholas	..	Willams for Nicholas
1 Jan	Tottenham H	H	L	1-2	..	..	..	..	..	..	Allinson	..	..[1]	..	..	
19 Jan	Chelsea	A	D	1-1	..	..	Sansom	..	..	Caton	Willams	..	..[1]	..	..	
2 Feb	Coventry C	H	W	2-1	..	..	..	..	..	..	..	..	Meade[1]	Allinson[1]	..	Nicholas for Caton
12 Feb	Liverpool	A	L	0-3	..	..	..	..	Adams	..	..	..	..	..	..	Nicholas for Alinson
23 Feb	Manchester U	H	L	0-1	..	..	Williams	..	Caton	..	Davis	..	Woodcock	Nicholas	Talbot for Davis
2 Mar	Woct Ham U	H	W	2-1	..	..	..	..	..	..	..	..	..	..	..	
9 Mar	Sunderland	A	D	0-0	..	..	Talbot	..	..	..	..	..	..	..	Meade for Woodcock
13 Mar	Aston Villa	A	D	0-0	..	..	..	..	..	..	..	..	..	Meade[1]	Talbot for Nicholas
16 Mar	Leicester C	H	W	2-0	..	..	Williams[1]	Adams	..	..	..	..	..[1]	..	Talbot for Davis
19 Mar	Ipswich T	H	D	1-1	..	..	..	..	..	Rix	..	..	..[1]	..	Talbot for Robson
23 Mar	Everton	A	L	0-2	..	..	..	O'Leary	..	..	Talbot	..	..	..	Allinson for Meade
30 Mar	Stoke C	A	L	0-2	..	..	..	..	..	..	Robson[1]	..	Talbot	..[1]	Allinson for Mariner
6 Apr	Norwich C	H	W	2-0	..	..	..	..	..	..	..	..	Allinson	..	..	
13 Apr	Nottingham F	H	D	1-1	..	..	..	..	..	..	..	..	..	..	..	

17 Apr	Tottenham H	A	W 2-0	..	..	..	..	..	..	..	..	..	..[1]	..[1]	Mariner for O'Leary
20 Apr	Q P R	A	L 0-1	..	..	..	..	Adams	..	..	..	..	..	..	Mariner for Adams
27 Apr	Sheffield W	H	W 1-0	..	..	..	..	O'Leary	..	..	..	Mariner[1]	..	..	Allinson for Robson
4 May	Luton T	A	L 1-3	..	..	..	Talbot	..	..	..	..	..	Allinson	..[1]	Davis for Caton
6 May	Southampton	H	W 1-0	..	..	..	..	Adams	Davis	..	..[1]	..	..	..	
11 May	W B A	A	D 2-2	..	..	opponents	..	O'Leary	Adams	..	..	..	Davis	..	Allinson[1] for Nicholas

FA Cup

5 Jan	Hereford (3)	A	D 1-1	Lukic	Anderson	Caton	Talbot	O'Leary	Adams	Robson	Willams	Mariner	Woodcock	Nicholas	Allinson for Nicholas
22 Jan	Hereford (3R)	H	W 7-2	..	..[1]	Sansom	..[2]	..	Caton	..	..	..[2]	..[1]	..[1]	
26 Jan	York C (4)	A	L 0-1	..	..	..	..	..	..	..	..	..	..	..	Allinson for Nicholas

Milk Cup

25 Sep	Bristol R (2)	H	W 4-0	Jennings	Anderson[1]	Sansom	Talbot	O'Leary	Caton	Robson	Rix	Mariner	Woodcock1	Nicholas[2]	
9 Oct	Bristol R (2)	A	D 1-1	..	..	..	..	..	..	..	..	..	..	..	
31 Oct	Oxford U (3)	A	L 2-3	..	..	..	..	..	..	..	..	Allinson[1]	..	..	Adams for Robson

Appearances (Goals)

Adams T 16 · Allinson J 27 (10) · Caton T 35 (1) · Davis P 24 (1) · Hill C 2 · Jennings P 15 · Lukic J 27 · Mariner P 36 (7) · Meade R 8 (3) · Nicholas C 38 (9) · O'Leary D 36 · Rix G 18 (2) · Robson S 40 (2) · Sansom K 39 (1) · Talbot B 41 (10) · Williams S 15 (1) · Woodcock T 27 (10) · Own goals 1 · Total: 18 players (61)

Position in League Table

	P	W	L	D	F:A	Pts	
Everton	42	28	8	6	88:43	90	1st
Arsenal	42	19	14	9	61:49	66	7th

1985-86

SEASON 1985-1986 FOOTBALL LEAGUE (DIVISION 1)

Date	Opponent	V	Res	Lukic	Anderson	Sansom	Williams	O'Leary	Caton	Robson	Allinson	Nicholas	Woodcock	Rix	Substitutions
17 Aug	Liverpool	A	L 0-2	Lukic	Anderson	Sansom	Williams	O'Leary	Caton	Robson	Allinson	Nicholas	Woodcock	Rix	
20 Aug	Southampton	H	W 3-2	..	..	..	..	..	..[1]	..[1]	..	..	..	..	
24 Aug	Manchester U	H	L 1-2	..	..	..	..	..	..	..	..[1]	..	..	..	Davis for Williams
27 Aug	Luton T	A	D 2-2	..	..	..	Davis	..	..	..	opponent	..	..	..[1]	Mariner for O'Leary
31 Aug	Leicester C	H	W 1-0	..	..	..	..	Mariner	..	..	..[1]	..	..[1]	..	
3 Sep	Q P R	A	W 1-0	..	..	..	..	O'Leary	..	..	..[1]	..	..	..	
7 Sep	Coventry C	A	W 2-0	..	..	..	..	..	..	..	..	..[1]	..[1]	..	
14 Sep	Sheffield W	H	W 1-0	..	..	..	..	..	..	..	..[1]	..	..	..	
21 Sep	Chelsea	A	L 1-2	..	..	..	..	..	..	..	..	..[1]	..	..	
28 Sep	Newcastle U	H	D 0-0	..	..	..	..	..	..	Rocastle	..	..	..	..	Whyte for Allinson
5 Oct	Aston Villa	H	W 3-2	..	..[1]	..	..	..	..	Whyte[1]	..	..[1]	..	..	
12 Oct	West Ham U	A	D 0-0	..	..	..	..	..	..	..	..	..	..	..	Rocastle for O'Leary
19 Oct	Ipswich T	H	W 1-0	..	..	..	..[1]	..	..	..	..	..	..	..	Rocastle for Nicholas
26 Oct	Nottingham F	A	L 2-3	..	..	..	..[1]	..	..	..	..	..	..	..[1]	Rocastle for Allinson
2 Nov	Manchester C	H	W 1-0	..	..	..	..[1]	..	..	Williams	..	..	..	..	Whyte for Allinson
9 Nov	Everton	A	L 1-6	..	..	..	..	..	..	..	..	..[1]	..	..	
16 Nov	Oxford U	H	W 2-1	..	..	..	..[1]	..	..	Robson	..	..[1]	..	Hayes	Allinson for Woodcock
23 Nov	W B A	A	D 0-0	..	..	..	..	Keown	..	..	..	..	..	..	Whyte for Hayes
30 Nov	Birmingham C	H	D 0-0	..	..	..	..	O'Leary	..	..	..	..	..	..	Allinson for Williams
7 Dec	Southampton	A	L 0-3	..	..	..	..	..	..	..	..	..	..	..	Allinson for Hayes
14 Dec	Liverpool	H	W 2-0	..	..	..	..	Keown	Allinson	..	..	..[1]	Quinn	Rix	
21 Dec	Manchester U	A	W 1-0	..	Caesar	..	..	..	..	..	..	..[1]	..	..[1]	
28 Dec	Q P R	H	W 3-1	..	..	..	..	..	..	..	..	..[1]	..	..[1]	Woodcock[1] for Robson
1 Jan	Tottenham H	H	D 0-0	..	Anderson	..	..	..	..	Robson[1]	..[1]	..	..		
18 Jan	Leicester C	A	D 2-2	..	..	..	..	..	..	Robson[1]	..	..	..		
1 Feb	Luton T	H	W 2-1	..	..	..	Rocastle	..	..	..[1]	Mariner	..	..		
1 Mar	Newcastle U	A	L 0-1	Lukic	Anderson	Sansom	Williams	O'Leary	Keown	Allinson	Rocastle	Nicholas	Woodcock	Rix	Mariner for Woodcock
8 Mar	Aston Villa	A	W 1-1	Wilmot	..	..	..	opponents	..	Hayes[1]	..[1]	..[1]			
11 Mar	Ipswich T	A	W 2-1	..	..	..	..	..	..	..	..[1]	..			Mariner for O'Leary
15 Mar	West Ham U	H	W 1-0	Lukic	..	..	..	..	..	..	..	..[1]			
22 Mar	Coventry C	H	W 3-0	..	Adams	..	opponents	..	..[1]	..	..[1]	..			
29 Mar	Tottenham H	A	L 0-1	..	Anderson	..	..	..	..	..	..	Quinn	..	Mariner for Quinn	
31 Mar	Watford	H	L 0-2	..	..	..	..	..	..	..	..	Mariner	..	Robson for Hayes	
1 Apr	Watford	A	L 0-3	..	..	..	..	Adams	..	Robson	..	Woodcock	..	Allinsonfor Williams	
5 Apr	Manchester C	A	W 1-0	..	..	..	Allinson	..	..[1]	..	..	Quinn	..	Mariner for Quinn	
8 Apr	Nottingham F	H	D 1-1	..	..	..	..[1]	..	..	..	..	..	..	Mariner for Rocastle	
12 Apr	Everton	H	L 0-1	..	..	..	..	..	..	..	Davis	..	..		
16 Apr	Sheffield W	A	L 0-2	..	..	..	..[1]	..	..	..	..	..	Woodcock	..	
26 Apr	W B A	H	D 2-2	..	..	..	..[1]	O'Leary	Adams	..[1]	..	Hayes	..	..	Quinn for Woodcock
29 Apr	Chelsea	H	W 2-0	..	..[1]	..	Keown	..	..	..	Nicholas[1]	..	..	Quinn for Rix	
3 May	Birmingham C	A	W 1-0	..	..	..	..	..	..	..	..[1]	..	..		
5 May	Oxford U	A	L 0-3	..	..	..	..	..	..	..	..	..	..	Allinson for O'Leary	

FA Cup

Date	Opponent	V	Res	Lukic	Anderson	Sansom	Davis	O'Leary	Keown	Allinson	Rocastle	Nicholas	Quinn	Rix	Substitutions
4 Jan	Grimsby T (3)	A	W 4-3	Lukic	Anderson	Sansom	Davis	O'Leary	Keown	Allinson	Rocastle	Nicholas[3]	Quinn	Rix[1]	
25 Jan	Rotherham U (4)	H	W 5-1	..	..	..	Rocastle	..	..	..[2]	Robson[1]	..[1]	..	..[1]	Woodcock for Robson
15 Feb	Luton T (5)	A	D 2-2	..	..	..	Williams	..	..	..[1]	Rocastle[1]	..	Woodcock	..	Mariner for Nicholas
3 Mar	Luton T (Extra Time 5R)	H	D 0-0	..	..	..	..	..	..	..	..	..	Mariner	..	
5 Mar	Luton T (5 2nd Rep)	A	L 0-3	..	..	..	..	..	..	..	..	..	..	Hayes	Quinn for Hayes

Milk Cup

Date	Opponent	V	Res	Lukic	Anderson	Sansom	Davis	O'Leary	Caton	Robson	Allinson	Nicholas	Woodcock	Rix	Substitutions
25 Sep	Hereford U (2)	A	D 0-0	Lukic	Anderson	Sansom	Davis	O'Leary	Caton	Robson	Allinson	Nicholas	Woodcock	Rix	Mariner for Robson
8 Oct	Hereford U (2 extra time)	H	W 2-1	..	..[1]	..	..	..	Whyte	..	..[1]	..	..	Rocastle for Davis
30 Oct	Manchester C (3)	A	W 2-1	..	..	..	..	..	..	Williams	..[1]	..[1]	..	
19 Nov	Southampton (4)	H	D 0-0	..	..	..	..	..	..	Robson	..	..	Hayes	Allinson for Hayes
26 Nov	Southampton (4R)	A	W 3-1	..	..	..	..	..	..	..[1]	..[1]	..	..[1]	
22 Jan	Aston Villa (5)	A	D 1-1	Wilmot	..	..	Rocastle	..	..	Allinson	..	Quinn	Rix	Woodcock for Robson
4 Feb	Aston Villa (5R)	H	L 1-2	Lukic	..	..	..	..	..	..	Mariner[1]	..	..	Woodcock for Allinson

Appearances (Goals)

Adams T 10 · Allinson I 33 6 · Anderson V 39 2 · Ceasar G 20 1 · Caton T 20 1 · Davis P 29 4 · Hayes M 11 2 · Keown M 22 · Lukic J 40 · Mariner P9 · Nicholas C 41 10 · O'Leary D 35 · Quinn N 12 1 · Rix G 38 3 · Robson S 27 4 · Rocastle D 16 1 · Sansom K 42 · Whyte C 7 1 · Williams S 17 · Wilmot R 2 · Woodcock T 33 11 · Own goals 3 · Total:21 players 49

Position in League Table

	P	W	L	D	F:A	Pts	
Liverpool	42	26	6	10	89:37	88	1st
Arsenal	42	20	13	9	49:47	69	7th

1986-87

SEASON 1986-1987 FOOTBALL LEAGUE (DIVISION 1)

Date	Opponent	V	Res	Lukic	Anderson	Sansom	Robson	O'Leary	Adams	Rocastle	Davis	Quinn	Nicholas	Rix	Substitutions
23 Aug	Manchester U	H	W 1-0	Lukic	Anderson	Sansom	Robson	O'Leary	Adams	Rocastle	Davis	Quinn	Nicholas[1]	Rix	Hayes for Rocastle
26 Aug	Coventry C	A	L 1-2	..	..[1]	..	..	..	..	..	..	..	..	..	Hayes for Rix
30 Aug	Liverpool	A	L 1-2	..	..	..	..	..	..	..[1]	..	..	..	..	Williams for Robson
2 Sep	Sheffield W	H	W 2-0	..	..	..	..	..	..[1]	..	..	..	..[1]	..	Hayes for Rocastle
6 Sep	Tottenham H	H	D 0-0	..	..	..	..	..	..	..	..	..	..	..	Hayes for Rocastle
13 Sep	Luton T	A	D 0-0	..	..	..	Williams	..	..	..	..	..	..	..	Groves for Rix
20 Sep	Oxford U	H	D 0-0	..	..	..	..	..	..	..	..	..	..	..	Groves for Rix
27 Sep	Nottingham F	A	L 0-1	..	..	..	..	..	..	..	..	..	..	Groves	Allinson for Nicholas
4 Oct	Everton	A	W 1-0	..	..	..	..	..[1]	..	..	..	Allinson	..	Caesar for Groves
11 Oct	Watford	H	W 3-1	..	..	..	..	..	..	..[1]	Groves[1]	Hayes[1]	Allinson for O'Leary
18 Oct	Newcastle U	A	W 2-1	..	..[1]	..	..[1]	..	..	..	..	..	Caesar for Quinn
25 Oct	Chelsea	H	W 3-1	..	..	..	..	..[1]	..[1]	..	..	..[2]	Allinson for Quinn
1 Nov	Charlton A	A	W 2-0	..	..	..	..	..	..[1]	..	..	..[1]	Caesar for Groves
8 Nov	West Ham U	H	D 0-0	..	..	..	..	..	..	..	..	..	..	
15 Nov	Southampton	A	W 4-0	..	..[1]	..	..	..	..	..[1]	..[1]	..[1]	Caesar for Rocastle

Date	Opponent		Res	Score	Lukic	Anderson	Sansom	Williams	O'Leary	Adams	Rocastle	Davis	Quinn	Nicholas	Hayes	Substitutes
22 Nov	Manchester C	H	W	3-0	..	..¹	..	..	..	..	..¹	..	..¹	Allinson	..	Merson for Hayes
29 Nov	Aston Villa	A	W	4-0	..	..	opponents	..	..	..	..	..¹	..	Groves¹	..¹	
6 Dec	Q P R	H	W	3-1	..	..	..	..	..	..	..	..	..	..¹	..²	Nicholas for Groves
13 Dec	Norwich C	A	D	1-1	..	..	..	..	..	..	..	..	..	..	..¹	Caesar for Groves
20 Dec	Luton T	H	W	3-0	..	..	..	..	..	..¹	..	..	..¹	..	..¹	Nicholas for Groves
26 Dec	Leicester C	A	D	1-1	..	..	..	..	..	..	..	..	..	..	..¹	Caesar for Groves
27 Dec	Southampton	H	W	1-0	..	..	..	..	..	..	..	..	..¹	Nicholas	..	Allinson for Hayes
1 Jan	Wimbledon	H	W	3-1	..	..	..	..	..	..	..	..	..²	..	..¹	Allinson for Rocastle
4 Jan	Tottenham H	A	W	2-1	..	..	..	..	..	..¹	..	..¹	..	..	..	Rix for Quinn
18 Jan	Coventry C	H	D	0-0	..	..	..	..	..	..	..	..	..	..	..	Rix for Hayes
24 Jan	Manchester U	A	L	0-2	..	..	..	..	..	..	..	..	..	..	..	Caesar for Nicholas
14 Feb	Sheffield W	A	D	1-1	..	Thomas	..	..	..	..	Groves	..	..¹	Rix	..	Allinson for Williams
25 Feb	Oxford U	A	D	0-0	..	Anderson	..	Thomas	..	..	Rocastle	..	..	Groves	..	Nicholas for Groves
7 Mar	Chelsea	A	L	0-1	..	..	..	..	..	..	..	Caesar	..	Allinson	..	Merson for Hayes
10 Mar	Liverpool	H	L	0-1	..	..	..	..	..	..	..	Groves	..	..	..	Caesar for Hayes
17 Mar	Nottingham F	H	D	0-0	..	..	..	Williams	Caesar	..	..	..	..	Nicholas	Thomas	Allinson for Groves
21 Mar	Watford	A	L	0-2	..	Caesar	..	Thomas	O'Leary	..	Allinson	Davis	..	..	Hayes	Rix for Quinn
28 Mar	Everton	H	L	0-1	..	Anderson	..	Williams	..	..	Rocastle	..	..	..	..	Groves for Hayes
8 Apr	West Ham U	A	L	1-3	Wilmot	..	Thomas	..	..	..	..	..	Groves	..	..¹	Rix for Hayes
11 Apr	Charlton A	H	W	2-1	Lukic	..	Sansom	..	..	..	..	..¹	Quinn	..	..¹	Groves for Quinn
14 Apr	Newcastle U	H	L	0-1	..	..	Thomas	..	..	..	..	..	Groves	..	..	Rix for Rocastle
18 Apr	Wimbledon	A	W	2-1	..	..	Caesar	..	..	..	..	..¹	Merson¹	..	Rix	Allinson for Rocastle
20 Apr	Leicester C	H	W	4-1	Wilmot	..	Sansom	..	..	Hayes²	..¹	..	..¹	..		Caesar for O'Leary
25 Apr	Manchester C	A	L	0-3	..	..	Thomas	..	Caesar	..	..	..	Quinn	..	Hayes²	Allinson for Merson
2 May	Aston Villa	H	W	2-1	..	..	..	..	O'Leary	..	Rocastle	..	Quinn	..	Hayes²	Groves for Quinn
4 May	Q P R	A	W	4-1	..	..	..	..	Caesar	..	Rix²	..	Merson¹	..	..¹	
9 May	Norwich C	H	L	1-2	..	..	..	..	O'Leary	..	..	..	..¹	..	..	Groves for Anderson

FA Cup

Date	Opponent		Res	Score	Lukic	Anderson	Sansom	Williams	O'Leary	Adams	Rocastle	Davis	Quinn	Nicholas	Hayes	Substitutes
10 Jan	Reading (3)	A	W	3-1	Lukic	Anderson	Sansom	Williams	O'Leary	Adams	Rocastle	Davis	Quinn	Nicholas²	Hayes¹	
31 Jan	Plymouth A (4)	H	W	6-1	..	..²	..	..	..	..	..¹	..¹	..¹	..¹	..	Groves for Hayes/Caesar for Groves
21 Feb	Barnsley (5)	H	W	2-0	..	..	..	Allinson	..	..	..	..	Groves	..¹		Nicholas¹ for Quinn/Thomas for Hayes
14 Mar	Watford (QF)	H	L	1-3	..	..	..	Williams	..	..	..	Groves	..	Allinson¹		Nicholas for Allinson/Thomas for Hayes

Football League (Littlewoods) Cup

Date	Opponent		Res	Score	Lukic	Anderson	Sansom	Williams	O'Leary	Adams	Rocastle	Davis	Quinn	Nicholas	Rix	Substitutes
23 Sep	Huddersfield T (2)	H	W	2-0	Lukic	Anderson	Sansom	Williams	O'Leary	Adams	Rocastle	Davis	Quinn¹	Nicholas	Rix	Groves for Quinn
7 Oct	Huddersfield T (2)	A	D	1-1	..	..	..	..	..	..	..	..	..	Allinson	Groves	Hayes¹ for Allinson
28 Oct	Manchester C (3)	H	W	3-1	..	..	..	..	..	..	..¹	..¹	..¹	Groves	Hayes¹	Allinson for Groves
18 Nov	Charlton A (4)	H	W	2-0	..	..	..	opponents	..	..	..	..	..¹	..	..	Allinson for Groves
21 Jan	Nottingham F (QF)	H	W	2-0	..	..	..	..	..	..	..	..	..	Nicholas¹	..¹	Rix for Quinn
8 Feb	Tottenham H (SF1)	H	L	0-1	..	Caesar	..	..	..	..	Groves	..	..	..	..	Thomas for Caesar/Rix for Nicholas
1 Mar	Tottenham H (SF2)	A	W	2-1	..	Anderson¹	..	Thomas	..	..	Rocastle	..	..¹	..	..	Allinson for Nicholas
4 Mar	Tottenham H (SFR)	A	W	2-1	..	..	..	..	..	..	..¹	..	..¹	..	..	Allinson1 for Thomas
5 Apr	Liverpool (F) (at Wembley)		W	2-1	..	..	..	Williams	..	..	..	..	..²	..	..	Groves for Quinn/Thomas for Hayes

Appearances (Goals)

Adams T 42 6 · Allinson I 14 · Anderson V 40 4 · Caesar G 15 · Davis P 39 4 · Groves P 25 3 · Hayes M 35 19 · Lukic J 36 · Merson P 7 3 · Nicholas C 28 4 · O'Leary D 39 · Quinn N 35 8 · Rix G 18 2 · Robson S 5 · Rocastle D 36 2 · Sansom K 35 · Thomas M 11 · Williams S 34 2 · Wilmot R 6 · Own goals 1 · Total: 19 players (58)

Position in League Table

	P	W	L	D	F:A	Pts	
Everton	42	26	8	8	76:31	86	1st
Arsenal	42	20	12	10	58:35	70	4th

SEASON 1987-88 FOOTBALL LEAGUE (DIVISION 1)

Date	Opponent		Res	Score	Lukic	Thomas	Sansom	Williams	O'Leary	Adams	Rocastle	Davis	Smith	Nicholas	Hayes	Substitutes
15 Aug	Liverpool	H	L	1-2	Lukic	Thomas	Sansom	Williams	O'Leary	Adams	Rocastle	Davis	Smith	Nicholas	Hayes	Groves for Rocastle
19 Aug	Manchester U	A	D	0-0	..	..	..	..	..	..	..	..	..	..	..	Groves for Nicholas
22 Aug	Q P R	A	L	0-2	..	..	..	..	..	..	..	..	..	..	..	Rix for Rocastle
29 Aug	Portsmouth	H	W	6-0	..	..	..	..	..¹	..¹	..	..¹	..³	Groves	Rix	Merson for Groves/Richardson for Rix
31 Aug	Luton T	A	D	1-1	..	..	..	..	..	..	..	..¹	..	..	..	–
12 Sep	Nottingham F	A	W	1-0	..	..	..	..	..	..	..	..¹	..	..	..	Hayes for Rocastle
19 Sep	Wimbledon	H	W	3-0	..	..¹	..	..	..	..	..¹	..¹	..	..	..	Merson and Richardson for Groves and Williams
26 Sep	West Ham U	H	W	1-0	..	..	..¹	..	..	..	..	..	..	..	..	Hayes for Rocastle
3 Oct	Charlton A	A	W	3-0	..	..¹	..	..	..	..¹	..	..	..	..¹	..	Hayes for Rocastle
10 Oct	Oxford U	H	W	2-0	..	..	..	..¹	..	..	..	..¹	..	..	Richardson	Hayes and Caesar for Rocastle and Smith
18 Oct	Tottenham H	A	W	2-1	..	..¹	..	..	..	..	..	..¹	..	..	..	Hayes for Groves
24 Oct	Derby C	H	W	2-1	..	..¹	..	..	..	..	..	..	..	..	..¹	Merson for Groves
31 Oct	Newcastle U	A	W	1-0	..	..	..	..	..	..	..	..¹	..	..	..	Caesar and Hayes for Williams and Adams
3 Nov	Chelsea	H	W	3-1	..	..	..°°	..	..	..	..	..	..	..¹	..²	–
14 Nov	Norwich C	A	W	4-2	..	..¹	..	..	..	..	..²	..	..	..¹	..	Caesar for Adams
21 Nov	Southampton	H	L	0-1	..	..	..	..	..	..	..	..	..	..	..	Quinn for Groves, Winterburn for Quinn
28 Nov	Watford	A	L	0-2	..	..	..	..	..	..	..	..	..	..	..	Hayes for Richardson
5 Dec	Sheffield W	H	W	3-1	..	..	..	..	..	..	..	Hayes	..	..¹	..¹	Merson¹ for Davis
13 Dec	Coventry C	A	D	0-0	..	..	..	..	..	..	..	Davis	..	..	..	Merson for Hayes
19 Dec	Everton	H	D	1-1	..	..	..	..	..	..	..¹	..	..	..	..	Merson for Richardson
26 Dec	Nottingham F	H	L	0-2	..	..	..	..	..	..	..	..	..	Merson	Quinn	Smith and Caesar for Merson and O'Leary
28 Dec	Wimbledon	A	L	1-3	..	..	..	..	Caesar	..	..	Hayes	..¹	..	..	Smith for Hayes
1 Jan	Portsmouth	A	D	1-1	..	..	Winterburn	..	..	..	..	Hayes	Smith¹	..	..	Smith¹ and Merson for Quinn and Groves
2 Jan	Q P R	H	D	0-0	..	Winterburn	Sansom	..	..	..	..	..	Smith	Merson	..	Groves for Merson
16 Jan	Liverpool	A	L	0-2	..	..	..	..	..	..	..	..	..	Quinn	..	Thomas and Groves for Caesar and Rocastle
24 Jan	Manchester U	H	L	1-2	..	Thomas	Winterburn	..	O'Leary	..	..	Rix	..	..¹	..	Groves for Rix
13 Feb	Luton T	H	W	2-1	..	Dixon	..	Thomas¹	..	..	..	Hayes	..	..	..	Caesar for Adams
27 Feb	Charlton A	H	W	4-0	..	Winterburn	Sansom	..¹	Caesar	..	..	..¹	..	Merson²	..	Davis and Quinn for Merson and Richardson
6 Mar	Tottenham H	H	W	2-1	..	..	..	..	..	..	..	..	..¹	Groves¹	..	–
19 Mar	Newcastle U	H	D	1-1	..	Dixon	Winterburn	..	..	..	..	Davis	..¹	..	Hayes	Quinn for Smith
26 Mar	Derby Co	A	D	0-0	..	..	..	..	..	..	..	..	..	..	..	Richards and Quinn for Rocastle and Smith
30 Mar	Oxford U	A	D	0-0	..	Winterburn	Sansom	..	..	..	..	..	..	..	Marwood	Merson and Quinn for Rocastle and Marwood

Date	Opp	V	R	Score	1	2	3	4	5	6	7	8	9	10	11	Subs/Notes
2 Apr	Chelsea	A	D	1-1	..	Dixon	Winterburn	Williams	..	..	..°g	..	Quinn	..	Hayes	-
4 Apr	Norwich C	H	W	2-0	..	Winterburn	Sansom	..	..	..	..	Smith1	..1	..	..	Merson for Groves
9 Apr	Southampton	A	L	2-4	..	..	..	..	Thomas	..	..1	..	..°g.	..	Merson	Richardson / Rix for Richardson
12 Apr	West Ham U	A	W	1-0	..	..	..	Thomas1	Adams	..	..	..	..	Merson	Richardson	Hayes for Richardson
15 Apr	Watford	H	L	0-1	..	..	..	..	..	..	..	..	..1	..	..	Hayes for Richardson
30 Apr	Sheffield W	A	D	3-3	..	..	..	..	..	..	..	..	..1	..2	Marwood	Richardson and Hayes for Davis and Winterburn
2 May	Coventry C	H	D	1-1	..	Dixon	..	..	..	..	..	..	..	..	..1	Hayes and Groves for Merson and Richardson
7 May	Everton	A	W	2-1	..	..	..	..1	..	..	..	..	Hayes1	..		Rix and Campbell for Caesar and Hayes

FA Cup

Date	Opp	V	R	Score	1	2	3	4	5	6	7	8	9	10	11	Subs/Notes
9 Jan	Millwall (3)	H	W	2-0	Lukic	Winterburn	Sansom	Williams	O'Leary	Adams	Rocastle1	Hayes1	Smith	Merson	Richardson	Groves for Merson
30 Jan	Brighton (4)	A	W	2-1	..	..	..	..	..	..	..	Rix	Groves1	Quinn	..1	Hayes for Rix
20 Feb	Manchester U (5)	H	W	2-1	..	..	..	Thomas	..	..°g	..	Hayes	Smith1	Groves	..	Rix for O'Leary
12 Mar	Nottingham F (6)	H	L	1-2	..	..	..	..	..	..	..1	..	..	..	..	Davis and Quinn for O'Leary and Hayes

Football League (Littlewoods) Cup

Date	Opp	V	R	Score	1	2	3	4	5	6	7	8	9	10	11	Subs/Notes
23 Sep	Doncaster (2)	A	W	3-0	Lukic	Thomas	Sansom	Williams1	O'Leary	Adams	Rocastle	Davis	Smith1	Groves1	Rix	Richardson and Quinn for Groves and Rix
6 Oct	Doncaster (2)	H	W	1-0	..	..	..	..	Caesar	..	..	..	..	..	Hayes	-
27 Oct	Bournemouth (3)	H	W	3-0	..	..1	..	..	O'Leary	..	..	..	..1	..	Richardson1	Merson for Groves
17 Nov	Stoke C (4)	H	W	3-0	..	..	..	..	..	..	..1	..	..	..	..1	Hayes for Groves
20 Jan	Sheffield W (5)	A	W	1-0	..	Winterburn1	..	..	..	..	..	Rix	..	Quinn	..	Groves for Quinn
7 Feb	Everton (SF)	A	W	1-0	..	..	..	Thomas	..	..	..	Hayes	..	Groves1	..	Caesar and Quinn for Rocastle and Smith
24 Feb	Everton (SF)	H	W	3-1	..	..	..	..1	..	..	..1	..	..1	..	..	Davis for O'Leary
24 Apr	Luton (F) (at Wembley)		L	2-3	..	..	..	..	Caesar	..	..	Davis	..1	..	..	Hayes1 for Groves

Appearances League only (Goals)

Lukic 40 · Rocastle 40 (7) · Adams39 (2) · Smith 39 (11) · Thomas 37 (9) · Groves 34 (6) · Sansom 34 (1) · Richardson 29 (4) · Williams 29 (1) · Davis 29 (5) Hayes 27 (1) · O'Leary 23 · Caesar 22 · Winterburn 17 · Merson 15 (5) · Quinn 11 (2) · Rix 10 · Dixon 6 · Marwood 4 (1) · Nicholas 3 · Campbell 1 · Own goals 3 · Total:21 players (58)

Position in League Table

	P	W	L	D	F:A	Pts	
Liverpool	40	26	2	12	87:24	90	1st
Arsenal	40	18	10	12	58:39	66	6th

SEASON 1988-89 FOOTBALL LEAGUE (DIVISION 1)

Date	Opp	V	R	Score	1	2	3	4	5	6	7	8	9	10	11	Subs/Notes
27 Aug	Wimbledon	A	W	5-1	Lukic	Dixon	Winterburn	Thomas	Bould	Adams	Rocastle	Davis	Smith3	Merson1	Marwood1	-
3 Sep	Aston Villa	H	L	2-3	..	..	..	..	O'Leary	..	..	..	..1	..	..1	Groves for Rocastle
10 Sep	Tottenham H	A	W	3-2	..	..	..1	..	..	..	..	..	..1	..	..1	Groves/Richardson for Rocastle/Marwood
17 Sep	Southampton	H	D	2-2	..	..	..	..	..	..	..	..	..1	..	..1	Hayes/Richardson for Davis/Merson
24 Sep	Sheffield W	A	L	1-2	..	..	..	..	..	..	..	..	..1	..	..	Groves for Merson
1 Oct	West Ham U	A	W	4-1	..	..	..	..1	Bould	..	..1	..	..2	Groves	..	Hayes for Groves
22 Oct	Q P R	H	W	2-1	..	..	..	..	..	..	..1	Richardson	..1	Merson	..	Groves for Merson
25 Oct	Luton T	A	D	1-1	..	..	..	..	..	..	..	..	..	..	..	
29 Oct	Coventry C	H	W	2-0	..	..	..	..1	..	..1	..	..	..	..	..	Groves/Hayes for Rocastle/Merson
6 Nov	Nottingham F	A	W	4-1	..	..	..	..1	..1	..	..	..1	..	..1	Hayes for Merson
12 Nov	Newcastle U	A	W	1-0	..	..	..	..1	..	..	..	..	..	Hayes	..	Merson for Rocastle
19 Nov	Middlesbrough	H	W	3-0	..	..	..	..	..	..1	..	..	..	Merson2	..	Hayes for Marwood
26 Nov	Derby Co	A	L	1-2	..	..	..	..1	..	..	..	..	..	..	Hayes	Groves for Richardson
4 Dec	Liverpool	H	D	1-1	..	..	..	..	..	..	..	..	..1	..	Marwood	Hayes for Marwood
10 Dec	Norwich C	A	D	0-0	..	..	..	..	..	..	..	..	..	..	..	Hayes for Marwood
17 Dec	Manchester U	H	W	2-1	..	..	..	..1	..	..	..	..	..	..1	..	
26 Dec	Charlton A	A	W	3-2	..	O'Leary	..	..	..	..	..	..	..1	..1	..2	
31 Dec	Aston Villa	A	W	3-0	..	..	..	..	..	..	..1	..	..1	..	..	Grovesi for Merson
2 Jan	Tottenham H	H	W	2-0	..	..	..	..1	..	..	..	..	..1	..	Davis/Groves for Richardson/Marwood
14 Jan	Everton	A	W	3-1	..	Dixon	..	Davis	O'Leary	Caesar	..	..1	..1	..1	..	Groves/Thomas for Merson/Marwood
21 Jan	Sheffield W	H	D	1-1	..	..	..	..	..	..	..	..	..	..1	..	Groves/Thomas for Caesar/Rocastle
4 Feb	West Ham U	H	W	2-1	..	..	Thomas	..	Adams	..	..	..1	..	Groves1	Bould/Hayes for O'Leary/Merson
11 Feb	Millwall	A	W	2-1	..	..	..	..	..	..	..	..1	..	Marwood1	Bould for O'Leary
18 Feb	Q P R	A	D	0-0	..	..	..	..	..	..	..	..	..	Bould/Hayes for Dixon/Merson
21 Feb	Coventry C	A	L	0-1	..	Bould	..	..	..	..	..	..	..	Hayes for Marwood
25 Feb	Luton T	H	W	2-0	..	..	..	..	..	..	..	..1	Groves1	..	Merson for Rocastle
28 Feb	Millwall	H	D	0-0	..	..	..	..	..	..	..	..	..	Merson/Dixon for Rocastle/Richardson
11 Mar	Nottingham F	H	L	1-3	Lukic	..	..	..	..	..	..	..1	..	Merson/Dixon for Bould/Groves
21 Mar	Charlton A	H	D	2-2	..	Dixon	..	Davis1	..	..	..1	..	Merson	Groves/Thomas for Richardson/Merson
25 Mar	Southampton	A	W	3-1	..	..	..	..	..	..1	..	Groves1	..	Merson1 for Groves
2 Apr	Manchester U	A	D	1-1	..	..	..	..	..1	..	..	Bould	Thomas/Merson for Davis/Marwood
8 Apr	Everton	H	W	2-0	..	..1	..	Thomas	..	..	..	Quinn1	..	Merson for Marwood
15 Apr	Newcastle U	H	W	1-0	..	..	..	..	..	..	..	..1	Merson/Groves for O'Leary/Rocastle
1 May	Norwich C	H	W	5-0	..	..	..1	..1	..	..	..1	..	Smith2	..	Merson	Quinn/Hayes for Bould/Merson
6 May	Middlesbrough	A	W	1-0	..	..	..	..	..	..	..	..	Hayes1 for Merson
13 May	Derby Co	A	L	1-2	..	..	..	..	..	..	..	..1	..	Hayes/Groves for Bould/Merson
17 May	Wimbledon	H	D	2-2	..	..	..1	..	..	..	..	..1	..	Groves/Hayes for Bould/Merson
26 May	Liverpool	A	W	2-0	..	..	..1	..	..	..	..	..1	..	Groves/Hayes for Bould/Merson

FA Cup

Date	Opp	V	R	Score	1	2	3	4	5	6	7	8	9	10	11	Subs/Notes
8 Jan	West Ham U (3)	A	D	2-2	Lukic	O'Leary	Winterburn	Thomas	Bould	Adams	Rocastle	Richardson	Smith	Merson2	Marwood	Davis and Groves for Bould and Marwood
11 Jan	West Ham U (3R)	H	L	0-1	..	Dixon	..	..	O'Leary	..	..	..	..	Davis and Groves for Rocastle and Marwood

Football League (Littlewoods) Cup

28 Sep	Hull C (2)	A	W	2-1	Lukic	Dixon	Winterburn[1]	Thomas	Bould	Adams	Rocastle	Davis	Smith	Groves	Marwood[1]	Hayes and Richardson for Groves and Rocastle
12 Oct	Hull C (2)	H	W	3-0	..	..	..	..	..	..	..	..	..[2]	Merson[1]	..	Hayes and Richardson for Davis and Marwood
2 Nov	Liverpool (3)	A	D	1-1	..	..	..	..	..	..	..[1]	Richardson	..	..	..	Groves for Merson
9 Nov	Liverpool (3R)	H	D	0-0	..	..	..	..	..	..	..	..	..	..	..	Hayes for Merson
23 Nov	Liverpool (3R2)	A	L	1-2	..	..	..	..	..	..	..	..	..	..[1]	..	Hayes for Marwood

Appearances League Only (Goals)

Lukic 38 · Rocastle 38 (6) · Winterburn 38 (3) · Thomas 37 (7) · Merson 37 (9) · Adams 36 (4) · Smith 36 (24) · Richardson 34 (1) · Dixon 33 (1) · Marwood 31 (9) · Bould 30 (2) · O'Leary 26 · Groves 21 (4) · Hayes 17 (1) · Davis 12 (1) · Quinn 3 (1) · Caesar 2 · Total: 17 players (73)

Position in League Table

	P	W	L	D	F:A	Pts	
Arsenal	38	22	6	10	73:36	76	1st

SEASON 1989-90 FOOTBALL LEAGUE (DIVISION 1)

19 Aug	Manchester U	A	L	1-4	Lukic	Dixon	Winterburn	Thomas	O'Leary	Adams	Rocastle[1]	Richardson	Smith	Merson	Marwood	Caesar/Groves for Adams/Merson
22 Aug	Coventry C	H	W	2-0	..	..	..	..[1]	..	..	..	..	..	..	..[1]	Groves for Rocastle
26 Aug	Wimbledon	H	D	0-0	..	..	..	..	..	..	..	..	..	..	..	Groves for Merson
09 Sep	Sheffield W	H	W	5-0	..	..	..	..[1]	..	..[1]	..	..	..[1]	..[1]	..[1]	
16 Sep	Nottingham F	A	W	2-1	..	..	..	..	..	..	..	..	..	..[1]	..[1]	Groves for Merson
23 Sep	Charlton A	H	W	1-0	..	..	..	..	..	..	..	..	..	..	..[1p]	Groves for Rocastle
30 Sep	Chelsea	A	D	0-0	..	..	..	..	..	..	..	..	..	Groves	Hayes	Merson for Rocastle
14 Oct	Manchester C	H	W	4-0	..	..	..	..[1]	..	..	..	..	..	..[2]	Marwood	Jonsson/Merson[1] for Richardson/Marwood
18 Oct	Tottenham H	A	L	1-2	..	..	..	..[1]	..	..	..	..	..	..	Hayes	Jonsson/Merson for Richardson/Smith
21 Oct	Everton	A	L	0-3	..	..	..	..	..	..	..	..	Quinn	Merson	..	Smith for Hayes
28 Oct	Derby Co	H	D	1-1	..	..	..	..	..	..	..	..	Smith[1]	Quinn	Merson	Jonsson/Campbell for Winterburn/Quinn
4 Nov	Norwich C	H	W	4-3	..	..[2,1p]	..	..	..[1]	..	..	..	..	..[1]	..	Groves for Merson
11 Nov	Millwall	A	W	2-1	..	..	..	..[1]	..	..	..	..	..	..[1]	Marwood	Groves for Quinn
18 Nov	Q P R	H	W	3-0	..	..[1p]	..	..	..	..	..	..	..[1]	..	..	Groves/Jonsson1 for Rocastle/Marwood
26 Nov	Liverpool	A	L	1-2	..	..	..	..	..	..	..	..	..[1]	..	Groves	Hayes/Jonsson for Quinn/O'Leary
3 Dec	Manchester U	H	W	1-0	..	..	..	..	..	..	..	..	..	Groves[1]	Marwood	Merson for Marwood
9 Dec	Coventry C	A	W	1-0	..	..	..	..	..	..	..	..	..	..	..	Merson[1] for Marwood
16 Dec	Luton T	H	W	3-2	..	..	..	..	..	..	..	..	..[1]	..	..[1]	Merson[1]/Jonsson for Smith/Groves
26 Dec	Southampton	A	L	0-1	..	..	..	..	..	..	..	..	..	Merson	..	Davis/Groves for Marwood/Merson
30 Dec	Aston Villa	A	L	1-2	..	..	..	..[1]	Groves	..	..	Bould	Merson		Rocastle for Bould
1 Jan	Crystal Palace	H	W	4-1	..	..[1]	..	..	..[1]	..	..	..[2]	..	..		Rocastle/Davis for Smith/Winterburn
13 Jan	Wimbledon	A	L	0-1	..	..	..	Davis	..	..	..	..	..	..		Caesar/Rocastle for O'Leary/Smith
20 Jan	Tottenham H	H	W	1-0	..	..	Davis	Thomas	..	..[1]	Rocastle	..	..	..	Groves	
17 Feb	Sheffield W	A	L	0-1	..	..	Pates	Davis	..	..	..	..	..	..	Merson	Caesar/Campbell for Pates/Richardson
27 Feb	Charlton A	A	D	0-0	..	..	Winterburn	Thomas	Bould	..	..	..	..	Merson	Marwood	Campbell for Marwood
3 Mar	Q P R	A	L	0-2	..	..	..	..	..	..	..	..	..	..	Groves	O'Leary/Campbell for Thomas/Smith
7 Mar	Nottingham F	H	W	3-0	..	..	..	..	..	..[1]	..	..	..	..	..[1]	Campbell[1]/O'Leary for Merson/Groves
10 Mar	Manchester C	A	D	1-1	..	..	..	..	..	..	..	..	..	Campbell	Marwood[1]	Hayes for Rocastle
17 Mar	Chelsea	H	L	0-1	..	..	..	..	..	..	..	..	..	..	Groves	Hayes/O'Leary for Rocastle/Campbell
24 Mar	Derby Co	A	W	3-1	..	..	..	..	..	..	Hayes2	..	..	..[1]	..	O'Leary/Ampadu for Bould/Campbell
31 Mar	Everton	H	W	1-0	..	..	..	..	..	..	..	..	..[1]	..	..	O'Leary/Ampadu for Richardson/Campbell
11 Apr	Aston Villa	H	L	0-1	..	..	..	..	..	..	..	O'Leary	..	..	..	Merson for Hayes
14 Apr	Crystal Palace	A	D	1-1	..	..	..	..	..	..	..[1]	..	..	..	..	Davis/Merson for Bould/Campbell
18 Apr	Liverpool	H	D	1-1	..	..	..	..	..	..	Davis	..	..	Merson[1]	..	Campbell/Pates for Groves/Bould
21 Apr	Luton T	A	L	0-2	..	..	..	..	..	..	..	..	..	..	Campbell	Hayes/Rocastle for O'Leary/Merson
28 Apr	Millwall	H	W	2-0	..	..	..	..	..	..	Rocastle	Davis[1]	..	..[1]	Marwood	Campbell/Richardson for Marwood/Thomas
2 May	Southampton	H	W	2-1	..	..[1p]	..	..	..	..	Richardson	..	..	..	..	Rocastle[1]/Groves for Richardson/Marwood
5 May	Norwich C	A	D	2-2	..	..	..	Hayes	..	..	Rocastle	..	..[2]	Campbell	Groves	O'Leary/Thomas for Bould/Davis

FA Cup

6 Jan	Stoke C (3)	A	W	1-0	Lukic	Dixon	Davis	Thomas	O'Leary	Adams	Quinn[1]	Richardson	Groves	Bould	Merson	Jonsson/Rocastle for Thomas/Merson
27 Jan	Q P R (4)	H	D	0-0	..	..	Winterburn	Davis	..	..	Rocastle	..	Smith	..	Groves	Thomas/Merson for Davis/Bould
31 Jan	Q P R (4R)	A	L	0-2	..	..	..	Thomas	..	..	..	..	..	..	..	Merson for Groves

Football League (Littlewoods) Cup

19 Sep	Plymouth (2)	H	W	2-0	Lukic	Dixon og	Winterburn	Thomas	O'Leary	Adams	Rocastle	Richardson	Smith[1]	Bould	Groves	Merson for Groves
3 Oct	Plymouth (2)	A	W	6-1	..	opponents	..	..[3]	..	..	..	..	..[1]	Groves[1]	Hayes	Caesar/Merson for Dixon/Groves
25 Oct	Liverpool (3)	H	W	1-0	..	..	..	..	..	..	..	..	Quinn	Merson	..	Smith1 for Hayes
22 Nov	Oldham (4)	A	L	1-3	..	..	..	..	..	..	..	..	Smith	Quinn[1]	Jonsson	Groves for Jonsson

FA Charity Shield

12 Aug	Liverpool (at Wembley)		L	0-1	Lukic	Dixon	Winterburn	Thomas	O'Leary	Adams	Rocastle	Richardson	Smith	Caesar	Merson	Marwood/Quinn for Caesar/Smith

Appearances (Goals)

Lukic 38 · Dixon 38 (5) · Adams 38 (5) · Smith 38 (10) · Winterburn 36 · Thomas 36 (5) · O'Leary 34 (1) · Richardson 33 · Rocastle 33 (2) · Groves 30 (4) · Merson 29 (7) · Bould 19 · Marwood 17 (6) · Campbell 15 (2) · Hayes 12 (3) · Davis 11 (1) · Quinn 6 (2) · Jonsson 6 (1) · Caesar 3 · Pates 2 (2) · Total: 19 players (54)

Position in League Table

	P	W	D	L	F:A	Pts	
Liverpool	38	23	10	5	78:37	79	1st
Arsenal	38	18	8	12	54:38	62	4th

SEASON 1990-91 FOOTBALL LEAGUE (DIVISION 1)

Date	Opponent		Res	Score	Seaman	Dixon	Winterburn	Thomas	Bould	Adams	Rocastle	Davis	Smith[1]	Merson[1]	Limpar	Substitutions
25 Aug	Wimbledon	A	W	3-0	Seaman	Dixon	Winterburn	Thomas	Bould	Adams	Rocastle	Davis	Smith[1]	Merson[1]	Limpar	Groves1 for Limpar
29 Aug	Luton T	H	W	2-1	..	..	..	..[1]	..	..	..	..	..	..[1]	..	Groves for Limpar
1 Sep	Tottenham H	H	D	0-0	..	..	..	..	..	..	..	..	..	..	..	Groves for Merson
8 Sep	Everton	A	D	1-1	..	..	..	..	..	..	..	..	..	..	..	Groves1 for Smith
15 Sep	Chelsea	H	W	4-1	..	..[1p]	..	..	..	..	..[1]	..	Groves	..[1]	..[1]	Campbell/Linighan for Groves/Bould
22 Sep	Nottingham F	A	W	2-0	..	..	..	..	..	..	..[1]	..	..	..	..[1]	Smith for Rocastle
29 Sep	Leeds U	A	D	2-2	..	..	..	Jonsson	..	..	..	..	Smith	..	..[2]	Hillier/Groves for Winterburn/Merson
6 Oct	Norwich C	H	W	2-0	..	..	..	..	..	..	..	..[2]	..	..	..	Hillier/Groves for Limpar/Merson
20 Oct	Manchester U	A	W	1-0	..	..	..	Thomas	..	..	..	..	..	..	..[1]	Groves for Rocastle
27 Oct	Sunderland	H	W	1-0	..	..[1p]	..	..	..	..	..	..	..	..	..	Groves for Rocastle
3 Nov	Coventry C	A	W	2-0	..	..	..	..	..	..	Groves	..	..	..	..[2]	Campbell/O'Leary for Smith/Groves
10 Nov	Crystal Palace	A	D	0-0	..	..	..	..	..	..	O'Leary	..	Campbell	..	..	Groves/Smith for Merson/Limpar
17 Nov	Southampton	H	W	4-0	..	..	..	..	..	..	Groves	..	Smith[2]	..[1]	..[1]	O'Leary/Campbell for Dixon/Groves
24 Nov	Q P R	A	W	3-1	..	..	..	..	..	..	..	..	..[1]	..[1]	..	Campbell1/O'Leary for Groves/Adams
2 Dec	Liverpool	H	W	3-0	..	..[1p]	..	..	..	..	O'Leary	..	..[1]	..[1]	..	
8 Dec	Luton T	A	D	1-1	..	..	..	..	..	..	..	..	..[1]	..	..	Groves for Limpar
15 Dec	Wimbledon	H	D	2-2	..	..	..	..	..	..	Groves	..	..	..[1]	..	O'Leary for Winterburn
23 Dec	Aston Villa	A	D	0-0	..	..	..	..	..	Linighan	..	..	..	..	..	Rocastle for Limpar
26 Dec	Derby Co	H	W	3-0	..	..	..	..	..	..	Rocastle	..	..[2]	..[1]	..	Campbell/O'Leary for Rocastle/Limpar
29 Dec	Sheffield U	H	W	4-1	..	..[1p]	..	..[1]	..	..	Groves	..	..[2]	..	..	Cole/O'Leary for Groves/Winterburn
1 Jan	Manchester C	A	W	1-0	..	..	..	..	..	..	O'Leary	..	..[1]	..	..	Hillier/Groves for O'Leary/Limpar
12 Jan	Tottenham H	A	D	0-0	..	..	..	..	..	..	..	..	..	..	..	Hillier/Groves for Davis/Merson
19 Jan	Everton	H	W	1-0	..	..	..	..	..	..	Groves	..	..	..[1]	..	Campbell/Hillier for Limpar/Bould
2 Feb	Chelsea	A	L	1-2	..	..	..	..	..	Linighan	Groves	..	..[1]	..	..	Hillier/Campbell for Bould/Limpar
23 Feb	Crystal Palace	H	W	4-0	..	..	..	..	..	..	O'Leary[1]	..	..[1]	..[1]	Campbell[1]	Pates/Rocastle for Linighan/Merson
3 Mar	Liverpool	A	W	1-0	..	..	..	..	..	Adams	..	Hillier	..[1]	..	..	Rocastle/Davis for Campbell/Adams
17 Mar	Leeds U	H	W	2-0	..	..	..	..	..	..	..	..	..	..	..[2]	
20 Mar	Nottingham F	H	D	1-1	..	..	..	..	..	..	..	Davis	..	..	..[1]	Groves/Limpar for Davis/Merson
23 Mar	Norwich C	A	D	0-0	..	..	..	Rocastle	..	..	..	..	..	Campbell	Limpar	Groves/Linighan for Limpar/Rocastle
30 Mar	Derby Co	A	W	2-0	..	..	..	Campbell	..	..	Rocastle	..	..[2]	Merson	..	Groves/Hillier for Limpar/Rocastle
3 Apr	Aston Villa	H	W	5-0	..	..	..	Hillier	..	..	Campbell[2]	..[1]	..[2]	..	..	Thomas/Groves for Hillier/Merson
6 Apr	Sheffield U	A	W	2-0	..	..	..	..	..	..	..[1]	..	..[1]	..	..	Groves/Thomas for Merson/Limpar
9 Apr	Southampton	A	D	1-1	..	opponents	..	..	..	..	..	..	..	Groves	..	Thomas/Merson for Hillier/Limpar
17 Apr	Manchester C	H	D	2-2	..	..	..	Thomas	..	..	..[1]	..	..	..	Merson[1]	Groves Limpar/O'Leary for Merson/Dixon
23 Apr	Q P R	H	W	2-0	..	..[1p]	..	Hillier	..	..	..	..	..	..[1]	Limpar	O'Leary/Groves for Merson/Limpar
4 May	Sunderland	A	D	0-0	..	..	..	..	..	..	..	..	..	..	Groves	O'Leary for Groves
6 May	Manchester U	H	W	3-1	..	..	..	..	..	..	..	..	..[3,1p]	..	Limpar	Thomas/O'Leary for Hillier/Limpar
11 May	Coventry C	H	W	6-1	..	opponents	..	..	..	..	..	..	..[1]	..	..[3]	Linighan/Groves1 for Merson/Campbell

FA Cup

Date	Opponent		Res	Score	Seaman	Dixon	Winterburn	Thomas	Bould	Adams	Rocastle	Davis	Smith	Merson	Limpar	Substitutions
5 Jan	Sunderland (3)	H	W	2-1	Seaman	Dixon	Winterburn	Thomas	Bould	Linighan	Groves	Davis	Smith[1]	Merson	Limpar[1]	O'Leary for Limpar
27 Jan	Leeds U (4)	H	D	0-0	..	..	..	..	..	Groves	O'Leary	..	..	..	..	Hillier/Campbell for O'Leary/Limpar
30 Jan	Leeds U (4R)	A	D	1-1*	..	..	..	..	..	Linighan	Hillier	..	..	..	..[1]	
13 Feb	Leeds U (4R/2)	H	D	0-0*	..	..	..	..	..	Groves	O'Leary	..	..	..	..	Campbell/Linighan for Groves/Limpar
16 Feb	Leeds U (4R/3)	A	W	2-1	..	..[1]	..	..	..	Linighan	..	..	..	..[1]	Campbell	
27 Feb	Shrewsbury T (5)	A	W	1-0	..	..	..	..[1]	..	Adams	..	Hillier	..	..	..	Rocastle for Merson
9 Mar	Cambridge U (6)	H	W	2-1	..	..	..	..[1]	..	..[1]	..	..	..	..	..[1]	Davis for Hillier
14 Apr	Tottenham H (S/F) (at Wembley) *after extra time		L	1-3	..	..	..	..	..	Campbell	Davis	..[1]	..	Limpar	Groves for Limpar

Football League (Rumbelows) Cup

Date	Opponent		Res	Score	Seaman	Dixon	Winterburn	Hillier	Bould	Adams	Rocastle	Davis	Smith	Merson[1]	Groves	Substitutions
25 Sep	Chester (2)	A	W	1-0	Seaman	Dixon	Winterburn	Hillier	Bould	Adams	Rocastle	Davis	Smith	Merson[1]	Groves	Cambell for Rocastle
9 Oct	Chester (2)	H	W	5-0	..	..	..	..[1]	..	..	..[1]	..	..	..[1]	..[2]	Campbell/O'Leary for Rocastle/Bould
30 Oct	Manchester C (3)	A	W	2-1	..	..	..	Thomas	..	..[1]	Groves1	..	..	..	Limpar	Campbell for Limpar
28 Nov	Manchester U (4)	H	L	2-6	..	..	..	..	..	..	..	..	..[2]	..	..	Campbell for Limpar

Appearances (Goals)

Bould 38 (5) · Dixon 38 (5) · Seaman 38 · Winterburn 38 · Davis 37 (13) · Merson 37 (13) · Smith 37 (22) · Limpar 34 (11) · Groves 32 (3) · Thomas 31 (2) · Adams 30 (1) · Campbell 22 (9) · O'Leary 21 (1) · Rocastle 16 (2) · Hillier 16 · Linighan 10 · Jonsson 2 · Cole 1 · Pates 1 · Own goals 2 · Total: 19 players (86)

Position in League Table

	P	W	D	L	F:A	Pts
Arsenal	38	24	13	1	74:18	83**	1st

**two points deducted

SEASON 1991-92 FOOTBALL LEAGUE (DIVISION 1)

Date	Opponent		Res	Score	Seaman	Dixon	Winterburn	Hillier	O'Leary	Adams	Campbell	Davis	Smith	Merson[1]	Limpar	Substitutions
17 Aug	Q P R	H	D	1-1	Seaman	Dixon	Winterburn	Hillier	O'Leary	Adams	Campbell	Davis	Smith	Merson[1]	Limpar	Rocastle/Groves for O'Leary/Campbell
20 Aug	Everton	A	L	1-3	..	..	..[1]	..	..	..	Rocastle	..	..	..	..	Groves/Linighan for Limpar/Hillier
24 Aug	Aston Villa	A	L	1-3	..	..	..	Linighan	..	..	..	..	..[1]	..	..	Groves/Thomas for O'Leary/Rocastle
27 Aug	Luton T	H	W	2-0	..	..	..	Thomas	Linighan	..	..	..	..[1]	..[1]	..	
31 Aug	Manchester C	H	W	2-1	..	..	..	..	..	..	..	..	..[1]	..	..[1]	Campbell/Pates for Rocastle/Limpar
3 Sep	Leeds U	A	D	2-2	..	..	..	..	..	..	O'Leary	..	..[2]	..	Campbell	Rocastle for Thomas
7 Sep	Coventry C	H	L	1-2	..	..	..	Campbell	..	..[1]	Rocastle	..	..	..	Limpar	O'Leary/Thomas for Limpar/Davis
14 Sep	Crystal Palace	A	W	4-1	..	..	..	Hillier	..	..	..	Groves	..[1]	..	Campbell[2]	Thomas[1]/O'Leary for Groves/Hillier

1991-92 continued

Date	Opponent	Result	1	2	3	4	5	6	7	8	9	10	11	Substitutions
21 Sep	Sheffield U	H W 5-2	..	..[1]	..	Campbell[1]	..	..	..[1]	Davis	..[1]	..	Groves[1]	O'Leary/Thomas for Winterburn/Groves
28 Sep	Southampton	A W 4-0	..	..	..	Thomas	..	..	..[1]	Wright[3]	..	..	Limpar	Campbell for Merson
5 Oct	Chelsea	H W 3-2	..	..[1p]	..	..	..	Pates	..	..[1]	..	Campbell[1]	..	Merson/O'Leary for Limpar/Wright
19 Oct	Manchester U	A D 1-1	..	..	..	Davis	Pates	Adams	..[1]	..	..	Merson	Campbell	
26 Oct	Notts Co	H W 2-0	..	..	..	..	..	..	..[1]	..	..	..	..	Limpar for Campbell
2 Nov	West Ham	H L 0-1	..	..	..	Thomas	..	Linighan	..	..	..	..	Limpar	Groves for Thomas
16 Nov	Oldham	A D 1-1	..	..	..	Hillier	Bould	..	..[1]	..	..	..	Pates	O'Leary/Groves for Bould/Pates
23 Nov	Sheffield W	A D 1-1	..	..	..	..[1]	..	..	..	..	..	..	..	O'Leary for Hillier
1 Dec	Tottenham H	H W 2-0	..	..	..	..	..	..	..[1]	..	..	..	Campbell[1]	Limpar/O'Leary for Wright/Rocastle
8 Dec	Nottingham F	A L 2-3	..	..	..	..	..	..	..	Campbell	..[1]	..[1]	Limpar	Carter/O'Leary for Limpar/Bould
21 Dec	Everton	H W 4-2	..	..	..	..	..	Adams	..	Wright[4]	..	..	..	O'Leary/Campbell for Rocastle/Merson
26 Dec	Luton T	A L 0-1	..	..	..	O'Leary	..	..	..	..	..	..	..	Campbell for Limpar
28 Dec	Manchester C	A L 0-1	..	..	..	..	..	..	..	..	..	..	Davis	Linighan/Groves for Bould/O'Leary
1 Jan	Wimbledon	H D 1-1	..	..	..	Hillier	Linighan	..	..	..	..	..[1]	Carter	Campbell for Wright
11 Jan	Aston Villa	H D 0-0	..	..	..	..	O'Leary	..	..	Campbell	..	..	..	Groves for Merson
18 Jan	Q P R	A D 0-0	..	..	..	Davis	..	..	..	Wright	..	..	..	
29 Jan	Liverpool	A L 0-2	..	..	..	Parlour	..	..	..	..	..	..	..	Bould/Groves for O'Leary/Parlour
1 Feb	Manchester U	H D 1-1	..	..	..	Hillier	Bould	..	..[1]	..	..	..	..	Pates/Limpar for Rocastle/Carter
8 Feb	Notts Co	A W 1-0	..	..	..	..	..	Pates	..	..[1]	..	..	Groves	Parlour/Campbell for Winterburn/Groves
11 Feb	Norwich C	H D 1-1	..	..	..	..	..	..	..	..	..	..[1]	Limpar	Campbell/Parlour for Limpar/Winterburn
15 Feb	Sheffield W	H W 7-1	..	..	..	..	..	..	Rocastle	..[1]	..[1]	..[1]	..[2]	Campbell[2] for Smith
22 Feb	Tottenham H	A D 1-1	..	..	..	..	..	Pates	..	..[1]	..	..	Campbell	O'Leary/Limpar for Hillier/Rocastle
10 Mar	Oldham	H W 2-1	..	..	..	..	..	Adams	..	..[1]	..	..[1]	Limpar	O'Leary for Limpar
14 Mar	West Ham U	A W 2-0	..	..	..	..	..	..	..	..[2]	..	..	Groves	Campbell/O'Leary for Smith/Groves
22 Mar	Leeds U	H D 1-1	..	..	..	..	..	..	..	O'Leary	..[1]	..	Campbell	Parlour/Limpar for Hillier/Rocastle
28 Mar	Wimbledon	A W 3-1	..	..	..	..	..	..	Parlour[1]	..[1]	Campbell[1]	..	Groves	Limpar/Lydersen for Groves/Merson
31 Mar	Nottingham F	H D 3-3	..	..[1p]	..	..	..	..	..[1]	Rocastle	..	..[1]	Limpar	Lydersen/Smith for Rocastle/Wright
4 Apr	Coventry C	A W 1-0	..	..	..	..	..	..	Lydersen	..[1]	..	..	..	Rocastle/Smith for Winterburn/Limpar
8 Apr	Norwich C	A W 3-1	..	O'Leary	Lydersen	..	..	..	Rocastle	..[2.1p]	..[1]	..	..	Morrow/Smith for O'Leary/Limpar
11 Apr	Crystal Palace	H W 4-1	..	Lydersen	Winterburn	..	..	..	..	..	..[1]	..[3]	..	Smith/Morrow for Limpar/Winterburn
18 Apr	Sheffield U	A D 1-1	..	..	..	..	..	..	..	Campbell[1]	Smith	..	..	Heaney for Limpar
20 Apr	Liverpool	H W 4-0	..	..	..	..[1]	..	..	..	Wright[2]	Campbell	..	..[1]	O'Leary for Lydersen
25 Apr	Chelsea	A D 1-1	..	Dixon[1]	..	..	..	..	..	..	..	..	..	Smith/Merson for Limpar/O'Leary
2 May	Southampton	H W 5-1	..	..	..	..	..	..	..	..[3.1p]	..[1]	..	..	Smith[1]/Parlour for Limpar/Merson

FA Cup

Date	Opponent	Result	1	2	3	4	5	6	7	8	9	10	11	Substitutions
4 Jan	Wrexham (3)	A L 1-2	Seaman	Dixon	Winterburn	Hillier	O'Leary	Adams	Rocastle	Campbell	Smith[1]	Merson	Carter	Groves for Campbell

Football League (Rumbelows) Cup

Date	Opponent	Result	1	2	3	4	5	6	7	8	9	10	11	Substitutions
25 Sep	Leicester C (2)	A D 1-1	Seaman	Dixon	Thomas	Campbell	Linighan	Adams	Rocastle	Davis	Wright[1]	Merson	Groves	O'Leary for Linighan
8 Oct	Leicester C (2)	H W 2-0	..	..	Winterburn	Thomas	Pates	..	..	Wright[1]	Smith	..[1]	Campbell	Groves for Writht
30 Oct	Coventry C (3)	A L 0-1	..	..	..	Davis	..	..	..	..	..	..	Limpar	Groves/Linighan for Limpar/Pates

FA Charity Shield

Date	Opponent	Result	1	2	3	4	5	6	7	8	9	10	11	Substitutions
18 Aug	Tottenham H (at Wembley)	D 0-0	Seaman	Dixon	Winterburn	Hillier	O'Leary	Adams	Rocastle	Davis	Smith	Merson	Campbell	Thomas/Cole for Rocastle/Campbell

European Cup

Date	Opponent	Result	1	2	3	4	5	6	7	8	9	10	11	Substitutions
18 Sept	FK Austria (1)	H W 6-1	Seaman	Dixon	Winterburn	Campbell	Linighan[1]	Adams	Rocastle	Davis	Smith[4]	Merson	Limpar	Groves for Limpar
2 Oct	FK Austria (1)	A L 0-1	..	..	..	Thomas	..	..	..	Campbell	..	..	O'Leary	Groves for Merson
23 Oct	Benfica (2)	A D 1-1	..	..	..	Davis	Pates	..	..	..[1]	..	..	Limpar	Groves/Thomas for Campbell/Limpar
6 Nov	Benifica (2)	H L 1-3*	..	..	..	..	..	..	..[1]	..	..	..	..	

*after extra time

Appearances (Goals)

Seaman 42 · Merson 42 (12) · Winterburn 41 (1) · Rocastle 39 (4) · Smith 39 (2) · Dixon 38 (5) · Adams 35 (2) · Campbell 31 (13) · Wright 30 (24) · Limpar 29 (4) · Hillier 27 (1) · Bould 25 (1) · O'Leary 25 · Linighan 17 · Groves 13 (1) · Davis 12 · Pates 11 · Thomas 10 (1) · Carter 6 · Parlour 6 (1) · Morrow (2) · Heaney 1 · Total 22 players (71)

Position in League Table

	P	W	D	L	F:A	Pts	
Leeds U	42	22	16	4	74:37	82	1st
Arsenal	42	19	15	8	81:46	72	4th

SEASON 1992-93 FOOTBALL LEAGUE (DIVISION 1)

1992-93

Date	Opponent	Result	1	2	3	4	5	6	7	8	9	10	11	Substitutions
15 Aug	Norwich C	H L 2-4	Seaman	Dixon	Winterburn	Hiller	Bould1	Adams	Jensen	Smith	Campbell[1]	Merson	Limpar	Wright for Merson
18 Aug	Blackburn Rov	A L 0-1	..	..	..	..	..	..	..	..	..	Carter	..	Pates/Groves for Jensen/Limpar
23 Aug	Liverpool	A W 2-0	..	..	..	..	Pates	..	..	Wright[1]	..	Parlour	..[1]	Merson for Limpar
26 Aug	Oldham	A W 2-0	..	..	..[1]	..	Bould	..	Parlour	..[1]	..	Merson	Morrow	Pates/Smith for Merson/Wright
29 Aug	Sheffield W	H W 2-1	..	..	..	..	..	..	Jensen	..	..	..[1]	Parlour[1]	Smith for Merson
2 Sep	Q P R	A D 0-0	..	..	..	..	..	..	..	..	..	..	..	Pates/Smith for Hillier/Merson
5 Sep	Wimbledon	A L 2-3	..	..	..	Pates	..	..	..	..[2]	..	..	..	O'Leary/Smith for Jensen/Adams
12 Sep	Blackburn Rov	H L 0-1	..	..	..	Selley	..	..	..	..	Smith	..	..	Campbell/Morrow for Parlour/Jensen
19 Sep	Sheffield U	A D 1-1	..	..	..	Parlour	..	..	..	..[1]	..	..	Limpar	Linighan/Flatts for Merson/Limpar
28 Sep	Manchester C	H W 1-0	..	..	..	Hillier	..	..	..	..[1]	..	..	Campbell	Limpar for Smith
3 Oct	Chelsea	H W 2-1	..	..	..	..	..	..	..	..[1]	..	..[1]	..	Limpar for Merson
17 Oct	Nottingham F	A W 1-0	..	..	..	..	..	..	..	..	..	..[1]	..	Limpar/Pates for Wright/Jensen
24 Oct	Everton	H W 2-0	..	..	..	..	..	..	..	..[1]	..	..	..	Pates/Limpar[1] for Dixon/Wright
2 Nov	Crystal P	A W 2-1	..	..	Morrow	..	..	..	..	..[1]	..[1]	..	..	Limpar for Wright
7 Nov	Coventry C	H W 3-0	..	..	..	..	..	..	..	..[1]	..[1]	..[1]	..[1]	Limpar for Campbell
21 Nov	Leeds U	A L 0-3	..	..	..	..	..	..	..	..	Campbell	..	Limpar	Parlour/Miller for Hillier/Seaman

28 Nov	Manchester U	H L	0-1	..	..	..	..	..	..	..	..	..	..	..	..	Parlour/Flatts for Jensen/Limpar
5 Dec	Southampton	A L	0-2	..	..	..	..	..	..	Parlour	..	..	..	..	Flatts	Jensen/Limpar for Dixon/Flatts
12 Dec	Tottenham H	A L	0-1	..	Lydersen	Winterburn	..	..	..	Jensen	..	..	..	..	Parlour	Limpar for Jensen
19 Dec	Middlesbrough	H D	1-1	..	..	..	..	Linighan	..	Flatts	..[1]	Smith	..	..	..	Jensen/Campbell for Merson/Parlour
26 Dec	Ipswich T	H D	0-0	..	..	..	..	Bould	Linighan	Jensen	..	..	..	Campbell	Flatts	O'Leary Limpar for Jensen/Campbell
28 Dec	Aston Villa	A L	0-1	..	..	..	..	..	..	O'Leary	..	..	..	..	Parlour	Flatts/Limpar for Parlour/Hillier
9 Jan	Sheffield U	H D	1-1	..	Dixon	..	..[1]	Linighan	Adams	Jensen	..	..	..	Merson	Limpar	O'Leary for Merson
16 Jan	Manchester C	A W	1-0	..	..	..	..	Bould	..	..	Campbell	..	..[1]	Flatts		
31 Jan	Liverpool	H L	0-1	..	..	..	..	Linighan	..	Carter	..	..	..	..	Parlour	O'Leary/Heaney for Hiller/O'Leary
10 Feb	Wimbledon	H L	0-1	..	Keown	..	..	..	..	Selley	Wright	..	..	Campbell		Carter/Morrow for Merson/Smith
20 Feb	Oldham A	A W	1-0	..	..	Morrow	..	..[1]	..	Jensen	Selley	Campbell	..	Limpar		Carter for Limpar
24 Feb	Leeds U	H D	0-0	..	..	Winterburn	..	..	..	Selley	Wright	Smith	..	..		Campbell for Limpar
1 Mar	Chelsea	A L	0-1	..	Dixon	Morrow	..	..	Keown	Jensen	Campbell	..	..	..	Flatts	Lydersen/Carter for Hillier/Campbell
3 Mar	Norwich C	A D	1-1	..	..	Winterburn	Davis	..	..	..	Wright1	Parlour	Carter	Limpar		Campbell for Limpar
13 Mar	Coventry C	A W	2-0	..	..	Keown	..	..	Adams	Parlour	..[1]	Campbell[1]	Merson	Morrow		Limpar/Hillier for Wright/Merson
20 Mar	Southampton	H W	4-3	..	Keown	Winterburn	..	..[1]	..	Carter[2]	Morrow	..	..[1]	Limpar		Hillier/Dickov for Davis/Limpar
24 Mar	Manchester U	A D	0-0	..	Dixon	Keown	Morrow	..	..	Jensen	Wright	..	..	Carter		Parlour/Hillier for Carter/Adams
6 Apr	Middlesbrough	A L	0-1	..	O'Leary	Winterburn	Hillier	..	..	..	..	Smith	Carter	Limpar		Morrow/Keown for Hillier/O'Leary
10 Apr	Ipswich T	A W	2-1	..	..	..	Morrow	..	Keown	..	Campbell	..[1]	Merson[1]	Carter		Adams/Parlour for O'Leary/Jensen
12 Apr	Aston Villa	H L	0-1	..	Dixon	..	Selley	Keown	Adams	Morrow	Wright	..	..	Campbell		Parlour/Linighan for Wright/Campbell
21 Apr	Nottingham F	H D	1-1	..	..	..	..	Linighan	Keown	Jensen	..[1]	..	Parlour	Carter		Adams/Campbell for Winterburn/Parlour
1 May	Everton	A D	0-0	..	O'Leary	Lydersen	Davis	..	Bould	Keown	Selley	..	Campbell	..		Jensen/Heaney for Lydersen/Carter
4 May	Q P R	H D	0-0	Miller	Dixon	Keown	..	..	Adams	Jensen	Campbell	..	Merson	Heaney		Carter for Merson
6 May	Sheffield W	A L	0-1	..	Lydersen	..	Marshall	O'Leary	Bould	..	Selley	..	Heaney	Carter		McGowan/Flatts for Jensen/Lydersen
8 May	Crystal P	H W	3-0	Seaman	Dixon	Winterburn	Davis	Linighan	Adams	Carter	Wright1	Campbell[1]	Merson	Parlour		Dickov[1]/O'Leary for Carter/Wright
11 May	Tottenham H	H L	1-3	Miller	Lydersen	Keown	Marshall	O'Leary	Bould	Flatts	Selley	Smith	Dickov[1]	Heaney		McGowan/Carter for Lydersen/Flatts

FA Cup

2 Jan	Yeovil T (3)	A W	3-1	Seaman	Dixon	Winterburn	Hillier	Bould	Adams	O'Leary	Wright[3]	Smith	Merson	Limpar	
25 Jan	Leeds U (4)	H D	2-2	..	..	..	..	Linighan	..	Jensen	Campbell	..	..[1]	Parlour[1]	Carter for Jensen
3 Feb	Leeds U (4R)	A W	3-2*	..	..	..	Selley	..	..	Morrow	Wright[2]	..[1]	..	..	Campbell/O'Leary for Parlour/Winterburn
13 Feb	Nottingham F (5)	H W	2-0	..	..	..	Hillier	..	..	Jensen	..[2]	Selley	..	Limpar	Campbell/Morrow for Wright/Limpar
6 Mar	Ipswich T (6)	A W	4-2	..	Opponents	..	Davis	..	..[1]	Carter	..[1p]	Smith	..	Morrow	Hillier/Campbell1 for Carter/Smith
4 Apr	Tottenham H (SF)	W	1-0	..	..	..	Hillier	..	..[1]	Parlour	..	Campbell	..	Selley	Smith/Morrow for Wright/Campbell
	(at Wembley)															
15 May	Sheffield W (F)	D	1-1*	..	..	..	Davis	..	..	Jensen	..[1]	..	..	Parlour	Smith/O'Leary for Parlour/Wright
	(at Wembley)															
20 May	Sheffield W (FR)	W	2-1*	..	..	..	..	..[1]	..	..	..[1]	Smith	..	Campbell	O'Leary for Wright
	(at Wembley)															

*after extra time

Football League (Coca-Cola) Cup

22 Sep	Millwall (2)	H D	1-1	Seaman	Dixon	Winterburn	Hillier	Bould	Adams	Parlour	Wright	Smith	Merson	Limpar	Campbell[1] for Limpar
7 Oct	Millwall (2)	A D	1-1*	..	..	..	..	..	..	Jensen	..	..	..	Campbell[1]	Parlour for Merson
	*(won 3-1 on penalties)															
28 Oct	Derby Co (3)	A D	1-1	..	Lydersen	Morrow	..	..	..	..	Campbell[1]	..	..	Limpar	
1 Dec	Derby Co (3R)	H W	2-1	..	Dixon	..	..	..	..	Parlour	Wright[1]	Campbell[1]	..	Flatts	
6 Jan	Scarborough (4)	A W	1-0	..	..	Winterburn[1]	..	..	..	O'Leary	..	Smith	..	Limpar	Campbell for Merson
12 Jan	Nottingham F (5)	H W	2-0	..	..	..	..	Linighan	..	Jensen	..[2]	..	..	..	Campbell for Limpar
7 Feb	Crystal P (SF)	A W	3-1	..	..	..	..	..	..	Selley	..[1p]	..[2]	..	Campbell	Morrow for Wright
10 Mar	Crystal P (SF)	H W	2-0	..	..	..	Davis	..[1]	..	Carter	..[1]	..	..	Morrow	Hillier/Campbell for Winterburn/Smith
18 Apr	Sheffield W (F)	W	2-1	..	O'Leary	..	Morrow[1]	..	..	Campbell	..	Davis	..[1]	Parlour	
	(at Wembley)															

Appearances (Goals)

Seaman 39 · Campbell 37 (4) · Adams 35 · Merson 33 (6) · Jensen 32 · Wright 31 (15) · Smith 31 (3) · Hillier 30 (1) · Dixon 29 · Winterburn 29 (1) · Bould 24 (1) · Limpar 23 (2) · Linighan 21 (2) · Parlour 21 (1) · Morrow 16 · Carter 16 (2) · Keown 16 · O'Leary 11 · Flatts 10 · Selley 9 · Lydersen 8 · Pates 7 · Davis 6 · Heaney 5 · Miller 4 · Dickov 3 · 2 · Marshall 2 · McGowan 2 · Groves 1 · Total:29 players (40)

Position in League Table

	P	W	D	L	F:A	Pts	
Manchester U	42	24	12	6	67:31	84	1st
Arsenal	42	15	11	16	40:38	56	10th

1993-94

SEASON 1993-94 FA CARLING PREMIERSHIP

14 Aug	Coventry C	H L	0-3	Seaman	Dixon	Winterburn	Davis	Linighan	Adams	Jensen	Wright	Campbell	Merson	Limpar	McGoldrick/Keown for Jensen/Dixon
16 Aug	Tottenham H	A W	1-0	..	Keown	..	..	..	..	..	..[1]	..	McGoldrick	Parlour	
21 Aug	Sheffield W	A W	1-0	..	..	..	..	..	..	..	..[1]	..	McGoldrick	Parlour	Merson for Parlour
24 Aug	Leeds U	H W	2-1	..	Opponents	..	Hillier	..	Selley	Merson[1]	..	..	McGoldrick	Parlour	Hillier for Davis
28 Aug	Everton	H W	2-0	..	..	..	..	..	Adams	Jensen	..[2]	..	..	..	Merson for Hillier
1 Sep	Blackburn Rov	A D	1-1	..	..	..	Merson	..	..	..	..	..[1]	..	..	Selley for Merson
11 Sep	Ipswich T	H W	4-0	..	..	..	Davis	..	..	..	..[1]	..[3]	Merson	McGoldrick	Hillier/Limpar for Jensen/Merson
19 Sep	Manchester U	A L	0-1	..	..	..	Hillier	..	..	..	..	..	..	..	Davis/Smith for Hillier/Merson
25 Sep	Southampton	H W	1-0	..	..	..	Davis	..	..	..	..	..	..[1]	..	Hillier for Davis
2 Oct	Liverpool	A D	0-0	..	Dixon	..	..	..	..	..	..	..	..	..	
16 Oct	Manchester C	H D	0-0	..	..	..	..	..	..	Heaney	..	Smith	Parlour	..	Campbell for Heaney
23 Oct	Oldham A	A D	0-0	..	..	..	..	..	..	Hillier	..	..	Merson	..	Campbell for Hillier
30 Oct	Norwich C	H D	0-0	..	..	..	..	Bould	..	Jensen	..	..	..	Limpar	Keown/Campbell for Winterburn/Smith
6 Nov	Aston Villa	H L	1-2	..	..	..	Selley	Keown	..	..	..[1]	Campbell	Merson	Limpar	
20 Nov	Chelsea	A W	2-0	..	..	..	Davis	Linighan	Bould	Keown	..[1p]	Smith[1]	..	Selley	Morrow for Winterburn
24 Nov	West Ham U	A D	0-0	..	..	..	Keown	..	..	Morrow	..	..	..	Limpar	Campbell/Miller for Limpar/Wright
27 Nov	Newcastle	H W	2-1	..	..	..	Morrow	Keown	..	Jensen	..[1]	..[1]	..	McGoldrick	
4 Dec	Coventry C	A L	0-1	..	..	..	Davis	..	Adams	Selley	..	..	..	..	Bould/Campbell for Adams/McGoldrick
6 Dec	Tottenham H	H D	1-1	..	..	Keown	Selley	Bould	..	Jensen	..[1]	..	..	Limpar	Campbell for Smith
12 Dec	Sheffield W	H W	1-0	Miller	..	Morrow	..	Keown	..	..	..[1]	..	..	..	Bould/Campbell for Keown/Merson

233

1993-94 League (continued)

Date	Opponent	V	Res	Sc	1	2	3	4	5	6	7	8	9	10	11	Substitutes
18 Dec	Leeds U	A	L	1-2	Seaman	..	Winterburn	..	Bould	..	..	..	..	Campbell[1]	..	Parlour/Morrow for Smith/Dixon
27 Dec	Swindon T	A	W	4-0	..	..	..	Parlour	..	..	..	..[1]	Campbell[3]	Hillier	McGoldrick	Merson/Keown for Parlour/Adams
29 Dec	Sheffield U	H	W	3-0	..	..	..	..	..	..	..	..[1]	..[2]	..	..	Merson/Keown for Wright/Parlour
1 Jan	Wimbledon	A	W	3-0	..	..	..	..[1]	..	..	..	..[1]	..[1]	..	..	Keown/Merson for Dixon/Jensen
3 Jan	QPR	H	D	0-0	..	..	..	..	..	..	..	..	..	..	..	Keown for Jensen
15 Jan	Manchester C	A	D	0-0	..	..	..	..	..	..	..	..	..	..	..	Merson/Keown for McGoldrick/Jensen
22 Jan	Oldham A	H	D	1-1	..	..	..	..	..	..	..	..[1p]	..	..	..	Merson/Keown for McGoldrick/Jensen
13 Feb	Norwich C	A	D	1-1	..	..	Davis	..	..	..	Campbell[1]	Smith	Merson	Parlour		
19 Feb	Everton	A	D	1-1	..	..	..	..	..	..	..[1]	..				Keown/Hillier for Adams/Jensen
26 Feb	Blackburn Rov	H	W	1-0	..	..	..	..	..	..	..[1]	..				
5 Mar	Ipswich T	A	W	5-1	..	opponents	..	Selley	..	..	Parlour[1]	Wright[3,1p]	..	Hillier	Limpar	Merson/Keown for Limpar/Hillier
19 Mar	Southampton	A	W	4-0	..	..	opponents	..	Keown	Linighan	..	..	..[3,1p]	Campbell[1]	Selley	Smith for Limpar
22 Mar	Manchester U	H	D	2-2	..	opponents	..	Davis	Bould	..	Jensen	..	Smith	Merson[1]	Selley	Campbell for Davis
26 Mar	Liverpool	H	W	1-0	..	..	Keown	Parlour	..	Linighan	..	Campbell	..[1]			Morrow/Smith for Jensen/Wright
2 Apr	Swindon T	H	D	1-1	..	..	..	Davis	Linighan	Adams	..	..	Smith[1]	..	Parlour	Campbell/McGoldrick for Merson/Jensen
4 Apr	Sheffield U	A	D	1-1	..	Keown	Winterburn	Parlour	Bould	..	Campbell[1]	..	..	Selley	McGoldrick	Dixon/Merson for Keown/McGoldrick
16 Apr	Chelsea	H	W	1-0	..	Dixon	Morrow	Hillier	Keown	..	Selley	..[1]	Campbell	Parlour	..	Smith for Hillier
19 Apr	Wimbledon	H	D	1-1	..	..	Keown	Davis	Bould[1]	..	Campbell	..	Smith	..	Selley	Flatts for Davis
23 Apr	Aston Villa	A	W	2-1	..	..	..	..	..	Linighan	..	..[2,1p]	..	Morrow	Flatts	Parlour for Davis
27 Apr	QPR	A	D	1-1	..	..	..	Morrow	Linighan	Adams	Flatts	..	..	Merson[1]	Parlour	Selley/McGoldrick for Flatts/Keown
30 Apr	West Ham U	H	L	0-2	Millier	McGoldrick	Winterburn	Davis	Bould	Linighan	Parlour	..	Campbell	..	Selley	Morrow/Dickov for McGoldrick/Merson
7 May	Newcastle	A	L	0-2	..	Dixon	..	..	..	Adams	McGoldrick	..	Smith	Morrow	Selley	Parlour/Linighan for Davis/Dixon

FA Cup

Date	Opponent	V	Res	Sc	1	2	3	4	5	6	7	8	9	10	11	Substitutes
10 Jan	Millwall (3)	A	W	1-0	Seaman	Dixon	Winterburn	Parlour	Bould	Adams[1]	Keown	Wright	Campbell	Hillier	McGoldrick	Merson/Jensen for Wright/Hillier
31 Jan	Bolton W (4)*	A	D	2-2	..	..	..	..	..	..[1]	..	..[1]	..		Merson	Smith for Parlour
9 Feb	Bolton W (4R)	H	L	1-3*	..	..	..	Hillier	..	..	Campbell	..	Smith[1]	Merson	Parlour	Keown/McGoldrick for Hillier/Wright

*aet

Football League (Coca-Cola) Cup

Date	Opponent	V	Res	Sc	1	2	3	4	5	6	7	8	9	10	11	Substitutes
21 Sep	Huddersfield T (2)	A	W	5-0	Seaman	Keown	Winterburn	Davis	Linighan	Adams	Jensen	Wright[3]	Campbell1	Merson[1]	McGoldrick	Hillier/Smith for Jensen/Merson
5 Oct	Huddersfield (2)	H	D	1-1	..	Dixon	..	Parlour	..	Bould	..	Smith[1]	..	Limpar	..	Selley/Heaney for Jensen/McGoldrick
26 Oct	Norwich C (3)	H	D	1-1	..	..	..	..	..	Adams	..	Wright[1]	Smith	Merson	..	Campbell/Davis for Merson/McGoldrick
10 Nov	Norwich C (3R)	A	W	3-0	..	..	Keown	Selley	..	Bould	..	..[2]	..	..[1]	Limpar	
30 Nov	Aston Villa (4)	H	L	0-1	..	..	Winterburn	Morrow	Keown	..	..	..	..	..	McGoldrick	Campbell/Davis for Jensen/Dixon

FA Charity Shield

Date	Opponent	Res	Sc	1	2	3	4	5	6	7	8	9	10	11	Substitutes
7 Aug	Manchester U (at Wembley)	D	1-1	Seaman	Dixon	Winterburn	Davis	Linighan	Adams	Jensen	Wright[1]	Campbell	Merson	Limpar	Keown/McGoldrick for Dixon/Limpar

European Cup Winners' Cup

Date	Opponent	V	Res	Sc	1	2	3	4	5	6	7	8	9	10	11	Substitutes
15 Sep	Odense (1)	A	W	2-1	Seaman	Selley	Winterburn	Davis	Linighan	Keown	Jensen	Wright[1]	Campbell	Merson[1]	McGoldrick	Smith for Wright
29 Sep	Odense(1)	H	D	1-1	..	Dixon	..	..	Keown	Adams	..	..	..[1]	..	..	Smith for Wright
20 Oct	Standard Liege (2)	H	W	3-0	..	..	..	..	..	..	..	..[2]	Smith	..[1]	..	Campbell/Linighan for Wright/Keown
3 Nov	Standard Liege (2)	A	W	7-0	..	..	..	..	..	..[1]	Selley[1]	..[1]	..[1]		Campbell[2]	McGoldrick [1]/Bould for Smith/Keown
2 Mar	Torino (3)	A	D	0-0	..	..	..	..	Bould	..	..	Campbell	..		Hillier	Selley for Davis
15 Mar	Torino (3)	H	W	1-0	..	..	..	..	..	..[1]	..	Wright	..		..	Selley/Keown for Hillier/Jensen
29 Mar	Paris	A	D	1-1	..	..	..	..	..	..	..	..[1]	..		Selley	Keown/Campbell for Davis/Smith St-German (SF)
12 Apr	Paris	H	W	1-0	..	..	..	..	..	..	..	..	..	Campbell[1]	Selley	Hillier/Keown for Davis/Winterburn St-German (SF)
4 May	Parma (F) (at Copenhagen)		W	1-0	..	..	..	..	..	..	Campbell	Morrow	..[1]	Merson	..	McGoldrick for Merson

Appearances (Goals)

Seaman 39 · Wright (39 23) · Campbell 37 (14) · Adams 35 · Winterburn 34 · Dixon 33 · Keown 33 · Merson 33 (7) · Jensen 27 · Parlour 27 (2) · McGoldrick 26 · Bould 25 (1) · Smith 25 (3) · Davis 22 · Linighan 21 · Selley 18 · Hillier 15 · Morrow 11 · Limpar 10 · Miller 4 · Flatts 3 · Dickov 1 · Heaney 1 · Own goals 3 · Total: 23 players (51)

Position in League Table

	P	W	D	L	F:A	Pts	
Manchester U	42	27	11	4	80:38	92	1st
Arsenal	42	18	17	7	53:28	73	4th

SEASON 1994-95 FA CARLING PREMIERSHIP

Date	Opponent	V	Res	Sc	1	2	3	4	5	6	7	8	9	10	11	Substitutes
20 Aug	Manchester C	H	W	3-0*	Seaman	Dixon	Winterburn	Jensen	Bould	Adams	Campbell[1]	Wright[1]	Smith	Merson	Schwarz	Keown/Dickov for Adams/Merson
23 Aug	Leeds U	A	L	0-1	..	..	..	..	..	..	..	..	..	..	..	Keown for Bould
28 Aug	Liverpool	A	L	0-3	..	..	..	Keown	..	..	..	..	..	..	..	Linighan/Davis for Jensen/Merson
31 Aug	Blackburn Rov	H	D	0-0	..	..	..	..	..	..	..	..	..	..	..	Dickov/Linighan for Merson/Adams
10 Sep	Norwich C	A	D	0-0	..	..	..	Selley	..	..	Parlour	..	..	Campbell	McGoldrick	Smith for McGoldrick
18 Sep	Newcastle U	H	L	2-3	..	..	..	Jensen	..	..[1]	..	..[1]	Smith	Merson		Selley/Campbell for Jensen/Parlour
25 Sep	West Ham U	A	W	2-0	..	..	..	Davis	..	..[1]	Selley	..[1]				Linighan for Keown
1 Oct	Crystal P	H	L	1-2	..	..	..	..	Linighan	..[1]						Campbell for Davis
8 Oct	Wimbledon	A	W	3-1	..	..	..	Jensen	Bould	..	Parlour	..[1]	..[1]	Campbell[1]	..	Hillier for Schwarz
15 Oct	Chelsea	H	W	3-1	..	..	..	..	..	..[2]	..	..[1]				Selley/Keown for Jensen/Adams
23 Oct	Coventry C	H	W	2-1	..	..	..	Selley	..	Keown	Campbell	..[2]		Schwarz	Parlour	McGoldrick for Wright
29 Oct	Everton	A	D	1-1	..	McGoldrick	.Jensen	Keown	Adams	Parlour	Campbell	..	Merson	Schwarz	Schwarz[1]	Selley/Linighan for Winterburn/Merson
6 Nov	Sheffield W	H	D	0-0	..	Keown	..	Selley	Bould	..	..	Dickov	..	Campbell	McGoldrick Schwarz	Campbell for Smith
19 Nov	Southampton	A	L	0-1	..	Dixon	..	..	..	..	Keown	..	Campbell	McGoldrick	Schwarz	Carter for McGoldrick
23 Nov	Leicester C	A	L	1-2	..	..	..	..	Linighan	..	Wright1p	Dickov	Carter			Campbell/Morrow for Linighan/Selley
26 Nov	Manchester U	H	D	0-0	..	..	..	Jensen	..	Adams	Morrow	..	Smith	McGoldrick	Carter	Dickov/Keown for Carter/Jensen
3 Dec	Nottingham F	A	D	2-2	Bartram	..	..	Davis[1]	..	Keown[1]	Parlour	Hillier	Campbell	Flatts	Schwarz	Shaw for Flatts
12 Dec	Manchester C	A	W	2-1	..	..	..	Morrow	..	..	Jensen	Campbell	Smith[1]	Parlour	..[1]	

17 Dec	Leeds U	H	L	1-3	..	..	..	..	..	..	..	..	..	..	..	Flatts/Linighan1 for Smith/Jensen
26 Dec	Aston Villa	H	D	0-0	..	..	..	..	..	..	Hughes	Dickov	Campbell	..	..	Flatts for Hughes
28 Dec	Ipswich T	A	W	2-0	..	..	..	Jensen	..	..	Campbell[1]	Wright[1]	Smith	..	..	Linighan/Dickov for Smith/Wright
31 Dec	Q P R	H	L	1-3	..	..	..[1]	..	..	..	..	..	..	..	..	Clarke for Smith
2 Jan	Tottenham H	A	L	0-1	Seaman	..	..	..	..	Linighan	Selley	..	Campbell	..	..	Smith for Selley
14 Jan	Everton	H	D	1-1	..	..	..	..	Keown	..	Hillier	..[1]	Hartson	..	..	Kiwomya/Morrow for Parlour/Jensen
21 Jan	Coventry C	A	W	1-0	..	..	Morrow	Keown	Bould	..	Campbell	..	..[1]	Hillier	..	Parlour/Kiwomya for Hillier/Wright
24 Jan	Southampton	H	D	1-1	..	..	..	..	..	..	Jensen	..	..[1]	Parlour	..	Hillier/Kiwomya for Keown/Parlour
4 Feb	Sheffield Wed	A	L	1-3	..	..	Winterburn	Jensen	Linighan[1]	Adams	Selley	Campbell	..	Merson	Kiwomya	Keown/Parlour for Jensen/Selley
11 Feb	Leicester C	H	D	1-1	..	..	..	..	..	..	McGoldrick	Selley	..	..[1]	..	Keown/Parlour for Selley/Jensen
21 Feb	Nottingham F	H	W	1-0	..	..	..	..	Bould	Linighan	..	Merson	Kiwomya[1]	Schwarz	Helder	
25 Feb	Crystal P	A	W	3-0	..	..	..	..	..	..	..	..[1]	..[2]	..	..	Morrow for Winterburn, then Parlour for Morrow
5 Mar	West Ham U	H	L	0-1	Bartram	..	..	..	..	..	Parlour	Wright	Helder	Merson	Schwarz	Morrow/Kiwomya for Jensen/Helder
8 Mar	Blackburn Rov	A	L	1-3	..	..	..	Morrow[1]	Linighan	Adams	..	Helder	Hartson	..	..	Wright/Bould for Hartson/Linighan
19 Mar	Newcastle U	A	L	0-1	..	..	..	Jensen	Bould	..	Morrow	Wright	..	..	Helder	Parlour/McGoldrick for Helder/Hartson
22 Mar	Manchester U	A	L	0-3	..	..	..	Morrow	..	Adams	Keown	..	Kiwomya	Merson	Parlour	Helder for Parlour
1 Apr	Norwich C	H	W	5-1	..	..[1]	..	..	..	opponents	Hillier	..	Hartson[2]	..[1]	Helder	Keown/Kiwomya for Morrow/Hartson
8 Apr	Q P R	A	L	1-3	Seaman	..	..	Schwarz	..	Adams[1]	Morrow	..	..	..	..	Hillier/Kiwomya for Morrow/Hartson
12 Apr	Liverpool	H	L	0-1	Keown	..	..	..	..	..	Hillier	..	McGoldrick	..	..	Parlour/Hartson for Merson/Helder
15 Apr	Ipswich T	H	W	4-1	..	Dixon	..	..	..	..	Keown	..[3]	Hartson	..[1]	..	Parlour/Kiwomya for Winterburn/Wright
17 Apr	Aston Villa	A	W	4-0	..	..	..	..	..	..	..	..[2,1p]	..[2]	..	Parlour	Hillier/Kiwomya for Parlour/Wright
29 Apr	Tottenham H	H	D	1-1	..	..	..	..	..	..	..	..[1p]	..	..	Helder	Parlour for Helder
4 May	Wimbledon	H	D	0-0	..	..	..	Jensen	Linighan	..	Parlour	..	..	..	..	Kiwomya for Hartson
14 May	Chelsea	A	L	1-2	..	..	McGowan	..	Bould	..	..	..	..[1]	..	..	Linighan/Dickov for McGowan/Helder
	*including an own goal															

FA Cup

7 Jan	Millwall (3)	A	D	0-0	Seaman	Dixon	Winterburn	Jensen	Bould	Linighan	Hillier	Wright	Smith	Parlour	Schwarz	Keown/Campbell for Jensen/Smith
18 Jan	Millwall (3R)	H	L	0-2	..	..	..	..	Keown	..	..	..	Campbell	..	Morrow	Adams/Flatts for Keown/Jensen

Football League (Coca-Cola) Cup

21 Sep	Hartlepool U (2)	A	W	5-0	Seaman	Dixon	Keown	Davis	Linighan	Adams[1]	Parlour	Wright[2]	Smith[1]	Merson[1]	Selley	McGoldrick for Smith
5 Oct	Hartlepool U (2)	H	W	2-0	..	..	Winterburn	..	Bould	Keown	..	Dickov[1]	Campbell[1]	Hillier	McGoldrick	
26 Oct	Oldham A(3)	A	D	0-0	..	..	..	Selley	..	Adams	..	Campbell	Smith	Merson	Schwarz	Keown/McGoldrick for Dixon/Campbell
9 Nov	Oldham A (3R)	H	W	2-0	..	Keown	..	..	..	..	..	Dickov[2]	Campbell	McGoldrick	..	Jensen for Selley
30 Nov	Sheffield W (4)	H	W	2-0	..	Dixon	..	Morrow[1]	..	..	Campbell	Wright[1]	Smith	..	..	Bartram/Dickov/Keown for Seaman/Morrow/McGoldrick
11 Jan	Liverpool (QF)	A	L	0-1	..	..	..	Jensen	..	Linighan	Hillier	..	Campbell	Parlour	..	Morrow/Dickov for Bould/Parlour

European Cup Winners' Cup

15 Sep	Omonia Nicosia (1)	A	W	3-1	Seaman	Dixon	Winterburn	Schwarz	Linighan	Keown	Jensen	Wright[1]	Smith	Merson[2]	Parlour	Morrow for Schwarz
29 Sep	Omonia Nicosia (1)	H	W	3-0	..	..	..	..[1]	..	Adams	..	..[2]	..	..	..	Hillier/Campbell for Jensen/Merson
20 Oct	Brondby (2)	A	W	2-1	..	..	..	..	Bould	..	..	..[1]	..[1]	Campbell	..	
3 Nov	Brondby (2)	H	D	2-2	..	..	..	Selley[1]	Keown	..	..	..[1p]	..	Merson	..	Campbell/Bould for Wright/Dixon
2 Mar	Auxerre (3)	H	D	1-1	..	..	..	Schwarz	Bould	..	..	..[1p]	Kiwomya	..	McGoldrick	Hartson/Parlour for McGoldrick/Kiwomya
16 Mar	Auxerre (3)	A	W	1-0	..	..	..	..	..	..	Keown	..[1]	Hartson	..	Parlour	Morrow for Hartson
6 Apr	Sampdoria (SF)	H	W	3-2	..	..	..	..	..[2]	..	Hillier	..[1]	..	..	..	Kiwomya/Morrow for Wright/Merson
20 Apr	Sampdoria (SF)	A	L	2-3*	..	..	..	..[1]	..	..	Keown	..[1]	..	..	Hillier	McGoldrick/Kiwomya for Hillier/Wright
	*Arsenal won 3-2 on penalties after extra time															
10 May (at Paris)	Real Zaragoza (F)		L	1-2*	..	..	..	..	Linighan	..	..	..	..[1]	..	Parlour	Morrow/Hillier for Winterburn/Keown
	*after extra time															

Appearances (Goals)

Winterburn 39 · Dixon 39 (1) · Schwarz 34 (2) · Bould 31 · Wright 31 (18). · Seaman 31 · Keown 31 1 · Parlour 30 · Adams 27 (3) · Merson 24 (4) · Jensen 24 (1) · Campbell 23 (4) · Linighan 20 (2) · Smith 19 (4) · Hartson 15 (7) · Morrow 15 (1) · Kiwomya 14 (3) · Selley 13 · Helder 13 · Bartram 11 · McGoldrick 11 · Hillier 9 · Dickov 9 (4) · Davis 4 (1) · Carter 3 · Flatts 3 · Hughes 1 · Shaw 1 · Clarke 1 · McGowan 1 · own goals 2 · Total:30 players (50)

Position in League Table

	P	W	D	L	F:A	Pts	
Blackburn R.	42	27	8	7	80:39	89	1st
Arsenal	42	13	12	17	52:49	51	12th

1995-96

SEASON 1995-96 FA CARLING PREMIERSHIP

20 Aug	Middlesbrough	H	D	1-1	Seaman	Dixon	Winterburn	Keown	Bould	Adams	Platt	Wright[1]	Merson	Bergkamp	Parlour	Helder for Parlour
23 Aug	Everton	A	W	2-0	..	..	..	..	..	..	..[1]	..[1]	..	..	..	Jensenw for Keown
26 Aug	Coventry C	A	D	0-0	..	..	..	..	..	..	..	..	..	..	..	Jensen/Helder for Dixon/Parlour
29 Aug	Nottm F	H	D	1-1	..	..	..	..	..	..	..[1]	..	..	..	..	Helder for Parlour
10 Sept	Manchester C	A	W	1-0	..	..	..	..	..	..	Jensen	..[1]	..	..	..	McGoldrick for Parlour
16 Sept	West Ham U	H	W	1-0	..	Dixon	..	Jensen	..	..	Parlour	..[1p]	..	..	Helder	
23 Sept	Southampton	H	W	4-2	..	..	..	Keown	..	..[1]	..	..[1]	..	..[2]	..	
30 Sept	Chelsea	A	L	0-1	..	..	..	..	..	..	..	..	..	..	Jensen	Helder/Linighan for Jensen/Keown
14 Oct	Leeds U	A	W	3-0	..	..	..	..	..	..	..	..[1]	..[1]	..[1]	Helder	
21 Oct	Aston Villa	H	W	2-0	..	..	..	..	..	..	..	..[1]	..[1]	..	..	
30 Oct	Bolton W	A	L	0-1	..	..	..	..	..	..	..	..	..	..	..	Platt for Keown
4 Nov	Manchester U	H	W	1-0	..	..	..	..	..	..	Platt	..	..	..[1]	..	Hartson for Wright
18 Nov	Tottenham H	A	L	1-2	..	..	..	..	..	..	..	Hartson	..	..[1]	..	Hillier for Helder
21 Nov	Sheffield W	H	W	4-2	..	..	..	..[1]	..	..	..	..[1]	..	..[1]	..	Dickov[1] for Helder
26 Nov	Blackburn R	H	D	0-0	..	..	..	..	..	..	..	..	..	..	Hillier	Helder/Dickov for Keown/Hartson
2 Dec	Aston Villa	A	D	1-1	..	..	..	Jensen	..	..	..[1]	Wright	..	Hartson	Helder	Morrow/Dickov for Helder/Hartson
9 Dec	Southampton	A	D	0-0	..	..	..	Keown	..	..	..	..	..	..	Jensen	Clarke for Hartson
16 Dec	Chelsea	H	D	1-1	..	..	..[1]	..	..	..	..	..	..	..	..	Helder for Jensen
23 Dec	Liverpool	A	L	1-3	..	..	..	Jensen	Keown	Linighan	..	..[1p]	..	Parlour	..	Marshall/Hartson for Parlour/Helder
26 Dec	Q P R	H	W	3-0	..	..	..	..	Adams	..	..[1]	..	..[2]	Dickov	Clarke	

Date	Opponent	V	R	Score	1	2	3	4	5	6	7	8	9	10	11	Substitutions
30 Dec	Wimbledon	H	L	1-3	..	..	..	..	..	Linighan	..	..¹	..	Bergkamp	..	Parlour/Dickov for Clarke/Jensen
2 Jan	Newcastle U	A	L	0-2	..	..	..	..	Keown	Bould	Adams	..	..	..	Parlour	Dickov/Clarke for Bould/Parlour
13 Jan	Middlesbrough	A	W	3-2	..	..	McGowan	Jensen	Keown	Adams	..¹	..	..¹	..	Helder¹	Dickov for Clarke
20 Jan	Everton	H	L	1-2	..	..	Winterburn	..	Linighan	Marshall	Clarke	..	..¹	..	..¹	Hughes for Jensen
3 Feb	Coventry	H	D	1-1	..	..	..	..	..	..	..	..	..	..¹		
10 Feb	Nottm F	A	W	1-0	..	..	..	..	Keown	Hillier	..	..	..¹			
24 Feb	West Ham U	A	W	1-0	..	..	..	Morrow	..	..	Hartson¹	..	Parlour			Platt for Hillier
2 Mar	Q P R	A	D	1-1	..	..	..	..	..	..	Platt	..	..¹			Rose for Morrow
5 Mar	Manchester C	H	W	3-1	..	..¹	..	Rose	..	..	..²	..				
16 Mar	Wimbledon	A	W	3-0	..	..	..¹	Marshall	..	..	..¹	Wright	..¹	Hartson		
20 Mar	Manchester U	A	L	0-1	..	..	..	..	..	..	..	..	..			Hillier/Helder for Bergkamp/Merson
23 Mar	Newcastle U	H	W	2-0	..	..	..	..	..	..	..¹	..	..			Parlour/Helder for Wright/Winterburn
6 April	Leeds U	H	W	2-1	..	..	..	..	..	..	..²	..	..			Rose/Shaw for Helder/Hartson
8 April	Sheffield W	A	L	0-1	..	..	Helder	..	..	..	..	..				Helder for Merson
15 April	Tottenham H	H	D	0-0	..	..	Winterburn	..	..	..	..	..				Rose/Shaw/Hartson for Morrow/Linighan/Wright
27 April	Blackburn R	A	D	1-1	..	..	..	Morrow	..	..	..¹p	..				
1 May	Liverpool	H	D	0-0	..	..	..	..	Marshall	..	..	Hartson				
5 May	Bolton	H	W	2-1	..	..	..	..	..	..	..¹	Wright	..¹	..		Shaw/Hartson for Marshall/Wright

FA Cup

Date	Opponent	V	R	Score	1	2	3	4	5	6	7	8	9	10	11	Substitutions
6 Jan	Sheffield U (3)	H	D	1-1	Seaman	Dixon	Winterburn	Jensen	Keown	Adams	Clarke	Wright¹	Merson	Hartson	Helder	
17 Jan	Sheffield U (3R)	A	L	0-1	..	..	McGowan	..	..	....	Platt	..	..	Bergkamp	..	Linighan/Clarke for Dixon/Jensen

Football League (Coca Cola) Cup

Date	Opponent	V	R	Score	1	2	3	4	5	6	7	8	9	10	11	Substitutions
19 Sept	Hartlepool (2)	A	W	3-0	Seaman	Dixon	Winterburn	Jensen	Bould	Adams²	Parlour	Wright¹	Merson	Bergkamp	Helder	
3 Oct	Hartlepool (2)	H	W	5-0	..	..	..	Keown	..	..	..³	..	..²	Jensen		Helder/Hartson for Merson/Bergkamp
24 Oct	Barnsley (3)	A	W	3-0	Seaman	..	..	..¹	..	..	Jensen	..	..¹	Helder		Hughes/Hartson for Jensen/Wright
29 Nov	Sheffield W (4)	H	W	2-1	..	..	..	Jensen	..	..	Platt	..¹p	..	Hartson¹		Helder for Bergkamp
10 Jan	Newcastle U (5)	H	W	2-0	..	..	..	Keown	..	..	..	..²	Merson	Helder		Jensen for Bould
14 Feb	Aston Villa (SF)	H	D	2-2	..	..	..	Jensen	Linighan	Keown	Hillier	..²			Parlour for Helder	
21 Feb	Aston Villa (SF)	A	D	0-0 (aet)	..	..	..	Morrow	..	..	Hillier	..	..	Parlour	Platt for Winterburn	

Appearances (Goals)

Seaman 38, · Dixon 38 (2), · Merson 38 (5), · Winterburn 36 (2), · Keown 34, · Bergkamp 33 (11), · Wright 31 (15), · Platt 29 (5), · Helder · 24 (1), · Parlour 22, · Adams 21 (1), · Bould 19, · Hartson 19 (4), · Linighan 18, · Jensen 15, · Marshall 11 (1), · Dickov 7 (1), · Clarke 6, · Hillier 5, · Morrow 4, · Rose 4, · Shaw 3, · McGowan 1, · McGoldrick 1, · Hughes 1 · Total: 25 players (48)

Position in League Table

	P	W	D	L	F:A	Pts	
Manchester U	38	25	7	6	73:35	82	1st
Arsenal	38	17	12	9	49:32	63	5th

SEASON 1996-97 FA CARLING PREMIERSHIP

Date	Opponent	V	R	Score	1	2	3	4	5	6	7	8	9	10	11	Substitutions
17 Aug	West Ham U	H	W	2-0	Seaman	Dixon	Winterburn	..	Bould	Linighan	Parlour	Morrow	Merson	Bergkamp1p	Hartson1	Wright/Dickov for Hartson/Bergkamp
19 Aug	Liverpool	A	L	0-2	..	..	..	..	..	..	..	..	..	..	..	Wright/Helder/Hillier for Bergkamp/Hartson/Morrow
24 Aug	Leicester C	A	W	2-0	..	..	..	..	..	..	..	..	..	..1p	..	Wright¹/Hillier for Bergkamp/Hartson
4 Sept	Chelsea	H	D	3-3	Lukic	..	..	..¹	..	..	..	..	..¹	..	..	Platt/Wright¹ for Bould/Hartson
7 Sept	Aston Villa	A	D	2-2	..	..	..	..	Morrow	..¹	Platt	Wright	..¹	..	Parlour	Hartson/Helder for Morrow/Bergkamp
16 Sept	Sheffield W	H	W	4-1	Seaman	..	..	..	Bould	..	..¹	..3,1p	..	Parlour	Hartson	Vieira for Platt
21 Sept	Middlesbrough	A	W	2-0	..	..	..	..	..	..	..	..1	Vieira	..¹		Adams for Dixon
28 Sept	Sunderland	H	W	2-0	..	..	..	..	Adams	..	..	..	..¹			Parlour¹/Shaw for ../Merson
12 Oct	Blackburn Rov	A	W	2-0	..	..	..	..	..	..	..	..²	..	..		Parlour for Hartson
19 Oct	Coventry C	H	D	0-0	..	..	..	..	..	..	..	..	..	..		Bergkamp for Hartson
26 Oct	Leeds U	H	W	3-0	..	..¹	..	..	..	..	..¹	..	Bergkamp¹	Vieira		Morrow/Garde for ../Wright
2 Nov	Wimbledon	A	D	0-0	..	..	..	..	..	..	..¹	..¹	..	..		Garde for Bergkamp
16 Nov	Manchester U	A	L	0-1	..	..	..	..	..	..	..	..	..	..		
24 Nov	Tottenham H	A	L	3-1	Lukic	..	..	..	..	..	..¹	..1p	..¹	..		Hartson/Parlour for Platt/Bergkamp
30 Nov	Newcastle U	A	W	2-1	..	..¹	..	..	..	..	..¹	..	Hartson			Linighan/Morrow/Parlour for Keown/Hartson/..
4 Dec	Southampton	H	W	3-1	Lukic	..	..	Linighan	..	..	..1p	..¹	..			Shaw¹/Parlour for Platt/Hartson
7 Dec	Derby Co	H	D	2-2	..	..	..	Linighan	..	..¹	..	..¹				Shaw for Linighan
21 Dec	Nottingham F	A	L	1-2	..	McGowan	..	Keown	..	Linighan	..	..¹	..	Bergkamp	Garde	Hartson/Parlour/Morrow for McGowan/Garde/Bergkamp
26 Dec	Sheffield W	A	D	0-0	..	Parlour			Adams							Shaw/Marshall for Keown/Platt
28 Dec	Aston Villa	H	D	2-2	..	..	..	..	..	Garde	..¹	..¹	..	Vieira		Morrow for Garde
1 Jan	Middlesbrough	H	W	2-0	..	..	..	..	..	..	..¹	..¹				Hartson/Morrow/Shaw for Garde/../Bergkamp
11 Jan	Sunderland	A	L	0-1	Seaman	..	..	..	..	..	Platt	Hartson	..			Hughes for ..
19 Jan	Everton	A	W	3-1	..	..	..	..	..	..	..	Wright	..¹	..¹	..¹	Dixon/Hughes for Platt/Wright
29 Jan	West Ham U	A	W	2-1	..	Dixon	..	Rose	..	..	Parlour1	..¹	..	Hughes		Hartson/Marshall/Morrow for Rose/Wright/Hughes
1 Feb	Leeds U	A	D	0-0	..	..	..	Marshall	..	..	..	Hartson	..			Wright for Hartson
15 Feb	Tottenham H	A	D	0-0	Lukic	..	..	Keown	..	..	..	Wright	Bergkamp	..		Hughes for ..
19 Feb	Manchester U	H	L	1-2	..	..	..	..	..	..	..	..	..¹			Hughes for Adams
23 Feb	Wimbledon	H	L	0-1	..	..	..	Garde	..	Marshall	..	..	..			Hughes/Morrow/Shaw for Garde/Bould/Parlour
1 Mar	Everton	A	W	2-0	..	..	..	Keown	Garde	..	Platt	..¹	Hughes	..¹		Morrow for Garde
8 Mar	Nottingham F	H	W	2-0	..	..	..	..	Marshall	Adams	..	Hughes	Merson	..2,1p	..	Morrow for Hughes
15 Mar	Southampton	A	W	2-0	Harper	Parlour	..	..	..	..	Shaw¹	Hughes¹	..			Garde for Shaw
24 Mar	Liverpool	H	L	1-2	Seaman	Dixon	..	..	..	..	Wright¹	..	..			Parlour/Garde/Shaw for Dixon/Marshall/Hughes
5 Apr	Chelsea	A	W	3-0	..	..	..	..	Bould	Garde	..¹	..¹	..	..¹		Parlour/Anelka/Selley for Wright/Hughes/Vieira

1996-97 continued

Date	Opponent				1	2	3	4	5	6	7	8	9	10	11	Substitutes
12 Apr	Leicester C	H	W	2-0	Seaman	..	..	..	..	Adams1	..[1]	..	..	..	..	Parlour for Hughes
19 Apr	Blackburn Rov	H	D	1-1	..	..	..	..	..	..	..[1]	..	..	..	..	Parlour for Hughes
21 Apr	Coventry C	A	D	1-1	..	..	..	..	..	..	..	..[1p]	Merson	..	..	Parlour/Anelka for Dixon/Merson
3 May	Newcastle U	H	L	0-1	..	..	..	..	..	..	..	..	..	..	..	Parlour/Anelka for Adams/Platt
11 May	Derby Co	A	W	3-1	..	..	..	..	..	..	..	..[2]	..	..[1]	..	Anelka/Parlour for Merson/Vieira

Football League (Coca-Cola) Cup

Date	Opponent				1	2	3	4	5	6	7	8	9	10	11	Substitutes
23 Oct	Stoke City (3)	A	D	1-1	Seaman	Dixon	Winterburn	Keown	Bould	Adams	Platt	Wright1	Merson	Bergkamp	Vieira	Hartson for Bergkamp
13 Nov	Stoke City (3R)	H	W	5-2	..	..	..	..	..	..	..[1]	..[2,1p]	..[1]	..[1]	..	Hartson/Morrow for Vieira/Bergkamp
27 Nov	Liverpool (4R)	A	L	2-4	Lukic	..	..	..	..	..	..	..[2p]	..	Hartson	..	Parlour/Morrow for Merson/Winterburn

FA Cup

Date	Opponent				1	2	3	4	5	6	7	8	9	10	11	Substitutes
4 Jan	Sunderland (3)	H	D	1-1	Lukic	Parlour	Winterburn	Keown	Bould	Adams	Morrow	Hartson1	Merson	Bergkamp	Vieira	Shaw for Morrow
15 Jan	Sunderland (3R)	A	W	2-0	Seaman	..	..	..	..	..	Platt	Hughes[1]	..	..[1]	..	
4 Feb	Leeds U (4)	H	L	0-1	..	Dixon	Morrow	..	..	..	Parlour	Wright	..	Hughes	..	Hartson for Hughes

UEFA Cup

Date	Opponent				1	2	3	4	5	6	7	8	9	10	11	Substitutes
10 Sep	Moenchengladbach	H	L	2-3	Seaman	Dixon	Winterburn	Keown	Linighan	Parlour	Platt	Wright[1]	Merson[1]	Bergkamp	Hartson	Helder/Bould for Parlour/Bergkamp
25 Sep	Moenchengladbach	A	L	2-3	..	Linighan	..	..	Bould	Adams	..	..[1]	..[1]	Vieira	..	Parlour/Helder for Linighan/Adams

Appearances (Goals)

Winterburn 38 · Wright 35 (23) · Bould 33 · Keown 33(1) · Dixon 32 (2) · Merson 32(6) · Vieira 31(2) · Parlour 30 (2) · Bergkamp 29 (12) · Adams 28 (3) · Platt 28 (4) · Seaman 22 · Hartson 19 (3) · Lukic 15 · Hughes 14 (1) · Linighan 11 (1) · Garde 11 · Marshall 8 · Morrow 14 · Shaw 8 (2) · Anelka 4 · Helder 2 · Hillier 2 · Dickov 1 · Harper 1 · McGowan 1 · Rose 1 · Selley 1 · Total 28 players (62 goals)

Position in League Table

	P	W	D	L	F:A	Pts	
Manchester U	38	21	12	5	76:44	75	1st
Arsenal	38	19	11	8	62:32	68	3rd

SEASON 1997-98 FA CARLING PREMIERSHIP

Date	Opponent				1	2	3	4	5	6	7	8	9	10	11	Substitutes
9 Aug	Leeds United	A	D	1-1	Seaman	Garde	Bould	Grimandi	Winterburn	Parlour	Vieira	Petit	Overmars	Wright[1]	Bergkamp	Platt/Hughes for Vieira/Overmars
11 Aug	Coventry City	H	W	2-0	..	..	Marshall	..	..	..	..	..	..	..[2]	..	Platt/Hughes for Petit/Overmars
23 Aug	Southampton	A	W	3-1	..	..	Bould	..	..	..	..	..	..[1]	..	..[2]	Platt/Marshall/Boa Morte for Grimandi/Petit/Overmars
27 Aug	Leicester City	A	D	3-3	..	Dixon	..	..	..	..	..	..	..	..	..[3]	Anelka/Platt/Hughes for Parlour/Overmars/Wright
30 Aug	Tottenham Hotspur	H	D	0-0	..	..	..	..	..	..	..	..	..	..	..	Platt/Anelka for Parlour/Petit
13 Sep	Bolton Wanderers	H	W	4-1	..	..	..	..	..	..[1]	..	..	..	..[3]	..	Platt/Boa Morte/Anelka for Parlour/Overmars/Wright
21 Sep	Chelsea	A	W	3-2	..	..	..	Adams	..[1]	..	..	..	..	..	..[2]	Boa Morte/Grimandi for Parlour/Overmars
24 Sep	West Ham United	H	W	4-0	..	..	..	..	..	..	..	..[2]	..[1p]	..[1]	..	Grimandi/Platt/Anelka for Dixon/Winterburn/Wright
27 Sep	Everton	A	D	2-2	..	Grimandi	..	..	..	..	..	..[1]	..[1]	..	..	Boa Morte/Platt/Garde for Parlour/Vieira/Wright
4 Oct	Barnsley	H	W	5-0	..	Dixon	..	..	..	..[1]	..	..[1]	..[2]	..	..	Platt[1]/Anelka/Boa Morte for Parlour/Overmars/Wright
18 Oct	Crystal Palace	A	D	0-0	..	Grimandi	..	..	..	..	Boa Morte	..	..	..	..	Platt/Mendez for Parlour/Boa Morte
26 Oct	Aston Villa	H	D	0-0	..	Dixon	..	..	..	..	..	..	..	..	..	Platt/Anelka for Parlour/Boa Morte
01 Nov	Derby County	A	L	0-3	..	..	..	..	..	..	Platt	..	Anelka			Boa Morte/Wreh for Winterburn/Anelka
9 Nov	Manchester United	H	W	3-2	..	..	Grimandi	..	..	..[1]	Platt[1]	Overmars	..	..[1]		Bould/Wreh for Vieira/Anelka
22 Nov	Sheffield Wednesday	A	L	0-2	..	..	Keown	..	..	Platt	Grimandi	..	..	Mendez		Hughes/Marshall/Wreh for Parlour/Grimandi/Mendez
30 Nov	Liverpool	H	L	0-1	..	..	..	..	Hughes	..	Petit	..	..	Bergkamp		Wreh/Grimandi for Hughes/Petit
6 Dec	Newcastle United	A	W	1-0	..	..	..	..	Parlour	..	..	..	..[1]	..		
13 Dec	Blackburn Rovers	H	L	1-3	..	..	..	..	..	..	..	..[1]	..	..		Vieira/Boa Morte for Parlour/Platt
26 Dec	Leicester City	H	W	2-1	..	..	Bould	Keown	..	Vieira	Platt[1]	..	..	..		Hughes/Anelka for Platt/Wright
28 Dec	Tottenham Hotspur	A	D	1-1	..	..	..	..	..[1]	..	Petit	..	Anelka	..		Grimandi/Hughes/Rankin for Dixon/Anelka/Bergkamp
10 Jan	Leeds United	H	W	2-1	..	..	..	..	..	..	..	..[2]	Wright	..		
17 Jan	Coventry City	A	D	2-2	..	..	..	..	..	..	..	Upson	Anelka[1]	..[1]		Grimandi/Boa Morte for Keown/Anelka
31 Jan	Southampton	H	W	3-0	Manninger	Grimandi	..	Adams[1]	..	..	Hughes	..	Overmars	..[1]	..[1]	Platt/Wreh for Hughes/Anelka
8 Feb	Chelsea	H	W	2-0	..	..	..	..	..	..[2]	..	..	..	..		Dixon/Wright/Platt for Grimandi/Overmars/Anelka
21 Feb	Crystal Palace	H	W	1-0	..	Dixon	Keown	Grimandi[1]	Upson	Venazza	Vieira	Hughes	Boa Morte	Platt		McGowan for Vernazza
2 Mar	West Ham United	A	D	0-0	..	..	..	Adams	..	Hughes	..	Petit	Overmars	..		Winterburn/Boa Morte for Upson/Platt
11 Mar	Wimbledon	A	W	1-0	..	..	..	..	Winterburn	Parlour	..	..	..	Wreh[1]	..	Garde/Hughes/Boa Morte for Parlour/Overmars/Wreh
14 Mar	Manchester United	A	W	1-0	..	..	..	..	..	..	..	..	..[1]	..		Anelka/Garde for Wreh/Parlour
28 Mar	Sheffield Wednesday	H	W	1-0	..	..	..	..	..	..	Hughes	..	..	..[1]		Garde/Anelka/Grimandi for Dixon/Parlour/Wreh
31 Mar	Bolton Wanderers	A	W	1-0	..	Grimandi	..	..	..	..	Petit	..	..[1]	Anelka		Hughes/Bould/Platt for Overmars/Wreh/Anelka
11 Apr	Newcastle United	H	W	3-1	..	Garde	Bould	..	..	..[1]	..	..	Anelka[2]	Wreh		Platt/Hughes/Boa Morte for Overmars/Anelka/Wreh
13 Apr	Blackburn Rovers	A	W	4-1	..	..	..	..	..[2]	..	..	..	..[1]	Bergkamp[1]		Platt/Hughes for Overmars/Anelka
18 Apr	Wimbledon	H	W	5-0	..	..	Upson	..[1]	..	..	..[1]	..[1]	..	..[1]		Dixon/Wreh[1]/Platt for Garde/Vieira/Anelka

Date	Opponent		Res	1	2	3	4	5	6	7	8	9	10	11	Substitutions/Notes
25 Apr	Barnsley	A W	2-0	..	Dixon	Keown	..	..	Platt	..	..	..[1]	..	..[1]	Wreh forAnelka
29 Apr	Derby County	H W	1-0	..	..	..	..	..	Parlour	..	..[1]	..	..	..	Wreh/Platt for Bergkamp/Anelka
3 May	Everton	H W	4-0	..	..	..	..[1]	..	..	..	..	..[2]	..	Wreh	Wright/Bould for Anelka/Wreh
6 May	Liverpool	A L	0-4	Manninger	..	Bould	Upson	Grimandi	..	Platt	Hughes	Boa Morte	Wright	..	Vieira/Mendez/Anelka for Parlour/Wreh/Wright
10 May	Aston Villa	A L	0-1	Seaman	Grimandi	Keown	Adams	..	..	Vieira	Petit	Overmars	..	Anelka	Platt/Wreh for Parlour/Wright

FA Cup

Date	Opponent		Res	1	2	3	4	5	6	7	8	9	10	11	Substitutions/Notes
3 Jan	Port Vale (3)	H D	0-0	Seaman	Grimandi	Keown	Bould	Winterburn	Parlour	Vieira	Petit	Overmars	Anelka	Bergkamp	Hughes/Boa Morte/Wreh for Parlour/Petit/Anelka
24 Jan	Port Vale (3R)	A D	1-1*	..	Dixon	Bould	Keown	..	..	Hughes	..	Wright	..[1]		Grimandi/Anelka/Boa Morte for Vieira/Overmars/Wright
*Won on penalties after extra time															
24 Jan	Middlesbrough (4)	A W	2-1	Manninger	..	..	Adams	..	..[1]	..	Petit	..[1]	Anelka	..	Grimandi for Dixon
15 Feb	Crystal Palace (5)	H D	0-0	..	..	..	Grimandi	..	..	Hughes	..	..	..	..	Vieira/Platt/Wreh for Bould/Hughes/Anelka
25 Feb	Crystal Palace (5R)	A W	2-1	..	..	Keown	Adams	Upson	Boa Morte	Vieira	Platt	Hughes	..[1]	..[1]	Overmars/Crowe for Upson/Bergkamp
8 Mar	West Ham (6)	H D	1-1	..	..	..	..	Winterburn	Parlour	Vieira	Petit	Overmars	..	..[1]	Wreh for Anelka
17 Mar	West Ham (6R)	A D	1-1*	..	..	..	..	..	Garde	..	..	..	..	..[1p]	Hughes/Wreh/Boa Morte for Petit/Overmars/Anelka
*Arsenal won on penalties after extra time															
5 Apr	Wolverhampton (SF) at Aston Villa	W	1-0	Seaman	Grimandi	..	..	..	Parlour	..	..	..	Wreh[1]	..	Bould/Hughes/Platt for Keown/Wreh/Anelka
16 May	Newcastle United (F) at Wembley	W	2-0	..	Dixon	..	..	..	..	..	..	..[1]	..	..[1]	Platt for Wreh

Football League (Coca-Cola) Cup

Date	Opponent		Res	1	2	3	4	5	6	7	8	9	10	11	Substitutions/Notes
14Oct	Birmingham City (3)	H W	4-1 (a.e.t)	Manninger	Dixon	Marshall	Grimandi	Upson	Mendez[1]	Platt[1]	Vernazza	Hughes	Wreh	Boa Morte[2]	Crowe/Muntasser for Dixon/Boa Morte
18 Nov	Coventry City (4)	H W	1-0 (a.e.t)	..	..	Bould	Keown	..	Parlour	..	Mendez	..	Anelka	Bergkamp[1]	Wreh/ Marshall for Mendez/Anelka
6 Jan	West Ham(QF)	A W	2-1	Seaman	Grimandi	Keown	Bould	Winterburn	..	Vieira	Petit	Overmars[1]	Wright[1]	..	Wreh/Hughes for Overmars/Wright
28 Jan	Chelsea (SF)	H W	2-1	Manninger	..	Bould	Adams	..	..	Hughes[1]	..	..[1]	Anelka	..	Platt for Grimandi
18 Feb	Chelsea (SF)	A L	1-3	..	Dixon	Grimandi	..	..	..	Vieira	..	..	..	..[1p]	Platt/Hughes for Winterburn/Parlour

UEFA Cup

Date	Opponent		Res	1	2	3	4	5	6	7	8	9	10	11	Substitutions/Notes
16 Sep	PAOK Salonika (1)	A L	0-1	Seaman	Dixon	Bould	Adams	Winterburn	Parlour	Vieira	Petit	Overmars	Wright	Anelka	Platt/Boa Morte/Wreh for Parlour/Overmars/Anelka
30 Sep	PAOK Salonika (1)	H W	1-1	..	..	..	..	..	..	..	..	..		Bergkamp[1]	Platt/Anelka for Parlour/Overmars

---

Appearances (Goals)

Winterburn 36 (1) · Parlour 34 (5) · Petit 32 (2) · Overmar 32 (12) · Vieira 33 (2) · Seaman 31 · Bergkamp 28 (16) · Dixon 28 · Adams 26 (3) · Wright 24 (11) · Bould 24 · Keown 18 · Anelka 26 (6) · Grimandi 22 (1) · Platt 31 (3) · Hughes 17 (2) · Wreh 16 (3) · Manninger 7 · Garde 10 · Upson 5 · Boa Morte 15 · Marshall 3 · Mendez 3 · Vernazza 1 · Rankin 1 · McGowan 1 · own goals 1 · Total 26 players (67)

Position in League Table

	P	W	D	L	F	A	Pts	
Arsenal	38	23	9	6	68	33	78	1st
Manchester U	38	23	8	7	73	26	77	2nd

Index

Page numbers in italic refer to captions

Adams, Tony 131, 156, 158, 160, 164, 165, 166, 168, 171, 175, 176, 177, 178, *179*, 180, 180, 181, 182, 183, *184*, 186, 187, 188, 192, 194, 196, 197
Aldridge, John 156, 163, 164, 201, 204, 205, *205*, 206, *206*
Allen, Clive 154, *161*
Allen, Paul 150
Allen, Jack *70*, 73, 74
Allen, Gubby 53
Allison, George 10, 17, 25, 31, *40*, 56, 57, 58, 59, 68, 70, 75, 76, 78, 82, 82, *85*, *89*, *92*, 96, 98, 99, 105, 113, *114*, 116, 184, *187*
Alsop, Gilbert 79, 80
Anderson, Bob 104
Anderson, Viv 151, 154, 156, 161
Anelka, Nicolas 195, 196, *196*, 199, 201, 202, 203, 204, 205
Armstrong, George 53, 124, 126, 127, 128, 130, 131, 132, 134, 137, 137, 139, 144, 146, 147, 150
Ashby, Gerald 196
Ashcroft, Jimmy 35, 36, 37
Asprilla, Faustino 180
Astle, Jeff 129
Austin, Dean 175

Bailey, Garry 150, *155*
Baker, Alf 10, *10*, *17*, *19*, *46*, 47, 53, 56, 56, 61, *61*
Baker, Joe 117
Ball, Alan 113, 146, 147, 149
Ball, Peter 158
Banks, Gordon 126, 127, 128, *131*, 132, 136, 147, 206
Barbour, H. 27, *28*
Barclay, Patrick 164
Barnes, John 163, 164
Barnes, Walley 99, 105, *108*, 109, 112,
Barnett, Geoff 119, 144, 147, 148, *148*
Barnett (Watford) 18
Barnwell, John 115
Bastin, Cliff 10, *10*, 12, *12*, *13*, 17, 18, 19, *19*, 20, 54, 60, 61, 61, 62, 63, 68, 69, *69*, 70, *70*, 73, 75, 76, 78, 79, 80, *80*, 81, 83, *83*, 85, 86, *86*, 87, 88, 89, 90, 91, *94*, 95, *96*, *96*, 98, 99, 152, 163, 198, *199*, 205
Bates, Mick 130
Bates, Morris 23, 25,27, 28
Beal, Phil 134
Beardsley, Fred 23, 24, 25, 25, 26, 27, *28*, 20
Beardsley, Peter 163, 164
Beardsley-Comer, RA 24
Beasley, Pat 73, 75, 85, 86, *87*, *89*
Beck, John 168
Bee, E. 27
Bell, Bunny 85
Bell, Colin *126*
Bell, Emily 176
Benali, Francis 198
Benson, Bob 37, 41
Bentley, Roy 104, 105
Bergkamp, Dennis .187, *191*, 192, *192*, 193, 195, 198, *198*, 199, 200, *200*, 201, 202, 203, 204
Berkovic, Eyal 203
Bernhard, Mickey *131*, *136*
Best, George 59
Bilic, Slaven 204, *205*
Birkett, Ralph 75
Black, Tommy 17, 79, 80
Blanchflower, Danny 59, 117
Blockley, Jeff 149
Bloomer, Steve 59
Bloor, Alan 131
Blyth, Billy 46, 47, 53, *54*, 56, *56*
Boa Morte, Luis 197
Bond, John 166
Bonetti, Peter 127
Book, Tony 126
Booth, Tommy *126*
Bose, Mihir 183
Bould, Steve 156, 158, 164, 181, 182, 186, 187, 188, 190, 203, 204, 205
Boulton, Frank *70*, 75
Bowden, Ray 75, *85*, 86, 87, *89*, 90
Boyle, John 33
Bradshaw, Frank *46*
Bradshaw, George 76
Bradshaw, Harry 31, 35, 36, 37
Brady, Liam 149, 150, 151, 157, 159, 178, 179, 184, 191, *195*

Brain, Jimmy 48, 53, 54, 55, 56, 56
Branagan, Keith 198
Bremner, Billy 123, 131, 132, 136
Briercliffe, Tommy 35
Bright, Mark 177, 178
Brook, Eric 85
Brolin, Thomas 180, 181
Brooking, Trevor 150
Brown, Tony 129, 130
Brown (1886) 25
Bruce, Steve 171
Bucci (Parma) 180
Buchan, Charlie 18, 20, 36, 48, 50, 50, 51, 51, 52, 53, 54, 54, 55, 56, 56, 58, 59, 82, 124
Buchanan, R. 33
Buckley, Chris 46
Buckley, Frank 22
Buist, Bobby 28
Buksh, Alf 175
Burgess, D. *46*
Burkinshaw, Keith *154*
Burnett, Frances 23
Burtenshaw, Norman 131, 132
Burtenshaw, Steve 149
Busby, Matt *81*
Butler, Jack *46*, 53, 54, 56, *56*

Caesar, Gus 156, 158
Calderhead, Dave 90
Caldwell, J. *33*
Callaghan, Ian 137
Campbell, Bobby 104, 149
Campbell, Kevin 168, 169, 171, 172, 174, 178, 179, 180, 184, 185, 187
Cantona, Eric 179, 180
Carr, Eddie 92
Carr, Franz 160
Carruthers, Frank 84
Carter, Raich 76
Cavey, Mr 29
Chapman, Harry 14, È
Chapman, Herbert 9, *9*, 10, *12*, 17, 19, 20, 25, 26, *36*, 41, *42*, 44, 45, 46, 47, *47*, 48, 49, 49, 50, *50*, 58, *59*, *61*, 69, 70, 72, 77, 80, *82*, 83, 87, 90, 91, *91*, 92, 93, 105, 114, 117, *117*, 149, 151, 152, 152, 183, *186*, *187*, 191, 206
Chapman, Keith 10
Chapman, Ken 18
Charlton, Bobby 59
Charlton, Jack 131, *136*
Cheesmuir, Fred 10
Chenhall, John 112
Childs, Arthur 61, *64*
Chivers, Martin 134
Christmas, A. 27
Clapton, Danny 116, *116*
Clapton, Dennis 116
Clarke, Adrian 188
Clarke, Allan *119*, 148
Clemence, Ray 137, *139*, 140, 141, *141*, 143, *157*
Close, Brian 109
Clough, Brian 184
Clough, Nigel 160, 170
Cole, Andy 185
Coleman, Eddie 75
Coleman, Tim 35, 37, 38
Collins, Peter 134
Collymore, Stan 185
Common, Alf 38
Compton Denis 91, 94, *97*, 98, 100, 101, *102*, 102, 104, 105, 106, 108, 109, 115, 196, 205
Compton, Leslie 75, 98, 100, 101, 102, 102, 104, 105, 106, *106*, *108*, 109, 111, 115
Connolly, Peter 27, 28, *28*
Conroy, Terry 125
Constantine, Learie 53
Cook, Henry *96*
Cook, A. Hunt 81
Cooper, Terry 118, 118
Cope, Horace 56, *56*
Coppell, Steve 184
Copping, Wilf 53, 63, 68, 75, 76, *85*, 86, 89
Corrigan, Joe 126
Cottee, Tony 154
Counley, F. F. *46*
Coupland, Ernest *46*
Court, David 120
Cox, Eileen 106, 111
Cox, Freddie 106, *108*, 109, 110, 111, 112
Crawford, Gavin *30*
Crayston, Jack *14*, 53, 68, 75, 86, *89*, 90, *114*, 115, *116*
Crew, Tom 12, *12*

Crighton (1886) 27
Crisp, C. *46*
Croker, Peter 100
Cross, Archie 35
Crozier (Brentford) *94*
Cruyff, Johan 121
Cullis, Stan 95
Cumbes, Jim 130
Cumner, Horace 98

Dalglish, Kenny 158,166, 169, 205
Daniel, Bobby *96*
Daniel, Ray 109, 111, 113
Danskin, David 23, 24, *24*, 25, *25*, 27, *28*, 30
Davidson, Bobby 91, *94*
Davies, Barry 141
Davives, Gordon 172
Davies, Len 57
Davies, Roy 110
Davies, F. W. *33*
Davis, Malcolm 42
Davis, Paul 156, 158, 165, 172, 174, 176, 177, 179, *181*
Davis, Richard 101
Davison (Newcastle) 73
Dean, Dixie 58, 78, 79, *90*
Dean, William 96
Dein, David 166, 173, 183
Devine, Andy 41
Di Matteo, Roberto 192
Dick, John 35
Dickov, Paul 188, 190
Dibble, Andyn 156, 163
Dixon, Lee 156, 160, 161, 164, 165, 166, 167, 170, 171, 172, 174, 180, 182, 183, 185, 188, 190, *192*, 194, *195*, 203, 205
Dobing, Peter 147
Dodds, Jock 86
Dodgin, Bill 113, 115
Dougall, Peter 76
Downsborough, Peter 121
Doyle, Mike *126*
Drake, Ted 18, 36, 54, 63, 76, 84, 85, 85, 86, *88*, 89, 90, 91, 92, *94*, 96, 98, 99, 152, 163, 205,
Drury, George 91, 98
Dublin, Dion 168
Ducat, Andy 37, *38*
Duncan (Hull) 61
Dunn, S. *46*
Dunne, Jimmy 75, 76
Durban, Alan 147
Dyson, Keith 128
Eastham, George *115*, 117, 147
Edinburgh, Justin 176
Edwards, J. J. *92*
Elcoat, George 35
Elder, Alex 147
Elizabeth, Queen 147
Elliott, A. 33
Elliott, Billy 102
Elliott, Matt *198*
Ellis, Arthur 111
Ellis (Barnsley) *87*
Emerson 192
Epstein, Jacob 9, *22*
Eriksson, Goran 181
Esnaider, Juan 185, *187*, 188
Evans, Alun 137
Ewan (1920) *46*

Fairclough, W. 55
Farquharson, Tom 55, *56*
Farrington, John 124
Ferguson, Hugh 55, 57
Fern, Rodney 124
Finney, Jim 124, 131
Finney, Tom 113
Fletcher, Paul 129
Forbes, Alex 102, 113, *113*
Ford, David 96
Ford, Trevor 113
Forrest, James 23
Foster Steve (Luton) 156
Fowler, Robbie 185, 196
Fatzeskos 199
Freeman, Bert 36, 27
Friar, Ken 166, 183
Fry (1886) 27
Furnell, Jim 118

Gabriel, Jimmy *134*
Gallgher, Hughie *72*
Garbutt, Bill 36, *36*, 37
Garde, Remi
Gascoigne, Paul 168, 169, 176, 185, 186
Geldard, Albert 105
Gellatly (1996) 25

Gemmill, Archie 170
George V, King 9, *10*, *11*, 12, *16*
George, Charlie *120*, 122, 123, 124, 126, 126, 127, 128, 129, 129, 130, 131, 132, 134, 135, *136*, *138*, 140, 141, 142, 143, *143*, 144, 147, *147*, *148*, 149, 157, 165
Gibson, Colin 172
Gibson (Hull) *64*
Giles, Johnny 131, *155*
Gilzean, Alan 134
Gladsone, William 23
Glanville, Brian 124
Glass, Hugh 96
Goodall, John 28
Goodall, Roy 10, 12, 59
Goodfellow, Derek 104
Gooing, Bill 35
Goring, Peter 102, 105, 107, *108*, 109
Gould, Bobby 118, 121
Graham, Alec 46
Graham, george 118, 120, 121, 123, 124, 132, *133*, 137, 140, 141, *141*, *143*, *144*, 146, 151, 152, 154, 156, 157, 158, 160, 161, 162, 163, 165, 166, 167, 168, 169, 170, 171, 172, 173, 174, 175, 178, 179, 180, 181, 183, 184, 185 187, *187*, 193, 194
Gray, Andy 206
Gray, Bill 118, 147
Gray, Eddie 131, 180
Greaves, Jimmy 59, 120
Green, Geoffrey 123
Green (Sheffield U) 58
Greenaway, D. *46*
Greenhof, Jimmy 125, 127, *131*, 132, 147
Greenwood, Ron 102
Gregory (1986) 27
Gribble, Leonard *96*
Griffiths, Bill 98
Griffiths, Mel 92
Griffiths, Tommy 85, *95*
Grimandi, Gilles 197, *197*, 201
Grimsdell, Arthur *50*
Grimes, Ashley 156
Grobbelaar, Bruce 154, *163*, 164, 165, *169*, 184, 206
Groves, Freddie *46*
Groves, Perry 154, 156
Gudmunsen, Arthur 99
Gullit, Ruud 182, 200

Hacking, Jack 68
Hall, William 39, *46*, *47*, 52
Halliday, David 60, 62, 63
Hancocks, Johnny 102
Handley, Bill 121
Hapgood, Eddie 10, 12, 16, *19*, 56, 57, 61, 63, *69*, 73, 75, 78, *80*, 81, *85*, 86, 89, 90, *90*, *92*, 96, 98, 205
Hardy, George 37, 41, *46*, *48*, 70
Hare, C. B. *33*
Harford Mick (Luton) 156
Harkes, John 174
Harland, Stan 121
Harper, Bill 52, 54, 63, 70, *70*
Harper, Bill (referee) 73
Harris, John 104, 192
Harrison, Reg 101
Hartson, John 183, 184, 185, *187*, 188, 190, 200, 203
Hauge, Rune 183
Harvey, Colin 123
Hayes, Matin 154, 156, 161
Heath, John 33
Hegel 59
Heighway, Steve 136, 137, *139*, 140
Heslop, George *126*
Hill, Jimmy *115*, 140
Hillier, David 180, 182, 185
Hill-Wood, Denis 117, 118, 146
Hill-Wood, Peter 160, 183, 191, 194
Hill-Wood, Samuel 52
Hinton, Alan 147
Hirst, David 176, 177, 181
Hoar, Syd *54*, 55, 56, *56*
Hoddle, Glenn 179, *193*
Hodgson (Grimsby) 86
Hollins, John 122
Hollis (1895) *33*
Holton, Cliff 99, 109, 111, 112, 116, 190
Homer, Harry *86*
Hornby, Nick 187
Horsington, D. *28*
Hopkins, Jimmy *46*
Houghton, Ray 165
Houston, Stewart 175, 184, *187*, 191, 193
Howatt, D. 27
Howcroft, Jack 37

Howe, Don 121, 124, *134*, 135, 140, 141, *144*, 146, 148, 150, 151, 152, 170
Howells, David 176
Howie, Jimmy 36
Howieson (Hull) 61
Howley, Kevin 133, 135
Hudson, Alan 150
Hughes, Emlyn 140, *141*
Hughes, Rob 165, 173, 174, 177
Hughes, Stephen 188, 196, 201, *201*
Hulme, Joe 10, 17, 18, 19, *19*, 20, 53, 54, *54*, 56, *56*, 58, *58*, 60, 61, 62, *62*, 63, *64*, 70, 73, 75, 76, 78, *80*, 81, 85, 86, *89*, 90, 91, *94*, 152, *155*, 163, 206
Humble, John 23, 24, 25, 25, 29, 30, *46*, 47
Hunt, George *85*, 91
Hutchins, Arthur *46*
Hutchinson, David 164
Hutchinson, Don 204

Inglis, Simon 93
Isaias (Benfica) 172
Islip (Huddersfield) 17

Jack, David 10, *10*, 11, 13, *17*, 18, *19*, 20, 54, 58, 59, *59*, 60, 61, *61*, 62, 63, 72, 73, 73, 75, 76, 77, 79, *79*, 80, 81, *81*, 84, 85, 86, *86*, 87, 89, 90, 90, 91, 95, 112, 115, 205
Jeffrey, William 35
Jenkyns, Caesar *33*, 34, 35
Jennings, Pat134, *137*, 150, 154
Jensen, John 173, 176, 177, 180, 183, 191
Jewett (1920) *46*
Jobey, George 41
John, Bob 10, *10*, 12, *19*, 47, 48, 53, 55, 56, *56*, 60, 63, 68, *70*, 73, 75, *77*, 78, 91
Johnson, Tom 86, *88*
Johnston, Craig 154
Jones, Bryn 91, 92, 93, 95, 95, 96, 100, 101, 105
Jones, Charlie 10, 54, 63, 68, *70*, 75, 76
Jones, Cliff 116
Jones, Lowerth 123
Jones, Leslie 91, 95
Jones, Mick 148
Jone, Paul 198
Jones, Robert 70
Jones, Stuart 161
Jordan, Joe *154*
Joy, Bernard 53, 59, 61, *61*, 63, 68, 70, 75, 83, 91, 92, 98, 99
Jugovic 182, 183
Julian, Bill 27, *30*, 31
Julian, J. W. 116
Juninho 192

Kay, George 106
Keane, Tom 105
Keenor, Fred 55
Kelly, Bob 12
Kelly, Eddie 120, 122, *122*, 123, 129, 132, 133, 136, 137, 140, 141, *141*, *144*, 149, 161
Kelly, Gary 192
Kelsey, Jack 113, 114, 115, 120, 121, 122, 125
Kelso, Phil 36, 37
Kempes, Mario 151
Kempton, A. *46*
Kendall, Howard 123, 204
Kennedy, Ray 122, *123*, 123, 126, 128, *131*, 134, 136, 137, *143*, *144*, 146, 147, 148, 149, 157
Kenny, Vince 105
Keown, Martin 174, 180, 182, 185, 188, *193*, *197*, 203, 205
Ketsbaia, Temur 205
Keyser, Gerry 63, 70
Kiezer, Piet 134, 176
King, Harry *37*, 41
Kinnaird, Arthur 152
Kinnear, Joe 134, *137*
Kirchen, Alf 75, 92
Kitson, Paul 200
Kiwomya 183, 184
Knighton, Leslie 38, 44, *45*, 46, *46*, 47, *47*, 48, *48*, 49, 49, 51, 52, 53, 56, *56*, 61, 69
Knowles, Cyril 134, *137*
Krol, Rudi 121
Kulkov (Benfica) 172
Kyle, Bob 51, *51*
Kyle, Peter 37

Lacey, David *123*, 156, 183
Lack, Leslie *96*

Lama, Bernhard 202
Lambert, Jack 10, *10*, 12, 13, *19*, 20, 54, 60, 62, *62*, 63, 64, 70, 75, 76, 78, *80*, 81, 91, 206
Langley, Ambrose 16
Lawler, Chris 137, 140
Lawton, tommy 99, 101, 113
Leboeuf, Frank 192
Lether, J. 35
Lewis, C. H. *46*
Lewis, Dan 12, 14, 54, 55, 56, *56, 57*, 61, *70*, 147
Lewis, David 41
Lewis, Reg 98, 99, 100, 101, 102, *102*, 105, *106, 108*, 109, 110, 111, 205
Liddell, Bill 101, 106, 109
Lightbown, Chris 118
Limpar, Anders 166, 172, 174, 176, 177, 178, *181, 182*, 188
Lindsay, Alex 137
Lineker, Gary 168, 169
Linighan, Andy 166, 172, 174, 176, 177, 178, *181, 182*, 188
Linward, Bill 35
Lishman, Doug 104, 107, 109, 110, *110*, 111, 112, 113, *113*
Livermore, Doug 175
Lloyd, Larry 140, 143, *143*
Lochhead, Andy 130
Lofthouse, Nat 113
Logie, Jimmy 100, 101, *104*, 108, 109, 110, *110*, 111, 112, 113, *113*
Lomas, Steve 202, 203
Lombardo, A. 183, *188*
Lorimer, Peter 130, 132, 148
Lovejoy, Joe 179, 181
Lukic, John 161, 165, 166, 190, *193*
Lydersen, Pal 185

McAllister, Gary 230
McAteer, Jason 196
Macaulay, Archie 53, 100, 102, 104, 107
McBean, John 27, *28, 30, 31*
McCracken, Bill 44, 61
McCulloch, Derek 82, 83
McDermott, terry 151
Macdonald, Malcolm 150, *152*
MacDonald, Ramsey 18
McEachrane, Roddy 35
McFaul, Iam 129
McGoldrick, Eddie 183
McGown, Gavin 188
McIlroy, Sammy 150
McInroy (Sunderland) *51*
Mackay, Dave *134*, 146
McKenna, John 38, 43, 44, 59
McKinnon, Angus 46
McLintock, Frank 117, 118, 120, 121, 122, *122*, 123, 125, 127, 128, *130*, 130, 131, 132, *134*, 135, *136*, 143, *143, 144*, 146, 147, 149, 152, 157, 206
McMahon, Steve 164
McNab, Bob 120, 121, 129, 131, 132, 136, *144*, 148, *148*
McPherson, Ian 100, 102, 107
McQueen, Gordon 150
McWilliam, Peter 48
Mabbutt, Gary *177*
Madeley, Paul 131
Mchoney, John 126, *127, 131*, 206
Male, George 63, *69, 70*, 73, 75, 79, 80, *85*, 86, *89*, 91, *97, 99*, 101, 104, 152, 205
Mancini, R. 182
Manning, L. V. 73
Manninger, Alex 201, 202, 203, *204*
Marden, Ben 112
Marinello, Peter *144*
Marks, George 96
Marshall, Scott 188
Martyn, Nigel 195
Marwood, Brian 156, 158, 161, 184, 185
Matthews, Stanley 59, 60, 98, 101
Mears, Gus 39
Medhurst, Harry 106
Mee, Bertie 118, 120, 121, 122, 123, 124, *124, 125, 126, 127*, 128, *131, 132, 134*, 135, 136, *138, 144*, 146, 149, 151, 205
Melia, Jimmy 106
Mendez, Alberto 197
Mercer, Joe 53, 99, 100, 101, 102, 104, 105, 106, *106*, 107, 108, 100, 111, 113, 114, 116, 152, 205
Merson, Paul 154, 158, 166, *166*, 167, 169, 170, 172, 174, *174*, 175, 176, 176, 177, 178, 179, *179*, 180, 181, *182, 182*, 185, 187, 188, *188, 191, 193*, 194, 197
Merton (Aston Villa) 85
Milburn, Jackie 111, *112*,

Miller, David 164
Mills, S. *33*
Mills (Hull) 62
Milne, Billy *69*, 76, 122
Milne, Jackie 94
Milton, Arthur 109, 110, 111, 112
Minotti (Parma) 249
Mitchell, Albert 110, 111
Mitchell, Bobby 111, 112
Mitchell, T. B. 35
Moffat, 'Midget' 48, 49
Moir, Willie 112, 113
Molby, Jan 170
Moore, Bernard 110
Moore, Bobby *134*
Moore, Brian 140
Morrell, George 37, *37, 38*, 41, 51
Morris, John 101
Morrisey, John 137
Morrow, Steve 174, 175, 176, 178, *179*, 181
Mortensen, Stan 98, 101, 104
Mortimer, P. *33*
Morton, Alan 59
Moss, Frank 10, 63, 68, *70*, 75, 76, 79, 84, *85*, 86, 101
Moy (1886) 27
Muhren, Gerrit 121, 146
Mulder, Jan 121, 122
Mullen, Jimmy 102
Mullery, Alan 132
Mulligan, Paddy *122*
Myrhe, Thomas 204

Napier, Charlie 90
Nayim 185, 186, 187, *188*
Neal, Phil *157*
Neighbour, Jimmy 134
Neil, Andy 53
Neill, Terry 80, 118, 120, *138*, 146, 149, 150, 151, *152*
Nelson, Sammy *144*, 150
Newton, Henry *123*
Newton, Keith *123*
Nicholson, Bill 117, 132, 135, 149
Nicholas, Charlie 151, 154, 163
Nicol, Steve 164, 165
Nixon, Bob 171
Norris, Henry 16, 25, 30, 37, *38, 43*, *46, 47, 48*, 51, *51*, 52, 53, *69*, 63
North, F. J. 46
Nayim 198

Oakes, Don 112
O'Brian Peter *33*, 35
O'Donnell (Preston) 69
Offer (1886) 27
O'Flanagan, Kevin 99
O'Leary, David 150, 151, 158, 160, *170*, 176, 177, 194
O'Neill, Martin 198, *198*
Osbourne, Roger 150, 178
Osgood, Peter 122
Overmars, Marc 197, 199, 200, 201, 202, 203, *203*, 204, 205, *205, 206*

Pagnam, F. *46*
Paine, Terry *134*
Paisley, Bob 106
Palmer, Carlton 175
Parker, Tom 9, 10, *10*, 14, *16, 17, 19*, 20, 54, 56, 56, 57, 59, 63, 74, *74*, 75
Parkinson Gary (Middlesbrough) 161
Parlour, Ray 198, 200, 202, 205
Parr, William *96*
Parry, Jack 105
Parry, Rick 183
Partridge, Pat 127, 131
Paterson, Jimmy *46*, 48
Paterson, W. *70*
Pates, Colin 172
Payne, Jimmy 106
Peachey, G. *46*
Pearce, Richard 23
Pearson, Stan 109
Peart, J. C. *46*
Pelé 122
Pepper, Guy 80
Pereira (Valencia) 151, *159*
Perryman, Steve *137, 151*
Peter, Jim *46, 47*
Peters, John 59, 70, 82
Peters, Martin 134
Petit, Emmanuel 197, *197*, 199, 201, 204, 205
Platt, David 182, 187, *190*, 191, 192, 199
Platt, Ted 109
Plumb (1920) *46*
Porteous (1886) 25, 27
Powell, Joe *33*
Poynton, Cecil 48

Preedy, Charlie 10, 12, *14, 15, 19, 20*, 61, *70*
Price (1886) 25, 27
Pugh, Sidney *96*
Pye, Jesse 101

Quinn, Niall 151, 152, 160
Quinton, John 184

Radcliff, T. P. 10
Radford, John 118, 120, *120*, 122, 128, 131, 132, *134*, 136, 137, 137, *138*, 140, 141, *143, 144*, 147, 148, *148*, 150, 157
Ramsay, Jimmy *51*, 53
Ramsey, Alf 120
Ratcliffe (1886) 25
Ratcliffe (1920) *46*
Ravanelli, Fabrizio 192
Rawlings (Southampton) 54
Reed, Mike 202
Reeves, Peter 180
Reid, Robert 184
Rep, Johnny 176
Revie, Don 121, 132, 147
Rice, Pat 91, 123, 124, 130, 136, 137, *139, 144*, 146, 150, *155*, 188, 191, 194
Richardson, Jimmy 73
Richardson, Kevin 156, 158, 160, 164, 165
Ridley, Ian 183
Rioch, Brue 157, 187, *187*, 188, 190, *190*, 191, 192, 193, *193*
Ritchie, John 126, 127, 131
Ritchie, Tom *184*
Rix, Graham 127, 150, 151, *155, 159*, 178
Roberts, Charlie 39, 44
Roberts, Herbie 10, 18, 54, 56, 63, 70, 75, *75*, 79, 80, 84, 86, *89*, 90, *90*, 91, *96*, 99
Roberts, John 123, 129, *144*
Robertson, B. 27
Robledo, George 111, 112
Robson, Stewart 188, *203*
Rocastle, David 154, 156, 157, 158, 160, 161, 164, *164*
Rogers, Don *118*, 121
Rooke, Ronnie 36, 98, 99, 100, 101, 102, 104, 105, 113, 205
Roper, Don 100, 101, 102, 104, 107, 109, 111, 112, 113
Rose (1920) 46
Rose, Matthew 188
Rosebotham (1920) 46
Ross, Jimmy, Jun 85
Rous, Stanley 122
Rowley, Jack 102
Royle, Joe 123
Ruffell, Jimmy 47
Rush, Ian 154, 163, 164, 177
Rutherford, Jock 41, *46*
Rutt, Bert *13*

Sagar, Ted 101
Salisbury, Lord 23
Sammels, John *120*, 122, 123, 127, 133, *144*
Sands, Percy 35, *75*
Sansom, Kenny 156
Satterthwaite, Charlie 36, *36*
Saunders, Dean 172
Scala, Nevio 181
Scales, Paul *166*
Schmeichel, Peter 199, 202
Schwarz, Stefan 182, 183, 187
Scott, Brough 176
Scott, J. L. 48
Scott, Laurie 98, 104, *108*
Scoular, Jimmy 116
Seaman, David 166, 171, 172, 181, 182, 183, 185, 186, 188, *188*, 190, 192, 106, 107, 200, 202, *£04*, 205
Seddon, Bill 10, *10, 14, 19, 56*
Seed, Jimmy 22, 48, 60, 91
Selley, Ian 176, 181
Sexton, Dave 118
Shankly, Bill 135, 136, 143, 148
Shanks, Tommy 35
Shannon, Les 118
Sharp, Jimmy 37
Sharpe, Lee 166
Shaw, Arthur 111
Shaw, Joe 37, 41, *44, 46, 47, 47, 48*, 70, 82, *82*, 83, 100, 115
Shaw, Paul 188
Shaw, W. 33
Shearer, Alan 185, 205
Sheedy Kevin 158
Sheppard, Billy 79
Sheringham, Teddy 199
Shilton, Peter *129*, 161, *164*

Shorthouse, Bill 101
Sidey, Norman 79, 80
Sidlow, Cyril *106*, 109
Simpson, Peter 121, 123, 134, 144, 147, 157
Skeels, Eric *131*
Skirton, Alan *115*
Smith, Alan 151, 154, 156, 157, 158, 161, 164, 165, 168, *168*, 171, 172, 174, 175, 177, 178, 179, 180, 181, 184, 185, *186*, 187
Smith, Bill *46*
Smith, David 148
Smith, Denis 125, *131, 148*, 170
Smith, Joseph 23, 27
Smith, Lionel 104, 111, *112*
Smith, Tommy 137, *139*, 140, *141, 143*
Smith, W. H. *11*
Smith (Sheffield U) 86, *88*
Souness, Graeme 169, 170
Spence (Huddersfield) *11*, 12
Spencer, Charlie 50
Sprake, Gary 129, 132
Standen, Jim 119, 122
Stapleton, Frank 149, 150, 155
Steel, Billy 101
Stein, Brian 156
Stephenson, Clem 18, 51, 59, 60
Stephenson, Roy 113
Stephney, Alex 138
Stevenson, R. L. 23
Stock, Alec 115
Stockill, R. *69*
Storer, Harry *33*, 34, 35
Storey, Peter 61, 123, *123*, 125, 125, 127, 129, 130, *131*, 132, 135, 136, 137, *144*, 147, 157, 206
Stringer, Dave 161
Strong, Geoff 117
Strong, Jim 102
Stubbins, Albert 101
Sugar, Alan 168
Suggett, Colin 129
Sunderland, Alan 150, *152, 155, 157*
Sutton, Chris 185
Suurbier, Wim 134, 176
Swindin, George *70*, 100, 101, 102, 104, 105, 106, *108, 109, 111, 112, 114*, 116, 117, *117*, 122

Talbot, Brian 150, *151, 152, 155, 157*
Taylor, Graham 173, 174
Templeton, Bobby 36
Thomas, Michael 156, 158, 160, 161, 164, 165, 167, *169, 171*, 206
Thomas, Mickey (Wrexham) 172
Thompson, Len 60
Thompson, Peter 137, *143*
Tinkler, Ray 129
Toner, Joe *46*
Tooze, Cyril *96*
Toshack, John 136, 137
Trebilcock, Mike 178
Tremelling, Dan 48
Turner (Huddersfield) 13

Ure, Ian 118, 120, 121

Vaessen, Paul *159*
Van Himst, Paul 121
Veitch, Colin 36
Venables, Terry 168, 185, *186*
Vialli, Gianluca 192
Vieira, Patrick 102, 191, *195*, 196, 197, *197*, 199, 200, 201, *202*, 203, 204, 205
Voysey, C. R. 46

Waddle, Chris 174, 176, 177
Wade, Joe 112,
Wainwright, Eddie 101
Wakeham, H. B. T. *82*
Walden, H. A. *46*
Wales, Prince of 72
Wales, Prince of (Edward VIII) 93
Walker, Billy *86*
Walker, Clive 156
Walker, Des 166, 197
Wall, Bob 58, 81, 100, 115
Wallace, Rod 195
Walley, Tom 191
Walsh, Charlie 79, 80
Walsh, Steve 200
Walton, 'Piggy' 24
Ward, A. *33*, 100, 115
Ward, Gerry 115
Warhurst, Paul 176, *181*
Waring, Pongo 63, 78
Warnes, Billy 79, 80
Watkin, Steve 172
Watkins, Elija 23, 25
Watt, Tom 187

Wayman, Charlie 114
Weaver, George 30, *30*
Webster, Tom 60, *78, 90*
Wells (1886) 27
Welsh, Don *97*
Wenger, Arsene 191, *193*, 191, 194, *194*, 195, *195*, 196, 197, *197*, 199, 200, 201, 202, 203, 204, 205
Westcott, Ronnie 84
White, H. A. *46*
Whitehead (1886) 25, 27
Whitehouse, Brian 146
Whittaker, Tom 9, 18, *19, 46, 47, 47*, 54, 56, 57, *57*, 60, 68, 69, *69*, 70, 73, *73*, 76, 79, 81, 82, 83, *85, 89*, 90, 92, *94*, 96, *96*, 99, 100, 101, 102, 104, 105, 109, 110, 111, 113, 114, *114*, 115, 116, 205
Wignall, Trevor *86*
Wilkinson, Howard 161
Williams, Joey 62, *64*
Williams, Steve 151, 154
Williamson, Ernie *46*
Wilson, Alex *69*, 70, 76, 86, *89, 90*
Wilson, Bob *119*, 121, 123, 125, 126, 127, *128*, 129, 131, 135, 136, 137, *139*, 140, 143, 144, 147, 148, 148, 152
Wilson, Danny 156
Wilson, David 37
Wilson, Hugh 146
Wilson, Tom 9, 10, *10*, 20, *28*
Winterburn, Nigel 156, 169, 161, *163*, 164, *166*, 170, 174,. 177, 190, *191*, 199, 205
Wise, Dennis 173, 192
Woan, Ian 170
Wood (1920) *46*
Woods, Chris 175, 176, 177, 178
Woolnough, Brian 175
Worthington, Frank 146, *188*
Worthington, Nigel 178
Wreh, Christopher 197, 202, 205
Wright, Billy 117, *117*, 118, 121
Wright, George *124*, 135, 140, *144*, 146
Wright, Ian 172, 174, 175, 176, 177, 178, 179, 180, *181, 182*, 183, 184, 185, 187, *187*, 188, 192, 193, 194, 197, 198, 199, *199*, 200, 201, 203, 206
Wright, Mark 229
Wright, Tommy 137

Young, Willie 150
Yorke, Dwight 188

Zagalo, Mario *122*
Zenga, Walter 182, 183
Zola, Gianfranco 192